routard

California Nevada & Arizona

Series director: Philippe Gloaguen
Series creators: Philippe Gloaguen and Michel Duval
Chief editor: Pierre Josse
Assistant chief editor: Benoît Lucchini
Coordination director: Florence Charmetant

Editorial team: Yves Couprie, Olivier Page, Véronique de Chardon, Amanda Keravel, Isabelle Al Subaihi, Anne-Caroline Dimas, Carole Foucault, Bénédicte Solle, André Poncelet, Jérôme de Gubernatis, Marie Lung and Thierry Brouard.

English translation: Carmona Translations
Managing editor: Liz Coghill
Editorial: Eileen Townsend Jones, Sarah Hudson, Penny Langton and Sofi Mogensen

Additional research and assistance: Kate Williams, Michael Hutchinson and James Miller
Proofreader: Hilary Hughes
Index: Indexing Specialists

We have done our best to ensure the accuracy of the information contained in this guide. However, addresses, phone numbers, opening times etc. do invariably change from time to time, so if you find a discrepancy please do let us know and help us update the guides. You can contact us at: hachetteuk@orionbooks.co.uk or write to us at Hachette UK, address below. Hachette UK guides provide independent advice. The authors and compilers do not accept any remuneration for the inclusion of addresses in this guide. Please note that we cannot accept any responsibility for any loss, injury or inconvenience sustained by anyone as a result of any information or advice contained in this guide.

Hotels, restaurants, B&Bs – price guide

Because of rapid inflation in many countries, it is impossible to give an accurate indication of prices in hotels and restaurants. Prices can change enormously from one year to the next. As a result we have adopted a system of categories for the prices in the guides: 'Budget', 'Cheap', 'Moderate', 'Chic' and 'Très Chic' (in the guides to French-speaking countries), otherwise 'Expensive' and 'Splash out' in the others. These categories do vary from guide to guide, however. If the 'Budget' or 'Cheap' hotels start at £2/$3 per night, then those costing £5/$7.50 per night will belong to the 'moderate' category and those costing £10/$15 and upwards will belong to the 'chic' or 'expensive' category. It therefore follows that in a guide where the 'Budget' option costs £10/$15 per night, the price ranges in the other categories will increase accordingly.

As prices may change so may other circumstances – a restaurant may change hands, the standard of service at a hotel may deteriorate since our researchers made their visit. Again, we do our best to ensure information is accurate, but if you notice any discrepancy, do let us know at the address already given above. The only thing we can't predict is when a hotel or a restaurant changes its standing (gets better or worse) and moves into a different category. If this happens, then we look forward to hearing from you, either by e-mail (see above) or by post (see below for address).

First published in the United Kingdom in 2001 by Hachette UK.

Distributed in the United States of America by Sterling Publishing Co., Inc.
387 Park Avenue South, New York, NY 10016-8810.

A CIP catalogue for this book is available from the British Library.

ISBN 1 84202 025 0

Typeset at The Spartan Press Ltd, Lymington, Hants.
Printed and bound by Aubin, France. E-mail: sales@aubin-imprimeur.fr

Hachette UK, Cassell & Co, Wellington House, 125 Strand, London WC2R 0BB.

Cover design by Emmanuel Le Vallois (Hachette Livre) and Paul Cooper.
Cover photo © Tony Stone. Back cover photo © Tony Stone.

routard

California Nevada & Arizona

The guides for travellers

CONTENTS

JUST EXACTLY WHO OR WHAT IS A ROUTARD?

You are. Yes, you! The fact that you are reading this book means that you are a Routard. You are probably still none the wiser, so to explain we will take you back to the origin of the guides. Routard was the brainchild of a Frenchman named Philippe Gloaguen, who compiled the first guide some 25 years ago with his friend Michel Duval. They simply could not find the kind of guide book they wanted and so the solution was clear – they would just have to write it themselves. When it came to naming the guide, Philippe came up with the term Routard, which at the time did not exist as a bona fide word – at least, not in conventional dictionary terms. Today, if you look the word up in a French-English dictionary you will find that it means 'traveller' or 'globetrotter' – so there you have it, that's what you are!

From this humble beginning has grown a vast collection of some 100 titles to destinations all over the world. Routard is now the bestselling guide book series in France. The guides have been translated into five different languages, so keep an eye out for fellow Routard readers on your travels.

What exactly do the guides do?
The short answer is that they provide all the information you need to enable you to have a successful holiday or trip. Routards' great strength however, lies in their listings. The guides provide comprehensive listings for accommodation, eating and drinking – ranging from campsites and youth hostels through to four star hotels – and from bars, clubs and greasy spoons to tearooms, cafés and restaurants. Each entry is accompanied by a detailed and frank appraisal of the address, rather like a friend coming back from holiday who is recommending all the good places to go (or even the places to avoid!). The guides aim to help you find the best addresses and the best value for money within your price range, whilst giving you invaluable insider advice at the same time.

Anything else?
Routard also provides oceans of practical advice on how to get along in the country or city you are visiting plus an insight into the character and customs of the people. How do you negotiate your way around the transport system? Will you offend if you bare your knees in the temple? And so on. In addition, you will find plenty of sightseeing information, backed up by historical and cultural detail, interesting facts and figures, addresses and opening times. The humanitarian aspect is also of great importance, with the guides commenting freely and often pithily, and most titles contain a section on human rights.

Routard are truly useful guides that are convivial, irreverent, down-to-earth and honest. We very much hope you enjoy them and that they will serve you well during your stay.

Happy travelling.

The Hachette UK team

SYMBOLS USED IN THE GUIDE

Please note that not all the symbols below appear in every guide.

- ■ Useful addresses
- Tourist office
- Post office
- Telephone
- Railway station
- Bus station
- Shared taxi
- Tram
- River transport
- Sea transport
- Airport
- Where to stay
- Where to eat
- Where to go for a drink
- Where to listen to music
- Where to go for an ice-cream
- ★ To see
- Shopping
- ● 'Other'
- Parking
- Castle
- Ruins
- Diving site
- Shelter
- Camp site
- ▲ Peak
- ● Site
- ○ Town
- Hill
- Abbey, chapel
- Lookout
- Beach
- Lighthouse

GETTING THERE

BY AIR

These days the West Coast of the US is one of the best connected and most popular air destinations in the world. Due to increased competition between airlines, fares to California and the West Coast have dropped drastically over the past decade. It is possible for travellers coming from Europe, for example, to find flights for under £200. There are also good deals available if you're travelling from Canada, Australia, New Zealand and South Africa, especially if you're willing to take slightly roundabout routes.

Los Angeles International Airport and San Francisco International Airport are the main destinations for international flights, although you can also find services to San Diego International Airport and Las Vegas McGarran International Airport.

The West Coast of the US is superbly connected, and once you're there, you'll find it fairly straightforward to visit as much of the country as you want. Travellers can fly, drive or take the legendary Greyhound bus or Amtrak train. *See* 'Transportation' for more details.

FROM THE UK

Flights to the US from Britain seem to get cheaper every year. Not only is the travel industry in the UK one of the most competitive in Europe, but the routes to the US are some of the most hotly contested. You'll find competitive prices, especially out of season, to Los Angeles, San Francisco and, increasingly, Las Vegas. It is possible to find flights advertised for as low as £200 return or less. However, the overwhelming choice of flights to the West Coast doesn't necessarily make things easier, and cheap deals often come with hidden catches, so here is some advice. Don't be pushed into buying if you're unsure – remember, reputable travel agents will hold flights for you free of charge to give you time to make up your mind. Make sure you shop around and always be careful to check all the details, especially taxes or any obligation to book certain accommodation or tours that might bump up the price.

Most importantly, make sure that you are buying from a travel agent that has been certified by ABTA (Association of British Travel Agents). If you choose one that isn't, you might get a fantastic deal, but if the company goes bankrupt in the meantime, you will have no way of getting your money back. Buying a ticket on a credit card can provide a limited amount of insurance, but you can't always rely on this.

FLIGHT-ONLY DEALS

There are flights to the US from many UK airports, but if you want to fly across to the West Coast, you'll have to fly from London (either Heathrow or Gatwick). As a general rule, it's the non-stop flights that leave from

Heathrow and the stopover flights from Gatwick. There are daily non-stop flights to LA and less frequent non-stop flights to Las Vegas and San Francisco, with occasional services to San Diego, as well as regular stopover flights to all of the major airports. Non-stop flight time is about 11 hours to LA or San Francisco. Many airlines do good deals on 'open-jaw' tickets, which are particularly good for anyone contemplating a fly-drive deal, as you can fly into one city and out of another.

The peak months for travelling to the US are June to August and at Christmas, but prices can still be high in May, September and around Easter. However, excellent deals are available in winter and it's still possible to find cheap flights at peak times by making use of the various discount schemes. The three main methods of getting reductions on standard tickets are: using the Apex system, taking advantage of airline price wars and by shopping around for tickets that have been offloaded and sold cheaply through discount travel agencies. Note that weekend departures cost around £20–£30 more than during the week. If you're under 26 or a student under 32, you can also take advantage of the deals offered through student travel services such as STA Travel, Campus Travel and Trailfinders.

Most airlines that serve California apply the Apex or 'advance purchase' system to their standard economy fares. Prices are lower if you buy your ticket more than seven days in advance, with the greatest reductions on tickets bought 21 days in advance. Apex fares differ between airlines and routes, but most impose similar restrictions on your stay.

By far the most dazzling array of flight deals can be found among those that have been offloaded by major airlines and travel companies to smaller agents. The classified sections in the travel pages of weekend broadsheet newspapers and TV's Teletext are good places to start looking. Surfing the Internet – especially 'last minute' sites – can yield some excellent bargains. Websites such as www.cheapflights.com, www.ebookers.com and www.dialaflight.com had good deals at the time of writing, but new Internet sites are opening up all the time so it's best to check the web regularly.

The best schedule deals are often to East Coast destinations, especially New York and Boston. Travellers with more time on their hands can usually buy cheap connecting flights to the West Coast from the UK, and many airlines issue air passes. *See below* for more details.

When buying flights, it is worth remembering the following points. Many flights sold as 'direct' do in fact stop at a number of airports before reaching their final destination. This can be especially time-consuming if you have to stop somewhere else in the US before reaching California, as you'll have to enter customs and go through all the formalities at that airport and then get back onto the plane again. Beware also of buying a one-way ticket. Not only will your visa requirements be more complex, but immigration officials in the US may refuse you entry on the suspicion that you are planning to stay for good. If this happens, you will have to buy a ticket home there and then, which will be expensive and you may have to stay in an immigration holding jail overnight until your return flight leaves for Britain – not an ideal introduction to America!

CHARTER FLIGHTS

California is an extremely popular destination for UK package tour operators and you'll find bargain flights all year round. They are sold either as part of a package holiday or as a flight-only option and often have fixed and unchangeable outward and return dates with a maximum stay of one month. Many flights are 'red-eye specials' that arrive early in the morning.

PACKAGE HOLIDAYS

For those who want a shorter holiday, it is worth checking the package holidays on offer in High Street travel agents. These all-in deals are nearly always cheaper than booking the elements separately. Prices start from about £450 a week, with especially good deals in connection with Disneyland.

Fly-drive packages – which offer free or cut-price car rental with a trans-Atlantic flight – are always popular. These packages give excellent reductions on car rental, but the flights can be more expensive, so shop around between airlines and travel agents to take advantage of promotional prices and deals. A return flight and a week's car rental in California can cost as little as £300–£350.

TOURING PACKAGES

California, Nevada and Arizona are among some of the most rewarding destinations for longer trekking packages. They provide an excellent way of experiencing the West Coast wilderness without the hassle. Tours can be as short as one week or as long as nine weeks and the price includes transport, accommodation (often in tents), a guide and some meals. **Trek America** (www.trekamerica.com) is very popular and is experienced in organizing treks to California (among other destinations). Once in America, **Green Tortoise**, a San Francisco-based company, comes highly recommended for treks to a range of destinations, including the Grand Canyon and national parks.

AIRLINES

- **American Airlines**: 45–46 Piccadilly, London W1V 9AJ. ☎ (020) 8572 5555 or (0345) 789789. Website: www.aa.com
- **British Airways**: PO Box 365, Harmondsworth, West Drayton, Middlesex UB7 0GB. ☎ (0345) 222111. Website: www.britishairways.com
- **Continental Airlines**: Beulah Court, Albert Road, Horley RH6 7H2. ☎ (01293) 776464 or (0800) 776464. Fax: (01293) 773726. Website: www.continental.com
- **Delta Airlines**: 10 Warwick Street, First Floor, London W1B 5LZ. ☎ (0800) 414 7667. Website: www.delta.com
- **Northwest Airlines**: ☎ (01424) 224400. Website: www.nwa.com
- **KLM UK**: Head Office, Endeavour House, Stanstead Airport, Essex CM24 1RS. ☎ (08705) 074074. Website: www.klmuk.com
- **United Airlines**: 7–8 Conduit Street, London W1S 2XF. ☎ (0845) 844 4777. Website: www.ual.com

• **Virgin Atlantic**: The Office, Crawley Business Quarter, Manor Royal, Crawley, West Sussex RH10 2NU. ☎ (01293) 747747. Website: www.fly-virgin.com

DISCOUNT TRAVEL AGENTS

• **USIT Campus**: 52 Grosvenor Gardens, London SW1W OAG. ☎ (0870) 240 1010. Website: www.usitcampus.co.uk. Branches across the country. Specialists in student/youth travel.

• **STA Travel**: Priory House, 6 Wrights Lane, London W8 6TA. ☎ (020) 7361 6262 (long-haul). Website: www.statravel.co.uk. Also student/youth travel specialists and discount fares.

• **Trailfinders** (for long-haul travel): 42–50 Earl's Court Road, London W8 6FT. ☎ (020) 7938 3366. Website: www.trailfinders.com

• **FlightBookers**: 177–178 Tottenham Court Road, London WC1H OTA. ☎ (020) 7757 2000 (SA department) or (0870) 010 7000 (customer services). Website: www.flightbookers.com. Discount flights.

Many of these travel agents hold details of recommended low-cost hotels and hostels. They can book these for you for a few nights while you find your feet.

SPECIALIST TRAVEL AGENCIES, TOUR AND TREK OPERATORS

The following UK-based companies are just a selection of those that offer trekking, touring and fly-drive packages to California, Nevada and Arizona:

• **American Adventures and Roadrunner International**: 64 Mount Pleasant Avenue, Tunbridge Wells, Kent TN1 1QY. ☎ (01892) 512700. They arrange touring, trekking and adventure holidays on the West Coast in small groups.

• **American Airlines Holidays**: PO Box 5, 12 Coningsby Road, Peterborough, Cambridgeshire PE3 8XP. ☎ (0870) 605 0506. Flight, accommodation and fly-drive deals to California.

• **Destination US**: 14 Greville St, London EC1N 8SB. ☎ (020) 7400 7000. Accommodation and fly-drive itineraries.

• **Explore Worldwide**: 1 Frederick Street, Aldershot, Hampshire GU11 1LQ. ☎ (01252) 319448. Hiking holidays in national parks on the West Coast.

• **Fly-drive USA**: PO Box 45, Bexhill-on-Sea, East Sussex TN40 1PY. ☎ (01424) 224400. Flights and accommodation or fly-drive deals.

• **North America Travel Service**: Kennedy Building, 48 Victoria Road, Leeds LS11 5AF. ☎ (0113) 246 1466. Tailored itineraries. Branches also in Nottingham and Manchester.

• **Top Deck Travel**: 131–135 Earl's Court Road, London SW5 9RH. ☎ (020) 7370 4555. Agents for trekking and adventure tours, with an excellent selection to California. Top Deck Travel has a particularly good range of Exodus tours.

• **Trek America**: 4 Waterperry Court, Middleton Road, Banbury, Oxfordshire OX16 4QB. ☎ (01295) 256777. Specialists in touring and adventure holidays.

• **Up and Away**: 19 The Mall, Bromley, Kent BR1 1TT. ☎ (020) 8289 5050. Fly-drives and other packages to California and the national parks.

• **USIT Now**: 13B Fountain Centre, College Street, Belfast BT1 6ET. ☎ (01232) 324073. Website: www.usitcampus.co.uk

FROM THE REPUBLIC OF IRELAND

Delta and **Aer Lingus** offer direct flights from Dublin to Los Angeles and San Francisco, but there were no direct flights to Las Vegas or San Diego at the time of writing. Apex fares can be as low as IR£400, while students and under 26s can get especially good deals from the travel agent **USIT Now**. The recent increase in competition between airlines flying between London and Dublin means that if you're flexible about when you travel, you can find return flights to the UK for as low as £30–£40. You may find it cheaper, therefore, to fly to London in the first instance and buy your onward flight to California from there.

• **Aer Lingus**: 40–41 Upper O'Connell Street, Dublin 1. ☎ (01) 844 4777 or (01) 886 8888. Website: www.aerlingus.com

• **Delta**: First Floor, 3 Dawson St, Dublin 2. ☎ (01) 407 3165. Website: www.delta.com

• **USIT Now**: 19–21 Aston Quay, O'Connell Bridge, Dublin 2. ☎ (01) 677 8117 or (01) 602 1600. Website: www.usitcampus.co.uk

FROM NORTH AMERICA

California is a popular destination for both business travellers and holidaymakers, so the flight connections from the rest of North America to the West Coast are usually excellent (*see* 'Domestic Flights and Flight Passes'). All US airlines operate daily flights to LA and San Francisco, with frequent flights to Las Vegas and San Diego as well as to Oakland International and San Jose airports. There are also frequent flights to the smaller airports in Orange County in California.

Fierce competition between airlines means that you won't find too much difference between published standard fares. Return flights between New York and Los Angeles start at about $300–$350, but you can get excellent discounts depending on the time and date you are travelling. The most expensive months for travel within the US are between June and August and around Christmas, with high prices still lingering in May, September and around Easter. Nevertheless, travellers can still get good deals in high season by using either the Apex system, taking advantage of airline price wars or by looking for tickets that have been offloaded and sold cheaply through discount travel agencies.

Most airlines running to California offer Apex discounts. Prices are lower if you buy your ticket 7, 14 or 21 days in advance, with the greatest saving obtainable on tickets bought 21 days in advance. Apex fares vary from one airline to another and on the route that you choose, but most airlines impose similar restrictions on your stay. For example, the 21-day Super Apex is valid for not less than seven days and not more than a month.

Airline price wars happen frequently, and without warning, so keep checking with the airlines themselves or with your travel agent. If two of you are travelling together, you may also find special deals.

DOMESTIC AIRLINES

Domestic airlines running frequent services from cities in North America to California include the following:

• **America West Airlines**: ☎ 1-800-2 FLY-AWA or 1-800-235-9292. Website: www.americawest.com

• **American Airlines**: ☎ 1-800-433-7300. Website: www.aa.com

• **Canadian Airlines**: ☎ 1-800-426-7000. Website: www.cdnair.com

• **Continental Airlines**: ☎ 1-800-525-0280. Website: www.continental.com

• **Delta Airlines**: ☎ 1-800-221-1212. Website: www.delta.com

• **Northwest Airlines/KLM**: ☎ 1-800-225-2525. Website: www.nwa.com

• **Southwest Airlines**: ☎ 1-800-435-9792. Website: www.swa.com

• **United Airlines**: ☎ 1-800-241-6522. Website: www.ual.com

• **US Airways**: ☎ 1-800-428-4322. Website: www.usairways.com

DOMESTIC FLIGHTS AND FLIGHT PASSES

Internal flights can be very cheap with the range of special deals on offer from transcontinental airlines. Alternatively, many travel agents in your home country can sell you connecting flights between cities. Flights between LA and San Francisco can be as low as $70 single, and at the time of writing, there were flights between New York and San Francisco selling for $180. Again, take advantage of price wars, out-of-season deals and group travel offers. Flights departing mid-week are less expensive and the further you book in advance the better the deals on offer. Phoning airlines direct can be a good way of getting cheap tickets, but it's always worth checking with a travel agent, either in your home country or the US, as there are plenty of charter airlines operating domestic flights that you can't buy independently.

Nearly all of the US domestic airline services offer Visit US flight passes to non-US citizens. These are essentially books of coupons and each coupon equals a flight. Prices and restrictions vary from airline to airline, but the general rule of thumb is that you'll get a better price if you have a planned itinerary to stick to. You normally need to buy them in conjunction with a flight to the US from another destination, although flights from Mexico and Canada are not always included in this. Some airlines, such as Northwest and Delta, offer passengers the possibility of flying standby. This means you can ring the airline a few days in advance and make a 'standby reservation' that puts you first in the queue. Thanks to the large number of domestic airlines, there's a wide choice of flight passes available, so it's worth shopping around to find the one that suits you best in terms of price and validity.

Try one of the following:

• **American Airlines**: You can buy the American Airlines Visit US pass outside the US in conjunction with an international flight from any destination except Canada and Mexico. You must give a date and destination for your first flight and stick to it, otherwise you will be fined. Flights must be reserved one day in advance.

• **Continental Airlines**: This flight pass must be bought in conjunction with an international flight (Mexico and Canada are not included) from outside the US. It is valid for 60 days after the first flight or 81 days after arrival in the US. You must confirm times and dates of flights when buying the pass, and if you change your mind you will be fined $50. High-season prices are around $479 for three flights or $769 for eight flights.

• **Delta Airlines**: For the Visit US pass you need to organize your itinerary in advance and stick to it. Delta also offer a Discover America pass in which each coupon is worth a standby flight to anywhere in the US. Prices are $550 for four flights and $1,250 for 10 flights.

DISCOUNT TRAVEL AGENCIES IN THE US

The following are just a selection of the wide range of discount travel agencies and travel clubs in the US, more can be found in the broadsheet newspaper travel sections and on the Internet. Travel clubs can also be worth investigating if you're planning on making a number of trips.

• **Council Travel**: 205 East 42nd Street, New York, NY 10017. ☎ (212) 822-2700 or 1-800-226-8624. Website: www.counciltravel.com. Specialist in student travel.

• **Last Minute Travel Club**: 100 Sylvan Road, Suite 600, Woburn, MA 01821. ☎ 1-800-LAST-MIN. Website: www.vacationoutlet.com. Travel club for standby deals.

• **STA Travel**: 10 Downing Street, New York, NY 10014. ☎ (212) 627-3111 or 1-800-777-0112. Website: www.sta.com. Other branches also. Specialists in youth and independent travel.

FROM CANADA

There is a wide choice of regular flights between Canada and California, including daily direct flights from Toronto and Vancouver and regular (usually connecting) flights from Montreal and other cities to LA and San Francisco. There are also frequent flights to Las Vegas and San Diego, while smaller Canadian towns are well connected to California by air, via connecting services. There is not as much competition on routes as you might think, however, and you may find that it's cheaper to travel or fly to an East Coast city in the first instance and buy an onward flight to the West Coast from there. Some of the best deals can be found by surfing Internet travel sites and checking out the travel pages of broadsheet newspapers, such as the *Toronto Globe and Mail* and the *Vancouver Sun*.

AIRLINES

Scheduled airlines running frequent services from cities in Canada include:

• **Air Canada**: ☎ 1-888-247-2262. Website: www.aircanada.ca

• **Air France**: ☎ 1-800-667-2747. Website: www.airfrance.com

• **British Airways**: ☎ 1-800-668-1059. Website: www.british-airways.com

• **Continental**: ☎ 1-800-525-0280. Website: www.continental.com

- **Delta Airlines**: ☎ 1-800-221-1212. Website: www.delta.com
- **Iberia**: ☎ 1-800-772-4642. Website: www.iberia.com
- **KLM**: ☎ 1-800-361-5073. Website: www.klm.nl

DISCOUNT TRAVEL AGENCIES

- **New Frontiers/Nouvelles Frontières**: 1180 Drummond Road, Suite 330, Montreal, Quebec H3G ES1. ☎ (514) 871-5100. Other branches too, including New York and Quebec City. French discount travel agency.

- **Travel Cuts**: 187 College Street, Toronto, Ontario M5T 1P7. ☎ 1-800-667-2887 or 1-888-238-2887 or (416) 979-2406. Website: www.travelcuts.com. Branches across the country. Specialists in student travel.

SPECIALIST TOUR AND TREK OPERATORS

- **Adventures Abroad**: 20800 Westminster Highway, Suite 2148, Richmond, BC V6V 2W3. ☎ (604) 303-1099 or 1-800-665-3998. Website: www.adventures-abroad.com

- **Worldwide Adventures**: 1170 Shepperd Avenue West, Toronto, Ontario M3K 2A3. ☎ (416) 633-5666 or 1-800-387-1483.

FROM AUSTRALIA

Travellers from Australia can either fly the Pacific route or the trans-Asian route to get to the West Coast of the US. Both routes, however, offer plenty of regular flights at a reasonable price. Flights over the Pacific are usually non-stop, taking about 12–14 hours from Sydney to LA, while those via Asia take a more circuitous route, which often requires a stop in the airline's home city and possibly spending a night there. For those with a little more time to spare, it is possible to find good deals including one night's accommodation in perhaps Tokyo with **JAL Japan Airlines**, or Manila with **Philippine Airlines** or Jakarta with **Garuda Airlines**.

Fares vary according to season, with the cheapest periods running from mid-January to the end of February and October to the end of November. Low season fares from Sydney to LA cost around AUS$ 2,000 return, with increases of AUS $200–$500 in peak season. Prices from other cities on the east coast of Australia to LA and San Francisco are usually a similar price and those from Perth cost about AUS $400–$600 more.

Australian travellers can also take advantage of the deals for US flight passes. These are books of coupons that you can exchange for flights within the US and are usually purchased with an international flight. Prices vary from airline to airline, but usually work out at just over $100 per coupon, with further deductions if you buy more. The minimum amount of tokens you can buy is generally three, with a maximum of 10. The flight passes from **Delta**, **Northwest** and **United Airlines** can work out as particularly good deals.

AIRLINES

Scheduled airlines running frequent services from Australia to California include:

- **Air New Zealand**: ☎ 13 476 or (02) 9223-4666. Website: www.airnz.com.au
- **Cathay Pacific**: ☎ 13 17 47. Website: www.cathaypacific.com
- **Delta Air**: ☎ 1-800-500-992. Website: www.delta.com
- **Garuda Indonesia**: ☎ 1-800-800-873 or (02) 9334-9944. Website: www.garuda-indonesia.com
- **JAL Japan Airlines**: ☎ (02) 9272-1111. Website: www.japanairlines.com
- **KLM and Northwest Airlines**: ☎ (02) 9231-6333. Website: www.nwa.com
- **Philippine Airlines**: ☎ (02) 9279-2020. Website: www.philippineair.com
- **Qantas**: ☎ 13 13 13. Website: www.qantas.com
- **Singapore Airlines**: ☎ 13 10 11 or (02) 9350-0100. Website: www.singaporeair.com
- **United Airlines**: ☎ 13 17 77. Website: www.ual.com

Reputable travel agents can often give better prices and special offers than the airlines themselves, but it is worth trying both. Either use a local agent, or one of the discounted travel companies listed below. Special youth offers are available to those under 26 or students under 32. STA Travel are experts in student discount fares, although many specialist and discount travel agencies also offer cheap student deals. Other good hunting grounds for cheap flights include the travel sections of the weekend broadsheet newspapers and 'last minute' sites on the Internet.

SPECIALIST AND DISCOUNT TRAVEL AGENCIES

- **Brisbane Discount Travel**: 260 Queen Street, Brisbane. ☎ (07) 3229-9211.
- **Flight Centres**: Level 13, 33 Berry Street, North Sydney 2060. ☎ (02) 9241-2422. Call 13 600 for your nearest branch or 1-300-131-600 for the 24-hour customer care line. Flight deals and special offers.
- **STA Travel**: Shop 3, 702–730 Harris Street, Ultimo 2011, Sydney. ☎ 1-800-637-444. Call 13 776 for your nearest branch and 1-300-360-960 for telesales. Website: www.statravel.com. Specialists in student travel.
- **Tymtro Travel**: 428 George Street, Sydney 2000. ☎ (02) 9233-2211. Good discounts, deals and special offers.

ROUND-THE-WORLD TICKETS

If you're planning to take in more of the world, it's worth considering the excellent deals on round-the-world tickets, especially as many of these include inter-US flights in the price. **Singapore Airlines** and **TWA** offer a particularly good itinerary for those wanting to spend longer touring the US. Their 'Easyworld' ticket includes stopovers, according to mileage, in all continents flown to by **Singapore Airlines** and its partner airlines, and eight stopovers within the US for just over AUS$3,000, plus airport taxes. For more details, check with your travel agent, visit the **Singapore Airlines** website at www.singaporeair.com.au or contact one of the regional offices below:

• 17–19 Bridge Street, **Sydney**, NSW 2000. ☎ (02) 9350-0100. Fax: (02) 9241-2046.

• 414 Collins Street, **Melbourne**, VIC 3000. ☎ (03) 9254-0300. Fax: (03) 9254-0326.

• **Adelaide**: ☎ (08) 8203-0800. Fax: (08) 8410-0523.

• **Brisbane**: ☎ (07) 3259-0710. Fax: (07) 3259-0717.

• **Cairns**: ☎ (07) 4031-7538. Fax: (07) 4031-7638.

• **Perth**: ☎ 13 10 11 or (08) 9265-0500. Fax: (08) 9265-0553.

If your itinerary includes fewer domestic US flights, you may want to look at the round-the-world passes offered by other airlines. The **Qantas** 'Global Explorer' pass, for example, allows 15 stopovers in all continents flown to by **Qantas** or its partner airlines (not South America) within a mileage of 27,000 miles. It costs from AUS$2,500 in low season, plus airport taxes and from around AUS$3,000 in high season, plus airport taxes. Check www.qantas.com or contact your travel agent or one of the **Qantas** offices below.

Other tickets worth considering are the 'World Navigator' from **Air New Zealand/ KLM /Northwest Airlines**, and the 'Globetrotter' from **Cathay Pacific/United Airlines**. Fares start at AUS$2,600 for about six stop-overs.

• **Cathay Pacific**: ☎ 13 17 47. Website: www.cathaypacific.com

• **KLM**: Level 13, 115 Pitt Street, Sydney, NSW 2000. ☎ (02) 9233-6255. Fax: (02) 9235-3908. Website: www.klm.com.au

• **Qantas**: Chifley Square, 70 Hunter Street, Sydney, NSW 2000. ☎ 13 13 13 or (02) 9951-4294; 50 Franklin Street, Melbourne, VIC 3000. ☎ (03) 9285-3000.

SPECIALIST TRAVEL AGENCIES, TOUR AND TREK OPERATORS

For organized tours, trekking packages and planned itineraries try:

• **Adventure World**: 73 Walker Street, North Sydney. ☎ (02) 9956-7766. Agents for tours and treks in small groups.

• **American Travel Centre**: Second Floor, 262 Adelaide Street, Brisbane. ☎ (07) 3221-4788. Flights, accommodation, fly-drives and tours.

• **Peregrine Adventures**: 258 Lonsdale Street, Melbourne, VIC 3000. ☎ (03) 9663-8611. Tours and treks in small groups.

• **Sydney International Travel Centre**: Reid House, Level 8, 75 King Street, Sydney, NSW 2000. ☎ (02) 9299-8000 or 1-800-251-911. Flights, fly-drives, planned itineraries and travel passes.

• **Top Deck**: Level 2, 123 Clarence St, Sydney, NSW 2000. ☎ 1-300-656-566. Agents for adventure tours.

FROM NEW ZEALAND

Like those from Australia, flights between New Zealand and the West Coast of the US either go via Asia or across the Pacific. Most flights leave from Auckland, with supplements of about NZ$100–$150 for departures from Christchurch or Wellington. **United Airlines** and **Air New Zealand** offer good deals on trans-Pacific routes, while travellers wishing to fly via Asia should try **Singapore** and **JAL Japan Airlines** for special deals. Flights begin at about NZ $2,000 in low season, rising to NZ$2,500–$3,000 in peak season.

AIRLINES

Scheduled airlines running frequent services from cities in New Zealand to California include:

- **Air New Zealand**: ☎ (09) 357-3000. Website: www.airnz.co.nz
- **Cathay Pacific**: ☎ (09) 379-0861. Website: www.cathaypacific.com
- **Delta Airlines**: ☎ (09) 379-3370. Website: www.delta.com
- **Garuda Indonesia**: ☎ (09) 366-1855. Website: www.garuda-indonesia.com
- **JAL Japan Air**: ☎ (09) 379-9906. Website: www.japanair.com
- **Singapore Air**: ☎ (09) 303-2129 or 0800-808-909. Website: www.singaporeair.com
- **United Airlines**: ☎ (09) 379-3800. Website: www.ual.com

SPECIALIST AND DISCOUNT TRAVEL AGENCIES

- **Auckland Flight Centre**: 205 Queen Street, Auckland. ☎ (09) 309-6171.
- **Destinations Unlimited**: 3 Milford Road, Auckland. ☎ (09) 377-7999.
- **STA Travel**: Travellers' Centre, 10 High Street, Auckland. ☎ (09) 309-0458. Website: www.statravel.com.au

ROUND-THE-WORLD TICKETS

A variety of airlines offer round-the-world tickets in partnership with other airlines. The 'Global Explorer Pass' from **Qantas** and partner airlines allows up to 16 stops in countries that they fly to (depending on mileage). There are different passes and prices, depending on where you want to fly to and whether you are travelling during the peak or off-peak season. Prices begin at about NZ $2,400 plus tax in low season and NZ$2,800 plus tax in high season.

For more information, check the website www.qantas.com, contact your travel agent or your local **Qantas** office.

- **Qantas**: Qantas House, 191 Queen Street, Auckland. ☎ (09) 357-8900.

FROM SOUTH AFRICA

Travellers from South Africa will find frequent flights to the US from Johannesburg and Cape Town. Flights to the West Coast of the US are less frequent than to the East Coast but there are good connecting flights available, so you may find it cheaper and easier to fly to an East Coast US destination first and then fly on from there. Flights from Johannesburg to San Francisco start at about $2,000 and from Johannesburg to New York at about $1,500. **American Airlines** and **South African Airways** run the most services while **STA Travel** is a source of good deals for students and young travellers.

- **American Airlines**: ☎ 1-800-433-7300. Website: www.aa.com
- **South African Airways**: ☎ (11) 978-1000. Website: www.saa.co.za
- **STA Travel**: 27A Mutual Square, Cradock Road, Rosebank, Johannesburg 2196. ☎ (11) 447-5414. Website: www.statravel.co.za

GENERAL INFORMATION

ACCOMMODATION

Americans are very hospitable. If you make friends with someone, it's not unknown to be loaned an apartment for the weekend. If you are a newly-married couple, be sure to say so as soon as possible as the Americans believe in treating honeymooners with the greatest care and attention.

You can find discount coupons for hotels and motels in some of the free newspapers. You can get *Traveler Discount Guides* either at a Visitors' Center, a newsagent, or a hotel. But in general you'll need to make reservations in advance.

The cost of breakfast is almost never included in the charge for a room, and very few hotels offer it.

Everything is subject to negotiation, especially the price of a room. Hotels frequently offer reductions, especially if you arrive at the close of the day. Remember to ask if they give a discount for cash.

In tourist areas, it is advisable to make your hotel reservations as far in advance as possible. Be ready to give your credit card details, and don't forget that if you decide not to take the room, you'll be charged all the same.

THE YMCA AND YWCA

The **YMCA** (for men) and **YWCA** (for women) charge very variable prices. You have to be a member of the relevant association (*see below* for addresses). The YMCA is relatively expensive, and charges in California can easily reach $42 in San Francisco and $55 in Los Angeles. There are some cheaper dormitories where you can expect to pay $20–$25, but these are increasingly rare. In Hollywood you might pay about $22. The YMCA is usually mixed, whereas the YWCA is always for females only.

A 'Y' is usually very centrally located. Many students, young local people and itinerant workers stay there, so this is a fast, certain way to learn about the city. The only problem with a 'Y' is that they are often full up, especially at weekends. Make your reservation before leaving the last place or as soon as you arrive in town, or try turning up around 11am, which is check-out time. You will then be in with a chance of getting one of the few rooms being vacated. In many smaller towns, if there's no more room at the 'Y' you can always go to a downtown hotel. These are sometimes cheaper than the 'Y', but might not be quite as clean.

Website: www.ymcausa.net

YOUTH HOSTELS

There are almost 200 youth hostels in the US, under the name of Hostelling International American Youth Hostels (or just plain Hostelling International). They are located in most of the big cities (including San Francisco, Los Angeles, San Diego and Phoenix) and some are out of town, sometimes in superbly renovated historic buildings.

The youth hostels have recently brought in preferential rates known as 'family specials', which apply in more than 100 establishments. In most big-city hostels, it's possible to reserve a bed by telephone or fax up to six months in advance, using your credit card. There's a charge of $2. For reservations in the US, call ☎ (202) 783-6161.

Reservations can also be made by calling the hostel direct, 7am–10am or 5pm–10pm. However, reservations will only be held until 10pm on the night you plan to arrive. If you fail to show up, you will still be charged for the room.

To make a reservation from Britain, call the International Booking Network (IBN) on ☎ (01629) 581418.

Hostelling International American Youth Hostels in the US

AYHI: 733 15th Street NW, Suite 840, Washington, D.C. 20005. ☎ (202) 783-6161. Website: www.hiayh.org

In the UK, the International Youth Hostel Handbook provides a complete list of hostels. A year's membership costs £12, which is about £5 cheaper than joining in America.

International Youth Hostel / Youth Hostel Association offices

England and Wales: Trevelyan House, 8 St Stephen's Hill, St Albans AL1 2DY (relocating to Matlock, Derbyshire in June 2001). ☎ (0870) 870 8808 (number will remain the same). E-mail: customerservices@yha.org.uk. Website: www.yha.org.uk

Scotland: 7 Glebe Crescent, Stirling FK8 2JA. ☎ (01786) 891400. Website: www.syha.org.uk

Republic of Ireland: An Oige, 61 Mountjoy Street, Dublin 7. ☎ (01) 830 4555. Website: www.irelandyha.org

Australia: Level 3, 10 Mallet Street, Camperdown, NSW 2050. ☎ (02) 9565-1699. Website: www.yha.org.au

New Zealand: PO Box 436, Christchurch. ☎ (03) 379-9970. Website: www.yha.org.nz

Canada: Hostelling International, 205 Catherine Street, Suite 400, Ottawa K2P 1C3. ☎ (613) 237-7884. Website: www.hostellingintl.ca

South Africa: Hostelling International, PO Box 4402, Cape Town 8001. ☎ (21) 424-2511. Website: hisa.org.za

In parallel with the youth hostels run by the official federation, Hostelling International, there is also the **American Association of Independent Hostels**. The advantage of the hostels belonging to this association is that they are open all day, so you aren't turned out between 10am and 4pm.

UNIVERSITIES

Halls of residence are run by colleges and universities. Foreign students can be accommodated during term-time, but this option is not always available. Contact each university direct.

CAMPGROUNDS

These are usually located close to tourist spots. They are cheap and quite well fitted out. You may find *Woodall's Camping Guide* useful, although backpackers will prefer to do without it as it's heavy! Once you're in America you can make reservations to camp in the national parks on freephone: ☎ 1-800-365-CAMP. You can book up to eight weeks in advance.

Some tour operators offer particularly well thought-out itineraries for camping tours. For suggested addresses *see* 'Getting There'.

Camping is possibly the best way to see America. Situated right in the middle of the countryside, campgrounds are nothing like what you get in Europe, and are usually vastly superior. The saving you'll make on the cost of accommodation will allow you to pay for a car, if you are in a group. In any case, it's virtually essential to have one in order to enjoy a camping tour. The locations involved are often difficult to reach by public transport. Some trailer parks don't accept tents.

There are two kinds of campgrounds:

NATIONAL AND STATE CAMPGROUNDS

These are the cheapest. You'll find them everywhere in the national parks, national monuments, national recreation areas, national forests and state parks. In national campgrounds you usually have to drop an envelope containing a few dollars in an urn, putting your name and address and the registration number of your car on the envelope. It's possible that you won't see anyone checking whether or not you have paid, because the US Constitution is based on honour and trust. Apart from being cheap, campgrounds are mostly situated in the nicest places, generally wooded.

The space between tents is very large as a rule, so if you make a noise you won't disturb everyone else. Each pitch has a table and a barbecue. There are always washbasins, but not always showers. Arrive between 10am and noon to reserve your location in the national parks. Remember to do your shopping in a supermarket before entering the park. Shops are either rare or quite expensive, and are not well stocked. And don't forget to take warm clothing. Many parks are at a high altitude, and even in September there can be an overnight frost.

In summer the campgrounds are often full, but it's still worth trying your luck as bookings are often made in the morning that are not taken up later on. A site at a national park campground costs on average $10–$20 per tent per night.

Destinet Reservation Center handles advance bookings for campgrounds in California, although not all the campgrounds in this state are hooked up with Destinet. Only some campgrounds are connected, especially those situated in the state parks. You pay by credit card, quoting your number over the telephone. This system is swamped with calls in summer, so try calling in the middle of the day, or mid-week. It's a freephone number: ☎ 1-800-444-7275. Open 8am-5pm (Pacific Time), seven days a week. Website: www.destinet.com

PRIVATE CAMPGROUNDS

These offer a certain number of convenient features, such as running water, electricity and sanitary facilities, as well as picnic tables and barbecue grills. There are also chains of campgrounds, such as KOA (Campgrounds of America), which are very luxuriously equipped with services without being all that expensive. They have space for caravans and campers, and offer washing-machines, self-service grocery stores, showers, amusement areas for children, picnic tables and even swimming pools. KOA publishes a brochure (available at all its sites) that lists all its sites, their exact locations in all the states, and a roadmap. Ask also for a membership card, which gets you a 10 per cent reduction.

Clearly, private campgrounds are superbly equipped, which is not always the case with government campgrounds. The prices reflect this fact: $13–$20 for two people in a KOA, which is a lot more expensive than a government campground.

BUS TERMINALS

It's still possible to sleep at bus terminals, especially if you arrive by bus in the middle of the night. It's not exactly peaceful, but it's useful if you're hard up and it's permitted on condition that you have a bus ticket. Many backpackers travel by Greyhound, whose terminals are supervised at night, and there are machines providing drinks and snacks. You'll see some strange people there, though. The chairs in these terminals often incorporate a TV set – pleasant if you can't sleep, but not terribly practical as a pillow. It's worth pointing out that bus stations are frequently situated in less salubrious parts of town, so it's often better to sleep in the station than take the risk of looking for a hotel in the surrounding area. If you're hoping to sleep in a terminal, it's wise to spend a few dollars on storing your belongings in the left-luggage, as too many people wake up in the morning to find they don't have much left.

Don't trust people who offer you accommodation in places such as bus terminals that are heavily frequented by tourists. They might just be members of some cult or other looking for new recruits.

MOTELS

These are useful in that you can take a single room and accommodate several people there, provided you don't draw too much attention to yourselves. Often located near a road or freeway, they are usually fairly anonymous and are open 24 hours a day. The two biggest chains of hotels and motels in the US are Holiday Inn and Howard Johnson (although the latter is mainly on the East Coast). Some of these hotels offer a reduction called 'Freedom USA', as long as you reserve several months in advance.

There are also chains of bargain motels: **Econo-Lodge** (mainly on the

East Coast) and **Motel 6** (mainly on the West Coast, particularly in California) are the least expensive. Most have a swimming pool, colour TV (films are available in the rooms), air-conditioning, private toilets, guarded parking, etc. Local calls and parking are free.

– **Motel 6** is a good bet. At the first one that you reach, ask for the Motel 6 directory of the US, as their establishments provide excellent value for money. Prices range from $24–$89 plus tax for one person, with a supplement of about $6 for each additional person (under 18s are free).

There are more than 750 Motel 6 establishments in the US, 250 of them in California and 40 in Florida. Situated on the outskirts of town (and thus quieter) and on main highways, they are easy to spot and access to them is very easy. For information and reservations: ☎ (423) 893-6481. Freephone: ☎ 1-800-466-8356. Fax: (423) 893-6482. Website: www.motel6.com

– **Econo-Lodge** is represented in London by Choice Hotel-International. There is a free number for reservations: ☎ (0800) 912424. Fax: (0207) 808 5601. Website: www.choicehotelseurope.com

These bargain motels, which are often more comfortable than hotels in the same category, have only one drawback. They are usually nowhere near the city centre.

• **Useful to know**

– **To get yourself back on form**: whenever you are exhausted, give yourself a night in a motel with a jacuzzi, a sauna, and washing and drying machines to take care of the laundry. It'll put new life into you!

– **Breakfast**: remember that this is rarely included in the price.

– **Phonecalls**: making telephone calls from a hotel costs more than phoning from a call-box or an office. When checking-in at most hotels, you have to pay the receptionist a deposit to cover any calls you may make from your room. This deposit may be payable in cash ($10 or $20). Usually, the receptionist will copy your credit card for security (in case you leave without paying for your calls). If you've made calls from your room, the charges for them will then be debited from your account. Remember when leaving to ask the receptionist to tear up the photocopy in your presence if you haven't made any calls.

Motel 6 establishments now sell prepaid cards bearing a code. These phonecards are sold at reception.

– **Negotiate**: always ask for a discount, especially if the hotel isn't full. Americans often do this and the manager won't mind, even though he may turn you down. It's much easier to negotiate after 9pm.

– **Check-out time**: finally, watch your check-out time, which is generally noon. If you haven't gone by that time you'll have to pay for another night.

– **On the highways**: be careful when using the rest areas on the highways. They're sometimes dangerous at night, so be sure to sleep in a locked vehicle. Next day, you'll be able to make good use of the toilet and washbasin facilities of the service stations.

- **Hotel terminology**

– *Single*:	single room
– *Double twin*:	room with two beds
– *Double queen*:	room with a double bed
– *Double king*:	room with a big double bed
– *European plan*:	room only
– *American plan*:	full-board
– *Modified American plan*:	half-board

RENTING AN APARTMENT

Many people at university sublet their apartments when they go off on holiday. The period varies widely, from three weeks to three months or more. You'll find advertisements in universities, usually under the heading 'Sublet'. Don't expect a great bargain, because it can be expensive. If you are in a group, however, this approach may be worthwhile.

Another useful arrangement is to look for advertisements for 'roommates', where you share an apartment with other students, paying a fairly low rent. Most likely to be a possibility in summer. This is also a good way to meet Americans.

BUDGET

It's difficult to make a decent budget forecast in a country as huge as this. However, there are always ways to make economies, whether it's on accommodation, food or transport.

– The first unknown is the exchange rate for the dollar. When planning your trip in March for departure in July, you can't predict the rate of exchange. In general, you should remember that the cost of living is lower in the US than in Britain. With the dollar converted at its 'normal' rate, i.e. around 60p sterling, this soon becomes obvious: a bed in a youth hostel, for example, costs $12–$15, a hamburger and fries $5 and a bus ticket $1, while petrol is two or three times cheaper than in Britain.

– **Mode of transport**: think carefully here. The size of your group, the cost and where you want to go are all important factors. For example, if there are four or five of you and you want to visit the national parks, a car is indispensable and will save you an awful lot of time and money. If there are two of you and you want to see the major cities only, a car is less relevant. You can use a plane or bus for long distances and local transport in the cities.

– **Accommodation**: it's difficult to quote an average figure. Tourists travelling by camper or car who camp in the national parks are pleasantly surprised by the low cost ($12–$15 for the pitch) and if you want to sleep in motels and hotels, you'll have to pay between $40 and $60 a night (for two), without breakfast. The different types of accommodation fall into the following approximate price bands:

- Extra Budget: up to $20 (single room)
- Budget: $20–$40 (double room)
- Moderate: $40–$90
- Expensive: over $90

– **Spending money on leisure**: Be aware of hidden extra costs, however. How, on a pleasant summer's afternoon, can you resist the call of the 'Big Splash'? It'll cost you $10–$15. If you pass through Las Vegas, even with the disdainful air of an intellectual who has only come 'to analyse the decadence of a bankrupt model', how will you be able to resist slipping a few coins into the slot machine? Allow at least $10! And that's before you even think about the museums, the galleries or the nightclubs. So, don't forget about all those extra little pleasures when preparing the budget for your trip.

– **Estimated overall budget**: excluding international flights, you can expect to spend on average a budget of £30 per day per person. This means £600 per person for 20 days, as long as you don't go too mad. If you could start off with £700 for the same period, you would have more of a margin. If you are a grass-roots nomad, or just a student, with very limited funds at your disposal, plan for about £15 per day – but not less.

CLIMATE

Due to the vastness of the territory, the climate varies a great deal. San Francisco experiences small variations in temperature from one season to another, frequent rainfall in winter and a fine general level of sunshine from April to September. The famous morning mist can be present all year round. In southern California the climate is more Mediterranean, with mild winters and dry, hot summers. On the West Coast, the sea barely reaches 66°F (19°C) even in the height of summer in Los Angeles and only 61°F (16°C) in San Francisco. To the northwest of Los Angeles, in the desert regions, the summer heat is overwhelming. It's best to visit Death Valley in autumn or spring. In Arizona, the summer temperatures are incredibly hot, but made bearable by the low humidity.

If you're visiting the national parks, you need to take care for several reasons. You'll need to take water, sunglasses and a hat, and cover yourself with a high-factor sunblock. It's extremely hot out there and you run a serious risk of sunstroke and/or dehydration if you don't take the proper precautions. At the other extreme, you should also carry a woollen sweater in winter, because the temperature drops very low on account of the altitude, and snow is common. In any event, get information before setting out, as some of the national parks are closed in winter.

– **Weather information**: ☎ 1-900-WEATHER. Useful when planning your driving or walking itinerary. Website: www.cnn.com/WEATHER/index.html

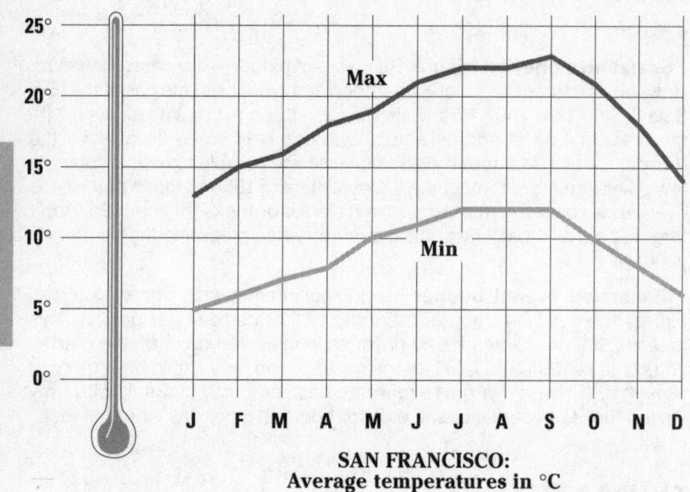

SAN FRANCISCO:
Average temperatures in °C

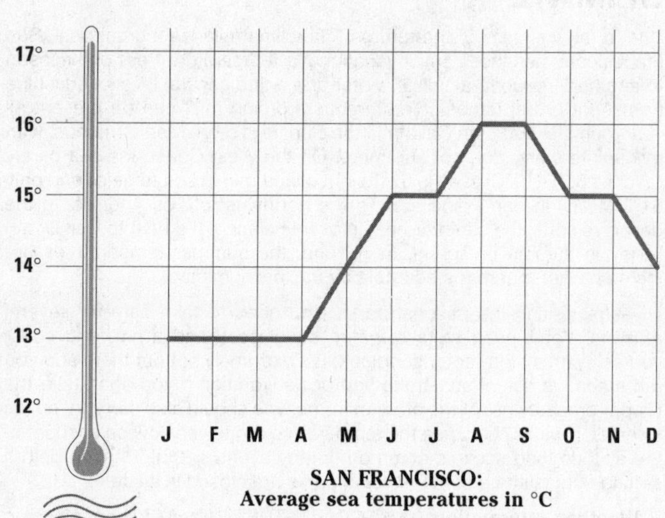

SAN FRANCISCO:
Average sea temperatures in °C

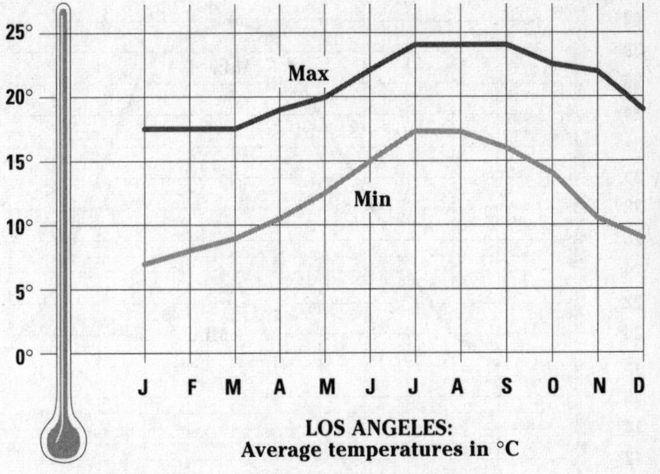

LOS ANGELES:
Average temperatures in °C

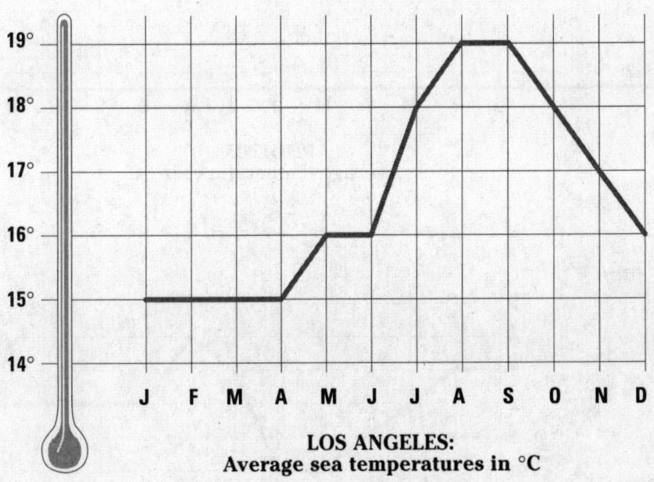

LOS ANGELES:
Average sea temperatures in °C

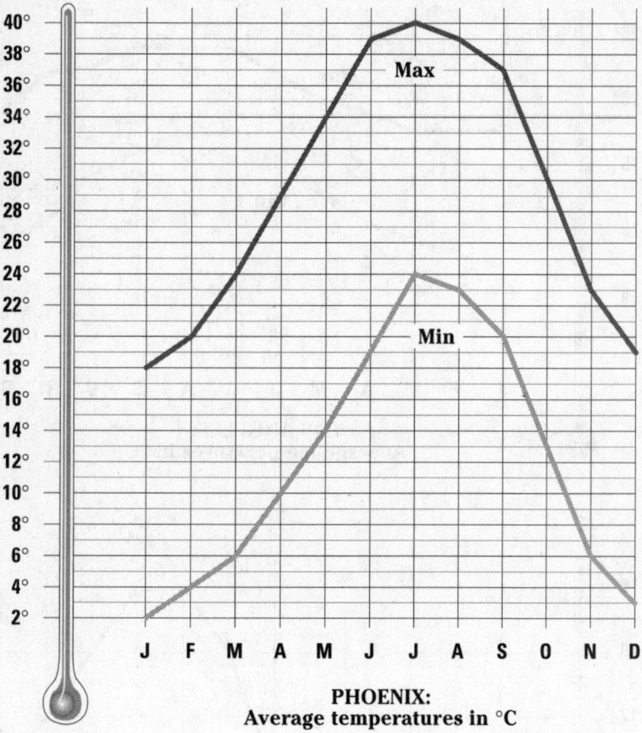

40°
38°
36°
34°
32°
30°
28°
26°
24°
22°
20°
18°
16°
14°
12°
10°
8°
6°
4°
2°
Max
Min
J F M A M J J A S O N D

PHOENIX:
Average temperatures in °C

5
4
3
2
1
0
DAYS
J F M A M J J A S O N D

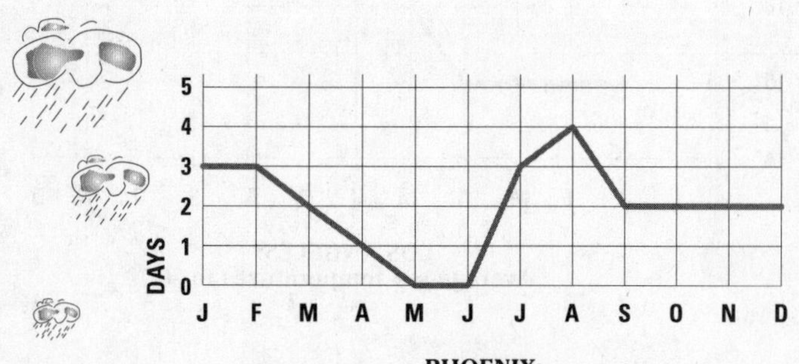

PHOENIX:
Number of rainy days

COMMUNICATIONS

POSTAL SERVICES

You can have your letters sent to the main post office in each city ('**poste restante**' is known in America as 'general delivery'). Envelopes should be addressed as: John Smith, General Delivery, Main Post Office, City, State, Zipcode. Alternatively, you can get your mail sent to American Express. The post office won't always keep your mail for longer than the legal maximum of 10 days.

Watch out when buying **stamps**. You can get them at post office (US Mail) counters, but buying from stamp machines will cost twice as much.

Post offices are open Monday–Friday 8am–5pm and on Saturday mornings for the sale of stamps and the handing in of letters and packages. They are not responsible for sending telegrams: this is the job of private companies.

USING THE TELEPHONE

CALLING THE US FROM ABROAD

First dial the international access code, followed by **1** (US country code), followed by the area code (omitting any initial zero), followed by the number. International access codes are:

From the UK: ☎ 00
From the Republic of Ireland: ☎ 00
From Canada: ☎ 011
From Australia: ☎ 0011
From New Zealand: ☎ 00
From South Africa: ☎ 09

CALLING ABROAD FROM THE US

Dial **011** followed by the country code, followed by the local area code (omitting any initial zero), followed by the number. The country codes are:

UK: ☎ 44
Republic of Ireland: ☎ 353
Canada: ☎ 1
Australia: ☎ 61
New Zealand: ☎ 64
South Africa: ☎ 27

CALLING FROM WITHIN CALIFORNIA

If you are dialling within California and you are unsure of the area code, call freephone ☎ 1-800-310 2535 for assistance from the Pacific Bell operator.

CALLING ANOTHER STATE

Dial **1** followed by the local area code followed by the number.

Local area codes (California):

Los Angeles: ☎ 213
Hollywood / East LA: ☎ 323
West LA: ☎ 310
East LA: ☎ 562
Pasadena / San Gabriel: ☎ 626
Burbank / San Fernando Valley: ☎ 818
Northern Orange County: ☎ 714
Southern Orange County: ☎ 949
San Bernardino / Riverside: ☎ 909
San Diego: ☎ 619
South-eastern California: ☎ 760
Santa Barbara / San Luis Obispo: ☎ 805
Monterey / Big Sur: ☎ 831
San Francisco / Marin County: ☎ 415
East Bay: ☎ 510
The Peninsula: ☎ 650
San Jose: ☎ 408
Wine Country: ☎ 707
Sacramento: ☎ 916
Gold Country: ☎ 209
Lake Tahoe / Northeastern California: ☎ 530

Local area codes (Nevada):

Las Vegas: ☎ 702

Local area codes (Arizona):
Phoenix: ☎ 602
Tucson / Bisbee / Tombstone: ☎ 520
Flagstaff: ☎ 520

Phoning home or even the US from a telephone box in the US is something of an ordeal unless you have a telephone card. Most telephone companies won't accept credit cards, while chip cards have yet to make an appearance in the US and hotels charge exorbitant amounts. This leaves you with only the reverse-charge (a 'collect call' in America) option.

One private telephone company has set up a system that will give you access to reduced American rates, using only your dialling finger and your credit card. The principle is simple – the company buys extremely large quantities of telephone minutes from the Big Three on the American market, thus obtaining ultra-low rates that it can then re-sell at very low prices. Just dial freephone: ☎ 1-800-232-6775 when you reach the US and the operator will tell you everything you need to know. Payment is by credit card.

USEFUL TIPS

– Information about **overseas calls**: ☎ **0-0** (a freephone number).

– The national telephone network is divided up into areas and to make a call from one area to another you have to dial **1** followed by the area code. Every area has an operator. So dialling **0** in one area won't get you information about subscribers in a different one. If you need information about another area, dial **1**, followed by the appropriate area code, followed by **0**.

– **Make maximum use of the telephone**: it'll save you a lot of time. If, for example, you get lost or dead drunk, just go into a telephone box and dial **0**: the operator will be able to tell you where you are! Look in the front of Yellow Pages and you'll find interesting information about transport (domestic and international), parks, sites of interest, museums, theatres, etc.

– **Use your home telephone chargecard**. In Britain, it is best to get a free BT Chargecard, which you can use to charge all calls made overseas to your home account. Call ☎ **150** for a card / further information.

In Australia, get a Telstra Telecard (☎ 1-800-626-008) or an Optus Calling Card (☎ 1300-300-300).

In New Zealand, get a New Zealand Telecom Calling Card. ☎ (04) 382-5818.

– **Use prepaid phonecards**: the use of coins to make calls from telephone boxes is being replaced by the system of prepaid phonecards, which are on sale more or less everywhere (shops, hotel reception desks, etc.) at various prices. The Motel 6 chain also issues its own prepaid phonecards at its reception desks. A guest can use the card to make local or international calls from the room at any time. There is a confidential code number recorded on the card, which has to be entered before a number can be dialled. The amount of credit left on the card is displayed automatically.

It's worth knowing that American phonecards don't incorporate electronic chips, so this can slow them down a bit.

– **Telekey card**: this is a very useful phonecard (one of many) letting you make calls very easily and cheaply to any part of the US, without cash and without a credit card. You can also extend your local credit by quoting your bank card number. It has one big plus: wherever you may be in the US, the Telekey card will let you receive telephone calls by dialling a freephone number.

– **Freephone calls**: all telephone numbers beginning with **1-800** are free and are generally provided by airlines, hotel chains, car-hire companies, etc. In America they are known as 'call-free' or 'toll-free' numbers – always ask whether there is one available, because it will save you money whenever you want to make a hotel reservation or get information (most tourist offices have a freephone number). If you telephone someone in a different state (or in Canada), remember to precede the number with **1**.

Be aware that the freephone numbers given out by smaller companies often work only within the same state. Freephone numbers are never free if you're making an international call.

TELEGRAMS

Western Union send telegrams. These take about eight hours to reach Europe. Look up Western Union in the telephone book, and choose the service you need. They can send money across the world for you too.

In general, Americans don't send many telegrams because long-distance telephone charges are not very high, especially at night and during the weekend.

ELECTRICAL SUPPLY

The electrical supply in the US is generally 110–115 volts, 60 Hz (in Britain it's 50 Hz). In the US, plugs have two flat pins. Buy an adaptor before you leave your country as they are hard to find in the US. Similarly, if you buy electrical devices, get a European adaptor at the same time. Otherwise, you may not be able to use whatever you buy for some time!

EMBASSIES AND CONSULATES

FOREIGN CONSULATES

United Kingdom: 1 Sansome Street, Suite 850, San Francisco, CA 94104. ☎ (415) 981-3030. Fax: (415) 434-2018. 1176 Wilshire Boulevard, Suite 400, Los Angeles, CA 90025. ☎ (310) 477-3322. Fax: (310) 575-1450.

Republic of Ireland: 44 Montgomery Street, Suite 3830, San Francisco, CA 94104. ☎ (415) 392-4214. Fax: (415) 392-0885.

Canada: 550 South Hope Street, 9th Floor, Los Angeles, CA 90071. ☎ (213) 346-2700. Fax: (213) 620-8827.

Australia: 7th Floor, 1 Bush Street, San Francisco, CA 94104-4413. ☎ (415) 362-6160. Fax: (415) 986-2775. Level 19, Century Plaza Towers, 2049 Century Park East, Los Angeles, CA 90067. ☎ (310) 229-4800. Fax: (310) 277-2258.

New Zealand: 12400 Wilshire Boulevard, Suite 1150, Los Angeles, CA 90025. ☎ (310) 207-1605. Fax: (310) 207-3605.

South Africa: 6300 Wilshire Boulevard, Suite 600, Los Angeles, CA 90048. ☎ (323) 651-0902. Fax: (323) 651-5969.

US EMBASSIES AND CONSULATES ABROAD

In the United Kingdom: 24 Grosvenor Square, London W1A 1AE. ☎ (020) 7499 9000. Fax: (020) 7409 1637.

In the Republic of Ireland: 42 Elgin Road, Dublin 4. ☎ (01) 668 8777. Fax: (01) 668 9946.

In Canada: 490 Sussex Drive, Ottawa, Ontario, K1N 1G8. ☎ (613) 238-5335. Fax: (613) 233-8511. PO Box 65, Postal Station Desjardins, Montreal, Quebec, H5B 1G1. ☎ (514) 398-9695. Fax: (514) 398-0973. 360 University Avenue, Toronto, Ontario, M5G 1S4. ☎ (416) 595-1700. Fax: (416) 595-0051.

In Australia: Moonah Place, Yarralumla, Canberra, ACT 2600. ☎ (02) 6214-5600. Fax: (02) 6214-5970; 553 St Kilda Road, Melbourne, Victoria 3004. ☎ (03) 9526-5900. Fax: (03) 9525-0769; MLC Centre, Level 59, 19–29 Martin Place, Sydney, NSW 2000. ☎ (02) 9373-9200.

In New Zealand: 29 Fitzherbert Terrace, Thorndon, Wellington. ☎ (04) 472-2068.

In South Africa: 877 Pretorius Street, Arcadia 0083, Pretoria. ☎ (12) 342-3006. Fax: (12) 342-2299; 1 River St, Killarney, Johannesburg. ☎ (11) 644-8000. Fax: (11) 646-6913; 7th Floor, Monte Carlo Building, Adderley Street, Cape Town. ☎ (21) 421-4351. Fax: (21) 425-3014.

ENTRY FORMALITIES

VISAS

The US was once notorious among travellers for complicated visa procedures and queues at immigration. However, the authorities have since made changes and travellers from outside the US should find the entry procedures reasonably straightforward.

Canadian citizens can enter the US without a passport, although it's a good idea to take it if you're travelling as far as California. If you're intending to stay for longer than 90 days, you'll need to apply for a visa from your nearest embassy or consulate and if you're intending to work in the US then you'll need the correct papers (*see* 'Working in the US').

Citizens of the **UK**, the **Republic of Ireland**, **Australia** and **New Zealand** may enter the US without a visa under a reciprocal visa-waiver scheme. To be eligible for this exemption, you must have a full, valid passport from your home country, a return ticket that is non-refundable and your stay must not last longer than 90 days. If you are intending to stay for longer than 90 days, or to work or study in the US, you must apply to the US Embassy in your home country (*see* 'Embassies and Consulates'). The rules governing different visas can be complex, especially for those wishing to work, so it's advisable to apply as far in advance as possible. In the UK, call ☎ (0891) 200290 in the first instance.

South African citizens were not included under the visa-waiver scheme at the time of writing. You'll need to contact your embassy or nearest consulate for a tourist visa, for which you'll require a passport that is valid for longer than six months and passport photographs. There are different visas for different types of stay and the lengths of time and the conditions are determined by US immigration authorities. One of the most common visas issued to citizens of South Africa and countries excluded by the visa-waiver scheme is a tourist multiple-entry visa, which is valid for a year or longer.

If you wish to stay for longer than 90 days or change your existing visa once you are in the US, then apply to your local INS (Immigration and Naturalization Service) office. Look in the local white pages telephone directory under US Government or call freephone ☎ 1-800-375-5283 for the nearest office. It's best to contact them as far in advance as possible, as the authorities will not look too kindly on you if you apply on or after the date stamped on your passport and you will probably have to provide evidence of funds at the very least.

If you are going to the US to work or study and you have a confirmed offer of a job or place in an educational institution, your visa requirements should be handled by the company or establishment concerned and you should contact them if you are concerned about your visa. If you are applying to work without a company to sponsor you or relatives in the US (including parents or children aged over 21), you'll have a difficult time convincing the INS to issue you with a visa.

IMMIGRATION

US immigration officials are some of the toughest in the world, so be prepared to answer a lot of questions if you're coming in for anything more than a two-week package stay. Those travelling on a one-way flight may have particular difficulties. Officials are looking for people who are intending to overstay or work illegally, so you may be asked about your plans and the money that you have with you. If you can show that you have about $400 for each week that you plan to stay in the US and a major credit card as well, you should have no problem. Don't over-emphasize friends or relations that you have in the US – this may persuade the official that you'll be tempted to stay. Travellers often find the East Coast immigration officers to be the most stringent (so beware if you are coming in via New York or another city on the East Coast). It may sound like a cliché, but being neat, polite and well dressed will encourage officials to look favourably on you. It might seem like an extra hassle to bring suitable clothing, but if you're not permitted entry, you'll have to buy a flight home on the spot – a considerably more expensive option in the long run.

The officials of the INS are also on the lookout for travellers with AIDS and tuberculosis. Being HIV-positive is not grounds for deportation, but it is grounds for 'exclusion' and officials may refuse you entry. You will not be tested on arrival, but if you answer 'yes' to the question on the immigration form 'Have you ever been afflicted with a communicable disease of public health significance' or you are carrying AIDS/HIV medicine, you will probably have to answer questions. Officials may also stop you if they think you look ill. If you are the spouse, parent, or child of a US citizen, or a Green Card holder, you cannot be excluded from entering the country on these grounds.

If you think that you may be prevented from entering for these or any other reasons, it's advisable to discuss your travelling plans with a qualified immigration lawyer. For information, contact:

The National Immigration Project of the National Lawyers Guild, 14 Beacon Street, Suite 602, Boston, MA 02108. ☎ (617) 227-9727. Fax: (617) 227-5495. Website: www.nlg.org

Immigration Legal Assistance Project, Los Angeles County Bar Association, 300 North Los Angeles Street, Room 3107, Los Angeles, CA 90012. ☎ (213) 485-1872. Website: www.lacba.org/community/ilap.html

CUSTOMS

All persons aged 21 and over are allowed to import one litre of spirits duty-free into the US. Those over 17 can bring in over 200 cigarettes. Non-US citizens are allowed to import $100 of gifts duty-free into the country. There is no legal restriction on money imported into the country, although large amounts will have to be declared. There are severe penalties for the import of illegal drugs and equipment that might be associated with drugs, so if you're taking any medicines that are even slightly different from the norm, it's worth taking a doctor's certificate with you, to avoid problems on immigration. Other items that will make you a candidate for deportation and possibly prosecution are illegal weapons and obscene publications. Lottery tickets, liqueur chocolates and pre-Columbian artefacts are also restricted.

US customs also prohibits the import of items from certain countries, and this varies according to worldwide diplomatic relations. If you're intending to carry anything with you from Iraq, Iran, Libya, North Korea and other countries with histories of diplomatic entanglements with the US, then you must contact your embassy or local consulate for assistance before departure. Relations with Cuba have improved significantly, but Cuban products can still be subject to restriction, especially cigars, so you should check this before departure.

Immigration officials are particularly strict on the import of fresh produce into California. You must dispose of any fruit, vegetables, bread and meat before entering the US. If in doubt about whether any gifts or other foods that you are taking with you constitute fresh produce, check with your embassy or consulate before leaving, or with customs officials on entry. If you come into California by road, you will be asked to surrender all fresh produce at special roadside stations.

Many travellers to California, Arizona and Nevada are tempted to pick up a few stones on their way, but doing so is not only ecologically unsound – it's also illegal. Customs officials don't look kindly on travellers they think are hoping to export objects from their national parks, even if they seem to come from areas that are not defined as protected. So – leave the Grand Canyon intact.

FESTIVALS – *SEE* 'PUBLIC HOLIDAYS AND FESTIVALS'

HEALTH

For medical emergencies: ☎ **911**.

The healthcare system is one of the most expensive in the world and it's therefore imperative to take out health insurance to cover you if anything does go wrong. Travel agents will usually advise you to buy the most expensive policy to cover US healthcare costs. *See* also 'Insurance'.

HAZARDS

California, Arizona and Nevada are not destinations that pose any particular hazard to personal health. However, there are a few things that you need to keep in mind.

Always be particularly careful of the strong **sun**. Use a high-factor sunblock and try to wear a hat and cover up your arms and shoulders. In Arizona and Nevada you should be particularly careful of **heat**

exhaustion and heatstroke. Drink plenty of water, watch your alcohol intake, carry water bottles on all walking trips and be careful of exercising too strenuously. Heatstroke, which occurs when the body's temperature reaches highly dangerous levels, must be treated in hospital. The best immediate treatment is to take the sufferer out of the sun, remove clothing, cover with a wet towel and fan continually.

The desert can get very cold at night and you should ensure that you have sufficient warm clothing and a good sleeping bag in order to avoid **hypothermia**. If this occurs, you should remove wet clothing, get near a fire or into a warm bath (if possible) and take hot liquids and high-energy foods such as chocolate or dried fruit. Do not give alcohol or rub anyone with hypothermia.

The air quality can be poor and **pollution levels** can be high in Californian cities, and asthma sufferers should be particularly careful in Los Angeles, where smog is a big problem.

Although most travellers don't get to altitudes that are high enough to risk severe **altitude sickness**, if you are going hiking in the mountains you should drink plenty of water, avoid alcohol and come back down again if symptoms such as headaches, sickness, fatigue and / or shortness of breath persist.

There are plenty of **poisonous animals and reptiles** in the desert (and in built-up areas as well), although most will not bite if left alone. The species of scorpions and spiders that live in the desert are not deadly, and their bites, although painful, will not cause any long-term damage to adults. If you are bitten, seek medical advice as soon as possible. There are rattlesnakes in the West Coast states, so watch where you step. Although their bite is very painful, it is rarely fatal as long as you seek medical help.

Bears are highly dangerous, of course. Anyone camping in the national parks should take care to keep food in bear-proof containers and away from the tent and car.

The deserts may seem potentially full of hazards, but if you're sensible about your limits you should avoid climate-related conditions and if you're careful about disturbing animals and their habitats, you should escape any serious bites or stings. Mosquitoes are more than just a nuisance. A great number of repellent sprays, creams and lotions sold in chain stores and even in pharmacies have very little or, indeed, no effect. According to specialists, the most effective products contain either 50 per cent DEET or 35/35. These are ingredients, not commercial names. Whatever you use, treat the exposed parts of the body at intervals of not more than four hours.

ID

Remember that you'll need proof of age to purchase alcohol in California, Arizona and Nevada (the legal age is 21), so it's worth taking some sort of photo ID with you to save you from having to take your passport with you on trips to clubs or bars.

Apart from the International Driving Permit (*see* 'Driving Licence' under

'Transportation') it's a good idea to take an International Student Identity Card (ISIC) or International Youth Travel Card, which not only gives you a photo ID but will also get you all kinds of discounts and advantages, both before you leave and once you're abroad.

Cards are arranged by the International Student Travel Confederation. Check out their website: www.istc.org for details.

INSURANCE

If you are travelling from abroad it is advisable to take out comprehensive travel insurance before visiting America, particularly as there is no public health service in the US. However, if you have house contents insurance, it is worth checking exactly what this covers as many policies now cover items lost when travelling. Likewise, many credit card companies offer some degree of travel insurance, particularly if you use their credit card to pay for the holiday.

Always check the small print to see exactly what your insurance policy covers, particularly if you are planning to take part in activities such as skiing, watersports, riding, etc.

Travel agents can arrange holiday insurance or you can contact insurance companies directly. The **Travel Insurance Agency** is based in the UK but covers non-UK residents at no extra premium. ☎ (020) 8446 5414. E-mail: info@travelinsurers.com

Canadians are covered by their home province's health insurance plan for up to 90 days after leaving the country. In Australia, contact the **Australian Federation of Travel Agents** on ☎ (02) 9264-3299 (Sydney) or log onto their website: www.afta.com

MONEY, BANKS AND CURRENCY EXCHANGE

– **Coins** come in the following denominations: 1 cent (a penny), 5 cents (a nickel), 10 cents (a dime – smaller than the 5-cent coin), 25 cents (a quarter), 50 cents (a half-dollar).

– **Banknotes** all carry the portrait of a US president or major historical figure: $1 (George Washington), $5 (Abraham Lincoln), $10 (Alexander Hamilton), $20 (Andrew Jackson), $50 (Ulysses S. Grant), and $100 (Benjamin Franklin).

Be careful – the notes are all the same size and colour, so they're easy to mix up. To check that a dollar bill is genuine, slightly moisten the green side and rub it against a piece of paper. The green colour should fade slightly (try not to do this in a bank!). A dollar is often called a 'buck'. This word goes back to the days of the trappers, who sold the skins of deer (bucks) for dollars.

– A basic piece of advice is to keep most of your money in the form of **traveller's cheques**, because thieves operate in the US just like they do anywhere else. In the event of loss or theft, the banks will reimburse you fairly easily. Reimbursement will be much easier if you carry traveller's cheques from an American bank (First National, Chase Manhattan, American Express and Bank of America are the four biggest). Note, too, that you don't have to go to a bank to exchange them for cash, as you would in Europe. Most big shops, restaurants and motels will accept them.

It's a good idea to provide yourself with US dollar traveller's cheques in small denominations ($20 for example), as these are accepted everywhere in lieu of cash, even in shops. Before you leave, it's also a good idea to try to get some coins in fairly small denominations.

One way to get cash when the banks are closed is to buy a hamburger or something small with a traveller's cheque. You'll get your change in cash.

– When you get back home, the rate of exchange on traveller's cheques is usually better than on cash.

It's important to note that you have to buy your dollars before leaving, since few banks in the US will exchange foreign currency (an exception is the Bank of America). It's even difficult to get them to accept Canadian dollars.

– **Bank opening times** are generally Monday–Friday 9am–3.30pm. Many banks now have a drive-through facility, which will be open longer hours, opening earlier in the morning and closing later in the evening. Be aware that it is not always very easy to change cash at a bank.

– **Credit cards** are sometimes referred to as 'plastic money'. Some credit cards, such as Diners Club, are not widely accepted by shops even though they are American (perhaps because the providers take a hefty commission on every purchase). One of the most useful cards in the US is the international Visa card, and American Express is also very widely accepted.

Your credit card will also allow you draw a cash advance in a bank or directly from a cash dispenser (ATM). One potential advantage is that you are not debited for at least a week, at the exchange rate then prevailing, which is useful if the dollar falls in value. There will be a commission charged, though. If you draw money in a Banking Center, don't forget that there is a limit on your card. Once you overstep your limit, you won't even be able to draw money from a cash dispenser with your card.

If you pay by card in a restaurant, don't forget to fill in the service box and write the total at the bottom. If you leave it blank, the staff could fill in this box themselves, setting you up to pay a sizeable tip.

– Should you urgently need cash (having lost your tickets, traveller's cheques and / or credit cards, or had them stolen), you can be rescued in a few minutes by **Western Union Money Transfer**. Call freephone: ☎ 1-800-325-6000.

NATIONAL PARKS

The national parks include areas of sea, mountain, desert and forest. In some, heat is a permanent feature while other regions are renowned for their constant coolness. The extreme physical and climatic diversity of this country all through the year makes it a really wonderful place for excursions of all kinds.

The Americans are well aware of this and, to encourage people to enjoy it, they have designated dozens of parks, routes – even entire regions – that are something really special. The state authorities have set up rigorous ways of protecting their parks, and very strict rules are in place to prevent too many human depredations (there's even a $50 fine if you're caught gathering dead wood). The result is fabulous. Yosemite, for example, is a marvellous enclosed area of natural beauty.

Yet they have somehow managed to incorporate every conceivable facility into their rural accommodation in an unobtrusive way, so it's possible to spend a night in a cabin (with bath, shower, kitchenette, TV, etc.), or a tent or caravan. If you fancy spending a night in a national park in summer, you'd be wise either to make a reservation some way ahead or get there very early in the morning to get whatever accommodation becomes available.

– **Admission charges**: the average admission charge to national parks is $15 per vehicle (not per person). Yellowstone and Yosemite parks charge the most ($25). The cheapest park, Great Sand Dunes (Colorado), costs only $5 per vehicle. Some national monuments, such as the Canyon de Chelly in Arizona, make no charge at all.

– **Golden Eagle Pass**: this costs only $50 a year for a car and all its occupants. This pass, which you can buy at the park entrances, gives you unlimited access to all national parks, national monuments and other sites controlled by the parks administration (i.e. it is not accepted in state parks). Since taking a car into any one park costs an average of $15, your pass will soon pay for itself. It also entitles you to a 50 per cent reduction on the charge for a campground and on admission charges to leisure facilities.

– **Visitors' Centers**: there is a Visitors' Center in every nature reserve, where you can get a plan of the park, a huge range of topographical maps (for hikers, horse-riders, cyclists, etc.), superb postcards and splendid books. This is the first place you should make for on arrival. It's often also the point of departure for organized visits and is always a mine of information.

The website for American National Parks is useful: www.reservations.nps.gov. It gives plenty of information and admission charges, as well as handling bookings for accommodation and excursions. Travellers' cheques in dollars are accepted readily in shops and restaurants (even when made out for small amounts).

ACRONYMS EXPLAINED

NM	National Monument
NP	National Park
NHP	National Historic Park
NHS	National Historic Site
NRA	National Recreation Area

PUBLIC HOLIDAYS AND FESTIVALS

Public holidays can vary from one state to another, but the 10 public holidays listed below are celebrated throughout the country. Virtually all shops are closed on these days.

– **New Year's Day**: 1 January

– **Birthday of Martin Luther King Jr**: around the third Monday in January – whichever date is nearest to the actual birthday on 15 January

– **Presidents' Day**: the third Monday in February, in honour of past American presidents

– **Easter**: the Monday is a holiday

– **Memorial Day**: the last Monday in May. In memory of all who died in combat

– **Independence Day**: 4 July

– **Labor Day**: the first Monday in September

– **Columbus Day**: the second Monday in October

– **Thanksgiving**: the last Thursday in November

– **Christmas Day**: 25 December

Although it's not a holiday, **Halloween** also deserves a mention. Developed from a Druidic tradition brought over the America by the Irish and the Scots, the night between 31 October and 1 November is given over mainly to kids, who dress themselves up in any number of gruesome witch and ghost costumes to knock on people's doors and demand 'Trick or treat?'

As well as these national days, many towns in the American West like to celebrate with some kind of big parade. The visitors' centre in each city will have dates of all the parades each year.

– **Chinese New Year and Golden Parade** (Los Angeles and San Francisco, mid-February to early March): with parades, firework displays and Chinese dragons, this is the most important oriental festival.

– **St Patrick's Day** (San Francisco, the Sunday closest to 17 March): the beer flows freely in all the Irish bars.

– **Cherry Blossom** (San Francisco, early April): Japantown celebrates the flowering cherry trees.

– **Cinco de Mayo** (Los Angeles and San Francisco, 5 May): this is the biggest Mexican festival, with singing and dancing in the streets until the small hours.

– **Gay Pride Day** (San Francisco, late June): this is *the* gay festival, with fantastic processions and decorated floats. A real carnival atmosphere and good music are guaranteed.

– **International Surf Festival** (Los Angeles, end of July): gathering of all the West Coast surfing community, with their beautiful bodies!

– **California State Fair** (Sacramento, mid-August to early September): the usual round of cattle, pigs and horses, plus rodeo contests and other shows.

– **Wine and Craft** (Napa Valley, early September): California's vineyards on show, with free tasting of the best vintages.

– **Oktoberfest** (Torrance, September–October): beer festival rather like the *Oktoberfest* held in Munich.

– **International Festival of Masks** (Los Angeles, last Sunday in October): a big community celebration, with colourful parades and processions.

– **Dia de los Muertos** (San Francisco and Los Angeles, 2 November): a Mexican festival where the dead come back to visit their families.

– **Hollywood Christmas Parade** (Hollywood Boulevard and Sunset Boulevard, first Thursday after Thanksgiving): the biggest showbiz parade of the year, where local people and visitors get to rub shoulders with the stars.

SHOPPING

Some things are particularly worth shopping for in the US, as their prices can be 30–60 per cent lower than in Britain, but they can still vary enormously from one shop to the next. It's worth going to the out-of-town factory outlets (*see below*) and the malls, which are enormous shopping centres located outside towns, as prices can often be much better than in tourist areas.

Remember that all your purchases (including your hotel bills) will have the local tax added. This will range from zero to 15 per cent, depending on the state.

Here are some examples of possible bargains:

– cameras and photographic accessories

– Californian wines

– jeans (Levi 501s, naturally)

– Oshkosh B'Gosh overalls for kids. These prized fashion items are 60–70 per cent cheaper than in Europe

– anything made of leather, particularly footwear (including boots), as well as Nike trainers

– pushbutton telephones, cordless telephones, calculators

– answering machines – but don't forget to ask for a transformer that will fit your system at home

– CDs. Much cheaper than in Europe, especially second-hand ones

– Native American crafts – these are frequently beautiful, but almost always very expensive. It's best to buy from the Native Americans themselves. The goods you find in shops are usually imported (e.g. carpets from Mexico)

Be careful with the following:

– American sheets. Many tourists like to bring these home, as they're very unusual, but there can be a problem with the dimensions. Even the pillowcases won't necessarily fit your pillows, so check the sizes carefully

CONVERSION TABLES

Men's sizes

Shirts

UK	USA	EUROPE
14	14	36
14½	14½	37
15	15	38
15½	15½	39
16	16	41
16½	16½	42
17	17	43
17½	17½	44
18	18	46

Suits

UK	USA	EUROPE
36	36	46
38	38	48
40	40	50
42	42	52
44	44	54
46	46	56

Shoes

UK	USA	EUROPE
6	8	39
7	9	40
8	10	41
9	10.5	42
10	11	43
11	12	44
12	13	45

Women's sizes

Shirts/dresses

UK	USA	EUROPE
8	6	36
10	8	38
12	10	40
14	12	42
16	14	44
18	16	46

Sweaters

UK	USA	EUROPE
8	6	44
10	8	46
12	10	48
14	12	50
16	14	52

Shoes

UK	USA	EUROPE
3	5	36
4	6	37
5	7	38
6	8	39
7	9	40
8	10	41

Temperature

- To convert °C to °F, multiply by 1.8 and add 32.
- To convert °F to °C, subtract 32 and multiply by 5/9 (0.55). 0° C = 32° F

US weights and measures

1 centimetre	0.39 inches	1 inch	2.54 centimetres
1 metre	3.28 feet	1 foot	0.30 metres
1 metre	1.09 yards	1 yard	0.91 metres
1 kilometre	0.62 miles	1 mile	1.61 kilometres
1 hectare	2.47 acres	1 acre	0.40 hectares
1 litre	2.11 pints	1 pint	0.47 litres
1 litre	0.26 gallons	1 gallon	3.79 litres
1 gram	0.035 ounces	1 ounce	28.35 grams
1 kilogram	2.2 pounds	1 pound	0.45 kilograms

– radios – avoid buying these (unless you don't want to receive anything on long wave)

– stereo equipment – because frequencies are different at home, and a transformer will only change the voltage. However, there are many adaptable models (cassette recorders, digital CD players, etc.) that won't give you any problems.

– video game consoles – these are unlikely to work when you get them back home (even if the salesperson swears they will). The electronic system is different. The same applies for video game cassettes.

– pre-recorded cassettes, whether audio or video. Don't but these – the American (NTSC) system is incompatible with ours, unless you have multiple-standard equipment (e.g. PAL + Secam + NTSC). Blank cassettes will work fine with your equipment.

FACTORY OUTLETS

These are factory shops, hugely sign-posted all along the highways, selling either clearance stock from previous years or 'seconds' (they're called 'irregular' items). Factory outlets often handle a number of brands, such as Ralph Lauren, Nike, Levi, Timberland, Osh Kosh, etc. If you examine anything you'd like to buy quite carefully, you'll find some items that are virtually perfect being offered at extremely competitive prices.

SMOKING

Smoking in public places (shops, buses, cinemas, theatres, museums, hotels, etc.) is prohibited in 30 states. Smoking on domestic flights is also forbidden. In 1998, California also banned smoking in restaurants, bars and casinos and the fines for breaking the law can range from $10 to $200.

TAX

Everywhere in the US, prices shown in shops, restaurants, etc. are pre-tax prices. Sales tax is added at the time of payment, the amount varies according to what state you're in. In the West, it ranges from 8.75 per cent in California to 5 per cent in Arizona and 6.5 per cent in Nevada. If you forget to allow for it in your budget, you're in for an unpleasant last-minute surprise.

TIME ZONES

There are five time zones in the US (or seven if you include Alaska and Hawaii). New York is located in the Eastern Time Zone, so times there are 6 hours behind GMT. California and Nevada are in the Pacific Time Zone, which is 9 hours behind GMT. Arizona is in the Mountain Time Zone, which is 8 hours behind.

Whichever state you are in, clocks go forward by one hour for Daylight Saving Time, from April to the end of October. Generally times are quoted using the 12-hour clock.

US TIME AT 12:00 GMT

TIPPING

Tipping is the inevitable consequence of the tax charged in restaurants, bars, etc. Waiters get a tiny fixed wage and most of their income comes from tips. So tipping in restaurants is a long-established institution, and if you don't tip, you'll be seen as a complete jerk. Some countries have a completely different view of restaurant service, and often there's a service charge included in the bill, so they don't leave anything extra. Even when they do, it's more likely to be 10 per cent. In the US, 15 per cent is traditional, and it's as well to get this one into your head. The exception here, of course, is if you're completely dissatisfied. Then you don't leave a tip – but make sure that it's the waiter you're dissatisfied with and not the chef or the proprietor!

If you pay a restaurant bill using a credit card, whatever you do, don't forget to complete the 'Tips' box yourself, otherwise you are leaving it open to the proprietor to fill it in himself. If he's dishonest, he can write in any amount he pleases. As a general rule, a tip should be at least one-and-a-half times the amount of tax.

Likewise, in the case of taxis, it's usual to give 10–15 per cent on top of what the meter shows. If you ignore this, you can expect a string of abuse from a discontented driver. Cab drivers make no bones about telling you the error of your ways!

TOILETS / COMFORT STATIONS

Americans have a wide range of ways of not saying 'toilet'. Comfort station is probably the most extreme, but you'll definitely come across 'restroom', 'bathroom' (even though there's no bath in sight) and 'powder room'. Alternatively there are those basics – the 'john' or the 'can'.

Public toilets are almost always free of charge and are often well maintained. You'll find them in bus stations, at service stations (ask for the key at the cashdesk), in buildings and cafeterias, or the lobbies of large hotels.

TOURIST OFFICES

To obtain tourist information for your trip to the US, contact the California Office of Tourism, 801 K Street, Suite 1600, Sacramento, CA 95814. ☎ 1-800-862-2543 or (916) 322-2881. Website: www.gocalif.ca.gov

It is also worth contacting the American embassy in your home country for more information (*see* 'Embassies and Consulates').

TRANSPORTATION

However little attention you paid to geography at school, you'll know that the US is a very big country, and distances there are large – very large. Travelling in a group (four being the magic number) is the cheapest way to discover the US. Renting or even buying a car doesn't cost a fortune when you share the cost among friends. You can also opt to spend the night in small motels off the main drag. Take a double room and, if it doesn't have two wide beds, split the only bed so that two can sleep on the mattress and two on the base of the bed. It's probably the only cheap way to explore the country.

HITCHHIKING

In many areas this just isn't done any more and it can be potentially dangerous. Hitchhiking is allowed in most states (except Washington, D.C., New Jersey, Pennsylvania, the Carolinas and Virginia), and in California there's no problem. It's very inadvisable for unaccompanied girls to hitchhike, for all the usual reasons.

You may make hitchhiking easier and reduce possible hassles, with the police in particular, by providing yourself with a big card, clearly marked with the word 'British', 'Scottish', 'English', 'Irish', 'Welsh', or however you want to be identified. Write your destination on the card, too, so everyone knows where you want to go. There's always the off-chance of being given a lift by someone who ordinarily wouldn't stop for hitchhikers but who once made a trip to Scotland, spent some time 'overseas' in England during the war, or reckons to have Irish ancestors. Tell them you are hitchhiking for the experience and in order to meet Americans.

In any university student centre or union, you are very likely to find what they call a 'Driving Board', dedicated to 'rides with shared expenses'. Further variants include sharing driving and 'sharing nothing but the company'.

Only rarely will you find someone to take you into another state, unless you approach one of the major universities (Harvard, Columbia, etc.). To locate the less well-known campuses, buy a map in the 'Buckle-up USA' series, which shows them in red. Finally, note that a student is not allowed to let you stay in his or her university room for more than four days.

When 'on the road', take some water and some snacks with you, in case you find yourself on a quiet stretch of road – and don't forget that a large part of the US is desert country. Try to present a clean and tidy image – it always helps to reassure drivers.

Truck drivers rarely pick up hitchhikers (and nor do trailers). Very few of them are covered by the necessary insurance in the event of an accident. Don't bother looking for lifts at truckstops because there are signs everywhere saying 'no hitchhikers', or words to that effect. Even thumbing for a lift at the exit from a truckstop is prohibited.

In some cities, especially on the West Coast, urban hitchhiking has become commonplace. If you feel you can do it, and your direction of travel is straightforward, just stick out your thumb while you're waiting for a bus. It generally gets you there much faster.

It's also difficult to hitch in the national parks. The sort of people who visit them often have the whole family on board, which doesn't leave much room for you.

– Hitchhiking is prohibited on the highways and at the big service stations beside the highways, but you can try for a lift on the slip-roads. Be careful, though: if a cop pulls over and tells you not to hitchhike, you'd better do what he says, because there's an excellent chance that he'll either come back to check, or tip off a colleague by radio.

BY TRAIN

The Amtrak train is neither the fastest nor the cheapest route to California from other parts of the US, but it provides a unique view of America for anyone with a bit of extra time and money. There are usually daily departures and you can make reservations up to 11 months in advance. Fares are either peak or off-peak, with the peak season running from 1 June to 5 September inclusive. One-way, cross-country fares cost about $270–$300, although there are often promotions and special deals available, especially if you book in advance.

Amtrak also offer 'Explore America' fares, which are zone-based and allow stopovers. An 'Explore America' pass covering Denver to the West Coast, for example, starts at about $200–$240 in the peak summer season. 'Explore America' passes covering the whole of the US cost around $320–$380. Prices vary according to the type of seating; sleeping cars with meals and bathroom included start from about $150 per person per night.

One of the most popular routes among travellers in California, Arizona and Nevada is the 'Sunset Limited' route (trains run three times a week), which starts in San Antonio, Texas and heads through New Mexico to Arizona (with connecting bus services to the Grand Canyon) and ends in Los Angeles. Another favourite is the 'Desert Wind', which runs between Chicago and Los Angeles via Denver, Colorado, Salt Lake City and Nevada. Shorter train journeys are also available – for example, the 'Coast Starlite' from Los Angeles to Oakland (with connecting services to San Francisco and Seattle), costing about $75 for a single.

For information about Amtrak fares and schedules and to make reservations, either call 1-800-USA-Rail, ask your travel agent or visit their website: www.amtrak.com.

Distances in miles	Grand Canyon	Las Vegas	Los Angeles	Monterey	Palm Springs	Phoenix	Reno Nevada	San Diego	San Francisco	San Jose	San Luis Obispo	Santa Barbara	Yosemite
Grand Canyon		275	507	760	525	223	720	510	800	750	635	600	608
Las Vegas	275		270	525	240	290	450	340	570	565	415	378	333
Los Angeles	507	270		330	103	390	470	130	390	360	203	96	337
Monterey	760	525	330		433	700	313	460	115	70	143	236	210
Palm Springs	525	240	103	433		280	510	134	503	460	305	200	408
Phoenix	223	290	390	700	280		730	350	760	710	570	470	728
Reno Nevada	720	450	470	313	510	730		554	220	255	424	536	270
San Diego	510	340	130	460	134	350	554		510	486	320	228	430
San Francisco	800	570	390	115	503	760	220	510		46	228	320	200
San Jose	750	565	360	70	460	710	255	486	46		182	275	185
San Luis Obispo	635	415	203	143	305	570	424	320	228	182		93	225
Santa Barbara	600	378	96	236	200	470	536	228	320	275	93		330
Yosemite	608	333	337	210	408	728	270	430	200	185	225	330	

DISTANCE CHART IN MILES

Non-US citizens (except Canadian citizens) can take advantage of Amtrak's rail pass system. The passes are available for either 15 or 30 days and are subject to the peak and off-peak fare system. A rail pass covering the whole of the US costs about £185 for 15 days or £275 for 30 days off peak, or £157 and £200 during peak season. A 30-day pass covering the West Coast is available, costing from £147 off-peak and £179 in peak season. These passes can be bought at all Amtrak stations, on production of a non-US passport or from specialist American travel agents. You can also buy Amtrak passes from agents specializing in US travel. Examples include:

In Britain: Destination USA, 14 Greville St, London EC1N 8SB. ☎ (020) 7400 7099 (reservations).

In Ireland: USIT Now, Campus Travel/Eurotrain, 19–21 Aston Quay, O'Connell Bridge, Dublin 2. ☎ (01) 602 1600.

In Australia: Walshes World. ☎ (29) 232-7499.

In New Zealand: Atlantic & Pacific. ☎ (09) 302-9720.

In South Africa: STA Travel, 27A Mutual Square, Cradock Road, Rosebank, Johannesburg 2196. ☎ (11) 447-5414.

BY BUS

The bus network covers virtually the whole country and there are agreements between regional bus companies that allow further ticket extensions. Greyhound alone serves 4,000 cities and towns.

• Package deals

– **Greyhound 'Ameripass'**: Greyhound offers 'Ameripass' package deals for four, five, seven or 15 days, one month and two months, the period starting on the date of first use of the ticket. The four-day package can only be used on Friday, Saturday and Sunday and, in contrast to the others, is non-refundable. The distance you travel with an Ameripass is unlimited. Booking and luggage handling are included in the charge. It's also possible to use these packages at three different locations in Canada – Toronto, Montreal and Vancouver. If you want to use Ameripass with a company other than Greyhound, you have to go to the counter to get your ticket, which will show the destination, the name of the company, and the fact that you have an Ameripass. The whole thing is free. One hundred and twenty small bus companies accept Greyhound packages.

For information, contact the international information offices located in the Greyhound terminals in LA or San Francisco.

The Ameripass takes the form of a printed card that you show to the driver on boarding the bus, telling him your destination. The driver then makes a note of your Ameripass number in his logbook. He'll want to see your passport. Don't have your pass laminated, or the adhesive will dissolve the wording on it!

You can't buy a point-to-point ticket while still in Britain – they have to be bought on the spot. But long distances work out more expensive than packages, which very quickly pay for themselves. You can get a reduction by reserving at least 14 days in advance.

Greyhound serves the Grand Canyon, although it charges a supplement, and drops passengers off at the entrances to the park.

– **Buying an Ameripass package**: if you're already in the US, you can reach the Greyhound information service by calling ☎ 1-800-231-222. This number allows you to find out about timetables without having to go back to the station. You can also get packages from agencies that stock them. If you know when and how you plan to travel, then buying an Ameripass while still in Europe saves you money as you then won't have to pay the state tax. However, there is no financial advantage in buying point-to-point tickets or bus passes in advance.

In Britain, Greyhound have an office at Sussex House, London Road, East Grinstead, West Sussex RH19 1LD ☎ (01342) 317317. Website: www.greyhound.com

– **Organized excursions**: backpackers who are dedicated independent travellers shouldn't turn their noses up at organized excursions, especially those run by Graylines Tours. They organize a number of trips, either around a city or to a tourist attraction, and these trips, costing only a few dollars, give you a good overall view without taking up much of your time, even if you go back later under your own steam to see a few places you particularly liked.

Along the same lines, East Coast Explorer offers services to New York, Boston and Washington, going via secondary roads and giving you the chance to discover sites of natural, cultural and historical interest. Reservations: ☎ (718) 694-9667 or freephone: ☎ 1-800-610-2680.

• Luggage

Try to keep an eye on your luggage, because stuff does occasionally go astray: you get to San Francisco but your luggage goes to New Orleans! This happens rather too frequently, so take your luggage with you whenever possible and put it in the rack above your seat.

To avoid paying left-luggage charges in the big cities, don't take your luggage with you when leaving the bus: it will be kept free of charge at the luggage counter. You can check in your luggage three days in advance. It's as well to know, though, that the Greyhound automatic lockers are cleared after 24 hours, and the contents are put into an office that's closed at night and on weekends.

The package express service will take items for you direct from one city to another by bus, even if you aren't taking the bus yourself. Useful, perhaps, for shopping freaks who don't want to be burdened, but it's not advisable for valuable merchandise. The luggage will be kept at its destination at a cost of $2 for a maximum of six hours, and $4 for the day. If you're buying a rucksack, even an American one, don't get it if it measures more than 32 in (82 cm) tall, as you won't get it into a luggage locker.

• Comfort

In addition to their speed, buses offer a fair level of comfort, and even have 'on-board' toilets. The buses are air-conditioned, which means they can be rather chilly. It's a good idea to take a sweater with you, especially if you intend to try and get some sleep.

Buses are particularly useful if you travel at night, as you can cover great distances while saving the cost of a room in a hotel. However, the seats don't recline very far. If you have long legs, try to get a seat on the aisle.

You can buy a small inflatable pillow at Greyhound terminals. It's even decorated with the Greyhound emblem, and makes a useful beach mat when deflated.

In theory, when a bus becomes full up, a second one is put on to take remaining travellers. This happens mostly at larger stations and less frequently at small stations. But in case you were thinking it would be a great idea to be able to stretch out in the second (half empty) bus, remember that, as soon as there is room in the first one, everyone will be asked to transfer to it. This is not fun in the middle of the night!

Avoid sitting in the front seat (the opening and closing of the door might bother you) or the back one (you'll get the smells from the toilet, and you can't recline the back seat).

- **Useful tips**

– Be aware of the differences between services: express, non-stop, local, etc. Compare the times of departure and arrival to find out which one is the fastest.

– Highway stations are good meeting points if you aren't familiar with a town, and they also offer a good place to clean up. The only problem is that they are often a long way from the town centre and the shuttle services stop at 10pm.

– If you plan to buy a pass in the US, you may find it cheaper in some places than in others.

- **City buses**

– One-day tickets, or season tickets valid for several days, soon pay for themselves.

– Buy tickets that offer transfers, whenever you can. These let you change buses within the same journey without having to buy another ticket.

– Bus drivers will rarely give change. Keep some coins on you, and pay the exact amount.

BY CAR

- **Basic rules of driving**

– **Minimum age**: in California, the minimum age for driving is 16 years with a driving school, or 18 years without.

– **The driving controls**: if you've never driven an automatic – and that's just about the only kind of car you're likely to come across – the various controls are identified as follows: **P** = Parking (select this when parking), **R** = Reverse, **N** = Neutral, **D** = Drive (select this to move off), **1**, **2** and **3**: these are used to select the gear manually. In order to combat your instinctive reflex actions, plant your left foot in the left foot-well, and don't let it move from there till you get to the end of your journey. Only the right foot is used, for both accelerating and braking.

– **Seat belts**: these are compulsory in front seats, and children under five or weighing less than 40 pounds (18 kilograms) must be in a child's seat.

– **Speed limits**: all roads have speed limits throughout the US, although the actual limits are decided on by individual states. The maximum speed on many roads is 55 mph (85 kph), although on the interstates the limit may be as high as 65 mph (104 kph). In cities it is 20–25 mph (30–40 kph). Stick to these limits because the police are very vigilant – they turn their sirens on at any excuse. It's useful to know, too, that a police car has the means to measure your speed even when it's travelling in the opposite direction.

– **Priority on the right**: this applies only if two vehicles arrive at a junction simultaneously. The one on the right then has priority. In all other cases, the first to arrive has the right of way. It's difficult to imagine this system working anywhere else!

– **Turning left when an oncoming vehicle is doing the same**: contrary to the practice in many countries, including Britain, you turn left at a junction by taking the shortest route. In other words, if an oncoming vehicle is turning left while you are turning left, you pass each other on the off-side instead of going around an imaginary roundabout at the centre of the intersection.

– **At an intersection**: in some states, if you are in the far right-hand lane, you can turn right on a red light after stopping and checking that the way is clear. This applies in California, but elsewhere you'd better be careful. And, of course, you can't do it if there's a sign saying 'No Red Turn'.

– **On a highway**: to join a highway, merge with the traffic as quickly as possible. Never stop on the access road. If you break down, stand on the right of the vehicle, open the bonnet (hood) and wait. The highway police will help you. On some highways, there are roadside telephones you can use to make an emergency call. The highways have plenty of parking areas where you can stop and take a rest.

– **On national routes and highways**: the lanes coming from the right have either a STOP or a YIELD sign, meaning 'look left'. Here, giving priority to the right is not compulsory.

– **Traffic lights**: these are positioned beyond the crossroads, not on the side that you'd expect, so, if you actually stop at the lights, you'll be right in the middle of the junction. Don't worry, though. You only have to mess it up once or twice to get it firmly implanted in your brain.

– **Roundabouts**: these are rare. The first vehicle to reach the roundabout has priority. Americans call them 'traffic circles'.

– **The car pool system**: some main highways have a designated car pool lane, which is reserved for cars containing two or more occupants. This, of course, makes them much less crowded than other routes, but they are as yet quite rare. Don't even think about using these lanes if you're driving on your own!

– **Parking**: be careful where you park your car or you may find your windscreen covered with parking tickets. Never park at a bus stop or, worse still, in front of a fire hydrant. Even if there is no 'Tow Away' sign there to threaten you, they'll take your car away very quickly indeed and there's a heavy fine. It's a good idea when parking in a city to make a note of the street number so that you have some chance of finding the car again. The parking problem is serious in big cities. It's best to find a 'park and ride', even though these are not cheap: these are large parking areas at bus and subway terminals and the big stations. They are usually shown on town plans. Get there early, because they soon fill up.

– **Parking meters**: the system for parking in town is complicated. The existence of a parking meter doesn't mean you can park there for as long as you like. You have to look carefully at the colour of the markings on the sidewalk: red (prohibited), white (only for dropping off passengers, such as at hotels), green (parking limited to 15 minutes), etc. As well as this, you should look out for little signs on the pavement telling you about restrictions such as street cleaning. At the times marked, you'd better not be there. This is by no means an exhaustive list, and you'll discover many more things to watch out for when parking. Generally speaking, Americans have a highly developed sense of civic responsibility and would never dream of blocking traffic by double-parking just to get a newspaper.

– **Parking tickets**: if you get a ticket on your rented car, it's best to pay on the spot rather than wait until you get home. The easiest way to pay is by money order at a post office. You can also pay by credit card – a telephone number for this is given on the back of the ticket.

– **School bus at a stop**: when a school bus stops (you can't miss them – they are all yellow) and its indicators are flashing, it's mandatory to stop. You must stop your car before pulling out to pass it, to allow the children to get off in complete safety, and if you are driving behind one, don't overtake it whatever you do. Don't forget this one – it's one of the most severely penalized driving offences in the US.

– **Give way to pedestrians**: respect for pedestrian crossings is not a mere form of words, and pedestrians really do have priority. Whenever a pedestrian looks like approaching the roadway, everyone stops. In the US, people show respect to each other and practice tolerance – best do likewise.

– A useful little book has been produced by Hertz, the car rental company. It's called *Driving in the USA* and contains many useful driving tips.

• Petrol

Fill your tank before setting out across uninhabited areas, because you'll find that some gas stations are closed at night and on Sunday. You can drive along a highway for hours before finding one. The cost of 'gas' varies, depending on the area, the brand and the quality. An American gallon, at just under 3.8 litres, is a good 17 per cent smaller than a British gallon, which is just over 4.5 litres. There are two types of petrol: there's unleaded, which comes as 'regular' or 'super' unleaded ('regular' is fine and costs less, but large American cars need 'super') and there's 'ethyl', which is the most expensive. There is also diesel, of course, although not many vehicles use it. Your filler cap will show clearly which fuel you should fill up with. You usually have to pay at the cashdesk first, then help yourself. All gas stations offer a wide variety of services: information and toilets, as well as food and drink. They also sell very good local and regional maps.

Service stations offer two service options: 'full-served' (you are looked after and they clean your windscreen) and self-service. Self-service petrol costs 10 per cent less. And you don't give tips at service stations.

An increasing number of service stations are fitting pumps at which you can pay by credit card. The pump will give you a receipt.

• Driving licence

A British driving licence is valid in the US if you have held it for a minimum of one year, but you also should take an international driving permit (IDP) with you. If you're thinking of hiring a car, you will need your British licence as well, as some agencies will ask for it.

In Britain, international driving permits are issued by motoring associations such as the Automobile Association, the RAC and Green Flag. You will need to produce your British driving licence and two passport-size photographs. The cost is very low (about £4).

• General state of the roads and road signs

In Europe, if you know the name of the city you're heading for, you can usually find your way. In the US, however, you have to know the name and number of the highway, and whether your destination lies to the north, south, east or west. The freeways, interstates and secondary roads are all indicated differently and these differences are pretty easy to understand. The main thing is to be aware of what point of the compass you are heading for.

• Road maps

There's not much point in buying detailed maps before leaving home. Almost all American gas stations will sell them to you at very affordable prices. The maps provided by car-hire offices are also very useful, as are those you can get from the tourist offices.

– Buy the *Rand MacNally Road Atlas*, which has one page for each state and is very well produced. It also shows the national parks and campgrounds. The *American Automobile Association Atlas* is not bad either.

– When you cross a state line, there's often a Visitors' Center where you can get free road maps of the state you have just entered. They will also give you a whole armful of brochures and other prospectuses.

– To get a town plan, ask in a car-hire agency. They always have some on the counter and they will rarely object to your taking one (they are free).

• Hiring a car

Cars are hired out by the day or week. Some companies hire them out by the hour, but the large agencies require a minimum hire period of one day. Car-hire prices are highly competitive and changeable. Prices can vary from one state to another and there is no easy way to compare UK and US prices.

Car-hire companies

In Britain: Alamo: ☎ (0990) 993000. Avis: ☎ (0870) 606 0100. Budget: ☎ (0541) 565656. Hertz: ☎ (0990) 996699.

In the Republic of Ireland: Avis: ☎ (21) 281 111. Hertz: ☎ (01) 676 7476.

In Canada: Avis: ☎ 1-800-272-5871. Hertz: ☎ 800-263 0600.

In Australia: Avis: ☎ 13 63 33. Budget: ☎ 1-300-362-848. Hertz: ☎ 13 30 39.

In New Zealand: Avis: ☎ (09) 379-2650. Budget: ☎ (09) 275-3025. Hertz: ☎ (04) 388-7070.

In South Africa: Avis: ☎ (11) 923-3685. Budget: ☎ (11) 392-3929. Hertz ☎ (21) 934-3913.

• Hiring a car in the US

Before deciding which agency to hire from, call them and compare their prices. Some may charge twice as much as others for the same service. If you don't plan to cover a great distance, your best bet is to take the most favourable daily rate, even if the cost per mile works out higher. For a very long journey, the 'unlimited mileage' option is generally better value, certainly if you intend to cover 150 miles (240km) or more per day. The cheapest hire cars are those called 'economy' and 'compact'. They are very good for up to three people. Next, in order of size, comes the 'sub-compact' and the 'mid-size'.

Car-hire companies frequently offer weekend reductions ('weekend fares'): from Friday noon to Monday noon. This gets you three days' hire for the price of two.

You also have to remember that the prices stated by car-hire companies need some interpretation. If they quote you a daily rate, there are still other costs to add on, such as comprehensive insurance and tax. Tax can be anything from 4 to 15 per cent, depending on which state you're in, and of course it's never included in the vouchers sold by travel agencies. None of these will ever be included in the advertised price.

Many companies will offer 'one-way rental', where you return the car to a different location, but you will then have to pay a drop-off charge.

There's a new concept in international car-hire. Autoescape is an international agency (based in France but serving customers worldwide) that takes block reservations on hire cars and is able to pass on some of the discounts obtained to its customers. The agency offers a free service, unlimited mileage – and they're very flexible. There are no extra charges if you have to make changes, and even a last-minute cancellation is OK. You'll get the best price if you make your booking in advance. They even have a special deal for drivers under 25 in the US. Contact them in France on ☎ 04-90-09-28-28 (the national code for France is 44) or visit the website: www.autoescape.com.

• Some general rules

– You won't be allowed to hire a car if you are under 21, or even 25 in the case of some of the larger companies.

– If your licence is less than three years old or you are under 25, car-hire companies will charge you extra by the day. Agencies will often refuse to hire you a car unless you have your British licence – an international permit is not enough by itself.

– Avoid hiring a car at airports, where only the large companies are represented. The cheaper ones are in town but, if you arrive by plane, they can deliver the car to you.

– You will need to take a credit card (Visa is accepted everywhere). Cash is only accepted very rarely, and you'll also be asked for a large deposit. If you have one of the more prestigious cards (gold or platinum ones), you will probably get the benefit of free insurance against theft and damage. They certainly don't give these cards away, but they will soon repay the investment if you hire your car for a fortnight or more.

– Always fill up before returning the car. Otherwise, they'll bill you at three times the price per gallon you'd pay at the pump.

– If you reserve in advance, you'll pay less than if you leave the arrangements to the last minute.

– The prices quoted are always 'before tax'.

– The lowest rates are the weekly ones.

– If an agency can't provide the category of car you reserved, they'll offer one of higher category without charging extra.

– Always ask for a reduction if you hire a car for more than two weeks. It may work.

– The amount of excess you have to pay if you make a claim on your car insurance varies from one company to the next.

– Car-hire agencies occasionally refund the taxi fare you had to pay to get to their office (ask the taxi driver for a receipt). Many offer a free shuttle service from the airports to the agency.

– Hire contracts only become binding after 24 hours. Within that period, you can change the car, or the options, or both.

– Almost all hire cars (99 per cent) are automatics. You'll soon get used to this.

– Most hire cars have air-conditioning, which is absolutely indispensable in summer.

– Many cars come equipped with a CD player as well as a radio.

• Insurance companies

There are many of these and it's easy to get confused between them. Every vehicle has obligatory minimum insurance. This is included in the charges quoted. With a 'top-of-the-range' credit card (Visa Premier, MasterCard Gold, etc.), there's no need to take out CDW (Collision Damage Waiver) or LDW (Loss Damage Waiver) insurance, since paying with one of these cards automatically entitles you to both. If this is the case, take out only the LIS (Liability Insurance Supplement) insurance.

– **Loss Damage Waiver (LDW) or Collision Damage Waiver (CDW)**: each of these is a form of comprehensive insurance. This is not compulsory, but it does provide extra cover against all kinds of damage (theft, fire, accident, etc., but not vandalism, so avoid running any risk of that) if you are the guilty party. However, it does not cover damage caused to a third party if you were responsible. Some credit cards provide this kind of insurance (though not for very large or deluxe cars), so check with your bank or credit card provider to avoid paying twice. For total cover, it is advisable to take out LIS (Liability Insurance Supplement) cover as well.

– **Liability Insurance Supplement (LIS)**: this is supplementary insurance that covers you if an accident is your fault. No credit card will include this in its cover. It's essential to have cover. You probably already know that if you run someone over in the US and they spend six months in hospital, your liabilities will be way beyond your income. Of course if you drive while drunk, this insurance policy won't cover you.

– **Personal Accident Insurance (PAI)**: this covers accidents involving injury and is not necessary if you have also taken out personal insurance cover that includes road accidents.

– **Personal Effect Coverage (PEC)**: this covers personal effects stolen from a car. This insurance is almost pointless, as you only need to keep your wits about you and don't leave anything valuable inside the car. There's a new law now that prohibits car-hire firms from marking their hired vehicles with stickers. It was felt that this was like manna from heaven for thieves, showing them which cars they should 'explore'!

- **The small companies**

Thrifty Rent-a-Car, Greyhound Rent-a-Car, Compacts Only, and others, are small local companies with a small fleet of cars.

If all you want is a U-drive (i.e. to return to your starting point), it's best to hire a car from one of these small local companies: it'll be noticeably cheaper and, at least in theory, they'll accept cash by way of deposit. And if you take the car back to where you hired it, there's a chance you'll pay less. This tends to be quite economical if you're visiting the national parks.

Here are some small companies, together with their toll free numbers (you can't call these numbers from outside the US).

– **Holiday Payless Rent-a-Car**: ☎ 1-800-237-2804

– **Cafla Tours**: freephone: ☎ 1-800-636-9683 and ☎ 818 785-4569. Fax: (818) 785-3964. This is an agency that negotiates the best rates from various car-hire companies, such as Alamo, Enterprise, Thrifty, etc.

– **Rent-a-Wreck**: ☎ 1-800-421-7253. Agency in Los Angeles: ☎ 478-0676. The name is a joke, of course. Some of their models are old, others are brand-new; all are cheap. One of the few companies that hire cars to people aged 23–25.

– **Dollar**: ☎ 1-800-800-4000. This company also hires to 23–25-year-olds.

– **Hertz**: ☎ 1-800-654-3131

– **Alamo Rent-a-Car**: ☎ 1-800-327-9633. One of the few companies that will accept traveller's cheques in payment of a deposit, but whoever hires the car must have their driving licence, a copy of their telephone bill and evidence that they are employed! Individually tailored hire contracts.

• **The big companies: Hertz, Avis, National, Budget, Alamo**

– The disadvantage is that these companies rarely accept a deposit in cash. You have to have a credit card.

– The advantage is that their cars are generally new, so mechanical problems are rare.

– If you do have a mechanical problem, the local representative of the company will exchange the car.

HIRING A MOTOR-HOME OR CAMPER

These vehicles are a cross between a caravan and a truck and they're widely used in the US.

– A **camper** is like a pickup truck fitted with a dwelling unit that does not communicate with the cab, so you have to use the back door to get into the living quarters. It's a medium-sized vehicle 11ft 6in to 16 ft long (3.5 to 5m) that sleeps four in comfort.

– A **motor-home** is a real truck-cum-caravan, very luxurious and well fitted. It even has a shower. This is the largest kind of travelling home, measuring 23ft to 29ft long (7 to 9m), and can accommodate up to six people in great comfort. It's also the most expensive of this type of vehicle, but, if you can divide the cost among up to six people, it becomes much more affordable.

– The cheapest kind of travelling home is without any doubt a **converted Volkswagen bus**, camper model. It is fitted with a kitchenette and a small refrigerator, a table and folding beds. You can house up to five people in one of these.

– A **caravan** is not advisable, because you have to hire a car to tow it around. Known as a 'trailer' in the US.

• **A few tips**

– When choosing a campground, always have two or three alternatives in mind, in a radius of about 50 miles (80km). That way, if you don't like the first site, you can chance your luck further on, but remember that it's against the law to park overnight anywhere except in a campground. Always try the national parks or state parks – they cost less and the site will always be interesting.

– The refrigerators generally run on gas, and gas bottles can be refilled in service stations.

– Besides all the standard accessories needed in a mobile home, you'll find the following very handy: axe, bucket, shovel, crockery, folding chairs, a full set of bedding and even a broom.

– Motor-homes are fitted with air-conditioning, which runs from the engine or is plugged into the hook-up (the service line in the campground).

– If you're interested, you'll do better to hire one before you leave Britain because it's very hard to get one on the spot in summer.

Although it's fashionable to hire a trailer when visiting the US, there are a few **drawbacks**.

– It's slow.

– You have to take it back to the point of origin or pay a $100 supplement.

– Petrol consumption is extremely high, between 20 and 45 litres per 60 miles (100 km) depending on the model.

– It's hard to find parking places in summer, especially in the national parks. You can't just park anywhere (and, in the big cities, your vehicle will be impounded within the hour). You'll have to spend the night on specially reserved sites (you get a directory with the vehicle): it costs $5–$12 for a space, plus water, electricity and gas. It is possible, all the same, to park on the parking lots of hypermarkets or shops, provided of course that you refrain from doing any unpacking and that you leave the area clean.

– You can't reserve a space in the national parks. The length of your stay is limited and you need to get there in the morning if you want a good space. But, in contrast to European campgrounds, which are jam-packed in the summer, sites in the US often give you the chance of some degree of isolation.

– It's expensive: it's sometimes less costly to hire an ordinary car and sleep in a motel.

– You can reserve a camper with a British travel agent, which is often cheaper and you eliminate the risk of not finding a vehicle when you arrive in the US.

– Some places prohibit campers – Death Valley, for example, where leisure vehicles are barred during the summer.

THE 'AUTO DRIVE-AWAY' SYSTEM

Drive-aways are organizations looking for young people (over 21) to drive a vehicle to its destination if its owner doesn't have the time to do so. With a little luck, you could be crossing the US in a Cadillac.

To be sure of getting a car (the competition is fierce), just keep phoning the company every day (no need to go down in person). After a few days, you'll get a car for the destination of your choice. If they offer you a car that suits, leave your name to reserve it and get down to the company office right way to prevent anyone else from taking your place.

A few tips

– Be clean and well-groomed when introducing yourself.

– You'll have to pay a deposit (depending on the distance), which will be repaid when you deliver the car.

– You only have to pay for petrol (the first tankful is sometimes refunded) and any tolls required.

– Your contract forbids you to pick up hitchhikers.

– Quite frequently, the itinerary and the time are stipulated and if you depart from it you will be in trouble.

– You can find the addresses of companies in Yellow Pages under the headings 'Automobile Transporters' or 'American Transporters'.

BY MOTORCYCLE

If you are taking your motorcycle with you, you'll have difficulty insuring it at home. In larger cities, some of the big stores offer insurance cover to foreigners. You can usually find their ads in the motoring section of local newspapers. Or you could just buy a bike (which will be half the price you'd pay for the same thing back home) and sell it again before you leave. You'll then have to get your bike registered, in order not to find yourself stuck in some Texas hamlet with a sheriff who doesn't like your Easy Rider style. Then you need to arrange for a safety check to be carried out by an authorized motorcycle dealer (one showing a yellow sign). Fit your bike with a fairing and windscreen to cope with the insects you'll encounter. Wearing a helmet is obligatory.

Other information should be available from any tour operator: some have brought out special brochures exclusively dedicated to travelling bikers.

BY AIR

Domestic flights are big business in the US and most airlines specialize in particular areas. Since the deregulation of fares, competition has become fierce. That's all to the good – not so good are the frequent delays.

You may have trouble finding your way through this jungle, as new fares appear just about every day. Packages cost a whole lot less if you buy them well in advance. Here are a few things that may be helpful:

Night fares:

– on some main routes, there are domestic companies that will give you a reduction of about 20 per cent if you travel at night (9pm–6am), but this is less common nowadays.

'Visit USA' fares

– Companies offering Visit USA fares: American, Continental, Delta, Northwest, US Air, TWA, United and Western.

– Valid up to two months (sometimes a year). Great variations between companies.

– Depending on the company, this rate may apply to a one-way, return or 'open jaw' ticket (where the route is interrupted) with no limit to the number of stopovers but only one stop per city (except in the case of a stopover).

'Pass' packages:

– basically, these are special rates granted by the airlines to passengers who live outside the US and hold a trans-Atlantic ticket. They reduce the cost per unit distance. You have to specify your itinerary before leaving, so it's best to include as many cities as possible. If you don't go to a particular place, you can skip it, but you can't add any more stopovers without paying an additional $20. The system works on coupons, and one journey doesn't necessarily equal one coupon, so be sure to find out the exact number of coupons required for each trip.

Here are details of the conditions applied by some airline companies offering the pass:

– **America West**: ☎ 1-800-2FLY-AWA or 1-800-235-9292. Fax: (480) 693-8020. There are no special conditions except that you must not be an American resident and you must have bought a trans-Atlantic flight.

– **American Airlines** (*see* 'Getting There'): offer packages with a minimum of three coupons for the US, with extensions to Canada, Hawaii, Mexico and the Caribbean. You must not be an American resident, and your stay must be for a maximum of 60 days. Valid only in conjunction with an American Airlines trans-Atlantic flight. You can buy a maximum of 12 coupons.

– **Delta Airlines** (*see* 'Getting There'): they sell the 'Discover America' pass. You have to buy at least three coupons; the maximum is 10. The pass must start within 60 days of a trans-Atlantic flight made with Delta, Sabena or Swissair. It's also valid on any other regular route, although the cost is more expensive. You have to specify the itinerary and reserve the first flight before you arrive in the country. The tickets must also be issued and paid for before you arrive. No supplement is charged for Mexico or Canada.

– **Northwest Airlines** (*see* 'Getting There'): in conjunction with a trans-Atlantic flight with Northwest or KLM. You have to buy at least three coupons. The first coupon must be reserved and the actual pass issued a minimum of seven days before you arrive in the US. You can't change the first coupon. The pass is valid for 60 days. You have to use one coupon per flight number, and a maximum of two stops is allowed for each city. Supplement for Mexico.

– **TWA** (*see* 'Getting There'): offer their 'Airpass', which is reserved for passengers who are non-US residents and who hold a TWA trans-Atlantic ticket. Their pass is valid for a maximum of 60 days throughout TWA's domestic network. Note that it's one flight per coupon, unless you transit through St Louis or New York (when you need just a single coupon for the whole journey).

– **United Airlines** (*see* 'Getting There'): reserved for passengers who are not residents of the US or Canada, and have bought a trans-Atlantic flight with United Airlines. Valid for up to 60 days. The first flight must be reserved before you arrive in the US (be careful, as there's a $75 penalty for changes to the first coupon). You have to buy a minimum of three and a maximum of eight coupons. The remainder of the journey can be left open but the whole itinerary must be specified before departure. It isn't possible, however, to return more than twice to a given city, although you can transit through it several times. Also valid for Mexico, Alaska (and Hawaii, on payment of a supplement that's lower than with the other companies). 'Open jaws' allowed.

– **US Airways** (*see* 'Getting There'): offers very interesting packages covering its domestic network. From two to eight coupons, depending on the area in which you use them. One coupon is equal to one flight (and here, too, there's a penalty for changes to the first coupon). Preferential rates for passengers travelling on a trans-Atlantic flight (scheduled or chartered) with US Airways. It's also possible to use it for Canada, the Bahamas, Puerto Rico and the Virgin Islands without supplementary charge.

– IMPORTANT: one thing to do before you leave home – if you made a series of reservations for air travel within the US, don't on any account forget to confirm them with your first carrier, including the return flight, at least 72 hours before departure time.

Smoking

Under a law passed by Congress in 1987, smoking is now forbidden on all flights, domestic and trans-Atlantic, with American airline companies. Any contravention of this regulation is punishable by a fine of $1,000 ($2,000 if you smoke in the toilet).

WORKING IN THE USA

The US government has very strict rules about foreigners trying to get casual work, and a standard visa expressly forbids you from taking work – if caught, you will be swiftly deported. California's proximity to Mexico has led to an influx of illegal immigrants filling the most menial jobs, and as a result, the government is cracking down hard on illegal workers.

If you're lucky, you might get bar or waitressing work because of the novelty of your English accent. However, legislation passed in the 1980s has made it an offence for an employer to employ illegal workers, so if you do apply illegally for a job, your chances of being taken on are slim. Legitimate employment must be arranged before you arrive in the US, and it is your employer's responsibility to get the correct visa.

The only alternative is summer / winter work through cultural exchange organizations such as **Camp America** and **Resort America**. Camp America is open to applications from many countries, while Resort America is only open to Europeans from the UK, Germany and Poland, and citizens of Australia, New Zealand, South Africa and Zimbabwe.

Camp America employs 'counsellors', who carry out a wide range of summer camp jobs, from cooking to supervising children's activities. Resort America places students as waiters, cleaners, receptionists, etc. in resorts, hotels and conference centres across the US.

To apply you must be aged 18 and over, speak fluent English, provide references and pass a rigorous interview. If you want to work for Camp America then an enthusiasm for working with children is obviously essential. Interviews usually take place in your home country, and the organizations often tour around colleges and universities.

For Resort America you must be between 18 and 25 years of age and you have to be either a full-time student or enrolled to be a student. Camp America requires you to work for at least nine weeks, from 1 June. Resort America employs students from the southern hemisphere to work the winter season – a minimum of 10 weeks from 9 December.

Making an application can be expensive. Camp America requires an initial deposit of $80/£51, a second deposit, on finding a work placement, of $110/£70, a medical insurance premium of $165/£105, a contribution towards airport taxes of $17/£11, and a Visa administration fee of $50/£32. However, there are major discounts available on flights to the States, and you get free food and accommodation once you are there.

What payment you receive is in the form of pocket money, ranging from a basic $310 up to $1,200 for counsellors who have worked for Camp America before and arrange their own flights.

Camp America and Resort America are best contacted via the Internet, where you can download application forms and all the relevant information. Websites: www.campamerica.co.uk and www.resortamerica.com.au

All applications to Camp America are processed through the London office.

Camp America and Resort America can be contacted at 37A Queen's Gate, London SW7 5HR ☎ (020) 7581 7373.

Resort America can also be contacted in:

Australia: 288a Whitehorse Road, Balwyn, Victoria, 3103. ☎ (03) 9836-0111. Fax: (03) 9836-0149.

New Zealand: PO Box 35–151 Naenae, Lower Hutt. ☎ (04) 567-1111. Fax: (04) 567-1111.

South Africa: PO Box 7134, Roggebaai 8012, or at 801 Pearl House, 25 Heerengracht, Cape Town 8001. ☎ (21) 419-5740. Fax: (21) 425-2703; Up & Away Employment Abroad, Suite 2/3 2nd Floor, Musgrave Office Tower, Musgrave Centre, 115 Musgrave Rd, Durban 4062 SA. ☎ (31) 222-815. Fax: (31) 222-853.

BACKGROUND

The US is a country with too much geography – and not enough history.

Anonymous, 1997

VITAL STATISTICS: THE UNITED STATES

– **Area**: 3,615,100 square miles (9,363,123 square kilometres), or 38 times the size of Great Britain.

– **Population**: 274 million

– **Capital**: Washington, D.C.

– **Official language**: English. Spanish is also widely spoken in Florida, California, Arizona, New Mexico and Colorado.

– **Currency**: the dollar (US$)

– **Type of state**: Federal Republic (50 states plus the District of Columbia)

– **Form of government**: Presidential democracy

VITAL STATISTICS: CALIFORNIA, NEVADA AND ARIZONA

– **Area**: California is the third-largest state, after Texas and Alaska, with an area of 163,707 square miles (424,002 square kilometres). Nevada measures 110,561 square miles (286,352 square kilometres) and Arizona covers an area of 114,000 square miles (295,260 square kilometres).

– **Population figures**: California is the state with the highest population, which totals 31,742,000 inhabitants. The population of Arizona is 3,665,230, while that of Nevada is 1,201,800.

HISTORY OF THE UNITED STATES

SIGNIFICANT DATES IN AMERICAN HISTORY

1000–1002: Leif Eriksson, son of Viking Erik the Red, explores Maine, Newfoundland and Labrador

1492: discovery of America by Christopher Columbus

1524: Giovanni da Verrazzano discovers the bay of New York

1585: first English colony founded on Roanoke Island

1607: Jamestown, Virginia founded by Captain John Smith

1613: Niagara Falls discovered by Samuel Champlain

1619: first black slaves brought into the plantations at Jamestown

1620: the *Mayflower* arrives at Cape Cod, carrying 100 pilgrims from Plymouth

1636: creation of Harvard University near Boston

1647: Peter Stuyvesant elected first governor of New York

1650: legalization of slavery

1692: witch-hunts in Salem, Massachusetts

1718: foundation of New Orleans

1776: Declaration of Independence on 4 July

1784: New York provisionally chosen as capital of the United States

1803: Thomas Jefferson elected first president

1830: Mormon Church founded by Joseph Smith

1831: two million slaves now in the United States

1843: invention of the typewriter

1847: jeans invented by Levi Strauss

1849: first year of the Gold Rush

1857: invention of the steam lift by E.G. Otis

1861–65: American Civil War

1867: Alaska bought from Russia by the United States

1871: creation of the Yellowstone National Park

1872: chewing-gum invented by T. Adams

1872: wireless telegraphy patented by Mahlon Loomis

1876: Tom Sawyer's *The Adventures of Mark Twain*; mechanical floor-sweeper invented by M.R. Bissell

1880: first steel-framed skyscraper built, in Chicago

1886: Coca-Cola invented by J. Pemberton; the Statue of Liberty, created by Frederic Bartholdi, is given to the US in recognition of Franco-American co-operation

1895: opening of Sea Lion Park, America's first theme park, at Coney Island

1903: teddy bears created by Morris Michtom. The name given as a nickname to Theodore Roosevelt after an incident with a bear

1906: San Francisco earthquake

1911: first movie studio at Hollywood

1913: construction of the Woolworth Building by Cass Gilbert – the highest of its era

1914: Paramount Studios founded

1916: first self-service food shop opened in Memphis, Tennessee

1921: first Miss America competition

1923: Warner Bros. founded

1924: Indian Citizenship Act gives American citizenship to Native Americans

1925: J. Edgar Hoover is first presidential candidate to use the radio in his election campaign

1927: film 'Oscars' created by Louis Mayer

1928: Walt Disney creates Mickey Mouse

1929: Wall Street Crash; opening of Museum of Modern Art in New York

1930: opening of the first supermarket, on Long Island

1931: construction of the Empire State Building in New York

1932: the 'New Deal' brought in by Franklin D. Roosevelt to get the economy back on its feet

1933: *Monopoly* invented by Charles B. Darrow

1936: black athlete Jesse Owens wins four gold medals at the Berlin Olympic Games

1937: first shopping trolley used, in a shop in Oklahoma City

1939: John Ford's *Stagecoach*, and *Gone With The Wind* by Victor Flemming, Sam Wood and George Cukor

1941: Japanese attack on Pearl Harbour on 7 December. United States declares war on Japan on 8 December. Germany and Italy declare war on United States on 11 December

1944: Allied landings in Normandy on 6 June; bombs dropped on Hiroshima and Nagasaki on 6 and 9 August

1946: start of the 'Cold War'. Winston Churchill coins the name 'Iron Curtain'

1948: first fast food introduced by Maurice and Richard McDonald

1949: first meeting of NATO (North Atlantic Treaty Organization) in New York

1950: beginning of the McCarthy anti-Communist crusade

1951: Frank Lloyd Wright's Guggenheim Museum opens in New York

1952: beginning of Abstract Expressionism or 'Action Painting', consisting of throwing liquid colour to create images and shapes

1953: execution of the Rosenbergs, accused of spying

1955: Disneyland California opens its doors

1960: 'Pop Art' launched by Andy Warhol

1962: death of Marilyn Monroe on 5 August

1963: assassination of President John F. Kennedy in Dallas, Texas on 22 November

1964: start of the Vietnam War

1966: foundation of the 'Black Panthers' by the friends of Malcolm X, in Oakland; the expression 'Black Power' coined by Stokeley Carmichael when campaigning to send blacks back to Africa

1968: assassination of Martin Luther King on 4 April and of Bobby Kennedy on 4 June

1969: Neil Armstrong takes the first steps on the Moon; Dennis Hopper's *Easy Rider*

1973: World Trade Centre built in New York; first black mayors elected in Los Angeles, Atlanta and Detroit

1974: 'Watergate Affair' brings down President Richard Nixon

1977: Concorde makes first trans-Atlantic crossing

1980: John Lennon murdered in New York

1984: the statue of Liberty is designated as a UNESCO World Heritage Site; Los Angeles Olympic Games boycotted by countries of the Eastern bloc

1987: creation of 'Act Up', the AIDS support and action-group

1991: Gulf War 17 January to 27 February

1992: election of Bill Clinton as president. Los Angeles riots (59 dead and 2,300 injured)

1994: 'Whitewater Affair', in which President Clinton's financial affairs are under scrutiny

1996: Bill Clinton re-elected. for second term of office

1998: the Monica Lewinsky affair implicates the President; he emerges unscathed

1999: death of John Kennedy Jr. and his wife in a flying accident

2000: end of Bill Clinton's term of office. Presidential election in November: Al Gore versus George W. Bush

THE AMERICAN DREAM

From the shanty-town dwellers in Asia to the intellectuals in the West, from the businessmen of Japan to the *apparatchiks* of the former Soviet Union, almost everyone has always had, tucked away inside, some part of the American dream. This rather extraordinary fascination, shared by so many, cannot be explained merely by America's industrial might or the strength of the dollar. It may be that most of us have a childlike dream of a 'new world' imprinted on our subconscious. And, as proof of this, Mickey Mouse and Westerns, those epitomes of American culture, have ended up as part of many cultures around the world.

THE BERING STRAIT

The early colonists called the Native Americans 'Redskins', not because of their natural skin colour (which is closer to yellow), but because of the red paint they used to decorate their faces.

Arriving from Asia in approximately 50,000 BC, the wave of immigration lasted until the 11th or 10th century BC. These first immigrants were able to cross the Bering Strait on foot, because the great ice fields of the north extended as far as the Strait. Travelling on the West Coast, along the Rockies, these prehistoric people gradually penetrated the American continent to the east and to the south. This great migration lasted 25,000 years, after which, as the climate changed, the Bering Strait was submerged once more. For a long time, the Native Americans in both the north and the south imagined that they were alone in the world, as they knew the vastness of the American continent and the enormous bodies of water that surrounded it.

Although other kinds of civilization developed in Mexico and South America, the Native Americans of North America were, with few exceptions, nomads – perhaps because of the abundance of the country's resources. It has long been thought that a nomadic lifestyle slows down society's evolution, since, in order to invent and evolve, man must not only be confronted with challenges, he must also be sedentary in order to understand the reason for conserving and developing his acquisitions. It has to be said, though, that although the early colonists described the Native Americans as 'savages', the current state of ignorance about them, although much reduced, is still astonishing.

There was never a 'Native American nation' per se, but a multitude of tribes spread across the whole of North America. The size of the continent is such that, before the arrival of the white man, there are thought to have been more than 1,000 Native American languages, each incomprehensible to members of any other linguistic group. Isolated from each other, they never saw the true extent of their diversity. Since the arrival of the 'Paleface', more than 300 languages have disappeared.

Lifestyles varied from tribe to tribe. Some were sedentary, like the Pueblos (named thus by the Spanish because they lived in villages), but the majority lived by fishing, hunting and food-gathering, moving around following the game animals and the seasons. It is impossible to guess how many of them there might have been before the arrival of the white man, but some ethnologists estimate that there were as many as 10 to 12 million.

THE DISCOVERY OF AMERICA

Leif Eriksson (the son of Eric the Red), a Viking, explored the east coast of the New World. In 1003, accompanied by 35 men, he departed from South Greenland and explored the entire coast from Newfoundland to

New England, spending the winter on an island he called Vinland (now thought likely to have been Martha's Vineyard). Other expeditions followed and there were some brief attempts at colonization, but the Vikings eventually returned home. This happened centuries before Christopher Columbus 'discovered' America.

Columbus was looking for a short route to the East Indies. Most of the educated men of his day had come to the conclusion that the Earth really could be round. There must, therefore, be another route to the treasures of the Orient apart from the one taken by Vasco da Gama, even if, paradoxically, it lay in the west. A native of Genoa, Columbus lived in Portugal, and so it was to King John of Portugal that he turned to finance his expedition. King John was not interested, and it was finally a Spanish monk, Perez, the confessor to Queen Isabella of Spain, who helped Columbus approach the Queen and gain finance for his expedition. (There's currently a move to canonize Perez for having made possible the Christianization of the Americas.) Columbus's ship, the *Santa Maria*, together with two other little caravels, sailed on 3 August 1492. The *Santa Maria*, being heavy, hard to manoeuvre and slow, was not the ideal vessel for this kind of expedition, but, two months later, on 12 October 1492, Columbus disembarked in the Bahamas, equipped with a letter of introduction . . . to the Grand Khan of China! In fact, as everyone now knows, the original inhabitants of the US got the name 'Indians' because Christopher Columbus had been misinformed.

Stories about Columbus's discovery travelled round Europe like wildfire, and the great wave of travel to the New World had begun. Even more important than this newly-discovered continent was the hope of finding a passage to China, and all the geographers of the time were unanimous on this point – such a passage had to exist! The French king François I sent Jacques Cartier off to have a look, and he made three voyages between 1534 and 1541. Cartier sailed up the St Lawrence River as far as Montreal, where rapids prevented his getting any further. These rapids were named 'Lachine' – since clearly China (*La Chine* in French) was bound to be just a little bit farther on!

A passage was discovered, in 1520, by Fernand de Magellan. The only passage that was feasible at the time was, of course, the route round Cape Horn. So the bitter experiences of the Native Americans and, indeed, the colonization of America, only happened because of that great push to find an easier route to Asia.

THE FIRST ATTEMPTS AT COLONIZATION

Juan Pons reached Florida in 1513, and took it to be an island; on 7 March 1524, the Florentine Giovanni Da Verrazzano, who had also been sent exploring by the French king François I, landed in the New World – which had by then been named America in honour of the explorer and geographer Amerigo Vespucci – and promptly renamed it Francesca in honour of his adopted homeland and the king he served.

From 1539 to 1543, Hernando de Soto discovered and explored such rivers as the Savannah, the Alabama and the majestic Mississippi, but he was finally defeated by the hostile environment. At around the same time, Francisco Vasquez de Coronado left Mexico, crossed the Rio Grande and traversed all of Arizona. Also during the same period, the missionaries of Santa Fe made their first attempt at converting the natives to Christianity, and were martyred for their pains. They died at the hands of the Pueblo tribe and, little by little, the Spanish attempt at conquest ran out of steam. They might not have hesitated if there had been gold and the other rich spoils of a sophisticated civilization to benefit from. As it was, the manpower resources needed for a proper colonization were not available and the Spanish crown soon became convinced that there was no need for Spain to spread its horizons quite that far.

THE ARRIVAL OF THE BRITISH

The first 'English' arrival, John Cabot, was not of English origin, but a Genoese who lived in Bristol. In 1497, he, too, had set out to look for a passage to the Orient and navigated along the coast, laying claim to North America for England. Although he failed to find a passage, Cabot's name was laid down for posterity when the practice of coastal navigation became known as 'cabotage'. His son, Sebastian, working for Spain, went on to explore the coast of Brazil in 1512.

Just as suddenly, America was abandoned again, just as it had been by the Vikings – but it was not left alone for very long. Three-quarters of a century had passed, England had grown prosperous, religious quarrels had died down, and Queen Elizabeth I had been on the throne since 1558. America's time had come. One Martin Frobisher attempted to circumnavigate Canada along the northern route on behalf of the Cathay Company and brought a few poor Native Americans back to London. Sir Humphrey Gilbert suggested the establishment of a colony in America which, when the time came, would be able to supply victuals to ships en route to China. Elizabeth granted him a charter, but the colony never materialized.

Another charter was granted, this time to his half-brother, Sir Walter Raleigh. He was the man behind two attempts at colonization. He dropped anchor near Roanoke Island, naming the land Virginia in honour of Elizabeth, the Virgin Queen. After their first winter, however, the colonists decided to return to England. The second attempt was made one year later and on 8 May 1587, 120 colonists landed. A symbolic event distinguished this second try, as, according to the ship's log, before it sailed away again, a child was born on the soil of the New World – the first 'American', a little girl called Virginia Dare (a fittingly dramatic name in the circumstances). But once again it ended in failure, and a tragic one – for when the ship returned in 1590, the colonists had disappeared without trace.

Despite this series of failures, New World 'fever' had entered the English imagination, although proper colonization did not really begin until the reign of Elizabeth's successor, James I.

On 26 April 1607, after a crossing that took four months, 144 men and women sailed up the James River in three ships and chose as their anchorage a place that they called Jamestown. These colonists were led by a 27-year-old merchant adventurer, Captain John Smith, who had fought in Europe and knew how to keep good discipline. He penetrated the country and made topographical studies. The presence of a strong leader was vital in this kind of situation, and there is a story that illustrates how true this is. John Smith was captured by the Native Americans, but his life was saved by Pocahontas, the daughter of King Powhatan. After spending some time living with this tribe, he realized that his colonists could survive only by growing 'Native American corn', or maize. He went back and suggested to the colonists that they cultivate maize from seed provided by the Native Americans. This met with resistance, because although they were happy to go hunting, search for gold, and barter with the Native Americans, the colonists had no desire to become farmers. Eventually, however, maize would go on to make a great contribution to American culture.

NEW ENGLAND

In 1620, a new colony was founded by the 'Pilgrims' who arrived on the *Mayflower*. These Protestant immigrants had set sail to escape from religious persecution in England. They aspired to a simpler form of Christianity – one without the relics of papistry that still, in their view, weighed heavily in the Anglican church. A total of 100 men and women, with 31 children, arrived at Cape Cod. Nothing had prepared these people for their American adventure. They had to fish – but they were not fishermen. Nor did they have many skills as hunters, and had inevitable difficulty in defending themselves against the Native Americans, whom they considered to be savage and dangerous. Worse still, although they had wanted to get to the comforts of Virginia, here they were in New England, a faraway place with a rough climate and barren soil.

Half of them did not survive the first winter. The next year, however, they celebrated the very first Thanksgiving, feasting on a wild turkey. These austere pioneers still represent something of an aristocracy to present-day Americans, and there are a good many people who claim to trace their ancestors back to the *Mayflower*. They were a people with tenacity, strong determination and an even stronger religious commitment – components that were to contribute to the success of the new colony. By the year 1660, their numbers had reached 20,000.

WILLIAM PENN AND THE QUAKERS

Another group of white settlers in America were the Quakers. Their faith was founded on a principle of non-violence, and they rejected the power of the church, doubting the need for a priest to act as intermediary between man and God.

George Fox, who originated these revolutionary and, at the time, subversive notions, was born in 1624. His writings led to the foundation of the Quaker movement. His belief was that all people, whether Christian or pagan, were a manifestation of God's divinity and as a result, must be respected. This was a radical attempt to place religious authority within the individual, and it was being expounded at just the time when both settlers and theologians were arguing that the Native Americans were neither human, nor entitled to occupy their land.

The name of William Penn is the first to be associated with the word 'Quaker'. Born in 1645, Penn was one of many children in an extremely affluent family that had substantial property in both England and Ireland. At the age of 13, he met a man who was to leave a mark on him for life –

Thomas Loe, a Quaker and a dazzling orator. The Quaker influence upset Penn's family, and he was rejected by them for a time. He professed the belief that all men were equal, and despite being imprisoned in 1668 at the age of 24, and persecuted, Penn was to publish 140 books and brochures and write more than 2,000 letters and other documents. *No Cross, No Crown*, published in 1669, became a classic of English literature.

On the death of his father, Penn inherited a considerable fortune, and was immediately able to offer his wealth to the service of his fellow believers. The Quakers had already begun to look towards the New World to flee from persecution, but the Puritans of New England saw the Quaker presence on their territory as an intolerable invasion, and anti-Quaker laws were passed. In 1680, after visiting the New World for himself, William Penn entered into negotiations with King Charles II, and, by way of settlement for the considerable sums owed by the crown to his father, obtained the right to found a new colony in a territory that was to become Pennsylvania ('Penn forest'). It had almost the same land area as England.

The Native Americans who occupied this new colony were the Lenni Lenape (or Delaware), who spoke Algonquin and were semi-nomadic. Penn and the Quakers succeeded in establishing a relationship of brotherly love with them. Penn learned their language as well as other Native American dialects. His house at Pennsbury Park often accommodated a strange crowd of people – and Native Americans arrived by the score, sometimes even by the hundred! The house was kept wide open for them yet no one was alarmed by their painted bodies and their weapons. They settled questions of mutual interest with the man they called 'Onas' (Algonquin for 'pen'). Considering that non-violence was a key element in Quaker principles, the Native Americans could have massacred the entire colony in the twinkling of an eye – instead the two communities co-existed in perfect harmony. The Quaker philosophy was even reflected in the name of their capital, Philadelphia, which derives from the Greek words for 'city of brotherhood'.

There are many tales about the relations between the Quaker and the Native American communities. One element that undoubtedly drew them to each other was a similar way of looking at things. For although, on the one hand, the Native Americans were very primitive in a material sense, their approach to life and their spirituality were very sophisticated. This point is perhaps demonstrated in the following story. A meeting of the Friends was interrupted by the arrival of an aggressive group of Native Americans. They were armed and ready to kill anyone who moved, but, impressed by the reverence and non-violence of these people, they sat down and took part in the service. At the end of the meeting, the chief pulled a white feather from one of his arrows and fixed it above the door. This was a signal to all Native Americans that this was the abode of friends.

THE 'BOSTON TEA PARTY' AND INDEPENDENCE

In 1763, a crisis arose between England and the new colonies, which had become increasingly prosperous. The result would be American independence. In 1773, the Crown imposed a series of highly unpopular taxes and restrictive measures, and nationalist feelings were aroused that culminated, on 16 December, in what became known as the 'Boston Tea Party'. Disguised as Native Americans, a group of colonists boarded three English ships in Boston harbour and threw their cargo of tea overboard.

This event was a landmark. Arms were taken up in 1775 and, on 4 July 1776, the Declaration of Independence was drawn up by Thomas Jefferson and adopted by all 12 colonies. The basis of the Declaration is a philosophy of natural rights that explains that God created an order, which we call the natural order, and that, because of the reason with which God endowed him, any man can discover its principles. Furthermore, all men are free and equal before these laws. On 3 September 1783, a peace treaty, negotiated in Paris, was signed between Britain and America. America later extended its territories, pushing the Native Americans farther and farther into the desert lands of the West, while France sold Louisiana, and a new conflict appeared on the horizon in the shape of the Civil War.

SLAVERY AND THE CIVIL WAR

The idea of slavery itself goes back to ancient times. The Greeks, renowned for their humanity during their golden age of civilization, never had any doubt that mankind was naturally divided into two classes – those whose duty it was to perform heavy labouring tasks and those who, relieved of the burden of such tasks, would be free to cultivate the arts, literature and philosophy.

The immorality of buying and selling people was not the real reason for the Civil War, despite popular belief. For Abraham Lincoln the main concern was not in ending slavery but in maintaining the Union. He is quoted as saying: 'My paramount object is to save the Union and not to save or destroy slavery. If I could save the Union without freeing any slave, I would do it; and if I could save it by freeing all the slaves, I would do it'.

The American Civil War is perhaps best described as a conflict of cultures. The Southern culture was aristocratic, with a foundation of 'easy' money, and was very Latin in feel, with many French and Spanish roots. It was a society with a distinct identity; its people were very attached to 'their' land. The Northern culture was hard-working and austere, its people were highly mobile in pursuit of opportunities of work. They had ideals of the glory of their nation but had little real feeling of attachment to the land. This civil conflict was the most serious in American history and even today is still present in the national consciousness.

It all began with the election of Abraham Lincoln. What resulted was a war that lasted from 1861 to 1865, in which a total of 630,000 died and 400,000 more were wounded. It was also the first 'modern' war – with battles involving armoured ships, repeater rifles and machine-guns. Two profound changes in American society resulted from the Civil War: the first was the abolition of slavery, and the second was the will of the Union to both symbolize and guarantee some form of democracy. Lincoln emerged from it with an enhanced reputation and became a national hero. His assassination on Good Friday in 1865 by John Wilkes Booth –

an actor whose intention was to avenge the South – 'canonized' him in his role as the 'father of the American nation'.

MASS IMMIGRATION

The call of the New World throughout the 19th century and the early years of the 20th century drew immigrants from all over the world, but predominantly from Europe. In 1790, there were 4 million inhabitants – by 1860, this figure had reached 31 million. Between 1865 and 1914, the population tripled, reaching 95 million. There are many historical reasons for this huge wave of immigration, but persecution – both religious and political – and poverty were the main underlying factors. In the main, the immigrants came from Russia, Central Europe, Italy and Germany; their religious roots lay in Judaism and Catholicism as well as the other religions of the West.

In 1973, when the effect of interracial marriages was less pronounced, the ethnic jigsaw was made up as follows: 88 per cent whites, 10.5 per cent African Americans, and 1.5 per cent Native Americans and East Asians. As for their countries of origin, 22 million were from Africa, 15 million from Britain, 7 million from Germany, 5.5 million from Italy, with 4.4 million Austro-Hungarians, 3.4 million Russians, 2.5 million Scandinavians, about 1 million Poles, 300,000 Japanese and 250,000 Chinese.

Today there are still bastions of a cultural group, like the 'Bible Belt', which extends across the centre of the US and is mainly German and British in origin and strongly Protestant. Some pure minority groups have tended to take over well-defined parts of the larger cities, creating such areas as Chinatown and Japantown.

But the American family tree is becoming an increasingly complex ethnic kaleidoscope, and it seems likely that, in the not-too-distant future, a new 'race', unique in the history of man, will be born from the American melting pot.

AMERICA JOINS THE GREAT POWERS

Immediately after the Great War of 1914–1918, the supremacy of Great Britain began to decline and the US became a player on the world's chessboard. A clear pattern of this rise to power can be seen in the dates of certain inventions. 1831: development of the McCormick harvester; 1835: invention of the revolver (Samuel Colt); 1843: invention of the typewriter; 1844: invention of the telegraph (Samuel Morse); 1874: invention of barbed wire; 1876: invention of the telephone (Alexander Graham Bell); 1878: invention of the incandescent lamp and the phonograph by Thomas Edison.

In 1919, came the era of 'Prohibition', and the 18th amendment to the constitution prohibited the manufacture, sale and transport of alcoholic beverages. The corruption that resulted from this ban was inevitable and it took many forms – fraud, illegal trafficking and even prostitution. It took until 1933 for the ban to be lifted. This was done by President Franklin D. Roosevelt, who abolished the amendment soon after his election, in an attempt to raise morale.

The 1920s were crazy years. While American intellectuals gathered in the bars of Paris, stock-market speculation gathered pace. America was dancing to a new kind of music that was to open up the way to a new kind of popular song – they called it jazz. Women had won the right to vote, thanks to the efforts of the suffragettes. But the great euphoria ended tragically in October 1929 with the Wall Street crash. The world was horrified to see pictures of ruined businessmen jumping to their deaths from skyscraper windows, and of marathon dance competitions in which contestants danced till they dropped for a prize of a few dollars.

The early 1930s was also a grim period for the small farmers of the Mid-West 'Dust Bowl', who had to leave their land in their thousands to escape from the drought exacerbated by the collapse of the economy. The author, composer and singer Woody Guthrie has left us a poignant testimony of the era. Force of circumstances made him a hobo and he spent the Depression years hitching rides on the long, slow trains that crossed the US. With his guitar as companion, he wrote songs about the everyday lives of the people of the time. His music became widely known, perhaps due as much to the social climate as to his talent, and he became a spokesman for rural America. A political activist on the extreme left (he was actually a Communist, although the party refused him membership because of his religious beliefs), the American government regarded him with suspicion. Fear of the 'Reds' was already beginning to emerge. Guthrie was the father of folk song; in the 1960s he was the inspiration for the protest movement and had a major influence on the folk music revival of the time. To Bob Dylan, and to many more besides, he was an idol.

MCCARTHY AND THE BLACKLISTS

Franklin D. Roosevelt's pre-war 'New Deal' had been the medicine that was to cure the American economy. It was already taking effect in the unhappy context of World War II, and an era of prosperity opened up with the arrival of peace. The 1950s were also the era of Senator Joseph McCarthy and his blacklists. Communism represented the total opposite of America's spirit of free enterprise and its values – everything that America had come to stand for. America was all the more apprehensive about a rise of Western Communism because it seemed as though the intellectuals of the time were fascinated by what they saw as a humanist and generous doctrine. McCarthy began a militant nationwide crusade against people, especially those in public positions, who had Communist leanings. Blacklists were drawn up and for a period of three years, the lives and careers of many were threatened as his Committee of Un-American Activities carried out their investigations. This created a climate of fear and malice, encouraging colleagues to inform on colleagues. By 1954, McCarthy had lost his seat in the Senate; his name remained in the American vocabulary in the word 'McCarthyism' – forever associated with the unfounded persecutions of the early 1950s.

WELL-FED REBELS

The 'Beat Generation' appeared in about 1960, led by writers and poets like Jack Kerouac and Allen Ginsberg. Rebellious, detached from the ownership of material goods and dedicated to the spirit of freedom, the Beat Generation hit the road in search of an alternative lifestyle. Affluent society had created a series of injustices that drove young people to reject the 'adult' world.

This breakaway from behaving like their parents resulted in the arrival of a whole new kind of music – 'young people's music'. At one end of the extreme it was gentle folk and protest songs – at the other end it was raw rock'n'roll. The early beatniks dreamed of rebuilding a fairer world as they listened to Bob Dylan and Joan Baez, the successors of Woody Guthrie. Rock'n'roll erupted in 1956 with the arrival of Bill Haley – then came Elvis Presley.

Both wanted to be a symbol of revolt, but in a form very different from that of the beatniks, yet while early rock'n'roll certainly expressed a rejection of institutional values, it offered no solutions, contenting itself with a condemnation of the adult world.

It was perhaps James Dean, in *Rebel Without a Cause*, who best expressed the malaise experienced by young people in general. Dean died in a violent car accident in 1955 at the age of 24 and was immediately elevated to cult status. For many years after his death he was the very embodiment of youthful rebellion.

The 1960s also saw the arrival of black music being sung by black people in what might best be described as the 'white charts'. Up to that time, there had been 'black' radio stations and 'white' radio stations, and 'black' hits crossed the cultural divide only when white singers brought out cover versions. It was possible for misunderstandings to ensue: Chuck Berry, arriving at a venue where he was booked to play, was refused admission by the organizer. The man hadn't for a moment thought that these songs, describing American youth so faithfully, could have been written and sung by a black man. The concert went ahead without him, with a white band playing and singing the material.

Elvis Presley, by contrast, owed a great deal of his success to the fact that he was a white boy singing with a 'black' voice, while Chuck Berry broke through the black–white barrier to reach the top because his material drew on white Country and Western culture.

As a side-note, County and Western – still America's most popular music by far – is largely rooted in the traditional songs of Europe, especially Ireland. Just voice and guitar, it captures a feeling of nostalgia for the old pioneering days of the Far West and there's a characteristic 'campfire' feeling to it. In the old days in the West, the Irish cowboys were highly prized because they could sing all night while minding the herd, which kept the cattle quiet!

SEGREGATION

The barriers of segregation officially began to break down in 1953, when the Supreme Court decided to put an end to segregation in the school system, but it took the civil rights movement, headed by Martin Luther King, to stir the national conscience. The white singer Pete Seeger (another disciple of Guthrie) did a lot for the African American cause with his witty lyrics condemning segregation.

The 1960s were a time of protest almost everywhere in the world. The assassination of President John F. Kennedy in Dallas in 1963 signalled the end of a healthy, young, dynamic vision of politics. A more Machiavellian era had dawned, illustrated perhaps by the death of Marilyn Monroe. With the benefit of 30 years of hindsight, it seems that her death may not have been the suicide it had appeared to be, but rather that her death was a consequence of her relationships with some high profile politicians. Someone perhaps felt that she was expendable.

Idealism was moving along, and by 1966, the beatniks were succeeded by the hippies, who rejected the political world in a desire to return to nature. Wearing ethnic clothes and letting their hair grow long, the hippies wanted to distance themselves from a society whose principles were becoming increasingly suspect. The use of soft drugs such as cannabis became commonplace, and hallucinogenic drugs also played their part in the everyday life of many young people. In the meantime, the war in Vietnam began in 1964. Many young Americans saw their peers being lost in a conflict that seemed both mindless and unnecessary, and people burned their military call-up cards in public demonstrations.

One consequence of the American defeat in the Vietnam War was the growing political awareness of young people. Their hunger for higher ideals set the scene for the downfall of President Richard Nixon, who in 1974 felt obliged to resign when the often-denied involvement of the White House in breaches of national security finally became public knowledge. The nation reverted to Democrat rule when President Jimmy Carter narrowly beat Nixon's deputy and successor Gerald Ford in 1976. Carter's air of informality and honest integrity gave him his appeal, but he came to be perceived as ineffective, as the country's economic position worsened, and he failed to handle well the hostage crisis in Iran where American embassy staff were held by Islamic fundamentalists. The America of that period showed to the world the face of a nation that had become the victim of its own contradictions, undermined by public opinion, and undergoing a headlong economic recession.

The 1980s ushered in a profound revival of American hearts and minds. The election of a former movie star (the Republican Ronald Reagan) in 1980 gave the country back its 'cowboy' image. New tax laws had the effect of widening the gap between the rich and the poor. Superficially, the recession slowed down and industry made a recovery. But the America of the losers was becoming ever more visible, with a shocking number of homeless people living below the world poverty level in a country that seemed to care little for social problems. The 'other America', in harmony with Reagan, had become obsessed by aerobics and healthy living. Finally, the emergence of AIDS was to put an end to years of sexual freedom.

WORLD ORDER AND NATIONAL DISORDER

The Gulf War, which was expected to bring a halt to the recession, only made it worse. And George Bush, who had served as Reagan's Vice-President for eight years before himself being elected, played the puppeteer, brandishing the hate figure of Saddam Hussein. Concentrating more than anything on America's world standing and the strategy of a 'new world order', Bush and the Republican administration forgot about their electors, extolling the virtues of democracy in the Third World while neglecting them at home.

While American soldiers were intervening in Iraq, living conditions in the US continued to deteriorate, with rising unemployment, the abolition of welfare assistance, growing violence, the spread of hard drugs, and the growing scourge of AIDS. Just one year after the Gulf War, the American homeland was itself a scene of violence with disturbances in Los Angeles and other cities. Disillusioned, the American people duly punished Bush in the presidential elections of November 1992.

The Democrats duly prevailed and the hero of this election, Bill Clinton, epitomized the complete opposite of everything that Reagan and Bush had stood for. He was young, sincere and approachable. In a way, he was the voice of the Vietnam generation, sharing its concern for the environment and reflecting its pacifist aspirations and its tendency, at all political and social levels, to give more responsibility to women and to the representatives of ethnic minorities. He had all the promise of a new breed of president – but Clinton's tenure was not to be easy.

He was convincingly re-elected in 1996, in a contest against the Republican senator Bob Dole, who people saw as being a throwback to the Reagan years, Since then, America has seen Bill Clinton's most private actions discussed throughout the world in the shape of the 'Monica Lewinsky Affair', from which he emerged with his reputation bruised but intact. Clinton's amatory adventures were followed by one of the most bizarre episodes in American electoral history. The presidential election of November 2000 was left in chaos as George W. Bush, the son of the previous president but one, and Al Gore, Clinton's Vice President, fought in the courts over a handful of disputed votes in the decisive state of Florida. The Supreme Court intervened, and Bush eventually emerged the victor.

THE NATIVE AMERICANS

Native Americans had no notion of property, and lived in close proximity to the earth both spiritually and mentally. Nor could they have any conception of the mentality or laws of the European newcomers. The pioneers took shameless advantage of the tribes, dispossessing them of their lands in return for simple gifts. The Native Americans were fascinated by the unfamiliar objects they received in exchange for something that they could not possibly imagine being treated as a commodity – their land. The white man, greedy for new land and riches, made little attempt to reach any understanding with the tribes and, since a rifle would always outshoot a bow and arrow, he could and did take possession of the land without compunction. The livelihood of the Native Americans was also threatened by the near extermination of the buffalo, an animal which provided sustenance in the form of meat and hide for clothing and teepees. They made use of every part of the animal, whereas the hunting of buffalo became something of a sport for the white man, with animals discarded and left rotting on the plains. William Cody, otherwise known as Buffalo Bill, was contracted to kill nearly 5,000 buffalo in just 18 months to feed workers on the Kansas Pacific Railway.

Had the Native Americans taken a more conventional, and, in European terms, proprietorial view of their territories, the virtual wholesale physical and cultural destruction of the tribes could have been avoided. The initial bands of pioneers who penetrated the tribal lands could have been repelled, but there was no resistance. It wasn't until the white man had become well-established, bringing in more and more of his own people to colonize the land and erect townships, that the Native Americans began to retaliate. But it was too late. Driven out of what, according to Native American creed, were lands that belonged to everybody, the tribes fought back and bitter conflict ensued, but by then the white man was just too well entrenched.

THE NATIVE AMERICAN WARS: 1675–1915

The Native American Wars lasted, technically, almost 300 years, although the Native Americans were inadequately equipped to fight and they lacked solidarity. Barely 50 years after the *Mayflower* had landed, Chief Massassoit saw the dangers presented by the growing number of ships arriving from Europe. As well as taking his people's land, the newcomers inflicted murderous acts of violence and rape on the Native Americans. His response was to gather together a confederation of the tribes in his region and they went on the warpath against the Puritans. This initial conflict cost the lives of 20,000 Redskins and 50,000 colonists.

This victory, however, was to little avail. The surviving Native Americans would later be sold into slavery in the West Indies. This battle, and all the ones that followed, was fought in vain. Only the Battle of Little Big Horn was a victory for the Native Americans, bringing death to the notorious General George Custer and the 260 bluecoats in his cavalry command on 25 June 1876. It was an empty victory though, as it led to the inexcusable butchery at Wounded Knee, Nebraska, on 29 December 1890, when the US Seventh Cavalry massacred hundreds of Sioux, including women and children. This act flew directly in the face of the standing agreement that the white flag of surrender would offer protection.

Always at odds with each other and often in rivalry, the tribes nevertheless went into combat unified. But the treacherous white man went on to find means other than warfare for wiping out the Native Americans. The list of outrages is a long one. Disease was a useful ally – officers at Fort Pitt, for example, distributed to the Native Americans gifts of handkerchiefs and blankets that had been obtained from a smallpox isolation hospital. And alcohol was another weapon, with even the 'great and good' Benjamin Franklin declaring that: 'Rum should be considered a gift of Providence for extirpating these savages and making room for the cultivators of the soil'.

ATTEMPTS AT ASSIMILATION

As the 20th century dawned, the Native American population had been reduced to 250,000 – and that was more by oversight than design. In 1920, the American government took up the challenge of the Native American question again, this time aiming for a 'melting pot' approach. They called it a policy of assimilation. Many attempts were made to get the Native Americans to leave their reservations and become integrated into the 'American way of life'. It was thought that the introduction of the Christian faith would help, and Christian missions were given special subsidies for this pioneering work. Inevitably, the use of the Native American languages was discouraged in favour of English.

Only one Native American symbol is used by the American nation and yet it's perhaps the most significant – the American eagle. This is an Iroquois emblem, and the arrows the eagle grasps in its talons represent the six Native American nations.

In 1924, the Native Americans were granted American citizenship – an honour not lacking in irony. To help the process of assimilation, the reserves were to be done away with. The tribal lands, which had been collective property, were divided up and shared out between all the families.

This was a serious sociological mistake, one of many made by the white man. It put an end to Native American hierarchies and privileges, and the great majority felt unable to exist once cut off from their roots and their culture. Just as the Native American was extremely vulnerable to diseases imported by the white man, there was no hope for him, either economically or socially, once isolated within a white society.

One of the greatest benefactors of the American Indian turned out to be President Richard Nixon. It was he who, with a single stroke of the pen, drew a line under this disastrous policy of assimilation.

A Native American reserve is, in some ways, a ghetto – but it is also a reserved territory, the private property of the Native Americans, where they can organize themselves in their own way, respecting their culture and traditions. Just occasionally, they have been known to take advantage of this quasi-autonomy, opening gambling casinos in states where this kind of business is ordinarily prohibited. There are more than a few Native American millionaires as a result.

It is not that the 20th-century Native American has rejected progress – he has simply refused to accept the structure of a society into which he cannot be integrated. There are currently 400 reserves for the 310 surviving tribes. In spite of this, it has been estimated that barely 10 per cent of the budget of the Bureau of Native American Affairs actually reaches these reserves. The Native American population is growing quite rapidly and is now approaching a total of two million. Incidentally, there are 14 Native American radio stations that you can easily pick up with your car radio: Navajo in Arizona, Zuni in New Mexico.

THE NATIVE AMERICAN: MULTIRACIAL, BUT NOT MULTICULTURAL

The Native American peoples, whose mobility was to be their misfortune for 400 years, were relocated and dislocated by the white man, with total lack of regard for any treaty. This mobility led to an intermingling of the tribes, with many interracial marriages. Today, Native Americans will opt for a free computer check before marriage. This is strongly advised, for the children of the marriage must not be left with less than the established minimum of one-eighth Native American blood. Once the blood is diluted this far, a person loses their Native American 'citizenship', and thus their rights inside the reserve. These 'rights' have been known to be substantial. For example, the Osage Native Americans of Oklahoma discovered oil on their territory, bringing royalties of $800 million between 1906 and 1972. Since shares are indivisible and passed on only by inheritance, an 'heir' always tries to marry an 'heiress' in order to prevent any dilution by non-Native American blood.

But, in spite of this, the Native Americans still remain the ethnic group with the lowest per-capita income and some of the most serious problems in the United States. It is estimated that as many as 40 per cent of the members of certain tribes are alcoholics. What's more, there are 700 lawyers of Native American race all apparently involved in litigation with the government on questions such as the violation of Native American cemeteries.

On a cultural note, it's worth knowing that many ruined Anasazi villages still exist in the West. The Anasazi once occupied the American Southwest and the Navajos claim descent from them. These villages, built in the canyons between 1100 and 1300 BC, can still be seen at the Navajo National Monument (Arizona) and, further afield, in Mesa Verde National Park (Colorado).

HUMAN RIGHTS

The federal constitution of the US allows individual states considerable freedom to determine their own laws and criminal justice systems. This makes it rather difficult to generalize, but it is safe to say that for a country with such long established democratic credentials, the human rights record of the USA is rather more questionable than one might expect.

Most significantly the USA is among the very small minority of developed countries that retains the death penalty and uses it on a regular basis. It is currently available in 38 States of the US, including California, where in 1999 there were 525 prisoners awaiting execution, Nevada where there were 85 and Arizona where there were 119. These states currently use lethal injection rather then the more barbaric electric chair. The question of racism adds another dimension to the capital punishment issue. A United Nations report in 1997 found that those from black or Hispanic ethnic groups were significantly more likely to receive a death sentence than whites. There has also been concern at the imposition of the death penalty on prisoners who were juveniles at the time of their offence. Despite these doubts, capital punishment has popular backing in the US and is supported by politicians keen to be seen as tough on offenders. There seems little immediate prospect of change.

The US has among the highest prison populations in the world, over 1.8 million, or one out of every 150 residents. Californian law requires that anyone convicted of three felonies be given a life sentence, and this has lead to such sentences being imposed on minor, but recidivist, offenders. Partly due to this, Californian prisons are operating at over twice their designed capacity, and as in other states, conditions in prisons are a cause for concern. There are frequent allegations of violence against prisoners by prison guards. As with the ethnic composition of death row, all US states have a disproportionate number of prisoners from ethnic minorities. For instance, while in the US as a whole, African-Americans amount to 12 per cent of the population, they compose 49 per cent of the overall prison population. While this is undoubtedly due to a combination of social and political factors, there is persistent evidence of racial bias in the criminal justice system, particularly by the police.

There are frequent allegations of police brutality, including unjustified shootings and severe beatings, allegations which are often inadequately investigated by the authorities. The federal Justice Department was sufficiently concerned that it initiated reviews of several police forces, including Los Angeles and Riverside in California, to investigate claims of a general pattern of abuse.

Reflecting its domestic record, at an international level, the US has been at best a lukewarm supporter of treaties designed to protect human rights. In addition to opposing treaties to ban the use of anti-personnel land mines, it recently aligned itself with some of the world's most repressive regimes to oppose the creation of an International Criminal Court, one of the principal roles of which would be the protection of human rights.

To find out more, contact **Amnesty International** at one of the following addresses:

– **UK**: 99-119 Rosebery Avenue, London, EC1R 4RE. ☎ (020) 7814 6200 (relocating in summer 2001).

– **Republic of Ireland**: Sean MacBride House, 48 Fleet Street, Dublin 2. ☎ (01) 677 6361.

– **Australia**: Private Bag 23, Broadway, NSW 2007. ☎ (02) 9217-7600.

– **New Zealand**: PO Box 793, Wellington. ☎ (04) 499-3349.

– **Canada**: 214 Montreal Road, Fourth floor, Vanier, Ontario, K1L 1A4. ☎ (613) 744-7667.

– **United States**: 322 8th Avenue, New York, NY 10001. ☎ (212) 807-8400.

FOOD AND DRINK

The popularity of fast-food chains and 'eat as much as you can' offers have contributed to the notion that the American diet comprises excessive amounts of unhealthy food. Whilst there are plenty of cheap snack bars selling hamburgers, fries, hot dogs and the like, there is much more to the American diet than first meets the eye. Those planning to travel around the States will quickly discover a wide variety of culinary delights from the cosmopolitan tastes of New York to the Creole cuisine of Louisiana. Renowned for its fresh fruit and high quality fish and meat, California is one of the healthiest states to eat in, with a tantalizing selection of organic, vegetarian and low-fat cuisine. Like all big cities, you'll also find a large range of international food such as Mexican, Spanish, Chinese and Thai.

Restaurant portions in America are usually very generous and the choice can be overwhelming. Prices tend to be fairly reasonable, but by the time you add the cost of drinks and the obligatory 15 per cent tip, the final bill may be more than you bargained for. If you're staying in a place for several days, you'll get more for your money if you buy your food from supermarkets such as Safeway, Vons, Whole Foods Market and Albertson's – many of which have a deli counter, where they prepare freshly made sandwiches and salads. For those wanting a snack en route, look out for restaurant chains such as Howard Johnson's and Holiday Inn; prices may be higher, but you'll find a more varied and enjoyable menu than in the average hamburger joint.

BREAKFAST

For breakfast, you may be served a really convivial meal that's copious and varied. The menu is frequently as long as your arm, with a choice of fruit juices, cereals, hash browns (potatoes, grated and grilled), pancakes or French toast, and, of course, eggs.

If you order an egg, the waitress will ask you how you want it. Scrambled, as an omelette or fried. A fried egg can be 'up' or 'over' (cooked on both sides). In the latter case, if you don't want the yolk to be over-cooked, ask for it 'over easy'. Eggs can also (of course) be boiled or hard-boiled. You can add ham, bacon, sausages, plenty of ketchup, a few slices of buttered toast, and French fries.

And then there's the muffins, flavoured with raspberries, blueberries or gooseberries, crisp and delicious. These are found chiefly in the coffee-shops. Doughnuts are also popular in America. The leading chain, **Dunkin' Donuts**, sells a huge range – from plain ones to ones baked with jam or cream, coated with chocolate, or sugar, or a pink icing.

Bear in mind that the **all-in breakfasts**, offered at hugely competitive prices, usually don't include a hot drink. Breakfast in America, however, still gives you one of the best combinations of quality, quantity and price in the world.

LUNCH

In some restaurants, particularly in large cities, the same meals cost much more in the evening than at lunchtime, especially if there's a good ambiance. Perhaps the thing to do is to eat a good lunch, and stick to toast in the evening!

– 'Today's specials' are served both at lunchtime and in the evening and frequently offer great value for money. There are usually two or three of them and you'll find them displayed at the entrance to the restaurant. A special usually includes a bowl of soup (New England clam chowder or minestrone, for example) or a salad, which will fill you right up for just a handful of dollars.

– If you're hungry but don't want to overindulge, try the salad bars. These often give you a buffet choice of vegetables and salads for a reasonable price and you can have as many helpings as you want. An example of a salad bar menu: melon, tomatoes, celery, radish, carrots, grated cabbage, green salad, fruit salad, beans, spaghetti salad, and sometimes cakes and fruit, etc.

The Americans have a large choice of dressings to accompany their salads, which make a change from the standard vinaigrette. These include Blue Cheese, Thousand Island, Ranch, Italian and Caesar (a terrific accompaniment for Caesar salad, the deluxe version of which is made from romaine lettuce, croutons, Parmesan cheese and sometimes roast chicken or sautéed shrimp).

– Then there are 'delis'. New York delis specialize in Jewish cuisine, but any American will tell you that a deli is a typically American invention and the word 'deli' (short for delicatessen) has passed into the language. You'll be offered the finest of sandwiches, with pastrami, corned beef or turkey, served on wholemeal bread with gherkins and the ubiquitous little cardboard pot of coleslaw.

– Some restaurants advertize 'all you can eat'. For a few dollars you can eat your fill – and that really means 'fill'. This is a great way to try everything. Freshness is guaranteed, although quality perhaps not always so. All the casinos in Las Vegas offer this deal in order to attract customers. Elsewhere, in the big cities, some restaurants do it once a week, on their slackest day. At any rate, it's nice and cheap.

BRUNCH

Brunch is great on Saturday or Sunday morning. After a long lie-in, it's too late for breakfast but you're too hungry to wait for lunch. Quite a number of restaurants serve brunch at around 11am. This is a proper meal, in fact, which consists of the dishes traditionally served for breakfast, with a hot drink in addition.

SPECIALITIES

– **Meat**: American steak is top quality. The best cut you can get is prime rib, which is the tenderest of meat. There is no direct equivalent in Europe, and you only have to try it once – and you're hooked. American cattle tend to be smaller in size than the European breeds, so you can tackle a T-bone steak (tenderloin with a T-shaped bone) with greater ease. You'll have to decide whether you want it well done, medium or rare, and you can even add a few extra nuances – medium rare, medium well, etc. It'll come served exactly the way you asked. The system used by chefs here is to insert a little thermometer into the meat to indicate how the interior of the meat is doing.

The West, with its cowboys and cattlemen, has provided America and the rest of the world with an indispensable recipe – the **barbecue**, and this comes accompanied by an array of bottled sauces. **Fried chicken** from Kentucky (or elsewhere) is another basic component of the American menu, and there's also a wide range of **seafood**.

– In America the **hamburger** doesn't suffer from the poor image that it has in Britain. Although fast-food outlets tend to serve up food at the bottom of the quality range, the genuine hamburger restaurants serve fresh, juicy, tender and savoury meat, enclosed in two slices of good fresh bread.

– There's more to learn about the **sandwich** than you might think. What Europeans think of as a sandwich is called a 'cold sandwich' in America. A 'hot sandwich', by contrast, is a real hot meal that might include a hamburger, French fries and salad, so it will be much more expensive. Lots of the bread in America seems to have the consistency of a marshmallow, but it is possible to buy breads with a more interesting texture such as barley bread, wholemeal bread, rye bread, etc. An alternative to the sandwich is the 'submarine', a soft roll served with a more elaborate filling than you'd find in the average 'cold sandwich'.

The term **hot dog** was supposedly coined in 1901 in America when a cartoonist overheard a street vendor selling sausages in rolls and calling them 'dachshund' sausages. Desperate for an idea for his cartoon strip and unable to spell dachshund, he called them hot dogs, the cartoon was a hit and the phrase stuck. Stories vary about how the hot dog came to be sold in a roll but the obvious attraction was that it was a quick, easy meal and the roll prevented people from burning their fingers.

– **Popcorn**: if you like your popcorn sweet, be sure to say so when buying it, otherwise it comes salted. You can also have it with melted butter.

– **Ice-cream and desserts** are sold in thousands of ice-cream parlours, like Dairy Queen, a national chain bearing a variety of names such as Baskin Robbins, where they offer a choice of 31 delicious flavours. An 'American Sundae', for example, involves strawberry, grated coconut, pineapple, caramel, or hot fudge, which is hot, thick, melted chocolate with added nuts. At Ben & Jerry's, you could also try the Chocolate Chip Cookie Dough, the Dilbery's World Totally Nuts (with sugared almonds), the Caramel Chew Chew, the Double Trouble (made with dark and milk chocolate) or the Rainforest Chunk (with cashews covered in caramel). They're all truly delicious. As well as making ice-cream, Ben & Jerry's is a 'good-citizen' enterprise, and very original. They employ people suffering hardship, and buy organic products from small farmers in Vermont. They are original in that the two hippies who founded the business back in 1963 in a milk-bar attached to a gas station in Vermont, are still thinking up great ideas such as the 'Economic Crunch' (an ice-cream launched on Wall Street on the day of the market crisis, 19 October 1987) or the 'Cherry Garcia', named in honour of the leader of the Grateful Dead.

USEFUL TIPS

– Generally, the cheapest restaurants (which are also often the best) are those run by immigrant families. Their origins vary from one region to the next, so there are lots of Mexican restaurants in the Southwest and Asian restaurants on the West Coast.

– Left-overs: if your eyes were bigger than your stomach, ask for a plastic 'doggy' bag to take away the left-overs. They're quite used to this. And frequently they have given you too much in the first place.

– Many newspapers include coupons in their Wednesday edition. These offer substantial reductions, especially in restaurants, supermarkets, etc. The savings are real. But be aware that many of these coupons are not valid on weekends, or in the summer months.

– Many restaurants offer a children's menu, even for breakfast.

– Most bars have a 'happy hour' (usually 4pm–6pm). In these periods of slack business, food is often free if you buy a drink. The idea of a happy hour is for you to have a drink and a nibble before dinner, which explains why there is often a restaurant next to the bar. On the California coast, this kind of meal is often called an 'early-bird special'.

– When eating somewhere 'chic', hold your fork in your right hand and rest your left hand on your knee, or you'll be taken for a real peasant! You have been warned.

– Except at truck-stops or cafeterias, you can't just take any table on arrival, unless there's a sign saying 'Please seat yourself'.

RESTAURANT CHAINS

Scattered all over the US, the well-known restaurant chains can at least assure you of the same quality for the same price – if you're in the mood for it. As well as the universal McDonald's and Wimpy, you could try Taco Bell (for Mexican fast food), House of Pancakes, and Dunkin' Donuts for small snacks.

As well as being more chic, Steak Houses and Seafood Houses are renowned for the freshness of their products.

DRINKING

Alcohol is probably more frowned upon in the US than in Europe. It does seem a bit odd that in a society where you can fairly easily buy a Kalashnikov and boxes of ammunition you will often be asked for proof of your age if you just want to buy a beer! Perhaps the legacy of the Prohibition and, of course, powerful religious lobbies, have been over-influential. It's probably best to always carry your passport, particularly if you look much younger than you are, because you'll be asked to show it at some bistros.

– **Minimum age**: in bars and some grocery stores, they won't serve you alcohol if you are a minor or can't prove your age. The drinking age is 21, but you can always try it on.

– **Sales and consumption**: drinking alcohol in the street is strictly prohibited. You can also be arrested if you have bottles in your car that have been opened. And don't forget that, on Native American reservations, the sale of alcohol is forbidden.

– **Wine**: despite the rules and regulations about their consumption, Californian wines are very good!

– **Cocktails**: the word 'cocktail' was invented in America, and not many people seem to know the origin of the word. Back in the olden days, cockerel feathers of different colours were attached to glasses so that drinkers could identify their drinks. The story goes that in 1779, during the War of Independence, American and French officers of the Revolutionary Army would meet each day in Betsy Flanagan's inn at Yorktown, Virginia. One evening, she said she intended to do away with a cockerel belonging to an Englishman that she hated. No sooner said than done: a few hours later, she returned with the cockerel's tail. To celebrate the event, they held a banquet, in the course of which the golden head feathers were used to decorate the glasses. Some great cocktails that are worth a try include: Manhattan (red vermouth and bourbon), Screwdriver (vodka and orange juice), Dry Martini (vermouth and gin), Bloody Mary (vodka and tomato juice) and Black Velvet (champagne and stout).

– **Bourbon**: it's worth remembering to try Bourbon – the American whisky. At least half of this is produced in Kentucky.

– **Soft drinks**: the Americans drink soft drinks (which they call 'sodas') all the time: Coca-Cola, Seven-Up, Dr Pepper, Fresca, Tab . . . and many more. An added bonus is that, in many fast-food outlets, coffee shops and other small restaurants, the sodas are free. To check this out, ask for a refill. Try iced tea, vegetable juices (tomato juice, V8, etc.), fruit juices and extra-light beer (which doesn't give you a hangover).

– **Iced water**: in restaurants, it is also customary to give every customer a glass of iced water. If you are broke, go into any building and you'll find a drinking fountain with delightfully cool water. Due to water shortages in some Southwestern states it may not be served automatically any more, but it is still free if you ask for it.

– **In the morning**: it's best to order coffee with breakfast rather than tea because, in principle, you can ask for more coffee as often as you like. Coffee here is generally not as strong as in Europe. You could buy some Nescafé and then strengthen your cup to taste. Espresso coffee has arrived in the US in a big way and it's widely available. Good coffee is available in the chain of coffee-shops called **Starbucks** where you'll also find a wide choice of cappuccino and mocha coffees, served hot or iced.

– **Root beer**: an acquired taste for foreigners, this unusual brew is adored by American kids. It's a drink that you have to try if you want to get a real flavour of America.

BOOKS

FICTION

– ***Erections, Ejaculations, Exhibitions and General Tales of Ordinary Madness*** (1972) Charles Bukowski; novel. Before being recognized for his poems and short stories, Bukowski had worked at every conceivable kind of job. Writing in the same tradition as Kerouac and Burroughs, his novels reflect his experiences at work, telling the inside story of a world of misfits and dropouts who refused to inhabit the boredom of the 'air-conditioned nightmare made in the USA'.

– ***Less Than Zero*** (1985) Brett Easton Ellis; novel. Twenty-year-old Ellis's debut novel. Nihilism and conspicuous consumption among LA's super-rich kids.

– ***Brown's Requiem*** (1988) James Ellroy; detective novel. A violent tale that doesn't leave private eye Fritz Brown unhurt. He takes us along with him in his dark wanderings from one murder to another, from Los Angeles to Tijuana, following the trail of a crooked cop, whose punishment leaves a bitter taste in the mouth.

– ***Amnesiascope*** (1996) Steve Erickson; novel. Very original, very slick, very LA, *Amnesiascope* is a visionary and surreal evocation of an apocalyptic Los Angeles overrun by a cast of desperate, confessional characters all seeking to give meaning to their lives while the city is slowly engulfed by the desert.

– ***Ask the Dust*** (1980) John Fante; novel. The main character, Bandini, an Italian immigrant in Los Angeles, is a failed writer as well as a pathetic lover. His misadventures take us to the core of Alternative America, inhabited by misfits and streetwalkers. Fante writes with the energy of despair and a particularly caustic wit.

– ***The Last Tycoon*** (1941) F. Scott Fitzgerald; novel. Fitzgerald's glittering, unfinished novel of Hollywood decadence, inspired by his experiences as a scriptwriter.

– ***Coyote Waits*** (1992) Tony Hillerman; detective novel. In the ancient canyons of Arizona something strange is going on. A maniac daubs the volcanic peaks of the holy mountains with streaks of white paint. The Navajo cop in charge of the investigation is found murdered in his car. At the scene of the crime, his partner Jim Chee arrests an old medicine man who, dead drunk, keeps on mumbling, 'My son, I am ashamed!'

– ***The Ghostway*** (1992) Tony Hillerman; detective novel. Jim Chee of the tribal police investigates a double murder and disappearance, using the ancestral methods of the Navajo Indians to track down present-day criminals. With a complex, exciting plot, this book is a wonderful opportunity to discover a people whose customs are very much alive, and a dry mountainous area whose charming beauty is celebrated by Hillerman.

– ***St Mawr and Other Stories*** DH Lawrence; novel. Lawrentian antics as the savagery of the American desert overwhelms his characters. Inspired by his time at Taos, New Mexico.

– ***The Nowhere City*** (1997) Alison Lurie; novel. In the 1960s, a young couple from Boston set up home in Los Angeles, the nowhere city of the title. The conflict between the East Coast and the West doesn't show any mercy for their marriage, which gradually disintegrates as one of the young pair is seduced by the Californian frenzy while the other remains attached to traditional values. The best novel about 1960s LA.

– ***Tales of the City*** (1994) Armistead Maupin; novel. Sexual antics in San Francisco in the late 1970s and early 80s.

– ***The Folded Leaf*** (1996) William Maxwell; novel. Maxwell's novel is one of those unique lost jewels on which time has bestowed a patina of indisputable lustre. In this novel about adolescence (a difficult genre in which J.D. Salinger and F. Scott Fitzgerald, among others, have excelled), you notice above all the accuracy of the emotions, its decency, and that murmuring simplicity of departing childhood.

– ***Vineland*** (1990) Thomas Pynchon; novel. Pynchon turns his self-reflective, post-modern paranoia onto 1980s California and the disintegration of the idealism of the Flower Power generation.

– ***Motel Chronicles*** (1983) and ***Hawk Moon*** (1981) Sam Shepard. Shepard presents his bleak, monochrome visions of an America eaten away by boredom, inhabited by anxious characters wandering along infinitely long highways and losing their identity in this enormous, soulless expanse.

– ***East of Eden*** (1952) John Steinbeck; novel. Transports the biblical story of Cain and Abel to the lettuce farms of Salinas. Alternatively, Steinbeck's ***Cannery Row*** (1945) is less ambitious, a sentimental evocation of the Monterey fisheries.

– ***Fear and Loathing in Las Vegas*** (1972) Hunter S. Thompson; novel. Journalist Thompson turns the American Dream inside out as he descends on Las Vegas, accompanied by his attorney and loaded with a fearsome arsenal of hallucinogenic drugs.

– ***King Blood*** (1987, out of print: try the Internet for a used copy) Jim Thompson; detective novel. Through the adventures of Critch King, who is being pursued by a pitiless murderer and is involved in mortal combat with his brethren, the not-so-distant life of the prairie is rediscovered, where everyday dangers are described in language of unadorned simplicity, but with the distancing effect of the author's humour.

– ***The Day of the Locust*** (1939) Nathaniel West; novel. The finest satire of early Hollywood. Also made into a film.

– ***The Electric Kool-Aid Acid Test*** (1968) Tom Wolfe; novel. Zany account of Ken Kesey and the Merry Pranksters in the early days of the psychedelic 1960s as they tried to take Aldous Huxley's LSD visions to the masses and get California to turn on, tune in and drop out.

– ***Gold*** (1925) Blaise Cendrars; a fictionalized biography. After falling into bankruptcy, General Suter flees the city of Rünenberg, in the Jura Mountains near Basle, and arrives in the American West as a down-at-heel pioneer, rich only in his appetite for life, his genius for intuition and his ability to bluff his way. This book, which found a place on the bedside table of none other than Joseph Stalin, brought worldwide fame to its author, who was himself a renowned adventurer.

NON-FICTION

– ***On the Road*** (1960) Jack Kerouac. With his friends Allen Ginsberg and William Burroughs, Kerouac, a vagabond writer, invented the Beat Generation 20 years before the hippies of the 1970s. *On the Road* was a seminal book for hippies, who set off for Kathmandu in search of enlightenment. Disillusioned with the American Dream, these rebels spurned conformism and the commercial relationships that governed the Western way of life, to glorify the present moment, the journey and its unforeseen encounters.

– ***The Dharma Bums*** (1961) Jack Kerouac. If you enjoyed *On The Road* then you'll love these accounts of Kerouac in California, climbing mountains in search of Zen-like inspiration before eventually cracking up under the pressure of his own myth.

– ***Ishi in Two Worlds*** (1988) Theodora Kroeber; ethnology. This book, subtitled *A Biography of the Last Wild Native American in North America*, is the deeply moving account of a man, Ishi, who was found exhausted, naked and almost dead of starvation in a California farm-yard in August 1911, as though he had come 'to surrender to civilization'.

– ***Big Sur*** (1957) Henry Miller; memoirs. It's not a little strange that Henry Miller, after spending most of his life reviling the US, ended up settling down on the California coast. *Big Sur* is a love song in praise of this, his chosen corner of the world: Miller revels in all its isolation – the wild nature, the birds and the giant sequoias.

– ***From Scotland to Silverado*** (first published between 1883 and 1895) Robert Louis Stevenson; a miscellany. On 7 August 1879, Robert Louis Stevenson embarked on the *Devonia* for a voyage that would take him from the Atlantic to the Far West and the disused silver mine at Silverado. *From Scotland to Silverado*, consisting of a journal, correspondence and an autobiographical narrative, reads like a novel.

SAN FRANCISCO, THE WINE ROUTE AND SILICON VALLEY

A BRIEF HISTORY

Although battles raged between the French and British in the eastern part of America, California remained unexplored for much longer and early colonists didn't fully establish themselves there until a great deal later. Was this because California was so hard to reach? You got there, after all, either by ship from the Pacific or you struggled over the Rocky Mountains. Whatever the reason, the region seems to hold interest only for the Spanish (many of whom eventually settled in Mexico) and, in the early 19th century, a handful of Russians. The latter are commemorated by the area of San Francisco known as Russian Hill.

In 1540, Hernando de Alarón became the first white man to set foot in Upper California – or what is now the State of California. Baja (or 'lower') California remained a Mexican state. It is thought that, at that time, the area supported a population of more than 300,000 Native Americans, who lived in as many as several hundred tribes – including the Pomo, the Miwok, the Chumash, the Gabrieleños and the Tulares. It was not until 200 years later, in 1769, that Father Junípero Serra built the first mission at San Diego. This marked the start of a series of missions that would reach 21 in number by 1823, strung out all along the coast between San Diego and Sonoma on a line roughly corresponding to today's Highway 101. These missions comprised a church, a school, buildings for the priests, dormitories for the converted and large pastures. The Native Americans provided the forced labour needed for the production of their crops.

But there were earthquakes and numerous Indian revolts to contend with, and supplies arriving from Mexico were unreliable. Disease laid waste to a large part of the community. By 1820, the population of incomers in California totalled only 3,500, by contrast to the colony on the east coast, set up by those who came on the *Mayflower*, which had a population of 20,000 as early as 1660. In 1822, Mexico liberated itself from the Spanish crown and proclaimed Upper California a Mexican province. In 1846, Mexico started a war with the United States that ended the following year, and under the Treaty of Guadeloupe Hidalgo in 1848, California finally became part of the United States.

By a curious throw of the dice of history, gold was first discovered that very same year. If the Mexicans had only known, things might have turned out very differently.

The Gold Rush immediately attracted pioneers in their thousands. Immigration took a different form some years later when large numbers of Chinese labourers were brought across the Pacific to build the railroads. Subsequently, black people abandoning the racist attitudes of the Southern states also swelled the population of California. More recent immigrants have included numbers of hopeful Mexicans, who cross the border illegally in search of work and a new life.

Will California be *the* place of the future? In just a few years, the East Coast has lost its economic supremacy little by little and California's wealth has grown and grown. If it were an independent country, California would number among the world's richest states, although its population is only just over half that of Great Britain.

Its main economic assets are tourism and the many faces of advanced technology – the latter demonstrated in Silicon Valley and by the presence of such companies as Hewlett-Packard, Intel, Apple, Dreamworks, etc.

Politically, California was for many years a Republican stronghold, under the likes of Ronald Reagan. In 1992, it swung firmly to the Democrat camp.

SAN FRANCISCO

AREA CODE: 415

San Francisco is 410 miles (660km) north of Los Angeles. Everything is different here. For many members of ethnic or social minorities, or others who also feel excluded from American society, this harbour city symbolizes a point of departure and hope for a better life. It differs from the rest of the United States in many ways – in its diversity, its tolerance and its outward-looking orientation. These factors are reflected in, among other things, the local lifestyle, the cultural scene and even its town-planning policies. The city centre contains relatively few skyscrapers in comparison with other cities, and those that do exist have had to comply with very stringent aesthetic standards that are costly for their developers. As well as all that, on the principle that the mingling of all classes and types of people is necessary if you want to create a living city, the authorities have tight control over rents, in the hope of maintaining the sociological balance of the city. It's a policy that should be offered as an example to many places worldwide.

In any case, San Francisco has got to be one of the most beautiful cities in the world. It's an enchanting place, built on a number of hills and famous for its incredibly steep streets (immortalized in movie car chases, in such films as *Bullitt* and *What's Up Doc?*). It has a wealth of delightful urban districts, which differ as much in their appearance and atmosphere as in the ethnic mix of the people who live there, and there are some magnificent and fascinating places that go to make up the great cultural resources of the city.

It's no surprise that the Americans call this place 'Everybody's Favorite City'. Unfortunately, nothing is perfect and it's also known as 'Fog City'.

It's cool, especially in the evenings and, during the summer, when temperatures barely rise above 68°F (20°C), the fog often prevents your enjoying the beauty of the city. The best time to come here is spring (which begins a little earlier than in Europe) or late autumn, when there are fewer tourists and less fog, and still some beautiful sunny days.

Compared with LA, this city is on a genuinely human scale. For one thing, it has a population of only 750,000 people. For another, you can move around on foot without attracting suspicion. In other words, San Francisco is a city where you can take a break away from 'America'.

A BRIEF HISTORY

In 1579, the English adventurer Sir Francis Drake reached the coast of California, close to what would later become San Francisco Bay, and took possession of the country on behalf of Queen Elizabeth I. California had been 'discovered' a little earlier by Hernan Cortés (who is said to have given it its name), but the Spanish had not yet explored the northern part. Curiously, it wasn't until the 18th century that Spanish missionaries discovered San Francisco Bay. Hidden by fog, it had been missed by all the previous explorers. St Francis of Assisi was the patron saint of these missionaries and the city was named San Francisco in his honour. The Presidio fortress was built at this time, as was the first church (also dedicated to St Francis), and Spanish colonists from Mexico began to settle in the area.

SAN FRANCISCO AND THE GOLD RUSH

In 1848, San Francisco was nothing more than a little fishing village with about 30 houses. Some 137 miles (220km) away, a man by the name of John Marshall brought his discovery of a gold nugget – the first ever found – to his boss, a landowner called John Sutter. The story goes that Sutter managed to conceal the discovery for some time, while continuing to work the gold. Inevitably the word got out, with someone turning up dead drunk one day on the streets of San Francisco shouting 'Gold! Gold!' and brandishing a bag full of gold.

That was the start of the growth of San Francisco. In less than two years, the whole region had been invaded by adventurers, miners, unemployed men, ladies of the night, traders and rascals of every kind from all over the world – and San Francisco positively mushroomed. The Golden Gate got its name because it led the way to the 'land of gold'.

Within 10 years, the seams of gold had run out, but – fortunately for everyone – silver was then discovered in the surrounding mountains. This time, however, it was investors and professional miners who came running, and the city gradually abandoned its Wild West ways and began to look more like a serious metropolis, with banks, shops and offices.

Even today, the incredible alchemy that blends immigrant ethnicities and social milieux in San Francisco continues to ensure that this remains a city with a pioneering spirit. It should be said, however, that the new Eldorado is founded not on gold, or silver, or even oil, but on computers. Silicon Valley has replaced the Sierra Nevada as the new land of plenty.

THE STORY OF BLUE JEANS

In 1847, a poor Jewish immigrant from Bavaria arrived in San Francisco, bringing a load of tarpaulins. Levi Strauss (for such was his name), finding himself unable to sell them as they were, cut them up and produced some pairs of work trousers, whose hard-wearing quality was quickly appreciated by gold prospectors. The fabric, imported from Nîmes in France, was called 'denim', a corruption of the French *de Nîmes* (meaning 'from Nîmes'). The word 'jeans' is said to be taken from Genoa, the Italian port that shipped the fabric to the United States.

Strauss' jeans derived much of their strength from the rivets that reinforced their seams. At one time, their strength was almost their undoing, as, in 1937, the parents of a group of schoolchildren asked for the hip pockets to be sewn without the rivets, because of the damage they did to benches and chairs – their request was granted.

During the Second World War, demand was such that Levi's jeans were sold only to military personnel.

Levi's are now such a well-known symbol of the United States that a pair is on display at the Smithsonian Institute in Washington. They, too, are part of America's heritage!

SAN FRANCISCO, HOME OF JACK LONDON AND THE BEATNIKS

It's no surprise that Jack London was born in the city of gold seekers. The son of a self-proclaimed astrologer who was permanently in debt (and who never acknowledged his son), London took his name from his mother's second husband. He spent an unhappy childhood in San Francisco, and joined the navy at the age of 15. Desperate to escape the labourer's fate that he seemed to be destined for, London tried out all kinds of adventures. He eventually succeeded in his aim, but not in the way he had envisaged – it was his talent as a storyteller that won him recognition, first as a journalist and then as a writer. His novels (*White Fang, The Call of the Wild,* etc.) have gone on to become classics, and made him one of the earliest millionaires in the history of publishing. Yet his fortune did not divert him from his political thinking. He was a militant socialist, and his political writings were frequently visionary.

One of London's spiritual inheritors shared his first name. Jack Kerouac was the author of *On the Road*, an influential work that inspired many wanderers. Like London, Kerouac (born in Massachusetts) hit the road very early and had all kinds of jobs before gaining recognition for his (largely autobiographical) novels, which included *The Lonesome Traveler*. But, although his life of restless wandering appears to have been inspired by that of London (one of whose earliest novels told of vagabonds riding the railroads), Kerouac went somewhat further in his revolt and his artistic quest. He was not alone, of course, and his many friends doubtless encouraged him in his desire to live life to the full.

San Francisco was the crucible of the 'beat' movement. The word, according to Kerouac, the movement's 'high priest', was derived from 'beatitude'. Its other connotations – heartbeat, musical beat, the state of being at the end of one's tether, etc. – are also relevant.

It all began in 1955, when Allen Ginsberg's recently completed poem *Howl* became the point of departure for an artistic breakaway movement as well as a rallying cry for those who denounced a lifestyle based on materialism. Ginsberg's public reading of his work was attended by a whole crowd of individuals, who, from that point onward, became the leading figures of the Beat Generation. They were Jack Kerouac, William Burroughs, Neal Cassady, Lew Welsh and Michael McClure. Lawrence Ferlinghetti, the founder of the City Lights Bookstore, immediately published *Howl,* which was soon regarded by some as a manifesto. The poem stood trial for obscenity, but was cleared. Newspaper headlines at the time warned that 'the cops won't allow no Renaissance in here!'.

A great friend of Ginsberg and Kerouac, and of equal importance as an innovative writer, was William Burroughs (who died in 1997) – another key figure in modern American literature. A notorious homosexual and junkie, Burroughs was the heir of a great family whose fortune had been made in the manufacture of adding machines. He was forced to flee Mexico after accidentally killing his wife there: it was reported that he had tried to copy the exploits of William Tell during the course of a slightly over-stimulated party. And if you're wondering what Burroughs was doing with a wife, it's said that the marriage was unconsummated.

While living in Tangiers, he compiled *The Naked Lunch*, a cult novel that used his innovative 'cut-up' technique. This book, which immediately achieved classic status, influenced many poets and writers (from Paul Bowles to Philippe Sollers) and rock musicians (such as Bob Dylan, the Beatles, David Bowie, Led Zeppelin, Patti Smith and Kurt Cobain), as well as contemporary painters (Keith Haring, Robert Rauschenberg). Film directors like Gus Van Sant, Robert Frank and David Cronenberg (the director of *Crash*), who made a screen version of *The Naked Lunch*, also drew inspiration from Burroughs' writings.

The beatnik movement, so named by Herb Caen, a San Francisco columnist and noted anti-Communist, was not a mere fashion or a new way of thinking. More than anything else, it was a new form of poetry-collecting and storytelling, inspired partly by the experiments of Rimbaud and the Surrealists, the novels of Joseph Conrad and, of course, jazz. By contrast, the 'hippie' era that was its spiritual successor did not stand up so well to the test of time. Indeed, since the hippie leaders were not writers, that movement contributed little of much substance to literature, although it had drawn inspiration from the beatniks.

It's still an undeniable fact that San Francisco is the most literary city in the United States. A key event in this respect was the renaming in 1988 of 12 streets in honour of writers and artists, all of whom either were natives of or had worked in San Francisco. Among these were Jack London and Jack Kerouac, together with Bob Kaufman, Samuel Beckett, Dashiell Hammett, Mark Twain and Isadora Duncan.

'IF YOU'RE GOING TO SAN FRANCISCO . . .

. . . be sure to wear some flowers in your hair.' The song made famous by Scott McKenzie lives on. For a whole generation, San Francisco was the city that symbolized hippie freedom and it was in the Bay Area that the movement took off, at two places whose names have become legendary – Berkeley University and the Haight-Ashbury district.

In 1963, during the protest marches of the Free Speech Movement, the young Joan Baez took the microphone at Berkeley to call for a struggle against censorship and in favour of freedom of speech. One year later, Timothy Leary, the intellectual agitator and high priest of LSD, accompanied by Allen Ginsberg, Jack Kerouac and William Burroughs, acting as representatives of the Beat Generation, officially announced the advent of the 'psychedelic revolution'. It was an intermediate stage between the beatnik movement and the 'hip' generation. The students at Berkeley took him at his word and christened their university 'Trip City'.

From 1965 onward, starting with a memorable 'Halloween Acid Party', these revolutionary views were widely propagated through music, thanks to the emergence of an incredibly active local scene – which was later to turn out in force to attend the Woodstock festival on the east coast.

Among the most significant groups from San Francisco were the Grateful Dead, pioneers of psychedelic rock (whose guitarist, Jerry Garcia, was known as 'Captain Trips'); Jefferson Airplane, whose vocalist, Grace Slick, was to become the bard of the hippie movement; Country Joe and the Fish (a group made up of Berkeley students opposed to the war in Vietnam) and Big Brother and the Holding Company, fronted by a singer by the name of Janis Joplin. Then there was another hero of mind-blowing rock – Carlos Santana, a young Mexican guitarist from the Mission district.

In 1966, the movement got its name: Hunter S. Thompson, writing in the San Francisco magazine *Rolling Stone*, was among the first to use the term 'hippies', derived from 'hip' (a slang word meaning 'in the know'). They found themselves a district of their own: Haight-Ashbury, immediately converted into 'Hashbury' and later known to the whole world as 'Hippieland'. Attracted by the old buildings that were available there at incredibly low rents, they took up residence on Ashbury Street in the wake of Jimi Hendrix, Janis Joplin, Grace Slick, Jerry Garcia and the writer Richard Brautigan.

Hip people read *Zap Comics*, which were sold on the streets of San Francisco. These comics were produced by the artists Robert Crumb (who also illustrated record sleeves for Janis Joplin) and Gilbert Shelton (the father of the Freak Brothers). In the evenings, members of the San Francisco scene would gather for big concerts organized at the Fillmore Auditorium by Bill Graham, the guru of the 'San Francisco Sound', and for the gigantic free festivals at Golden Gate Park, the 'Human Be-Ins'. In 1967, the 'summer of love' attracted more than half a million expectant visitors to San Francisco. These runaways arrived from everywhere, fleeing their homes in the Far West or the reactionary South loking for a taste of the wine of freedom that the city seemed to promise. They came for music, love, and also for hallucinogenic drugs: LSD had just been banned, but it was sure to be available here – even though a newly elected right-wing Senator, one Ronald Reagan, was watching over the 'happenings'.

Abuses of every kind, combined with disillusionment, got the better of the movement after 1969, immediately after the Woodstock festival and two grievous losses took place in the same year – the deaths of Janis Joplin and Jimi Hendrix. Some hard-liners, however, kept the 'peace and love' flame burning; one such was Carlos Santana, whose pacifist message has never changed. The Grateful Dead have been playing to millions of nostalgic fans for the past 30 years, despite the death of Garcia, to the point where they became the top dollar-earning American band for live gigs. This paradoxical achievement has never affected their music, which is as mind-blowing as it ever was.

EARTHQUAKES

San Francisco (and all of California, in fact) is located on the San Andreas Fault, which gives it an unstable foundation, to say the least. The massive earthquake of 1906 destroyed 28,000 houses (80 per cent of the city). But the city recovered very quickly and by the following year, 6,000 buildings had been rebuilt and several thousands of others were under construction. The reason for this swift recovery was a decision by a low-ranking judge, who found that the major destruction was due to the three-day fire that had swept through the city – and not the earthquake itself. The insurance companies, which had been very reluctant to pay for the damage, were thus put on formal notice to honour everyone's fire insurance policies.

Religious leaders and Puritans of the day claimed that the catastrophe was a well-deserved punishment from on high for the decadent city. Indeed, the city was primarily a great port, and a place where gambling and prostitution naturally flourished (. . . and this was long before the 1960s).

One is inclined to wonder how they would have interpreted the earthquake of 1989, which caused the dramatic collapse of the Bay Bridge? Was this a belated punishment for the wild ways of the American West, or was it more specifically aimed at motorists, dozens of whom perished beneath thousands of tons of concrete? The strict standards that governed the construction of buildings to make them earthquake-resistant were totally vindicated and very few people in the city itself fell victim.

But there's no need to worry if you're thinking about visiting San Francisco in the near future. If you believe in statistics, a calculation based on simple probability shows that the area is not due for its next big heave until around the year 2070.

ARRIVING BY AIR

FROM SFO

From San Francisco International Airport (SFO), there are five ways to get Downtown. The best way is probably the Airport Shuttles.

– **Airport Shuttles**: for less than $10 per person, these minibuses drop you off directly (and quite quickly) at your hotel. There are several companies operating, almost all at the same prices. You should note that you can often find coupons giving fare reductions, inside tourist brochures such as the *Bay City Guide*, which is available at the airport information desk.

• **Super Shuttle**: 700 16th Street. ☎ 558-8500. Round the clock. Credit cards accepted.

• **American Airporter Shuttle**: 95 Berry Street. ☎ 546-6689. Round the clock. Credit cards accepted.

• **Bay Shuttle**: 2202 Judah Street. ☎ 564-3400. Book by phone to get to SFO or Oakland Airport.

• **Quake City Shuttle**: 1379 Folsom Street. ☎ 255-4899. Possible reduction for several people.

– **Samtrans**: take the local bus – No. 3B, 7B or 7F. It's faster than the shuttles, but you can only take hand-luggage on board. ☎ 1-800-660-4BUS. The bus leaves every half hour, 5.45am–1.30am. For the city centre, get off at the intersection of Mission Street and 5th Street. Charges are very reasonable. You can take the 3B as far as the BART station at Daly City. Make sure you have some change. The journey takes about one hour.

– **SFO Airporter**: ☎ 495-8404. The fastest shuttles from the airport for Downtown, running every 10–20 minutes, 5am–11pm, with two lines. The Red Route serves the centre (in front of the Hilton on the corner of Mason and Ellis Streets). Take the Blue Route if you're going to the youth hostel at Fort Mason, and get off at Fisherman's Wharf. This is more expensive than the Red Route. No reservations.

– **Taxis**: fairly expensive (about $30 to get Downtown), but it costs the same as the shuttles if you share among three or four. The main advantage is that they drop you off at your hotel.

– **Hire cars**: you'll find all the big hire companies at the airport terminal. To get to the city centre, ask the hire company to mark the route on a map for you. It isn't complicated, in any case. Take Highway 101, then Highway 80 for Downtown. Exit at 5th Street, Mission and Market Street.

A note about parking: If you hire or use a car in San Francisco, you must remember to turn the wheels in towards the sidewalk when parking on the sloping streets, otherwise you'll get fined! It's often hard to get parked in any position at all, mind you, even if the traffic isn't in gridlock, and it always ends up costing you! What's more, you almost always have to pay to use a hotel parking lot. If you're staying in San Francisco (or in the surrounding area), it's better to use public transport: this is much more practical and makes it far easier to explore the city.

FROM OAKLAND AIRPORT

– **BART (Bay Area Rapid Transit)**: the local railway service. Take a 'Bartair' shuttle and it'll get you to Coliseum Station in 10 minutes. From there it takes another 30 minutes to get to the city centre. The most central station is Powell.

– **Airport shuttles, taxis and hire cars**: *see above*. To get to the city centre in a car, take Highway 880, then Highway 580 and finally Highway 80. You'll then enter San Francisco by the Bay Bridge.

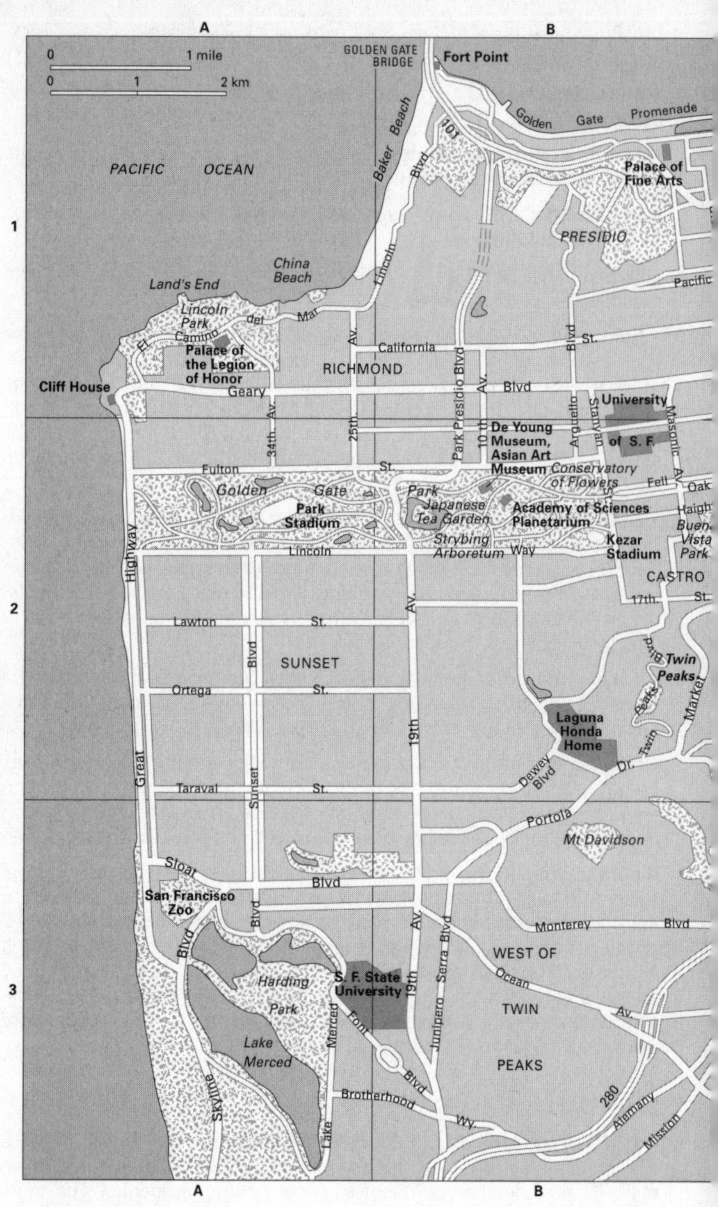
A
B
1
2
3
0
1 mile
0
1
2 km
GOLDEN GATE BRIDGE
Fort Point
Golden Gate Promenade
PACIFIC OCEAN
Baker Beach
101
Blvd
Palace of Fine Arts
PRESIDIO
Pacific
China Beach
Land's End
Lincoln
Lincoln Park
El Camino del Mar
Palace of the Legion of Honor
Cliff House
California
St.
RICHMOND
Blvd
Geary
Blvd
University of S. F.
Av.
34th. Av.
25th.
Park Presidio Blvd
10 th Av.
De Young Museum, Asian Art Museum
Arguello
Stanyan
Masonic Av.
Fulton
St.
Conservatory of Flowers
Fell
Oak
Golden Gate Park
Park Stadium
Japanese Tea Garden
Academy of Sciences
Planetarium
Haight
Buena Vista Park
Highway
Strybing Arboretum
Way
Kezar Stadium
Lincoln
CASTRO
17th. St.
Lawton St.
Twin Peaks
Blvd
SUNSET
Ortega St.
Laguna Honda Home
Market
Twin Peaks Blvd
19th
Great
Taraval St.
Sunset
Dewey Blvd
Dr.
Portola
Mt Davidson
Sloat Blvd
San Francisco Zoo
Blvd
Monterey Blvd
Blvd
WEST OF
Ocean Av.
Harding Park
S. F. State University
19th Av.
Junipero Serra Blvd
TWIN
Font Blvd
Lake Merced
Merced
PEAKS
Skyline
Brotherhood Wy.
280
Atemany
Mission
Lake

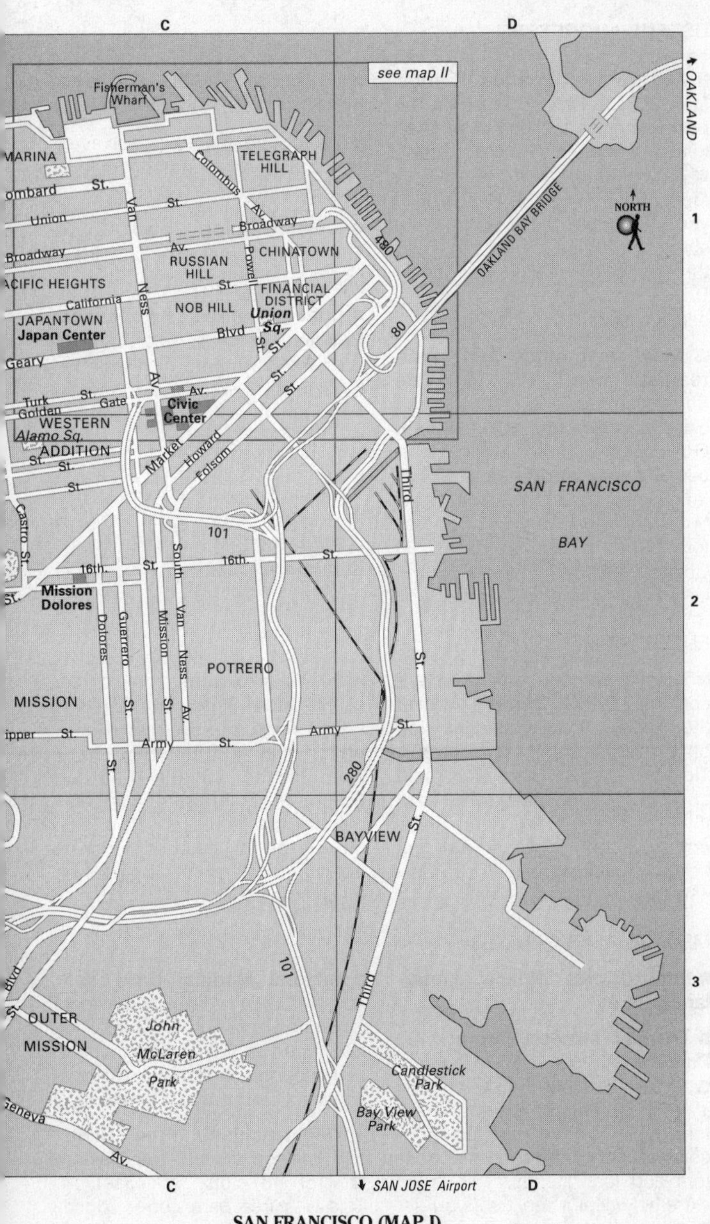

SAN FRANCISCO (MAP I)

SAN FRANCISCO

USEFUL ADDRESSES

Visitors' Information Center (map II, C3): Hallidie Plaza (in the basement), on the corner of Market Street and Powell Street. ☎ 391-2000. Open 9am–5pm (3pm Saturday and Sunday). If you want to see the maximum in a short time, there's a driving route through the city (called 'the Scenic Drive') that gives you a comprehensive tour.

✉ **Main post office and poste restante** (map II, B3): 101 Hyde Street, on the corner of Golden Gate Avenue and Hyde Street. Open 6am–5.30pm Monday–Friday. **Other post offices**: 150 Sutter Street (Downtown, 8.30am–5pm Monday–Friday), 867 Stockton Street (and Clay Street in Chinatown), 1640 Stockton Street (and Filbert Street in Northbeach), and Rincon Center (Embarcadero).

■ **Telephone**: there's one on every street and cards are on sale in grocery stores.

■ **Western Union** (map II, C3, **5**): 734 Market Street, near Grant. For sending telegrams.

■ **United States Appraisers Building** (map II, C2, **6**): 630 Sansome Street, Immigration Service (Room 107). ☎ 705-4411. Open Monday, Tuesday, Thursday and Friday 7am–3.30pm; closes 2.45pm Wednesday. For visa extensions. Go there a week before the expiry date. Best time is around 3pm, when there will be fewer people.

ENTERTAINMENT

■ Theatre and concert tickets are sold at **BASS Center**, behind the Union Square parking lot, on Stockton Street. ☎ 762-2277. Tickets for some shows are sold at half-price on the same day (there's a list on the right of the entrance door). You can also get tickets at **Ticketron**, in the Emporium store on Market Street.

■ **TIX**: Union Square, on the corner of Stockton Street. ☎ 433-7827. Open Tuesday–Thursday 11am–6pm; Friday and Saturday 11am–7pm. Theatre, dance and concert tickets at half-price for performances the same day, but you have to pay by cash. Also tickets at full price, which can be paid for by credit card.

MEDICAL EMERGENCIES

■ **Emergencies (Police, Ambulance)**: ☎ **911**.

■ **Traveler Medical Group**: 490 Post Street, Suite 225, Downtown. ☎ 981-1102. Open 24 hours. This is a care centre especially for tourists, and it works in conjunction with hospitals, specialist doctors and laboratories. This is an extremely useful service if you get into difficulties. They speak several languages and will come to visit you where you are staying. Credit cards accepted.

■ **In-Hotel Medical Care**: ☎ 1-800-DOCS-911. This is the local emergency medical service. They will attend to you in your hotel in response to a simple call. 24-hour service. Credit cards accepted.

■ **Haight-Ashbury Free Clinic**: 558 Clayton Street (and Haight). ☎ (415) 487-5632 or 431-1714. This is a free care centre (donations gratefully accepted). In an emergency, they will be able to direct you to other, more specific centres.

CURRENCY EXCHANGE

■ **At the airport**: Bank of America, in Central Terminal. Counter open 7am–11pm. ☎ 742-8079.

■ **Pacific Foreign Exchange Inc.** (map II, C2, **7**): 527 Sutter Street. ☎ 391-2548. Open Monday–Friday 9am–6pm, Saturday 10am–3pm. All the world's currencies bought, so they'll undoubtedly take yours. Traveller's cheques also accepted.

■ **Bank of America** (Foreign Currency Services; map II, C2): 345 Montgomery Street, Financial District. ☎ 622-2451. Open Monday–Friday 9am–6pm. You can get cash using your Visa card. Other banks also offer this service.

■ **Thomas Cook Foreign Exchange**: 75 Geary Street. ☎ 622-2451. Open Monday–Friday 9am–6pm, Saturday 10am–3pm, closed Sunday. All currencies accepted, even precious metals (!), but only Thomas Cook traveller's cheques.

■ **American Express** (map II, C2, **8**): 455 Market Street (Financial District). Freephone: ☎ 1-800-461-8484. Open Monday–Friday 8.30am–5.30pm, Saturday 9am–2pm, closed Sunday. There are also American Express currency exchange offices on the corner of Geary and Stockton, on the corner of California and Kearny and at Fisherman's Wharf.

■ **Macy's California**: Stockton and O'Farrell. On the 4th floor of the biggest shop in the city. ☎ 397-3333. Open Monday–Saturday 10am–8pm, Sunday 11am–7pm.

EMBASSIES AND CONSULATES

See 'Getting There' section

NEWSPAPERS

– ***The San Francisco Book***: this is a very well-produced free newspaper published by the Visitors' Office. Full of addresses, maps, practical information, timetables and fares for visits, and coupons giving a reduction on some services and attractions.

– ***Bay City Guide***: same sort of thing as above, but not as comprehensive.

– ***The San Francisco Examiner***: a newspaper whose Friday edition gives details of all the events, shows and demonstrations for the following week in San Francisco and surrounding area.

– ***The San Francisco Chronicle***: on Sunday, it includes *The Datebook*, a listing of all the films of the week, plays, concerts, etc.

– ***Visitors' News***: free monthly that lists the exhibitions, films, theatres and sporting events, and has a map of San Francisco.

– ***The Bay***: information for gays and bisexuals.

– ***The Bay Area Reporter*** and ***San Francisco Sentinel***: two free weeklies for gays. You can find copies in some clothes shops, particularly those on Haight Street.

– ***Visitors' Guide***, or the ***S.F. Weekly***: this free newspaper lists everything that's going on in the city. Get your copy at the cable-car departure point, on California Street or Ghirardelli Square, at Fisherman's Wharf.

– ***The San Francisco Bay Guardian***: free left-wing, trendy newspaper. Available at the entrance to some bars or restaurants, in vending machines or in shops. Gives comments on restaurants, shops, etc., plus discount coupons. It also contains the programmes of all the cinemas and jazz spots on the Bay.

- ***The Spectator***: interesting for its wild small ads.

- ***Travelhost*** and ***Key***: two free weeklies that you'll find in all the hotels.

HOW TO GET AROUND SAN FRANCISCO AND ITS ENVIRONS

INTERCITY TRANSPORT

Greyhound (map II, C2): at Transbay Terminal, 425 Mission Street, between Fremont Street and 1st Street, a few blocks from Downtown. Freephone: ☎ 1-800-231-2222. Open 24 hours. Left-luggage service.

Amtrak (map II, D2): Ferry Building, in the port, at the top of Market Street. Freephone: ☎ 1-800-872-7245 or 1-800-USA-RAIL.

■ **Green Tortoise**: 494 Broadway. ☎ 956-7500. Freephone (in the US and Canada): ☎ 1-800-867-8647 (TORTOISE). E-mail: info@greentortoise.com. Open daily, 8am–10pm. This is an alternative travel agency, set up during the hippie era. They use converted school buses, but with good drivers. Links with LA (Friday at 8pm), Seattle (twice weekly), Yosemite (every weekend), New York and Boston. Also with Northern California (Big Sur, Monterey, etc.), Grand Canyon, Alaska, the national parks, plus, in winter, Baja California, Guatemala, Costa Rica, etc. It's a good way to make acquaintances, as you sleep in the bus. There's music and lights to read by. Left luggage in the terminal. Great, typically-Californian atmosphere.

VEHICLE HIRE

■ **Cafla Tours**: ☎ (818) 785-4569. Freephone: ☎ 1-800-636-9683. Fax: (818) 785-3964. Run by a team of energetic French people, this agency undertakes to dig out a car for you that's no more than six months old at the best price, i.e. at lower rates than the big American hire companies charge for similar vehicles. No need to go there (the agency is a long way away) – you can do it all by phone and your car will be waiting for you at the airport. You can also hire a Harley-Davidson.

■ **Dollar Rent-a-Car**: 346 O'Farrell Street (and Mason) and at the airport. ☎ 771-5301 or 244-4130. Freephone: ☎ 1-800-800-4000. You must be at least 21. Unlimited mileage. Often offers promotions and useful reductions (especially with the coupons from the *Bay City Guide*).

■ **A One Rent-a-Car**: 320 O'Farrell Street. ☎ 292-1000. Open Monday–Friday 8am–6pm (5pm weekends). In principle, they will hire to under-21s, but there's no unlimited mileage. You must return the car to San Francisco.

■ **Automated Auto Transport International, IWC AAA**: 1300 Bayshore Boulevard, Suite 199, Burlingame, CA 94010. ☎ 342-9611. Call at least a week in advance. In the southern suburbs of San Francisco. A very likeable drive-away place, but it's a long way from the city.

■ **National Car Rental, System Inc.**: 550 O'Farrell Street. ☎ 474-5300. You can hire a car to drive in states other than California, which is something you can't do with every company.

URBAN TRANSPORT

– There are several kinds of **pass** that you can use on all forms of city transport, except BART. The daily one ($6) is not very cost-effective. Take the three- ($7) or seven-day pass ($15) or a monthly one ('fast-pass', $35) if you're planning to stay that long. It's very economical, particularly if you take the cable-car, because the shortest trip costs $2. You can buy a pass either at the Visitors' Center (Market Street) or at the cable-car departure point on Powell Street (and Market Street). In addition, it gives you reductions on most of the city's museums.

– **Cable-cars**: San Francisco would lose much of its flavour without its cable-cars. Each car has a grip that hooks onto a steel cable that runs in a dip in the ground between the rails: it's pulled up the hills and then freewheels down them, being restrained only by a handbrake. Since the slopes can have a gradient of as much as 21 per cent, that's some feat of engineering!

Your ticket entitles you to change lines. You then have to ask the conductor for a transfer. It's a good idea to expect a long wait when you're at the end of a line. The thing to do is buy your ticket and climb a few blocks on foot, to pick up the tram at an intermediate stop.

There's a museum that exhibits the machinery used for the operation of all the city's cable-cars. It's located at 1201 Mason Street, near Washington Street. Admission is free.

You absolutely must take a cable-car on the Powell-Hyde line, which is probably the most spectacular on the network. It takes you down the most winding and steepest streets in the city, finishing at Fisherman's Wharf.

– **MUNI public transport**: ☎ 673-6864. This is a group of five subway lines, all starting from Van Ness, which follow the same route to Embarcadero as do all the bus routes within the city. If you're leaving from Embarcadero, as many as six carriages may be uncoupled after Van Ness, so you need to keep an eye out for where you're going.

One interesting feature: on lines J, K, L and M, which serve Church Street, the carriage steps reappear when the subway train comes out above the surface, transforming it into a trolley. Going the other way, of course, the steps disappear. To tell the driver you want to get off at the next stop, you need to pull the cable that runs along the windows. On both the cable-cars and the MUNI, it's not unusual for the driver to get off to go for a coffee or a chat with someone! It's a long way from the stress of the big cities here.

– **BART**: the local railway system, is quite recent and therefore comfortable. It even has fitted carpets. ☎ 992-BART. Open Monday–Friday 4am–midnight (6pm Saturday, 8pm Sunday). Useful for getting from Oakland Airport to Downtown San Francisco. Take a bus between the subway station and the airport.

To get to Berkeley, you can also take Bus F from Transbay Transit Terminal, which goes to University Avenue.

You can get a 'discount' ticket at stations. This allows you to make two bus journeys for the price of one 'from BART/to BART'.

Microcomputers have been installed at many stations to provide information about transport, the subway, shows, etc. You can also take your bike on the BART outside rush hours and all day on weekends. Ask for a permit.

REGIONAL TRANSPORT

The buses that serve the East Bay Area (Berkeley, Oakland) can be caught at the Transbay Terminal, on the corner of 1st and Mission, near Embarcadero. They're cheaper than BART, they go further and run until 2am. ☎ 839-2882 (AC Transit).

– **Golden Gate Transit** buses serve the north of the city (Sonoma County, Sausalito, San Rafael, etc.) and depart from the Transbay Terminal. ☎ 923-2000.

– **Samtrans** serves the communities located between San Francisco and Palo Alto. Freephone: ☎ 1-800-660-4BUS.

BY BIKE, ROLLER SKATES, SCOOTER OR MOTORBIKE

You need a driving licence to ride a scooter here.

SAN FRANCISCO

■ **American Rentals**: 2715 Hyde Street, in the Fisherman's Wharf district. ☎ 931-0234. Open daily, 8am–10pm. This is a large, well-organized company that hires bikes of all kinds: children's bikes, mountain bikes, tandems, etc. Also scooters and motorbikes, including some Harley-Davidsons. Hire is by the hour, day or week. They'll supply you free of charge with a helmet, antitheft device, saddlebags and maps.

■ **Waller Sport**: 1749 Waller Street (and Stanyan). ☎ 751-7368. Open daily, 9am–7pm. They hire bikes and roller-blades. Everything you need for a trip round Golden Gate Park.

■ **Lincoln Bicycles**: 772 Stanyan. ☎ 221-2415. Nice reception and professional service. The proprietor is of Dutch origin, which means he knows a thing or two about bikes.

■ **Fog City Cycles**: 3430 Geary Boulevard. ☎ 221-3031. Open 10am–6.30pm (5pm Saturday).

ON FOOT

San Francisco is one of the few American cities that can – and should – be explored on foot. To help you to estimate distances, you need to know that block addresses go in hundreds. But it's not always advisable to walk in the evening. Avoid the parks and certain districts, including South of Market (SOMA) and Tenderloin.

USEFUL INFORMATION

– **Map S.F.** offer a free map of the city, with an index of the streets, activities and places of interest. You can even have this map sent to your home address. ☎ 474-3126. It can also be ordered from their website: www.mapwest.com.

– A useful tip: almost all the **museums** in San Francisco (which are generally quite expensive) are free on one day each month, e.g. on the first Tuesday or second Wednesday of each month. Find out the current state of play at the Visitors' Office or contact the museum direct.

– **Shopping**: be careful when buying electronic items – many tourists just buy their way into problems. As a general rule, you should avoid shops in Chinatown or on Market Street. When you buy electronic equipment (phones, computers, etc.) insist that it meets international standards, check that the guarantee is not limited to United States territory, and ask for mains adaptors, otherwise you won't be able to use it when you get home.

– **Good local radio station**: KSAM, on 107.7 FM. The best of rock, perfect if you're off to have a look around the surrounding area in a car.

WHERE TO STAY

With only a few exceptions, all the hotels covered here are within the area of Downtown. To give you an idea of the cost of an overnight stay in San Francisco, some price ranges are given below. Remember that prices can vary widely depending on how full the hotel is. Outside the tourist season (July and August), you'll find it easier to haggle in most establishments.

– **Youth hostels**: $12–20 per person per night
– **Budget**: $50–70 for a double room for one night
– **Moderate**: $70–90 for a double room for one night
– **Expensive**: $100–200 for a double room for one night
– **Splash Out**: $150–250 for a double room for one night

PRIVATE YOUTH HOSTELS, YMCAS AND 'OFFICIAL' YOUTH HOSTELS

☗ **Pacific Tradewinds Guesthouse** (map II, C2, **22**): 680 Sacramento Street (between Montgomery and Kearny). ☎ 433-7970. Fax: 291-8801. Website: www.hostels.com/pt. Very small private youth hostel, well situated right in the middle of Chinatown. The entrance is difficult to find, between two Asian restaurants ('Henry' and 'Hunan'). You have to give your name on the intercom before they let you in. Open 8am–midnight. Only 32 beds. Note: they don't take reservations in summer, so phone from 10.30am onwards to find out if they have any room. Rooms are well kept and quiet. There's a kitchen available, plus free tea and coffee. Ironing, left-luggage, fax service. Very good atmosphere and lots of information for backpackers.

☗ **International Guesthouse**: 2976 23rd Street and Harrison Street (Mission District). ☎ 641-

1411. Not really in the centre, but reasonably accessible. Nevertheless, it's preferable to have a car. Situated in a popular area that has a large Mexican population, South of SOMA. This place will be interesting to those who love places well off the established routes and who want to get a feel for the real social makeup of the city. This excellent private youth hostel has been set up in a beautiful Victorian residence, that was renovated with great taste, back in 1978. It was probably the first private youth hostel in San Francisco with 'aspirations'. There's a pretty mural on the inside staircase. Minimum stay is five nights. Don't forget to book or phone them before turning up. It's not too crowded, but you never know. They have small four-bed dormitories or rooms for two at unbeatable prices, and it's cheaper if you stay for a month. Sheets are supplied. There are two well-fitted kitchens, a TV (with 36 channels), and plenty of excellent information.

☗ **Green Tortoise Hostel** (map II, C2, **21**): 494 Broadway (and Kearny). ☎ 834-1000. Fax: 956-4900. Same team as for the bus tours (*see* 'Intercity Transport'). A very busy youth hostel (come early in the morning) with a relaxed backpacker atmosphere. Dormitories for three to eight people; some rooms for two (not many, so more expensive). The place is oldish, but clean. It's large, with 200 beds, but the atmosphere is not industrial. There's a kitchen and laundry. Left-luggage service. The communal parts are spacious and comfortable, with billiards, TV on a giant screen, and music.

☗ **Easy Goin' Guesthouse**: 555 Haight Street (Lower Haight). ☎ 552-8452. Fax: 552-8459. E-mail: diego@easygo.com. One of the few lodging houses in Lower Haight, this is a small private youth hostel. The atmosphere is nice and the prices are lower than in many other youth hostels. Dormitories and double rooms. Two nights minimum. The reception desk closes at 7pm. It's essential to book, as they only have 35 beds. They also operate a travel agency, and there's a fax service and mailbox. Bike hire is possible. Visa cards accepted.

☗ **San Francisco International Student Center** (off map II along C3, **23**): 1188 Folsom (Downtown). ☎ 255-8800. Fax: 487-1463. Fairly recent private youth hostel. Excellent and comfortable. There are 16 clean, well-tended rooms (each with three to five beds) all reasonably priced. Prices are reduced if you stay for a week. There's a quiet room with chess sets, and a nightclub on the ground floor. Take your pick.

☗ **Globe Trotters' Downtown Hostel** (map II, C3, **24**): 225 Ellis Street (and Mason). ☎ and fax: 346-5786. Small youth hostel with a relaxed atmosphere, offering an ideal location a short way from Union Square and the cable-car departure point. There are only 15 rooms in all, some private and some for four people. It's a bit grubby and rather small, though. Very young clientele, mostly the backpacking type. The dormitories are very cheap and the private rooms are not expensive either. Communal bathroom, kitchen and TV room. Lots of information available. Best to book in advance.

☗ **Globe Hostel** (map II, off C3, **25**): 10 Hallam Place. Entrance is on Folsom. ☎ 431-0540. Fax: 431-3286. Between 7th and 8th Streets. Open 24 hours. Private youth hostel in the same group as the Venice Beach Hotel in LA. Quite clean. Rooms for four with bathroom, and dormitories for up to eight people, smoking and non-smoking. Pleasant, cheap cafeteria, small lockers, free coffee and tea. Laundry. Common-room with TV and billiards. Nice, welcoming atmosphere. No reservations by phone – you have to write.

New Central Hostel (off map II along B3, **26**): 1412 Market Street (and Fell). ☎ 703-9988. Fax: 703-9986. Near the subway. This former hotel, with 150 rooms and communal bathrooms, has been turned into a youth hostel. The whole place is ultra-simple and quite grubby. No breakfast. The only advantage is the price.

San Francisco International Youth Hostel (map II, A1): in Fort Mason (Building 240, right at the back, slightly to the left). Entrance on the corner of Bay Street and Franklin Street. ☎ 771-7277. Open 7am–1pm and 2pm–1am. Get there at 7am in summer if you want a bed. From the Greyhound terminal, take the MUNI Bus 42 to Freemont. It's a magnificent location facing San Francisco Bay and the Golden Gate Bridge, with a big park all round. You have the option of doing your own cooking. Rooms have anything from four to 24 beds. Breakfast is included in the price. There's left-luggage, a laundry, billiards, and a free parking lot. Maximum stay 14 nights. No curfew. Quite a nice atmosphere, but you must do a housework task (10 minutes a day). A few minutes on foot takes you to Fisherman's Wharf, from where the cable-car will take you to the city centre.

San Francisco Central YMCA (map II, B3, **28**): 220 Golden Gate Avenue (and Leavenworth). ☎ 885-0460. Open 24 hours. Has 105 rooms for one, two or three people. Breakfast (coffee and muffins) included. Shuttle to the airport. They sell phone cards and offer a left-luggage facility. A bit of a Boy Scout atmosphere. Many activities are on offer, including swimming pool, sauna and weights room, but it's only a few dollars less than you'd pay at a small hotel.

Hostelling International (San Francisco Downtown; map II, C3, **29**): 312 Mason Street (one block from Union Square). ☎ 788-5604. Freephone for reservations: ☎ 1-800-444-6111. Fax: 788-3023. This is a recent official youth hostel, right in the centre. Approximately 240 beds in rooms for two or six people. Lockers and fully-equipped kitchen. Open 24 hours. Prices are higher for non-members.

☆ BUDGET

The majority of hotels are located in the Downtown area, i.e. right in the centre. You need to be aware that some streets in the district are still a place where street people and homeless people gather, particularly in the Tenderloin district. However, this district is part of the city and its life, and there are positive qualities to Downtown – its liveliness by day and its useful central position.

Verona Albergo Hotel (map II, B3, **30**): 317 Leavenworth Street (and Eddy). ☎ 771-42-42. Freephone: ☎ 1-800-422-3646. Fax: 771-3355. You can't get more central than this! Situated in the Tenderloin district between Union Square and the Civic Center, the hotel dates from 1908, and has been entirely renovated in its original style. There are some rooms for four and for families, with or without private bathroom. Colour TV, direct-dialling phone, coffee along with as many donuts as you want for breakfast, etc. Good atmosphere. It's a fairly run-down district, and full of atmosphere in the eve-

NORTH
Marina Green
Fort Mason
Fisherman's Wharf
Maritime
Cannery
Ghirardelli
MARINA
COW HOLLOW
Octagon
PACIFIC HEIGHTS
California Historical Society
Lafayette
Alta
NOB HILL
RUSSIAN HILL
FILLMORE
JAPANTOWN
Japan Center
St Mary's Cathedral
WESTERN ADDITION
Jefferson
Alamo
Federal
State Building
Veterans Building
City
Civic Center
Library
Opera
Auditorium
Davies
U.S.S.
San Francisco
Grace

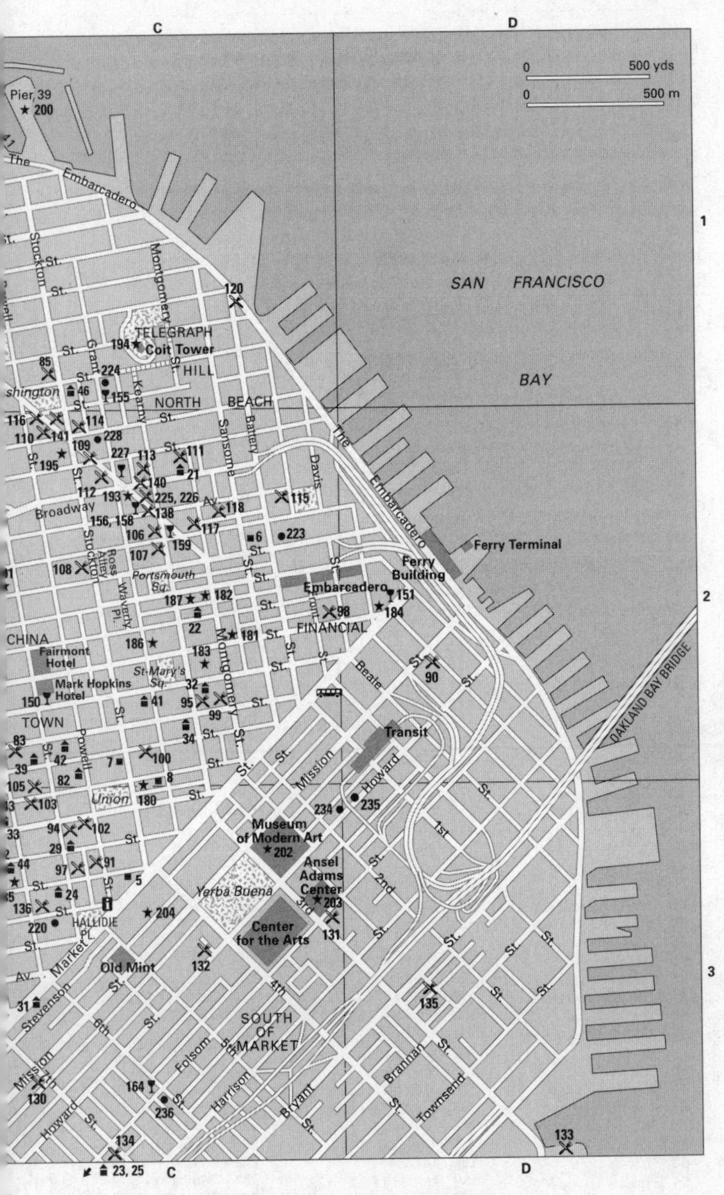

DOWNTOWN SAN FRANCISCO (MAP II)

SAN FRANCISCO

■ Useful Addresses

- i Visitors' Information Center
- ✉ Main Post Office and poste restante
- Greyhound
- 5 Western Union
- 6 United States Appraisers Building
- 7 Pacific Foreign Exchange Inc.
- 8 American Express

Where to Stay

- 21 Green Tortoise Hotel
- 22 Pacific Tradewinds Guesthouse
- 23 San Francisco International Student Center
- 24 Globe Trotters' Downtown Hostel
- 25 Globe Hostel
- 26 New Central Hostel
- 28 San Francisco Central YMCA
- 29 Hostelling International
- 30 Verona Albergo Hotel
- 31 Aida Hotel
- 32 Temple Hotel
- 33 The Adelaide Inn
- 34 Alisa Hotel
- 35 Pensione Internazionale
- 36 The Ansonia Hotel and B&B
- 37 Brady Acres
- 38 Atherton Hotel
- 39 Sheehan Hotel
- 40 Maxwell Hotel and San Remo Hotel
- 41 Grant Plaza Hotel
- 42 Cornell Hotel of France
- 43 The Fitzgerald Hotel
- 44 Best Inn & Suites
- 45 Jackson Court
- 46 The Washington Square Inn
- 47 The Mansion Hotel
- 48 The Majestic
- 49 Monroe Residence Club
- 50 The Kenmore Residence Club
- 51 The Harcourt Residence Club
- 52 Baker Acres
- 53 Marina Motel
- 54 Holiday Lodge Motel
- 55 Vagabond Inns

✕ Where to Have a Good Breakfast

- 80 Dottie's True Blue Cafe
- 81 Raphael's House (Brother Juniper's Restaurant)
- 82 Doidge's
- 83 Yakety Yak
- 84 Home Plate
- 85 Mama's

✕ Where to Eat

- 90 Rincon Center
- 91 Lori's Diner
- 92 Tommy's Joynt
- 93 Vietnam II
- 94 Cafe Mason
- 95 Cafe Bastille
- 96 Hard Rock Cafe
- 97 New Delhi
- 98 Tadich Grill
- 99 Plouf
- 100 Anjou
- 101 California Culinary Academy
- 102 Sushi Bune Restaurant
- 103 Postrio
- 104 Stars
- 105 Farallon
- 106 House of Nanking
- 107 Sam Lok
- 109 US Restaurant
- 110 L'Osteria del Forno
- 111 The Helmand
- 112 The Stinking Rose (A Garlic Restaurant)
- 113 Enrico's
- 114 Caffe Sport
- 115 MacArthur Park
- 116 Il Pollaio
- 117 Cypress Club
- 118 Bix
- 120 Fog City Diner
- 122 Wraps
- 123 Mel's Drive Inn
- 124 Baja Cantina
- 125 Cassis
- 126 Prego
- 127 Betelnut Peiju Wu
- 128 Scott's
- 129 Zuni
- 130 Cafe do Brasil
- 131 Max's Diner
- 132 Cadillac Bar
- 133 The Ramp
- 134 Julie's Supper Club
- 135 South Park Cafe
- 136 Original Joe's
- 137 Thai Stick
- 138 Brandy Ho's
- 139 Nob Hill Cafe
- 140 Little Joe's
- 141 Rose Pistola
- 142 Lou's
- 143 Scoma's
- 144 The Elite Cafe
- 157 Harry's Bar

Where to Have a Drink

- 151 Equinox
- 152 Cityscape
- 154 Art Institute Cafe or Pek's Cafe
- 155 The North End Caffe
- 156 Royal Oak Saloon
- 157 Cafe Trieste
- 158 Vesuvio
- 159 San Fransisco Brewing Company
- 161 The Grove
- 162 Coffe Bugatti's
- 163 Bepple's Pie Shop
- 164 Brainwash Laundromat

★ What to See

- 180 Circle Gallery Building
- 181 Wells & Fargo Bank History Room
- 182 Pacific Heritage Museum
- 183 Bank of California
- 184 Hyatt Regency
- 185 Glide Memorial Church
- 186 St Mary's Church
- 187 Chinese Historical Society of America Museum
- 188 Lombard Street
- 190 Grace Cathedral
- 191 Cable-Car Museum
- 192 St Mary's Cathedral
- 193 City Lights Bookstore
- 194 Coit Tower
- 195 North Beach Museum
- 200 Pier 39
- 201 Alcatraz
- 202 SFMOMA
- 203 Ansel Adams Center
- 204 Cartoon Art Museum

San Francisco by Night

- 157 Harry's Bar
- 220 Club 181
- 221 Red Room
- 222 Blue Lamp
- 223 Punch Line
- 224 Savoy Tivoli
- 225 The Spec's
- 226 Tosca Cafe
- 227 1232 Saloon
- 228 Lost & Found Saloon
- 230 Blues
- 231 Perry's
- 232 Royal Oak Saloon
- 233 Bus Stop
- 234 Caribbean Zone
- 235 Mercury SF
- 236 1015 Folsom Street

ning. If you're going out on foot, ask for the best route at night so as to avoid the meaner streets. They also rent out apartments by the month. Free parking lot for backpackers (subject to availability).

Aida Hotel (map II, C3, **31**): 1087 Market Street (and 7th). ☎ 863-4141. Freephone from California: ☎ 1-800-863-AIDA. Fax: 863-5151. 174 rooms and recently refurbished. The rooms are spacious and light. Bathrooms are shared by 74 of the rooms, which are therefore cheaper. Free coffee and tea available all day. You can hire a car or reserve a seat on the airport shuttle.

Alisa Hotel (map II, C2, **34**): 447 Bush Street. ☎ 956-3232. Very well located, at the entrance to Chinatown and beside the Cafe de la Presse. Small building with a certain charm, thanks to its 'period' entrance and oak stairway. About 50 entirely renovated rooms, 30 of them with bathroom. Also operates as a boarding house, by the week or by the month.

Temple Hotel (map II, C2, **32**): 469 Pine Street (and Kearny), at the entrance to Chinatown. ☎ 781-2565. Open to 10pm. A small, well-positioned hotel that has kept its 1960s feel, so the rooms are quite old-fashioned. The cleanliness is spot-on, though. The rooms that overlook the courtyard can be a bit noisy as the place is next to a disco. Hospitable staff. All in all, a good quality-to-price ratio.

The Adelaide Inn (map II, C3, **33**): 5 Isadora Duncan (small cul-de-sac off Taylor Street, between Post and Geary), Downtown. ☎ 441-2261. Fax: 441-0161. A well-located small hotel with 16 neat and tidy rooms, communal bathrooms and a collective kitchen. Will suit anyone who appreciates a peaceful family atmosphere. The surroundings are a bit old-fashioned, but the clientele's young and the rooms are very quiet, which is rare in the city centre. Consider booking, as it's often full.

The Ansonia Hotel and B&B (map II, B3, **36**): 711 Post Street. ☎ 673-2670 and 673-7232. Fax: 673-9217. Freephone: ☎ 1-800-221-6470. Near Union Square. This fairly old-fashioned but well kept hotel has 145 decent rooms. They have two rates: with communal or private bathroom. Some rooms have an old-style bathtub. In the basement there's a dining room, TV, plus machines for washing and drying your things. More expensive than the ones above, but an American breakfast and dinner are included. The snag is that the cooking is not brilliant, and the hotel sadly doesn't offer the option of dining elsewhere. Reception average.

☆☆ MODERATE

A word of warning: curiously enough, even in the smarter establishments in this category, hotel rooms may share a bathroom. On top of that, they often have no parking lot or, if they do, you have to pay for it.

Brady Acres (map II, B3, **37**): 649 Jones Street (between Post and Geary). ☎ 929-8033. Freephone for reservations: ☎ 1-800-627-2396. Fax: 441-8033. Website: www.bradyacres.com. Very well situated (six or seven blocks from Chinatown, and three from Union Square). This is a charming little place where it's usually necessary to book. The 25 rather small rooms are stylishly furnished, each with its own personality. Very comfortable (most rooms have a bar, refrigerator, microwave, TV, stereo, private phone, free local calls, etc.). You can wash and dry your clothes. Discount if you stay a whole week (one night is free). Loads of information about the city. They're really obliging – nothing's impossible here.

☗ **San Remo Hotel** (map II, C3, **40**): 2237 Mason Street. ☎ 776-8688. Fax: 776-2811. Freephone: ☎ 1-800-352-REMO. E-mail: info@sanremohotel.com. In the picturesque North Beach district, very close to the cable-cars, four blocks from Fisherman's Wharf and Telegraph Hill. Charming hotel in Italian-Victorian style dating from 1906 that has retained an old-fashioned atmosphere. Nice, very well-kept rooms, with brass bedsteads and antique furniture and fittings. Communal outside bathrooms (which are also rather charming). The rooms do lack sound insulation, but there's a family atmosphere and the welcome is warm. Paying parking lot.

☗ **The Fitzgerald Hotel** (map II, C3, **43**): 620 Post Street (between Taylor and Jones). ☎ 775-8100. Fax: 775-1278. Freephone for reservations: ☎ 1-800-33-HOTEL. 47 rooms, which aren't big but are pretty and very well kept, with TV. Excellent value for money. Continental breakfast included. You can use the swimming pool at the Sheehan Hotel (*see below*). Paying parking lot.

☗ **Pensione Internazionale** (map II, B3, **35**): 875 Post Street. ☎ 775-3344. Fax: 775-3320. Freephone: ☎ 1-800-358-8123. The front of the building is not very inviting, but the recently renovated interior is cosy. Rooms on the ground floor are a bit dark. Those upstairs are small but comfortable, even snug. A shade noisy, though. Two rates: with or without bathroom. Continental breakfast included, and as much coffee as you can drink during the day. Family atmosphere and cordial reception.

☗ **Atherton Hotel** (map II, B3, **38**): 685 Ellis Street (between Larkin and Hyde), Downtown. ☎ 474-5720. Fax: 474-8256. Freephone: ☎ 1-800-474-5720. Located beside the Civic Center. Large, quite luxurious hotel with 75 rooms, offering good value for money. Free for children under 12. They serve breakfast plus on Sunday there's champagne brunch and on Tuesday, it's wine-tasting.

☗ **Sheehan Hotel** (map II, C2, **39**): 620 Sutter Street (between Taylor and Mason), Downtown. ☎ 775-6500. Fax: 775-3271. Freephone for reservations: ☎ 1-800-848-1529. Former luxury hotel, superbly renovated and offering a very attractive range of prices. There are 71 rooms, the cheapest of which share one bathroom between three. Those that have private bathrooms are immense but more expensive. The interior decoration is in very good taste, with fresh colours and handsome furniture. Expensive, but some 'twin economy' rooms at more attractive prices. Continental breakfast included. Covered, heated swimming pool, of dubious cleanliness (non-residents come to swim there), and free gymnasium. Parking lot, but it costs extra. Often full.

☗ **Grant Plaza Hotel** (map II, C2, **41**): 465 Grant Avenue (between Pine and Bush). ☎ 434-3883. Freephone: ☎ 1-800-472-6899. Fax: 434-3886. Located at the entrance to Chinatown. This is not a luxurious grand hotel, no matter what its name seems to imply! Good location, though. The 75 rooms are not very big, but they are pleasant enough. Those looking onto the interior courtyard are dark but very quiet, the others open onto Chinatown, which is a lively district. Often fully booked.

☗ **Cornell Hotel of France** (map II, C2, **42**): 715 Bush Street (between Powell and Mason). ☎ 421-3154. Freephone: ☎ 1-800-232-9698. Fax: 399-1442. Hotel with 60 pleasant rooms (each with TV) run by a French couple. The various floors are named after painters, who are represented by framed posters that decorate the rooms and corridors. All mod cons, and immaculate decor (they are all non-smoking). On the premises is the Jeanne d'Arc restaurant. Good traditional French cooking (Loire Valley duck, marengo veal, sautéed rabbit, delicious pastries, etc.). Breakfast included. Optional half-board at lower prices (but only by the week).

☗ **Best Inn & Suites** (map II, C3, **44**): 415 O'Farrell Street (between Jones and Taylor). Three blocks from Union Square. ☎ 928-6800. Freephone: ☎ 1-800-BEST-INN. Fax: 928-3354. Website: www.bestinn.com. The 60 rooms are comfortable but small, old-fashioned and a little noisy. Prices include buffet breakfast. Direct phone line, coffee machine and TV in each room. Paying parking lot.

☆☆☆ EXPENSIVE

☗ **The Red Victorian Bed and Breakfast**: 1665 Haight Street. ☎ 864-1978. At the heart of the former hippie district, now the artistic and de luxe Bohemian quarter, lies this astonishing B&B with its unusual character and incredible charm. The proprietor, Sami Sunchild, herself an artist, had the great idea of creating a B&B above her Global Village Bazaar. To add to its incomparable reception, she has decorated the 18 rooms in a very personal way. You almost feel you want to try them all. Perhaps the 'Rose Garden' for its pastoral atmosphere or 'Gigi's', the 'Japanese Tea Garden' or the 'Peace Room'. Don't forget to pay a visit to the 'Aquarium Bathroom': the toilet cistern is full of fish! The more affluent owe it to themselves to plump for the 'Redwood Forest' or, even better, the 'Peacock Suite', the craziest, most eccentric of all the rooms (and also the most expensive, of course!). Allow $86 and up for a double. On the weekend, the minimum stay is two nights. Note, no smoking anywhere.

☗ **Jackson Court** (map II, A2, **45**): 2198 Jackson Street (between Laguna and Buchanan). ☎ 929-7670. In Pacific Heights, near Union Street. This is a lovely place if you love B&Bs, with 10 spacious, very elegant (not to say luxurious!) rooms with a certain charm, although the reception area is surpisingly drab. Two nights minimum at weekends. If you have the means, spoil yourself with the 'Executive Room', a suite decorated like a house, with fireplace and library.

☗ **The Washington Square Inn** (map II, C1, **46**): 1660 Stockton Street. ☎ 981-4220. Freephone: ☎ 1-800-388-0220. Fax: 397-7242. Small hotel of great charm, very well situated at the intersection of North Beach and Telegraph Hill, overlooking Washington Square Park. Handsome lobby with fireplace. With its 15 rooms, it's closer to a B&B than a traditional hotel, but the rooms are exquisitely decorated, with antique British and French furniture. Elegant fabrics. The cheaper rooms share a bathroom. Other rooms have a shower or bath and a lounge. Excellent comfort and fresh flowers. Continental breakfast and afternoon tea with cakes. Good reception.

Maxwell Hotel (map II, C3, **40**): 386 Geary Street (and Mason), Downtown. ☎ 986-2000. Fax: 397-2447. Freephone: ☎ 1-888 SF-4-MAXX. Right in the centre, one block from Union Square. Beautiful, classy building dating from 1908, in the 'theater deco' style (a mixture of art deco and Victorian). Entirely renovated, the 153 rooms have all mod cons, are impeccably decorated and very well equipped (with Nintendo, hair dryer and ironing board!). Some are very beautiful. Lovely view from the upper floors. Several rates, going from single to double. On the ground floor is Gracie's Restaurant, a pleasant American brasserie.

☆☆☆☆ SPLASH OUT

The Mansion Hotel (map II, A2, **47**): 2220 Sacramento Street. ☎ 929-9444. Level with Laguna Street (Pacific Heights). This manor house, straight out of a horror movie, conceals a hotel that's one of a kind. It has a unique, strange interior and a very special atmosphere reigns in the evening. The reception rooms are little museums of horror and kitsch: you can find pigs as well as portraits of Napoleon. You'll even meet Clinton's double on the stairs! But don't worry, the rooms are genuine cosy little nests: breakfast in bed, flowers in the rooms. All 21 rooms are different. The smallest costs $129, the largest includes two bathrooms, two fireplaces and a library of 2,000 books, but all the same, at $350 it's a teensy bit on the expensive side. They claim Barbra Streisand once stayed here. There's a small cabaret room, in which the proprietors organize displays of magic every evening. The cost of a room includes breakfast and a seat for the show. Very good restaurant (sophisticated and expensive). You can see the show for about $10 if you aren't staying at the hotel.

The Majestic (map II, B3, **48**): 1500 Sutter Street, on the corner of Gough. ☎ 441-1100. Freephone: ☎ 1-800-869-8966. Fax: 673-7331. Built in 1902, this very handsome Victorian hotel withstood the earthquake. Magnificently situated at the top of a hill, the Majestic is in the centre while far enough away from any noise and pollution. Superb lobby. Rooms have radio, colour TV, direct phone line and bathroom (some have four-poster beds). The decor and the antique tapestries create an atmosphere that is simultaneously old-fashioned and elegant. Nevertheless, it's very expensive – the cheapest rooms start at $160.

SAN FRANCISCO

HOTELS BY THE WEEK AND BY THE MONTH

Here are some establishments that offer rooms by the week and by the month at very attractive prices. All are relatively close to the centre.

Monroe Residence Club (map II, B2, **49**): 1870 Sacramento Street between Van Ness and Franklin. ☎ 474-6200. Fax: 346-1870. E-mail: monroe@sirius.com. This historic building survived the 1906 earthquake without a scratch. It looks unremarkable from the outside, but the interior is beautiful, with a lot of charm. Spacious, remarkably well-kept, quiet rooms (single or double, with or without bathroom). Breakfast (copious) and dinner are optional. Rooms by the week, fortnight or month. Reservations very advisable in summer, as it fills up quickly; there's a booking deposit of $50. Laundry. Terrace for sunbathing. Billiards and table-tennis.

☗ **The Harcourt Residence Club** (map II, B3, **51**): 1105 Larkin Street and Sutter. ☎ 673-7720. Fax: 474-6729. This has 100 rooms that aren't among the most luxurious, but they're clean and quiet and all have a phone. The (very low) prices include breakfast and an evening meal. There's a pleasant terrace with solarium, a games room (with library and TV) and a laundry.

☗ **The Kenmore Residence Club** (map II, B3, **50**): 1570 Sutter Street. ☎ 776-5815. Fax: 776-9659. E-mail: kenmoesf@aol.com. 79 slightly old-fashioned rooms, with or without private bathroom, at almost all prices, depending on the level of comfort provided. The price includes breakfast and dinner (brunch on Sunday). Games room, TV room and laundry.

☗ **Baker Acres** (map II, off A2, **52**): 2201 Baker Street and 3000 Jackson. ☎ 921-3088. A little place in the smart residential district of Pacific Heights. To get there, take a No. 3 bus for Jackson (the stop before Baker Acres). Single rooms only, and the minimum stay is two weeks. Communal bathroom. Quiet. Breakfast and dinner included in the price, but this is still high compared with some others on offer.

CAMPING

☗ **Anthony Chabot Campground**: excellent campground in the Anthony Chabot Regional Park, 50 minutes from San Francisco (by car). East Bay Regional Park, PO Box 5381, Oakland, CA 94605-5369. Open April–September, and booking is recommended: ☎ 562-2267. When you make a booking, they'll send you a map of how to access your site, which is, incidentally, among eucalyptus trees which smell great. Spacious sites, hot showers, barbecue, lake, footpaths for strollers, and peace! After a heavy day downtown, it feels wonderful to get away from the noise. To get there: from Downtown, take the Oakland Bay Bridge, at the exit from the bridge take Interstate 580, then Freeway 24 (towards Berkeley), and then Freeway 13 (towards Hayward), exiting at Redwood Road. After 10 miles (16km) of bends, you arrive at the entrance to the park. It's possible to get to the centre of San Francisco in 30 minutes by BART (nearest station to the campground is Hayward). You can register after 2pm but as the gate closes at 10pm you can alternatively get there between 5pm and 10pm and register for the following day. Don't get back too late from your day out – or you'll find the gates closed.

MOTELS

In the Marina district, Lombard Street has lots of motels (as does Van Ness). Practical if you arrive in San Francisco at night from the North (Highway 101) and want to put your luggage down before venturing Downtown. There's a wide choice, but not all motels are worthwhile and the street is noisy. Those listed below stand out from the rest. Note that motels in San Francisco are more expensive than in other US cities.

☗ **Marina Motel** (map II, A2, **53**): 2576 Lombard Street (corner of Divisadero). ☎ 921-9406. Fax: 921-0364. For anyone wanting to be fairly near Fisherman's Wharf. Handsome old-style motel, opened in 1939 (at the same time as the Golden Gate Bridge). One of the nicest in the Van Ness / Lombard district. Attractive, well-ventilated rooms, with kitchen and spacious bathroom, and you can park your car immediately outside your room!

☗ **Holiday Lodge Motel** (map II, B1, **54**): 1901 Van Ness. ☎ 776-4469. Freephone: ☎ 1-800-367-8504. Fax: 474-7046. Attractive place, with an internal courtyard with palm trees and a large swimming pool. Quite pleasant rooms and all mod cons. For (affluent) visitors there's an immense, quite astonishing suite, with microwave and a TV with a really giant screen.

☗ **Vagabond Inns** (map II, B2, **55**): 2550 Van Ness Avenue, on the corner of Filbert. ☎ 776-7500. Freephone: ☎ 1-800-522-1555. Fax: 776-5689. A large, quite luxurious motel. Not a great deal of charm, but the rooms on the 5th floor have a pretty view of the Golden Gate Bridge. Don't take a room on the lower floors unless you don't mind the street noise. Heated swimming pool and free parking lot. Impeccable rooms with air-conditioning and TV. Ground-floor restaurant open 24 hours.

WHERE TO GET A GOOD BREAKFAST

An American breakfast is much bigger and more varied than its average British counterpart (for example: eggs, bacon and toast, filled omelettes, sausages, turkey, sautéed potatoes, chips, pancakes, muffins, scones, waffles with maple syrup . . .). Coffee is often free. The restaurants listed here are specialists in providing great breakfasts. They open early (useful if you want to get to know the Americans living or working in the district, who assiduously hang out in such places), and they close in the early afternoon. Whether you are an early riser or late to bed, this is something you shouldn't miss, as it's part of San Francisco life. It's also a cheap way to fill up.

✕ **Dottie's True Blue Cafe** (map II, B3, **80**): 522 Jones Street (and Geary), Downtown. ☎ 885-2767. Open 7.30am–2pm. Closed Tuesday. Acknowledged as one of the best places for breakfast. Neat and tidy premises, all in blue as you'd guess from the name. Cosy family atmosphere. The food here is well prepared and absolutely fresh. Try the maple cornmeal, oatmeal raisin muffins, fruit pancakes and delicious home-baked bread. For lunch, copious sandwiches, jack and pepper quesadilla, Caesar salad. It's crowded on Saturday and on Sunday mornings, and the 15 little tables quickly fill up.

✕ **Raphael House, Brother Juniper's Restaurant** (map II, B3, **81**): 1065 Sutter Street (between Hyde and Larkin), Downtown. ☎ 474-4621. Open 7am–2pm (1pm Saturday). Closed Sunday. Located in the centre, this association, created in 1971, helps the homeless. You can enjoy an excellent breakfast here to the sound of classical music. There's nothing special about the decor but the welcome is warm. Many options, including a decent breakfast with three eggs, sausages, mushrooms, tomatoes, cheese and hash browns (grated potatoes). The pancakes are huge. As much coffee as you can drink is included.

✕ **Yakety Yak** (map II, C2, **83**): 679 Sutter Street. ☎ 885-6908. Open daily, 7am–9pm (8am Sunday). Near to most of the hotels, the Yakety Yak offers a very simple and cheap breakfast menu (giant glass of orange juice, delicious cakes) that you can put together yourself in a radically different atmosphere from the places mentioned above. The place has an art-student atmosphere and it's somewhere you can wake up gently in the company of some friendly locals.

✕ **Doidge's** (map II, B2, **82**): 2217 Union Street. ☎ 921-2149. Open 8am–1.45am (2.45am weekends). An early-morning restaurant that's very popular in the district, especially with the middle-classes. The proof is that it's full at brunch time! They specialize in omelettes, which you create yourself from a very comprehensive list of ingredients. Excellent chef.

✕ **Spaghetti Western**: 576 Haight Street (and Steiner), Haight-Ashbury. ☎ 864-8461. Open daily, 8am–3pm (4pm weekends). Easily recognizable: the front is decorated with an immense cactus. The interior is in *cantina* style, but more colourful. Not necessarily the best but without doubt the most copious breakfast in San Francisco, with no fewer than 30 different dishes to choose from. And, if that isn't enough, you can add the ingredients of your choice for a small additional charge. If you've never tasted a snapper 'n' eggs at dawn, this is your chance. This fresh Pacific mullet is cooked with a delicious sauce of white wine, garlic and tomatoes. Also recommended, the zydeco breakfast (Cajun brawn with eggs and black beans), Mama Cruz's *huevos rancheros* or *wham-bam-thank-you-Scram* (sorry, we aren't going to list the ingredients here!). All this in a picturesque atmosphere in which neo-grunge students mix with local employees and latter-day cowboys.

✕ **Home Plate** (map II, A2, **84**): 2274 Lombard Street (between Steiner and Pierce), Pacific Heights. ☎ 992-HOME. Open daily, 7am–4pm. Warm little place, a step or two from Union Street. People come here mainly for the eggs, which are cooked in every way imaginable. You can create your own omelette, for example, starting from about 30 different ingredients! Among their other specialities: Eggs Benedict, with poached eggs and muffins, covered with mustard sauce (ask to have it separately), turkey or ham, and grated potatoes. The coffee is extra. Homemade bread, and all dishes are served with a scone.

✕ **Mama's** (map II, C1, **85**): 1701 Stockton (and Filbert), North Beach. ☎ 362-6421. Open 8am–3pm. Closed Monday out of season. Very well located, opposite the pretty park on Washington Square. Well known for more than 20 years, this is a beautiful restaurant specializing in breakfasts. Wide choice of omelettes, pancakes, sandwiches and they also do salads and vegetarian dishes. A little more expensive than the previous entries, but it's still reasonable. Credit cards are not accepted.

SAN FRANCISCO DISTRICT BY DISTRICT

San Francisco is made up of around 15 districts, each very different from the others. Below are some tips on what there is to see and do.

– **Castro and Upper Market**: San Francisco's gay community, with bars, restaurants, shops and gymnasia. *(Good to go day or night.)*

– **Cole Valley**: family atmosphere, quiet and charming. Not much for tourists. *(Go during the day.)*

– **Chinatown**: interesting, commercial, overpopulated and touristy. *(Go during the day.)*

– **Downtown (and Tenderloin)**: hotels, shops, deluxe restaurants and down-and-outs. Something you shouldn't miss. *(Go during the day.)*

– **Financial District**: banks and offices, as the name indicates. Nothing much to see except skyscrapers and white collars. *(Go during the day, Monday–Friday.)*

– **Fisherman's Wharf**: what was once the port, although now only a few old boats remain; otherwise, there are shops selling T-shirts, seafood restaurants and other tourist traps. OK for blowing a few dollars while you wait for the ferry to Alcatraz. *(Go during the day.)*

– **Haight-Ashbury**: this is 'hippieland', with motley houses, revolutionary murals, 'smoke-shops', and shops selling CDs, records and second-hand books. Cool and original. *(Go during the day.)*

– **Lower Haight**: cradle of the counter-culture. Some nice bars and good restaurants. *(Go in the evening.)*

– **Mission**: lively and relaxed Mexican district. *(Go during the day for the coffee-shops and to see the murals. Go during the evening for the bars and trendy restaurants.)*

– **Noe Valley**: quiet, yet a bustling shopping area at the same time; gay and family atmospheres. *(Go during the day.)*

– **North Beach and Telegraph Hill**: pretty and touristy. A huge number of restaurants and cafes. *(Go in the evening, when it's much livelier.)*

– **Pacific Heights and Marina**: the most middle-class district in the city. You can take an architectural stroll or look at the smart shops. *(Go preferably during the day.)*

– **The parks**: for bike rides or roller-skating, for the museums and the beautiful Baker Beach. *(Go during the day only.)*

– **Russian Hill and Nob Hill**: two smart residential districts. Beautiful houses, some beautiful viewpoints, and extremely steep streets. *(Go during the day.)*

– **South of Market (SOMA)**: bars, nightspots, gay clubs and trendy restaurants. *(Go during the evening only.)*

RECOMMENDED SIGHTS

– **Not to be missed**: North Beach, Russian Hill, Haight-Ashbury, Castro and Golden Gate Park.

– **See if you can**: Fisherman's Wharf, Financial District, Nob Hill and Chinatown.

– **Perfect for backpackers**: Mission, SOMA, Lower Haight, Cole Valley and Noe Valley.

★ DOWNTOWN AND THE FINANCIAL DISTRICT

All along Market Street, starting from Van Ness, there is a series of districts with totally individual features. Beyond the monumental **Civic Center** is the old district of **Tenderloin** (now in the early stages of restoration), Union Square (with the best-known big stores) and the Financial District. In the north, are **Chinatown**, then **Northbeach** and **Fisherman's Wharf**.

In **Downtown** or, more precisely, beside Tenderloin, you'll be struck most of all by the number of homeless people. A long queue usually waits for a bowl of soup or some kind of work in front of the **Glide Memorial Church** (300 Ellis Street).

> **TIP**: there are **Free Walking Tours**, organized by the friends of the SF Public Library (Paul and Market Street). A superb programme each month, on such subjects as the murals on 24th Street, the Japanese churches, the mansions of Pacific Heights or the Roof Gardens and open spaces. The guides are enthusiastic volunteers who love their city. It's free, although no contribution is ever refused! Information: ☎ 557-4266.

SAN FRANCISCO

WHERE TO EAT DOWNTOWN

☆ BUDGET

✕ **Rincon Center** (map II, D2, **90**): 101 Spear Street and Mission. Open at lunchtime during the week only. A 'food court' right in the heart of the Financial District where the white-collar workers squeeze in together. In quite a luxurious and noisy setting there are 15 inexpensive little restaurants offering everything from Thai and Italian, to Chinese and Indian. There's also a post office and an international bookshop in the centre.

✕ **Lori's Diner** (map II, C3, **91**): 149 Powell Street (between O'Farrell and Ellis). ☎ 677-9999. Open daily, 6am–10pm. This is an American restaurant equipped with every cliché: red neon signs, big banquettes, retro petrol pumps, a bi-plane and a superb Indiana Jones motorbike hanging from the ceiling, hits from the 1950s blaring, etc. The menu is in the same style as the decor: blueberry pancakes, Mexican omelette, hamburgers and Caesar salad. A good place for breakfast. Two other branches, although smaller, are at 500 Sutter and 336 Mason.

✕ **Tommy's Joynt** (map II, B3, **92**): 1101 Geary Boulevard, on the corner of Van Ness Avenue. ☎ 775-4216. Open daily, 10am–1.40am. You pay cash at this self-service place. It's very well known and has been open since 1949. To start with, the decor is quite entertaining – the proprietor has hung everything he could find on the walls and ceiling: flags, sporting trophies, antique photos. The place has a warm atmosphere, and it feels intimate and colourful. Renowned for its buffalo stew, this being the only place you can get it in the city. The buffalo chilli is a delight. Also the astonishing steam beer (naturally fermented beer without any use of carbon dioxide), as well as world beers ranging from Chinese Tsingtao to Yugoslav Niksicko, including Norwegian Aass and O.B. from Korea; Steam and Hamm are on draught. Italian–American cuisine. The waitresses are in caps and gingham aprons.

✕ **Vietnam II** (map II, B3, **93**): 701 Larkin Street (and Ellis). ☎ 885-1274. Open daily, 8am–midnight. Curious name as there is no Vietnam I! There's a small fountain with goldfish, revolving trays and beautiful mother-of-pearl panels. You'll rarely get a smile from the waiters, however. The cuisine is a blend of Chinese and Vietnamese. Excellent value for money and a very long menu with 170 dishes. There's a large Asian contingent – always a good sign. The seafood is particularly good and very fresh. Delicious spring rolls, as well as Five Spices Chicken, Vietnam II Sizzling Seafood and curried goat stew.

✕ **Cafe Mason** (map II, C3, **94**): 320 Mason Street (between Geary and O'Farrell). ☎ 544-0320. Very near Union Square, this bar-restaurant is open 24 hours. A tiny bit reminiscent of Mel's Drive Inn (*see below*) with its green-and-red neon signs running along the spangled banquettes, an old Wurlitzer and intermittent fountains, but the feel is not quite as authentic. Various menus (the coffee is extra and the cups are not very big), and there's a good choice of omelettes, burgers, sandwiches and quesadillas.

✕ **Original Joe's** (map II, C3, **136**): 144 Taylor Street (and Eddy). ☎ 775-4877. Open daily, 10.30am–12.30am. Run by the same family for 60 years. Large cafeteria-style restaurant with loyal regulars. You can eat very well here for under $15. Since opening, they've served more than eight million customers. Another good sign: the waitresses and cooks have all been here for anything from 10 to 40 years. Italian specialities. The 'dish of the day' is copious, with a wide choice of sandwiches (including the famous Joe's JR) and pasta dishes, as well as steaks, etc.

✕ **Thai Stick** (map II, B3, **137**): 698 Post Street. ☎ 928-7730. Open Monday–Thursday 11am–3pm, 5–10pm, Friday–Saturday 11am–11pm, Sunday 11am–10pm. Serves good Thai food at really moderate prices. Excellent reputation. The high spots on the menu are the seafood, the chef's specials, the curries and the 'clay pots'. Many vegetarian dishes.

SAN FRANCISCO

☆☆–☆☆☆ MODERATE TO EXPENSIVE

✕ **Cafe Bastille** (map II, C2, **95**): 22 Belden Place (a small street between Kearny and Montgomery, and between Bush and Pine). ☎ 986-5673. Open 11.30am–11pm, 11.30am–2am Saturday. Closed Sunday. A real French restaurant with a Parisian ambiance: old lamps, subway-type tiling, etc. There's a little terrace that quickly fills up in fine weather. Very much appreciated by French people who live in San Francisco. They love backpackers here. Specialities include mussels, shepherd's pie and black pudding. Also on the à la carte menu are pancakes and Californian dishes such as grilled tuna and salad. Jazz evenings from time to time and dance-parties some Saturday nights.

✕ **Tadich Grill** (map II, C2, **98**): 240 California Street. ☎ 391-1849. Open Monday–Saturday 11am–9.30pm. In the Financial District, this old restaurant stands out in the middle of all the modern buildings. It's California's oldest restaurant, having been in existence since 1849. The present-day setting dates from the 1920s. A big room, like a brasserie, and with an enormous counter. Some tables at the side in little private areas. Good menu, based on fish and seafood. Renowned for its grilled crawfish and its seafood *Cioppino*, which is not cheap but includes clams, scallops, shrimps, crab and white fish. For smaller budgets, there's a very good, filling clam chowder. No reservations. Busy at lunchtime, quieter from 3pm.

✕ **New Delhi** (map II, C3, 97): 160 Ellis Street (between Mason and Powell). ☎ 397-8470. Open Monday–Saturday 11.30am–2pm, 5.30–10pm. Closed Sunday. Not far from Union Square. Very large room with smart yet plain decor. Shades of brown and red brick dominate, with curious Corinthian columns. Good specialities: tandoori, fish tikka, curry, chicken tikka masala. Some particularly well-prepared old recipes: *Kofta Shah Jahani* (stuffed lamb meatballs, the favourite dish of Shah Jahan, who built the Taj Mahal), and *Murg Akbari* (apparently much favoured by the Emperor Akbar). At lunchtime, they offer an inexpensive menu or a buffet lunch (10 dishes, with salad and *nan* bread) for under $8.

✕ **Plouf** (map II, C2, **99**): 40 Belden Place (between Bush and Pine, Kearny and Montgomery). ☎ 986-6491. Open Monday–Friday 11am–midnight, Saturday lunchtime only. The kitchen closes at 10.30pm, the bar at 11pm. Right beside the Cafe Bastille (same proprietor). When the modern is transformed into the ancient – that is, when Californian cuisine is reworked by a French restaurateur – what you get is a seafood bistro. This is a traditional brasserie put together using modern materials (the bar is imitation marble, there's a metal ceiling and wood-and-steel furniture). À la carte there are oysters, fried mussels and fish from the Pacific. Carnivores will still be able to devour a rack of lamb, a steak or a chicken. Prices are reasonable.

✕ **Hard Rock Cafe** (map II, B2, **96**): 1699 Van Ness Avenue, on the corner of Sacramento. ☎ 885-1699. Open 11.30am–11pm (midnight Friday and Saturday). Some 10 blocks north of the Civic Center. Those who don't like a crowd, or noise or industrial cuisine will avoid it – but Elvis fans will revel in his Golden Discs, the poster for *Jailhouse Rock* and his cape, donated by Priscilla. Admission is free, but do be careful: the consumption of alcoholic drinks is severely regulated. Under-21s are advised to abstain. A huge room with loads of miscellaneous objects: a Vespa scooter on the ceiling, a Cadillac sliced in two, rock-star guitars. And all the trimmings that you see in all the other Hard Rock Cafes across the world! 1960s nostalgics can admire old cars and juke-boxes. There's always a queue after 6pm, but they're often people who just want to buy the famous T-shirt. If you plan to eat there, wait inside and they'll give you a beeper that vibrates when it's your turn to sit down at a table.

☓ **Anjou** (map II, C2, **100**): 44 Campton Place (a back street connecting Stockton and Grant, between Sutter and Post). ☎ 392-5373. Open 11.30am–2.30pm, 5.30–10pm. Closed Sunday and Monday. Reservations are strongly recommended. This is a small restaurant where the customers appreciate the French touch. Setting fresh and pleasant. The French cuisine has a good reputation and the prices aren't too prohibitive. Grilled meat dishes (lamb chops, steak, salmon), shrimp and scallops, fish, medallions of sautéed veal, etc. Quite formal.

☓ **California Culinary Academy** (map II, B3, **101**): 625 Polk Street (and Turk). ☎ 1-800-BAY-CHEF. Reservations: ☎ 771-3536. Open Monday–Friday noon–1.30pm, Monday–Thursday 6–8pm, Friday 6–8.30pm (buffet). Note, however, that they have a great many private parties and theme parties at which prices are very high (phone and ask for the month's schedule). Why not eat in one of the most famous cookery schools in California? Besides, you'll love the retro setting of the Carme Room, an enormous and luxurious room that was once a theatre, where you can watch the training going on behind a big window. The tables are well separated, and there's a hushed atmosphere that's occasionally a touch austere. Here, you have to accept the rules of the game: the dishes may be sublime, or simply adequate, occasionally mediocre. But there are usually nice surprises (all the more so since the 'students' are occasionally chefs who are already in business). On Sunday, brunch 10.30am–2.30pm. Reservation is essential.

☓ **Sushi Bune Restaurant** (map II, C3, **102**): 389 Geary Street (between Powell and Mason). ☎ 781-5111. Opposite the Maxwell Hotel. Open daily, 11am–11pm. Pleasant Japanese restaurant with some tables but mainly a huge circular bar around which you sit. In the middle, waiters prepare sushi, then put them on little boats that sail around the bar, so that customers can help themselves. The colours of the plates correspond to certain sushi and thus to a price. At the end of your meal, the waiter calculates your bill from the empty plates. Be careful if you have a big appetite or you may end up with quite a hefty bill! The best place around the bar is definitely where the boats begin their voyage: otherwise, all you get to choose from are the sushi that nobody else wants!

☆☆☆☆ SPLASH OUT

☓ **Postrio** (map II, C3, **103**): 545 Post Street (and Taylor). Two blocks from Union Square. ☎ 776-7825. Open daily, 10am–midnight. One of the most sophisticated restaurants in San Francisco – you often see film stars eating here. On three levels, the restaurant provides exceptional spaciousness and superb decor – it's resolutely modern, yet fresh and warm. Smart clientele but, curiously, the atmosphere isn't stilted. The bar is one of the 'hottest' meeting places for trendies, and *antipasti* and delicious pizzas washed down with a glass of wine will not break the bank. It's different at the tables, of course: the dishes start at $20. But they're well worth it if you have the means. Californian cuisine with inspired ideas. Lots of different hors-d'oeuvres like giant smoked-salmon blinis, fresh cream and caviar, tuna *sashimi*, smoked golden trout, etc. Or try roasted Sonoma lamb, Chinese-style duck with stoned fruit, and astonishing mixtures such as pan-roasted quail with cornbread, *andouille* stuffing, mushroms and *foie gras*, etc. Service is occasionally a little slow, though staff on the whole are friendly and smiling. They serve breakfast during the week, and a sumptuous Sunday brunch.

✕ **Stars** (map II, B3, **104**): 150 Redwood Alley (McAllister and Golden Gate). Right next to the Civic Center. ☎ 861-7827. Open Monday–Friday noon–11pm. Stars is the great competitor to Postrio. It has a certain advantage in terms of 'seeing and being seen' as here virtually everyone is represented. Not so much the trendy set, more like industrialists and politicians. The cuisine is equally famous. The decor consists of large posters, souvenir photos and paintings. Piano bar. You can eat at the counter, opposite a big, open kitchen. Menu a little short. At lunchtime, there's an affordable lunch and copious salads. In the evening, it's twice the price. Seafood, grilled meat, dishes of French inspiration and superb desserts. Wines are expensive, apart from the chianti *classico*, but they do serve wine and champagne by the glass. Reservations essential.

– Adjacent to the main room, **JT's Bistro** (entrance at 555 Golden Gate Avenue, on the corner of Polk) offers dishes at more affordable prices.

– Otherwise, one block from there, the **Star Cafe** (500 Van Ness and McAllister Street) is an annexe where you can eat more intimately, as well as more quickly, away from society events. It's just as good as and much less expensive than Stars. Italian and Californian cuisine. Delicious baskets of fried seafood.

✕ **Farallon** (map II, C2–3, **105**): 450 Post Street. Just seconds away from Union Square. ☎ 956-6969. This is the city's top restaurant. Every evening, you see businessmen, top models and loaded trendies flock religiously to this enormous room with its subdued lighting, accompanied by the rustling sounds of stunning, but not always the most tasteful, evening gowns, and suits and ties in the latest fashion. In short, it's a spectacle in itself. People also come here for the cuisine, which is excellent, although the fish and seafood specialities are expensive. As for the decor, which was inspired by the film *20,000 Leagues Under the Sea* – the investors are said to have spent $4 million on it.

SAN FRANCISCO

WHERE TO HAVE A DRINK DOWNTOWN

🍸 **Cityscape** (map II, C2, **152**): on the 46th floor of the Hilton at 333 O'Farrell (and Mason). Open daily, 5pm–12.30am (opens 10am Sunday). Take any of the battery of lifts at the right-hand rear of the hotel. San Francisco Bay certainly looks beautiful when you see it from the 46th floor. The city stretches out below you in all directions. The bar is quite traditional, and the cocktail menu not very inventive. Unfortunately the tables nearest the windows are reserved for dinner (allow for more than $50 per person). That said, buying a drink entitles you to a full range of free snacks and even a *tapas* buffet.

🍸 **Equinox** (map II, D2, **151**): 5 Embarcadero Center, at the top of the Hyatt Regency Hotel. ☎ 788-1234. Open daily, 4pm–midnight (Saturday noon–1am). This is the city's only revolving bar, giving you a 360 degree view of the Bay Bridge, Treasure Island and the city. Over 40 cocktails on the menu, the house speciality being the well-named 'Souvenir' (you get to keep the glass!) based on rum and fruit juice. The beers are reasonably priced, but the rest is naturally expensive. The food is very expensive – of course, the clientele is not made up of backpackers. The view is superb, especially in late afternoon.

WHAT TO SEE DOWNTOWN

★ **The Civic Center**: station Civic Center, MUNI subway or a No. 5 or 21 bus. City Hall is built around a large square, in the classical 17th-century French style and with a dome that is 301ft (92m high). Opposite it are: the Opera, then the Davies Symphony Hall (a beautiful rotunda), the Civic Auditorium, the Public Library, State and Federal Buildings.

★ **Union Square**: the centre of San Francisco, with all the big shops including Macy's, Saks, Fifth Avenue, Neiman Marcus, and smart hotels, e.g. the St Francis and the Sir Francis Drake. Nearby is Powell Street, with its cable-car. Union Square is full of life – and it all kicks into action at sunrise. The grass there is great for a siesta.

★ **Circle Gallery Building** (map II, C2–3, **180**): 140 Maiden Lane (a minor road linking Stockton and Kearny, between Post and Geary). The building served as a first draft for the Guggenheim Museum in New York and was designed by Frank Lloyd Wright in 1948. See it chiefly for the architecture.

★ **The Financial District**: it's best to visit here on a working day (11am–3pm); in the evening and the weekend it's completely dead. At lunchtime, you'll marvel at the spectacle of the golden boys dashing for something to eat. Many of them go to the Crocker Galleria, which connects Sutter and Post Streets between Montgomery and Kearny. This is a very smart shopping arcade with a glazed semi-circular roof, from where you can get a beautiful view over the surrounding buildings. On the second floor there are lots of self-service places at prices that are still quite reasonable. The banking district, as you might expect, includes some lovely pieces of architecture. It has undergone much more development than the city centre, due in part to its proximity to the port.

★ **Wells Fargo Bank History Room** (map II, C2, **181**): 420 Montgomery Street, level with California Street. ☎ 396-2619. Open Monday–Friday 9am–5pm. Admission is free. There are two floors devoted to souvenirs of Wells Fargo, particularly the famous stagecoaches that contributed so much to opening up routes to the West. You can gaze in wonder at the Concord Coach, which carried as many as 18 people, nine of them on the roof! There are free brochures telling the history of the bank. Its founders were two New York financiers, Henry Wells and William George Fargo. The museum is almost on the exact spot where the bank opened in July 1852. By 1855, Wells Fargo already had 55 branches, and by 1890 this had grown to 2,600. You can't help being reminded of the house slogan in the middle of this period of growth, which ran: 'Work is a very necessary and good habit'. On the first floor, there's an exhibition of mock-ups and a photograph of Black Bart (a gentleman robber), who between 1875 and 1883 attacked no fewer than 27 stagecoaches. Wells Fargo put up a $250 reward for his capture (a large sum at the time). Today, Wells Fargo is the third biggest bank in California and the 10th biggest in the United States.

★ **Pacific Heritage Museum** (map II, C2, **182**): 608 Commercial Street (and Montgomery). ☎ 399-1124. Open Monday–Friday 10am–4pm. Admission free. An interesting museum about the cultural and economic links between the shores on both sides of the Pacific. There are temporary exhibitions and a permanent display that explains the history of American currency. The present building was constructed in 1875 to replace the first US Mint. It was seriously damaged by the 1906 earthquake, and then reconstructed using parts of the former structure (including the iron pillar in the main hall). There are many documents and photos of the construction techniques in use at the time.

★ **Montgomery Street and Jackson Square**: it's impossible to mention all the architectural landmarks of the Financial District, but here are a few of the best. The houses in the 700s on Montgomery Street (between Jackson and Washington) are quite remarkable. They include some of the oldest buildings of the Gold Rush period. On the corner of Montgomery and Washington, there's an elegant building dating from 1905. Next to it, No. 708 was erected after the great fire of 1906. No. 722 dates from 1851, No. 728, a brick building in Italianate style, was built in 1853, and No. 732 in 1852. At No. 552 you can see the opulent architecture of the Bank of San Francisco (1908).

Historic **Jackson Square** is in the 400s on Jackson Street. At No. 472 you'll find the Solari Building, in brick and cast iron, dating from 1850. Next door is the Larco's Building (1852). Nos. 440–444 were originally stables. No. 441 dates from 1861; Nos. 445, 451, 463 and 473 make up the Hotaling complex, built during the 1860s. No. 432, one of the loveliest buildings on the street, was built in 1906. Nos. 415–431 are where the first Ghirardelli chocolate factory stood in 1853. At No. 407 is a three-storey building from 1860. At No. 408 is a modern (1953) building that fits in well with the environs – and there are many more.

★ **Transamerica Pyramid**: 600 Montgomery, on the corner of Washington. The city's tallest and most astonishing building, its slender shape is recognizable from several miles away. In principle, it is not open to visitors (it only contains offices), but you can always try your luck! If the guards let you in, take the lift to the 27th floor, from where there's a fantastic panorama across the city.

★ **Bank of California** (map II, C2, **183**): 400 California Street. This is a superb building dating from 1907 – an immense temple whose front is adorned with Corinthian columns. Its height was raised in 1967. Today it's owned by the Japanese (a sign of the times . . .). In the basement is a small **Museum of the Currency of the American West** (open Monday–Friday 10am–3.30pm).

★ **Hyatt Regency** (map II, D2, **184**): at the end of Market Street, near the Embarcadero. Don't confuse this with the Grand Hyatt, located on Union Square. You don't have to have studied architecture to appreciate the beauty of this hotel. It is the interior that's great. The atrium is 17 floors high. The elevator attendants have been replaced by magnetic cards, so you can no longer take the interior lift to get a vertiginous view, unless you're staying at the hotel. This is where Mel Brooks filmed *High Anxiety*.

★ **Glide Memorial Church** (map II, C3, **185**): 330 Ellis Street. Small district Methodist church famous for its Mass with music. Really not to be missed, if only to get an idea of America's astonishing religious practices. Service at 9am every Sunday. Get there early if you want a seat. There's a chorale with gospels, and an extraordinary reverend preacher. In the pews, everyone repeats the words in a chorus while linking hands. The words appear on a giant screen, just like in a karaoke bar! CDs are on sale of some of the church's choral offerings.

– **Line F**: historic tramway line on Market Street. Brought into service in September 1995, it links Downtown to Castro. The trams come from all over the world: Italy, Japan, Australia, as well as from many other cities in the US. The motors and axles have been adapted for their new route, but the colours of the trams and the advertising posters of the era have been retained. This is a very practical way to get from Market to Castro. The line operates daily, 6.30am–12.30am and you can use the same ticket as the bus.

DOWNTOWN BY NIGHT

– **Club 181** (map II, C3, **220**): 181 Eddy Street (and Taylor). ☎ 673-8181. Open daily to 2am. A trendy supper-club in the Tenderloin district. Fills up very quickly at weekends. Decor very cosy, all in red with sofas, billiard tables and a magnificent curved bar. People go there mainly to dance to techno, funk, hip-hop and also (depending on the evening) to Latino, salsa, etc. A jacket is recommended, and it's best to go there by taxi, as the district is not very safe at night.

– **Red Room** (map II, B2–3, **221**): 827 Sutter Street (on the ground floor of the Hotel Commodore). ☎ 346-7666. Open daily, 5pm–2am. Nob Hill doesn't get to bed very early thanks to bars like the Red Room, which is famous for its superb decor – red from floor to ceiling! Good music, good prices.

– **Punch Line** (map II, C2, **223**): 444 Battery Street (between Clay and Washington). ☎ 397-7573. One of the most famous comedy clubs. Shows are generally at 9pm and 11.30pm (7pm on Saturday). You'd better practise listening to rapid-fire American, otherwise you may miss some of the gags. It's advisable to book.

– **Blue Lamp** (map II, B–C3, **222**): 561 Geary Street. ☎ 885-1464. Pleasant pub adorned by a small stage on which good rock, blues and country groups appear. Mixed clientele.

– **The Fillmore**: 1805 Geary (and Fillmore). ☎ 762-2277. The legendary concert hall where the whole hippie scene took off in the 1960s. Top-of-the-bill acts on a world tour still come here: the big rock groups, and also the new techno scene and the stars of world music. In short, they still have quality programmes almost every evening. The programmes are detailed in the free cultural newspapers.

★ CHINATOWN

The main entrance to Chinatown, Chinatown Gate, is at the intersection of Grant Avenue and Bush Street. With its 100,000 inhabitants San Francisco's Chinatown is the second-largest Chinese city outside Asia, after New York. In fact, if you go there on Saturday and Sunday mornings (about 10am is a good time), when everyone is out shopping, you could be forgiven for thinking you're in China!

Their ancestors started arriving in 1848, fleeing famine and the aftermath of the First Opium War, and they established a colony around Portsmouth Square that numbered close to 4,000 in 1850. They either went into gold mining or set up in various trades (each clan having its own) – all the ones you'd expect, like the clothing industry, restaurants, fishing and laundries.

The great cohesion of this community and their mode of dress, among other things, gave rise in the early days to feelings of distrust, and later, to strong hostility, and these attitudes were reflected in such anti-Chinese laws as the Chinese Exclusion Act of 1882. Such laws only began to fall into disuse after World War II, as Japan had become the common enemy of both the Americans and the Chinese.

WHERE TO EAT IN CHINATOWN

☆ BUDGET

✕ **House of Nanking** (map II, C2, **106**): 919 Kearny Street (between Columbus and Jackson). ☎ 421-1429. Open 11am–10pm (open 4pm on Sunday). This place isn't hard to spot, as there's usually a queue of at least 10 people outside. Inside are a few tables in a tiny room with minimal decor. The reason it's included here is because it provides the best value for money of all the city's cheap Chinese restaurants (the tributes covering the walls will convince you of this). The shrimp cake is delicious. The cuisine really is excellent and the portions are large. Note that this is a very small place – tricky if there are more than four of you.

✕ **Brandy Ho's**: 217 Columbus Avenue. ☎ 788-7527. Open daily, 11.30am–11pm (midnight Friday and Saturday). Very well-run restaurant, serving fine Chinese cuisine. During the week, the menu has unbeatable prices. Meticulous cooking and large servings. They specialize in duck and smoked chicken dishes. There's even a sign up on the wall to the effect that the restaurant doesn't use monosodium glutamate (MSG). There's another Brandy Ho's at North Beach (*see below*).

✕ **Sam Lok** (map II, C2, **107**): 655 Jackson Street. ☎ 981-8988. Open daily, 11am–11pm. One of the finest for Chinese cuisine. Their special lunch is very reasonably priced, served until 3pm (try succulent caramelized chicken with lemon sauce). Excellent specials such as baked lobster, spiced salt-baked crab and dry braised flounder. The crab comes straight out of a holding tank. A long menu and a good welcome.

WHAT TO SEE AND DO IN CHINATOWN

Chinatown is built up around Grant Avenue, which is like the backbone of this district. Here you'll find the greatest number of tax-free shops plus plenty of restaurants. It's worth leaving Grant Avenue to 'go native' on Stockton Street, Clay Street and Sacramento Street.

★ **St Mary's Church** (map II, C2, **186**): on the corner of Grant Avenue and California Street. The first cathedral in San Francisco, built in 1854 by Chinese workers. It withstood the earthquakes of 1906 and 1989, and some say this is because it is made of bricks and granite from China. In the entrance are interesting old photos of the district, mostly taken in 1854 and 1906.

★ **Chinese Historical Society of America Museum** (map II, C2, **187**): 50 Commercial Street. ☎ 391-1188. Open Tuesday–Saturday 1pm–5pm. On display is a collection of many interesting photographs showing the history of the Chinese in the American West and in San Francisco.

– For an original and inexpensive gift, if you're in Grant Avenue, you can have your name, or a friend's, written in Chinese characters.

– The curious can watch people doing Tai-Chi in the open air, and other martial arts also take place in the park on Clay Street, right in the middle of Chinatown. Best times are very early in the morning and in the evening. Best not to bring a camera – gang warfare is still rife in San Francisco.

★ If you're interested in architecture, have a look at the **Old Chinese Telephone Exchange Bank of Canton** at 743 Washington Street, a superb building dating from 1909. Also the **Ying on Labor and Merchant Association** at 745 Grant Avenue, with its beautiful Chinese front.

– There is also a large, picturesque fresco representing musicians at the intersection of Columbus and Broadway.

★ RUSSIAN HILL AND NOB HILL

Russian, Nob and Telegraph – these three are San Francisco's most famous hills. Many find **Russian Hill** to be a rather mysterious district, with its narrow, shady passages, wooden stairways, and its beautiful but austere houses, some of them locked up. As for the inhabitants, they seem to be a mixture of young trendies, Chinese and art students.

Nob Hill can be summed up by its three main features: plump little 'palaces', historic hotels like the Fairmont and the Mark Hopkins . . . and jam-packed cable-cars.

WHERE TO EAT IN NOB HILL

✕ **Nob Hill Cafe** (map II, B2, **139**): 1152 Taylor. ☎ 776-6500. A small and rather pretty Italian restaurant offering reasonably priced dishes. They have some delicious specialities: *penne bettola, linguine aglio ollio, tortellini Vitello, lasagne al forno.* They also do pizzas.

WHERE TO HAVE A DRINK IN RUSSIAN HILL

🍸 **Art Institute Cafe** or **Pek's Cafe** (map II, B1, 154): 800 Chestnut Street. The cafe of the San Francisco Art Institute (*see below* under 'What to See'). Open Monday–Thursday 8am–9pm, Friday 9am–4pm, Saturday 9am–2pm. From the terrace, there's a beautiful view of North Beach and Alcatraz. Frequented by art students, of course. The atmosphere is hip.

WHAT TO SEE

RUSSIAN HILL

Russian Hill is one of the city's most elevated residential districts, with extensive panoramas over the Bay. This is a good time to park your car and alternate between the cable-car and walking. Russian Hill got its name from the time when this wild and semi-rural hill was used as a burial ground for Russians working for a trapping company.

The steepest street is Filbert, which has a slope of 32 per cent (between Leavenworth and Hyde). There's a beautiful Edwardian house with elegant bow windows on the corner of Filbert and Hyde and other interesting ones on the corner of Union and Leavenworth.

★ Kerouac fans should call at **29 Russell Place** (Hyde and Union). This is where he wrote *On the Road, Doctor Sax* and *Visions of Cody*. He lived in the attic of Neal and Carolyn Cassady's villa.

★ **Green Street**: for urban trekkers, a delightful walk that lets you discover some superb houses. No. 1088 is a listed building from 1908, while No. 1067 is one of the most original of buildings, the **Feusier Octagon House** (1860). In principle, this is open to the public on the first Sunday and the second and fourth Thursday of each month (1–4pm). Nos. 1055 and 1045 are houses dating from 1866. No. 1039 is a house with an outside staircase, dating from 1885. Nos. 1011, 1030, 1040 and 1050 are also worth seeing, towards the end of the walk. No. 1050 is especially elegant.

Continue along Macondray Lane (between Union and Green). On the corner of Jones there is a 1908 Edwardian-style residence.

Vallejo and Jones Streets merge at the highest point on Russian Hill. This is an area full of pretty cul-de-sacs and alleys (notably Florence Street).

★ **Lombard Street** (map II, B1, **188**): 'The Crookedest Street in the World', between Hyde and Leavenworth is one of the world's most famous and probably most winding streets (you've probably already seen it in at least one screen car-chase sequence). It is absolutely full of flowers. There is a particularly beautiful house at 1100 Lombard, and one block away, at Chestnut and Jones, is the San Francisco Art Institute, built in Spanish-Colonial style. If you go down Lombard Street on foot, don't be alarmed if you hear a crunching sound – it's just the paving stones shifting!

★ **San Francisco Art Institute** (map II, B1): 800 Chestnut Street (and Jones). Open daily, 8am–9pm. It has a rather dull appearance from outside because of the exposed concrete, but as soon as you cross the threshold, it's like being transported into a Spanish *hacienda*, with a beautiful square arcaded courtyard with a central fountain. The entire building is open to visitors and you can walk through the various studios, taking care not to interrupt any classes. Two exhibition spaces show the work of artists who have already made their name. There's a pleasant cafe at the back of the Institute (*see* 'Where to Have a Drink').

NOB HILL

This district is roughly bounded by Bush and Broadway (to the south and north respectively) and Powell and Van Ness (to the east and west).

★ Don't miss **Grace Cathedral** (map II, B2, **190**), neo-Gothic in style, and the **Huntington Hotel** at 1075 California Street, which is an interesting piece of architecture dating from 1924. From the top, you can get a unique panorama over the whole city. Nearby is the **Masonic Museum**, at 1111 California. This is the museum of Californian Freemasonry (open 10am–3pm), and it's a modern building with a large auditorium.

★ **Cable-Car Museum (Powerhouse and Car Barn)** (map II, C2, **191**): Washington and Mason. ☎ 474-1887. Open daily, 10am–5pm (6pm April–October). This is the nerve centre of the cable-car operation and dates back to 1907. Admission is free. There's a photographic exhibition, some scale models and even some old cable-cars, plus a 15-minute film.

★ **St Mary's Cathedral** (map II, B3, **192**): on the corner of Geary and Gough Street (west of Van Ness and Nob Hill). In principle, open daily, 7am–5pm. The cathedral was built in 1970 and has a fabulous interior. There are four slender archways, clad in travertine stone from Italy (the same as was used for the Coliseum in Rome), and these join at the top, 196ft (60m) above the ground, to form a cross decorated with stained-glass windows.

★ NORTH BEACH AND TELEGRAPH HILL

The area around Columbus Avenue and Broadway. This was the place where the Italian immigrants settled. There were 5,000 Italians living here in 1889 and 60,000 by 1939. Interestingly, although it's well known that Haight-Ashbury was at the centre of the hippie movement, not many people remember that the Beat Generation was born in North Beach.

The wealthier Italians moved out of North Beach to the suburbs in the 1950s, leaving behind a lot of inexpensive housing. Young beatniks then settled into this lively, hospitable district and it became the headquarters of a literary and musical Bohemia following the same pattern as Greenwich Village in New York and Venice in Los Angeles. The white-haired dropouts who haunt certain bars are there as a reminder of that time, even though the district has been gradually taken over by gilded youth. It's also still one of the most interesting districts for going out in the evening, with an impressive number of trendy restaurants and bars.

Before you venture in, be warned that North Beach is the most nightmarish district in San Francisco for parking. It's best to go by taxi.

WHERE TO EAT IN NORTH BEACH AND TELEGRAPH HILL

☆–☆☆ BUDGET TO MODERATE

✕ **US Restaurant** (map II, C2, **109**): 431 Columbus Avenue and Stockton Street. ☎ 362-6251. Open Tuesday–Saturday 7am–9pm. Closed the second half of July. Very simple environment, with Formica tables. The cuisine is affordable and unpretentious. Weekday specials (on Friday, you can combine two of them at a reduced price) and a different speciality daily. On Saturday there's the house *osso buco*, and good minestrone on Tuesday, Wednesday and Saturday. On Friday, try the fried squid. Inexpensive Italian wines served by the glass.

✕ **L'Osteria del Forno** (map II, C2, **110**): 519 Columbus Avenue (and Green). ☎ 982-1124. Open daily, except Tuesday 11.30am–10pm (10.30pm Thursday and Friday). A small Italian restaurant. The menu includes Parma ham fondant, salads, sandwiches, pizzas and four or five dishes of the day (generally pasta, but also more unusual dishes). Good value, so it's full practically all the time.

✕ **Il Pollaio** (map II, C2, **116**): 555 Columbus Avenue. ☎ 362-7727. Closed Sunday. A little take-away that's very popular in the area. They do a good grilled chicken at a really cheap price, plus various kinds of soup, salads, sausages, hamburgers, etc. For dessert, there's fabulous ice-cream nearby at Ben & Jerry's.

✕ **Brandy Ho's** (map II, C2, **138**): 450–452 Broadway (and Kearny). ☎ 362-6268. Open daily, 11.30am –midnight. The same proprietors have the one in Chinatown (*see* 'Chinatown'). This is a small, modern room – very clean and fairly smart. A varied menu at very fair prices, where you can find traditional Hunan dishes including soup, rice with shrimps, pork and vegetables. Their speciality is smoked poultry. The lunch menu is very inexpensive.

✕ **Little Joe's** (map II, C2, **140**): 523 Broadway. ☎ 433-4343. Open Monday–Friday 10.30am–10pm, Saturday 11am–11pm, Sunday noon–10pm. Big, welcoming room offering Italian–American cuisine: minestrone soup, parmesan chicken, pasta, all at very fair prices. Interesting daily specials, like the fried squid and the *caciucco* (house speciality). The servings are very large, so you can easily order one dish between two.

✕ **The Helmand** (map II, C2, **111**): 430 Broadway (and Montgomery). ☎ 362-0641. Open Monday–Thursday 5–10pm, Friday and Saturday to 11pm, Sunday 6–10pm. The parking lot at 468 Broadway is free if you're eating in the restaurant. This place is a very good way to discover Afghan cuisine, which is halfway between Indian and Near Eastern, with some unique aromatic dishes. Among the finest dishes are *aushak* (beef ravioli with spiced tomatoes and mint yoghurt) and *dwopiaza* (marinated lamb with peas, onions and twice-cooked rice with cumin and oil). The decor's dull but the service is charming.

✕ **The Stinking Rose (A Garlic Restaurant)** (map II, C2, **112**): 325 Columbus Avenue. ☎ PU1-ROSE. Open 11am–11pm (midnight Friday and Saturday). This unusual restaurant puts garlic in all the sauces and all the dishes – which are delicious and quite original. The decor's great. You can even get a garlic-flavoured ice-cream for dessert! Not surprisingly, there aren't many vampires among their customers. And if the food isn't enough, there's a shop on the premises where you can buy all sorts of garlic-based products. Mouthwash is *not* supplied.

☆☆–☆☆☆ MODERATE TO EXPENSIVE

✕ **Rose Pistola** (map II, C2, **141**): 532 Columbus Avenue. ☎ 399-0499. Open daily, 11.30am–5pm, 5.30pm–1am. Rose has found a formula that works with the trendies of San Francisco, so the place is filled with smart young people every evening, attracted by the warm decor and the meticulous Italian cuisine, served at prices that are more reasonable than those of most other fashionable restaurants. The menu includes fried seafood, swordfish with celery, gnocchi with squid, ricotta ravioli with fennel and fish of the day prepared as you choose (you pay by weight). Impeccable service. Jazz every evening at 9pm (10pm weekends). If you want to have a conversation without shouting, try to get a table on the street.

✕ **Enrico's** (map II, C2, **113**): 504 Broadway Street (and Kearny). ☎ 982-6223. Open daily, 11.30am –2am. A bit like the Rose Pistola. A large, curved room with a huge French window. Some tables outside on Broadway, which can be noisy. The place operates as a bar, restaurant and supper-club, with jazz every evening around 8pm. Specialities include *tapas, prosciutto*, salmon *tartare*, cod *gratin*, crab pudding and oysters served with champagne. Also pasta, burgers and pizzas. Self-denial is hard in a place like this.

SAN FRANCISCO

☆☆☆ EXPENSIVE

✕ **MacArthur Park** (map II, C2, **115**): 607 Front Street (Jackson Square). ☎ 398-5700. Open 11.30am–3.30pm, 5–10pm (11pm Friday and Saturday). Closed at lunchtime on Sunday. Established in a former warehouse this is a smart, very Californian place sporting a blend of bricks and modern paintings. The clientele are mostly business people. The speciality dish is ribs. The portions aren't very large, though, and the cuisine occasionally suffers from a mood swing. A good selection of grilled meats and chicken, plus sandwiches and burgers, salads, and fish and chips with shrimps, salmon and mullet. Good house desserts.

✕ **Caffè Sport** (map II, C2, **114**): 574 Green Street, near Columbus Avenue. ☎ 981-1251. Open lunchtime and in the evening to 10.30pm. Closed Sunday and Monday. An improbable North Beach restaurant whose tables and chairs are painted, as is the ceiling, with all the kitsch grandeur of Sicilian art. It would be difficult to find anything more excessive. There are cooked meats hanging all over the place, so this is not a place for vegetarians! The dishes are large but sadly the management is not fond of people who share one. Specialities include pasta with seafood or vegetables: *calamaris, melanzane*, mussels, lobster, etc. It's quite expensive for just pasta. Get there in the early evening or you won't get in. The owner, Antonio La Tona, has been awarded a variety of distinctions for the quality of his pasta. Quite touristy.

☆☆☆☆ SPLASH OUT

✕ **Cypress Club** (map II, C2, **117**): 500 Jackson Street. ☎ 296-8555. The decor is original and sophisticated. You just have to close your eyes to dream up a Cotton Club ambiance, especially on Friday evening, which is jazz night. There are unusual pillars and enormous lamps. The bar is astonishing. On the menu is crisp salmon with jasmine rice and a pair of oysters, rabbit with wild mushroom ravioli, loin of lamb with garlic confit. Savour the desserts, which are real works of art. Expensive (with some dishes around $25) and sophisticated; a good place for a special party. Service with a smile.

✕ **Bix** (map II, C2, **118**): 56 Gold Street (little alley linking Montgomery and Sansome Streets, between Jackson and Pacific Avenue). ☎ 433-6300. Open Monday–Thursday 11.30am–11pm (midnight Friday and Saturday), Sunday 6–10pm. Set in what was a brick-built warehouse, this restaurant has charming decor. It's an immense room with pillars and stained-glass ceiling which, lit from above, diffuses a gentle orange glow and there's a crescent-shaped mezzanine with an intimate atmosphere that's ideal for romantic dinners. The style of service is designed to suit a distinguished clientele. As is often the case in this kind of place, the cuisine is French-inspired with some American ideas. Lots of grilled meats, skilfully cooked fish and a delicious *filet mignon*.

WHERE TO HAVE A DRINK IN NORTH BEACH AND TELEGRAPH HILL

San Francisco seems to have retained a lot of old bars whose proprietors haven't changed a single thing about them. Each of the coffee-shops listed is an experience, and some have even banded together into an association that publishes *Cups*, a little newspaper. There's an ever-growing number of sidewalk cafes around, so it all feels quite southern European.

🍸 **Cafe Trieste** (map II, C2, **156**): 609 Vallejo Street, on the corner of Grant Avenue. ☎ 392-6739. Open 6.30am–11.30pm (12.30am Friday and Saturday). A genuine Italian cafe where the espresso is excellent. The North Beach 'in' crowd take breakfast here, so you can sometimes meet poets, writers and philosophers: people, in fact, who would normally be at the Vesuvio or Spec's but have been crowded out from both of those places by tourists! Good sandwiches and pastries. At lunchtime on Saturdays you might even find some nostalgic Italians playing the mandolin. *Mamma mia!*

🍸 **Vesuvio** (map II, C2, **158**): 255 Columbus Avenue, level with Kerouac Street. ☎ 362-3370. Open daily, 6am–2am. Located just beside the City Lights Bookstore, this bar has been open since 1907 and is still as it was. Delightful decor, with Tiffany lustred glass, paintings, yellowing photos, miscellaneous souvenirs, collages. This is where all the big names of the beatnik era used to come drinking and Dylan Thomas even used to write poems here. They serve wine and cocktails and you can even bring a sandwich.

🍸 **San Francisco Brewing Company** (map II, C2, **159**): 155 Columbus Avenue, on the corner of

Pacific Avenue. ☎ 434-3344. Open 11.30am–1.45am (noon Saturday and Sunday). Interesting for its beer, which is brewed at the back of the shop and is really quite acceptable. Big, varnished wood counter. The heavy fan in itself is worth the trip. Quite quiet during the day. Students come to play music in the evening (Monday–Wednesday and Saturday).

🍸 **The North End Caffe** (map II, C1, **155**): 1402 Grant Avenue (and Green). ☎ 956-3350. Open 7.30am–midnight (11pm Sunday). A simple, quite small coffee-shop with a peaceful atmosphere and the sort of place where you can relax and enjoy an ice-cream or a beer after climbing Telegraph Hill.

🍸 **Royal Oak Saloon** (map II, B2, **232**): 2201 Polk Street. ☎ 928-2303. Open daily, 11am–2am. This saloon with its somewhat surprising collection of green plants fits perfectly into the nice ambiance of the street (with decor as rococo as anything). Beautiful woodwork, old carpets, warm colours. Very agreeable place for having an evening drink. Young people bring their pizzas here and sink into the soft, comfortable armchairs.

WHAT TO SEE IN NORTH BEACH AND TELEGRAPH HILL

★ **City Lights Bookstore** (map II, C2, **193**): 261 Columbus Avenue (and Jack Kerouac Street). ☎ 362–8193. Open daily, 10am–midnight. Opened in 1953, this bookshop must count as a historic monument because it was a focal point for the 'Beat' movement (*see above*: 'A Brief History').

SAN FRANCISCO

It all began in 1955, when Allen Ginsberg's poem *Howl* became the launching point for a breakaway movement and a rallying cry for those who chose to denounce materialistic lifestyles. Ginsberg's public reading of his work was attended by a whole crowd of individuals who soon grew to be the Beat Generation's figureheads: Jack Kerouac, William Burroughs, Neal Cassady, Lew Welsh and Michael McClure. Lawrence Ferlinghetti, the founder of the City Lights Bookstore, immediately published *Howl*, which was soon regarded as a manifesto.

Ginsberg is now regarded as a 'classic' of American literature, like his friends Kerouac and Burroughs. So it's hardly surprising that this bookshop has become a cult place, frequented by intellectuals and alternative beings of every style, children of the counter-culture in general and the beatnik culture in particular. Here you can find all the works of the alternative society, whether Buddhist, psychologist, anti-imperialist, ecologist, New Age travellerist, feminist, drug culturist or sexual liberationist.

They also stock posters and picture postcards of writers. From time to time there are poetry readings and debates. City Lights is also a bold publishing house whose authors, besides the works of the Beat Generation, include a variety of American and European writers who are philosophically in tune with the movement.

★ **Coit Tower** (map II, C1, **194**): Telegraph Hill Boulevard. From here you get a wonderful panorama over the city and the Bay. To reach it, take a No. 39 bus. The people of San Francisco like to tell the story of this tower. It was built in 1933 by a rich lady, Lillie Hitchcock Coit, after she was saved from certain death by the fire brigade. She developed a crush on the boys of the fire brigade and decided to have a monument built in their honour. It was to symbolize the fireman's tool – namely the fire hose. The problem is that, as the tower was named after the lady, there's the possibility of a misinterpretation, and some make no bones about calling it the 'Coit Erection'. The firemen's museum (*see below*) contains a large section devoted to their benefactor. On the way you can stroll down the stairs on Filbert to the Napier cul-de-sac, where pretty Victorian houses and small gardens make this one of the city's most charming residential areas.

★ **North Beach Museum** (map II, C2, **195**): 1435 Stockton (and Columbus). Open 9am–4pm. Closed Saturday and Sunday. This tiny museum consisting mainly of old photographs of the North Beach area, has been set up on the first floor of the Eureka Bank for anyone wanting to know more about the neighbourhood.

SHOPPING IN NORTH BEACH

Tower Records: on the corner of Columbus Avenue and Bay Street, near Fisherman's Wharf. Open daily, 9am–midnight. A large store with a huge choice of CDs, videos, etc. They frequently have sales, some of which are worth a look, and there's a classical annexe opposite.

Quantity Postcards: 1441 Grant Avenue ☎ 986-8866. Open daily, noon–11pm. There's no sign but you'll recognize the shop by its window display, which is usually completely outrageous. A crazy selection of postcards.

Patagonia: 770 North Point Street. ☎ 771-2050. This shop carries the famous brand that's well known to all walkers. Come and browse through the wide choice of quality shoes and clothing.

NORTH BEACH AND TELEGRAPH HILL BY NIGHT

Savoy Tivoli (map II, C1, **224**): 1434 Grant Avenue (and Union). ☎ 362-7023. Open daily, 5pm–2am. Closed Sunday. Handsome pub with two big bars, three billiard rooms and metal palm trees contrasting with the blood-red ceiling. Jam-packed on weekends, and you'll meet a mixed crowd having a great time.

The Spec's (map II, C2, **225**): 12 William Saroyan Place (formerly Adler). In a tiny passage opening onto Columbus. ☎ 421-4112. Open daily, 5pm–2am. Set back beside the Tosca Cafe. With its over-ornate decor, smoky atmosphere and liberally-flowing beer, Spec's has been pulling in the writers and artists of North Beach for more than 20 years. Right at the beginning it was a Chinese temple, after which it spent some time as a belly-dancing club. The walls are covered with memorabilia. You'll be lucky to find a place at the bar.

Tosca Cafe (map II, C2, **226**): 242 Columbus Avenue, not far from Broadway. ☎ YU6-9651. Open 5pm–2am. Very dark, with an antique coffee machine, a wood-and-aluminium counter and imitation leather benches. Drink the house cappuccino at the bar: it's a mixture of hot chocolate and brandy, a speciality of the house. It's best to come only on Monday and Tuesday evenings; on other days, from 10pm onward the tables shake with the sound of music from the Palladium, a nightspot located immediately below. It would be a shame not to be able to appreciate in peace the operatic arias played on the 1960s jukebox.

🍸 **1232 Saloon** (map II, C2, **227**): 1232 Grant Avenue. ☎ 989-7666. Open noon–2am. An old pub that's been in business since 1861. No one can prove it's been repainted since then. Opened by Ferdinand E. Wagner, who immigrated to the United States from Alsace in 1836. The building survived the 1906 earthquake and is thought to be one of the oldest in North Beach. Very dark and very smoky. Most customers are in their thirties or forties and really into their drink. There's a band almost every evening. Rock from the 1960s or scorching blues.

🍸 **Lost & Found Saloon** (map II, C2, **228**): 1353 Grant Avenue, near Green Street. ☎ 392-9126. Open 6am–11pm. Intimate, comfortable, warm. Excellent rock and blues groups Tuesday–Saturday. Small dance floor. Cover charge Friday and Saturday.

★ FISHERMAN'S WHARF

Once a district of fishermen and food industries, the wharf has been transformed and in recent years has become a formidable tourist trap that attracts millions of visitors every year. If there's still a reason for going to Fisherman's Wharf, it's probably to get across to Alcatraz.

WHERE TO EAT IN FISHERMAN'S WHARF

☆☆ MODERATE

✕ **McCormick and Kuleto's** (map II, B1): Ghirardelli Square, 900 North Point Street (corner of Beach and Larkin). ☎ 929-1730. Open 11.30am–11.30pm. This restaurant in a very pleasant setting is a large room on several levels with a view over the Bay. It still has its reputation for being a place for good fish and seafood and there's plenty of choice on the menu. The dishes are quite expensive, but if you ask for the **Crab Cake Lounge** menu, which in no way differs from the rest of the restaurant, you'll get the same quality while paying less – you just don't get a view of the Bay.Tucked away in a corner of the menu is a 'lunch and lite' at a low price, and it's served most of the day. Don't miss McCormick's Clam Chowder, the Dungeness Crab Cakes, the Crayfish Cake, the Swordfish Kebab, and the Cajun Fish Tacos. For the less affluent, very good pizzas are cooked on a wood fire. Good wine list, and wines can be ordered by the glass.

✕ **Fog City Diner** (map II, C1, **120**): 1300 Battery Street. ☎ 982-2000. Open 11.30am–11pm (midnight Friday and Saturday). This is one of the city's most popular diners. It has modern brasserie-type decor and the atmosphere is quite casual and easy-going. Constant good quality has ensured its success for a number of years and booking is necessary at weekends. The menu has a wide range of prices, from very reasonable to quite high, and specialities include seafood that's on view in the refrigerated displays. The crab cakes here are famous and there's a good selection of salads and an oyster bar. Austere service, however.

✕ **Lou's** (map II, B1, **142**): Pier 47. ☎ 771-0377. Very popular restaurant in the port. The setting and cuisine are typically American.

Dishes are of respectable quality and at prices that are attractive for the area. There's a choice of breakfast, soup, salad, burgers, pasta, seafood and fish and chips.

Blues gigs daily, starting at 4pm (noon at weekends), so there's an admission charge at concert times. If you're eating in the restaurant, your first drink is free.

☆☆☆ EXPENSIVE

✗ **Scoma's** (map II, B1, **143**): Pier 47 (opposite Jones Street, on the corner of Jefferson). ☎ 771-4383. One of the most highly reputed restaurants in the district, Scoma's is set up right in the port and stretches out along the wooden pontoons overlooking the moored yachts. It's always crowded at meal times: you take a ticket on arrival and wait until the waitresses come and seat you – but they're pretty efficient. Wide choice of fresh-caught fish, with the full list marked up at the entrance. Scoma's claims to serve the freshest fish on the Wharf. It's probably true, given the success of the place.

WHERE TO HAVE A DRINK IN FISHERMAN'S WHARF

🍸 **Buena Vista** (map II, B2): 2765 Hyde Street (facing the cable-car stop). ☎ 474-5044. Open 9am–2am. An old pub with an almost British atmosphere that's warm and lively. Always crowded in the evening and it's sometimes hard to get to the long bar, but it's basically a nice place. Famous for its Irish coffee – this was the first place to introduce it to America in 1952. It is delightful, even if you have tasted better in Ireland! On average, 3,000 coffees are served here daily. You can also get a huge breakfast.

WHAT TO SEE IN FISHERMAN'S WHARF

★ **On Taylor and Jefferson**: several dozen fish and seafood restaurants and lots of shops. Very touristy, frequently pretentious and therefore quite expensive. This is a suitable place to overdose on fashion shops, souvenirs and T-shirts.

★ **Between Jones and Hyde**: you can see what remains of the San Francisco fishing fleet here. Out of the hundreds of boats that were in business 30 years ago, fewer than 50 are still in operation. If you want to watch fish being landed and sold, you'll have to come very early in the morning, as it's all over by 9am.

★ **Ghirardelli Square** (map II, B1): North Point Street (and Larkin). It's a safe bet that old Domingo Ghirardelli, who began making chocolate in 1850, at the time of the Gold Rush, wouldn't recognize his old business today. He started off working in little workshops on Jackson Square and later his children built the Ghirardelli chocolate factory on the site of the Old Woollen Mill in 1893. The last building to be added to the premises was the Clock Tower on the corner of North Point and Larkin. It's said that the architect's design for this was inspired by the chateau at Blois in France. Nowadays, all that's left is a little shop with a tea-room where you can have the pleasure of contemplating immense vats filled with chocolate!

At one point the factory was threatened with redevelopment into apartments, but fortunately a millionaire had taken a fancy to this remarkable architectural feature in red brick, and he bought it and converted it into a shopping complex. All he added were a few green terraces and some minor buildings, the essentials being retained. A stroll through the 50 shops and dozen restaurants is very interesting and will help you form your own judgement of this post-industrial architectural adaptation. Don't miss the beautiful interior decoration in the Mandarin restaurant.

★ **National Maritime Museum** (map II, B1): 900 Beach Street, Aquatic Park, at the bottom of Polk Street (west of Ghirardelli). ☎ 556-8177. Open daily, 10am–5pm. Free admission. This is a very handsome museum, well presented, which will fascinate lovers of ships and shipping. It is divided into a number of sections, covering yachting, steam, whaling, Cape Horn, shipbuilding, etc. There are relics of old ships from the great days of sail, as well as scale models, including one of the *Snark*, the vessel built for Jack London to sail around the world. Also on display are beautifully carved and painted ships' figureheads, charts, panoramic photos of San Francisco in 1851 (just after the Gold Rush), articles made by seamen, etc. There is also a large terrace looking out over the Bay and the port and across to Alcatraz. On the top floor you'll find an observation tower that's as well equipped as a ship's bridge. When you look at it from the outside, you'll see that the overall shape of the museum is like that of a ferry-boat.

– Between the museum and the port there's a pleasant walk at the water's edge. Along the way there's a big solarium on several terraces, a quiet garden and a (rather grubby) little beach patrolled by seagulls. Curiously, there are usually only a few people – which is quite astonishing for a big city. Some very clued-up students come here to do their reading, while young fanatics dash up and down on rollerskates and the occasional local (or perhaps that should be loco) plucks up the courage to take a dip.

★ **Historic Ships (San Francisco Maritime National Historical Park)** (map II, B1): on Hyde Street Pier. ☎ 929-0202. Open daily, 9.30am–5pm. Admission charge (half-price for children). The port features a superb line-up of wonderfully restored historic ships, so don't miss it if you like that kind of thing. The *C.A. Thayer* is a superb schooner that once carried timber for construction. Go into the hull to admire the splendid structure and spot the differences in comfort between the captain's cabin and those of the mates. Then there's the paddleship *Eureka*, which was once the world's largest ferry-boat (it could carry 2,300 passengers and 120 vehicles). On the first floor, you can put a quarter into any of the old slot-machines to see gripping shots of the earthquake of 1906. Then on to the *Balclutha*, a splendid three-master. The captain's quarters are truly palatial, and everything's in varnished wood. Other vessels are still being restored. At Pier 45, don't miss a visit to the USS *Pampanito*, a former World War II submarine.

★ **The Cannery** (map II, B1): Leavenworth and Beach. Not a cannery any more, of course. Only a few of the original brick walls have been retained – all the rest is new. The result is a shopping centre that's a great success. It's worth climbing to the top for the view. Nearby is Haslette Warehouse, a fine example of an early 20th-century warehouse.

The picturesque terminus of the Hyde Street cable-car line is here. You could also indulge in a ritual Irish coffee at the Buena Vista!

★ **Pier 39** (map II, C1, **200**): this is the most recent of the shopping centres. Open 10.30am–8.30pm (some restaurants stay open until 11.30pm). Stretching out into the sea, it's wood all the way. It could almost be mistaken for a little town, a worthy feature in the finest Westerns. Everything is tailored to the tourist trade, but here it's cleverly done. There's always something going on in summer: clowns, jugglers, etc. A colony of seals has made their home here, to the great delight of tourists, basking on the pontoons that were once only used by sailors. Pier 39 is also the point of departure for seaplane tours of the city with San Francisco Seaplane Tours ☎ 332-4843 (*see* 'Sausalito').

★ Fort Mason houses other museums: the **San Francisco African American Historical and Cultural Society** (☎ 441-0640), the **Mexican Museum** (☎ 441-0445), the **San Francisco Craft and Folk Museum** (☎ 775-0990), and the **SS *Jeremiah O'Brien***, one of the last of the 2,751 Liberty Ships of World War II (☎ 441-3101). For information and timetables, go to the tourist office or phone direct.

★ **Alcatraz** (map II, C1, **201**): To visit this legendary island, head for the Blue & Gold Fleet ticket booth on Pier 41, adjacent to Fisherman's Wharf. You are advised to buy your tickets in advance, and you can either buy or book tickets in person, or call the ticket hotline on ☎ 705–5555 (there's a small charge for credit card reservations by phone). Website: www.blueandgoldfleet.com. You can choose to purchase a standard ticket, or one that includes the audio tour. (Don't worry if you decide not to opt for the audio tour and change your mind once you get there – you can always purchase it once you have arrived on the island.) Boats leave every 30 minutes at the weekend, and every 45 minutes during the week, from 9.15am–4.15pm in the summer and 9.30am–2.15pm in the winter. Be sure to arrive at least 15 minutes before your boat sails. It's jam-packed on summer weekends, when you'll have to book at least a week in advance. During the week, however, you'll only need to book your place the day before. Allow a good 2 hours 30 minutes for the visit (including the ferry journey). The same company also offers combined visits to Alcatraz and Angel Island. Warm clothing is recommended, as it can get very chilly on board.

Discovered in 1775 by Spanish explorer Juan Manuel de Ayala, who named the island after the pelicans living there, Alcatraz has been the focus of much interest over the years. After California was annexed by the United States in 1847, the island was fortified, in order to protect San Francisco Bay. The famous lighthouse was constructed in 1854, and has been in operation ever since. Advances in technology slowly rendered the fort obsolete, and during the Great Depression the Bureau of Prisons began to take an interest in the island as an ideal location for a high-profile, maximum-security jail. In 1934 the military buildings were converted into the notorious prison.

Nicknamed 'The Rock', this must be the most famous penitentiary in the United States. Designed to take on the most hardened criminals – those with reputations for causing trouble and trying to escape – it was the prison most feared by offenders, and was one from which they said escape was impossible. It took on even more notoriety when, in 1934, it housed Public Enemy Number One, Al 'Scarface' Capone, and gave him cell number AZ 85. Alcatraz housed many other heavyweight criminals, including George 'Machine Gun' Kelly, and the famous 'Birdman of Alcatraz', Robert Stroud. There were about 14 escape attempts in all, the most famous of which was the attempt by Frank Morris and the Anglin brothers, who were never seen again (except to be recreated in the Clint Eastwood movie *Escape from Alcatraz*). No one knows whether their bodies were carried away by the freezing currents, which made any escape practically impossible, or whether they made it and are still alive today. Whatever happened, they are still officially on the FBI's 'Wanted' list.

As you will discover, the audio tour comes in various languages (you get your own tape player with headphones), and incorporates interviews with former prisoners talking about the conditions they experienced in the penitentiary, against a background of clashing tin plates and slamming doors. The recording really does help bring the place to life, and the voices of the former inmates send shivers down your spine . . . In addition, a 12-minute film is shown, giving an overview of the island's history, and the park rangers give talks and lectures about certain aspects of life on the island – you will be told about the day's programme when you arrive. You may also meet ex-inmate Jim Quillen, who served 10 years here. He often comes to autograph his book, *Alcatraz: From Inside*.

Discipline in the prison was extremely harsh: talking was forbidden, only one prisoner to each cell and one warder to every three prisoners. There were never more than 250 prisoners at any one time, occupying the four blocks, A to D, the latter comprising mainly solitary confinement cells. There were 336 cells available, and prisoners spent up to 23 hours a day locked up. The luckiest prisoners spent only 17 hours under lock and key, and worked during the day in the dining room or the library.

Alcatraz served as a federal penitentiary from 1934 until 1963, when Robert Kennedy closed it down. Possession of the island was claimed by a group of Native Americans in 1969, who occupied it for 19 months, attracting media interest and public support. They were cleared out by the government in 1971, and in 1972 Alcatraz was made part of the Golden Gate National Recreation Area.

Note the fantastic views of the Bay, and of the San Francisco skyline as you cross over to Alcatraz on the ferry – don't forget your camera! If you're on a tight budget, and can't afford to visit Alcatraz, take a trip on the ferry that goes across to Sausalito. You still get a great view of the Bay, the Golden Gate Bridge and Alcatraz.

★ Between 111 and 175 Jefferson Street, there's the **Medieval Dungeon**, the **Fun House**, the **Wax Museum** ☎ 202–0400, (all owned by the same company) and the **Believe It or Not! Museum** ☎ 771–6188, all strictly for visitors who love touristy stuff!

★ PACIFIC HEIGHTS AND THE MARINA

Located between the Presidio and Russian Hill, **Pacific Heights** is certainly the most expensive, the smartest and the most upper-crust district in San Francisco, as it has been for almost a century. This is where the *nouveaux-riches* came to settle in the late 19th century, when Nob Hill and Russian Hill had become overcrowded with buildings. The move was a fortuitous one as it turned out, as they escaped the fires that followed the earthquake of 1906. If you take a walk round this district, which is bounded by Van Ness Avenue to the east, the Presidio to the west, and California Street to the south, you'll see some astonishing villas in a multiplicity of architectural styles.

The Marina is situated at the bottom of Pacific Heights. The Panama Pacific International Exhibition was held there in 1915, when the people of San Francisco went all out to show the world that their city was no longer in ruins. After the exhibition, Italian families came in and gave the place a Mediterranean cachet that is still noticeable. The area suffered badly in the 1989 earthquake and was immediately rebuilt in the same style as before.

WHERE TO EAT IN PACIFIC HEIGHTS AND THE MARINA

☆ BUDGET

✕ **Wraps** (map II, A2, **122**): California Street (and Fillmore). ☎ 931-0100. New-style fast food popular with the trendy young: exotic, organic and vegetarian sandwiches. The principle is similar to the Mexican tacos or the *paninis* that are all the rage with lunchers in Europe. The sandwiches are huge. Before opening one, it helps to read the instructions on the wrapper, because there's a special art to eating Wraps – if you don't, you may be taken for a *gringo*. There are two other Wraps in the city: at 465b Castro Street and 1909 Union Street.

✕ **Mel's Drive Inn** (map II, A2, **123**): 2165 Lombard Street (and Fillmore). ☎ 921-3039. Open 6am–1am (3am Friday and Saturday). A real diner, one of the oldest in the city. (There's also one in Los Angeles and another in San Francisco, on Van Ness Avenue.) Straight out of *Happy Days* or *American Graffiti*, with everything in chrome and Formica, mini jukeboxes on the tables and old photos on the walls. They sell the usual range of burgers, salads, daily specials, standards like Mel's Spring Chicken, Grandma's Turkey Meatloaf, Homemade Texas Chili, New York Steak. It's a hangout for young people, as you might expect, but also a few nostalgia types hoping to recapture a little of their lost youth. Good milkshakes and sundaes and a wide choice of breakfast dishes. Madly crowded at brunch at weekends.

✕ **Whole Foods Market**: 1765 California Street. ☎ 674-0500. This is not a restaurant but an organic supermarket, with appetizing displays of fruit and vegetables, fresh fruit juices, delicious cakes, etc. Ideal if you're renting an apartment, camping or planning a picnic. There's a little cafeteria in the basement.

SAN FRANCISCO

☆☆ MODERATE

✕ **Baja Cantina** (map II, A2, **124**): 3154 Fillmore Street (and Greenwich). ☎ 885-BAJA. Open daily, 11.30am–11pm. Excellent Mexican food. Not hard to spot, thanks to the boar's head over the entrance and the aircraft on the ceiling! Two rooms: one is the restaurant and the other is a restaurant and bar combined. It's nicer to eat in the second, which is much more welcoming. They offer a dozen different margaritas, served in precise measures in enormous glasses, and about 30 tequilas to choose from. The enormous fiesta dish is a mix of the house specialities.

✕ **Cassis** (map II, A2, **125**): 2120 Greenwich (and Fillmore Street). ☎ 292-0770. Open Tuesday–Saturday 5.30–10pm. This pleasant authentic Provençal restaurant has a warm and friendly ambiance.

All the food is fresh, simple, of high quality and very well prepared by the chef, who does his own shopping in the morning (that's why they're closed at lunchtime). Very good value for money.

✕ **The Grove** (map II, A1, **161**): 2250 Chestnut Street (and Avila). *See* 'Where to Have a Coffee'.

☆☆☆ EXPENSIVE

✕ **The Elite Cafe** (map II, A2, **144**): 2049 Fillmore Street (and California). ☎ 346-8668. Open Monday–Saturday 5–11pm, Sunday 10am–11pm. The kind of place that lives up to its name and the waitresses could just as easily find jobs in a model agency. But despite the pronouncedly elite tone of the place, this trendy restaurant has an elegant setting and a pleasant atmosphere. The cuisine is excellent, mainly seafood and Cajun specialities from Louisiana. Lunch prices are affordable but dinner is much more expensive.

✕ **Prego** (map II, A2, **126**): 2000 Union Street. ☎ 563-305. Open daily at lunchtime and in the evening until midnight. The setting is simple and the emphasis is on the food. Plenty of locals. The Italian–American cuisine has a good reputation. The prices are the same at lunchtime and in the evening. Specialities include pizzas made on a wood fire, *carpaccio Cipriani,* house pasta, *agnolotti d'Aragosta*, and *gnocchi alla Sorrentina.*

✕ **Betelnut Pejiu Wu** (map II, A2, **127**): 2030 Union Street (and Laguna). ☎ 929-8855. Open daily, 11.30am–11pm. Large, dark, elegant room where red and brown predominate. Smart colonial Singaporean ambiance. The menu mostly consists of Chinese and Vietnamese dishes. The sea-bass with ginger on a bed of cucumber is a real pleasure. The steamed dishes are also recommended.

✕ **Scott's** (map II, A2, **128**): 2400 Lombard Street. ☎ 563-8988. Open daily, 11.30am–10pm. A traditional place for fish and seafood for many years. The setting is quite plain, and engravings of fish and boats set the tone. Friendly welcome and excellent specialities such as fettuccine with mussels and scallops (or salmon), crab tortellini, grilled squid from Monterey Bay, sautéed scallops, Scott's *cioppino* with fish and shellfish. Delicious clam chowder. The wine list contains almost exclusively white wines.

SAN FRANCISCO

WHERE TO HAVE A COFFEE IN PACIFIC HEIGHTS AND THE MARINA

🍸 **The Grove** (map II, A1, **161**): 2250 Chestnut Street (and Avila). ☎ 474-4843. Open daily, 7am–11pm (midnight Friday and Saturday). One of the best places on Marina. A big coffee-shop where all is luxury, peace and comfort. You can have just a coffee or a salad. They also offer some simple hot dishes, and quite a few vegetarian specialities.

🍸 **Coffee Bugatti's** (map II, A2, **162**): 3001 Webster Street (and

Filbert). ☎ 922-4888. Open daily, 7am–6pm. Another coffee-shop that's full of charm. They serve French-style *crêpes.*

🍸 **Bepple's Pie Shop** (map II, A2, **163**): 1934 Union Street (and Laguna). ☎ 931-6225. Open 7am–11pm (midnight Saturday and Sunday). Nice tea-room with a wide choice of tarts and cakes. Or you can call in just for a *caffè latte.*

WHAT TO SEE IN PACIFIC HEIGHTS

Pacific Heights is the district to visit on foot if you'd like to see some of the city's finest residences. Around Lafayette Park, the following in particular stand out:

– 2150 Washington Street (and Laguna) which was once the Mayor's Palace during the office of Mayor J.D. Phalam (1894–1902).

– 2080 Washington Street (and Octavia) the **Spectrels Mansion**, home of the former administrator of what is now the California Palace of the Legion of Honor.

★ **Octagon House**: 2645 Gough Street (and Union). ☎ 441-7212. Open noon–3pm on the second and fourth Thursday and the second Sunday of each month. Closed January and on public holidays. One of the last two octagonal houses to be built, this one was designed and furnished in colonial style.

★ You must see the **Haas-Lilienthal House** at 2007 Franklin Street (and Jackson). ☎ 441-3004. Open Wednesday noon–4pm and Sunday 11am–4.15pm. There's an admission charge and it's guided tours only. This magnificent villa in Victorian style was one of the few to escape the fire of 1906. It's of exceptional size and is the only one open to the public. Superb furniture.

PACIFIC HEIGHTS AND THE MARINA BY NIGHT

🍸 **Harry's Bar** (map II, A2, **157**): 2020 Fillmore Street. ☎ 921-1000. Open daily, 3.30pm–2am. Beautiful place, very classy, yet warm and intimate. Blue ceiling and a bar made of superb wood, which is reputed to come from an old saloon in Alaska. Ideal for having a drink late in the evening. Live music on Friday and Saturday evening: jazz, soul, blues, even rhythm 'n' blues. Some evenings, the customers just push the tables back so they can dance. You can also dine here.

🍸 **Blues** (map II, A2, **230**): 2125 Lombard Street (and Fillmore). ☎ 771-2583. Open daily, 8pm–2am. Like a concert hall with a bar. Extremely informal, it's a young, jam-packed place where you dance in front of a stage. Very good atmosphere.

🍸 **Perry's** (map II, B2, **231**): 1944 Union Street. ☎ 922-9022. Open daily, 9am–11pm. Pleasant little terrace that's usually crowded. For 20 years, this place was considered to be one of the liveliest bars in the area. A one-time temple of cruising that has since cooled down considerably, it retains the good reputation it has always had. You can get good brunches here, and the menu includes burgers, a variety of salads, sandwiches and grilled meats. The welcome is completely charming. The average age is about 40.

🍸 **Bus Stop** (map II, A2, **233**): 1901 Union Street (and Laguna). ☎ 567-6905. Open daily, to 2am. The sports bar *par excellence.* There are TV sets almost everywhere and the place is full of happy Americans on match days. On such occasions, the beer flows freely in a delightful ambiance. The bar is rather traditional otherwise. Two billiard rooms out back.

★ HAIGHT-ASHBURY

This legendary district of the hippie movement has witnessed the growth of a very large number of cultural movements – first the hippies, then skinheads and now raves. At the beginning of the new millennium, Haight-Ashbury is again seeking to become the centre of the world by the renewal of the hippie movement and by the very special philosophy that characterizes the area – tolerance.

In the late 19th century, this was an upper-crust residential district that the richest families invested in, attracted by the proximity of Golden Gate Park. Handsome residences that survived the earthquake and huge fires of 1906 are there for you to admire, particularly on Waller Street and Page Street. After World War II, Haight-Ashbury lost favour with the upper-classes because of the growing size of the black community. Rents tumbled in the early 1960s, attracting the first hippies fleeing from North Beach, which had become too expensive and too touristy. A house in Haight-Ashbury for a dozen squatters could be had for less than $60 a month. Food, hallucinogenic drugs and concerts were freely available, in accordance with the slogan of the Diggers, 'The World is Yours'. In 1967, Haight-Ashbury experienced its apotheosis in the Summer of Love, a festival of concerts that attracted half a million young people from all over America. Very shortly after, however, it sank into problems of violence associated mainly with heroin.

Today what's left in the district is coffee-shops, small, inexpensive restaurants and clothes shops. Unemployed young people beg on the street and the cynics say that the slogan is no longer 'The World is Yours' and 'Make love, not war' but 'Spare some change?'.

WHERE TO EAT IN HAIGHT-ASHBURY

☆–☆☆ BUDGET TO MODERATE

✕ **Squat 'n' Gobble Cafe**: 1428 Haight Street (and Masonic). ☎ 864-8484. Open daily, 8am–10pm. Big cafe full of local colour, in a pleasant setting. Perfect whether you want a snack or a filling meal. All kinds of inexpensive dishes: sandwiches, generous salads, soup of the day, omelettes, bagels, exotic pancakes and big cakes. There's another on Lower Haight.

✕ **Taquería El Balazo**: 1654 Haight Street. ☎ 864-8608. Open 10am–11pm (1am Saturday and Sunday). Mexican self-service place with decor entirely in red and yellow. Good specialities at low prices: burritos, tacos, tamales (served with guacamole) and good *ceviche* (raw fish marinated in lemon juice).

✕ **Cha-cha-cha**: 1801 Haight Street (corner of Shrader). ☎ 386-

5758. Open daily, 11.30am–11pm (11.30pm Friday and Saturday). Surprising decor, offering specialities from the Caribbean, plus such things as tapas, Cajun sandwiches, steak sandwich chacha, squid fried with garlic mayonnaise, vegetarian dishes, classic American burgers and sandwiches. Brick walls, painted black and hung with little altars and masks. Good ambiance.

✕ **Escape from New York Pizza**: 1737 Haight Street (between Cole and Shrader). ☎ 668-5577. Open 11.30am–2pm. The name is a cover for one of the best pizzerias in the area. It's a small, anonymous room where customers come to get enormous pizzas straight out of the oven. They use natural products, fresh vegetables and serve big portions (the '20-inch' one has at least 12 slices) at very good prices. The big meat combo is good. This is a more of a take-away than somewhere you sit and eat in, as there are only a few tables. Rock fans will have a great time putting names to the many stars whose pictures are pinned on the walls. There are autographed photos of Van Halen, REM, Metallica, Chris Isaak, Leonard Cohen, David Byrne, the Ramones, to name but a few.

✕ **People's Cafe**: 1419 Haight Street (and Masonic Avenue). ☎ 553-8842. Open 7am–10pm. A big self-service cafe, cleaner and quieter than its competitors. The menu consists of soup and salad, and they do a good selection of coffees, so it's ideal for breakfast, especially given their wide choice of egg dishes.

✕ **Kan Zaman**: 1793 Haight Street (and Shrader Street). ☎ 751-9656. Open noon–midnight. Closed Monday. The decor is worth a look: floor-cushions, low tables under tents, hookahs. They serve food from the Middle East, of course, and there's a very interesting menu with six entrées. You absolutely must try the hot wine. Very nice waiters. Also Arab music and belly-dancers.

SAN FRANCISCO

WHERE TO HAVE A COFFEE IN HAIGHT-ASHBURY

🍸 **Jammin Java Coffee House**: 701 Cole Street (and Waller Street). ☎ 668-5282. Open daily, to 11pm. Very simple: some little wooden tables, with music playing in the background – and very good coffee. This is a coffee-shop in pure San Francisco style in a quieter street than Haight. Some tables outside.

🍸 **Cafe Cole**: 609 Cole Street (and Haight). ☎ 668-7771. Open daily, 7am–8pm (8am–9pm weekends). A beautiful room, with tables outside too. The *caffè latte* is delicious.

🍸 **Cafe Echo-Coffee House**: 1409 Haight Street (and Masonic Avenue). ☎ 863-2443. Open daily, 7am–midnight. For a long time this was the best-known coffee-shop in the district and one of those most representative of San Francisco's district cafe 'culture'. The patrons have changed, but the place has remained a good spot.

A SHORT ARCHITECTURAL WALK AROUND HAIGHT-ASHBURY

It would be difficult to list all of the elegant Victorian residences in the district. Here are some of the finest:

★ On the corner of **Haight and Masonic**, an attractive group of five houses. On **Haight**, the Red Victorian B&B (one of the most colourful frontages) at No. 1665; a former cinema at No. 1660; the oldest house on the street at No. 1779. Between **Lyon and Baker**, there's an interesting series of frontages at Nos. 1128, 1132 and 1144: note the workmanship of the windows and the bays. At No. 1080, the most imposing, there's some sumptuous exterior decoration to admire. Of the many others in the street and the surrounding area is one, on the corner of **Lyon and Oak**, that belonged to Janis Joplin from 1967 until her death in 1970. No doubt Janis would be happy to learn that since 1999, her house has been in use as a rehabilitation centre for homeless drug-addicted mothers and their children.

★ On the corner of **Broderick and Fulton** there's another beautiful terrace. In a continuation of Fulton, you get to **Alamo Square**, a charming place that will definitely make you wish you lived in San Francisco. Interesting views from the topmost point. This is where you'll find the city's famous 'Painted Ladies'.

★ Return to **Haight (and Baker)** for a stroll in **Buena Vista Park** (not advisable at night). Take the stairs to get a great view of the city.

★ Finally, for anyone who doesn't have too much time, take a last wander along **Waller Street**. Near the intersection with **Masonic** there are many more houses with special exterior features.

★ 710 Ashbury Street is the house of the **Grateful Dead**, the legendary San Francisco rock group.

★ Other houses with star associations include **Jefferson Airplane's house** (130 Delmar), the house where **Jimi Hendrix** lived for a short period (142 Central), great journalist-writer **Hunter S. Thomson's house**, where he wrote his book on the Hell's Angels (318 Parnassus), and storyteller **Richard Brautigan's house** (2500 Geary). **Courtney Love** (singer, actress and widow of Kurt Cobain) is said to own a house in Hayes Street.

★ On the corner of **Cole and Haight** is a mural depicting the evolution of the universe from the original chaos to the one still awaiting us. From a distance, it looks like a rainbow. From close up, there are many details that jump out at you: religious symbols, animals, monsters, etc.

★ **Wasteland** at **1660 Haight Street** is a former cinema that has gone through a variety of incarnations and is currently a clothes shop. The architecture is very unusual.

SHOPPING ON AND AROUND HAIGHT STREET

Amoeba Records: 1855 Haight Street (and Stanyan). ☎ 831-1200. Converted bowling alley that just might be the world's largest and most extensive record store.

Music factory: 573 Hayes Street. ☎ 487-8680. A vinyl record shop specializing in house, jungle and techno. Various local bands available on compilation cassettes.

Recycled Records: 1377 Haight Street, level with Masonic. ☎ 626-4075. Open 10am–10pm (8pm Sunday). Buy and sell second-hand or hard-to-find discs. A lot of old vinyl and a few CDs.

Reckless Records: 1401 Haight (and Masonic). ☎ 431-3434. Open 10am–10pm (8pm Sunday). Good prices for discs, new or second-hand. Wide choice of collectors' items, original film soundtracks, posters, T-shirts, musical magazines, videos, postcards, etc.

Held Over: 1543 Haight Street. ☎ 864-0818. Open 10am–7pm (open 11am Sunday). Great variety of clothing, from very standard to more original.

Austen Books: 1687 Haight Street. ☎ 552-4122. Open daily, 11am–6pm. An international bookshop that has the odd shelf of second-hand books. They also have some comics. They buy, sell and exchange.

Bound Together Books: 1369 Haight Street. ☎ 431-8355. Old anarchist bookshop that has kept its revolutionary atmosphere intact. Mostly books on history and politics, but also some anarchist posters, discs and amusing postcards.

Pipe Dreams: 1376 Haight Street. ☎ 431-3553. Open daily, 10am–7.50pm (6.50pm Sunday). A tobacco shop with a hippie ambiance. An astonishing choice of pipes, carved into amusing faces and monsters.

HAIGHT STREET BY NIGHT

– **Club Deluxe**: 1511 Haight Street (and Clayton). ☎ 552-6949. Open to 2am. Pleasant jazz club, occasionally invaded by big bands that fill the room, creating a marvellous ambiance.

★ LOWER HAIGHT

Ten blocks away from Haight-Ashbury, around the 500s, this district is similar to and yet different from Upper Haight. They have shared similar pasts: bourgeois residences at the start of the century, crises during the 1930s, World War II, and the building of black ghettos in the neighbourhood, which drove district rents downward.

The difference lies in the fact that, in contrast to Haight-Ashbury, which thrived during the hippie movement of the 1960s, Lower Haight didn't achieve its fame until the 1970s, with the arrival of avant-garde artists, apostles of the counter-culture, members of Generation X and followers of Jack Kerouac. Today these varied groups are joining up and there's a certain feeling of insecurity after dark – a sort of grungie counter-culture. The many underground bars and shops are less commercial than those on Upper Haight.

WHERE TO EAT IN LOWER HAIGHT

☆ BUDGET

✕ **Squat 'n' Gobble**: 237 Fillmore Street (between Haight and Waller). ☎ 487-0551. Open daily, 8am–10pm. There's a branch on Upper Haight. Delicious pancakes and extraordinarily good omelettes accompanied by sautéed potatoes. Vast portions and excellent value for money. Friendly setting, with big wooden tables.

✕ **Axum Cafe**: 698 Haight Street (and Pierce). ☎ 252-7912. Open daily, 10am–11pm. A nice Ethiopian restaurant that's very inexpensive. Some vegetarian dishes. All the dishes are quite spicy. Something you could try out is the N'Yoma beer, all the way from Togoland.

☆☆ MODERATE

✕ **Indian Oven**: 233 Fillmore, almost on the corner of Haight. ☎ 626-1628. Open daily, 5–11pm. Good Indian restaurant where they've opted for style while maintaining a relaxed atmosphere. Minimal decor and an intimate ambiance. A good menu, including chicken or salmon tandoori, chicken tikka (marinated with spices and yoghurt), tandoori fish, lamb vindaloo (very spicy), seafood biriyani (fish, squid and shellfish, cinnamon and cardamom with basmati rice), vegetarian dishes, etc. There's also a good-value buffet-lunch menu.

✕ **Thep Phanom**: 400 Waller Street (and Fillmore). ☎ 431-2526. Open daily, 5.30–10.30pm. A smallish room with a hushed atmosphere. The waiters wear traditional Thai costume. This is one of the best Thai restaurants in San Francisco, and it's listed in all the American gastronomic guides. Enough shrimps and other seafood for you to gorge yourself. It's best to book, especially at the weekend.

WHERE TO HAVE A COFFEE OR A SNACK IN LOWER HAIGHT

SAN FRANCISCO

🍸 **Cafe International**: 508 Haight Street. ☎ 552-7390. Open daily, 8am–11pm. A big, relaxed coffee-house, frequented by artists and students. After the climb up Haight Street, come in and slump down on one of the sofas or on the patio. The place seems like a little oasis decorated with a beautiful 'world music' fresco that perfectly sums up the spirit of the house. Excellent music (reggae, African, etc.). Snack on a few delicious dishes from the Middle East: houmous, tabouleh, falafel and creamy cheese bagels.

🍸 **Horse Shoe Coffee-House**: 566 Haight Street. ☎ 626-8852. Open 6am–1am (2am Friday and Saturday). A nice homely sort of place where you can enjoy a good read or play a game of chess. Students often come here to do their exam revision. The speciality of the house is *toranis* in more than 30 flavours: these are cordials that you can take as an Italian soda or put in your coffee.

🍸 **Bean There**: 201 Steiner Street (on the corner of Walles, a street running parallel to Haight). ☎ 255-8855. Open daily, 8am–10pm. A coffee-shop definitely for anyone looking for peace and quiet as it's less heavily frequented than the others. Exhibition of paintings inside, chess sets and rock music. Some tables outside.

WHAT TO SEE AND DO IN LOWER HAIGHT

★ **Duboce Park**: on Duboce Avenue (take Steiner Street from Haight Street). This is a charming little park where you can stretch out in the sun. Three culs-de-sac (Carmelita, Pierce and Potomac) enclose the park and are all safe to stroll in.

SHOPPING IN LOWER HAIGHT

Used Rubber: 597 Haight Street (and Steiner). ☎ 626-7855. Open daily, noon–6pm. Shop specializing in recycled products: diaries, bags and belts made from old tyres! They sell some beautiful products that are well finished and original too.

LOWER HAIGHT BY NIGHT

DRINKING

Noc-Noc: 561 Haight Street. ☎ 552-1090. Open 5pm–2am. One of the most original bars in San Francisco. The decor is strange, yet somehow it works – it's like *Mad Max* revisited by Gaudí, or Warhol reincarnated as a cyberpunk, with grotto walls, disembowelled TV sets, Zulu furniture, low lighting, and so on. The sounds are either all-pervading, mind-blowing techno music, or music for the wee small hours, depending on the time.

The Mad Dog in the Fog: 530 Haight Street (and Fillmore). ☎ 626-7279. Open 11.30am–2am. Opposite the Noc-Noc, this is quite a lively British bar. Very, very noisy and smoky. Good choice of beers (more than 50 labels), darts, etc. You can also have breakfast, lunch or dinner there from an inexpensive menu.

DANCING

– **Nickie's**: 460 Haight Street. ☎ 621-6508. Open daily, 10pm–2am. A little club that presents one of the best selections of DJs in the city.

SAN FRANCISCO

★ COLE VALLEY

Quite close to Haight-Ashbury, between Carl Street and Belgrave Avenue, this district is symbolic of San Francisco: beautiful houses, quiet and shaded, a suburban lifestyle, coffee-shops, a beautiful view from the top of Tank Hill, and few tourists.

WHERE TO EAT IN COLE VALLEY

☆ BUDGET

Crêpes on Cole: 100 Carl Street. ☎ 664-1800. Open daily, 10am–8pm. Big wooden room, some tables outside. Omelettes, delicious *crêpes* and gigantic salads (one's enough for two people). Menu very similar to that of the Squat 'n' Gobble. Definitely a success.

WHERE TO HAVE A COFFEE IN COLE VALLEY

Tassajara Cafee and Bakery: 1000 Cole Street (and Parnassus). Open daily, 8am–11pm. A popular place, where vigorous discussions take place among students and intellectuals of every shade. Some sandwiches and other pastries provide the sustenance.

WHAT TO SEE IN COLE VALLEY

You can have a peaceful stroll along Cole Street and Belvedere Street and see beautiful houses level with Grattan Street.

★ **Tank Hill Park**: get here on foot or by car via Belgrave Avenue. One of the peaks of San Francisco, it isn't as high as Twin Peaks but has the advantage of providing a beautiful view of Golden Gate Bridge and another of Downtown, SOMA, Mission and Castro. Much less heavily frequented than Twin Peaks.

★ CASTRO AND NOE VALLEY

Castro is a Mecca for gays: the Gay Village is located on Market Street, from Church up to 17th Street and, of course, on Castro and adjacent streets.

Noe Valley is the stretch of 24th Street between Douglas Street and Dolores Street. The district has bars, shops and gyms, and a character that's all its own (which is a fairly sensible one).

THE GAY COMMUNITY IN CASTRO

Originally, the density of the gay population was no greater in California than anywhere else, but Californian attitudes have made life a lot easier here than in, say, Texas . . .

At the last count, 25 per cent of the city's total population was gay, and Castro has become one of the city's liveliest districts. Between the early 1970s and the early 1980s, the gay community underwent a transformation and overcame many hostile attitudes. In 1972 for example, San Francisco became the first American city to pass a law prohibiting any discrimination in employment or housing on the basis of someone's chosen lifestyle or sexual orientation. In 1973, the American Psychiatric Association deleted homosexuality from its list of mental illnesses!

Of course, AIDS has changed many things: in March 1989 it claimed a historic high of 100 victims. But even though the community has been badly shaken by the ravages of AIDS, it has reacted energetically, pulling out all the stops to provide information and to advise on prevention. Counselling services have been strengthened, and the various organizations that provide assistance for those most seriously affected have been expanded. It is felt that the availability of information and community solidarity enables people not just to survive, but also to live with the virus. Although some streets or parts of streets have been won back by the 'straights', the ratio of political forces remains virtually unchanged. And these days, it's usual for several militant activists, well-known gay personalities, to be elected or re-elected to important posts, such as education boards.

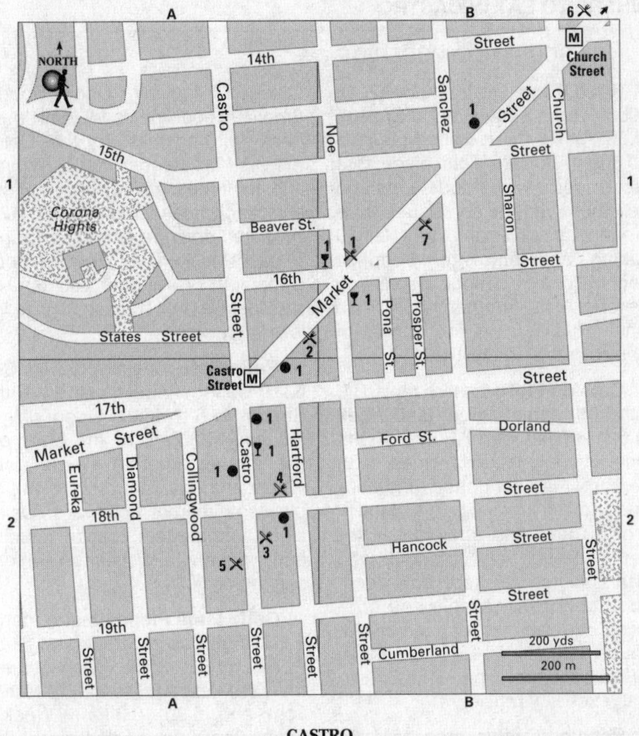

CASTRO

✗ **Where to Eat**

1 Cafe de Flore
2 Pozole
3 Patio Cafe
4 Khun Phoa
5 Caffe Luna Piena
6 Zuni
7 2223
11 The Castro Cheesery
12 Metro

Where to Have a Drink

10 Josie's Cabaret and Juice Joint

By Night

10 Josie's Cabaret and Juice Joint
15 The Cafe
16 Castro Station
17 The Midnight Sun
18 Cafe du Nord
19 Castro Theater

WHERE TO EAT IN CASTRO

☆–☆☆ BUDGET TO MODERATE

✕ **Khun Phoa** (Castro map, A2, **4**): 4068 18th Street (and Castro). ☎ 863-0679. Open daily, 11.30am–10.30pm. A little Thai place that serves curries, seafood soups and delicious vegetarian dishes that are not at all expensive. Restful setting and authentic Buddhist decor. You'd almost think you were in Asia. Another Khun Phoa isn't far away, on the corner of Castro and Market Street.

✕ **Cafe de Flore** (Castro map, B1, **1**): 2298 Market Street (and Noe). ☎ 621-8579. Open 7.30am–10pm. One of the nicest terraces, with perhaps the best coffee (and cappuccino) in the city. A motley crowd, gays and straights all together. Decor very colourful, with lush plants, relaxed ambiance. Food is healthy, simple and copious: big sandwiches, pancakes, soups, substantial dishes, salads, all self-service. The whole thing with excellent music.

✕ **Pozole** (Castro map, A1, **2**): 2337 Market Street. ☎ 626-2666. Not far from Castro subway station. Open noon–11pm (midnight weekends). Decor is particularly original and very colourful, and is changed regularly. Good South American cuisine and delicious fresh fruit cocktails. Try the 'California Wrap' (tender cactus, spinach, tomatoes, grilled chicken, rice and black beans), with *quesadilla catalana, pollo de la antigua Guatemala* (chicken with cocoa and cinnamon) or, madder yet, *potaje de Fidel Castro*! They specialize in low-fat cuisine.

✕ **Patio Cafe** (Castro map, A2, **3**): 531 Castro Street (and 18th Street). ☎ 621-4640. Open daily, 8.30am–10.30pm. At the back of the little arcade, an inexpensive American restaurant overlooking a pleasant internal courtyard. Delicious hamburgers, pasta, salads and more exotic dishes too, which change daily.

✕ **Caffe Luna Piena** (Castro map, A2, **5**): 558 Castro Street (and 18th Street). ☎ 621-2566. Open during the week (except Monday) 11am–3pm and 5.30–10.30pm. Weekends 9am–3pm. Specializes in dishes based on chicken, pastries and salads. Tempting menu. There's a very quiet garden here. It's more expensive than the Patio Cafe.

☆☆☆ EXPENSIVE

✕ **Zuni** (map II, off B3, **129**; Castro map, off B1, **6**): 1658 Market Street (and Rose). ☎ 552-2522. Open 11am–midnight (11pm Sunday). A new restaurant, very much in vogue. You come here primarily to be seen rather than to eat since, in culinary terms, the place is a little overrated – and they don't exactly give the food away! That said, this is an ideal place for encounters and it's considered OK to chat from table to table. They've gained some reputation for their oysters (from both California and the East Coast), which you order singly. Beautiful wine list. You are advised to book ahead, because it's always crowded.

✕ **2223** (Castro map, B1, **7**): 2223 Market Street. ☎ 431-0692. Open to 10pm during the week (11pm weekends). Quite a trendy restaurant and quite gay. Setting modern and warm. Very good food, particularly the fish, the grilled sonoma lamb chops and the grilled Angus New York strip, which are succulent. Service is stylish! Often packed, so it's best to book.

WHERE TO EAT IN NOE VALLEY

In Noe Valley, there are lots of coffee-shops and few restaurants. But there's one good place for lunch:

☆ BUDGET

✕ **Savor**: 3913 24th Street (and Sanchez). ☎ 282-0344. Open daily, 8am–11pm (10pm Sunday, Monday and public holidays). Trendy and cheap student canteen, packed in the evening. Vegetarian menus, pancakes, salads, sandwiches and omelettes.

– If you prefer to picnic, there's an organic supermarket nearby (Real Food Company) that sells very fresh products of good quality.

WHERE TO HAVE A DRINK IN CASTRO

Josie's Cabaret and Juice Joint (Castro map, B1, **10**): 3583 16th Street (and Market). ☎ 861-7933. Open 11am–8pm (11pm Saturday and Sunday). A large, pleasant and airy room with a mezzanine. It's a lush green setting with a relaxed ambiance, making it a nice staging-post for a good coffee accompanied perhaps by a quiche or a salad. Check out the 'smoothies' (fruit juice, yoghurt and fresh fruit). Gay cabaret after 8pm (*see* 'By Night'). Little terrace at the back for when the weather's fine.

Cafe de Flore (Castro map, B1, **1**): 2298 Market Street (and Noe); *see* 'Where to Eat'.

The Castro Cheesery (Castro map, A2, **11**): 427 Castro Street (and Market). ☎ 552-6676. Open daily, 8am–10pm (9am–8pm Sunday). A take-away cafe that treats the area around the corner of Castro and Market to the aroma of its coffees, which come from all over the world. Also sells tea and – yes – cheese.

Metro (Castro map, B1, **12**): 3600 16th Street and Market. Open daily, 2.30pm–2am (opens 1pm weekends). Near the Cafe de Flore, this first-floor bar is an ideal viewpoint on Upper Market. Sophisticated setting.

WHERE TO HAVE A COFFEE IN NOE VALLEY

There are many coffee-shops on 24th Street, but none of them has any real character. Two are listed here, however, because of their particularly good coffee.

Starbucks Coffee: 3995 24th Street (and Noe). Open 5.30am–10pm (11pm Friday and Saturday). This popular chain generally offers good coffee. Hospitable staff. They have a few tables, where you can try their delicious home-made cakes.

Martha and Bros Coffee Company: 3868 24th Street (and Vicksburg). Open to 10pm. A very small shop, with some benches in the sun (a rare feature in San Francisco).

WHAT TO SEE IN CASTRO AND NOE VALLEY

★ **Castro Street**: the section of Castro between Market Street and 20th Street is considered to be the centre of the gay community. The rainbow flag flies from the balconies of the houses. Despite the dramatic situation in which the gay community finds itself, it has managed to retain some of its former sparkle and liveliness. In particular, many shops sell really fine goods, although they tend to be expensive. It's worth the walk for those who complain that the nicest colours always seem to be reserved for women's clothing.

At 249 **Castro** is a cinema with its original architecture. The front is impressive, and the interior is in Spanish mission style.

★ **Names Project AIDS Memorial Quilt**: 2362 Market Street. This project, begun in 1987, aims to draw everyone's attention to the gravity of the AIDS situation and calls upon the friends and families of victims to put together a piece of patchwork quilt (measuring 6ft by 3ft / 1.8m by 0.9m) bearing the name of the deceased. Each piece is then incorporated into a quilt that is becoming immense. Initially made up of a few dozen, a few hundred, then a few thousand pieces of cloth, this impressive patchwork was laid out for the first time on Capitol Mall in Washington in October 1987, and its 1,920 individual pieces covered the equivalent of two football fields. It was subsequently exhibited in other cities across the country, growing continually as new contributions came in. This enormous effort to promote public awareness of AIDS has now brought the number of pieces in the quilt to a total of more than 29,000.

When fully laid out, it has a psychological impact worthy of the gravity of the disease. It's also a particularly effective cultural weapon in fighting for funds to carry on medical research and provide help for the sick. The quilt now weighs more than 34 tons and, laid out end to end, is 30 miles (50km) long. It has had more than five million visitors. For further information: ☎ (415) 882-5500 and 863-1966. Fax: (415) 882-6200.

SAN FRANCISCO

★ **Cruisin' the Castro**: 400 Castro Street (and Market Street). ☎ 550-8110. An interesting four-hour walk across the district organized by Trevor Hailey, who has lived there since 1972. Booking is essential, and you can go as either individuals or groups of six. Maximum group size is 12. Expect to spend about $35 (including brunch). The tour generally starts at 10am from Harvey Milk Plaza (near Castro Street MUNI Station). No tour on Sunday or Monday.

★ **A brief architectural tour of Noe Valley**: South of Castro, its spine formed by 24th Street and Church Street, stretches Noe Valley, a series of hills covered with old wooden houses, chalets and little traditional shops. This is a mixed district of gays, old working-class families, retired people, and has a reputation for peace and quality of life.

On Liberty Street, between Noe and Castro (Nos. 539–575), are some fine rows of houses with elegant verandas and tall staircases.

On Castro, at Nos. 713–733, there's another superb architectural line-up.

★ Finally, spend some time following the winding road to **Twin Peaks**, from where you'll get probably the best overall panorama of the city. Located west of Castro, between Portola and Clarendon.

OTHER GAY AREAS

The only district standing up well to the AIDS crisis is Castro and Market. The other former high spots of the gay community have gone downhill, as happened with Polk Street which seems to have totally imploded. There's some semblance of life between Geary and Sacramento but actually, all you'll find there now are drag queens and hustlers.

The Giraffe (between Sutter and Polk) is one of the few Downtown video-bars still in existence. As for the Folsom district in South of Market (SOMA), which was the temple of the leather bars, some survivors are still holding out, notably the **Stud Bar** and **Eagles** (*see* 'By Night').

CASTRO BY NIGHT

Castro, of course, is a lively district at night, every night. In general, the bars of Upper Market have a younger clientele than those on Castro.

🍸 **The Cafe** (Castro map, A2, **15**): 2369 Market Street. Open 12.30pm–2am. On the first floor. No admission charge. A modern, nightclub setting: all aluminium stools, leatherette, blue neon and loud music. The dance floor is very small and fills up quickly. Two bars and a few pool tables. A varied clientele: gay, straight, tourist. A good place for watching the streetlife, too. Good cocktails. The ambiance hots up from midnight on. It's worth noting that the toilets are bi!

🍸 **Castro Station** (Castro map, A2, **16**): 456B Castro Street. One of the most popular gay cafes in the area. The extremely loud sound system will hit you as you enter.

🍸 **The Midnight Sun** (Castro map, A2, **17**): 4065 18th Street (and Castro). Open noon–2am. One of the best gay video-bars in the city. But even so, it isn't crowded every night.

🍸 **Josie's Cabaret and Juice Joint** (Castro map, B1, **10**): 3583 16th Street (and Market). ☎ 861-7933. Open daily, from 11am. This starts off as a peaceful little cafeteria and then, from 8pm onward, it's transformed into a gay comedy cabaret. Excellent programming, in a great setting. Clientele both gay and straight. There's occasionally a gig around 10pm. The current heirs of Lenny Bruce will make you curl up. Little terrace out the back for when the weather is fine.

🍸 **Cafe du Nord** (Castro map, B1, **18**): 2170 Market Street. ☎ 861-5016. Open daily, to 2am. Jam-packed at weekends. In this very beautiful jazz spot, you'll discover a rather schmaltzy and downright retro side of San Francisco. Big dance floor. Hetero ambiance.

– **Castro Theater** (Castro map, A2, **19**): 429 Castro Street (and Market). ☎ 621-6120. Website: www.thecastro.com. A large neighbourhood cinema with an absolutely magnificent auditorium dating from the 1920s. The only problem is, so do the seats. The programme includes European films and Hollywood classics. You can see two films for just under $7. Be sure to get there early in order not to miss the performance on the organ that precedes the evening's film show. It's really worth seeing.

GAY FESTIVALS IN CASTRO

– **The Gay and Lesbian Freedom Day Parade** (last Sunday in June): for anyone who still doubted the existence of the gay community, this will be one of the liveliest, craziest days you ever see in San Francisco. It involves thousands of people every year.

– **The Castro Street Fair** (first Sunday in October): another gay festival with a great reputation. Many attractions, the length of Castro Street.

– **Halloween**: this isn't specifically a gay festival, of course, but Castro is famous for the magnificent Halloween processions that take place there on 31 October.

★ MISSION

Historically, the Mission District is the first district of San Francisco. In 1776, in fact, Spanish Franciscans founded the Dolores Mission there while the military set up shop in the Presidio fortress. Today, the district's Hispanic character is all around, the result of waves of immigration from South America and Mexico.

Mission lies between Church Street and Harrison Street, and between 16th and 26th Streets. One of the largest districts in the city, one of the liveliest and one of the most colourful. Don't miss the murals. It's certainly one of the most authentic and exotic areas that you'll go into. It's even quite common to meet people who don't know more than three words of English!

Over the last few years, certain streets have become very trendy (Valencia in particular), especially with a youthful Bohemian and intellectual crowd. As a result, it's becoming a little gentrified, but the advantage is that you'll find a lot of good restaurants and nice places to go in the evening here. All of this makes it a great place to be.

Where to Eat

1 Bougaloos
2 Taquería Pancho Villa
3 Puerto Alegre
4 The Rondalla
5 Nicaragua
6 New Dawn Cafe
7 Herbivore
8 Esperpento
9 Mangia Fuoco
10 Ti Couz
11 Cafe Picaro
12 Firecracker

Where to Have a Coffee

20 Cafe Macondo
21 Cafe Istanbul

By Night

25 Jack's Elixir
26 Elbo Room
27 Roxie

Shopping

30 Good Vibrations

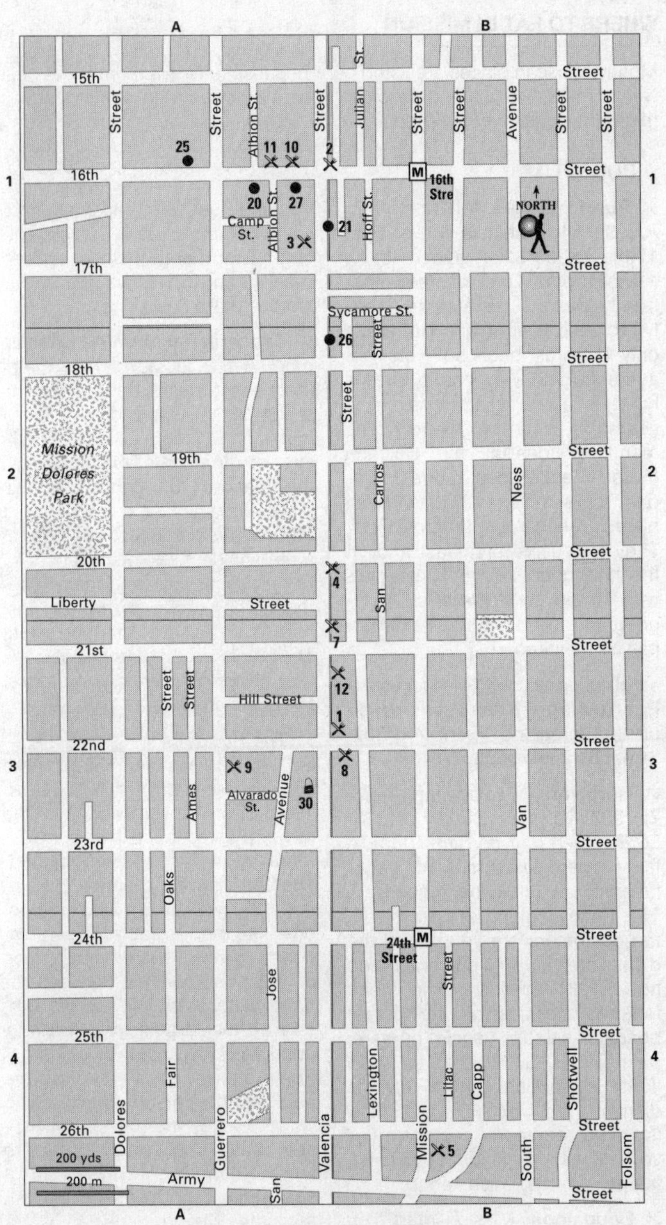

SAN FRANCISCO – MISSION

WHERE TO EAT IN MISSION

Mostly Mexican places are listed here because eating in them is the best way to meet the local population and get to know better a district that you might otherwise have missed.

☆ BUDGET

✕ **Puerto Alegre** (Mission map, A1, **3**): 546 Valencia Street (and 17th). ☎ 255-8201. Open daily, 11am–11pm. One of the most trendy Mexican restaurants. Madly crowded every night. But that's only natural because you get authentic and very cheap cuisine here, in a warm ambiance. The setting is kitsch but friendly. The menu includes all the Chicano classics: enchiladas, tacos, tostadas, chile rellenos, quesadillos, bistec rancheros, burritos, etc. They also serve breakfast and, at the bar, good margarita specials with lemon or strawberry. Party-goers in groups buy their margaritas by the pitcher!

– Following up on their success, a **Puerto Alegre II** has been opened on the corner of Bryant and 25th Street (☎ 285-7063).

✕ **Herbivore** (Mission map, A–B3, **7**): 983 Valencia Street. ☎ 826-5657. Open daily, 11am–10pm. A fairly recent restaurant, for vegetarians, as you will have guessed. The trendy setting is ultra-clean, the customers are young and the dishes are very well presented and not at all expensive. The menu features classics of the genre: beautiful salads, veggie burgers, pasta, etc. But there are also some tempting more exotic dishes: red curry, *pad Thai* (smoked sautéed noodles, flavoured with all kinds of spices), falafel, burritos, shish kebab.

✕ **Bougaloos** (Mission map, B3, **1**): 3296 22nd Street (and Valencia). ☎ 824-3211. Open 5–10pm (11pm Friday and Saturday). Closed Monday and Tuesday. A little local bar with a colourful, noisy, lively setting. The menu includes grilled meats, sandwiches and salads, all starting at modest prices.

✕ **Taquería Pancho Villa** (Mission map, A–B1, **2**): 3071 16th Street (between Valencia and Mission). ☎ 864-8840. Open daily, 10am–midnight. Big room with a high ceiling and murderous lighting for this, the cheapest Mexican self-service place in the city. As a real bonus, it attracts all sorts so you get to meet a really wide range of local people. Generous portions and free excitement. Their motto is: 'You eat fast here, but it isn't a fast-food joint.' Their burritos are famous, as are their chile rellenos, tacos, tostadas, fajitas and tamales.

✕ **The Rondalla** (Mission map, A–B2, **4**): 901 Valencia Street (and 20th Street). ☎ 647-7474. Open 11am–3am. Closed Monday. One of the most popular Mexican restaurants in the Mission district. There's a mixed clientele of *gringos* and *chicanos.* Two rooms: one is the restaurant section, cooler in atmosphere, with photos of the boss and his hunting trophies. The other houses the bar, where the traditional *mariachi* band spends most of its time. Some tables are set up at the back of the bar for patrons who want to enjoy the music, but they are usually occupied. If they're taken when you get there, find a seat at the bar. They serve all your favourite Mexican beers (Carta Blanca, Bohemia, Corona, Pacific, etc.) and house wines . . . and the best margaritas!

In the restaurant, the menu is well stocked and the prices are very reasonable. They have the standard items, of course: chile rellenos, enchiladas, tostadas and burritos. Some highly successful dishes are: *birria de Chivo* (grilled goat), *platillo a la michoacana, steak a la tampiqueña,* fajitas (strips of grilled beef with onions, guacamole and tomatoes), combinations of various sizes, depending on your appetite, *caldo de res* (succulent beef soup) on Sunday. Note that they only take cash.

✕ **Nicaragua** (Mission map, B4, **5**): 3015 Mission Street (and 26th Street). ☎ 826-3672. Open 11am–9.45pm (10.45pm weekends). Quite far from the centre, at the heart of the Hispanic district. The tablecloths are plastic, the lighting a little dim, the setting nondescript, but what they give you to eat is a copious serving of Nicaraguan dishes – quite distinct from Mexican food. Try their *Indio Viejo, chancho con yuca* (fine strips of pork with manioc), tamales, ceviche. Modest prices.

✕ **New Dawn Cafe** (Mission map, A1, **6**): 3174 16th Street. ☎ 553-8888. Open Monday–Tuesday 8.30am–2.30pm, 8.30pm Wednesday–Sunday. Nice for breakfast and lunch. The decor is completely screwy, what with the armless, headless mannequins, mutilated dolls emerging from vases, and the statue of Jesus presiding over the coffee machine. The burgers are juicy with tasty recipes such as patty melt or chicken slit. Delicious soup, vegetarian menu, meatloaf sandwich, salads. It's a young clientele, dropouts, Bohemians. For spiritual nourishment, there's a good bookshop nearby.

☆☆–☆☆☆ MODERATE TO EXPENSIVE

✕ **Esperpento** (Mission map, B3, **8**): 3295 22nd Street (and Valencia). ☎ 282-8867. Open daily, 11am–3pm and 5–10pm (closed Sunday). Pleasant Spanish restaurant in typical *bodega* style. Naturally, what they offer includes *tapas, paellas, jamón serrano,* salads and *tortillas.* All of this is washed down with some very good, copious house *sangría.*

✕ **Mangia Fuoco** (Mission map, A3, **9**): 1001 Guerrero Street (and 22nd Street). ☎ 206-9881. Open daily, 5.30–10.30pm (11pm Friday and Saturday). Closed Tuesday. A new-style Italian restaurant with a Bohemian, cool, trendy ambiance – more evidence of the 'gentrification' of the district. The house pastas are divine. The menu has *carpaccio,* ravioli *a la ricotta* and with spinach. The service is excellent, so it's a good place from any point of view.

✕ **Ti Couz** (Mission map, A1, **10**): 3108 16th Street. ☎ 25-CREPE. Open 11am–11pm, from 10am Saturday, and to 10pm Sunday. A Breton *crêperie*, for anyone who fancies a change from American cuisine and a taste of the fine specialities of Brittany without spending too much cash. The atmosphere and the welcome are both warm. It's often packed on weekend evenings.

✕ **Cafe Picaro** (Mission map, A1, **11**): 3120 16th Street (and Valencia). ☎ 431-4089. Just next to the Ti Couz. Open daily, 11am–2pm and 5pm–10pm (11pm Friday and Saturday). Same proprietor as the Esperpento, so you'll find more or less the same dishes here, more vegetarian *tapas.* Other dishes include seafood, fish and good paella. They also serve brunch from 11am–3pm. The decor is elegant and trendy, with a little touch of Joan Miró. It's OK to just have a drink.

✕ **Firecracker** (Mission map, B3, **12**): 1007 Valencia (and 21st Street). ☎ 624-3470. Open noon–3pm and 5.30–10.30pm (11pm Friday and Saturday). Closed Monday and Tuesday, plus Wednesday lunchtime. Despite its name, this little room, for all its trendy airs, is a cover for a restaurant of high repute. They offer Chinese cuisine that is spicy, flavoursome and highly inventive. Specialities include Rangoon crab and dishes based on asparagus. Very reasonable prices.

WHERE TO HAVE A COFFEE IN MISSION

Cafe Macondo (Mission map, A1, **20**): 3159 16th Street (and Guerrero Street). ☎ 863-6517. Open daily, 9am–11pm (11am weekends). Very beautiful room where the atmosphere is a mixture of Hispanic, jazz, and intellectual. Green plants, books and people playing chess.

Cafe Istanbul (Mission map, A–B1, **21**): 552 Valencia Street (and 17th Street). ☎ 863-8854. Open daily, 3–11pm (noon–midnight Friday and Saturday). They've succeeded in capturing the atmosphere of a real Turkish cafe with its low tables and cushions, and serve inexpensive sandwiches and hot dishes. A very small place.

WHAT TO SEE IN MISSION

This district is best seen on foot, although it's a little risky to move away from the main streets in the evening. Enjoy a walk there by day, but carry your camera in a bag rather than slinging it over your shoulder.

★ **Dolores Mission** (San Francisco of Assisi): 320 Dolores Street (and 16th Street): Open daily, 9am–4pm (except public holidays). Worth a visit, especially for the chapel and the little cemetery where approximately 5,000 Native Americans are buried. The chapel, built in 1782, is the oldest place in San Francisco. Very beautiful altar. In among the rosebushes in the cemetery, there are tombstones bearing many Irish and French surnames.

★ **Dolores Park**: two blocks south of the Mission, and still on Dolores Street, there's a beautiful view of Downtown and its skyscrapers.

★ **Murals**: the speciality of this district, which contains lots of very beautiful examples.

– **Balmy Alley**: a little alley between 24th and 25th Streets, parallel with Harrison Street. This has the greatest concentration of murals in the city. Absolutely superb.

– **24th Street and South Van Ness Avenue**: mural entitled *Carnival.*

– **23rd Street and Capp Street**: a mural made up of portraits. There's also a beautiful church opposite this mural. The Community Music Center Orchestra frequently plays there.

– **Mission and Clarion Alley**: between 17th and 18th Streets. A fabulous self-portrait. In the next side-alley (Sycamore) is a mural of Asian inspiration, featuring the Ying and Yang symbols.

– **18th Street and Lopidge Street** (parallel with Valencia): a wild mural covering three floors.

SHOPPING IN MISSION

Good Vibrations (Mission map, A3, **30**): 1210 Valencia Street. Freephone: ☎ 1-800-289-8423. Open daily, 11am–7pm. Actually, this is a sex shop. But it isn't just any old sex shop. Fine-looking, neither sordid nor of ill-repute, it has been a San Francisco institution for more than 20 years. Everybody knows about it! Even middle-class ladies do their shopping here!

The founder, Joani Blanks, a writer of books on sex, has become the bard of sexual liberation and the blossoming of the body. You'll find 'educational' videos here, practical manuals on subjects that moralists long kept suppressed, and beautiful books of photos. You'll also find condoms for all tastes, erotic CDs and a unique collection of sex toys. The funniest thing is to watch very serious young couples trying the gear on, and elegant ladies hesitating with no apparent embarrassment over which vibrator to choose. In short, a visit here is as instructive as it is amusing, shedding a bit of light on the contradictions and fantasies of San Francisco society, which is quite unlike any other.

MISSION BY NIGHT

– **Jack's Elixir** (Mission map, A1, **25**): 3200 16th Street (and Guerrero). ☎ 552-1633. Open daily, to 2am. More than 60 different draught beers. The waiters are really friendly: they offer you three or four different beers in little glasses to taste before you order the one you like best. Super ambiance at the weekend.

– **Elbo Room** (Mission map, A–B2, **26**): 647 Valencia (and Sycamore, between 17th and 18th Streets). ☎ 552-7788. Open daily. A big American bar on two floors, with billiard tables and videos. There are gigs upstairs every evening at 9pm or 10pm (admission charge): rock, blues, Latino, etc.

– **Roxie** (Mission map, A1, **27**): 3117 16th Street (and Valencia). ☎ 863-1087. A former fleapit that's been converted and now shows only art movies and try-outs. The programme is often themed, with seasons on forgotten or as yet undiscovered directors, Third World cinema, etc. Take one of their beautiful programme posters away with you.

★ SOMA (SOUTH OF MARKET STREET)

South of Market Street has been experiencing a second youth since the construction of the G.R. Moscone Convention Center, but it has also benefited from the recent construction of the Museum of Modern Art and its companion, the Yerba Buena Gardens. Even though there are still some dilapidated warehouses, as well as a few dark little streets and homeless people, this district has become a target area for the yuppies to explore, so you'll find restaurants, bars (jazz or otherwise) and fashionable nightspots. The place is really alive at night.

The latest trend has been the development of small, specialist on-line information and website design companies. As a result of this multimedia hub, San Francisco has awarded itself the grand title of 'capital of digital media', while South of Market has been nicknamed the 'multimedia gulch'.

One of the city's wildest festivals is held here every year – the **Folsom Street Fair**. It takes place on the last Sunday of September, when about 300,000 people crowd into Folsom Street, which gets blocked off between 4th and 11th Streets. There are concerts of every kind plus processions of outrageously garbed young people (there's a distinct tendency towards body-piercing, gay hardcore and sado-masochism). It may look alarming, but it's funny at the same time, lively and completely over-the-top: some people stroll along completely naked, some carry whips, others are in cages. There are stands selling jewellery, tattooists, and food from all over the world. Some people see this as American decadence, while others see it as an expression of total freedom, of people thumbing their noses at society.

WHERE TO EAT IN SOMA

☆–☆☆ BUDGET TO MODERATE

✕ **Cafe do Brasil** (map II, C3, **130**): 104 7th Street. ☎ 626-6432. Open 7.30am–10.30pm. In a simple setting, a warm, Brazilian-style welcome. At lunchtime, they offer a mini *feijoada*, the Brazilian national dish. Also pizzas that you can take away. In the evening, the menu is a little more extended and the prices go up a few dollars.

✕ **Max's Diner** (map II, C3, **131**): 3rd Street (and Folsom). ☎ 546-MAXS. Open 11.30am–10pm (midnight Friday and Saturday, 11pm Sunday). One of the most popular diners. Very large room, with an interesting collection of photos of other diners in the 1950s. Rock music in the background. American cuisine with a wide range of sandwiches (cold, hot or grilled), burgers and salads. To finish with, the inevitable sundaes. Family-type clientele. Believe it or not, the waiters are also singers. It's worth noting that under Article 20 of the house rules, if you arrive alone and a waiter is tactless enough to ask you 'Just one?', the meal comes free of charge! The dishes are enormous, but if you can't finish it all, they'll give you a doggie bag. If nothing else, this is one way of feeding some of San Francisco's homeless, and it's a habit that's become quite accepted.

✕ **Cadillac Bar** (map II, C3, **132**): 1 Holland Court (between 4th Street and Howard). ☎ 543-TACO. Open 11am–11pm (midnight Friday; noon–midnight Saturday, noon–10pm Sunday). A vast, warehouse-style room, very colourful, with classic Mexican food. When the place fills up, the atmosphere becomes really noisy. Apart from the traditional burritos and tacos, there are some dishes that are out of the ordinary, such as *surtido* platter for two (with a half-lobster, shrimp, prawns, *ceviche*, fish, various crustacea, rice and vegetables). Also *pollo Yucatán, burro combinado*, pasta Vera Cruz, chilli burger, etc.

✕ **Hamburger Mary's**: 1582 Folsom Street (and 12th). ☎ 626-1985. Open 11.30am–1am (2am

Friday and Saturday). The setting is unusual, to say the least (there's a urinal hanging on the wall and there are paintings more or less everywhere), but the atmosphere is warm and the clientele is quite a mixture. Depending on whether you come at lunchtime or in the evening, the atmosphere is very different. In the afternoon, it's mostly just regulars. In the evening, it's packed solid. You may have to wait half an hour, sometimes longer. The food is decent, though. Try the fantasy omelette, the Maryburger with avocado or bacon, steak 'n' eggs, homemade beef chilli, a variety of salads and vegetarian dishes. Or you can just come to have a drink at the bar (it's called **Mary's Backside**). Good beers: Sierra Nevada Ale, Henry's Private Reserve, Newcastle Brown, Red Hook.

✕ **The Ramp** (map II, D3, **133**): 855 China Basin Street. ☎ 621-2378. Open 8am–3.30pm, closed evenings in the week, Saturday and Sunday 8am–7.30pm. South of SOMA. Follow 4th Street, go under the highway and continue as far as 3rd Street, which follows the port. Level with Mariposa, you'll find the end of China Basin and The Ramp, which bears no resemblance to a ramp but looks more like a large shack at the water's edge. Nice restaurant and bar in one of the most difficult to get to places in the city, so it's only accessible to those with a car. Then you find you're on a country terrace in the middle of dockland. It gets pretty full, not surprisingly, when the weather is fine. During the week, they serve breakfast from 8am in a relaxed atmosphere: homemade corned beef hash, Italian sausages and eggs, Denver omelette, etc. Lunch consists of soups, clam chowder, salads, sandwiches, burgers, fish and chips. On Saturday and Sunday brunch is served, then it's barbecues until 7.30pm. From April to October there's open-air rock and blues, generally on Friday, Saturday and Sunday 3–8pm.

☆☆☆ EXPENSIVE

✕ **Julie's Supper Club** (map II, C3, **134**): 1123 Folsom Street (and 7th Street). ☎ 861-0707. Open Monday–Saturday 11am–2am. Colourful setting, rock'n'roll style, with a touch of the 1950s. It's a bar (a very handsome one), a restaurant and jazz club (free of charge). Try the salmon and the marinated lamb.

✕ **South Park Cafe** (map II, D3, **135**): 108 South Park. ☎ 495-7275. Open daily until 10pm (closed Sunday). A smartish restaurant with a Californian-style cuisine, although there are also some French influences. Dishes include black pudding with potatoes, duck with honey, roast salmon, blanquette of veal and some tempting pastries. The setting is quite serious and tasteful. Good selection of wine at reasonable prices. Booking is advised for dinner. The welcome is charming.

SAN FRANCISCO

WHERE TO HAVE A DRINK IN SOMA

🍸 **Brainwash Laundromat** (map II, C3, **164**): 1126 Folsom Street (and 6th Street). ☎ 255-4866. Open 7am–11pm (1.30am weekends). Such a simple idea: have a drink and listen to some music while doing your washing. This launderette has become something else altogether, but it's still a launderette! Things have recently undergone a few changes, to conform with regulations, so the setting is less unorthodox and there are fewer gigs, but the place has remained very convenient for a drink or a snack. And the crazy thing is that people actually still come here to do their washing!

WHAT TO SEE IN SOMA

★ **SFMOMA (San Francisco Museum of Modern Art)** (map II, C3, **202**): 151 Third Street. ☎ 357-4000. Admission charge. Open daily except Wednesday, 11am–6pm, Thursday to 9pm. Very close to the Yerba Buena Center, this is the latest of San Francisco's museums and one of the most successful. The exterior is rather forbidding – a windowless brick facade – but the interior is something else altogether. It's gigantic and lit from a central lightwell. There are four floors of exhibitions, some permanent, like the one on the second floor dedicated to paintings from the 1910 Fauvists with their hot colours to the Minimalist abstractions of the mid-1970s. The galleries are huge and well designed for the display of modern works.

On the first floor are works by Henri Matisse, Pablo Picasso and Paul Klee (who gets a room all to himself), André Derain, Georges Braque, Jean Dubuffet, Alberto Giacometti, Joan Miró, Max Ernst, Salvador Dalí– to mention only the best known. These are followed by several rooms of Californian art from the 1950s onwards, especially enlivened by canvases by Richard Diebenkorn.

The third floor is dedicated to photographs, from 1843 to the present day and including works by Louis de Clercq, Man Ray, Henri Cartier-Bresson and Andy Warhol.

There are concerts from time to time. This private museum, which has brought in more than $90 million in sponsorship, is the result of San Francisco's wish to regain its position as artistic capital of California. You'll probably agree it has been a success!

NB: the cafe at the Yerba Buena Center is much more peaceful than the one at SFMOMA (which is expensive, in any case) and the view is also better.

★ **Martin Luther King Memorial** (map II, C3) in Yerba Buena Gardens, between 3rd and 4th Street. The garden is open every day from sunrise to 10pm and it's a good place for a quick stroll when you come out of the SFMOMA. The memorial dedicated to the Reverend Martin Luther King is made of glass-and-granite panels engraved with some of the great man's sayings, all translated into the various different languages that are spoken in San Francisco.

★ **Ansel Adams Center** (map II, C3, **203**): 250 4th Street (between Howard and Folsom). ☎ 495-7000 and 495-7242. Open 11am–5pm. Closed Monday. Admission charge (free on the first Tuesday of the month). Very interesting photographic art centre. There's a room with a permanent exhibition of photos by Ansel Adams and some superb temporary exhibitions.

★ **Cartoon Art Museum** (map II, C3, **204**): 814 Mission and 4th Streets. ☎ 227-8666. On the second floor. Open Wednesday–Friday 11am–5pm,

Saturday 10am–5pm, Sunday 1–5pm. Admission charge. A comic-book museum that's unmissable if you're a fan of such things. This is one of the leading cartoon collections in the US. You can see some original pre-war plates, including Popeye (1934), Dick Tracy (1938) and a display of contemporary American comic books. There's a good shop, too.

★ **South Park**: between Second and Third Streets and Bryant and Brannan Streets. A nice little park, full of people.

SHOPPING IN SOMA

Esprit factory: 499 Illinois and 16th Streets. ☎ 957-2550. Open daily. This renovated warehouse right at the bottom of SOMA (quite a long way from Market Street) offers discounts of at least 25 per cent on the whole Esprit range of clothes and accessories for women and children only. The choice can sometimes be limited, but one thing they have lots of is T-shirts.

SOMA BY NIGHT

Don't cross SOMA on foot at night after the clubs close. Go by car or taxi, because the district isn't always very safe. You can get a taxi on Folsom Street, close to 7th Street.

WHERE TO HAVE A DRINK

– **Caribbean Zone** (map II, C3, **234**): 55 Natoma, behind the DV8, under the highway bridge. Open at lunchtime during the week and 5–11pm every evening (midnight Friday and Saturday). This is, perhaps, less of a place to be, more of a place to see. They've installed an aircraft fuselage on one side of the room, so you can have a drink while watching (through the portholes) a TV film, the location of which . . . is an aircraft. On the other hand, you *can* also eat here.

– **Paradise Lounge**: 308 11th Street and Folsom. ☎ 621-1911. Open 5pm–2am. Several rooms and two stages, providing lots of good music, with several bands each night (cover charge: $8–11, depending on the evening).

– **Holy Cow**: 1535 Folsom Street. ☎ 621-6518. Open Wednesday–Sunday 5pm–2am. No admission charge. Good music in a big room with an oval bar at the centre. Wooden decor. Theme evenings and dance music. Liveliest at weekends.

WHERE TO GO DANCING

– **Mercury SF** (map II, D3, **235**): 540 Howard. ☎ 777-1419. Open Wednesday–Saturday. Enormous nightclub with dance-floors on two levels. A certain amount of weeding out of would-be customers takes place at the entrance (especially on weekends). Inside, the spaces are beautifully designed.

– **Slim's**: 333 11th Street. ☎ 255-0333. Between Folsom and Harrison. Admission charge. Gigs five or six times a week. An enormous space offering mainly alternative music. Occasionally a bit grubby, so it's not the place to wear your best clothes. No smoking.

– **The DNA Lounge**: 375 11th Street. ☎ 626-1409 or 626-2532. Open every evening to 2am (4am weekends). Admission charge. Fashionable for some years and still doing well with local young people. Immense room with a mezzanine all the way round. Good music (house, techno, etc.). Three or four gigs a week, starting at 10pm.

– **1015 Folsom Street** (map II, C3, **236**): 1015 Folsom Street (and 6th Street). ☎ 431-BOYS. Open 10.30pm–6am (or later). Admission charge. Over the last four years, this place has acquired a great reputation for its late-night clubbing and a varied crowd. It occasionally has gay events. Lively and very smoky. Techno trance and house music. Quite frequently, admission to gigs is free for the first 50 people to arrive.

– **The Stud**: 399 9th Street. ☎ 863-6623. Open 5pm–2am. For over 30 years, this has been one of the pillars of Folsom. But the decor's getting a little dated. This is a gay disco and bar. Oldies night on Wednesday (the music, that is!).

– **Eagle**: Harrison and 12th Streets. ☎ 626-0880. Open 4pm–2am. On Sunday afternoon this is a meeting place for bikers in leathers. The clientele is gay – and into leather and muscles.

SAN FRANCISCO'S PARKS, GARDENS AND OTHER PLACES OF INTEREST

SAN FRANCISCO

There are three large parks within San Francisco: from north to south, they are the Presidio, facing on the Golden Gate Bridge, Lincoln Park and Golden Gate Park. Within each, there are a number of things to see and do.

★ **Golden Gate Bridge**: the most famous suspension bridge in the world, the Golden Gate Bridge was designed and built in less than five years, opening in 1937. The architect even gave it a subtle touch of art deco. Since the completion of a major lead-free repainting project in 1995, the bridge's famous 'International Orange' paintwork has been regularly maintained by a team of 38 painters.

Vehicles pay $3 to enter the city, but there's no charge to leave. Joggers take the bus to get to the stop after the bridge and then jog back across. From the bridge, the view of the Bay is quite superb – unless there's fog. You can return by the Sausalito ferry, but remember that the last one leaves at about 5pm and Sausalito is 3 miles (5km) away from the bridge. You can also cross the bridge by bike, carry on to Sausalito, and come back on the ferry.

To get to the Golden Gate Bridge, take the bus marked 'Golden Gate Bus Transit' close to the Civic Center (Market and 7th Streets). Or take the northbound 30 Stockton for Chestnut and Laguna, then the southbound 28 to Toll Plaza.

If you have a car, you really should go by the panoramic route north of the Golden Gate Bridge. There's a fantastic view of the bridge, with San Francisco in the background. Leave Highway 101 just after the Golden

Gate Vista Point, and follow the signs for 'Golden Gate National Recreation Area'. Another ideal viewpoint for admiring the sun setting over the bridge is at the end of Baker Street, near the Palace of Fine Arts (bus No. 30).

Or you may find the San Marin Vista Point quite good enough: turn right at the exit from the bridge.

★ **The Presidio**: at the tip of the Golden Gate is an immense park that covers 148 acres (66 ha – or more than 2 square miles). It takes its name from the fort built there by the Spanish in 1776. This strategic installation guarded the entrance to San Francisco Bay and was occupied by the military until October 1994.

There are some exquisite views of the Golden Gate Bridge and the old military barracks all along the hike-and-bike path and you pass through groves of pine, cypress and eucalyptus. As you travel along the coastal path and pass under the Golden Gate Bridge, you'll reach the place where Kim Novak plunged into the Bay in the Hitchcock film *Vertigo*. Then, just over a mile (2km) further on, you reach Baker Beach. The rangers say that this park is pretty safe during the day.

To get there by bus from Downtown, take a No. 45 ('NW bound') for Kearny right to the end of the line.

While you're there, you can also visit the following places (depending on your taste and motivation).

– **The Presidio Army Museum**: corner of Lincoln and Funston. ☎ 561-4331. Open 10am–4pm. Closed Monday and Tuesday. Free admission.

– **The Fort Point National Historic Site**: Long Avenue. ☎ 556-1693. At the foot of the south pillar of the Golden Gate Bridge. Apparently it's the only building of its kind west of the Mississippi, and it was built in 1853. Admission is free. Open Wednesday–Sunday 10am–5pm.

★ **Exploratorium**: 3601 Lyon Street, at the end of Marina Boulevard, next to the Presidio. Located within the Palace of Fine Arts, which is one of the last remaining traces of the 1915 Universal Exhibition. A No. 30 (Stockton) MUNI bus runs from the corner of Market and Kearny Streets all the way to the terminus. ☎ (415) 563-7337. Website: www.exploratorium.edu. Open Tuesday–Sunday 10am–5pm (9.30pm Wednesday). Closed Monday (except during school holidays). Admission charge (free on the first Wednesday of the month). Reduction for students. This is quite a well known science museum located in a huge old warehouse, where you can experience many scientific effects in a way that's interactive and therefore fun. The place is very popular with children and science students.

Physics takes pride of place, with sections on sound, vibration, light, magnetism, climatic phenomena, etc. If you pay an additional (and quite heavy) charge, you can go off on an adventure under the tactile dome, where you rediscover the sense of touch in the dark. Advance booking is needed for this.

★ **The California Palace of the Legion of Honor**: in Lincoln Park (34th Avenue and Clement Street). ☎ 863-3330 or 750-3600. By bus, take the No. 38 to 33rd Road and Clement, then the No. 18 to the museum. Open Tuesday–Sunday 9.30am–4.45pm (8.45pm on the first Saturday of each month). Admission charge (reductions for young people and the elderly). Free admission on the second Wednesday of each month.

The architecture of this very beautiful art museum was freely inspired by the building in Paris that houses the museum of the *Légion d'honneur* (whence the name of its American counterpart). At the entrance, the sculpture known as *The Thinker* heralds one of the world's finest collections of the works of Auguste Rodin. The museum is largely dedicated to French art: medieval, religious sculpture and tapestries, but the Dutch and Flemish Masters are also well represented. The combination of its exceptional location in Lincoln Park, the architecture of the building and the wealth of its collections make it probably one of the most beautiful museums in San Francisco.

It was built in 1920 and renovated, enlarged and strengthened against seismic attack in 1995. There are now new rooms in the basement for temporary exhibitions and there's even a pyramid not dissimilar to the one at the Louvre in Paris. Guided visits on Saturday only.

The rich collection of European paintings includes important works from the 14th to the 20th centuries. Paintings on display include works by El Greco, Fra Angelico, Tiepolo, Bruegel the Elder, Frans Hals, Rubens, Rembrandt, Fragonard, Watteau, Gainsborough, Constable, Courbet, Tissot, Degas, Manet, Renoir, Sisley, Cezanne, Monet, Bouguereau, Matisse, Van Gogh and Picasso.

The European Decorative Art collection includes furniture and other decorative items as well as sculpture. Highlights include French baroque inlaid furniture and 18th-century English porcelain. The gallery is world famous for its collection of sculptures by Rodin, including the original cast of *The Thinker*.

Famous works include: *The Empire of Flora* by Tiepolo, Rubens' *The Tribute Money*, with its remarkable effects of light, El Greco's *St John the Baptist* and Fra Angelico's *The Meeting of St Francis and St Dominic*. Also Van Gogh's *Montmartre*, and *Water Lilies* and *The Grand Canal, Venice* by Monet.

★ **Golden Gate Park**: 2 miles (3km) west of the Civic Center. Bordering the Haight-Ashbury district, this magnificent park is 3 miles (5km) long and nearly a mile (800m) wide. To get there, take a No. 5 or 21 bus from Market Street to the intersection of Fulton Street and 8th Avenue. The No. 71 Haight bus goes along Haight Street and finishes at Stanyan (east of the park). The No. 5 westbound Fulton bus goes there, too.

An Explorer Pass, available from the Visitors' Information Center, gives adults a discount of 25 per cent on admission charges to the Asian Art Museum, the California Academy of Science, the Japanese Tea Garden and the De Young Museum, and entitles you to a plan of the park.

This place is even more beautiful than Central Park in New York. Created in 1868 in an area previously covered by dunes, it contains no fewer than 6,000 varieties of plants from all over the globe. The landscapers, whose ambition was to outdo the Bois de Boulogne in Paris, planted a million trees. The most interesting section is the eastern one (between Stanyan and Stow Lake). This has more than 6 miles (10km) of tracks that you can hike along. But the park is too big to walk around in one go. There are bikes (hundreds of them) for hire on Stanyan. The only problem is that theft is commonplace, so you have to plan to padlock the bicycle to something – it's essential.

– The main entrance is on Oak and Stanyan and there's a map of the park at McLaren Lodge. A little further on are the Camellia and Fuchsia Gardens. These are followed by the Flower Conservatory. Built in 1878. Splendid Victorian architecture. After you reach the three giant ferns (like beautiful exotic trees), you'll reach the place with the rhododendrons that John McLaren, the great Scottish landscape gardener, was so fond of.

– In the **Japanese Tea Garden** (open 9am–6:30pm; October–February 8.30am–5.30pm), you can relax with a cup of jasmine tea in a really nice spot, surrounded by streams and little bridges, pagodas and bonsai trees. There's dancing to the latest hits on Sundays – it seems to be popular with all ages. Admission charge.

– The **Music Concourse** is where free rock (or brass band) concerts are held, generally on Sunday around noon–2pm.

– Opposite, are the museums of the **California Academy of Sciences**: the **Natural History Museum**, the **Morrison Planetarium** and the **Steinhart Aquarium** (☎ 750-7145). Open daily, 10am–5pm (6pm in summer). Admission charge. At the Natural History Museum, you can experience an earthquake. In the evening, there are laser shows at the Planetarium. The Steinhart Aquarium is well worth a look, with its 600 species of fish and many species of marine mammals. You can even watch the penguins' feeding time, 11.30am–4pm.

– The **National AIDS Memorial Grove** is to the southeast of the California Academy of Sciences, at the Middle Drive East and Bowling Green Drive intersection. The memorial is dedicated to people who suffer from, or who have died from, AIDS and is of particular note because it is, in effect, a 'living' tribute. Every third Saturday of the month, 100 to 200 volunteers assemble to mow, weed and plant up this section of the park, which previously offered little of interest. The garden was initially created on an informal basis by people touched in some way by the disease. It has now become a focus for people's memories and seems to exude a poetic serenity. It has a certain social significance as a result of the mass participation in its upkeep. At the foot of an incline, there's a circular beige granite plaque engraved with the names of AIDS victims.

– Near the Japanese Tea Garden are what are probably the two most beautiful museums in San Francisco: the **De Young Museum** and the **Asian Art Museum** (*see below*).

– Level with 12th Street there is a Rose Garden.

– To the south of the Japanese Tea Garden is the **Strybing Arboretum and the Botanical Gardens**, 19th Avenue and Lincoln Way, ☎ 661-1316. Open 8am–4.30pm (10am–5pm Saturday, Sunday and public holidays). This is a fabulous oasis with a number of themed gardens. There's a Garden of Fragrances with signs in Braille, a Moon-viewing Garden, a Biblical Garden and so on. Visitors are even invited to taste the spices.

– On **Stow Lake**, canoes and pedal boats are available. The lake is dominated by Strawberry Hill, an artificial hill that stands 460ft (140m) high. Around the lake are waterfalls, and dense acacia and eucalyptus groves. Higher up are the Rainbow Falls.

– In the western part of the park is the **Buffalo Paddock** and there are other small lakes before you finish up at the **Tulip Garden**.

– If you'd like to do some horseback riding in the park: ☎ 668-7360.

★ **M.H. De Young Memorial Museum**: 75 Tea Garden Drive, Golden Gate Park. ☎ 863-3330. Open Wednesday–Sunday 9.30am–4.45pm. Admission charge (reductions for young people and the elderly). Free admission on the first Wednesday of each month (and that day it stays open until 8.45pm). Pedestrian access to the museum is via Fulton and 10th Avenue. By bus from Union Square, take No. 38 to 6th and Geary, then No. 44 to the museum. This marvellous place has one of the most beautiful and wide-ranging permanent collections, from the art of Ancient Greece and Rome through European 17th-century paintings to 20th-century American art. There are also prestigious temporary exhibitions.

– **American late-19th-century art** includes works by Hobart, John Singer Sargent, Edward Hopper, Metcalf and Whistler.

– **20th-century art** offers Man Ray, Yves Tanguy, Wayne Thiebaud, John Kock, George Grosz (a splendid *Lower Manhattan*), Diego Rivera and many others.

– The examples of **English art** include works by Joshua Reynolds, Turner, Gainsborough and Constable.

– There's a superb and very pleasant open-air cafe around a pool that's decorated with bronze cherubs. Also an excellent bookshop.

★ **Asian Art Museum**: in the west wing of the De Young Museum. Same timetable and prices (one ticket gets you into both museums on the same day). ☎ 379-8800. Website: www.asianart.org. The museum will be open until October 2001, after which it is scheduled to move to a new location in autumn 2002.

One of the most fantastic museums of its kind, covering 6,000 years of Asian art and great if you're interested in the subject, otherwise it can be a bit overwhelming. It's impossible to describe everything. About half the rooms are devoted to China, where you can admire splendid jade and no less admirable paintings, miniatures and calligraphic manuscripts. Superb bronzes, Buddhist votive steles, earthenware and porcelain.

On the first floor are exhibits from Japan, Korea and Tibet, including an admirable *taima mandala* from 14th-century Japan, carved wooden items and beautiful Tibetan jewellery and bronzes.

★ **San Francisco Fire Department Museum**: 655 Presidio Avenue (and Bush). ☎ 861-8000 (ext: 365). Open Thursday–Sunday 1–4pm. Closed public holidays. An interesting exhibition of photos (many of the fire that ravaged San Francisco following the earthquake of 1906), hand pumps, fire engines and souvenirs of Lillie Hitchcock Coit, who metaphorically burned with passion for her heroes (*see* 'Coit Tower' under 'North Beach and Telegraph Hill').

★ **Cliff House**: around Nos. 1066–1090 on Point Lobos Avenue. Take a No. 38 bus from Geary Street to the Point Lobos terminus. While you're in the area of the California Palace of the Legion of Honor, you should take the opportunity to see one of the finest views of the cliff, the Pacific and Seals Rocks, right at the end of Geary Avenue. This is a favourite family walk. There's a delightful pedestrian route between Cliff House and the Golden Gate Bridge, where you can admire a rocky coast and beautiful houses. Allow two or three hours.

The first Cliff House was built in 1863. A boat was wrecked against the cliff and its cargo of dynamite exploded, taking part of the house with it. A few years later, the remainder of the house burned down on Christmas Day. At the end of the 19th century, it was rebuilt by Adolphe Sutro, but burned down again shortly afterwards. A new Cliff House emerged in 1909, but it subsequently underwent so much alteration and reconstruction that the present building is of little interest. Restaurants around here are expensive, touristy, and of debatable quality. On the other hand, you won't risk spending much if you only have breakfast, and you'll get the benefit of the beautiful view of Seals Rocks.

At the **Parks and Forests Office** you can pore over old photographs of the site and read a few anecdotes associated with it. There's a little **Museum of Tools and Mechanical Toys** (admission free), where some of the items on exhibit are quite rare, and are still working.

AROUND SAN FRANCISCO

★ ANGEL ISLAND

The biggest island in the bay is often ignored, being somehow overshadowed by Alcatraz, its better-known neighbour. Also a former military camp, Angel Island is now a park that's open to visitors. It's ideal for bike excursions, walking or even kayaking. The island also has nine campgrounds and some great viewpoints taking in the whole of San Francisco Bay. Access is by ferry only, from San Francisco or Tiburon. Angel Island is a tremendous green haven. ☎ 4435-1915 or 897-0715. If you are taking the boat from San Francisco, check out the Blue & Gold Fleet on Pier 41 (for reservations ☎ 705-5555), which offers a combined ticket for Alcatraz too.

★ SAUSALITO

This district is north of San Francisco, at the other end of the Golden Gate Bridge, It was once famous for its hippies, although today you're more likely to find people pretending to be hippies, yuppies in search of peace and quiet, and an ever-increasing number of tourists. The area is pretty, the shops sell mostly luxury goods, and the restaurants can be unaffordable.

Window-shopping is good at the Village Fair (777 Bridgeway). This is a complex of shops set up in a former opium den.

A striking addition here are the famous houseboats, of all sizes and colours, which form a floating village. Some distance from the city centre, they are level with the slip-road to the highway and you have to travel along the seafront for a good half-hour before you find them. Take the Golden Gate Transit bus to get there.

HOW TO GET TO ANGEL ISLAND AND SAUSALITO

It's a good idea to leave San Francisco by bus in the morning via the Golden Gate Bridge, while the Bay is under fog, then come back on the ferry. Take a No. 10, 20 or 50 bus from the corner of Market Street and 7th Street (the Golden Gate Transit). The ferry is just as much fun as a boat trip round the Bay, and it costs less. Allow 30 minutes for the crossing.

BY FERRY

• **Golden Gate Ferries**, Ferry Building, at the start of Market Street. ☎ 923-2000. Leaves San Francisco about every 90 minutes during the week, 7.40am–8pm; six departures per day (seven in summer) on Saturday, Sunday and public holidays, 11.30am–6.55pm (8.05pm in summer). Leaves Sausalito 7.05am–7.20pm during the week, and 10.50am–6.10pm on Saturday, Sunday and public holidays (until 7.30pm in summer). No boats on Thanksgiving, Christmas or New Year's Day. Fares are reasonable.

• **Red and White Fleet**, Fisherman's Wharf, Pier 43. ☎ 546-2700. Up to six daily departures for Sausalito. A bit more expensive than Golden Gate Ferries. Weekend departures to Angel Island twice a day.

• **Angel Island Tiburon Ferry**, 21 Main Street, Tiburon. ☎ 435-2131. Website: www.angelislandferry.com. Hourly departures seven days a week, 10.00am–4pm weekends and 10.00am–3pm, Monday to Friday.

WHERE TO STAY IN ANGEL ISLAND AND SAUSALITO

If you want to stay on Angel Island there is a selection of small campsites to choose from. Staying in Sausalito and visiting San Francisco puts the icing on the cake: it would be hard to find a more luxurious place. There are not many hotels, so they're often full up well in advance and, most of all, they tend to be very expensive.

The Continental Alta Mira Hotel: 125 Bulkley Avenue, on the heights (follow Princess Street to Bridgeway Avenue). ☎ 332-1350. Fax: 331-3862. Open all year round except early-January. There's an exceptional view of San Francisco Bay from here, and if you can't afford to stay here, have a drink or brunch on the terrace and enjoy the panorama. The rooms are quiet, with an old-fashioned charm, and some are more like small private apartments. Price range from \$80–\$190. The cheaper rooms don't have the view.

WHERE TO EAT IN SAUSALITO

Everything is very expensive in this area. If you're low on dough, get your provisions in the little supermarket located on California Street.

Bridgeway Cafe: 633 Bridgeway. ☎ 332-3426. Open 7.30am–5pm. In the village itself, right in the centre. Good sandwiches and burgers. Without doubt the cheapest breakfast with a view over the Bay – and, what's more, there's plenty of it. The 'Urban Tarzan', for example, combines hamburger, eggs, toast and sautéed potatoes. Now *there's* something to start your day on!

Giovanni's: 629 Bridgeway. ☎ 332-4418. Open to 9pm. Tiny pizzeria in an arbour, whose walls are decorated with old black-and-white photos. Their pizzas are excellent, especially the garlic pizza. The 'small' pizzas are generally too much for one person. Excellent sausage and green pepper, and they do a vegetarian menu.

Bayside Cafe: Harbor Center (exit north of Sausalito, just by the houseboats). ☎ (415) 331-2313. Open 7am–4pm. A little restaurant where you can get a good, inexpensive breakfast (but only until 10am during the week) or lunch. Wide choice of omelettes served with toast and potatoes. Behind the restaurant there's a pleasant little walk, from where you get a great view of the houseboats. Many of the customers are regulars, and prices are very reasonable.

✕ **Caffè Trieste**: 1000 Bridgeway. ☎ (415) 332-7770. Open 7am–11pm (1am Friday and Saturday). Just two small rooms with an nice Italian atmosphere. A good place to have breakfast (continental only) or a pizza. Good coffee. Prices very affordable. Some tables on the street.

WHAT TO DO AND SEE IN THE AREA

– **A flight over the city in a seaplane**: San Francisco Seaplane Tours organizes flights over the city. ☎ (415) 332-4843. Freephone: ☎ 1-888-SEAPLANE. E-mail: sfseaplane@aol.com. Website: www.seaplane.com. Three points of departure: San Francisco (at Pier 39), Lake Tahoe, and Sausalito (the most popular). From San Francisco, take the Golden Gate Bridge and continue on Highway 101. Leave at Stinson Beach–Mill Valley. Take a right immediately into a little road at the beginning of the exit road. You'll see the seaplanes alongside Highway 101, on the right.

The Golden Gate Tour, which lasts 30 minutes, is about enough to help you find your feet. There's something magical and unique about this flight over San Francisco, because it's very unusual to be able to fly above a city at this altitude. The alignment of the streets and the various districts are clearly visible. You also fly over Alcatraz and the Golden Gate Bridge (at very close range), then you climb north, where you see from on high the marvellous islands of Tiburon, the hills around Mill Valley, and Muir Beach. Flights are in a Cessna 172, which can carry three passengers, or a Beaver (one of only two in California), which can carry seven.

Obviously, this won't be cheap, but you won't be disappointed. Whatever you do, don't forget your camera! If you're in love, you can book the 'Champagne Sunset Flight' (40 minutes) with champagne, followed by sunset over the Golden Gate Bridge (if the sky isn't clouded).

★ **Point Bonita**: the lighthouse of the same name at the southwest end of Marin County is the nearest one to San Francisco. You get to it by crossing the Golden Gate Bridge, then taking the Alexander Avenue exit just after the bridge. Continue along Conzelman Road, a magnificent road that overlooks the whole entrance to the Bay. The last 500 (450 metres) yards up to the lighthouse have to be covered on foot. This is one of the wildest, most romantic places on this stretch of the coast. Open every weekend 12.30–3.30pm and any night there's a full moon if you book ahead. Call the Headlands Visitors' Center on ☎ 331-1540. The lighthouse is still in operation, but it has been automated since 1981. There's a lot of wind and it's foggy in summer, so cover up well.

★ SAN RAFAEL

San Rafael is a pleasant city about 10 miles (16km) north of Sausalito. It was founded in 1817, along with the mission at San Rafael Arcángel and is known for its picturesque Main Street, which was chosen by George Lucas when he was filming scenes for *American Graffiti* in 1972. Gastronomes will find 175 restaurants there, while aesthetes will note the charming Victorian districts, as well as the famous **Marin County Civic Center**, the work of Frank Lloyd Wright – an ultra-futuristic piece of architecture, that really should be in a science-fiction movie. There's tennis and a swimming pool at McNear's Beach.

– To get there, take the **Golden Gate Ferry** ☎ 923-2000. The ferry leaves from the Market Street wharf for Larkspur Terminal, south of San Rafael. There are twelve departures each day (five on Saturday, Sunday and public holidays).

– **Marin County Visitors' Office**: Avenue of the Flags. ☎ (415) 472-7470. Plenty of information about the city and the region.

WHERE TO STAY IN SAN RAFAEL

Villa Inn: 1600 Lincoln Avenue. ☎ (415) 456-4975. Fax: 456-1520. Located not far from Downtown. To get there from Highway 101, take the Lincoln Avenue or Central San Rafael exit. The bus for San Francisco (Golden Gate Transit) passes this way. The rooms are pleasant and comfortable. Continental breakfast is included in the price. Two major advantages are the swimming pool and the spa. Friendly welcome.

Colonial Motel: 1735 Lincoln Avenue. ☎ (415) 453-9188. Freephone: ☎ 1-800-554-9118. Not far from the previous entry, this is another nice motel with similar prices. It's quite small, with 20 neat rooms that are fairly spacious, with refrigerator, TV and cable; some with kitchenette. Try to avoid those that look out onto the avenue, as they're noisy. No breakfast, but there's coffee in your room. Nice welcome.

WHERE TO EAT IN SAN RAFAEL

✕ **Bay Thai**: 809 4th Street (and Lincoln). ☎ (415) 458-8845. Open Monday–Saturday 11am–4pm and 5–10pm; closed lunchtime on Sunday. A tiny little restaurant (seats only 14), serving good and inexpensive Thai cuisine. Try the Thai curry noodle (with coconut milk), red curry seafood (with broccoli and pasta) and *rad na talay* (seafood sautéed with spices). They don't take credit cards.

✕ **Double Rainbow**: 860 4th Street. ☎ (415) 457-0803. Open 8am–11pm (noon Sunday). An ice-cream parlour in true Haägen-Dazs style, with a fantastic choice of flavours (including peanut and chocolate brownie). Ask to try them before making up your mind – they're very happy to let you do this. There's also a wide choice of sandwiches and salads, and beautiful cakes.

AROUND AND ABOUT IN SAN RAFAEL

★ **Mount Tamalpais**: north of San Francisco, accessible via Highway 101, this peak offers a magnificent view over the whole of San Francisco Bay and is a point of departure for local tours. Lots of marked footpaths in a very agreeable setting. Be aware that in summer, the highest section is often closed off because of the risk of fire. Check before you go.

WHERE TO GO SWIMMING IN SAN RAFAEL

– **Muir Beach**: you need a car to get here (by bus, it's pure torture), but it's definitely worth the visit. Not far from Muir Woods (*see below*), north of San Francisco. If you have a car, take Highway 101 and leave at Mill Valley–Stinson Beach. At the first big intersection (after going back under Highway 101), take a left and continue along the same road. It winds over some marvellous hills. The view is captivating. At the bottom of the valley, a little sign on the left points the way to the beach.

On the right of the big beach, past the rocks, there's a smaller stretch of sand where you can strip off entirely.

– **Tennessee Valley Road**: take the Mill Valley exit and go north. Immediately after passing under the bridge, take the second on the left, as though you were going to Mill Valley. After a few hundred yards, there's a sign on the left for Tennessee Valley Road. From there, a little road winds up until you reach a parking lot. From that point onward the road is closed to traffic and becomes a paradise for joggers and cyclists, leading to a charming steep-sided beach about 2 miles (3km) further on. The landscape and the stroll are both pleasant, except for those times when the mist doesn't lift, and then you get total, unadulterated peace.

– **Stinson Beach**: further up the coast. This superb beach, just over a mile (2km) long, is the best-known beach and is the most highly prized by San Franciscans. Its facilities are much better than at the others. There may be a lot of people there on summer weekends, but they're really friendly. All you need is an ice-cream parlour, a game of volleyball and some suntan lotion. All of this area to the north of San Francisco can occasionally escape the blanket of fog that covers the city on certain summer days.

If you're hungry, try the brunch at the Parkside, near the parking lot.

★ BOLINAS

Some 20 miles (32km) north of Stinson Beach, to the left of Highway 1, Bolinas is not at all obvious when you're looking for it, because the inhabitants regularly take the road signs away. It's a little game they like to play in order to avoid being disturbed!

The village of Bolinas is in fact a haunt of former hippies, one of California's legendary places and probably the only one to have remained intact. The old houses have been preserved and peace reigns over this little village of die-hards, set in a superb location on the shore of a lagoon that has been taken over by birds, with the mountains in the background. Add to this a few fishermen's houses on stilts, and you'll understand why the lucky devils who live here don't want any tourists, despite the presence of a museum and a handful of art galleries. So, don't come here unless you're prepared to leave behind all tourist trappings and have no intention of behaving like someone visiting a zoo.

WHERE TO STAY AND EAT IN BOLINAS

Smiley's Schooner Saloon & Hotel: 41 Wharf Road, the main street, right in the centre. ☎ (415) 868-1311. The slogan of this establishment, set up in 1851, says it all: 'Before Lincoln was president, before baseball was a game, before 'Jingle Bells' was a song, there was Smiley's!' It's an authentic saloon, worthy of a part in a Western, with a few rooms above the bar that are basic but full of charm. You'll pay about $75 a night (more on weekends). Even if you don't sleep there, go and have a drink at the bar – it really is worth it. The clientele are regulars, and there are some colourful personalities.

✕ **The Shop Cafe**: opposite Smiley's. Open 9am–2:30pm Tuesday and to 9pm Wednesday–Sunday. Closed Monday. Its little terrace is well located at a strategic intersection. They serve a little of everything, at very modest prices: breakfast, burgers, Mexican dishes, salads, chicken, dishes of the day and ice-cream. Or there's a grocery store nearby if you'd prefer a picnic.

WHAT TO SEE IN BOLINAS

★ **Bolinas Museum**: opposite Smiley's Saloon. Open 1–5pm Friday–Sunday. There are two little rooms devoted to painting and, behind, another building that concentrates on the history of the region, with an exhibition of seafaring souvenirs, implements used at the time of the pioneers, and so on.

AROUND AND ABOUT BOLINAS

★ Continuing along Highway 1 to the north, you come to **Bodega Bay**: there's more about this in 'The Wine Route'.

★ BERKELEY

To the east of San Francisco (East Bay), Berkeley is home to one of the world's most celebrated universities and holds the record for the greatest number of Nobel prizes per unit area. Not surprising, really – an average of 25,000 students each year must help with the odds!

The Berkeley campus also won fame as the hotbed of the protest movement during the 1960s (*see* 'A Little History' at the beginning of 'San Francisco'). Things have cooled down a lot since then, but Berkeley remains extraordinarily young and lively, full of good restaurants and interesting shops, often cheaper than those in San Francisco.

But the main point of being here is you're either studying or partying, especially in the fraternity and sorority houses where the students live. These use letters from the Greek alphabet for their names, and are usually single-sex establishments. All summer long, these houses are the scene of immense parties to which associations of the opposite sex are invited. Often enough, some outsider will manage to slip in (it could be you – with a little luck and a lot of determination!).

If you come in September, don't miss the beer festival which usually takes place on the third weekend: it includes concerts, home-brewing displays, tastings, cigar sales, etc., all of it obviously going on in a very well-irrigated atmosphere! Information is available by phone: ☎ 510-THE-ROCK or on the website at www.realbeer.com/berkeleybeerfest.

Throughout the year there are rock concerts on certain evenings at the Greek Theater, right in the middle of the university. This theatre, which was a gift from the tycoon William Randolph Hearst, is worth seeing as an example of what you can do when you have no ideas, but plenty of cash!

There's always something going on at Berkeley. Perhaps the best reason for going there is to enjoy meeting people and getting to see how the young people of California live these days.

HOW TO GET TO BERKELEY

Berkeley is on the other side of the Bay from San Francisco, about 9 miles (15km) away. The easiest way is to take the BART from the bottom of Powell Street (in the centre of San Francisco) towards Richmond, as far as Berkeley Station (on Shattuck Avenue). It runs until midnight. By car, cross the Bay Bridge (toll-free in this direction) and take Highway 80 East. Be aware that it's hard to find a parking space and even when you do, it will not be cheap.

Alternatively, there's the bus: take lines F or T at San Francisco's Transbay Terminal (corner of Mission and 1st Streets). The bus company is AC Transit. ☎ 817-1717.

BERKELEY DISTRICTS

There are three avenues to explore, each representing a district of a different kind.

The best-known one is **Telegraph Avenue** (south of the university), a truly crazy street with bars, restaurants, new and second-hand record shops, bookshops, second-hand clothes shops, hippies selling jewellery, etc. The ambiance is one of a world where youth rules.

Euclid Avenue (north of the university), frequented by students for its peaceful and intimate character (surrounded by residential streets), is more conducive to reading and study.

Shattuck Avenue is a series of shops and restaurants for the finer palate, known as the 'Gourmet Ghetto'.

USEFUL ADDRESSES IN BERKELEY

Visitors' Office: 2015 Center Street (between Shattuck and Melvia). ☎ 549-7040. Freephone: ☎ 1-800-847-4823. Open Monday–Friday 9am–5pm. Excellent welcome. Lots of information on the city and a free map that's well produced. The office also has a hotline: ☎ (510) 549-8710, from which you can get full information about events in the city, timetables for museums, public transport, accommodation, etc.

WHERE TO STAY IN BERKELEY

☆☆ MODERATE

Berkeley Downtown YMCA: 2001 Allston Way (and Milvia Street). ☎ (510) 848-9622. Fax: (510) 848-6835. This YMCA is immense, occupying a whole block. Use the entrance marked 'Residence'. This is undoubtedly the city's cheapest place to stay. The accommodation is mixed, but men and women are on different floors. There are 80 tiny rooms for one or two people. Not expensive compared with the Y in San Francisco, but it's a bit old-fashioned, and the decor is minimalist. There are no dormitories, and showers and toilets are on the landing. The communal parts have no charm but they are clean. You get access to a fitness club with three pools, weight-training, etc. The nearby parking lot is not too expensive.

International House Berkeley: 2299 Piedmont Avenue. ☎ (510) 642-9490. Fax: (510) 643-8157. This hospitable university residence has a few rooms that are let by the night or by the week to non-students. Booking is advisable at any time except during the summer. It costs almost double the price at the YMCA, but the rooms are really small studio flats, with bathroom, phone and office. You can even have one with a sitting room, although this costs more. The building has a TV room, sports room, bookshop, international newspapers and a pub. It also has a restaurant and a big cafe-grill. The ambiance is relaxed and the staff are very friendly. The house organizes many events and activities, generally free to residents: theme banquets, slide shows, debates, dances, concerts, guided walks, etc. It's a chance to meet lecturers, researchers, students and their families who are living in the establishment.

☆☆☆☆ SPLASH OUT

Bancroft Hotel: 2680 Bancroft Way (and College Avenue) ☎ (510) 549-1000. Freephone for reservations: ☎ 1-800-549-1002. Fax: 549-1070. Website: www.bancrofthotel.com. This is a very handsome hotel in the style of a grand Italian villa; it was built in 1928 and is now a listed building. There are 22 comfortable and very clean standard rooms, though they are a little small. Expect to pay about $100, with breakfast included. The 'deluxe' rooms are very nice, with balconies offering a view of the trees or the university.

The French Hotel: 1538 Shattuck Avenue (between Vine and Cedar Streets). ☎ (510) 548-9930. A nice hotel with 18 light, spacious rooms. The decor is tasteful, and rather high-tech. Avoid the rooms on the street, as they can be noisy. Charming welcome. On the ground floor there's a busy cafe where you can get a continental breakfast. Parking near the hotel.

The Beautiful Sky Hotel: 2520 Durant Avenue. ☎ (510) 540-7688. E-mail: beausky@emf.net. This large, all-white Victorian house has 20 spacious and pleasant rooms. Try to get a room with a balcony. It's well positioned, very close to the campus – and therefore to the fun. Expect to pay at least $68, and $85 for a standard room.

WHERE TO EAT IN BERKELEY

ON TELEGRAPH AVENUE (SOUTH OF THE CAMPUS)

✕ **Cafe Intermezzo**: 2442 Telegraph Avenue. ☎ 849-4592. Open Monday–Friday 10am–9pm. A student meeting-place where people come to eat enormous salads (served in bowls) and impressive sandwiches in a very friendly ambiance. It's a large room that's light and airy, and it's ideal for meeting new people – especially when queuing, as it's frequently full. Very cheap.

✕ **The Blue Nile**: 2525 Telegraph Avenue. ☎ 540-6777. Open daily, 11:30am–10pm (5pm Sunday). Here they serve Ethiopian cuisine in an exotic setting – not the sort of food you see very often, so grab the chance. The lower room has intimate little cubicles with rush curtains. Special lunch 11am–4pm. The dishes are copious and cheap. Try *kitfo* (mince with pepper and spices), *yé siga tibs* (beef, rice and vegetables), *yé doro tibs* (chicken, rice and vegetables).

✕ **Kips**: 2439 Durant Avenue, near Telegraph Avenue. ☎ 848-4340. Open daily, 11am–1am. A very American cafeteria, complete with team pennants, although it's run by Asians. Lots of Italian specialities on the menu, and the place was voted by the *Daily Californian* as the restaurant that makes the best pizza this side of Shattuck Avenue. They also do delicious hamburgers. It's often crowded, and justly so. Superb 1950s jukebox.

ON EUCLID AVENUE (NORTH OF THE CAMPUS)

✕ **La Val's**: 1834 Euclid Avenue. ☎ 843-5617. Open daily, 11am–11pm (10pm Sunday and Monday). This restaurant, which has been around for about 20 years, has become an institution. People come here for the excellent pizzas, pastas and sandwiches. Every Thursday, Friday and Saturday, at 8pm, there's a show in the basement theatre. Some evenings there are concerts. There's another **La Val's** on Durant Avenue, and it's much cheaper.

✕ **The Little Market (Northgate Food Fair)**: 2507 Hearst Avenue, corner of Euclid Avenue. Arranged along a charming timber arcade there are several small yet unpretentious exotic restaurants, offering Chinese, Japanese, Korean, Lebanese and other cuisines. There's something for every taste here, and within the reach of most pockets. Particularly nice in summer, but note that it all fills up quickly, and there are only a limited number of seats on the terrace.

ON SHATTUCK AVENUE (NORTH SHATTUCK VILLAGE)

✕ **Saul's**: 1475 Shattuck Avenue. ☎ 848-DELI. Open daily, 8am–9.30pm. A delicatessen (and grocery and restaurant) with a good reputation for excellent breakfasts, including Napa Valley chicken, apple sausage and eggs, or just Challah French toast (which you can have covered with strawberries and Chantilly cream, at a small extra cost). A very popular place. Nice setting and inexpensive, with an Early Bird menu Monday–Friday 4–5pm. Great omelettes and well-stocked menu (soup, salads, bagels, deli sandwiches and old-fashioned deli platters).

– **The Cheeseboard**: 1504 Shattuck Avenue. Practically opposite Chez Panisse. Open daily from

10am. Closed Sunday. Not a restaurant; but an authentic cheese shop, where any cheese buff can satisfy their hunger for bleu d'Auvergne, Brie, Cantal, goat's cheese, Bougon as well as many varieties of Italian and Dutch cheese. They make their own bread, too, which is on sale from 8.30am.

– Connoisseurs can supplement their gastronomic shopping with a little bottle of something from **North Berkeley**, just opposite.

☆☆☆☆ SPLASH OUT

✕ **Chez Panisse**: 1517 Shattuck Avenue. ☎ (510) 548-5525. Open daily, 11.30am–3pm, 5–10.30pm (11.30pm weekends). Closed Sunday. This smart Italian–Californian restaurant, in a sort of chalet, has been fashionable for several years. On the ground floor there's a very classy dining room with a unique menu in the evening, costing $38–68 depending on the mood of the chef, and for that you have to book well in advance. So it's probably not the ideal backpacker spot, especially as the cuisine can be a bit pretentious, despite their excellent reputation. Upstairs, on the other hand, the layout is like a brasserie, more friendly and less expensive, but you can't book and it's often necessary to queue.

WHERE TO HAVE A DRINK IN BERKELEY

🍸 **Caffè Strada**: 2300 College Avenue (and Bancroft). ☎ 843-5282. Open 6.30am–11.30pm (7.30am Sunday). A coffee-shop full of students, with a large terrace that's very popular. Good coffee and excellent pastries. A really pleasant place, ideal for making new acquaintances.

🍸 **Caffè Mediterraneum**: 2475 Telegraph Avenue. ☎ 549-1128. Open daily, 7am–11.30pm. One of the least expensive cafes in the district. Omelettes, burgers, snacks. Excellent espresso as only the Italians know how to make it. Cool ambiance, with an arty, neo-hippie feel.

🍸 **Juice Bar**: 1807 Euclid Avenue. ☎ 540-8865. Fax: 540-8090. Open 7am–7pm (6pm Friday and Saturday). Bar combining brick decor and pretty engravings. Quite smart. Wide choice of coffees and smoothies, a typically Californian beverage (fruits and iced fruit juices with honey). Pastries, too.

🍸 **Triple Rock**: 1920 Shattuck Avenue (one minute from the intersection with University Avenue). ☎843-2739. Open 11am–1am daily. Every kind of beer, including the famous Red Rock, is all they serve, and much of the stuff is produced in the brewhouse that you can see from the bar. You can eat here, too (sandwiches, nachos, etc.). Customers are mainly students, as you might expect.

WHERE TO HEAR MUSIC IN BERKELEY

– **Blake's**: 2367 Telegraph Avenue. ☎ 848-0886. Restaurant open 11.30am–10pm (11pm Saturday, 9pm Sunday). Bar open to 1.30am, with billiard table and videos on a giant screen. You can eat here, too: snacks, salads, barbecue chicken, vegetarian lasagne, burgers, etc.

Setting warm and very colourful. Good blues programme starting at 9.30pm in a basement room.

WHAT TO SEE IN BERKELEY

★ **Berkeley Art Museum (BAM)**: 2626 Bancroft Way (another entrance at 2625 Durant Avenue). ☎ 642-0808. Website: www.bampfa.berkeley.edu. Open 11am–5pm. Closed Monday, Tuesday and public holidays. Admission charge. Free admission Thursday 11am–noon, 5–9pm. One of the most important university galleries in the world, with rich art collections that extend from the Renaissance to the 20th century. There are interesting exhibitions of contemporary art. On permanent display are works by Raymond Saunders, Sylvia Lark, Nancy Spero, Mark Rothko and Francis Bacon, as well as Joan Mitchell, Sam Francis, Richard Diebenkorn and Elmer Bishoff.

One extraordinary room contains a collection of work by Fernand Léger, Roberto Matta, Pierre Alechinsky, Asger Jorn, Tadeusz Kantor, René Magritte, Paul Klee, Henri Matisse, Joan Miró, Georges Rouault, Max Beckmann, George Grosz . . . and Pablo Picasso.

A room devoted to Hans Hofmann (1880–1966) contains many works by this inventive painter who expressed himself in blazing colour, sometimes in the style of Jackson Pollock.

The R. and R. Swig Gallery has another fine mixture, including works by Daumier and Boudin, and ink drawings by John Singer Sargent. Beautiful landscapes by Albert Bierstadt, a curious self-portrait by Joseph Ducreux, *Madonna and Child* by Titian, plus a remarkable *Road to Calvary* by Rubens and Renoir's *Sleeping Woman*.

✕ You can get refreshments at the **Cafe Grace**, a quiet little cafe with a sun-filled terrace and some seats in the museum's sculpture garden. Open 11am–4pm. Good cookies.

★ **Pacific Film Archive**: in the same building as the Berkeley Art Museum. Same hours and prices. Richly stocked film library with more than 7,000 titles, with thematic programmes. Information: ☎ 642-1124. At the entrance (on Durant Avenue) are petrified rocks that serve as armchairs. There's a free magazine, which contains details of the film programmes. The bookshop is open to the public.

★ **Phoebe Hearst Museum of Anthropology**: 103 Kroeber Hall, Bancroft Way and College Avenue. ☎ 642-7648. Open 10am–4.30pm (7pm Thursday). Closed Monday, Tuesday and public holidays. Low admission charge. A small museum, but one of great interest to any lover of ethnographic collections. A section is devoted to Ishi (the last of the Yahi tribe), with handicrafts, beautiful basketwork, Mojave pottery, jewellery, ornaments and toys. Some unusual items include a mummified crocodile, a ceremonial receptacle (of the Kwakiutl tribe) in the shape of an eagle, a royal lion from Dahomey, an Etruscan tomb, and much more.

★ **Lawrence Hall of Science**: Centennial Drive (under Grizzly Peak Boulevard, northeast of the campus). ☎ 642-5132. Open daily (except public holidays) 10am–5pm. Admission charge. A fascinating port-of-call if you have an interest in scientific museums. This one has all the best technological and pedagogical equipment.

★ **Museum of Paleontology**: 1101 Valley Life Sciences Building, near Oxford and University Avenue. ☎ 642-1821. Open Tuesday–Friday 8am–9pm. Free admission. One of the largest collections of fossils in North America. Among the treasures of the museum are the complete skeleton of a *Tyrannosaurus Rex*, impressive dinosaur skulls, a baby dinosaur and the world's oldest bird, the *archaeopteryx*. It's a pity that most of the collections are reserved for researchers. But the most spectacular items can be seen in the atrium.

★ **Tours of the campus** are available during the week (usually around 1pm). Information from the UC Campus Visitors' Center, at the entrance to the university on the Bancroft Way side. It is worth a visit if you've ever wondered what an American campus is like. In fact, it's like a city, with streets, parks, a stadium, swimming pools, tennis courts, museums, libraries – even a hospital. Nothing short of the ideal place to study, if you have the means. Students here pay $10,000–$15,000 per term!

If you walk around the campus, you may come across some astonishing characters, all well known to the students. There's Stancy the comedian (a hilarious political satirist), and a mad singer who thinks he's Frank Sinatra and has spent years singing every day in front of Sather Gate.

It's worth climbing up the Sather Tower on campus. It doesn't cost much and is worth doing (it closes at 3pm).

★ **People's Park**: Telegraph and Haste. A large militant fresco (somewhat the worse for wear) greets you in the street at the bottom of the park. It was here, on this legendary esplanade, that the big protest gatherings were held in the 1960s. Nothing much remains of the spirit of those times – just a few semi-abandoned kitchen gardens, and a few placards. It's now a refuge for the homeless and some student associations run soup kitchens here. The municipality, however, as well as a few promoters, have their eyes on this huge space right in the city centre, but they haven't dared to touch it yet for fear of reawakening the old demons. It should be said that, in spite of the apparent political apathy of the students and lecturers, many still appear to value this symbolic site. Recent threats to the People's Park provoked a great deal of interest.

★ **Berkeley Rose Garden**: on Euclid Avenue and Eunice Street. Open May–September. This floral park, located on the heights north of campus, displays hundreds of different rose species. From here there's also a magical panorama of the Bay, Marin County and the Golden Gate Bridge.

SHOPPING IN BERKELEY

Shakespeare and Co: 2499 Telegraph Avenue, on the corner of Dwight Way. ☎ 841 8916. Bookshop open daily, 10am–9.45pm. Offers over 100,000 used and remaindered volumes. Subjects include art, humanities and fiction titles.

Cody's: 2454 Telegraph Avenue. Open 10am–10pm (10.45pm Friday and Saturday). The biggest and best bookshop in Berkeley. Books in various languages upstairs.

Moe's Books: 2476 Telegraph Avenue, level with Dwight Way.

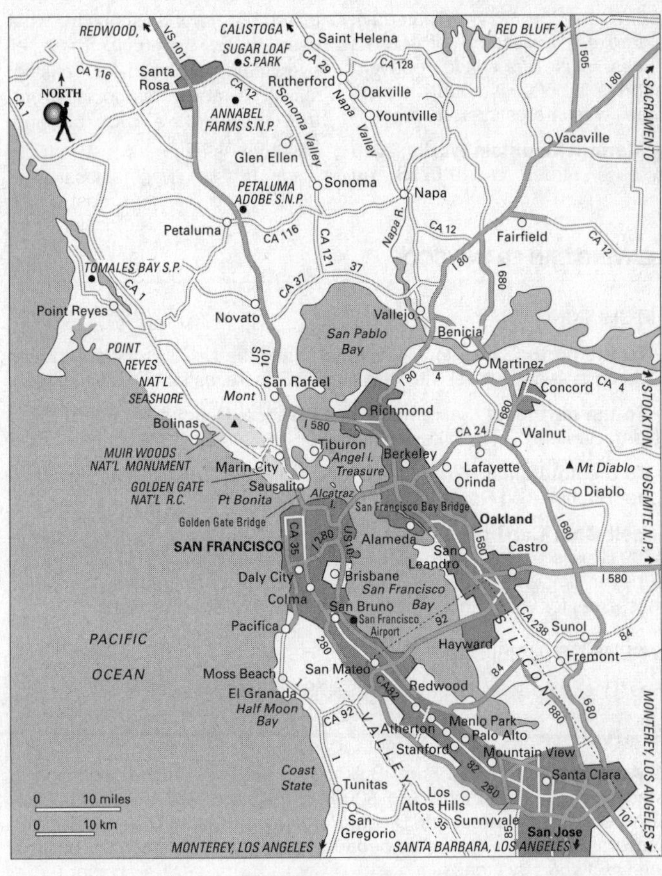

SAN FRANCISCO BAY

☎ 849-2087. Open daily, 10am–11pm (midnight Friday and Saturday). A bookshop where you just have to dive in. Four floors of new and second-hand books, with a section of rare books on the fourth floor.

Rasputin: 2401 Telegraph Avenue. Open daily, 10am–11pm. Enormous record shop (new and second-hand) that also sells videos. Great building with original architecture.

Collector's Realm: 2566 Telegraph Avenue. Here they sell everything for teenage collectors: posters, videos and a large stock of photos autographed by the stars.

International News: 2444 Durant Avenue. In a small shopping gallery, a big selection of newspapers and magazines in several languages.

Bill's Men's Shop: 2386 Telegraph (and Channing Way). ☎ 848-5636. Open 10am–6pm

(5pm Sunday, 8pm Thursday). Complete collection of Clarks shoes, plus Timberland footwear and the famous Frye boots, sometimes with interesting reductions.

Marmot Mountain Works: 3049 Adeline Street. ☎ 849-0735. An incredible sports shop in what used to be a church. They sell everything you need for trekking, skiing, climbing, camping – and they make their own clothing. Competent staff.

LEAVING SAN FRANCISCO

HITCHHIKING

– **To the north** (Sausalito, Wine Valley): take the No. 30 Stockton bus to Columbus Avenue, level with Washington Square, as far as Marina Green.

– **To the northeast** (Sacramento, Lake Tahoe, Reno): take the BART to 'North Berkeley'. Hitchhike on Route 80.

– **To the southeast** (Yosemite, Fresno): take the BART to the 'Hayward' stop. Hitchhike on Route 580, then Route 205.

– **Half-Cost Car-Pool Transit Systems**: 2720 Grove, Berkeley. ☎ 845-1769. This is an organization which, for the small sum of $10, will find you a driver or some passengers, help you with a drive-away car, take messages for you, and perform a whole heap of other services.

BY BUS OR (HIRE) CAR

See 'Useful Addresses' at the start of 'San Francisco'.

BY TRAIN

Amtrak (map II, D2): Ferry Building, in the port, at the beginning of Market Street. Freephone: ☎ 1-800-872-7245 or 1-800-USA-RAIL. Daily service to Los Angeles, San Diego, Portland and Seattle. Also to Merced (Yosemite), Fresno, etc. Three departures daily for Sacramento. The fares are OK if you buy a pass.

BY AIR

Bus Terminal for getting to the airport: corner of Ellis Street and Taylor Street, near Union Square. Departures every 15 minutes.

– Many of the shuttles to the airport will pick you up at your hotel. For a list of companies, *see* 'Useful Addresses'.

– **Door-to-Door Airport Express**: 865 Post Street. ☎ 775-5121. Every half-hour, 5.30am–10.30pm. Call 24 hours ahead to book.

BY DRIVE-AWAY CAR

– **Auto Drive-away Co.**: 350 Townsend Street. ☎ (567) 777-3740.

BY SECOND-HAND CAR

Many sales outlets in the area known as **Daly City**, on Mission Street (from No. 6600 up).

MUIR WOODS PARK

Muir Woods is a superb little nature park in the hollow of a valley close to the Pacific coast and about 18 miles (30km) north of San Francisco. It has a splendid forest of giant sequoias, some of which reach 230ft (70m). There's a small Visitors' Center at the entrance, and you now have to pay an admission charge, but it's not very much. A footpath allows you to take a stroll among these ancient trees.

A visit to this charming park can ideally be combined with a day on Muir Beach or Stinson Beach (both quite busy in summer) only a few miles away. One way to cover both things would be to leave San Francisco in the morning, walk in the park for an hour or two, then go off for a picnic on the beach of your choice.

A note about John Muir and the sequoias . . . A philosopher, humanist and an ecologist who was very much ahead of his time, John Muir had a strong interest in nature. When he left school he embarked on several lengthy journeys, allowing him to contemplate man's relationship with nature, and he concluded that all life forms are important in their own right, and all have an equal right to exist. He went on to gain public acceptance of environmental conservation and was the inspiration for generations of natural ecologists. Muir Woods were named after John Muir at the bequest of Congressman William Kent, who bought 245 acres of Redwood Creek within Muir Woods in 1905. In order to protect the land from the clearances that had begun to sweep through California, Kent donated it to the Federal Government, and in 1908 President Theodore Roosevelt declared it a national monument. Roosevelt suggested the area be named after William Kent, but Kent's nomination fell on Muir instead.

Despite Muir's efforts, there are now no more than one-twentieth of the sequoias still standing that were growing in his day. Demand is so strong, and the felling companies are so powerful, that ecologists are finding it extremely difficult to hold on to this particular piece of heritage. Demonstrators have reportedly chained themselves to trees as the lumberjacks arrive and sit-ins have been held high up amid the sequoia branches. This conflict is unlikely to be settled soon.

HOW TO GET THERE

You'll need a car to get there, as there's no public transport. The park is 12 miles (19km) to the north of the Golden Gate Bridge. Take Highway 101 north, exit at Mill Valley–Stinson Beach and follow the signs for Highway 1.

THE WINE ROUTE

North of San Francisco you enter Wine Country, which actually consists of two little valleys with a big reputation – Sonoma Valley and Napa Valley. There's great walking to be done round here, thanks to the huge diversity of the landscape. Wine-lovers, of course, will be fascinated by this area, as will those who've read any Jack London, who got his artistic inspiration living in this area.

You need to allow a full day for an excursion from San Francisco, and don't bother to go there at weekends as it gets very crowded. If you fancy staying overnight, you'll soon find that prices in the region are rather high. In fact, it's more for affluent travellers, especially ones with cars.

CALIFORNIAN WINE

Winemaking began in the region thanks to the vine-growing skills of the excitingly-named Agastón Harászthy, a Hungarian who moved to California from Wisconsin to establish a fruit farm back in 1849. Over the next few years he imported vine cuttings from Europe and planted them in Sonoma, Northern California and is generally regarded as the founding father of the Californian wine industry. Serious winemaking began in 1857 but the spread of a deadly root disease called phylloxera curtailed initial endeavours. The devastating root disease was finally banished, allowing wine production to flourish up until the 1990s, when it struck again, this time leading to the development of improved rootstocks and higher density vineyards. Today the USA is the fourth largest producer of wine in the world and California produces 90 per cent of all wine made in the United States. These so-called 'New World Wines' (along with their Australian, New Zealand, South American and South African cousins) are now regularly drunk throughout the world and their popularity is growing.

Those of you who fancy 'doing' the Californian wine route and stashing a few cases in the trunk of your Mustang convertible will find that vineyards stretch right down the coast through the central valley, reaching as far as Santa Barbara in the South. The largest producing region is the South Central Coast but the prestigious Napa Valley is at the centre of the wine industry in California, producing impressive Cabernets and Chardonnays, some of which fall into the class of the most expensive wines in the world. Dwarfing neighbouring Sonoma Valley, Napa is home to the greatest concentration of vineyards in California; its warm dry summers and cool wet winters providing the perfect environment for Chardonnay grapes (which are the leading white variety) and red wine varieties of grapes (notably Cabernet Sauvignon and Merlot). Wines made in the region are notorious for their high levels of alcohol (up to 15 per cent), which may come as a bit of a surprise if you are used to drinking French wine, so watch you don't overdo it!

Tastings are occasionally free in Napa, but more often than not there is a charge. You may also spot signs for swanky designer restaurants in the area, which offer upmarket environments in which to taste wines and sample the cuisine – all for a hefty price of course.

SONOMA

AREA CODE: 707

There's a twice-daily Greyhound service from San Francisco to Sonoma – a charming, peaceful little town in Mexican *pueblo* style. Think of a large square with an island of green in the centre (a bit like the one in the film

Back to the Future), and four streets that form the nerve centre of the city, with nice hotels, beautiful shops and lots of art galleries. All the places listed as worth visiting lie around this square, which has been superbly restored.

USEFUL ADDRESS

Visitors' Office: in the central square. ☎ 996-1090. Established in a little grey house that's squeezed in between the Hotel Toscano and the Cheese Factory. Open daily, October–April, 9am–5pm (7pm in summer). The staff are very knowledgeable. Free plan of the valley.

WHERE TO STAY

El Pueblo Inn: 896 West Napa Street. ☎ (707) 996-3651. Freephone: ☎ 1-800-900-8844. Five minutes from the centre on the road to Santa Rosa. This little motel is attractively built in timber and brick. There are 41 spacious rooms, with TV, phone and coffee-maker (just as well, as they don't serve breakfast). Super swimming pool. Not cheap for a motel, but the prices are still very fair for what you get.

Swiss Hotel: 18 West Spain Street, in the plaza, near the cheese shop. ☎ 938-2884. Five rooms, tastefully decorated and all different, with friezes, flowery bedspreads and antique furniture. Refrigerator, mosquito screen and ice-bucket in every room. Impeccable, luxurious bathrooms. No. 5, which is extremely spacious, has a fan and a terrace overlooking the square. Prices start at $110 including breakfast (more expensive on weekends). There's also a restaurant and a good bar: you can enjoy your pizza, pastries, etc. on a pretty veranda. Overall, a cosy, refined atmosphere.

Sonoma Hotel: 110 West Spain Street. ☎ (707) 996-2996. Freephone: ☎ 1-800-468-6016. On the corner of the square. There are 17 charming late-19th-century rooms on two floors. The family suites are on the second floor – all flowery and furnished in the old-fashioned way, and all with bathrooms. The third floor has mostly washbasins in the rooms and communal bathrooms on the landing. The decor's positively rococo. The welcome here is warm. Prices are about the same as for the Swiss Hotel and they even have a half-bottle of wine waiting for you in your room! There's a restaurant, plus concerts on Friday and Saturday evenings.

WHERE TO EAT

Basque Cafe: 460 First Street East. ☎ (707) 935-7687. Open daily, 7am–6pm. Good bakery with homemade bread and a wide choice of excellent pastries: cookies, muffins, cinnamon rolls, cakes and even croissants. Some tables outside, facing the square. Ideal for having a small lunch or snack – a Basque omelette (with potatoes) for example. There's also a dish of the day, savoury tarts and salads.

The Coffee Garden: 415 and 421 First Street West. ☎ (707) 996-6645. Open Sunday–Thursday 7am–9pm (10pm Friday and Saturday). A little shop, a little cafe, and a superb flower-filled patio with a fountain and a honeysuckle-covered arbour right at the back. This is a real oasis of freshness where you can enjoy a sandwich or a small salad.

✕ **Sonoma Cheese Factory**: 2 Spain Street. ☎ (707) 996-1931. Open every day 8.30am–6pm (7pm on weekends). Large grocery store, heavily frequented by locals. Here you can taste pure Californian cheese, made on the spot, with a choice that includes such things as onion, chilli and hot pepper. To try a sample, you just open up the plastic boxes provided. At the back of the shop, a large window gives you a glimpse of what's going on behind the scenes. They also sell wine, sausages, various salads, pastries, ice-creams and some cooked food. You can picnic at tables provided under a long arbour, or in the park just across the way, where there are wooden tables and you can walk on the grass.

WHAT TO SEE AND DO

★ **San Francisco Solano Mission**: this building was the last mission to be built in California and it's now a museum. An exhibition of watercolours shows the various missions around the state, although the outside is probably more interesting than the interior.

★ **The miniature train**: at the south entrance to the city. So-so: not a lot to see because there aren't many houses built along the track.

★ **Cycling in the valley**: bike hire at the Sonoma Valley Cyclery. ☎ 935-3377. Open daily, 10am–6pm (4pm Sunday). There's a good choice: tandems, mountain bikes, etc.

GLEN ELLEN

AREA CODE: 707

A little village located a few miles north of Sonoma. Its main interest (and quite a major one) is that Jack London stayed here for a while. Don't miss a visit to the Jack London State Historic Park.

From San Francisco, take the Golden Gate Bridge going north and follow Highway 101. Shortly after the Ignacio exit (which you don't take), take Highway 37 and then, after a few miles, Highway 121 on the left. This will take you to Sonoma via Highway 12. Glen Ellen is a little further to the north.

Useful as a place to stop for the night or to have a meal, although it can be quite expensive. It's amusing to see the most insignificant hotels and restaurants taking advantage of the great writer's name!

WHERE TO STAY

☗ **Jack London Lodge**: 13740 Arnold Drive (just before the entrance to the park, on the right). ☎ 938-8510. If you fancy spending some time in this area, this motel has 22 rooms on two levels. The rooms are large and pleasant and have TV. The river runs very close by and there's a small swimming pool. Prices are fair: $50 on average, $75 in summer.

☆☆☆☆ SPLASH OUT

Gaige House Inn: 13540 Arnold Drive. ☎ 935-0237. Fax: 935-6411. Freephone: ☎ 1-800-935-0237. At the Glen Ellen exit, shortly after the Glen Ellen Inn, on the left. A charming place: in a superb 19th-century house, entirely modernized, there are eight very comfortable guest rooms, with impeccable decor. For honeymoon couples there's the luxurious Gaige Suite, which has an immense four-poster bed draped in white lace, superb paintings and a gigantic blue bathroom with a jacuzzi. The three cheapest rooms are on the ground floor, looking out over the swimming pool. But it'll cost you: they charge $135–200, depending on the season, breakfast included. The price of the suite isn't worth talking about!

WHERE TO EAT AND WHERE TO HAVE A DRINK

Jack London Saloon: Arnold Drive, near the Jack London Lodge. This brick-built house, dating from 1905, reveals a Wild West-style saloon, with a large, comfortable main room and a clientele of regulars. As you would expect, Jack London features prominently on the walls. There are also a few concessions to the modern world: fans, a billiard table and a giant screen where you can watch baseball games. Whisky lovers will find a wide choice. Food at the bar.

Glen Ellen Inn: 13670 Arnold Drive. ☎ (707) 996-6409. Open Tuesday–Friday 11.30am–2.30pm, and 5.30–9.30pm; Saturday and Sunday 5.30–9.30pm. A delightful little restaurant run by a charming young couple; the place consists of a main dining room and a terrace. Good, inventive dishes (lobster ravioli and Californian jambalaya, for example) and everything's very fresh. Not the cheapest place going, but they take good care of you and the welcome is great.

WHAT TO SEE

★ JACK LONDON STATE HISTORIC PARK

Access via London Ranch Road. Signposted from Glen Ellen. Not far from the centre. Entry to the park costs $6 per car. Buy a map of the park at the reception office. Museum open daily, 10am–5pm (park closes 7pm). Closed Christmas, Thanksgiving and New Year's Day.

It was in the Valley of the Moon that Jack London, one of America's greatest writers, chose to settle down. Finding a spot surrounded by superb hills and in a serene setting, he took the decision in 1905, at the age of 29, to set down his pack right here. He wrote to his friends: 'I am really going to throw out an anchor so big and so heavy that all hell could never get it up again.' The former adventurer, gold prospector, fisherman and journalist now wanted to be a farmer. He had a huge residence built – a kind of ranch-house made of great blocks of lava, a combination of enormous uncut rocks and timber. In August 1913, just before he and his wife were to take up residence at Wolf House, as he named it, the whole place burned to the ground. London had sunk his entire fortune into the house and it was not covered by insurance. Sadly, he didn't have time to rebuild the house, as he died on 22 November 1916. The successful author of *The Call of the Wild, White Fang* and *The Valley of the Moon* . lived to the age of just 40 years.

Created in 1959, this beautiful park houses a museum dedicated to London, as well as the ruins of his house and his tomb. There are plenty of footpaths allowing many walks. Not far from the house is the timber cottage that he lived in for several years, and some farm buildings.

Apart from the many souvenirs connected with the writer, the park is also a place that offers lots of different excursions into the wild.

★ **The museum**: open daily, 10am–5pm. Located in the house built by London's wife Charmian in 1919 in memory of her husband and where she lived until her own death. Smaller than the house that burned down, but in the same style, this is now a museum displaying many of the writer's personal belongings.

In the museum are photographs, a model of his boat, the *Snark* (on which he and his wife visited the islands of the Pacific), souvenirs from the Solomon Islands, original furniture, and a reconstruction of his office complete with his portable typewriter, a Dictaphone, shellfish, a paddle, and so on. One of the showcases displays a letter of rejection of one of his early manuscripts! There's a short, touching, silent film show that was made just six days before his death, in which the writer is seen playing with some piglets. An exhibition contains some of his books, which were translated into as many as 29 different languages. Upstairs is a reconstruction of his bedroom and a superb collection of lances, as well as a map of the world marked up with his long journeys. There are plenty of other items on display, including documents showing the development of the writer's socialist thinking.

★ **The ruins of Wolf House**: along a little path, about a mile from the museum (the walk there and back takes about an hour). Of this imposing ranch-house, hidden in a grove of sequoias, there now remain only the high stone walls, but you can still visualize the layout of the rooms. At the top of the staircase that leads up to a timber gallery, you can inspect the original plans of the house as designed by London, in which it is clear that he intended his bedroom to be located in a tower.

★ **The tomb**: a few hundred yards from his former house, on a little hill. A simple monument, whose only feature is a large block of stone taken from the ruins of his home.

★ **The cottage**: follow the map for directions. It was here, from 1911 until his death, that Jack London wrote his most famous novels. This rather modest little timber house is therefore a more realistic part of the writer's existence than the legendary Wolf House, where he never actually lived. Unfortunately, it isn't open to visitors.

Around the cottage there are barns, an old distillery and a stable. There's a picnic area above the parking lot.

– **Jack London Bookstore**: 14300 Arnold Drive. ☎ (707) 996-28-88. Open 10.30am–5pm (closed Tuesday). At the entrance to Glen Ellen, on the left if you're coming from Sonoma. A bookshop from another age, which has been run for over 20 years by some rather quaint Jack London enthusiasts. The shop has first editions, manuscripts, photos, works in various languages, and posters. This is also a research centre.

WHAT TO SEE NEARBY

★ **Petrified Forest**: 17 miles (27km) from Glen Ellen, on the road to Calistoga, a group of fallen sequoias that were petrified by a flow of lava. A little disappointing. Just before you get to Calistoga, there's a geyser that erupts every 7–15 minutes.

NAPA VALLEY

The Napa Valley lies to the east of Sonoma Valley. The estates in the Napa Valley between Napa and Calistoga stretch for more than 30 miles (50km) along Highway 29. Less wild and less beautiful than Sonoma, this valley is mostly given over to wine production. To some extent, this region is to California what the Bordeaux area is to France. But it's as well to note that you aren't surrounded by philanthropists here: the big houses and the winery buildings battle to outdo each other – in a frenzy of luxury that seems like madness. Some growers have no qualms about spending a real fortune on their 'baby', as Robert Mondavi famously did with his Opus One.

Don't visit Napa Valley on a Sunday in July or August – there are far too many people.

Did you know?
It seems that the French champagne producers Moët et Chandon, probably alarmed by what they see as competition from American winegrowers, have bought some land in the Napa Valley. There, they produce a wine known as *Domaine Chandon* using the traditional 'champagne method'. Champagne-drinkers won't be disappointed: it has plenty of nose, but is less full than real (i.e. French) champagne. Still, it makes an interesting comparison.

Did you know?
The **Beaulieu** winery was one of the few in this region to be allowed to continue producing wine during the Prohibition era. The proprietor (a Frenchman of course) managed to convince the authorities that his product was needed for the celebration of Holy Mass . . .

USEFUL ADDRESS

🅸 **Visitors' Information**: Napa town centre. Well signed from the entrance to the city. ☎ 226-7459. Open 9am–5pm. Lots of information. Get a copy of the free newspaper, *Inside Napa Valley*, which is very practical, with a map of the region and a complete list of the wineries.

THE VINEYARDS

– **Robert Mondavi**: 7801 St Helena Highway, Oakville (on the road to Rutherford). ☎ (707) 226-1335. Open 10am–4.30pm. Tours of the cellars and vineyards, and tastings: in theory you have to book. Well known for his Opus One, but also his Cabernet Sauvignon and his Pinot Noir (the 1990 was excellent). Also owns Vichon, between Yountville and Oakville, on the left.

– **Clos Pegase**: 1060 Dunaweal Lane (on the right, just before you get to Calistoga). ☎ (707) 942-4981. Open 10.30am–5pm. Some very good wines, but you have to pay to get a taste.

– **Newlan Vineyards**: 5225 Solano Avenue (halfway between Napa and Yountville, on the left). ☎ (707) 257-2399. Open 10am–5pm. Has been awarded several gold medals for its Pinot Noir. You have to pay for a taste, but then they give you the glass!

– **Beaulieu Vineyards**: 1960 St Helena Highway (in the vicinity of Rutherford). ☎ (707) 967-5230. Open daily, 10am–5pm. You are welcomed with a glass of wine at the entrance. The visit and the tasting are free!

– **Domaine Chandon**: 1 California Drive, at the entrance to Yountville (on the left when you're coming from Napa). ☎ 944-2280. Offers tours and tasting sessions. Admission charge.

WHERE TO STAY

☗ **Tall Timber Chalets**: 1012 Darms Lane. To the west of Highway 29, just before you get to Yountville. ☎ (707) 252-7810. Fax: 252-1055. Eight pretty and very comfortable chalets that can accommodate four persons (two in a fold-out bed) in a nice environment surrounded by vineyards. Each has a fitted kitchen, with champagne in the fridge! Ask for the chalet with a veranda, which has a swing-seat for candlelit dinners! Costs about $105 a day (it goes up to $150 on weekends). Best to come in winter, when the prices fall to $75. Included is a map of the valley showing the location of every winery (Newlan is quite nearby). Information is also available from the Adelaide Inn (☎ 441-2261) in San Francisco, run by the proprietor's husband.

☗ **Napa Valley Railway Inn**: 6503 Washington Street, Yountville. ☎ (707) 944-2000. Behind the Overland Sheepskin Co. shop. Very poorly signed, this deluxe hotel looks nothing like a hotel! In fact, it is a 'railway inn' with six rooms, established in a train that has been disused since the end of the 19th century. The 'rooms' are practically suites (one per coach) with every convenience and a drawing-room area. The rooms aren't all that spacious (it is a train, after all) but the furniture is of the period, with brass bedsteads. Expect to pay a bit over $100 per night. Note that practically the whole village of Yountville is a very successful shopping centre.

BODEGA BAY

AREA CODE: 707

Right at the edge of the ocean, 50 miles (80km) north of San Francisco, taking Highway 101 north and then Highway 1. If you arrive at Bodega Bay by night, you might think you've come to the end of the world, because this little fishing village is a sleepy place, often shrouded by fog. But when the fog lifts, you can see that the natural environment here is superb. It is quite unspoiled, with sand dunes, cliffs overlooking the sea, coves, wild flowers and birds of prey. Built around a bay, the village is really pretty, with its little port and old-style houses.

This is an ideal place for the travel-weary to recover, or if you've had enough of big cities. The ecologically minded executive natives of California love to come and relax at Bodega Bay, because it has so many different sporting activities on offer, including fishing and surfing. There are several beaches and you can even go whale-watching just a few miles away. You'll need some warm clothing, as the evenings are quite chilly. Note that the hotels are often fully booked on weekends and during holiday periods.

Bodega Bay is also a legendary place for movie buffs: this is where Hitchcock filmed *The Birds*. The house that featured in the film lasted well for a time, but the great director's many souvenir-hunting fanatical followers chipped away pieces of the building and it finally had to be demolished.

USEFUL ADDRESS

Visitors' Center: Bodega Bay Area Chambers of Commerce, 850 Coast Highway 1. At the entrance to the city, near the Unceal 76 service station. ☎ 875-3422. Freephone: ☎1-800-905-9050. Plenty of info. When the building is closed, you can get a map of the city, which gives useful addresses including hotels and restaurants, from a box outside.

WHERE TO STAY AND WHERE TO EAT

There are only about 20 places to choose from where you can stay, ranging from a motel B&B to a deluxe inn, a cottage and a house for rent. The problem is that everything is quickly booked up, and the prices reflect this. There are quite a few good restaurants where you can try the seafood that has given Bodega Bay its reputation. Note that they don't stay open far into the evening.

WHERE TO STAY

Campgrounds: there are several of these, located in the nature parks around the bay. Information on them is obtainable at the Visitors' Center. The setting is delightfully wild – actually it's even a bit on the windy side. Take a good coat and a warm sleeping bag. The campgrounds are inevitably pretty full in summer and at weekends. Supermarket 10 minutes away.

Bodega Harbor Inn: 1345 Bodega Avenue. ☎ 875-3594. A

charming, old-fashioned little inn. These are the cheapest rooms in Bodega Bay, at around $50. For twice that price you can have a room with a fireplace, kitchen, jacuzzi – and view of the bay.

☗ **Valley Ford Hotel**: 14415 Coast Highway 1, Valley Ford. ☎ (707) 876-3600. Freephone: ☎ 1-800-696-6679. Fax: 876-3603. Located 7.5 miles (12km) from Bodega Bay in a beautiful setting. An elegant residence dating from 1864, with characterful rooms costing around $100 (more at weekends). There's a large garden and a Basque-style restaurant. Breakfast is included in the price. Note that house rules are 'no smoking' and 'no young children'.

WHERE TO EAT

✕ **The Sandpiper**: at the port. ☎ 875-2278. Open daily, 7am–8.30pm. A modest inn, cheap for the area and in an ideal location. Big, friendly dining room and a menu for all budgets, offering breakfast, sandwiches, burgers, soup and salads. Especially renowned for its seafood dishes and fish from the Pacific, including red snapper, halibut and sole.

✕ **The Inn at the Tides**: 800 Coast Highway. ☎ 875-2751. Deluxe hotel, but the restaurant is especially recommended (if you can afford it) for its view of the bay, elegant setting and excellent cuisine. Local specialities, based on fish and seafood, are well prepared. Dinner by candlelight – the service is perfect. The clientele is very smart, as you might expect.

SILICON VALLEY

A lot of places try to imitate the Valley, but none of them has ever made it.

Marc Andreessen, *founder and chairman of Netscape*

The road maps almost never show it, and guidebooks rarely mention it – but Silicon Valley, 50 miles (80km) long and 6 miles (10km) wide is no mirage but a genuine economic miracle – and a Mecca for any traveller who is intoxicated by high technology. It's hardly a valley, either – more of an extended plain between San Francisco in the north, the famous bay to the east, San Jose in the south and a chain of hills to the west looking every bit like the hills you've seen in the movies. Beyond this lies the Pacific Ocean.

Who, in the post-war years, could have imagined that within 40 years this rustic hinterland of prairies and orchards would become the cradle, heart, brains and engine of the American electronics and computing industry? Today, thanks to the 7,000 or so companies that have been established here, this part of California, its name now legendary, is chalking up the highest rate of economic growth in the US and probably the world. Like the Seven Wonders of the Ancient World, or the Valley of the Kings in ancient Egypt, Silicon Valley is already set to become a third-millennium landmark.

Where did the name come from? In case you were in any doubt, it has nothing to do with the 'silicone' that's used in breast implants, but derives from the word 'silicon', which is a non-metallic element derived from sand. This is the base material used in the manufacture of microprocessors or 'chips', which are among the chief products of the electronics industry in this valley.

WHAT DOES SILICON VALLEY LOOK LIKE?

Seen from an aeroplane, this crucible of revolutionary world technology doesn't look anything like the endless, deadly dull, grey concrete industrial estate that you would imagine – quite the opposite, in fact. More than anything else, it resembles a pleasant Mediterranean landscape, complete with eucalyptus and cypress groves, parks and gardens, red roof-tiles and a bright blue sky, into which some mischievous giant has tipped the internal components of a transistor radio. These are the company buildings and research laboratories, of every shape and colour, and they stretch out as far as the eye can see.

From San Francisco Airport to San Jose, Highway 101 passes through some 30 small towns (San Mateo, San Carlos, Palo Alto, Menlo Park, Cupertino, Sunnyvale, Santa Clara, and so on) but the same unchanging vista stretches out along both sides of the road, where glass-and-steel buildings house a myriad of these research and development laboratories. Not one building is more than three storeys high and each is surrounded by plenty of space and all manner of greenery. Overall, it's a strange blend of science park and industrial estate.

Twenty per cent of the world's Top 100 high-tech companies are located in Silicon Valley, including Apple and Hewlett-Packard (computers), Intel (microprocessors), Sun Microsystems, Netscape (software), Cisco Systems – and many that are less famous. There are also hundreds of other companies, even some foreign firms such as the Japanese firm Sony and Acer, from Taiwan, all attracted to this location by the Californian goose that lays the golden eggs.

HOW DOES IT WORK?

First, there's Stanford University, renowned the world over for the quality of its teaching, particularly in the domain of electronics and computing. It acts as a brain-powered breeding ground, a hothouse–incubator for ideas and concepts. Most of the young geniuses who are now responsible for the prosperity of the valley's firms were raised and still are raised on this immense and wealthy campus. Examples include Messrs Hewlett and Packard. These two, when they were still at college, made a brilliant discovery in a garage in Palo Alto (*see* 'Palo Alto') and set up their electronics company right then and there.

Several companies were set up around the campus thanks to a Stanford professor who encouraged young graduates to set up in the local area, instead of relocating to the East Coast. This had a snowball effect and hundreds of other companies went on to be created in proximity to the famous university until the sector found itself transformed into one

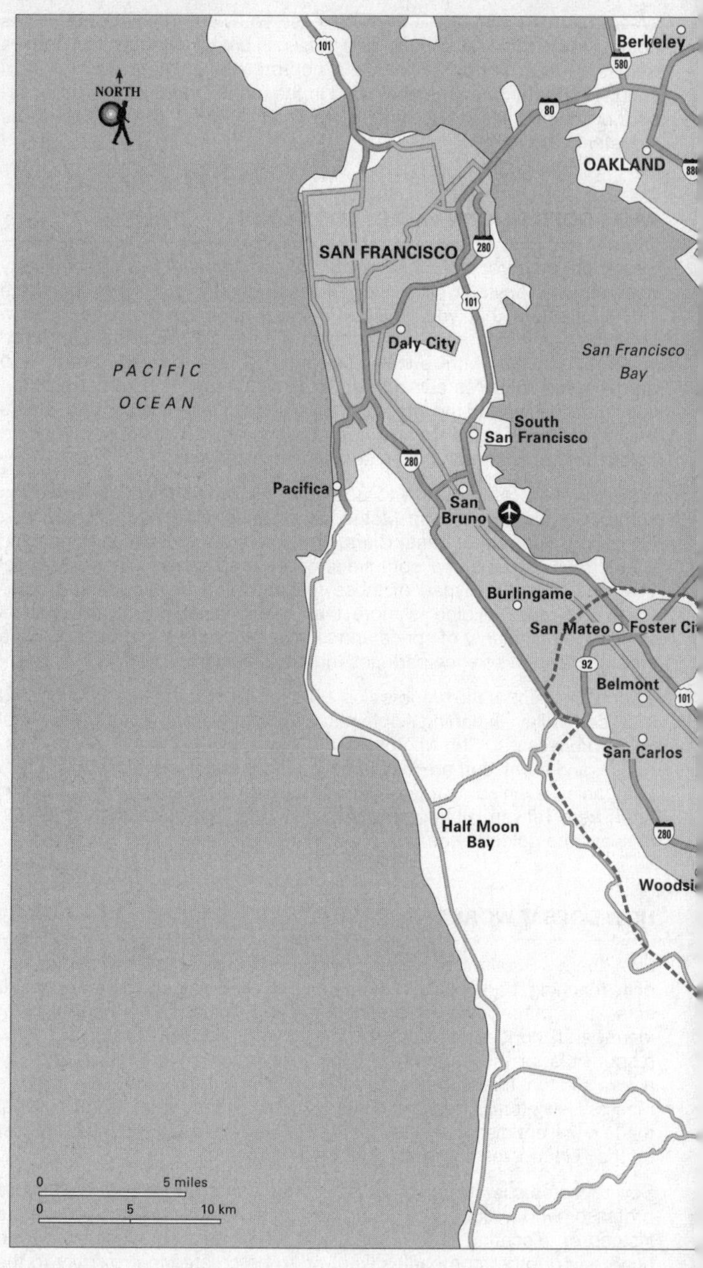
NORTH
101
Berkeley
580
80
OAKLAND
880
SAN FRANCISCO
280
101
Daly City
San Francisco
Bay
PACIFIC
OCEAN
South
San Francisco
280
Pacifica
San
Bruno
Burlingame
San Mateo
Foster Ci
92
Belmont
101
San Carlos
Half Moon
Bay
280
Woodsi
0
5 miles
0
5
10 km

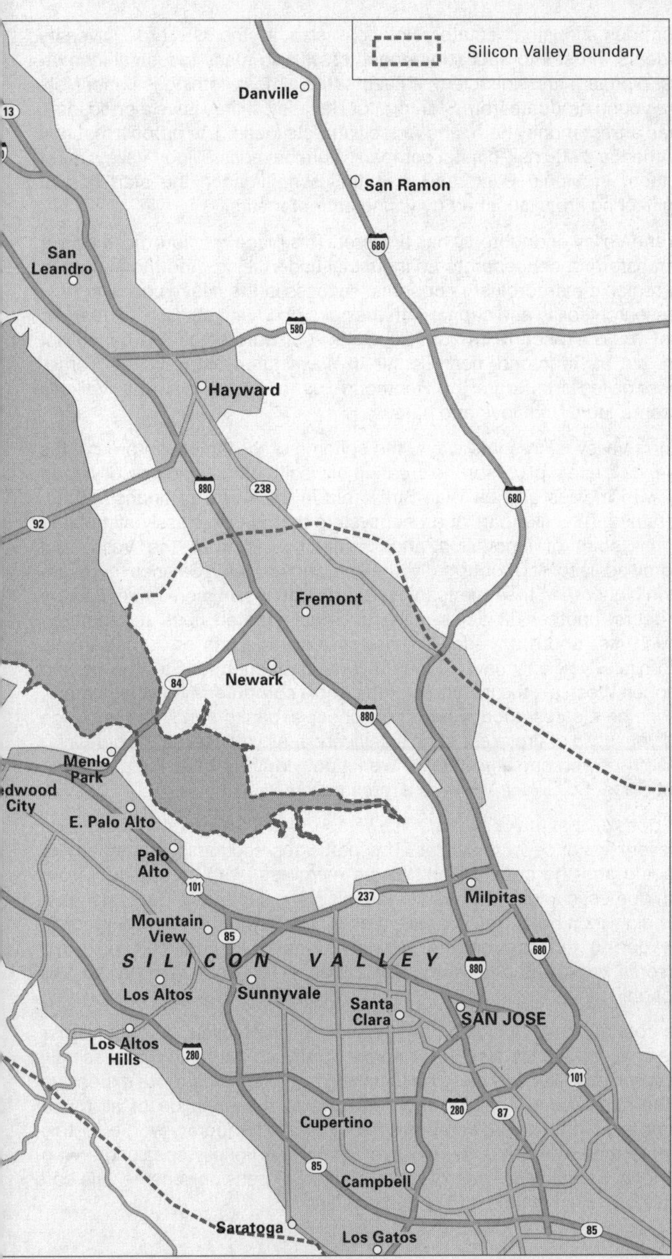

SILICON VALLEY

enormous industrial estate. Nowhere else in the US are university students thrust into such close contact with so many industrial innovators, pioneers and financiers. It seems that almost nothing is impossible for a young graduate from Stanford, or Berkeley, if they have a good idea. Ideas attract money here, and money attracts ideas. The proof is that half of America's 600 risk-capital companies are based in Silicon Valley, most of them in Menlo Park, and it is they who finance the start-ups of engineering firms launched by young entrepreneurs.

For the Valley undoubtedly has a secret. This place is unique in its power to transform a concept into an industrial undertaking. And the source of the region's extraordinary economic success is the heavy concentration of research ability and capital with the spirit of adventure. But, contrary to what you'd expect, Microsoft, Bill Gates' software empire, is based not here but at Redmond, near Seattle in Washington State. Gates, sometimes called the 'ogre of Redmond', is a figure that the Valley's entrepreneurs both love and hate.

Silicon Valley is, in some ways, the epitome of the American dream. It's America's latest place for the creation of wealth, benefiting as Hollywood did with movies and as Wall Street did in the world of finance. Here, everything runs like part of an ecosystem that is ceaselessly stimulated by the spirit of innovation and competition. And is the Valley the 'promised land'? Undoubtedly the answer is 'yes'. Salaries here are much higher than the American average and they rise more rapidly. Every 24 hours, another 62 dollar-millionaires are created here. It seems as though just about any idea created in a garage can be turned into a goldmine – you only have to look at what happened for Steve Jobs and Stephen Wozniak, the inventors of the Apple computer. And what's more, no one here cares about your ethnic or social background, and your age and your style of dress are of no significance. All you need is the right kind of brain-power, and if your mind works powerfully and fast, you're in the right place. So Silicon Valley is a meritocracy.

But does all that make it a paradise? Nope. There's a less salubrious side to every instance of success. The battle for economic supremacy is ongoing and the competition can be merciless, with competition from both domestic and Asian rivals – especially the Japanese. So, although a new high-tech company is created every five days (this is a US record), only one in ten manages to stay in business. In addition, you need personal energy and a Herculean capacity for work in order to win through.

The cost of living, including house prices and rent levels, is much higher here than anywhere else in California. Traffic is becoming increasingly heavy while space seems to be shrinking and becoming more expensive at the same time. That's before you get to the question of all those temporary staff. The area employs about 30,000 temporary workers – this is more than four times the US average, proportionally speaking – who are not covered by any sort of social security or pension scheme. Life can be difficult even in the Land of Opportunity.

PALO ALTO

AREA CODE: 415

The cradle and the heart of Silicon Valley is Palo Alto (56,000 inhabitants), just 30 miles (50km) south of San Francisco and 15 miles (24km) from San Jose. This beautiful and little-known city has ended up holding a US record – there's so much grey matter in harness here and so much energy and money invested in local high-tech enterprises, that people here earn the highest average annual family income for any city of more than 50,000 inhabitants. At the time of writing, that was in the region of $62,000 (about £38,000).

Laid out like a chessboard, spacious, green and with a provincial feel, the city stretches out between San Francisco Bay and a line of hills that remind you of the Mediterranean. Through the centre runs El Camino Real ('the royal road'), an expressway with a portentous name that marks out a sort of boundary between the city centre and the immense campus of Stanford University, the Valley's breeding-ground. This is where it all began.

On one side of the Camino Real, students pore over their books. On the other side, they live, eat, sleep and go out at night (when they have the time). And all around, in the factories and research and development labs, people are working hard, inventing the future of electronics and computing that will run the world of tomorrow. That sums up Palo Alto – and it makes a good base from which to explore Silicon Valley.

A few miles away is East Palo Alto, which is a far cry from its opulent neighbour.

A BRIEF (AND VERY RECENT) HISTORY

Apart from the century-old Stanford University, everything is new and everything happens very fast. They're already well into the third millennium here. But it's important to take a short trip into the past in order to understand a few things. From the outset, Palo Alto was the first city in Silicon Valley to get the benefit of the whirlwind of technological innovation that centred on Stanford during the 1940s. Its economic growth, like that of the whole valley, was broadly stimulated by the extraordinary concentration of capital, research and entrepreneurial spirit in this place. Many of the students and professors at Stanford live in Palo Alto. There's even a district called Professorville, which is now listed as an historic area.

David Packard and **William Hewlett** once lived in Palo Alto. In 1938, these two young Stanford graduates put together their first electronic audio oscillator in an old garage on Addison Avenue. This garage is now regarded as the birthplace of Silicon Valley (*see* 'What to See'). In the last 40 years, the Hewlett-Packard Company has become a giant in the highly competitive field of electronics – and their headquarters at Palo Alto now employs 5,000 people.

Steve Jobs and **Stephen Wozniak** worked at Hewlett-Packard in the early 1970s, meeting up at the city's Homebrew Computer Club, a rendezvous for computer buffs. In April 1976, these two unknowns invented the first microcomputer (the Apple I) in the garage of Jobs's parents, also in Palo Alto. This was the ancestor of the Macintosh. Nowadays, Apple headquarters are at Cupertino, but other firms, such as Digital Equipment, Varian, Sun Microsystems and the research and development laboratory of Xerox, are in Palo Alto.

USEFUL ADDRESSES

Chamber of Commerce (Tourist Office): 325 Forest Avenue. ☎ (415) 324-3121. Open Monday –Friday 9am–noon, 1–5pm.

– **City of Palo Alto** website: www.city.palo-alto.ca.us

WHERE TO STAY IN THE CITY

Most of the motels in Palo Alto are located on El Camino Real, the expressway that separates the city from the Stanford University campus. Coming from the city centre, turn left before the entrance to the campus and follow El Camino Real for a few miles towards San Jose. There are many motels along the road.

A motel room for two in Palo Alto costs an average of $60, including tax. There's nothing any cheaper.

National 9 Inn: 3339 El Camino Real. ☎ (415) 493-2521. Fax: 493-2747. Freephone: ☎ 1-800-524-9999. The cheapest motel in Palo Alto. Nothing out of the ordinary, but clean.

Mayflower Garden Motel: 3981 El Camino Real. ☎ (415) 493-4433. Fax: 493-1120. Around 40 very plain rooms, a little faded, with TV. Choose from rooms 130–140 for preference, as they're a little further away from the road.

Imperial Inn: 3945 El Camino Real. ☎ 493-3141. Fax: 493-3144. Freephone: ☎ 1-800-900-0524. Nothing very imperial here, but the place is decent. Motel run by Indians (from India), with about 60 pleasant and spacious rooms: thick carpet, TV, microwave, mini-fridge, kitchenette. Choose from rooms 127–130 or 227–230, which are the quietest. Continental breakfast.

Coronet Motel: 2455 El Camino Real, on the corner of Sherman Avenue. ☎ (650) 326-1081. The decor of the 22 rooms is a little old-fashioned but they're very spacious; although it's beside the road, the rooms are relatively well insulated against noise.

Hotel California: 2431 Ash Street. ☎ (415) 322-7666. Fax: (415) 321-7358. E-mail: desk@hotelcalifornia.com. Coming from Stanford via El Camino Real, four blocks before the Oregon Expressway, turn left on California Avenue. The hotel is located on the corner of the first street on the right (Ash Street). A charming little hotel of only modest size, with 20 smallish rooms, but all well kept and furnished with antique furniture. The meticulous decor reminds you of the interior of a B&B. There's a small courtyard where you can read in peace while sipping a drink. A place tucked away from the traffic, run by friendly people. About $70 for a room for two, breakfast included.

WHERE TO STAY IN THE SURROUNDING AREA

Hidden Villa (Los Altos Hills): Moody Road, in Los Altos Hills. ☎ 949-8648. Closed Monday. From Palo Alto, follow El Camino Real towards San Jose. In Los Altos, take El Monte Avenue going south and cross Interstate 280. Continue on El Monte. At Foothill College, take Altamont Road on the left and continue to the intersection with Moody Road. The youth hostel is approximately 1.5 miles (2.5km) beyond this intersection. Tucked away in a peaceful valley, surrounded by cultivated fields and woods, Hidden Villa is indeed a well-hidden farm – an oasis of peace that lives up to its name. They operate an organic farm here, but they don't take backpackers from June to the end of August as this period is reserved for groups of teenagers doing a training stint in the countryside. Accommodation in dormitories. The place is not accessible by public transport.

WHERE TO EAT

On University Avenue, Palo Alto's main street, are several simple and inexpensive places, in particular **Starbucks** (which serves delicious coffee), as well as some cafes and fast-food restaurants.

Peninsula Fountain & Grill: 566 Emerson Street, at the Hamilton intersection. ☎ (415) 323-3131. An old (1923!) cafe with jukebox, leatherette benches, fans and old-fashioned speakers and TV sets. It's clean and the service is efficient. Cafe cuisine: sandwiches, burgers, soup, salads. A good port-of-call for breakfast.

Miyake: 261 University Avenue. ☎ (415) 323-9449. Open daily, 11.30am–10pm. This Japanese restaurant is in a long, narrow room with, at the bar, an amusing arrangement of sushi-carrying boats. Be careful if you have a large appetite and are easily tempted: you'll be clobbered by the bill. There's a wide choice on the menu and overall it's good value.

WHAT TO SEE

★ **The birthplace of Silicon Valley**: 367 Addison Avenue. At the rear of the garden of this private house with wood-shingle walls there's a garage, now partly hidden by climbing plants with blue flowers. Two Stanford students, David Packard and William Hewlett, invented their first audio oscillator here in 1938, and that was the start of an industrial adventure that has transformed the valley in the last 60 years. A plaque on the front of the house proclaims it to be 'The Birthplace of Silicon Valley'.

A display tells about the important role played by Fred Terman, a professor of electrical engineering at Stanford. He encouraged the two students to create their electronics company in the Valley instead of moving to the East Coast to look for employment with existing companies. Terman, a truly visionary patron, even lent Hewlett and Packard $538 so that they could give it a try. Great inventions are often born in unexpected places! And since Steve Jobs and Stephen Wozniak also put together their first Apple microcomputer in a garage, it's clear that history loves to repeat itself.

★ **The Barbie Doll Hall of Fame**: 433 Waverly Street. ☎ (415) 326-5841. Open Tuesday–Saturday, 1.30–4.30pm; also Saturday morning, 10am–noon. This famous young lady probably needs no introduction. A place for true fans.

STANFORD UNIVERSITY

Looking at the red tiles under an azure sky, you have to remember that this isn't the Costa del Sol but Stanford University, 34 miles (56km) south of San Francisco at the exit from Palo Alto. This is probably the most beautiful campus in the US, if not the world. There's very little concrete – almost everything is built in real stone, a rich ochre in colour, in a style that reminds you of the Spanish-influenced missions in California that date from the time when the state was part of Mexico. It looks as though the founder was aiming at an immortal monument that tied in with its Hispanic heritage.

From the top of the Hoover Tower you get a superb view of this immense 100-year-old university, all nestling in greenery, and a distant glimpse of the little city of Palo Alto flanked by the last range of wild hills before you hit the Pacific. There's a host of buildings of every shape and size, set among eucalyptus groves and avenues of cypresses that create a really Mediterranean feel. The place is spacious, there's no graffiti, no cigarette ends lying around – everything is clean, functional and efficient. It's obvious that here they do everything to encourage highly intelligent people to work in the quest for excellence.

STANFORD – JUST THE OPPOSITE OF BERKELEY

Students in T-shirts go to class by bike, on skateboards or on roller-blades. As well as the 14,000 students (most of whom live in university accommodation), the university has 7,250 employees, so Stanford is run like a private enterprise and administered like a small city. The quality of life has always been extremely good because the campus is twice the size of Berkeley's while catering for only half the number of students. In spring and summer, lessons are often given outside and, if you walk towards the classroom behind the 'quad', you may find students sitting on the grass around their teacher, just as they did in ancient Greece at the time of Aristotle.

Another big difference, of course, is that Stanford is a private establishment, whereas Berkeley is publicly funded. The cost of study is among the highest in the US, not to mention the world, with fees set at approximately $21,000 (around £14,000) a year. Without very affluent parents or a sizeable scholarship, studying at Stanford is not an option.

A BIT OF HISTORY

It all began with the death of a 15-year-old boy, Leland Stanford Junior, who died on 13 March 1884, carried off by typhoid fever while travelling in Europe. For his parents this was a terrible tragedy, all the more so since they had had to wait 18 years before Leland came along. Stanford Senior had been Governor of California and he had amassed a considerable fortune during the Gold Rush. A natural philanthropist, he declined to spend his life in bitter regret but instead used his millions to invest in the future and in the young people of California. 'California's children shall be our children', he declared. So Stanford bought a huge estate of 8,085 acres (3,272ha) – the Palo Alto Stock Farm.

In 1891 it became the site of Stanford University, an establishment that was to be considerably in advance of the ideas of its day. It was co-educational at a time when most private universities were reserved for men only, and it was a lay establishment when most others were supported by the churches. The university's original aim has been maintained: 'to produce cultivated citizens, useful to society'. Stanford is generally regarded as a breeding ground for the American elite.

And it was at Stanford, in 1969 (soon after the Woodstock festival and the American moon landing), that the first historic **Internet** link was established between computers respectively located at the University of California at Los Angeles (UCLA) and the Stanford Research Institute. The experimenting teams who found themselves able to chat through the intermediary of machines were every bit as excited as those first moon-walkers.

SOME STANFORD CELEBRITIES

THE PROFESSORS

Twelve Nobel Prize-winners (mostly in the fields of physics, chemistry and economics) and four Pulitzer Prize-winners currently teach at Stanford. In addition, another 194 professors are members of the prestigious American Academy of Arts and Sciences. If it were necessary, these statistics give some idea of the calibre of Stanford's teaching staff.

THE STUDENTS (PAST AND PRESENT)

More than 300 high-technology enterprises based in Silicon Valley have been set up and are now run by former Stanford students, such as **Scott MacNealy**, president of Sun Microsystems, **John Chambers** of Cisco Systems, **Marc Andreessen** of Netscape and **Eric A. Benhamou**, President of 3Com.

But Stanford doesn't just produce good mathematicians. Olympic athletes, politicians, writers and artists have also studied there, including the actress **Sigourney Weaver**. **Chelsea Clinton**, always escorted by her bodyguards, is undoubtedly the most closely monitored student in the history of the campus! Surprisingly, and contrary to popular belief, Microsoft's Bill Gates didn't study at Stanford.

USEFUL ADDRESSES

🛈 **Visitors' Information Center**: on the left, on Galvez Street, opposite the Ford Center, just after the intersection of Galvez and Memorial Way. Also quite close to the visitors' parking lot on Memorial Way). ☎ 723-25-60. Not to be confused with the Stanford Information Center, which is an information centre for students. In summer, the Visitors' Information Center consists of a piece of wood laid out on a pair of trestles out in the open air in the shade of the trees, in front of the Ford Center. Here you'll find information, a map of the campus and a detailed guide for visitors on foot.

– **Guided visits to the campus**: daily, 11am and 3.15pm (it's free and no booking is necessary). Details from the Visitors' Information Center.

– **Stanford visitors' website**: www.stanford.edu/home/visitors/ provides links to other websites internal to the university.

WHERE TO EAT AND WHERE TO HAVE A DRINK

✕ **Bon Appetit**: a very large cafe located in the Tressider Union building in the middle of Stanford campus, with large terraces that are crowded whenever the weather's fine. There's a nicely varied buffet, plus salads, soup, sandwiches and coffee. Good value.

WHAT TO SEE

★ **The Quad**: located behind the main courtyard (The Oval) and at the foot of the Hoover Tower. This is the heart of the campus, consisting of a dozen buildings fringed by Spanish-style arcades, dating back to the university's foundation.

★ **The Hoover Tower**: open to the public daily, 10am–4.30pm, except during the end-of-year examinations and on some public holidays. It's a sort of large campanile, 280ft (85m) high, which houses, on the ground floor, the library of the Hoover Institute. Admission charge. Take a lift to the top, where you get a 360° view of the campus and part of Silicon Valley. Coins thrown by superstitious visitors (there are more of them than you might think!) can be seen under the clock in the middle of the platform.

★ **Rodin Sculpture Garden**: there are several original sculptures by Rodin on Lomita Drive (access via Campus Drive West), near Stanford Museum. The famous replica of *The Thinker* stands in the centre of the campus in front of the Meyer Library, as an inspiration for study and reflection.

★ **Memorial Church**: built by Jane Lathrop Stanford as a memorial to her husband, who died in 1893. Inside, there's an organ with no fewer than 7,777 pipes.

– **Graduation ceremony**: if you ever find yourself at Stanford around mid-June, don't miss the graduation ceremony, which attracts more than 20,000 people every year. You'll be able to watch a procession of some 4,000 young graduates dressed in black gowns and mortar-boards, in the purest American tradition.

FROM SAN FRANCISCO TO LOS ANGELES VIA THE COASTAL ROUTE

If you travel from San Francisco to Los Angeles by road, you have a choice between the famous Highway 1, the faster route that takes you inland, or the Coast Road, which is a series of pretty curves that crosses an area of magnificent cliffs. It is possible to cover most of this distance by bus, but the ideal thing is to go by car. Hitching a ride isn't too easy and to try it, you need to have plenty of time to spare, as the road is anything but direct.

SAN JOSE

AREA CODE: 408

A city of 835,000 inhabitants (more than San Francisco) and about 44 miles (70km) south of San Francisco, San Jose is the official capital of Silicon Valley. In reality, this large, flat and octopus-like conglomeration at the bottom of San Francisco Bay, is nearer to being the start – or finish (depending on which way you're facing) of the famous valley of technology. This city has developed at a phenomenal speed, driven on by the region's explosive economic expansion. Don't miss the astonishing Winchester Mystery House.

HOW TO GET THERE

BY CAR

From San Francisco, take Freeway I-280 south. This road, which is slightly longer than Highway 101, is generally faster. Leave at San Jose–17th Street or Stevens Creeks Boulevard. Bear in mind that the high volume of traffic means that the trip by car from San Francisco takes approximately 1 hour 30 minutes.

BY TRAIN

Take the Cal Train. ☎ 1-800-660-4287. The fastest link between San Francisco and San Jose. Journey time is 1 hour 20 minutes. About 40 departures daily, one every 15 minutes. The San Jose station for the Cal Train is at 65 Cahill Street, just south of The Alameda.

WHERE TO STAY

– There are few hotels in San Jose city centre, and these are expensive. You have to leave the city to find more practical prices.

– Motels charging sensible prices are along The Alameda, between the city centre and the University of Santa Clara. To get there, take Santa Clara Street going west. This street later becomes The Alameda.

AROUND SAN JOSE

Sanborn Park Hostel: 1508 Sanborn Road. ☎ (408) 741-0166. Call before you go to check on their opening hours. From San Jose, take Saratoga Avenue for about 11 miles (18km). From the village of Saratoga, continue for 2.5 miles (1.5km) and you'll find yourself right in the middle of the forest at an intersection. Just before a little bridge on this curve, turn left (onto Sanborn Road) and continue for 1.25 miles (2km), then follow the 'Hostel' sign on the right. Nature-lovers won't want to miss this stopover, which is a favourite place for backpackers who love the natural environment. It's a really exceptional spot, right in the middle of the forest, with sequoias all around.

The house is magnificent – built entirely from logs, it holds up to 39 people. Built in 1908 and once a judge's residence, it looked as if it had come straight out of the film *Judge Roy Bean*. Yet only 15 years ago it was on its way to becoming a ruin. Then, thanks to the tenacity of a lady named Sylvia, it was saved from destruction by becoming listed and was turned into a youth hostel. All this was worth the effort: the interior is beautiful – timber throughout, and a superb staircase with treads made from split logs. There's a volleyball pitch, a table-tennis table and, of course, nature paths for walkers. You cook your own food (kitchen equipment is provided), but remember to take supplies with you: the nearest shop isn't very close. Good prices and a very warm welcome.

WHERE TO HAVE A DRINK AND WHERE TO EAT

☆☆ MODERATE

The Pavilion: 150 South First Street. ☎ (408) 286-2076. San Jose Live: ☎ (408) 294-5483. Right in the centre, not far from Gordon Biersch, this is a complex that includes a cinema, five clubs or discos and a sports bar the size of a landing-strip.

Gordon Biersch Brewery Restaurant: 33 E. San Fernando Street. ☎ (408) 294-6785. Open seven days a week, lunch and dinner. Right in the city centre, a huge restaurant-brasserie with an interior courtyard with brick walls. The atmosphere on summer evenings is great. Clientele tends to be young and trendy. The ambiance is one of Silicon Valley residents out relaxing after a day's work. Light dishes are served at lunchtime: pizza, satay, sandwiches and salads. In the evening what's on offer is more elaborate. Service is efficient and the welcome is good. They serve excellent home-brewed German-style beers. Live music (jazz and R'n'B) from April to September.

WHAT TO SEE

★ **The Tech Museum of Innovation**: 145 W. San Carlos Street. ☎ 279-7150. Website: www.thetech.org. Open Tuesday–Sunday, 10am–5pm. Great if you're into technology: microcomputers, or anything from space exploration to high-tech bicycles, robotics and biotechnology. This is a museum where you can have fun and learn at the same time, interactively, of course.

★ **Winchester Mystery House**: 525 South Winchester Boulevard. ☎ (408) 247-2101. Open daily from 9am (last admission 4.30pm). Admission price is expensive. The guided visit lasts an hour.

The story? Sarah was the widow of the famous Winchester rifle manufacturer. A superstitious woman, she spent her life completely under the influence of a medium. During a seance, the medium commanded her to build a room for every person who had been killed by a Winchester! The medium predicted that Sarah would live as long as the sound of building work could be heard – but if it ceased, she would die. For 38 years, workmen laboured round the clock to enlarge her house, which, as a result, has 160 rooms. The interior is an astonishing labyrinth of rooms of all sizes. Some of them are interlinked, some have cupboards lining the walls to serve as traps for evil spirits; there are even staircases that don't lead anywhere.

In total, Sarah Winchester spent $5 million and her heirs, seeing her squandering her fortune, tried to have her locked away. Then in 1922, a violent thunderstorm struck the whole region and the workers who were finishing the roof dispersed. And lo and behold, exactly as predicted, Sarah died the very same night. Is it only a legend? Whatever the truth, the Americans have certainly worked out how to exploit it. It's really very touristy, with odd little souvenir shops and loads of visitors all shuffling along in a line.

★ **The Great America Amusement Fair**: along Highway 101, Great America Parkway exit. Speaks for itself. Worth the trip.

MONTEREY

AREA CODE: 408

Monterey sits on the slope of a hill, with a blue bay below it and with a forest of tall dark pine trees at its back.

John Steinbeck, *Tortilla Flat*

A seaside resort of some 33,000 inhabitants, 124 miles (200km) south of San Francisco, Monterey is also a fishing port – but the main thing you see here are tourists, who come to spend their dollars and to visit the Monterey Bay Aquarium, which is thought to be the finest in the US. The Cannery Row district, which at one time was an area peopled by fishermen and the sardine industry, and held dear by the writer John Steinbeck, is now nothing more than a tourist trap.

TIP: avoid coming here on weekends (especially in August): the motels are packed and prices seem to double.

– **Jazz Festival**: this famous event takes place each year in September.

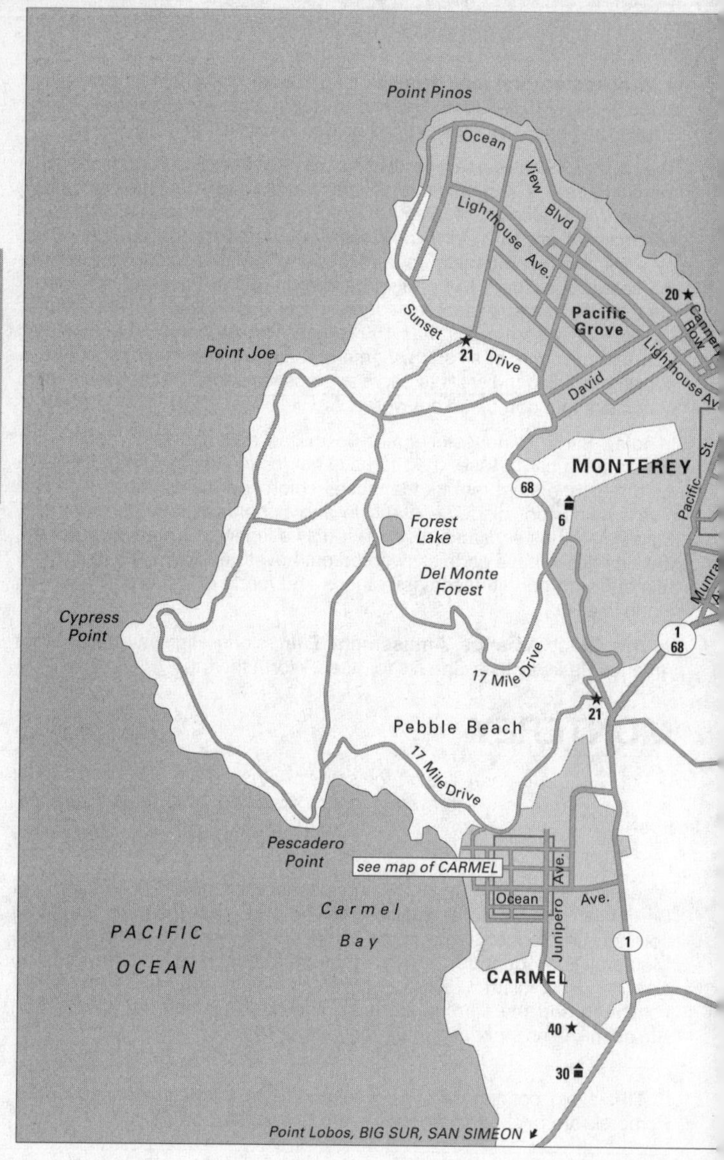

Point Pinos
Ocean View Blvd
Lighthouse Ave.
20
Pacific Grove
Sunset Drive
21
Point Joe
David
Lighthouse Ave
MONTEREY
St.
Pacific
68
6
Forest Lake
Del Monte Forest
Cypress Point
1
68
17 Mile Drive
21
Pebble Beach
17 Mile Drive
Pescadero Point
see map of CARMEL
Ocean
Ave.
Junipero Ave.
Carmel Bay
PACIFIC OCEAN
1
CARMEL
40
30
Point Lobos, BIG SUR, SAN SIMEON

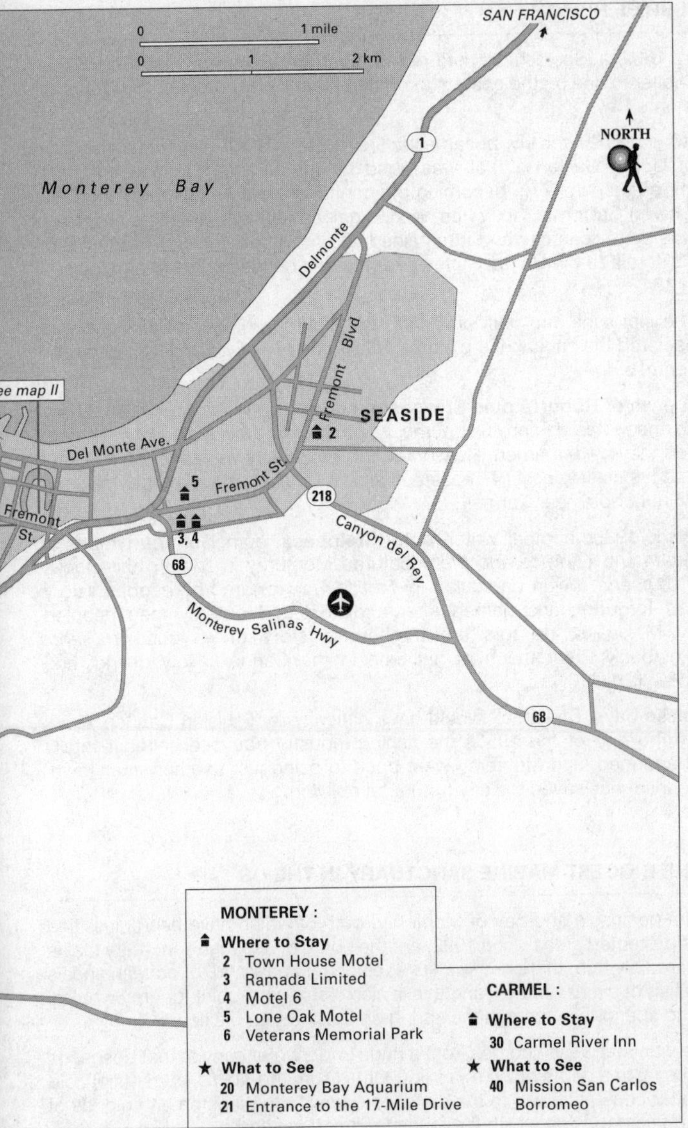

MONTEREY AND CARMEL (MAP I)

A BRIEF HISTORY

In 1602 a Spanish adventurer, **Sebastián Vizcaíno**, discovered this sheltered site on the coast and named it after his protector, the Count of Monte Rey.

Around 1770, the city became the first *presidio* of Alta California, the area of Upper California that was ruled by the Spanish. It took on more importance in 1775, becoming the capital of both Alta (Upper) and Baja (Lower) California. So, when Mexico gained its independence, Monterey was a Mexican city and it remained so until a peace treaty granted Alta California to the United States after the war between the US and Mexico in 1842.

The city sank into oblivion during the Gold Rush, when San Jose was declared the capital of the state of California. Finally, San Francisco took centre stage.

The writer **Robert Louis Stevenson** stayed at Monterey in 1879. There he encountered Fanny Osbourne, whom he had previously met in France, and they were married. He worked for the local newspaper and it is said that his classic novel, *Treasure Island*, was inspired by the peninsula of Point Lobos, near Carmel.

In the 1930s another writer, **John Steinbeck**, author of *The Grapes of Wrath* and *Of Mice and Men*, featured Monterey in some of his books – *Cannery Row* in particular. In *Tortilla Flat*, inspired by people history had forgotten and named after a district in Monterey then peopled by Mexicans, he told the tragi-comic story of a young *paisano*. Steinbeck spent much of his time in the Cannery Row district and knew it well.

These days, Steinbeck would have difficulty recognising Cannery Row. By the end of the 1950s the fishing industry had been almost totally abandoned, and Monterey went back to being just another small town. Tourism has saved the city from total oblivion.

THE BIGGEST MARINE SANCTUARY IN THE US

The peninsula and bay of Monterey, both of which have been classified as protected areas since 1992, are the home of a marine sanctuary that is incredibly rich: there are sea-lions, elephant seals and, of course, shoals of fish of every variety – and this is also a stopping-point for grey whales, who spend time there in the spring on their way to Mexico.

This animal wealth comes from a huge underwater canyon that descends steeply to a depth of 2.5 miles (4,000m). From this abyss, currents of cold water constantly rise to the surface, loaded with plankton and clouds of organic debris on which the fauna feed and multiply.

The researchers at the oceanographic centre attached to the aquarium have a particular interest in conserving the strange creatures that populate the bay between the depths of 3,000 and 13,000 feet (1,000 to 4,000m). To do this, they use the very latest high-tech equipment, highly efficient robots, and the *Alvin*, a submarine that was used to photograph the wreck of the *Titanic* for the first time. Their task is a difficult one, for the creatures living in the great depths usually die as soon as they are brought to the surface. They are very much adapted to living in an extreme environment of darkness and cold, withstanding huge pressures and the absence of oxygen.

USEFUL ADDRESSES

Visitors' Information Center (map II, **B2**): corner of Del Monte Avenue and Camino el Estero Street. ☎ 649-1770. Open daily, 9am–6pm (5pm Sunday). A very friendly welcome and all kinds of useful information: maps of Monterey and Cannery Row, tons of brochures about the city and the region.

– **Monterey City website**: www.montereybay.com

Greyhound Bus: 1042 Del Monte Avenue. Two buses daily to Los Angeles and San Francisco. Tickets are available from Mr B's Mini Market at the Exxon service station.

■ **Freewheeling Cycles**: 188 Webster Street. ☎ 373-3855. Open daily, 9am–5pm. Bike hire.

■ **Monterey Moped Adventures**: 1250 Del Monte Avenue. ☎ 646-0505 or 373-2696. Moped and bike hire.

PUBLIC TRANSPORTATION

– **The Wave (Visitor Shuttle)**: open daily, 24 May to 1 September, 9am–6.30pm. $1 per passenger per trip. This very practical bus serves a number of routes. Line A: Monterey Aquarium to Del Monte Center (departs every 10–12 minutes), Aquarium to Pacific Grove (departs every 30 minutes) and Aquarium to Downtown Monterey.

WHERE TO STAY

Monterey really doesn't have any cheap hotels.

AWAY FROM THE CENTRE

☆☆ MODERATE

Paris Motel: Fremont Street, near Motel 6 and the Vagabond Inn, opposite the Best Western. They have a sign claiming 'Lowest rates', and it's true: this is the cheapest motel on Fremont Street, charging around $65 for a room for two. Small L-shaped building with a parking lot. Rooms are pretty standard and they're clean.

Motel 6 (map I, **4**): 2124 N. Fremont Street. ☎ 646-8585. East of the city and not far from the intersection with Highway 1. About 50 rooms, and recently renovated. There's a swimming pool. Prices may be a little higher than those at other Motel 6 establishments.

☆☆☆ EXPENSIVE MOTELS

Town House Motel (map I, **2**): 1106 Fremont Boulevard, Seaside. ☎ 394-3113. Pastel walls, salmon pink doors, gallery with climbing plants. Clean little motel run by nice people. Good value.

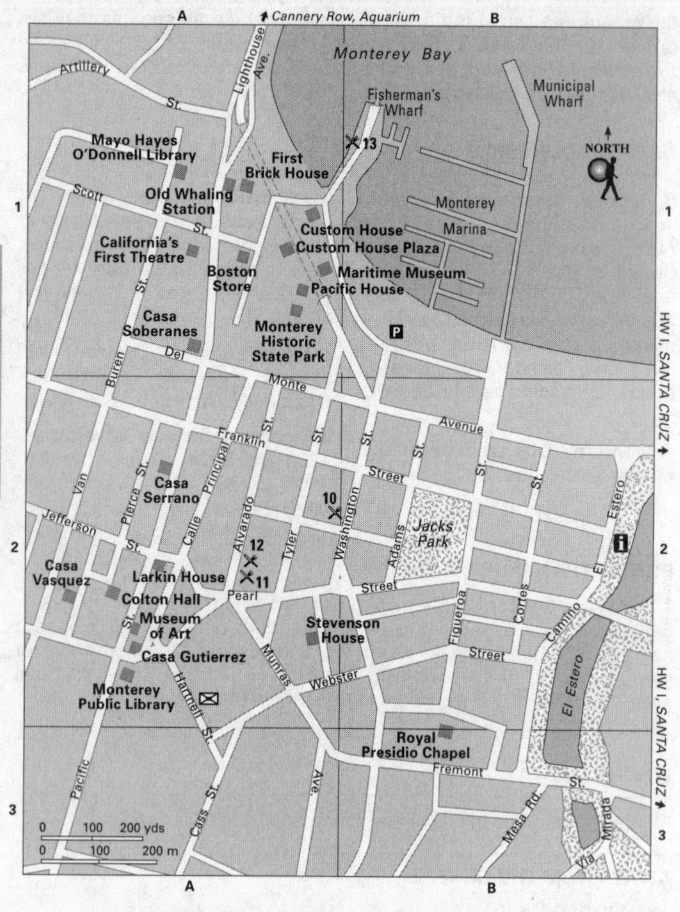

MONTEREY – TOWN CENTRE (MAP II)

■ **Useful Addresses**

- Visitors' Information Center
- Post office

Where to Eat

- 10 Paris Bakery
- 11 Old Monterey Café
- 12 The Mucky Duck Pub
- 13 Old Fisherman's Grotto

Ramada Limited (map I, **3**): 2058 N. Fremont Street. ☎ 375-9511. Not far from the intersection with Highway 1. Decent and a good welcome. High prices ($120 in summer), but a continental breakfast is included.

Lone Oak Motel (map I, **5**): 2221 N. Fremont. ☎ 372-4924. There are 47 rooms, some of them with fireplace, others with jacuzzi. The welcome is average.

CAMPGROUND

Veterans Memorial Park (map I, **6**): at the end of Jefferson Street, as you come from Monterey, or you can get there via Highway 68 West. ☎ 646-3865. Turn right at Skyline Forest, then left at the bottom of the hill, or take a No. 3 bus from the city centre. The only campground in Monterey, so try to get there fairly early. They only have 40 positions, but they're all nicely shaded.

WHERE TO EAT

☆ BUDGET

Paris Bakery (map II, A2, **10**): 271 Bonifacio Plaza, corner with 444 Washington Street. ☎ 646-1620. A French bakery-patisserie also operating as a cafe. Many varieties of bread: cinnamon, herbal, sesame, and currant buns. Also soup, salads, sandwiches, *caffè latte* or cappuccino. Everything that you need for a quick breakfast without paying ruinous prices.

Old Monterey Cafe (map II, A2, **11**): 489 Alvarado Street. ☎ 646-1021. Closed Tuesday. Excellent little restaurant at the top of the main street of old Monterey. Copious breakfasts, soup, salads, sandwiches. Ambiance and service rather nice, and prices are reasonable for the quantity of food you get.

The Mucky Duck Pub (map II, A2, **12**): Alvarado Street. British-style pub but with Californian ambiance. Lots of people in the evening, coming straight from work. They serve drinks, beers and simple dishes such as sandwiches, salads and soup.

☆☆ MODERATE

Old Fisherman's Grotto (map II, B1, **13**): Fisherman's Wharf. ☎ 375-4604. Good fish-and-clam chowder, and one of their specialities is *bouillabaisse à la marseillaise*. Lavish starters for the seriously hungry. There's always a queue, but the service is efficient. You may find it interesting to know that the restaurant once belonged to Sabu, an actor of Indian origin who appeared in a number of films in the 1940s, notably under the director Alexander Korda. There's a statue of him hovering modestly at the entrance.

The Fontana (map I, **7**): 2030 North Fremont Street. ☎ 646-1330. Dinner at prices that are still reasonable. Pleasant setting. Good pasta, seafood and grilled meats. At lunchtime they serve pizzas, burgers, sandwiches, plus a salad bar. You can also have breakfast there, and they serve good cinnamon rolls.

WHAT TO SEE

★ **Fisherman's Wharf**: very, very touristy. A series of timber houses at the edge of the sea, built in the 19th century by whalers and sardine fishers. As you might expect, the whole place has been transformed over the last decade or so into souvenir shops and expensive restaurants. There are still things to see, however, because the restoration work has been quite successful. Seals come right up to the end of Fisherman's Wharf, where tourists feed fish to them – this makes for a lovely, if improvised, attraction.

★ **Maritime Museum**: open daily, 10am–5pm. Near Fisherman's Wharf. Here you can see a vast Fresnel lens that was once used in a lighthouse on the coast of Big Sur, south of Carmel.

★ **Monterey Path of History**: if you're staying a few days and would like to explore the historic houses of the city centre, the tourist office can give you a map showing the main points of interest.

★ **Stevenson House**: 530 Houston Street (between Pearl and Webster Streets). Closed Wednesday. The house where Robert Louis Stevenson and his wife spent some months, late in 1879. The place contains some souvenirs, but there's nothing very exciting. Nevertheless, the house itself remains a place of pilgrimage for admirers of the great writer-traveller.

CANNERY ROW DISTRICT

★ **Monterey Bay Aquarium** (map I, **20**): 886 Cannery Row. ☎ 648-4888. Website: www.mbayak.org. Open daily, 9.30am–6pm in summer, 10am–6pm out of season. Admission $14. Note that in summer there's sometimes a very long queue. You can get a ticket the day before from the special 'Advance Tickets' office on Cannery Row, opposite Hovden Way. ☎ 1-800-756-3737.

It all began with a generous idea that occurred to David Packard, the co-founder of the electronics firm Hewlett-Packard (*see* 'Palo Alto'). An industrialist and philanthropist, Packard set up the aquarium in 1984 on the site of a former cannery facing Monterey Bay, the richest haven for marine life in the US. The investment of many dollars and just as many ideas has brought the aquarium huge success, and two million visitors a year pass through the gates. Millions of cubic feet of seawater are pumped in direct from the bay, and the aquaria are designed so that you feel as though you're underwater.

Every species in the bay is represented here. Starting with the kelp – these are giant algae that form a kind of cathedral of vegetation in a pool that's 30ft (9m) deep. This is the first time that kelp has grown on such a scale in an enclosed environment. You can get a close look at the sharks, rays, octopuses, seals and many other species large and small alike. In some halls you can even touch them, which pleases the kids. What's unmissable are the banks of silvery anchovies that swirl around in a dome-shaped aquarium. This is something you won't have seen anywhere else.

The big hit of your visit will be the red jellyfish. Under orange-ochre lighting and against a blue interstellar background, these strange creatures float around behind the glass of a giant aquarium, accompanied by some very Zen music. Consisting of 95 per cent water, these creatures are particularly difficult to breed. The simple act of touching the glass of the pool is enough to tear them apart. To prevent them sticking to the walls, a series of water jets propels them continuously away from the sides.

★ If you go along the coast, just after Monterey Bay Aquarium you'll be able to see a multitude of **seals** close to the shore. This show is free!

★ **Cannery Row**: of the 18 old canneries, only one is still working. The rest have been converted into restaurants and a variety of shops. Many unsuspecting Steinbeck readers still come to try and rediscover the atmosphere of his stories. Sadly, they're doomed to be disappointed, though a John Steinbeck Bookstore and Museum does exist at 551 Foam Street. ☎ 646-9117.

AROUND AND ABOUT

★ **17 Miles Drive** (map I, **21**): a coast road, 17 miles (27km) long as its name suggests, going around the peninsula. It gets very busy in summer, but the viewpoints are superb. There's an admission charge for vehicles, but it's free for cyclists (*see above* for hire of bikes and mopeds). There are many splendid villas, no doubt belonging to millionaires, along the road, but they are often well screened.

From the shore road there's a superb view of shimmering cypresses. Stop at Seal and Bird Rocks, where you can see pelicans and cormorants as well as seals, which frisk about on the rocks just a few feet from the shore.

– If you continue by car going south, remember to fill your tank as you leave Monterey. There are not many service stations on Highway 1, though it's a beautiful road with many great viewpoints.

CARMEL

AREA CODE: 408

Carmel is a lovely village just 4.5 miles (7km) south of Monterey. A seaside resort with barely 5,000 inhabitants, it owes some of its fame to movie star Clint Eastwood, who was the mayor there from April 1986 to 1988.

Here, all is prosperity and affluence. If it isn't paradise, it's as near as you'll get. Carmel's opulence extends over ravishing hills covered with pine, cypress and eucalyptus groves that roll down to the ocean and culminate at the beach.

The area is probably better protected than the Acropolis and there's a long-standing ban on neon signs, parking meters, advertising hoardings and traffic lights, none of which is considered to be visually attractive. The houses don't have letterboxes, which are considered aesthetically deplorable: instead, everyone goes to fetch their mail from the poste restante! There's a law against cutting down trees and at one time there was a regulation prohibiting the eating of ice-cream cones in the street. But Eastwood got rid of that one.

A BRIEF HISTORY

The writer Jack London often came to Carmel to see his novelist friends, George Sterling, Mary Austin and Sinclair Lewis. He wrote and rested there, camping wild and bivouacking in the woods. Henry Miller, author of *The Tropic of Capricorn*, didn't live there much either, contrary to popular belief, far preferring the pure and severe wilderness of Big Sur to the over-comfortable and excessively expensive bijou environment of Carmel. Today his children, Tony and Valentine Miller, live there, but then, they're richer than their father.

USEFUL ADDRESS

🅸 **Visitors' Center** (Carmel map, A1): Carmel Business Association, in the Eastwood Building on San Carlos Street, between 5th and 6th Streets, above the Hog's Breath Inn (the Eastwood restaurant). ☎ 624-2522. Fax: 624-1329. E-mail: carmel2@aol.com. Website: www.chamber.carmel.ca.us. They're efficient and can give loads of information. If you call them in summer, they'll tell you what hotels have rooms available. There's also a Carmel Heritage Walking Tour brochure to help you explore the city on foot.

WHERE TO STAY

There are about 50 hotels (mostly rather nice B&B-type, at the deluxe end of the market) in Carmel itself, and nearly 1,000 rooms in the entire area. Everything is very expensive in Carmel: there's nothing for less than $75 a night for two people and the only two places with moderate prices are outside Carmel. The backpacker solution is to sleep in Monterey and spend a few hours in Carmel during the day.

☆☆ MODERATE

▲ **Carmel River Inn** (map I, **30**): Highway 1 (at the Bridge), at the south entrance to the city and near the mission. ☎ 624-1575. A small motel with 19 rooms; a bit on the expensive side, but clean. Swimming pool. Also some cottages to rent. Bookings are for two nights minimum.

▲ **Saddle Mountain Campground**: from Highway 1 South, turn onto Carmel Valley Road and carry on for 5 miles (8km) to Shulte Road, where you turn right and drive a further 1.25 miles (2km). The campground, which has 25 places, is located on a hill right in the middle of Mother Nature. Swimming pool. Note that it's a very long way from the centre.

☆☆☆ EXPENSIVE

▲ **The Homestead** (Carmel map, A2, **10**): Lincoln Street and 8th Avenue. ☎ 624-4119. One of the cheapest B&B places in Carmel. A room with twin beds and bathroom costs $75 (for two). This is a charming timber house, very flowery, surrounded by a garden and run by a nice lady whose favourite colours (and you can't miss them) are carmine and burgundy. The thickly carpeted rooms 2 and 3, in

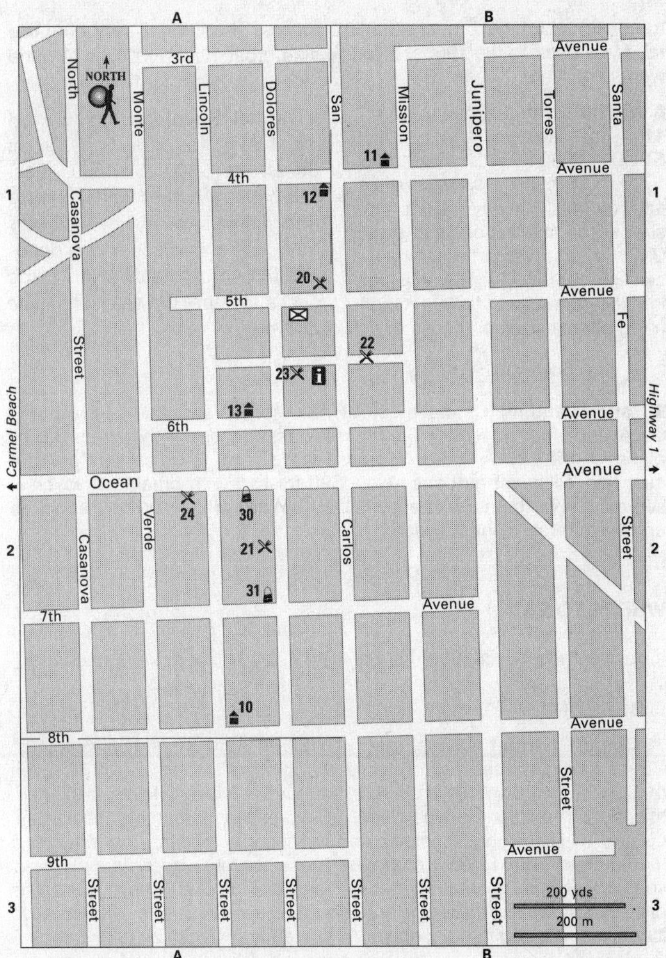

CARMEL (TOWN CENTRE)

Useful Addresses

- Visitors' Center
- Post office

Where to Stay

- **10** The Homestead
- **11** Wayfarer's Inn
- **12** Carmel Fireplace Inn
- **13** Happy Landing

Where to Eat

- **20** China Gourmet
- **21** Toots Lagoon
- **22** Jack's London
- **24** Chez Christian
- **23** Hog's Breath Inn

Shopping

- **30** Boatworks
- **31** Wings America

the basement, have a decor that'll take you back to the 1960s, if you were ever there.

Wayfarer Inn (Carmel map, B1, **11**): 4th Avenue and Mission Street. ☎ 624-2711. Fax: 625-1210. Website: www.wwsites.com/ca/inns. Away from the shops and the action, this pretty B&B is quite smart and has a certain charm. There's a sunny interior garden; a timber colonnade offers covered access to the rooms. The interior very comfortable, spacious, and light. Around $90–100 a night for two.

Carmel Fireplace Inn (Carmel map, A2): 4th and San Carlos Street. ☎ 1-800-634-1300. Fax: 625-5443. Another lovely house with flowers everywhere. Every room has a fireplace and is decorated in an individual style. Same prices as the Wayfarer Inn (*see above*).

☆☆☆☆ SPLASH OUT

Happy Landing (Carmel map, A2, **13**): Monte Verde (between 5th and 6th Avenues). ☎ 624-7917. For the more affluent, one of the prettiest B&B places in the city. A real dolls' house that seems to be straight out of a fairy tale. Pleasant gardens. Allow $90 for two with breakfast, which is served in your room. Frequently full, in summer, with every room booked up two to three months ahead.

WHERE TO EAT

It goes without saying that there are not many inexpensive restaurants!

☆ BUDGET

✕ **China Gourmet** (Carmel map, A1, **20**): on 5th Street, between San Carlos and Dolores, just opposite the post office. ☎ 624-3941. Even though the bright orange leatherette banquettes look a little old-fashioned, this small restaurant is vindicated by two essential features: successful cuisine (Chinese in this case) and reasonable prices. The chef is a Vietnamese from Hong Kong. The menu is very varied: soup, meat, seafood dishes, vegetarian dishes, excellent chicken chow mein. The dishes cost $6–10 on average and this is very rare in Carmel. They also do lunch specials and family dinners. And, in addition, you can take it away.

☆☆ MODERATE

✕ **Toots Lagon** (Carmel map, A2, **21**): on Dolores, between Ocean and 7th Street. ☎ 625-1915. At this trendy address, only the pizzas, the soup and the salads could be described as inexpensive. The other dishes (pastries and meat) are at the normal rates for Carmel.

✕ **Jack's London** (Carmel map, B1, **22**): on San Carlos Street, opposite the Visitors' Center. This is a pub in honour of the famous writer (there's a photo of him in the window), where they provide food and drink. Bar cuisine, simple and not very expensive: sandwiches, burgers, pizzas, Mexican dishes.

✕ **Hog's Breath Inn** (Carmel map, A1, **23**): 3 San Carlos Street and 5th Avenue. ☎ 625-1044. For 20-odd years, this was Clint Eastwood's bar and restaurant, so all American and foreign tourists wanted to stop here. After being closed for all of 1999, it reopened in 2000 under new ownership. Very few changes, apparently, but only time will tell. In the Eastwood days, it never emptied, and you had to queue. The setting is pretty: a shaded interior courtyard dominated by a mural representing a hilly landscape. In this terrace garden, there's a scarcity of seats, particularly in the two small pubs where the customers chatter in the shadows close to the fire.

✕ **Chez Christian** (Carmel map, A2, **24**): Ocean Avenue, between Lincoln and Monte Verde, in the courtyard of the Golden Bough. ☎ 625-4333. Open Friday–Sunday 11.30am–2.30pm, and daily (except Monday) 5–9.30pm. This little restaurant is run by a young Frenchman and serves some dishes that are unusual in the US: frogs' legs *à la provençale*, chicken *cricri*. But there are also salads, burgers and pastries. Best to go at lunchtime – it's more expensive in the evening.

BOUTIQUES AND SHOPS

The shops in Carmel are among the most beautiful and, of course, the most expensive in California. The display windows here are arranged like works of art, while the interiors are as meticulous as those in *Vogue* or *Harper's*. Everything that's for sale has to be sophisticated and totally original, so it's worth looking at closely, even if you aren't buying.

Here are some places that repay a quick look:

Boatworks (Carmel map, A2, **30**): corner of Ocean Avenue and Lincoln. ☎ 626-1870. Superb shop specialising in things associated with the sea: models of boats and lighthouses, books, posters, paintings, maritime objects and clothing.

Wings America (Carmel map, A2, **31**): corner of Dolores and 7th Streets. ☎ 626-9464. This shop is to aircraft and the sky what Boatworks is to ships and the sea. Marvellous shop that's worth going out of your way to see, if only to have a look at the pretty models hanging from the ceiling. Everything is expensive.

Tuck Box English Tea Room: on Dolores, between Ocean and 7th Streets. Snow White would like living in this dolls' house with its beams and quirky shape. A great little shop behind the tea room that looks as though it came from one of the *Tales of Beatrix Potter*.

WHAT TO SEE

★ **The San Carlos Borromeo Mission** (map I, **40**): south of Carmel on Rio Road. Open 9.30am–4.30pm (10.30am Sunday). This was the second mission to be established in California (on 3 June 1770) and it's certainly one of the prettiest. The superb restoration was the work of Sir Harry Downie, who dedicated 50 years of his life to it.

The tour explores the various rooms, including the kitchen and the priests' common-room, as well as the first US library. You then pass into a room containing a memorial to Junípero Serra, the Spanish friar who set up the mission, and then finish up in the superb church, which was elevated to the rank of basilica by Pope John XXIII. Finally, there are the gardens and a little pavilion dedicated to Harry Downie, with his studio and various models, including his first, which he made at the age of 12.

AROUND AND ABOUT

★ **Point Lobos**: open 9am–4.30pm. Ask for the detailed brochure at the entrance. This nature reserve, a few miles south of Carmel, is well worth the 17 Miles Drive. Admission is $7 for a car and two persons. It's best to go by bike or on foot as the narrow roads end up as small footpaths that run along the seashore, giving access to the prettier sites – promontories dominating the Pacific. The peninsula is one of the last wild places in California and it is strictly protected. Here you'll find groves of Monterey cypress – a rare species of tree that hangs onto the cliffs and is twisted by the wind and the sea spray. You can observe many seabirds and animals here, including otters and seals.

The rocks at Sea Lion Point are a gathering place for sea-lions that have the peculiar characteristic of 'barking'. The first Spanish sailors to discover the region took the sound to be the howling of wolves, and so wrongly named the place *Punta de los lobos marinos* ('sea-wolves point'), hence the name Point Lobos.

In December and January, grey whales travel along the coast from north to south and, in March and April they return the other way. They can reach a length of 50ft (15m) and weigh up to 40 tonnes. Their annual journey totals nearly 10,000 miles (16,000km), which is the longest recorded migration distance for a mammal.

★ Don't miss **Bird Island**. There are several beaches and picnic areas and the squirrels will come and keep you company.

– Finally, it's interesting to know that it was on the wild site at Point Lobos that Robert Louis Stevenson, who was based in Monterey in 1879, is supposed to have found the inspiration for his adventure story, *Treasure Island*.

> **TIP**: Beware of poison oak, a shrub whose shining leaves resemble those of the oak. It secretes an oil that causes rashes and unbearable itching.

BIG SUR

AREA CODE: 831

You just have to look at this country to want it to stay intact.
This is the spiritual reserve of some rich and luminous spirits.

Henry Miller, *Big Sur and the Oranges of Hieronymous Bosch*

This is an area much appreciated by backpackers who are keen on wild nature and freedom. Magnificently preserved, it offers on the one hand rocky coves battered by the ocean waves and, on the other, forests filled with sequoias. Sometimes it feels like the Mediterranean and at other times the resemblance is more to the coasts of Scotland or Scandinavia. In short, it's a genuine paradise for hikers, for there is a huge number of footpaths – all of which can be walked free of charge.

It's hardly surprising that many artists have been inspired by this place. One such was the writer Henry Miller, who wrote in the 1950s: 'This is the California that men dreamed of years ago, this is the Pacific that Balboa looked out on from the peak of Darien, this is the face of the earth as the Creator intended it to look.'

TIP: the best months to come here are October (when the temperature averages 75F°/25°C) and April. In general, between November and February the weather is cool and invigorating, with a clear sky and a sun that's still quite hot.

A BRIEF HISTORY

Apart from Jack London, who explored the region on horseback from the Valley of the Moon, the general public remained unaware of Big Sur until 1937, when the road from Carmel to San Simeon was opened. This runs along the Pacific Coast for a good 60 miles (100km). In 1960, another Jack (Kerouac – a turbulent writer and inveterate drinker) came to this wild area to be detoxified from a wild session that had lasted for three years. For him, Big Sur wasn't paradise but hell. Feeling as he did, like the morning after the night before, the place seemed to him to be a place of terror, with what he described as 'black rocks' and a 'devastating sea'. He didn't even want to meet Henry Miller.

The golden days of Big Sur seem now to be a thing of the past. Since the 1980s, the penniless artists and bohemians have given way, little by little, to residents that are increasingly affluent and, accordingly the place has become gentrified.

TOPOGRAPHY

Big Sur is neither city nor village. It's a micro-region which, in the words of Henry Miller: '. . . roughly comprizes an area two to three times the size of Andorra.' This wild enclave begins a little way north of the River Sur at Malpaso Creek and extends south to Lucia and east to Salinas Valley. There isn't a real centre (*see* map), but a living environment that's crumbling, with houses either scattered along the road, buried deep in the woods or clinging to the hillsides.

HENRY MILLER AT BIG SUR: A DEVIL IN PARADISE

After years of poverty in Paris, where he wrote *Tropic of Cancer*, and wanderings in Greece, Henry Miller returned to America during World War II and took up residence in California. Alarmed by the 'air-conditioned nightmare' that his country had become, the writer, who was still subject to censorship, decided to flee as far as possible from the consumer society that he detested. The discovery of Big Sur, an unpopulated area, was a revelation for him. 'For the first time in my life . . . I am in love with my home, the first real home I have known.'

In February 1947, the nomad hung up his boots on Partington Ridge, in a little house clinging to a sheer drop plunging to the Pacific Ocean. 'It is all thrown at you pell-mell: landscapes, seascapes, forests, streams, birds of passage, weeds, pests, rattlesnakes, gophers, earwigs, misfits, vagabonds, sunsets, rainbows, yarrow, hollyhocks and that leech of the plant world called the morning-glory. Even the rocks are seductive and hypnotic.' But there was a price to pay for this solitude: poverty and discomfort. At the beginning, his house had no gas, electricity, telephone, fridge, heating or sewerage. His mail came just three times a week and he had no vehicle except a little cart that he loaded with food and, almost naked, pulled like a mule.

For a long time, in order to survive, he sold his paintings at the side of the road. Many admirers also sent him gifts, donations and money through the mail. Success came. His books sold well, and he could finally buy his house. He became less and less solitary.

Well before the hippie era, Big Sur had become the refuge of a community of artists and non-conformists, impoverished but with a strong sense of solidarity, resolved to remain far from the din of the modern world. Miller divided his time between writing (he wrote *Big Sur and the Oranges of Hieronymous Bosch* here), walking, visiting friends (especially Emil White) and bathing in the sulphurous waters of Slade's Spring.

It was in this paradise at once so splendid and so terrible, a haven of peace and solitude, that Miller the devil became Miller the buddha – a great artist illuminated from within and ceaselessly creative. He enjoyed the companionship of various women, and, above all, his children, Tony and Valentine (both of whom now live in Carmel).

Miller lived at Big Sur from 1947 to 1962. He then moved to Pacific Palisades, near Los Angeles, where he remained until his death in 1980. Curiously, he was quite gloomy about the future of the area which, according to him, '. . . may rapidly develop into a suburb [of Monterey] with . . . all the odious claptrap that makes suburbia so horrendous.'

USEFUL ADDRESSES

🛈 **Big Sur Station**: ☎ 667-2315. Open daily, 8am–6pm. On the left of the road as you come from the north, 4 miles (6.5km) before the Henry Miller Library. This place gives you all the information you need for exploring this area and finding places to stay and eat. What's more, the welcome is warm.

✉ **Post office**: near the Big Sur Bazaar, which is the 'centre' of Big Sur.

■ **Grocery store, provisions**: at the Fernwood Motel, and at the Big Sur Bazaar, which also functions as a minimarket.

■ **Big Sur Health Center**: on Highway 1, between Big Sur Campground and The River Inn. Open Monday–Friday 10am–5pm. ☎ 667-2580.

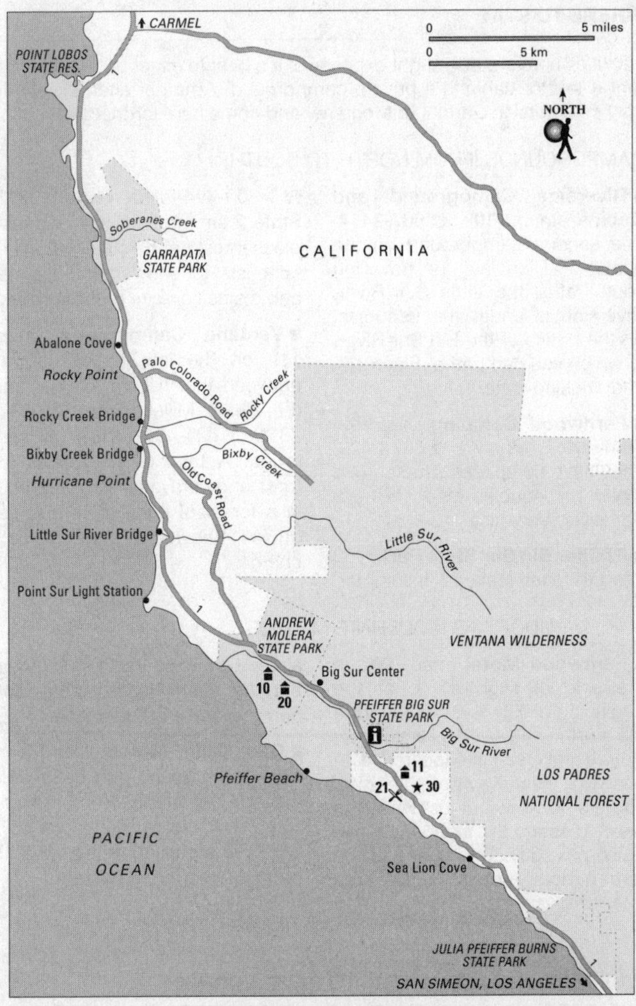

BIG SUR AND HIGHWAY ONE

Useful Address

Big Sur Station (Tourist Office)

Where to Stay

10 Riverside Campground and Cabins
11 Ventana Campground
20 Fernwood Motel

Where to Eat

21 Nephente Restaurant

What to See

30 Henry Miller Memorial Library

WHERE TO STAY

Facilities here are downright expensive! It's best to either put up a tent or rent a tent or cabin in a private campground. A further alternative is to stay in a motel in Carmel or Monterey and come here for the day.

CAMPGROUNDS (FROM NORTH TO SOUTH)

Riverside Campground and Cabins (map, **10**): ☎ 667-2414. The second campground on the right of Highway 1, travelling south, after the Little Sur River, Riverside is under the sequoias, on the banks of the Big Sur River, in which you can bathe. Electricity and drinking water.

Fernwood Camping: near the Fernwood Motel. ☎ 667-2422. They have 60 spaces situated in a forest of sequoias along the Big Sur River. Very nice.

Pfeiffer Big Sur State Park: you need to reserve ahead in summer. ☎ 1-800-444-PARK or 667-2315. State campground, the biggest, pleasantest and cheapest (218 spaces). Hot showers, launderette and a small on-site grocery store.

Ventana Campground (map, **11**): on the left, about halfway between the Visitors' Center and the Henry Miller Library. ☎ 667-2331 or 624-4812. Open all year round. A total of 75 spaces for tents and caravans are spread out in a forest of eucalyptus and sequoias. Showers are subject to a charge.

☆–☆☆ BUDGET TO MODERATE MOTELS

Fernwood Motel (map, **20**): at the side of Highway 1, at the beginning of Big Sur, coming from the north. The rooms, which are simple and clean, are located in an annexe a little away from the road. There's no view, but just what you need to spend the night and leave again next day. This is one of the rare budget motels in the area (there are very few). The Fernwood also runs a restaurant (you can get burgers, sandwiches, tacos and burritos) and a grocery store.

Glen Oaks Motel: after Riverside Campground and before the Visitors' Center, on the left of Highway 1, heading south. ☎ 667-2105. A pleasant motel with 15 rooms at moderate prices.

WHERE TO EAT AND WHERE TO HAVE A DRINK

> **TIP**: why not buy food at the grocery store and then have a picnic out in the open? This is both inexpensive and will allow you to soak up a few rays of sunshine.

☆☆ MODERATE

Coast Gallery: Highway 1, Big Sur, 1.25 miles (2km) south of the Henry Miller Memorial. ☎ 667-2301. Closes at 6pm. A gallery of paintings and sculptures with works by Miller and many photographs. On the first floor is a pleasant cafe with a view to the horizon. Fresh food, snacks, sandwiches, salads at moderate prices. A hippie, rather bohemian atmosphere.

✕ **Nephente Restaurant** (map, **21**): ☎ (408) 667-2345. Restaurant open daily, 11.30am–10pm. This was once a lodge, the property of Orson Welles until 1947. He gave it to his wife, the actress Rita Hayworth, who never came here (what a drag to have a superstar for a husband!). In any case, the pair didn't waste much time before getting divorced. Jack Kerouac lived here in the 1950s, drunk, as he often was, and terrified by the infernal beauty of Big Sur. Kerouac described this place as 'A magnificent restaurant perched at the top of the cliff and provided with a huge patio'. The Nephente was transformed into a restaurant for tourists in a hurry, but it's nice all the same, with a splendid view of the coast, the wooded mountains and the Pacific Ocean 1,000ft (300m) below. Reasonable prices. The **Kevah Cafe**, outside, serves bar food and drinks from 9am to 4pm, weather permitting.

WHAT TO SEE

GOING FROM NORTH TO SOUTH

★ **Bixby Bridge**: approximately 2 miles (3km) south of Rocky Point, this bridge crosses Bixby Creek. Its construction in 1937 made possible the opening of Highway 1, linking Monterey with San Simeon via the coast. Up until then, these stretches of the coastline were the wildest and most inaccessible places in California.

★ **Andrew Molera State Park**: the biggest nature park in Big Sur, located on the coastline. A path just under a mile (1km) long leads to a beach of fine sand. An ideal place for a picnic.

★ **Pfeiffer Big Sur State Park**: another state park, this one is 800 acres (324 hectares) in size. Admission charge. There's a campground and a holiday village consisting of a series of bungalows.

★ **Big Sur Station**: This is the tourist office for Big Sur (*see* 'Useful Addresses' above).

★ **Pfeiffer Beach**: approximately 0.75 miles (1km) off to the left of Highway 1, after Big Sur Station, Sycamore Canyon Road leads you the 3 miles (2km) to Pfeiffer Beach. Note that this is a narrow, bumpy road, prohibited to campers and large vehicles. There is a very small parking lot at the end.

★ **Henry Miller Library** (map, **30**): on the left of Highway 1, in a curve. ☎ 667-2574. Website: www.henrymiller.org. Open Thursday–Sunday 11am–6pm. No, it isn't a mausoleum but a pretty, modest rustic timber residence, surrounded by sequoias and fronted by a lawn that serves as an exhibition space for the artists of Big Sur. The house was once the hideaway of Emil White, Henry Miller's best friend. Today it is a museum and bookshop dedicated to Miller the writer, the man, his life, work, and genius. The collection includes a large part of his library, signed works, posters, photos, his Underwood typewriter, etc. A donation of $1 to the Foundation is requested.

The first shack in Anderson Canyon, where Miller started off his time at Big Sur, is now part of the most beautiful property in the region. His second house, the more comfortable one in Partington Ridge where he spent more time, is also private and no longer open to visitors. From the road, though, you can see where it is set, above a sheer 1,000ft (300m) drop to the ocean. Read his book *Big Sur* before coming here, and everything will fall into place.

★ **Julia Pfeiffer Burns State Park**: contains the Mac Way Falls, the only waterfall on the Californian coast. The water falls from a height of 50ft (15m) straight into the ocean.

HEARST CASTLE (SAN SIMEON CASTLE)

AREA CODE: 805

This gigantic former residence of the newspaper proprietor William Randolph Hearst, 230 miles (370km) from San Francisco and 240 miles (390km) from Los Angeles, was begun in 1922 but never completed.

Hearst laid down one simple principle for the construction project: 'Time and money don't count.' He entrusted the materialization of his dream to Julia Morgan, a graduate architect from Berkeley and the École des Beaux-Arts in Paris. Even so there were some rooms that he didn't like and he had them rebuilt several times. He was a purist who made no compromises – or that's what the guides who take you round will tell you.

Hearst, who had previously lived on the East Coast, was something of a countryman and so decided on the construction of his 'ranch' here. His wife refused to move west and they separated. Hearst was then joined by Marion Davies, a shapely Hollywood starlet. She had played some minor roles in silent films, but a stammer meant that she would have no future once the talkies arrived. She moved in – and remained at Hearst's side for 30 years, until his death.

What was life really like in the mansion? How much of what we know was reality play and how much was speculation is hard to say. Hearst was a strangely ambiguous person: he forbade his guests to bring their lovers – or alcohol, for that matter – yet he never actually married Marion Davies. His political ideas tended towards the reactionary, yet his newspapers assiduously dug out every scrap of scandal.

This extravagant residence is still the world's most expensive house, although you may well agree that, if money can't buy you love, it won't necessarily help you buy any taste either! With so much money at his disposal, it is quite amazing that Hearst managed to build such an uninhabitable house. Even if the works of art stacked floor to ceiling are priceless, their poor arrangement in the various rooms robs them of much of their value.

USEFUL INFORMATION

Note: if you want to visit Hearst Castle you'll have to book, except out of season. There are three ways to do it:

– Phone Destinet, the telephone booking system. Freephone: ☎ 1-800-444-4445. From abroad: ☎ 1-619-452-8787. You'll need your Visa or MasterCard handy. This service is open daily, 9am–9pm. Specify which guided tour you have chosen (No. 1 is the best if it's your first visit, *see* below).

– Go to the Holiday Inn at San Simeon, a city located a few miles south of Hearst Castle. They may have tickets for the following day. It's cash only.

– You can also turn up 'on spec' at the ticket office at the entrance. The chances of getting a ticket for the next tour are unpredictable. But you never know your luck.

THE TOUR

The tours generally run from 8am–4pm, but these times vary over the year. They begin with a 15-minute bus run along the private road, 5.5 miles (9km) long, that leads to the castle. The best views are to be had from the right of the bus. Note that the conditions for visitors are stringent. In no way are you allowed to smoke, chew gum or even stroll along by yourself. You'll be hemmed in by the guide and a security guard, who will call you to order if you try to slip away. So be warned!

Four options are available, each lasting 1 hour 45 minutes (including the bus ride). Each option takes in the two beautiful swimming pools – the 'Neptune', a magisterial outdoor pool, all in marble and in Graeco-Roman style, with a temple and statues, and the equally grandiose 'Roman', an indoor pool where the walls are covered by a blue-and-gold mosaic that makes the whole thing reminiscent of the bathouses of Ancient Rome.

– **Tour 1** seems the most appropriate for getting an overall view. After the Neptune swimming pool, you go to the Casa del Sol guest rooms, where some have coffered ceilings and others are in Spanish style. After crossing a garden with an art-deco fountain, a baroque gate and a classical column, you finally enter the 'Casa Grande'. Its facade is a jumble of all known styles. Inside, you can marvel at the chilly dining room with its coffered ceiling, banners and enormous silver chandeliers, and then move on into the billiard room. From there on to the theatre, where you will be shown a short film featuring the notable guests who came here: Charlie Chaplin, Greta Garbo, Clark Gable, Cary Grant and many others of the period. Finally, you end up at the Roman swimming pool, which is so enormous that Hearst had two tennis courts installed on the roof.

– **Tour 2** concentrates more on the 'Casa Grande', with, in particular, the library and its 5,000 rare volumes (which Hearst is said never to have read).

– **Tour 3** includes a visit to the Casa del Monte and a video about the construction of the 'ranch'.

– **Tour 4** is devoted to the gardens, the cellar, with its 3,000 bottles of

European and Californian wines, and the Casa del Mar, where Hearst lived for some years before his death.

You'll then be marshalled back into the bus to return to the point of departure. In passing, you'll be able to glimpse the cages of Hearst's private zoo. If you still have time, there are several exhibition rooms dedicated to Hearst and his family, as well as the incredible empire he built up during his lifetime: 26 daily newspapers, four weeklies, 11 radio channels and a cinema production company. This last visit is free of charge and unrestricted.

To broaden the context, it's worth having another look at *Citizen Kane*, made by and starring Orson Welles, which gives quite a faithful picture of Hearst's life and entourage. Hearst himself detested the film, which was produced by RKO and was the property of millionaire Howard Hughes.

WHERE TO STAY SOUTH OF HEARST CASTLE

SAN SIMEON (2.5 MILES/4KM)

San Simeon isn't really a village at all, but a collection of motels, at a variety of prices, strung along the road. The big motel chains (Best Western, Quality Inn, etc.) are all there.

☗ **Jade Motel**: Highway 1. ☎ (805) 927-3284. Located at the right-hand exit of the hotel area, as you travel south towards Los Angeles. Simple and clean. View out over a meadow, and a little glimpse of the ocean in the background.

☗ **Motel 6**: 9070 Castillo Drive. ☎ 927-8691. Fax: 927-5341. The least expensive in this area, in true Motel 6 tradition. This one has 100 decent rooms and is set back from Highway 1. The advantage here is that these rooms are larger than average for a Motel 6. Some face the rear and are consequently quieter. There's a restaurant and bar. Booking ahead is essential.

☗ **San Simeon Lodge**: 9520 Castillo Drive. ☎ 927-4601. Fax: 927-2374. There are some decent rooms in this blue-and-white building. It has no particular charm but is away from the road with views out over a lawn. There's a restaurant and swimming pool.

☗ **San Simeon State Park**: campground south of San Simeon, 0.75 miles (1km) before you get to Cambria, alongside the Highway, 750 Hearst Castle Road. ☎ 927-2068. Open all year round. Spaces for 240 on a huge estate that's right in the middle of the countryside. Not much shade. The charge for a space covers up to eight persons. In summer, it's vital to book several weeks ahead.

CAMBRIA (11 MILES/18KM)

The hotels here are more expensive, but they enjoy a peaceful setting and a terrific view of the ocean.

Castle Inn: 6620 Moonstone Beach Drive. ☎ 927-8605. Small motel with 25 pleasant and comfortable rooms. Beautiful swimming pool. Courteous welcome.

Sea Otter Inn: 6656 Moonstone Beach Drive. ☎ 927-5888. A motel in the English style. No view of the ocean, but it's very close by. The 25 rooms have meticulous decor, though they're all identical. Fireplace, swimming pool and jacuzzi.

White Water Inn: 6790 Moonstone Beach Drive. ☎ 927-1066. Freephone: ☎ 1-800-995-1715. Little bungalows sitting side by side, with cosy decor. Not very luxurious. Rooms start at $100 for two, breakfast included.

CAYUCOS (25 MILES/40KM)

Seaside Motel: 42 South Ocean Avenue. ☎ (805) 995-3809. Freephone: ☎ 1-800-549-0900. Impeccable little motel; some rooms have a 'cute' interior decor magazine sort of feel. Patio garden at the back.

Seagull Motel: 51 South Ocean Avenue. ☎ (805) 995-1600. At the intersection with Pacific Avenue. Little motel with white walls and a tiled roof. Good welcome. Rooms are simple and clean; quite atractive.

MORRO BAY (30 MILES/48KM)

The Golden Pelican Inn: 3270 North Main Street. ☎ 772-7135. Leave the main road at Yerba Buena Street. Small, inexpensive motel. Good pancakes and excellent welcome. The basic dish, two eggs and two pancakes, costs just $1.

Motel 6: 298 Atascadero Road, opposite the High School. ☎ 772-5641. Fax: 772-3233. Exit 41 (signposted for Los Angeles) on the right. This road, going north from the city, runs towards the ocean. There are 72 rooms. Coffee's always available at reception, as is an agreeable welcome. Small swimming pool.

Pacific Cottage Motel: 2830 Alder Avenue. At the south exit from the city. ☎ 772-2959. Coming from the north, turn left at San Jacinto. The 15 rooms are a little old-fashioned. Some have a kitchenette. Clean and inexpensive. The welcome's good.

SAN LUIS OBISPO

AREA CODE: 805

Medium-sized city with 43,000 inhabitants, 45 miles (70km) south of Hearst Castle, in a markedly Spanish style. The streets are laid out like a chessboard and the ambiance is young.

USEFUL ADDRESS

Visitors' Center: 1039 Chorro Street. ☎ 781-2777. Open Tuesday–Friday 8am–8pm, Saturday 10am–8pm. Serious and efficient. Complete information on the city.

WHERE TO STAY

★ **Madonna Inn**: 100 Madonna Road. ☎ 543-3000. Freephone in California: ☎ 1-800-543-9666. Fax: 543-1800. To the south of the city, very near Highway 101, Madonna Road exit. Unique and unbelievable at the same time. Imagine a hotel designed by Walt Disney for honeymooners. Lovers need not necessarily be either young or married, but they do have to book well in advance. The dominant colour is pink. Created in 1958 by the Madonna family, their first 12 rooms were so successful that they enlarged the place, and it now has 109 rooms, each with its own specific decoration. You can choose between a cavern, a cathedral crypt, an Indian tepee and a safari tent, and, yes, you *can* have a waterfall in your room. All of the rooms feature on pretty and inexpensive postcards that you can buy at the reception desk! Rooms start at $97 for a double; the Rock Room is $145.

The most fantastic place, without any doubt, is the restaurant (not the cafe). Everything is pink, everything is (of course) baroque kitsch. Try the cocktails, which are just as schmaltzy. Don't worry about your open-mouthed stares: they're used to it there! Even the toilets are fantastic: the men's room features a waterfall, while the ladies features large mirrors and padded doors. The restaurant isn't too expensive, given the setting . . . and credit cards are accepted.

☆☆ MODERATE

Budget Motel: 345 Marsh Street. ☎ 543-6443. Freephone in California: ☎ 1-800-458-8848. One of the least expensive of the standard motels. The welcome is average. Not far from the Madonna. If you're coming from Highway 101, take the exit at Marsh Street.

☆☆☆ EXPENSIVE

Apple Farm: 2015 Monterey Street. ☎ 544-6100. (Freephone in California): ☎ 1-800-374-3705. Very handsome Victorian hotel and much more expensive: rooms start at $100 for a double. There are 103 rooms, all different, with every detail of decor taken to the limit: it's a bit like something out of *Alice in Wonderland*. Breakfast, however, is delicious. The restaurant is affordable, and also serves good food.

WHERE TO EAT

☆ BUDGET

✕ **Art of Sandwich Delicatessen**: 717 Higuera Street. Very good sandwiches made to order from French-style baguettes with a variety of ingredients. A good place to go at lunchtime. Sensible prices.

☆☆ MODERATE

✕ **SLO Brewing Co**: 1119 Garden Street. Between Higuera and Marsh Streets. ☎ 543-1843. The nicest place in the city. There's a big room on the first floor with beer barrels and a stage for musicians. Live music with groups several evenings during the week. Enhanced bar cuisine: salads, burgers, soup, specialities. Happy hour: 4–5.30pm.

✗ **Tortilla's Flat**: 1051 Nipomo Street. ☎ 544-7575. Open 11am–9pm. One of the best of the Mexican restaurants, with some excellent specialities such as their *chimichanga* – an enormous tortilla stuffed with beef or chicken, cheese, onions, olives, tomatoes, etc. and accompanied by rice and guacamole. The room is vast and colourful. One of the favourite rendezvous spots for the young. Fiesta Hours are Monday–Friday 4–6pm. Sunday Champagne Brunch 10am–2pm. From 9pm–2am, it becomes a nightspot with a DJ.

✗ **China Bowl**: 685 Higuera Street. An 'all you can eat' restaurant serving Chinese and Japanese dishes. On the left as you go in is the Santa Veggie, styled as a smart cafe. On the right is the China Bowl. Customers serve themselves. Prices are reasonable.

WHAT TO SEE

★ **The San Luis Obispo de Tolosa Mission**: on the corner of Monterey and Chorro Streets. Open 9am–4pm (5pm in high season). Founded in 1772, this was the fifth mission in California. Built by Father Junípero Serra and almost entirely destroyed during the earthquake of 1830. Some minor renovation work was done in the late 19th century, transforming it into the Victorian style that was fashionable at the time, and taking away much of its charm. It contains several exhibition rooms, some of them – the most interesting ones – devoted to the Chumash Indian tribe. Or you could have fun exploring the creekside paths just opposite the mission.

★ **Historical Museum**: 696 Monterey Street (beside the mission). Open Wednesday–Sunday 10am–4pm. Free. A small museum covering the history of the county. First came the Native Americans, of course, then the Mexicans, with a special exhibit, the sombrero of Pio Pico, the last Mexican governor of California. Another room presents temporary exhibitions. Very warm welcome from the staff, who are all volunteers.

★ **Bubblegum Alley**: on Higuera Street, between Garden and Broad. On the left coming from Garden. This is a narrow alley with a brick wall on each side to which passers by have stuck thousands of pieces of chewing gum. Names, hearts, drawings, graffiti, you name it. This is America in all its extravagance and bad taste.

★ **The market**: Higuera Street. Open Thursday 6–9pm. This is the market for the farmers of the area and gives all the city's inhabitants a chance to meet up. The street is closed entirely to traffic, access from the cross streets being barred. Vegetables, fruit, pastries and barbecues where you can buy a meat-filled sandwich or a sausage. A friendly, good-natured ambiance. The shops in the street stay open, and after the market closes, everyone meets up again to have a drink or a dance, often at F. McLintock's Saloon (686 Higuera Street), where good rock and country groups play.

SOLVANG

AREA CODE: 805

Between San Luis Obispo and Santa Barbara, Solvang is a little detour if you have a bit of time to spare. A curious village, established in 1911 by a colony of Danes and built entirely in the style of that country, it has some interesting and unusual architecture, as well as beautiful windmills. The village is carefully tended, very colourful and, of course, rather touristy. It's also a good opportunity to taste some good Scandinavian pastries, particularly in the *Dansk Bageri Kafe og Conditori* on Alisal Road, the one leading to Frederick's Court.

USEFUL ADDRESS

Conference and Visitors' Office: Mission Drive. ☎ (805) 688-6144. Open daily, 10am–4pm. The smiling welcome is pleasing.

WHERE TO STAY

Flying Flags: 180 Avenue of the Flags, 93427 Buellton. ☎ 688-3716. Just 2 miles (3km) from Solvang along Highway 101. A very beautiful campground, recently established and not expensive. Open all year round and well shaded. Facilities are very clean. Jacuzzi, big heated swimming pool. Good capacity for both tents and mobile homes.

Solvang Gaard Lodge: 293 Alisal Road. ☎ 355-4404. Fax: 688-4404. At the edge of town, this is a peaceful, well-kept motel with a spacious garden. Always plenty of folk, because many visitors are regulars and some take rooms by the month. Booking ahead is necessary. Prices are very reasonable.

Viking Motel: 1506 Mission Drive (on the main street). ☎ 688-4827. Very good value for money. The 12 rooms are a little old-fashioned, but the charge includes breakfast, which you take in the Danish bakery opposite after picking out the pastry you want.

Three Crowns Inn and Cottages: 1518 Mission Drive. ☎ 668-4702. Fax: 688-6907. A little more expensive than the previous entry, but the 32 rooms are more spacious. There are also some cottages with air-conditioning. The price of a room varies according to size and comfort: the cheapest ones cost less than $50. Breakfast is included.

Hamlet Motel: 1532 Mission Drive. ☎ 688-4413. Fax: 686-1301. Another small motel with very well kept rooms (showers only). Breakfast is included, and you take it in the patisserie opposite the hotel.

WHERE TO EAT

The Dane: 485 Alisal Road. ☎ (805) 688-8348. On the first floor of a building located at the back of Frederick's Court. Run by a couple of authentic Danes. Good Danish sandwiches with shrimps, salmon and roast beef.

Andersen: at the exit from Highway 101, turn left immediately. The restaurant is a few hundred yards along on the right. This restaurant chain, established in 1924, is quite popular and has a good reputation for its pea soup: take as much as you can eat – the record is 70 bowls! Ask for the 'additionals' (pieces of ham, cheese, bacon cubes, onions) and your soup will be transformed into a Danish *gazpacho*.

LOS ALAMOS

AREA CODE: 805

On Highway 101, halfway between San Luis Obispo and Santa Barbara. A stopping place for stagecoaches in the 19th century, then a depot for the Pacific Coast Railroad, which at one time linked North and South California, Los Alamos ended up being totally forgotten for a number of years. The result is that the town has retained a certain charm. It offers two hotels, a small supermarket, a gas station, some antique shops (most of them housed in the former Pacific Coast Railroad station), plus a small Mexican restaurant and another, more typically American, restaurant.

WHERE TO STAY

☆☆☆☆ SPLASH OUT

Union Hotel: 362 Bell Street. ☎ 344-2744. Open all year round. Old timber-built hotel dating from 1880 that has retained all of its picturesque attributes. You can dine superbly in the evening, Wednesday to Sunday, and it's also open to people passing through. Old furniture, beautiful objects, huge, magnificently decorated rooms. Among the things worth seeing are the dining room, the billiard room and the table tennis room, which has the finest table you could ever dream of playing on. The 13 rooms run from $80 (with shared bathroom) to $150 (plus tax). The very copious breakfast is included. Swimming pool in the garden and jacuzzi. Peace is guaranteed. Saloon-type bar with a cheering and definitively 'old-time' atmosphere. You may get a slight case of *déjà vu*: the hotel served as a backdrop for the video of *Say, Say, Say* by Paul McCartney and Michael Jackson.

Close by, for more affluent readers, is the **Victorian Mansion**. Six nutty theme rooms: the '50's Drive Inn' (where you sleep in a Cadillac), the 'Gypsy', the 'Roman', the 'Egyptian', the 'French', the 'Pirate'. Each room is knee-deep in electronic gadgets (in the Egyptian room, the entrance to the bathroom is a surprise!). We aren't going to spoil the fun by telling you all the little features! Rooms cost $240 (plus tax), but the experience is one of a kind.

WHAT TO SEE

★ **The Santa Inés Mission**: at the eastern exit from the city, on the right. Open 9am–4.30pm (7pm in summer). Founded in 1804 by Estevan Tapis. Several rooms contain displays of priestly robes and old implements retracing life on the mission since the 17th century. Then come the Chapel of the Madonna and the church, with its charming paintings. The tour ends in the small garden. The story goes that the mission was saved from complete destruction in 1824 thanks to a young Native American girl, Tulares, who warned Father Francisco (who, in turn, had previously saved her from certain death) that her tribe was going to burn the mission down. The Father, who (as luck would have it!) had been a soldier before becoming a missionary, managed to save some of the buildings. A model at the entrance shows the mission as it originally was.

SANTA BARBARA

AREA CODE: 805

This seaside resort (with approximately 90,000 inhabitants), 93 miles (150km) north of Los Angeles and 335 miles (535km) south of San Francisco, has a high reputation on the Californian coast for its exceptional climate, with fine weather for 84 per cent of the year. It has been appreciated since the start of the 20th century for its healthy atmosphere.

The city has retained some traces of its Spanish past, particularly its adobe (sun-dried clay-brick) houses, arcaded squares and little streets that invite strolling – it's a jewel of an American city.

Paradoxically, the people here so assiduously preserve their way of life and their environment that nothing ever changes. Real-estate speculators and promoters are kept at a distance. The effect is that there are some rather impoverished streets and poor segments of the population, even in the city centre. Add to that a certain number of street people who have discovered that the climate suits them as much as it does the rich, and you get a city that is filled with interesting contradictions. Many actors and singers have chosen to live in this area, including Michael Jackson, Kevin Costner, Karl Malden, Priscilla Presley, Steve Martin, Michael Douglas and many others.

A LIVELY CITY

Contrary to what many people think, Santa Barbara is a young, even a very young city. It contains a university, the UCSB (University of California at Santa Barbara), the SB City College, and Brooks, a photography school of high repute.

The life of the city is concentrated on State Street, level with the Paseo Nuevo Mall, which is between Canon Perdido and Ortega Streets. There's a mass of restaurants and shops, ranging from department stores to tiny corner places. All the well-known American stores are here: Gap, Eddie Bauer Furniture, Banana Republic, Macy's, Victoria Secret, etc. There's also a large number of second-hand clothes shops and 'antique' shops, as well as military surplus stores and cafes with terraces. This is also the location of the Tuesday afternoon 'Farmer's Market', which is also held on Saturday morning in the area around 700 Santa Barbara Street, not far away. Here you can buy vegetables and fruit, fresh shrimps, crab, flowers, and even natural body oils.

'THE SEVENTH ART' HITS THE BEACH

When the cinema arrived, early in the 20th century, Santa Barbara became for a very brief period the capital of the Seventh Art, before Hollywood took over. A huge studio belonging to the American Film Company was located at that time on the corner of State and Mission Streets. It was thought to be the largest film studio then in existence. More than 1,200 films, most of them Westerns, were made there over a period of 10 years.

But the supremacy of Hollywood quickly eclipsed the early success of Santa Barbara. The seaside resort said goodbye to the production side of the industry and opened its arms to Hollywood stars when they came in quest of peace and sunshine. Douglas Fairbanks and Mary Pickford had a property here in the 1920s. In 1928, a young millionaire called Charlie Chaplin had the Montecito Inn built, which became a refuge for the stars of the Roaring Twenties.

The famous German director Friedrich W. Murnau, who had made *Nosferatu* and then went to work for the Fox company, died in Santa Barbara in a car accident in 1931. According to legend, this was in fulfilment of a curse he incurred by violating the religious taboos of Bora-Bora while making the film *Tabou* that same year, with his eminent American co-director, Robert Flaherty. The actor Ronald Colman bought the very Spanish San Ysidro Ranch in 1935, which provided a hideaway for such celebrities as Bing Crosby, Jack Benny, Audrey Hepburn and Groucho Marx. Vivien Leigh and Laurence Olivier got married here and, in 1953, John and Jacqueline Kennedy came here to spend part of their honeymoon.

The TV series *Santa Barbara* has made the city famous to soap fans the world over, although ironically, most of the scenes were filmed in a studio in Los Angeles. The beach scenes, however, were authentic: there's no denying that this beach is fantastically beautiful!

HOW TO GET THERE

BY TRAIN

Connections daily with the entire 'Pacific Coast Route' with Amtrak. Information: ☎ 1 (805) 963-1040 or Freephone: ☎ 1-800-USA-RAIL. Or ask at the station for timetables.

BY BUS

🚌 Airbus provides a connection with Los Angeles in both directions. ☎ 964-7759. The Airbus stop in Santa Barbara is in front of the Sheraton Hotel at 1111 East Cabrillo Boulevard. Santa Barbara Airbus: 5755 Thornwood Drive, Goleta CA 93117.

🚌 The Greyhound company also provides a bus service. ☎ 965-7551. 34 Castillo Street, near the Transit Center. Several buses for San Francisco (with a journey time of 6 hours 30 minutes) and Los Angeles (a journey time of 2–3 hours).

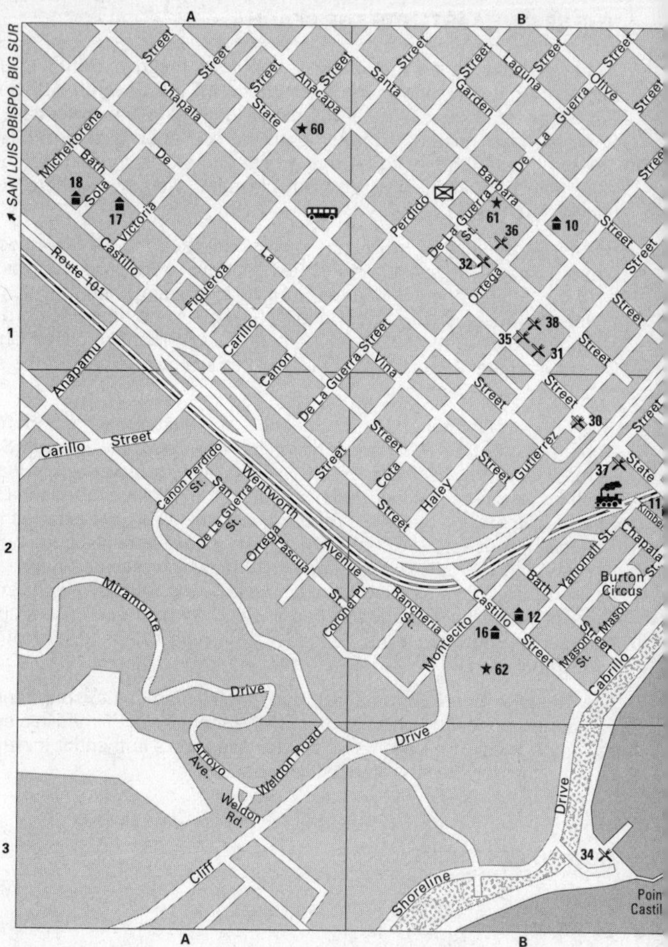

■ Useful Addresses

- Visitors' Information Center
- Post office
- Greyhound Bus Station
- Amtrak Rail Station

Where to Stay

10 Banana Bungalow Hostel
11 Hotel State Street
12 Colonial Inn
13 Motel 6
14 Pacific Crest Inn
15 Cabrillo Inn
16 Tropicana Inn
17 The Glenborough Inn
18 The Ivanhoe
19 Old Yacht Club Inn

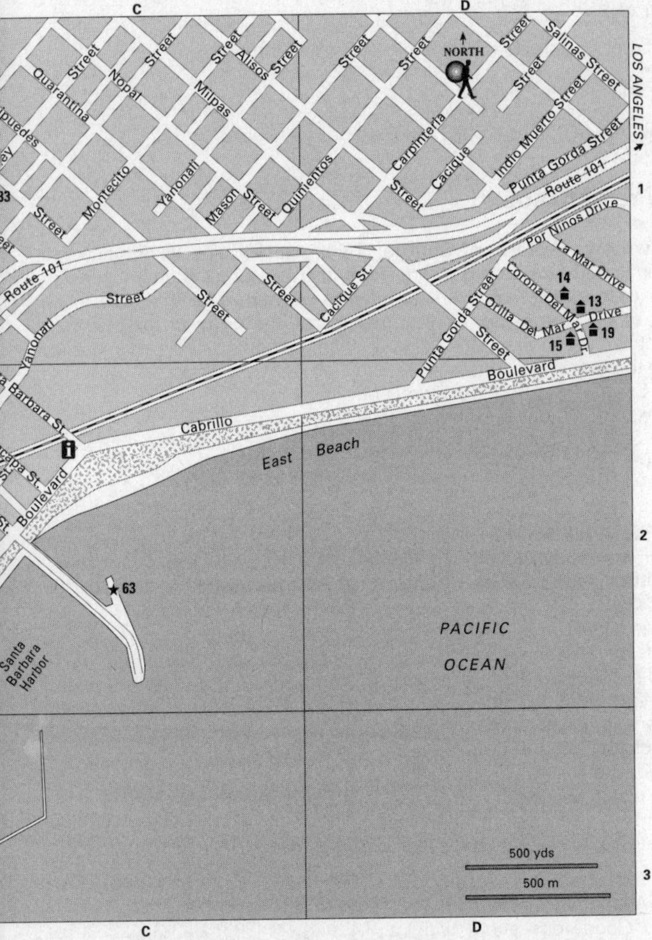

SANTA BARBARA (TOWN CENTRE)

Where to Eat

30 Essau's
31 Pierre Lafond Deli
32 Le Pacific Crepes
33 Roses Cafe
34 Brophy
35 The Natural Cafe
36 Paradise Cafe
37 The Enterprise Fish Co.
38 The Palace Cafe

Where to Have a Drink

50 Bar Californian Hotel

What to See

60 Santa Barbara Museum of Art
61 The History of the City Museum
62 The Stagecoach, Wagon and Cart Museum
63 Santa Barbara Sea Center

BY PLANE

The airport is approximately 8 miles (13km) north of Santa Barbara.

BY CAR

Via Highway 101, from San Francisco or Los Angeles.

HOW TO GET AROUND

– **Downtown-Waterfront Shuttle**: a little electric bus takes you from Upper State Street to the beach. From there, another shuttle takes you either to the West Beach Area, as far as the port, or to the East Beach Area, as far as the zoo. Don't forget to ask the driver of the bus from Downtown for an extension ticket so that you can continue your journey along the waterfront. This is very handy, as well as cheaper: 25 cents one way. Shuttles run from 10.15am–6pm (the Downtown one runs to 8pm Friday and Saturday in summer). You can also hire a bike at the bottom of State Street. The bicycle is one of the favourite means of transport for Santa Barbara residents.

USEFUL ADDRESSES

Visitors' Information Center (map, C2): 1 Santa Barbara Street, Cabrillo Boulevard. Near Stearns Wharf. ☎ (805) 965-3021. Open Monday–Saturday 9am–5pm, Sunday 10am–5pm. In December and January, it closes at 4pm. In summer, closing time is 6pm. A well-organized office. Free information, road plans and maps of Santa Barbara on sale. Telephone hotline for last-minute hotel reservations.

■ **Pacific Traveller Supply**: 12 West Anapamu Bar. ☎ (805) 963-4438. Good bookshop with a choice of books and maps aimed at travellers.

Amtrak Station (map, B2): 209 State Street. ☎ (805) 963-1015. Open 7am–10pm. Counters closed between 1.30 and 2.30pm, 6.30 and 7pm, and after 9.30pm. There's an Amtrak Bus Connection for Los Angeles, San Luis Obispo and Bakersfield.

Greyhound bus station (map A1): 34 West Carillo Street. ☎ (805) 965-3971.

Nearby, there's the **Santa Barbara bus terminal**. 1020 Chapala Street. ☎ (805) 683-3702. Buses for Goleta, Montecito, Carpinteria, etc.

WHERE TO STAY

Bear in mind that it's best to avoid hotels near the beach, except from May to early October. On the approaches to the beach there's fog, it's colder, and there's sometimes a lot of wind, which is frankly unpleasant. In summer and on weekends, Santa Barbara is invaded by tourists from all over California. The hotels are generally full, so reserve your room ahead, and expect room prices to increase by approximately 20–30 per cent. Out of season, you can negotiate a better price for a longer stay, i.e. one lasting three days or more.

CAMPGROUNDS

A list of campgrounds is available from the tourist information office.

Carpinteria Beach State Park: at Carpinteria, approximately 10.5 miles (17km) south of Santa Barbara on Highway 101. ☎ 684-2811. Reservations from Mistix. ☎ 1-800-444-7275. Take Carpinteria Street, exit at Palm Avenue. This is the closest campground to Santa Barbara.

El Capitan Beach: at El Capitan, 18 miles (29km) northwest of Santa Barbara via Highway 101. ☎ 1-800-444-7275.

Cachuma Lake: 20 miles (33km) northwest of Santa Barbara via Highway 154. ☎ 688-4658.

☆–☆☆ BUDGET TO MODERATE HOTELS

Banana Bungalow Hostel (map B1, **10**): 710 East Ortega Street. ☎ (805) 963-0154. A dormitory with 30 bunk beds and a room with six beds. Many young people, both European and American. Expect to pay $14–18 a night. The showers and toilets are clean. You must vacate your room by 10am. Backpacker ambiance.

State Street Hotel (map B2, **11**): 121 State Street. ☎ (805) 966-6586. Fax: (805) 962-8459. Allow approximately $65 for a double in summer, $10 less out of season. Breakfast included. Special prices for a stay of 15 days or more from 1 October to 15 June, and good prices for a stay of one month. This might interest you if you plan to stay for a while in Santa Barbara, as it would be difficult to find alternative decent accommodation in the city for less than $600 a month. Very central – opposite the Amtrak station. Built early in the 20th century, this was one of the best known 'railroad' hotels in the American West. Impeccably clean. The decor retains the original charm, but do note that trains pass close to the hotel, the first at 7.30am and the last about 11pm. In between those times, you can only sleep if you strap the pillows against both ears!

They make you very welcome, however, and the owners can give plenty of information about the city and the area. Several types of room: the simplest have washbasins and shared toilets. Only one room has a bathroom (No. 12), and it also has two corner windows and a double bed.

Motel 6 (map D1, **13**): 443 Corona del Mar. ☎ 564-1392. Fax: (805) 963-4687. A few steps from the beach. Facilities are what you'd expect from this chain of motels. Small swimming pool. Particularly sought-after because of its location. Booking is essential.

If you're travelling by car out of season, you'd do better to try the **Motel 6** on Upper State Street (3505 State Street). ☎ (805) 687-5400. It's warmer there and you can enjoy the swimming pool from April onwards. There's no charge for a child (under 17) accompanied by its parents.

☆☆–☆☆☆ MODERATE TO EXPENSIVE HOTELS

Colonial Inn (map B2, **12**): 206 Castillo Street. ☎ 963-4317. On one of the streets going down to the ocean, the Colonial is busy, but there isn't too much noise despite this. Very well kept. You'll pay twice as much for a room as in the hotels above, but there's a heated and sun-soaked swimming pool.

Days Inn: 116 Castillo Street. Close to the Stagecoach, Wagon and Cart Museum and the port. Good welcome and comfortable rooms. Very affordable for a motel in the vicinity of the beach but, as everywhere, the Days Inn raises its prices in season and on weekends. Room 20 can take six people, and you can negotiate for a good price. Rooms with shower only. Same prices as the previous entry, but no swimming pool.

Pacific Crest Inn (map D1, **14**): 433 Corona del Mar Drive (East Beach). ☎ 966-3103. Just behind the Cabrillo Inn on Cabrillo Boulevard (the road down to the sea). A standard motel in quite a peaceful place, offering very decent rooms. You get a direct outside phone line, a kitchenette in some rooms, laundry and swimming pool.

Cabrillo Inn (map D1, **15**): 931 East Cabrillo Boulevard. ☎ 966-1641. Freephone: ☎ 1-800-648-6708. A step or so from the beach and five minutes' drive from Montecito. Comfortable rooms. The ones with an ocean view are quite expensive, but others are affordable. Two swimming pools, one of them heated. Approximately $30 more is charged in summer. The hotel also has a colonial cottage nearby, which you can rent by the week (maximum five persons) or by the month.

Tropicana Inn (map B2, **16**): 223 Castillo Street. ☎ 966-2219. Freephone: ☎ 1-800-468-1988. Fax: 962-9428. An attractive motel and it's non-smoking. Rooms are very comfortable, with interior decor in a pleasant 'French country' sort of style. There are several rooms that can hold four or six people, and a penthouse for eight with dining room, kitchen and a beautiful view of the mountains. Heated swimming pool and jacuzzi. Also some suites. Prices go up slightly from 25 May to 7 September.

BED & BREAKFAST

Located in some beautiful old houses in peaceful areas, these B&Bs are as expensive as the hotels in the moderate price category. (The adjacent cottages are larger and listed under 'Expensive'.) Rooms are tastefully decorated and many have a garden where it's nice to have breakfast. Breakfast is included in the room price, as is a glass of Californian wine and the evening's cocktail snacks, which are served in the garden around 5pm.

The Glenborough Inn (map A1, **17**): 1327 Bath Street. ☎ 966-0589. In a beautiful house dating from 1880, with a peaceful, cosy atmosphere. Charming welcome. Individually styled rooms at a wide range of prices and all with names like 'Aurelia's Fancy', 'French Rose' and 'Country'. There's even a gracious 'Garden Room' with a brass bedstead, at a very affordable price (but the bathroom's on the landing). Rooms cost the same in high season and on weekends, all year round. The 'full gourmet breakfast' is something special. As in all B&B places, the minimum stay is two nights on weekends and three nights on summer weekends. There's a garage.

Not far away, at 1720 Bath Street, is another B&B, **The Bath Street Inn**, which is just as delightful, with a beautiful little garden and parking at the back. ☎ (805)

682-9680. Similar prices. Reduced prices October to May.

☗ **The Ivanhoe** (map A1, **18**): 1406 Castillo Street (and Sola). ☎ 963-8832. Just the name is enough to set you dreaming. This charming residence was built in about 1880 by a retired Danish captain. Superb fireplace, antique furniture, warm decor. All the rooms or cottages can accommodate between one and three couples. The 'Captain's Quarters' cover an area of nearly 1,080 square feet (100 square metres) and occupy virtually the whole ground floor ($100 for two and $150 for four). Booking is definitely required.

☗ **Old Yacht Club Inn** (map D1, **19**): 431 Corona del Mar Drive. ☎ (805) 962-1277. Fax: 967-3989. Freephone: ☎ 1-800-549-1676 (in California) and 1-800-676-1676 (in the US). A residential district close to the ocean, not far from the Cabrillo Inn and the Sheraton. It's actually two houses side by side, the Old Yacht Club and Hitchcock House, which are furnished in exquisite taste, with warm colours and a crackling fireplace. There are 12 rooms at a wide range of prices, each with a different style. Courteous welcome. Special prices midweek and from October to May. Beach towel and bicycle provided. Private courtyard parking lot.

☗ **The Parsonage**: 1600 Olive Street. ☎ (805) 962-9336. Built in 1892 to serve the Trinity Episcopal Church as a boarding school, this large Victorian residence is now a comfortable B&B in a peaceful environment five blocks from the city centre. The five rooms all differ in size but each is decorated in cosy English style. The best is the Honeymoon Suite, which has a large corner bedroom with a superb view of the city and the ocean, a big drawing room and a bathroom with jacuzzi.

SAN FRANCISCO TO LOS ANGELES

☆☆☆ EXPENSIVE

☗ **The Cheshire Cat Inn**: 36 West Valerio Street. ☎ (805) 569-1610. Fax: (805) 682-1876. This is the most elegant B&B in the city and staying here will cost you anything between $140 and $270. The rooms are decorated in 'English country' style and the general atmosphere is smart and tasteful. The medium-priced rooms have a balcony and the more expensive ones are located in the two bungalows facing the main building. Pleasant, handsome garden with a pavilion in the middle containing a jacuzzi.

– The same proprietors have another B&B in much the same spirit, though it's not so smart – not so expensive either – two blocks further down: **The Secret Garden Inn and Cottages**, 1908 Bath Street. ☎ (805) 687-2300.

☗ **Simpson House Inn**: 121 East Arrellaga Street. ☎ (805) 963-7067. A magnificent Victorian house dating from 1874 and surrounded by a delightful garden. The rooms are certainly what you'd expect from the look of the place. It's even more expensive than the Cheshire Cat Inn, with prices going as high as $350. Bicycles provided.

WHERE TO EAT

If you like Mexican food, you've hit on exactly the right place. There are excellent restaurants and cafes and the prices are unbeatable.

☆ BUDGET

✕ **Esau's** (map B2, **30**): 403 State Street. Open Monday–Friday 6am–1pm, weekends 7am–3am. An extremely lively coffee shop that serves up good and copious food: omelettes, pancakes and French toast . . . It's the most popular place in the city, charging fair prices, and it's *the* place to go for breakfast. What more could you ask?

✕ **Joe's Cafe**: 536 State Street. ☎ 966-4638. Opened in 1928. A typically American place – the kind that campaigning politicians like to visit (Bob Dole came here on one of his tours). Long counter and checked oilcloth on the tables. The food is nothing out of the ordinary. The place is mainly popular as somewhere to drink, as the cocktails have a good reputation. It's quite lively at weekends.

✕ **Pierre Lafond Deli** (map B1, **31**): 516 State Street. ☎ 962-1455. Open daily, 7am–8pm. Terrace on the street and deli inside. Very wide range of sandwiches and vegetarian dishes, at lowish prices.

✕ **Maikai Cafe-Restaurant** (map B2, **32**): 217 State Street. ☎ 963-9276. Next to the station and near the large parking lot, this place has palms planted all around it. A central place, nice and inexpensive. Serves dishes based on fish, some of which have a vaguely Polynesian style. You order your meal, then pick it up at the counter. Pay before you eat, as in a fast-food restaurant. Decorated in the style of a Pacific beach with fans, aquariums and TV screens. Some tables on a terrace for taking the sun and dreaming of a Polynesian island.

✕ **Roses Cafe** (map C1, **33**): 424 East Haley Street. ☎ 966-3773. Open 7am–9.30pm. One of the best Mexican restaurants in the city. The setting is simple yet cosy at the same time. Counter with stools for enjoying a good selection of burritos, enchiladas, tacos, chilli, and so on.

✕ **La Super Rica**: 622 North Milpas (and Alphonse). ☎ 963-4940. Open 11am–9pm. Run by the same family since 1980, this Mexican *taquería* in the style of a large canteen is lasting well and keeping its reputation intact. The *verde* and *picante* sauces have a real taste of the country, as do the tacos. The dishes are copious and inexpensive, the daily special is often good, and the drinks are exotic, including tamarind and *horchata*. And, of course, there are Mexican beers: Bohemia, Tecate, etc. Plenty of people at lunch, but the district is a little tense in the evening, with gangs of young Mexicans misbehaving. Milpas, along with Haley Street, is the hot point of the city, one of those places where you don't go for a late-night stroll.

✕ **Sushi Go Go**: 119 Harbor Way. ☎ (805) 962-6568. The boss is called Bruce Lee, and sharing his name with the King of Kung Fu is a bit of a joke for him. His small snack shop, right beside Brophy's, has a good reputation even in the ultra-smart Montecito, and that says it all. His good humour and kind nature have a lot to do with it. His Fisherman's Sushi (four kinds of sushi and four Californian rolls), as well as his Tako Salad (octopus, cucumber and seaweed) and his Korean Bowl (barbecued beef on rice) are a bargain. A minuscule terrace lets you dine while relishing a view of the sun setting over the port and the Santa Ynez mountains.

✕ **Be Bop Burgers**: 111 State Street. ☎ (805) 966-1956. More interesting for its decor than its burgers, which are routine, but kids love it. There are old posters on the walls, red benches, miniskirted waitresses, music from the 1950s and 1960s, a big 1950s-style car (a different one each month). The set burger meal (burger, coke and chips) is really inexpensive. At weekends, many families come along with their kids, so it can be noisy.

✕ **Fatburger**: 718 State Street. ☎ (805) 962-8955. Who makes the best burger in the city? Everyone has their own answer to this controversial question, but many would vote without hesitation for this place. Fatburger with cheese, egg-burger, chilli-burger . . . whichever one you pick, it'll have the two virtues that make this place stand out – generous size and low price.

☆–☆☆ BUDGET TO MODERATE

✕ **Brophy** (map B3, **34**): in the fishing port. ☎ 966-4418. If you come in at the bottom of Castillo Street, turn right into Shoreline Drive, then into Harbor Way. This port bistro, located on the first floor of a dock building, is of interest as much for its cuisine as for its lively, sometimes rip-roaring atmosphere. The seafood obviously takes place of honour and the star is the famous clam chowder, a dish that gained its reputation on the East Coast. Also on offer are beer-boiled shrimps, mussels cooked in wine American-style, and there's always a 'fish of the day', which might be Atlantic salmon or shark. There's a balcony on the small terrace, which tends to fill up quickly because of the lovely view by day and by night. In the bar on the ground floor, which has a tiny terrace, you can enjoy small snacks (fish 'n' chips, fried squid or Brophy's fried shrimp).

✕ **Tutti's Bakery**: 129 East Anapamu Street. ☎ (805) 962-2089. From the terrace, there's a pleasant view of the gardens of the Court of Justice, which are just a minute or two away. Up until 11.30am you can get a generous and inexpensive brunch of excellent quality, choosing from such items as eggs Benedict, smoked salmon omelette or strawberry waffles. On the menu there's every imaginable kind of egg and omelette, plus a large selection of teas and herbal teas.

✕ **Mona Lisa Cafe**: 12 West de La Guerra. ☎ (805) 564-8783. At the heart of the Paseo Nuevo, the liveliest shopping centre in the city. Californian cuisine that lightly mixes the tastes and colours of Europe with those of Asia and Latin America. Take a seat in the patio to get the sun and watch the action. The sandwiches and salads are very tasty.

✕ **Playa Azul Cafe**: 914 Santa Barbara Street. ☎ (805) 966-2860. Very close to the Presidio. Lovely terrace with a holiday atmosphere. The food is Chicano-Mexican, and while they don't reach any great culinary heights, you can eat generously here. Successes include: steak *ranchera*, *chimichanga* (fried burrito with meat, beans and cheese), *carne asada* (minced meat, marinated and grilled, served with perfect corn pancakes) and tacos *de pescado*. Prices are lower at lunchtime, 11.30am–4pm.

✕ **The Natural Cafe** (map B1, **35**): 508 State Street. ☎ (805) 962-9494. Open daily, 11am–11pm. Good natural food at reasonable prices. The speciality is chilled fruit juice with a large choice of fruits including peach, banana, blueberry, pineapple and papaya.

☆☆–☆☆☆ MODERATE TO EXPENSIVE

✕ **Bucatini**: 436 State Street. ☎ (805) 957-4177. Take a seat on the patio and order either a pizza (10 or so to choose from) or such pasta dishes as *penne alla puttanesca* (spiced tomato sauce, black olives, capers), *rigatoni al pomodoro* (with tomato sauce and basil), which are cooked *al dente*. At lunch (11.30am–2.30pm) there are several dishes of the day as well as Italian-style snacks. Italian wines are sold by the glass. The service is cheery.

✕ **Piranha**: 714 State Street. ☎ (805) 965-2980. This Japanese place, with its sparse, modern decor and sushi bar with designer seats, may appear a little cold at first, but with good music in the background (jazz, blues, R'n'B, hip-hop) and the quality of the sushi, it doesn't take long for the atmosphere to warm up.

✕ **The Enterprise Fish Co.** (map B2, **37**): 225 State Street. ☎ 962-3313. Huge room in a former warehouse built of timber and corrugated iron. There's a bar at the entrance for drinks when you arrive, and you can watch the chefs preparing the food. The decor is suitably fishy, with nets and seascapes. The fish, all of which is fresh, is listed on hanging boards. The cuisine here is decent and it's a good place for seafood. Expect to pay $20 on average for a good meal. The service is excellent.

✕ **Paradise Cafe** (map B1, **36**): 702 Anacapa Street. ☎ 962-4416. Open 11am–11pm. Sunday brunch from 9am. The decor here is very Californian. The bar is one of the best known in Santa Barbara. The clientele isn't even slightly of the backpacker type – in fact quite the opposite: they're the smart and cool set. The place has a good reputation for its cocktails and fine wines. The cuisine is appreciated locally, though it's nothing special. They do a very reasonable *gazpacho* and good grilled fish. Terrace for fine weather. Cheerful service.

☆☆☆☆ SPLASH OUT

There's no shortage of smart restaurants in Santa Barbara.

✕ **Oysters**: 9 West Victoria Street. ☎ 962-9888. Quite a sober environment. The place has an excellent reputation for seafood and fish dishes, and some worth mentioning are: spaghetti with lobster, cream and mild peppers, linguini with clams, scallops with bacon and garlic, Cajun fillet steak with cornbread, grilled leg of lamb.

✕ **The Palace Cafe** (map B1, **38**): 8 East Cota Street (and State). ☎ 966-3133. Open daily, 5.30pm–midnight. Closed lunchtime. They have an elegant setting and a relaxed atmosphere, and specialize in Cajun and Creole cuisine, sprinkled with Italian touches. Enticing menu: some items stand out, include braised crawfish, blackened *filet mignon* and Louisiana barbecued shrimp. Desserts come in the form of such good Southern specialities as sweet potato pecan pie and key-lime pie. And the bill stays reasonable. Try the Cajun Martini as an aperitif – it'll certainly give you a twinkle!

WHERE TO HAVE A DRINK

🍸 **Bar Californian Hotel** (map C2, **50**): 35 State Street. ☎ (805) 966-7153. On the ground floor of an expensive but well-situated hotel, this is the liveliest bar in the city centre. Musical groups nearly every evening in summer.

🍸 **Santa Barbara Brewing Company**: 501 State Street. ☎ (805) 730-1040. Quite lively in the evening, especially at weekends. Eight TV screens tuned to non-stop sport channels combine with the special house beers to ensure its popularity. When a big American football game is on, it's pandemonium! The house brews about a dozen kinds of beer each year, including a spring beer and one for Christmas.

WHERE TO EAT IN THE AREA

✕ **Pane e Vino**: 1482 East Valley Road, Montecito. ☎ (805) 969-9274. If you enjoy *Hello!*-type gossip magazines, this Italian trattoria is definitely the place to visit. Michael Douglas eats here regularly, as do many of the showbiz personalities living in the area. The Italian cuisine is good but the prices tend to match the financial means of its ultra-smart clientele. The terrace is highly prized, and is screened from onlookers. Booking is essential.

✕ **Cold Spring Tavern**: 5995 Stage Coach Road. ☎ (805) 967-0066. In San Marco Pass, in the mountains overlooking Santa Barbara, about 10.5 miles (17km) from the centre of Santa Barbara. Take Highway 154 towards Lake Cachuma – it's well signed. This was once a stagecoach point on the old route that once linked Santa Barbara with places inland. There are two timber houses in the middle of the forest, so the tavern has hardly changed in the last 100 years and still has that feel of the Old West. The cuisine is good. Daytime snacks might include such things as venison hamburgers. On the (quite expensive) evening menu: sauteed medallions of rabbit, grilled fillet of New Zealand venison, fresh pastries, fish of the day. Booking is recommended for the evening meal and it's essential at weekends. Live music on Wednesday evenings and at weekends.

WHAT TO SEE AND DO

★ **State Street**: the backbone of the old city. Just about everything takes place right here. Strolling along a dozen blocks or so of its length is enjoyable by day or by night. Combine this with taking the **Red Tile Walking Tour,** which lets you take a look at the old adobe buildings in the area bounded by State, Anapamu, de la Guerra and Santa Barbara streets.

★ **El Presidio de Santa Barbara State Historic Park**: 123 East Cañon Perdido Street. ☎ (805) 965-0093. Open daily, 10.30am–4.30pm. Free admission. Founded in 1782, the Presidio Real de Santa Barbara was the last of a series of four fortified towns built by the Spanish along the

California coast – the others were at San Diego, Monterey and San Francisco.

The presidios played a vital role in the colonization of New Spain. They protected the missions and the newly-arrived colonials against attack by Indians or other invaders.

The Presidio de Santa Barbara was the seat of government for the whole region and stretched from the southern limit of the present county of San Luis Obispo to the village of Los Angeles. The whitewashed walls are built of adobe – a kind of masonry made from sun-dried clay bricks. Several earthquakes in 1806 and 1812 damaged the structure and the Presidio was in ruins by the time the Americans occupied California in 1846. Only some portions of the area survived when the city was rebuilt in accordance with the American plan in 1850.

Nowadays, all that remain are two of the original buildings: El Cuartel, the house of the officer responsible for the western gate, and another building, called 'Canedo adobe', which is used as an exhibition room for the park. The chapel, the monks' accommodation and the commandant's quarters have recently been reconstructed. There is a plan to rebuild something like a quarter of the original building.

The Presidio contrasts strongly with the surrounding buildings and you really get the impression you've arrived on the site of an archaeological dig. In fact, the digging is still going on. Inside are objects, paintings and costumes of the period, a genealogy of the people living in the Presidio, a model of the site, and posters explaining the digs and the reconstruction project. In the yard, which is planted with orange trees, you almost expect a sudden appearance by Zorro. In the chapel is a 17th-century tabernacle and a painting of Santa Barbara from 1785. The consumer society of the US seems like another world.

★ **Santa Barbara Museum of Art** (map A1, **60**): State and Anapamu. ☎ 963-4364. Fax: 966-6840. Open 11am–5pm (9pm Thursday), Sunday noon–5pm. Closed Monday. Free admission on Thursday and the first Sunday of the month. From its original area of 44,000 square feet (4,100 square metres), the museum has grown to 55,000 square feet (5,100 square metres), and understandably, everything is in a state of turmoil. At the time of writing the restructuring work was still underway. On the first floor is a remarkable Asian section; it contains pretty golden statuettes of the goddess Tara, a symbol of compassion and wisdom, a 19th-century Thai banner showing Buddha in every possible pose, an 18th-century Chinese lacquer screen depicting the lives of women in a palace, a Japanese kimono casket – all simply lovely examples of workmanship. This department is unlikely to move, although other works in the collection may have been put into storage awaiting the final reorganization. Other notable exhibits include a marble statuette by Auguste Rodin and canvases by Frederic Remington, the famous painter of the American West. A cafe and an interactive space for children are to be added to the space.

This new museum is likely to give more room to 19th-century Californian art (photography, painting, etc.), as well as to their collection of 20th-century art. There will continue to be a number of temporary exhibitions. The museum's permanent collection includes works by Sisley, Picasso,

Matisse, Monet, Dalí, Chagall, Kandinsky, Homer, Calder, Cole and Rivera.

★ **The History of the City Museum** (map B1, **61**): 136 East de la Guerra Street. ☎ 966-1601. Open 10am–5pm (noon on Sunday). Closed Monday. Free admission. Guided tours Wednesday, Saturday and Sunday at 1.30pm. In the former residence of an aristocrat, the Casa Grande, built in 1819 in brick and adobe, this is one of the finest buildings of its type in California. Souvenirs of the Casa and the de la Guerra family are on display, including religious statuary, historic manuscripts, Spanish embroidered clothing, a superb Chinese carved and gilded altar, the remarkable painting *Stormy Voyage around the Horn* by Franck W. Thompson, and numerous engravings and watercolours. In addition there is a reconstruction of a pioneer's house, old cowboy saddles, a collection of dresses from the early 20th century, and illustrations of the *Tales of Old California* by Charles C. Park.

Two adobe buildings also form an integral part of the museum: Casa de Covarrubias at 715 Santa Barbara Street, and Historic Adobe next door. As you leave the museum, there's a small cigar store opposite.

★ **The Santa Barbara Mission**: at the end of Laguna Street (and Los Olivos). ☎ 682-4713. Open daily, 9am–5pm. Closed Easter, Thanksgiving and Christmas. Small admission charge. Self-guided tour $3. One of the 10 Franciscan missions in California, it's home to 25 brothers. Built in 1786 and called the 'Queen of the Missions', it suffered two devastating earthquakes in 1812 and 1925. It was for a long time the parish church of the Chumash Indians and became a theological school, closing in 1986. To aid your visit, there's a small but comprehensive leaflet.

The collection includes a miscellany of exhibits, including souvenirs of the construction of the mission, examples of Chumash craft products, statues that adorned the pediment until the 1925 earthquake, tools belonging to the monks who operated the forge, the mission kitchen, an 18th-century altar, some wooden statuary, a catechism in Indian dialect and a beautiful figure of Christ in Philippine mahogany.

★ **Museum of Natural History**: 2559 Puesta del Sol Road. ☎ 682-4711. Open daily, 9am–5pm (10am Sunday and public holidays). Free admission on the first Sunday of the month except if this is a public holiday when the free day will be on the second Sunday. One of the most highly reputed museums in the country, although less prestigious than the one in Los Angeles. There is a large section devoted to the life of the Native Americans in prehistoric times, a skeleton of a huge blue whale, a fossil dwarf mammoth found at Santa Ana, as well as a planetarium.

★ **County Courthouse**: 1100 Anacapa Street. ☎ 681-4200. Open 8am–5pm (10am weekends and public holidays). Free admission. Guided tours Friday 10.30am and Saturday 2pm. A small palace built in 1926 in dazzling Spanish-Moorish style, containing many frescoes, carved doors and paintings. The gardens are very beautiful and it's worth climbing the tower to get the fine panorama of the city.

★ **Botanic Garden**: 1212 Mission Canyon Road. ☎ (805) 682-4726. Open November–February, Monday–Friday 9am–4pm, Saturday and Sunday 9am–5pm; March to October 9am–5pm, Saturday and Sunday 9am–6pm. Next to the mission. Here is a splendid panorama of

Californian flora, from cacti through to redwoods, with more than a thousand plants, including rare indigenous species.

For any addicts, the biggest fig-tree still standing in the US is the one at Moreton Bay, planted in 1874 and to be found at the intersection of Chapala Street and Highway 101.

★ **Santa Barbara Zoo**: 500 Ninos Drive. ☎ (805) 962-5339. Open daily, 10am–5pm (last tickets 4pm). This small zoo is obviously no rival for the one in San Diego, but the advantage is that you don't have to queue for hours here. It's considered by Americans to be a model for other zoos of the same size and it's very well kept and is well integrated into its environment. There are about 600 animals, some 100 of which can be viewed. Elephants, giraffes, gorillas, otters, leopards, etc. are each allotted a space that resembles their natural habitat as far as possible, and yet with some of the animals, it's possible to get right up close.

★ **Arlington Theatre**: 1317 State Street. Built in 1875, this was initially a hotel that was partially destroyed by the earthquake in 1925 and demolished in 1926. Since the colonial style had come back into fashion, it was rebuilt in its former style but this time as a theatre. The building's primary function today is as a centre for the performing arts rather than a cinema, and it presents a varied programme of concerts and dance performances. A popular film festival also takes place each year. If you find the colonial-style exterior extravagant, you'd better hold your breath for the interior, where Mexican village decor adorns every wall and the ceiling is painted to look like a starry sky. As a bonus, there's a large movie screen and comfortable seats. If you go to see a film, the admission charge is halved for the 4pm show.

★ **The Stagecoach, Wagon and Cart Museum** (map B2, **62**): 129 Castillo Street. ☎ 569-2077. Open Sunday 1–4pm. Some of these vehicles are more than 300 years old. They are dusted off every August for the big parade in celebration of Old Spanish Days.

★ **Santa Barbara Sea Center** (map C2, **63**): Stearns Wharf. ☎ 963-1067. Open June–September, Monday–Thursday and Sunday 10am–5pm, Friday and Saturday 10am–9pm; October–May, Monday–Friday noon–5pm, Saturday, Sunday and public holidays 10am–5pm. Closed Thanksgiving and Christmas. Displays on the marine fauna of Santa Barbara Channel.

★ **Santa Barbara Winery**: 202 Anacapa Street. ☎ 963-3633. Open daily, 10am–5pm. Guided tours 10am–5.30pm. There's a tour of the production facilities for the wines of Santa Ynez Valley, including Chardonnay, Sauvignon Blanc, Pinot Noir, Cabernet Sauvignon, etc.

– **Cruises on board the Harbor Queen**: designed to let you enjoy the view of palm-lined beaches, the Spanish architecture and the magnificent mountains of Santa Ynez. Departures are from Stearns Wharf. For information: ☎ 969-5217.

WHAT TO SEE IN THE AREA

★ **Montecito**: a very pretty little town situated several miles to the east of Santa Barbara, between the luxuriant hills and the Pacific Ocean, and also known as the 'little Beverly Hills' of Santa Barbara. Charlie Chaplin had the Montecito Inn built in 1928 and it became a refuge for Hollywood stars. It's still there now, at 1295 Coast Village Road. The lift is the original one – 1920s vintage. The swimming pool is strangely small for a hotel of this standing. Prices are those of a four-star hotel. ☎ 1-800-843-2017 or (805) 969-7854. Fax: (805) 969-0623.

★ **Channel Islands**: there are eight islands, the largest of which is Santa Cruz, 23 miles (37km) off the coast. It takes only 20 minutes by plane from Camarillo Airport to get to Anacapa Island and it's also possible to make an impromptu trip to any of the islands. The boats leave from Ventura.

★ **The Railroad Museum**: 300 North Los Carneros Road, at Goleta (the little town just before Santa Barbara University). ☎ 964-3540. Open Wednesday–Sunday 1–4pm. You can see the old goods depot, station building and Southern Pacific carriages; there's also a wonderful miniature train and the usual shops, etc. To get here, take a No. 11 bus.

★ **Whale-watching**: from mid-March to late April. The small grey whales arriving from Canada pass by the coast of Santa Barbara on their way to the warm waters of Mexico. In summer, it's the turn of the large blue whales. During these periods, several boats leave each day to watch them, and the voyage lasts approximately 2 hours. Generally, the explanations given by the skippers are good. Catch a boat on the dock at Stearns Wharf, but call ahead, because timetables can vary. In summer, because of the volume of trade, the prices soar.

★ **The Wine Route**: the vineyards are located to the northwest of Santa Barbara, around Santa Ynez, Los Olivos and Santa Maria, where about 30 winegrowers produce Californian wine from the Chardonnay, Pinot Noir, Riesling, Sauvignon Blanc, Cabernet Sauvignon and Gewürztraminer grape varieties. A certain number of wine cellars are open to visitors. A list and map of the wine cellars and the vineyards (the Santa Barbara County Wineries Touring Map) is available from the tourist information office.

LEISURE ACTIVITIES AND FESTIVALS

Nightlife is quite brisk. It does no harm to remember that the Santa Barbara police are extremely severe on drink-driving. For a complete schedule of festivals, buy a copy of *The Independent.*

– **Old Spanish Days Festival**: this fiesta is held at the beginning of August and consists of five crazy days with a parade of old buggies, a rodeo, mariachi singing, and dancing in the crowded streets. If you want accommodation during this period, you'll need to book several months ahead, and expect to pay up front.

– **The University of California of Santa Barbara** organizes excellent concerts and dance shows. Combine this with a visit to their Museum of Art, which has a number of interesting works. For information ☎ 961-2951.

– **Summer Solstice Parade**: a big, extremely colourful festival is held on the Saturday closest to 21 June (the longest day of the year).

– **International Film Festival**: takes place in March, in the old and charming Arlington Theatre.

– **French Festival**: held on the weekend nearest to 14 July (Bastille Day), at Oak Park. Take Highway 101, and exit at Pueblo or Mission. Admission free. This is the biggest French celebration on the West Coast, with dancing, music, street acrobats, French cuisine and, of course, French being spoken.

SHOPPING

The Santa Barbara Supply Sergeant: 631 State Street. ☎ (805) 963-3868. You'll find all sorts of things here. Complete survival equipment, Harley-Davidson boots, Carhartt jackets (not expensive), rain gear, outsize shirts, military trousers, all at prices that are definitely attractive for Europeans.

INLAND CALIFORNIA (THE SIERRA NEVADA)

SACRAMENTO

AREA CODE: 916

Between San Francisco and South Lake Tahoe lies the old city of Sacramento. It's been rebuilt pretty much as it was in the days of the Wild West. Magnificent steam trains carrying passengers still call at the railroad station on the banks of the Sacramento River, leaving you with the feeling that you were in the middle of a film set – or transported back in time.

– There's a **Train Museum** in the old city, where you get a real Hollywood-type show. Admission is not expensive. Other things to see include the **Capitol**, the **Automobile Museum**, and the **paddleboats**, which have been converted into a museum.

– From Sacramento, take Highway 50 if you want to get to South Lake Tahoe. It's a very pretty, scenic drive.

WHERE TO STAY

☆ BUDGET

International Hostel: 900 H Street. ☎ 443-1691. A nice youth hostel located in an old Victorian house. Reception open 7.30–10.30am and 5–10pm. Choice between dormitories and private rooms. There's a launderette and the place has plenty of information. The downside is that you are not allowed in during the day (9.30am–5pm).

WHERE TO EAT

☆☆–☆☆☆ MODERATE TO EXPENSIVE

✕ **River City Brewing Co.**: Downtown Plaza, near K Street. ☎ 447-2739. Definitely the liveliest place to go in the evening. The restaurant is definitely worth going out for – they serve good American cuisine with Caribbean, Hispanic and Asian influences. You wait at a large bar, equipped with a portable gizmo that vibrates when your table's ready! Good local beers. Expect to pay about $18 for a meal and a beer.

WHAT TO SEE

★ **Sutter's Fort State Historic Park**: at the intersection of 27th and L streets. ☎ 455-4422. Right in the heart of the city is the old fort of John Sutter, which has been fully restored and is now brought to life by actors in period costume. The admission charge is quite expensive.

John Sutter's life was quite a story. Born in Switzerland in 1803, Sutter left his wife, five children and plenty of debts behind him and emigrated to America in 1834. He worked in New York, travelled through Missouri and Kansas, sailed to the Hawaiian islands, and finally landed in California in July 1839, hoping to make his fortune. The Mexican government of the day granted him some land and a Mexican passport, and he became a new pioneer of the West, dreaming of founding 'New Helvetia' on American soil. Somehow, he achieved this goal and became the biggest landowner in the West. In 1848, he employed a man named Marshall to build a watermill at Coloma, on the South Fork River, and it was here that Marshall discovered gold. The Gold Rush was sparked off at that moment, but, ironically, Sutter not only didn't get a penny from it but was in fact ruined. He died in poverty while waiting for compensation from the federal government. The fort that he had built was his headquarters for many years.

SOUTH LAKE TAHOE

AREA CODE: 916 (CALIFORNIA SHORE), 702 (NEVADA SHORE)

South Lake Tahoe is a holiday resort on the southern edge of the large lake that links California and Nevada. The lake, with its azure blue waters, is surrounded by lovely forests of fir-trees. A panoramic driving route skirts the edge of the lake. The waters are incredibly blue and the beaches feel really Mediterranean, with a sky every bit as blue as in Greece – so much so that you'd think you were down at sea level. Yet Lake Tahoe is a mountain lake, an astonishing 6,125ft (1,867m) above sea level. Of course, you can't expect such a natural wonder as this to remain untouched, considering how close it is to the large cities on the Californian coast. Tourism is well developed here, and advancing at lightning speed.

The climate here is very sunny, but it's not overwhelming, mainly because of the altitude. There are lots of things to do, including watersports, boat rides and bathing, and plenty of forest walks.

In winter, this is a really good place for skiing. It's very well equipped and Valley Springs, which was an Olympic site, is just a short distance away.

LAKE TAHOE

– **Origin**: this is not a volcanic lake but more of a bowl formed by the collapse of the underlying rock strata.

– **Dimensions**: it's the third deepest lake in North America (1,617ft/493m) and stretches 22 miles (35km) from north to south and 12 miles (19km) from east to west.

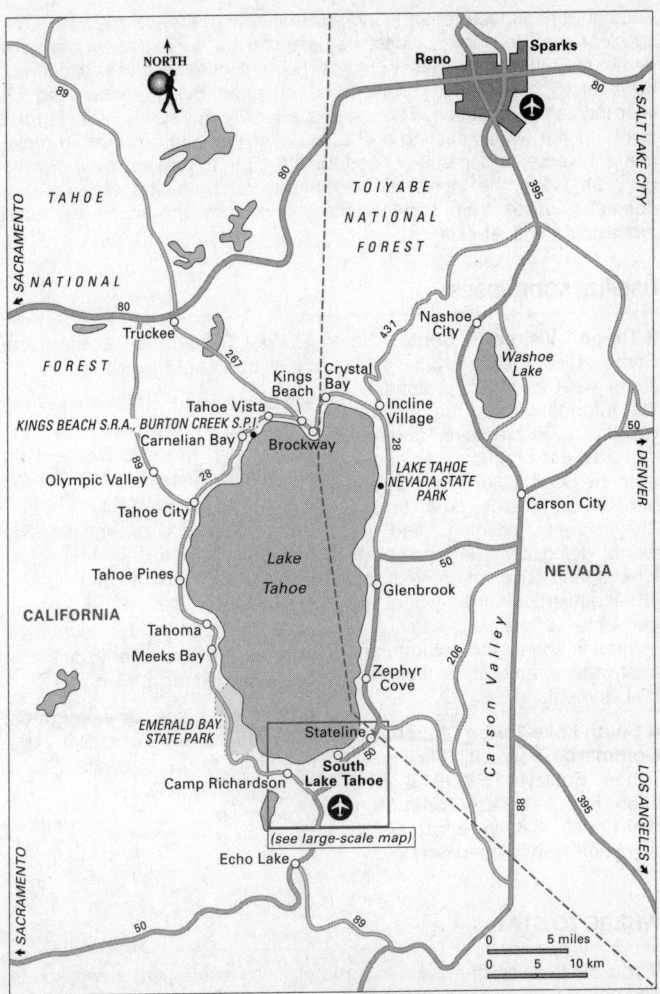

LAKE TAHOE

– **The waters of Lake Tahoe**: the lake is fed by rain and meltwater from the snow and ice on the mountains all around, although interestingly, not a single drop of the water from Lake Tahoe ever reaches the ocean. A minor tributary, the Truckee River, branches off it, running down to Reno and eventually reaching Pyramid Lake, in the Nevada desert. The average temperature of the water fluctuates around 70°F/20°C in summer along the shore, where you can bathe, falling, of course, as you move further away from the shore.

Another curious feature is the incredible clarity of the waters, which are so clear that, in some places, objects can be seen underwater at a depth of 72ft (22m). This purity is becoming seriously endangered, however, because of a proliferation of algae being encouraged by ever-increasing pollution. The algae are slowly but surely reducing the clarity of the water, casting a shadow over the lake bottom. To make matters worse, and in spite of serious attempts to prevent it happening, pollution is on the increase, with the worst problems coming from domestic waste from local houses, and from the many outboard motorboats and jet-skis.

USEFUL ADDRESSES

Tahoe Visitors' Center: at Camp Richardson, 1.25 miles (2km) west of the city along US 89. Information on the environment is available here; and you can also get practical information from the South Lake Tahoe Chamber of Commerce (*see below*). They're very obliging, and it's worth going for the chance to look at their observation point, cut into the riverbank, from where you can observe the fish, particularly salmon in spring and autumn, and freshwater creatures in their natural element.

■ **South Lake Tahoe Chamber of Commerce** (map, **2**): 3066 Lake Tahoe Boulevard. ☎ (916) 541-5255. Fax: 541-7121. Open Monday–Friday 8.30am–5pm, Saturday 9am–4pm. Closed Sunday.

✉ **Post Office**: Park Avenue, one block north of Highway 50.

Greyhound: 1099 Park Avenue, east of the city, near the border with Nevada. The building is located between the Harrah Hotel and the Embassy. The entrance is on the parking lot side (Harrah's Casino Entrance) – just look for the Transportation Office. ☎ 1-800-231-2222. Buses depart from the parking lot alongside. The bus for Sacramento and San Francisco leaves at 6am.

■ **Hire of bikes and mopeds**: 3131 Highway 50. ☎ 544-7160. Opposite the El Dorado campground. They also hire out small motorboats.

WHERE TO STAY

If you are thinking of staying in a motel, don't come here at weekends. The prices soar horrendously and it's difficult to find a room.

☆ BUDGET

Doug's Mellow Mountain Retreat (map, **11**): 3787 Forest. ☎ 544-8065. About 1 mile (2km) from the casinos, and 0.5 miles (1 km) from the lake, Doug's is a private youth hostel in the woods. It has billiards, skis and gym apparatus. Sleeping accommodation is in small dormitories each with three or five beds. There's a well-fitted kitchen, plus drawing room with divans and TV. An excellent place for backpackers.

Pioneer Inn Motel (map, **12**): 3863 Pioneer Trail. ☎ 544-5728. Situated among the trees at the edge of the road. Excellent welcome. Parking lot in an interior courtyard. The rooms are large and impeccable, with fan, shower and WC, TV. This is the motel offering the best value for money in the whole of South Lake Tahoe.

☆☆ MODERATE

Rodeway Inn: 3520 Highway 50. ☎ 544-1177. Fax: 541-3983. Timber building with 33 rooms. Warm welcome, clean, quiet rooms with telephone and TV. Free coffee provided. Small swimming pool.

Lazy S Lodge (map, **13**): 609 Emerald Bay Road. ☎ 541-0230. Fax: 541-2503. Surrounded by trees and set away from the road, this place has bungalows and nicely appointed rooms at fair prices. You get a shower and WC, fan, kitchenette. There's a parking lot at the back. Also a swimming pool and lawn. Excellent welcome.

Sunshine Inn Motel (map, **14**): 1184 Emerald Bay Road. ☎ 542-3500. Set among trees, about 300 yards (275 metres) from the big 'Y-junction'. The place has less charm than the Lazy S Lodge, and no swimming pool, but prices are very reasonable and you can park.

Motel 6 (map, **15**): 2375 Lake Tahoe Boulevard. ☎ 542-1400.

INLAND CALIFORNIA

☆☆☆ EXPENSIVE

Royal Valhalla Motor Lodge (map, **16**): 4104 Lakeshore Drive. ☎ 544-2233. A fairly upmarket motel at the edge of the lake in a peaceful and green little spot, situated not far from the casinos. Spacious, classically comfortable rooms.

CAMPGROUNDS

Eldorado: at the western entrance to the city. Situated in a pretty pine forest, about 100 yards (90 metres) from the lake. Quite expensive. Avoid positioning yourself too close to Highway 50 – it may be noisy.

Campground By The Lake (map, **10**): ☎ 542-6096. Behind the Chamber of Commerce offices, on the edge of Highway 50, but pretty quiet. Hot showers and well-equipped washing facilities.

Eagle Point Campground: approximately 4 miles (7km) northwest of South Lake Tahoe on Highway 89. Reservations from Destinet: ☎ 1-800-444-7275 or (916) 541-3030. Superb site (the nicest one around the whole lake) overlooking Emerald Bay. The individual spaces are spread out in a wood that looks out over a lovely creek with a small island in the middle, and you share the space with the squirrels. The pitches with the best view are numbers 54–70, at the far end of the campground.

D.L. Bliss State Park Campground: on Highway 89, about 6 miles (10km) west of South Lake Tahoe, after Emerald Bay. ☎ 525-7277. Another very nice campground, on a slightly less sloping site than the Emerald Bay State Park, but the positions are shaded and well spaced. Also, there's a Mediterranean-style beach, picnic spots and miles of paths for hiking. Occasionally, bears drop in to visit.

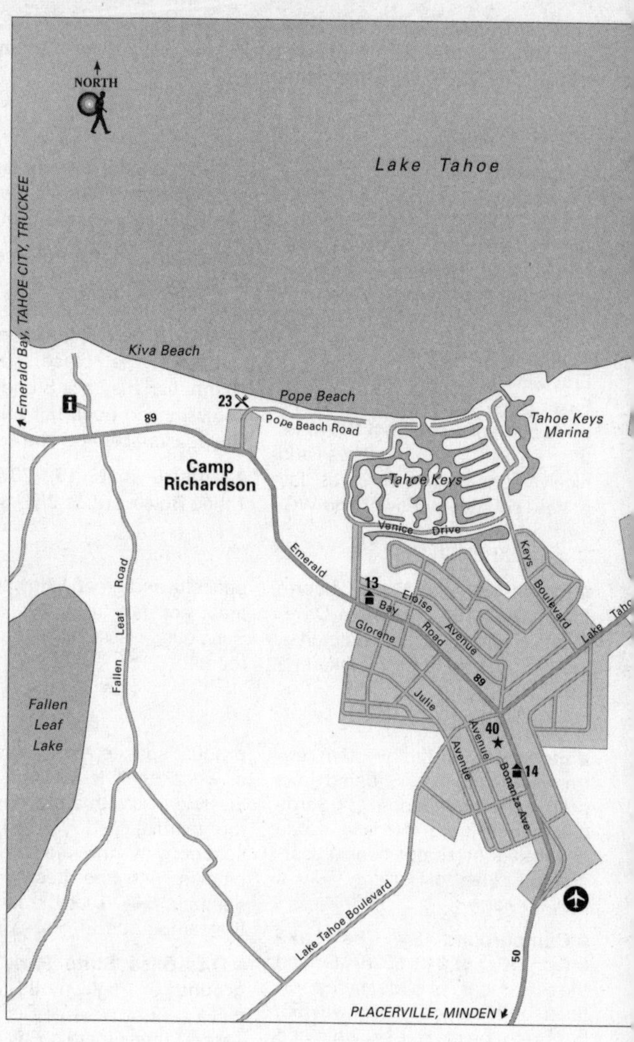

Useful Addresses

- Tahoe Visitors' Center
- 2 South Lake Tahoe Chamber of Commerce

Where to Stay

- 10 Campground By The Lake
- 11 Doug's Mellow Mountain Retreat
- 12 Pioneer Inn Motel
- 13 Lazy S Lodge
- 14 Sunshine Inn Motel
- 15 Motel 6
- 16 Royal Valhalla Motor Lodge

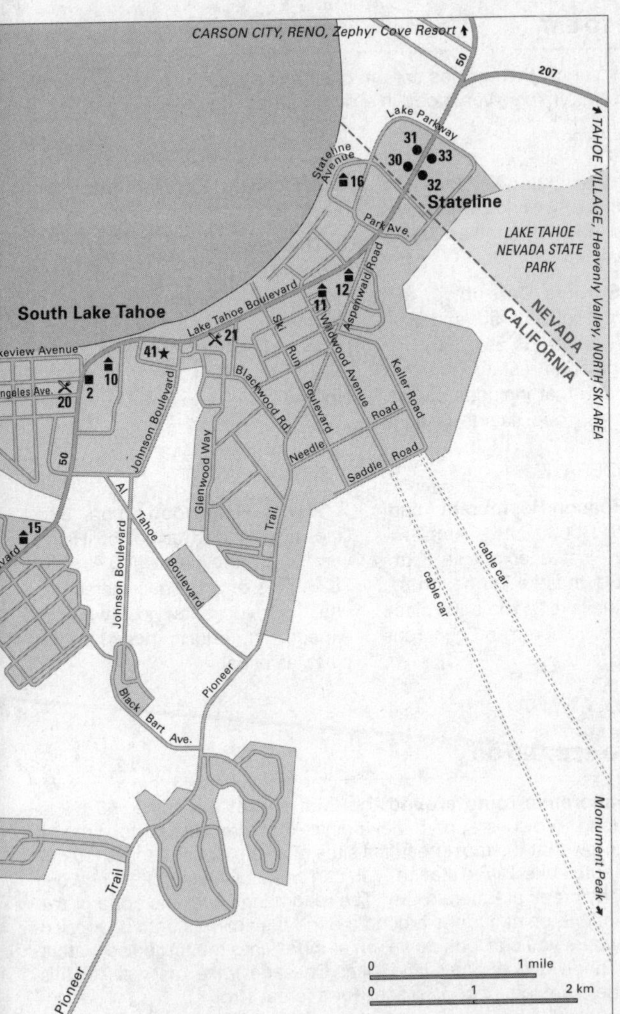

SOUTH LAKE TAHOE

Where to Eat

- 20 The Sprouts Cafe
- 21 The Brewery
- 23 The Beacon Restaurant
- 33 Planet Hollywood

Casino-hotels

- 30 Harvey's
- 31 Horizon
- 32 Harrah's

General

- 40 Shopping mall
- 41 Safeway

INLAND CALIFORNIA

WHERE TO EAT

As in Las Vegas, the casinos are the cheapest places to eat: they make sure that everything's very good in order to attract gamblers.

☆ BUDGET

✕ **Harvey's** (map, **30**): this is a casino that's well known for its delicious and affordable Graveyard Breakfast.

✕ **The Sprouts Cafe** (map, **20**): corner of Highway 50 and Alameda Avenue. ☎ 541-6969. A small vegetarian restaurant with a varied menu that includes bagels, sandwiches, soup, salads, lasagne and houmous. Excellent place for breakfast.

✕ **The Brewery** (map, **21**): on Highway 50, opposite the entrance to Lakeland Village. This is a cafe for good snacks. It makes its own beers – six different varieties. Less expensive and better than Planet Hollywood.

☆☆ MODERATE

✕ **The Beacon Restaurant** (map, **23**): ☎ 541-0630. At Camp Richardson, just over a mile (2km) west of South Lake Tahoe, on the edge of the lake. A romantic place with a nice welcome and generous portions.

✕ **Planet Hollywood** (map, **33**): Caesar's Tahoe Casino, 55 Highway 50, Stateline. ☎ (702) 588-7828. One of a famous restaurant chain, so you know just what to expect. The music plays at full blast, as usual.

WHAT TO SEE AND DO

★ **The panoramic route around the lake shore**: this route, 68 miles (110km) long, provides superb viewpoints; if you're pushed for time, it helps to know that the most beautiful sites of all are about 6 miles (10km) west of South Lake Tahoe station. You can hire a bike and take a ride out to the pretty creek at Emerald Bay. The road hangs over the edge of the lake and at one point, it goes around a bend then climbs onto a wooded hill from where you can look down, on all sides, into the turquoise waters of Lake Tahoe and another little lake, Cascade Lake, as well. In this vicinity, there are lots of good places for a forest stroll.

★ **The casinos**: these will be of interest only if you haven't already been to Las Vegas, as they have neither Vegas's splendour nor its excesses. On the eastern edge of the city.

★ **Lake Cruise**: three departures per day (11am, 1.30pm and 4pm); the Tahoe Queen, a Mississippi-style paddleboat, goes out along the lake as far as Emerald Bay, on a trip that lasts for 2 hours.

★ **Seaplane flight over the lake**: San Francisco Seaplane Tours (☎ 583-0673) organizes 30-minute flights over part of the lake, especially the southern end, and gives you a good chance to see Emerald Bay from the air. It's a memorable experience but it does cost about $90 per person. Departures are from Tahoe City Marina, in Tahoe City, next to the lake

(700 North Lake Boulevard). The plane is parked in front of the **Grazie** restaurant.

★ **Parasailing on the lake**: departures from the Ski Run Marina, in the centre of South Lake Tahoe.

YOSEMITE NATIONAL PARK

AREA CODE: 209

'This sierra shouldn't be called snowy (Nevada) but luminous.'

John Muir, *A Summer in the Sierra*

Some 317 miles (510km) north of Los Angeles and 180 miles (290km) east of San Francisco is this magnificent park, the first place in the world to be made a protected area – in 1864 – by a decree signed by Abraham Lincoln himself.

This valley was given the name of Yosemite (pronounced *yossemittee* with the stress on the second syllable) in memory of a Native American tribe, the Uzumatis, who were destroyed in the mid-19th century. Yosemite Park covers thousands of acres of forest, part of it devastated by a fire in August 1990, and towering mountains where the altitudes vary from 1,000 feet to 13,000 feet (600m and 3,960m). This is one of the great sanctuaries for the fauna and flora of the American continent. Yosemite Valley, right in the centre of the park, is one of the most beautiful examples of a glaciated valley in existence anywhere, and its two fantastic monoliths, El Capitán and Half Dome, are quite unlike anything else. The valley's main characteristic is its high, steep sides and its flat bed, along which the Merced River flows – all that now remains of the floor of the glacier.

Right at the heart of the Sierra Nevada is a vision of greenery and mountains, where the giant sequoias, the incredible landscapes and panoramas will take your breath away. The animals that live here are entirely free – the wolves, the bears, the deer and the squirrels that come to beg for food at your feet.

TIP

Since the park is home to lots of bears, you must put all your food (as well as everything that smells good, like soap, aftershave or shaving foam) into one of the large iron boxes that you'll find at every camping space. Generally speaking, the bears are not aggressive but may be if provoked.

The park really is immense and, since the roads are winding and there are often motor homes to slow the traffic down, you should expect to take 1 hour 30 minutes to 2 hours to cross it, without stopping, from west to east.

For full information: ☎ 372-0200. Website: www.nps.gov/yose. For practical information and reservations, use this website: www.nps.gov/parks.html.

In the park itself, at Yosemite Village, there's a supermarket, post office, garage, service station, deli and grocery store, shops, restaurants and a museum behind the Visitors' Center. You can also get a free brochure at the Visitors' Center (*see* 'Useful Places and Information').

As far as climate goes, it's best to book your trip to Yosemite for the summer months. It can get very cold, even in April.

HOW TO GET THERE

BY BUS

– **Travelling from the west**: Greyhound buses only go as far as Merced, west of the park. To get from Merced to Yosemite, take a YARTS or a VIA bus, which connect with the Greyhound service.

An **Amtrak** train, ☎ 1-800 USA-RAIL, will take you from San Francisco to Merced, from where you can catch a connecting YARTS or VIA bus to Yosemite.

VIA Charter Lines (☎ 722-0366) provide two buses daily to the park, leaving from Merced. The trip from Merced to Yosemite takes 2 hours 30 minutes.

Grayline (☎ 558-9400 in San Francisco) will give you a connection with Amtrak departing from San Francisco. Fares are high: $130 per adult for a return ticket. Call them 24 hours in advance.

– **Travelling from the east**: Greyhounds stop at Lee Vining. Then you take a **Yosemite Transportation System** bus, but these only run from 1 July to 10 September and there's only one bus per day. Booking is mandatory in summer. Note that this route goes through the Tioga Pass, which, because of snow, is open only from June to October – and not always then, as it still depends on the weather!

– **From San Francisco**: if you don't have a lot of time, you can take a one-day trip organized by **Tower Tour**, 77 Jefferson Street, ☎ 434-8687. This agency has an office on Fisherman's Wharf, in the Travelodge Hotel. A trip lasting approximately 13 hours costs $99 and runs three days a week.

BY CAR

– **There are four entrances**, including two from the west, that are easily accessible from San Francisco. If you come from Las Vegas, note that the eastern entrance is often closed (best to call beforehand).

– **Travelling from the south**: if you are coming from LA, turn right immediately after the park entrance in order not to miss the sequoias.

USEFUL PLACES AND INFORMATION

ℹ On arrival, you must stop at the **Visitors' Center**, where you'll find friendly rangers who will give you a map showing the roads, walking paths and cycle tracks. There's also a small, well-produced park newssheet that shows the level of difficulty of the various walks, the average time you can expect to take, etc. The rangers can also tell you the state of availability in every campground and will direct you to

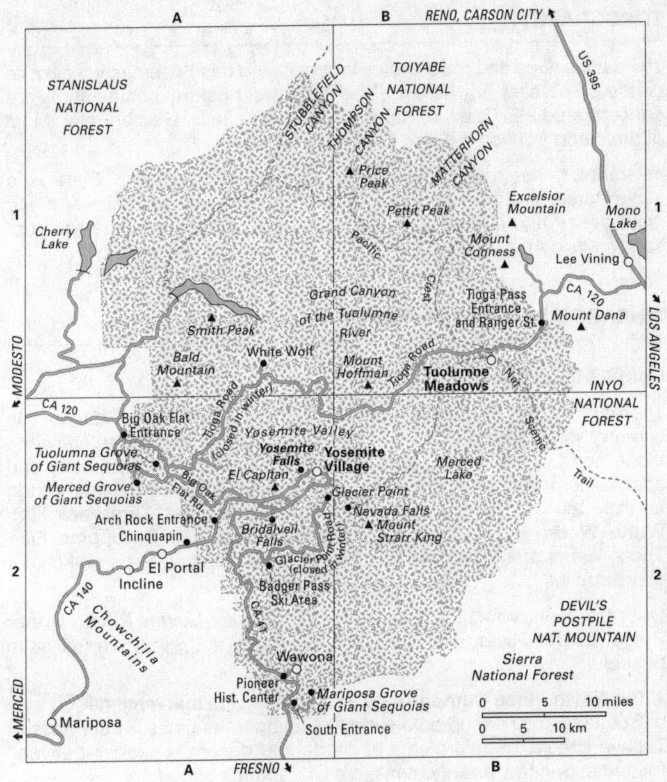

YOSEMITE NATIONAL PARK

the ones that still have sites available. They will be able to tell you about the kind of facilities at the campgrounds (water, shower, barbecue, etc.).

Information on the park: ☎ (209) 372-0200. Website: www.nps.gov/yose.

– **Admission charge**: $20 per vehicle, valid for seven days; $10 on foot or by bicycle. The 'Golden Eagle Pass' is on sale on the spot, costing $50 per vehicle and it also gives you access to all the other national parks.

– As in all national parks, the ideal place to spend the night is a **campground**, not only because it's the cheapest solution (though it is!), but also because it's the only way to live in harmony with nature while exploring its treasures. Even though the centre of the park (the Valley) is often full up in high summer, it's still possible to find a place.

TOPOGRAPHY

The park is huge and roughly oval in shape, and has Yosemite Valley at its centre. The Valley is where the park's greatest natural beauty spots are concentrated – El Capitán, Half Dome, Nevada Falls, Glacier Point. Most of the campgrounds are also located here.

In summer, the area is completely packed with people. There is a supermarket and parking lots – and a constant flow of vehicles. If you want peace and a more intimate experience, avoid the high season or camp outside the valley.

WHERE TO STAY IN THE PARK

CAMPGROUNDS

The park has 15 or so campgrounds with varying levels of comfort. In summer, it is advisable to avoid those in the Valley and give preference to those north of the Valley (even if some are quite rough-and-ready and accessible only if you have your own vehicle). The following are not too far from the western entrance to the park: **Crane Flat**, **Tamarack Flat**, **White Wolfe** and, further on, **Yosemite Creek** and **Porcupine Flat**. These last two and Tamarack Flat have no drinking water, so take your own supplies.

Out of season, you can camp at the Valley sites: **Lower Pines**, **Upper Pines**, **Lower River**, etc. There's often space and everything is more peaceful.

☗ The **North Pines Campground** is in a landscape that reminds you a bit of Scotland. You set up on a sandy area under the pines on the edge of Tenaya Creek. There's plenty of shade and generous spaces between the tents. Sanitary arrangements are OK, if rather antiquated.

– The best way to be sure of having a space is to book several weeks ahead. **Reservations**: the number for international calls: ☎ (301) 722-1257. Freephone: ☎ 1-800-436-7275. Or you can book through the website, www.reservations.nps.gov. It's usually still possible to find a camping space at the last minute, if you don't mind being on a campground outside the Valley – you just have to get there early, like before 10am. Look on the map distributed by the rangers. In any case, five of the campgrounds operate on a first-come-first-served basis and don't take reservations. As a last resort, if everything is full, you can still ask people to share their site: try looking for individuals or couples who have a small tent.

■ **Yosemite National Park Campgrounds Office**: ☎ (209) 372-8502.

THE LODGES

– To book a lodge inside the park, write to **Yosemite Park Central Reservations**: 5410 E Home, Fresno, CA 93727. ☎ (209) 252-4848. You have to pay a deposit equivalent to the charge for one night. From June to September, there's a good chance that the answering machine will tell you everything is sold out because, in principle, you have to book in advance! But, while the message is rattling on, you're told to try all the same (by pressing button 1 or 3 on your phone). Your call is then diverted to Yosemite reservations for tent cabins or cabins without bath: these are reservations that haven't been taken up.

Canvas Tent Cabins: at Curry Village. Offer tents with two beds, so you'll need a sleeping bag. Right in the middle of the forest. There's a chance you'll find a place without booking – if you get there by 6am!

Cabins Without Bath: at Curry Village and Yosemite Lodge. The walls are solid, but you're still very close to the campground. Costs about the same as a moderate-price motel.

WHERE TO STAY AND WHERE TO EAT OUTSIDE THE PARK

LEE VINING

Approximately 10 miles (16km) from the eastern (Tioga Pass) entrance to Yosemite Park, on Highway US 395. This is a pretty, peaceful village overlooking the magnificent Lake Mono, with the ghost town of Bodie only 25 miles (40km) away. One disadvantage: until spring arrives, you may find the Tioga Pass from Yosemite closed because of snow. If that happens, there's no access to the park from the east: you have to go around the park via the north (which is a whole day's trip) to reach the western gate. There are several motels, but nothing cheap at Lee Vining. Everything fills up quickly in summer, so book. If everything is full, go to Lone Pine (*see below*) rather than Bridgeport.

Mono Lake Information Center: on Highway 395, level with 3rd Street. ☎ (760) 647-6595. Website: www.monolake.org. Open daily in summer 9am–10pm. Plenty of information about tours in the Lee Vining and Lake Mono area. They organize guided canoe tours of the lake.

Mono Vista RV Park Campground: at the northern exit from the village. ☎ (619) 647-6401. Pretty lawns, very green (even in summer), and very clean sanitary facilities. Nights here can be freezing cold.

The Inn at Lee Vining: 2nd Street and Mono Lake Avenue. In the centre, but away from the main road. ☎ (619) 647-6300. A pretty little motel, the least expensive in the village. The welcome is excellent and the rooms are decent enough. Some have kitchenettes and cost a moderate price (around $70 for two). Free coffee.

Murphey's Motel: Main Street (US 395). ☎ (619) 647-6316. Freephone: ☎ 1-800-334-6316. Good welcome and clean rooms with TV and phone, some with jacuzzi. More expensive than the previous entry.

Gateway Motel: Main Street. ☎ (619) 647-6467. Charming timber-built house with terraces facing Lake Mono and its astonishing limestone formations. A little more expensive than its neighbours, costing about $100 for two.

Yosemite Trails Inn: a good restaurant run by Native Americans and located in the main street, across from the Trading Company shop. ☎ (619) 647-6369. Open 6am–10pm. The cuisine is simple and informal: steaks, soup, salads, burgers. The breakfast is really good and the evening menu is copious and cheap. Native American craft products on display on the walls.

BRIDGEPORT

Some 30 miles (50km) from the eastern (Tioga Pass) entrance to Yosemite Park.

☗ **Virginia Creek Settlement**: Highway 395. ☎ 932-7780. Just 20 miles (33km) north of Lee Vining and 5 miles (8km) south of Bridgeport. The boss of this restaurant, motel and campground is a humorous guy, and puts up notices like the one that says: 'In 1897, nothing happened here!' There are two rooms in the motel and a campground museum in the garden; you sleep in a teepee or covered wagon at the water's edge. There are also some tents. The place also operates a restaurant where they serve pizza, pasta and salads. Prices are reasonable.

MAMMOTH LAKES

On US 395 south of Lee Vining, 35 miles (57km) from the eastern (Tioga Pass) entrance to Yosemite Park (approximately 45 minutes by car). This is a big ski resort in winter, remaining very lively in summer. Out of 37 restaurants, only four are fast-food outlets, which must say something.

☗ **Motel 6**: 3372 Main Street. ☎ (619) 934-6660. Rooms are quite cheap. If this place is full, there are other inexpensive motels on the same side of the road.

☗ **Swiss Chalet Motel Lodge**: 3776 Viewpoint Road. ☎ 1-800-937-9477 or (760) 934-2403. Around $65 a night for two. Rooms are quite well kept, with balcony and view. Swiss chalet decor, as you might guess from the name. Excellent welcome.

✕ **Breakfast Club**: on Main Street. On the right as you go down, beside the Shell station. Look for the black-and-white bar stools at the entrance. Serves good breakfasts: *huevos rancheros*, club burrito, scrambled eggs, omelettes and pancakes.

✕ **Perry's Pasta and Pizza**: Main Street, level with Motel 6. ☎ 934-6521. A cool little terrace on summer evenings, and a bar – this is a good place for an Italian meal without bankrupting yourself. Practical for anyone staying at the Motel 6 on the other side of the road.

✕ **Gringo's Mexican Food y Cantina**: in the main street, facing the Fire Department. Open from 4pm. Decent cuisine, copious and inexpensive.

OAKHURST (SOUTHERN ENTRANCE)

South of Yosemite Park on Route 41. Several motels, slightly more upmarket than those at Lee Vining.

☗ **White Chief Mountain**: at Fish Camp. ☎ 683-5444. At the southern entrance to Yosemite Park going toward Oakhurst. A very hospitable motel, deep in the woods. Pleasant restaurant serving good cuisine. Closed in winter (opens 1 April); closed Sunday and Monday in season.

☗ **Apple Blossom B&B**: 44606 Silver Spur Trail, at Ahwahnee, a village on Route 49, 8 miles

(13km) north of Mariposa. ☎ (209) 642-2001 or 642-3880. Just 45 minutes from the southern entrance to the park, this is a charming place run by nice people. Beautiful rooms for two or four. Excellent breakfast. Jacuzzi in the garden.

MARIPOSA (WESTERN ENTRANCE)

Southwest of the park on Route 49. Western-style village with more character than Oakhurst. You'll find a dozen hotels there, plus a good youth hostel, the Yosemite Bug Hostel.

Yosemite Bug Hostel: 6979 Highway 140. Located 11 miles (18km) north of Mariposa at Midpines, on the road to Yosemite Park (Arch Rock entrance). ☎ (209) 966-6666. Fax: 966-6667. Website: www.yosemitebug.com. On the VIA bus, ask the driver to call at Whispering Pines. At long last there's a youth hostel in this region. It's flagged by a green-and-white sign, 11 miles (18km) from Mariposa, to the left of Route 140 as you go towards Yosemite Park. The hostel is at the far end of a little path, a long way from any noise, in the middle of the countryside. It's run by really nice young people who seem to be full of ideas. Several bungalows are scattered across the hillside and contain dormitories with six or 12 beds for $12. The interior is clean, with views of the hills. Private rooms available at $18. You can also camp, for $2 per tent. The Recovery Cafe serves breakfasts, simple dishes, beer and wine. There's a launderette, and sheet hire. They also hire mountain bikes and snowshoes and organize trips in the Sierra.

Mariposa Lodge: 5052 Highway 140. ☎ 1-800-341-8000. Fax: (209) 742-7038. Located away from the highway, so you'd expect it to be peaceful. Nicer than the Sierra Motel, with enclosed parking lot. They offer two types of room: the cheaper ones are just bedrooms, while the other kind have a sitting area too. The welcome is nice.

EC Yosemite Motel: 5180 Jones Street. ☎ (209) 742-6800 or 1-800-321-5261. Fax: 742-6719. On the right at the exit from the city towards Yosemite Park. The exterior isn't bad, and the interior is fine. Nice welcome. Small heated swimming pool. All rooms have twin beds.

Sierra View Motel: 4993 7th Street. ☎ 966-5793. Freephone: ☎ 1-800-627-8439. The setting is charming, with a small garden. The proprietress is very friendly. Rooms have air-conditioning and TV. Moderate price. Note that they're usually full up at weekends.

Gold Rush Grill and Saloon: 5109 Highway 140. ☎ 742-2100. At the exit from the village. A small room with wooden seats and benches. Efficient service. Very good meat dishes, served with Californian wines. Taste their pepper steak covered with herbs, accompanied by the Silver Fox red wine. This is really a restaurant for the evening.

BETWEEN MODESTO AND THE PARK (NORTHWEST ENTRANCE)

Approximately 22 miles (35km) from the northwest (Big Oat Flat) entrance to Yosemite Park, Groveland is the next-to-last village on Route 120, as you come from Modesto. This is a good place to stop if you left San Francisco late in the day.

Westgate Motel: 7647 Highway 120, at Buck Meadows. ☎ (209) 962-5281. Fax: 962-5285. Very decent rooms with air-conditioning, quiet in spite of the highway alongside. Swimming pool and jacuzzi. There's also a restaurant here, or, as an alternative, there's a place selling snacks 500 yards away.

LOCAL TRANSPORT

■ **Bike hire**: at Yosemite Lodge (the best one) and Curry Village. Open March–October / November. There are several routes reserved for bicycles – in particular the run of 4.5 miles (7km) that gets you to Mirror Lake (northeast of Curry Village).

A free bus shuttles between the campgrounds and the two villages. In summer: 7.30am–10pm, every 10 minutes.

■ **Horse hire**: near North Pines Camping. ☎ 372-1248. Available March–November. Accompanied trips last either two hours, a half-day or a full day. (It takes two hours to get to Yosemite Falls or Mirror Lake.)

WHAT TO SEE IN THE PARK

★ There are two superb **viewpoints** when you arrive in the Valley by car from the western and southern entrances – in each case it's just after the tunnel. You get scenic views of the waterfalls and rocky summits.

★ As you arrive, you very soon see **El Capitán**, a gigantic face which, at 2,950ft (900m), is the highest cliff in the world. This is a meeting-place for free climbers from all over the world.

★ Almost opposite is the **Brideveil Fall**. The name is supposed to evoke the motion of the spray as it flies away in the wind.

★ A little further on are the **Yosemite Falls**, the highest falls in the park.

★ The **Half Dome**, with its recognizable shape, has become the symbol of the park. You can see its silhouette from practically everywhere.

★ The famous **giant sequoias**: at Wawona and Mariposa Grove, south of the park, and Tuolumne Grove to the west (near Crane Flat). These trees sometimes grow to more than 20ft (6m) in diameter and can be as much as a staggering 2,700 years old.

The most photographed curiosity in the park until recently was the Wawona tunnel tree, 233ft (71m) high and 2,100 years old, whose trunk had room for a tunnel accommodating a two-lane road. Unfortunately, very heavy snowfalls loaded its top to such an extent that, one fine day in the winter of 1968–69, the giant tumbled over, leaving tourists nothing to look at but its impressive body, which will lie outstretched on the ground for some years to come. In order to see it, you have to park your car and take the passenger truck that actually makes the tour.

Fortunately, the park still contains much older sequoias, such as the giant Grizzly, which has been standing for 2,700 years. To see this one, you have to walk just over a mile (2km) from the parking lot.

★ At the mouth of Merced Canyon, at the southeast corner of Yosemite Valley, there's a rocky outcrop from which, at **Glacier Point**, you can see what has to be the best ever viewpoint. There's a magnificent view of Yosemite Valley, Merced Canyon with its waterfalls, and the High Sierra.

★ Southeast of Yosemite, **Devil's Postpile National Monument**: here, if you're interested in rocks and volcanic phenomena you can study at first hand the finest, largest and most regular basalt columns in the world.

★ **Tuolumne Meadows**: 19 miles (30km) west of the Tioga Pass entrance (which is the only eastern entrance to the park), on Route 120 (or Tioga Road), Tuolumne Meadows is a large sub-alpine prairie situated at a high altitude, and is as wild as you could wish for. This is the place for the most rugged landscapes in the Sierra. The woods are sparse here, because of the climate and the altitude (8,460ft/2,580m), giving way to meagre but tenacious alpine vegetation. The rangers at the Visitors' Center will give you any information you need about the various routes. One easy tour to make, a round-trip of 7 miles (11km), goes to Elizabeth Lake (with mosquitoes in summer), where you can bathe – though the water's very, very cold.

TREKKING

Yosemite is interesting above all for its hiking routes. If you are a keen trekker, you absolutely must look at the Yosemite newspaper. It's very detailed, giving routes, distances, altitudes, typical weather, etc. The itineraries are innumerable and suitable for all levels of effort. If you want to go off for more than one day, you must ask for a wilderness permit at the Visitors' Center. This is free of charge and the rangers will then know where you are: the bears are numerous and not anywhere near as nice as those in Disney movies. Every year there are attacks on hikers, so don't leave a trail of food when you camp. In addition, freak weather conditions, such as snow, can be extremely dangerous. **Make sure you tell a ranger your intended route**.

– **Three-hour trek** (one of many): one of the most beautiful (and most frequented) trips is to leave from Upper Pines Camping and go as far as Vernal Fall. The path runs alongside the river. You can make this journey on horseback. Braver souls will then continue to Nevada Fall (it's a climb, but it's really worth the effort). Remember to take a waterproof to protect yourself against the inevitable shower from the waterfall.

– **Two-day trek**: follow the same itinerary as above. Then, from Nevada Fall, continue along the path and camp in Little Yosemite Valley, approximately 1.5 miles (2.5km) from the falls. Don't forget to ask for a wilderness permit before leaving. The site is fantastic, but the night can be uncomfortably cold, as you're up at nearly 6,560ft (2,000m)! Next day, retrace your steps as far as Glacier Point. The view here is amazing. Then go back down to Yosemite Village on the Four Miles Trail.

– **To go for a dip**: go to either the River Merced, which flows along the valley floor (but there are lots of people here in summer), or Mirror Lake (departing from Upper Pines Campground). A short (30-minute) walk. Just before Mirror Lake, which is nearly dried-up, there's another nice little lake where you can dive off the big rock in the middle.

– **For real trekkers**: there are dozens of other circuits lasting two to 10 days. Ask the rangers.

– **A few tips**: You can leave your things in the lockers near the Registration Office in Curry Village, although they are often full up. It's absolutely forbidden to damage or cut the trees, whether they're alive or whether they're dead! Don't even think about doing a trek in winter (from November onward).

WHAT TO SEE IN THE AREA

★ **Mono Lake**: from Lee Vining, go south on US 395. After 6 miles (10km), turn left (to the east) on Route 120. Follow this road for approximately 4.5 miles (7km). The tourist information office for the lake is housed in a little shack, and you can get all the information you need there. Mono Lake is one of the oldest lakes in America: over 700,000 years old; it's isolated in a sublime desert of sagebrush, with the snowy peaks of the Sierra Nevada in the background. Sadly, since the 1960s, the springs feeding it have been diverted off to serve Los Angeles, and as a consequence, it's on the way to drying up. But this is where its charm lies, for as it dries out, limestone formations become exposed. These are 13,000 years old and form an unusual lunar landscape.

The walk to reach these formations is superb. It's very quiet and you can even enjoy a dip. In summer, there's a tour of the lake with a guide and in the evening you can stargaze. The salt level of the lake has tripled, and it rather resembles the Dead Sea. This makes bathing a pleasure and you can read a newspaper while bobbing about in the water.

For more information contact **Mono Lake Information Center**, at Lee Vining (*see* 'Where to Stay' and 'Where to Eat Outside the Park').

★ **An unusual tomb**: at the intersection of Route 395 and Route 120 (towards the southern shore of the lake) there's a weird tomb, now covered with a pile of miscellaneous objects – cigarette packets, beer bottles, old shoes, helmets, graffiti, etc. – suggesting some kind of strange cult. Some people say that it contains the body of one Mono Joe (1676–1723), an unknown pioneer and great friend of the Native Americans. Others say, more bluntly, that it's a fake tomb and Mono Joe never existed.

★ **Saddlebag Lake**: some miles from the eastern exit from Yosemite. To get here, take Highway 120, which crosses Yosemite from west to east (but remember that it's often closed in winter). First you go through some fields, then you start to climb, and leave the park via the main road. When the road starts to descend again, you'll find on a curve in the road that another road on the left goes off towards Saddlebag Lake. This turns into a track, though it's a very good one, after about 2.5 miles (4km).

You then come to a superb alpine lake that's sometimes fished for trout. There's a mountain refuge-style timber shack that operates as a cafe and grocery store. There are paths going around the lake, and one that takes you to the passes that overhang it. Canoeists are often to be found out on the lake and if you really want peace and quiet, there's a campground next to the cafe.

Note that the lake is at an altitude of between 8,200 and 9,840ft (2,500 and 3,000m), and it gets cold very quickly after the sun has set.

SEQUOIA NATIONAL PARK

About 80 miles (128km) south of Yosemite and with an average altitude of 6,500–8,200ft (2,000–2,500m), the Sequoia National Park is a breathtaking region that incorporates imposing peaks of granite, deep gorges, lakes, rivers, and forests of ancient trees. These trees include the giant sequoias, and one example of these 2,000-year-old monsters is the celebrated 'General Sherman Tree'. The circumference of its trunk is 102ft (31m), making it the world's largest living thing.

Don't try to come here before June – the roads are still snowed up. And another tip: if your main interest is in experiencing the beauty of the giant sequoias themselves, there's no need to go to Yosemite, because the trees in the Sequoia National Park forests are the most majestic of all. But on the other hand, the landscape and the mountain backdrop are most spectacular at Yosemite.

– Admission charge: $10 per vehicle; $5 per person in you're travelling on foot, by bike or on a bus.

USEFUL ADDRESSES

Information about the park: ☎ (209) 565-3341. Website: www.nps.gov/seki. For practical information and reservations, go to: www.reservations.nps.gov.

Lodge reservations: ☎ (209) 335-5500.

Foothills Visitors' Center: at the southern entrance to the park, coming from Three Rivers. ☎ 565-3134. Open 8am–5pm.

Lodgepole Visitors' Center: several miles from the Giant Forest and General Sherman. ☎ 565-3782. Open daily in summer 8am–6pm.

– Other services at Lodgepole include a post office, launderette, grocery store (where they sell equipment for trekkers and campers), snack-bar.

WHERE TO STAY

THREE RIVERS

Sequoia Motel: 43000 Sierra Drive, Highway 198, Three Rivers. ☎ 561-4453. Three miles (5km) from Three Rivers, on the road to the park, on the right. this is a small motel with two timber buildings, quite peaceful, not far from a stream. Clean. Air-conditioning, small swimming pool. Prices very reasonable. Approximately 1.25 miles (2km) away is a good restaurant with grilled meats and real bread. Nice environment.

Three Rivers Motel and RV Park: 43365 Sierra Drive. ☎ (209) 561-4413. Between the road and the river, this site is well shaded. The rooms are in timber bungalows with shower, WC and (pretty pointless!) carpet. Air-conditioning is provided, because it gets hot in summer. The whole thing is simple but clean. Costs around $45 for two.

WHAT TO SEE

★ **The General Sherman giant sequoia**: this star of the forest is in Giant Forest, on the right of General's Highway, which crosses the park from south to north. Approximately 2 miles (3km) before Lodgepole Visitors' Center. It's very well signposted. The General is known to be between 2,300 and 2,700 years old, making it not quite the oldest known living tree on the planet. That honour still goes to the Bristlecone pines in the east of the Sierra Nevada.

If the General could speak, he would probably have a few things to say about the genius of some (those who protect him) and the stupidity of others (there are those who dream of transforming him into a heap of planks . . .). He is 272ft (83m) high, the height of a 27-storey building, but that still doesn't make him the biggest of all the living sequoias. There's one that's taller – in northern California. Nor is General Sherman the biggest in terms of trunk base diameter (36ft/11m), but he does hold the world record for tree mass – that is, his volume in timber.

If General Sherman ever has the misfortune to lose a branch, it feels like a national disaster. This happened once, in 1978, when the fallen branch was 138ft (42m) long, with a diameter of 6ft (1.8m). It's difficult to get a decent photograph, unless you have a wide-angle lens.

★ **The General Grant sequoia**: yet another well-conserved old patriarch, located in Grant Grove at the western exit from the park. This one, too, is very well signposted. This one is a direct competitor with the General Sherman sequoia, as it's neither as old nor as tall, but it is 4ft (1.2m) wider at the base, with a diameter of 40ft (12.3m).

BODIE

At the time of the Gold Rush, Bodie had a sordid reputation for being a hangout for 'desperados'. The word was that when people were travelling to Bodie, they would say: 'Goodbye God, I'm going to Bodie'. In order to rid the place of this profane image, a collection was made for the building of a Methodist church, but it was hard to get pastors to come here because, it was said, all the money came from brothels and opium bars. It seems that there was one death per day and the miners would joke: 'Well – have we got a man for breakfast this morning?'

The city was abandoned by government order in 1942, 10 years after it was more or less completely destroyed by a huge fire that had been lit by a small boy. All the same, there are quite a few houses remaining intact after being renovated, along with the old mine. The whole city and its surroundings are classified as a State Park.

There's a fascinating old cemetery, where many were buried still with their boots on and prostitutes were buried under tombstones with no inscription. The city has managed to retain the spirit of the old days: at least, that's how it feels. Situated in a desert landscape, the impression is rather ghostly. What remains is quite interesting – the bank and the prison, plus parts of Chinatown and the houses where the gold-panners lived.

PRACTICAL INFORMATION

Bodie is on Route 270, away from Highway 395, between Carson City and Bishop. No local service! The simplest thing to do if you want to stay somewhere is to stop at Lee Vining, 26 miles (42km) south of Bodie. There are several relatively cheap motels here (*see above* 'Where to Stay and Where to Eat Outside the Park' under 'Yosemite Park').

– **Bodie State Historic Park**: There's an admission charge. Open 8am–7pm in summer (6pm out of season).

Visitors' Center: in the same building as the museum. On the corner of Green Street and Main Street. ☎ 647-6445. Open 9am–4pm. Organizes guided tours of the Standard Stamp Mill ($3), for a minimum of 20 people.

THE STORY OF THE GHOST TOWNS AND THE GOLD RUSH

In 1848, a young man named Marshall, who was working in the watermills of Sacramento Valley, discovered some gold nuggets in the South Fork River near Coloma. On that exact spot, by the side of Route 49, tourists now come to visit the Marshall Gold Discovery State Historic Park.

The rumours travelled as fast as Wells Fargo stagecoaches. There was an immediate inrush of cardsharps, bar girls and desperados of all kinds, and dozens of towns sprang up out of the desert. Saloons sprang up like mushrooms and the ever-thirsty gold-seekers would swallow their beer standing in front of a huge mirror in order to see what was happening behind their backs.

The mill where the great discovery was made belonged to one John A. Sutter, a Swiss adventurer who had become a colonist in the service of Mexico, and had founded Sacramento (*see* 'Fort Sutter' under 'Sacramento'). He had explored and went on to administer a large part of the region. Unfortunately, this landowner made the grave mistake of not surrounding his land with barbed wire. The law of the time held that unenclosed territory belonged to no one, and in just a few days, the unfortunate Sutter was stripped of all his property. Despite many court battles, he never regained possession, and died a pauper in 1871.

This marked the beginning of a fantastical era. Anyone in the United States who had dreamed of making his fortune went into action. Some took ships from the great ports on the East Coast, went round Cape Horn or crossed the isthmus of Panama on foot, while others travelled across the continent in long wagon trains that departed from St Louis, on the Missouri.

When the seams of gold ran out, the cities that had been built were abandoned as quickly as they had been set up. Some have now been extremely well restored, with the result that in many parts of the Californian hinterland, the ghost towns and former Gold Rush settlements now hold a degree of interest for tourists, who only know of the existence of such places through Hollywood movies.

LONE PINE

AREA CODE: 619

On Highway 395, at the junction of the road to Death Valley and not much visited by tourists, this little western city is famous for having been one of Hollywood's most important locations.

Most of the great Hollywood classic Westerns and adventure films were made in the desert and the surrounding mountains, and the area around Lone Pine was used, across the movie-making generations, in many films including *The Charge of the Light Brigade*, *The Bengal Lancers*, *Star Trek* and *Nevada Smith*. When you walk into Lone Pine, just remember that you're stepping in the footprints of John Wayne (who filmed here four times), Gary Cooper, Errol Flynn, Cary Grant, Douglas Fairbanks Jr., Humphrey Bogart, Anthony Quinn, Rita Hayworth, Kirk Douglas, David Niven, Spencer Tracy, Lee Marvin, Tyrone Power, and goodness knows who else.

USEFUL ADDRESS

Visitors' Center: as you leave the city, where Route 136 branches off for Death Valley. There's a map of the area that shows all the big movie locations. They have an interesting bookshop that sells books on Western movies, Native Americans, the fauna and flora of the West etc., as well as information on Death Valley.

WHERE TO STAY

Boulder Creek Campground: 2550 South, about 2 miles (3.5km) south of Lone Pine, on the left of Route 395 if you're going in the direction of Death Valley. ☎ 876-4243. Fax: 876-5253. The terrain is hard if you're using a tent but the welcome is good, and there's a swimming pool. Kitchen provided and breakfast is available.

The Portal Motel: Main Street. Decent rooms with two double beds. Cheaper than the Dow Villa Motel.

☆☆ MODERATE

Dow Villa Motel: 310 South Main Street. ☎ 876-5521. Formerly a hotel and built to house the film crews, this is now a clean motel, with swimming pool. Friendly welcome and as much coffee and tea as you can drink. The place has recently been renovated. The rooms above the restaurant are cheaper.

Trails Motel: Highway 395, 633 South Main Street. Freephone for reservations: ☎ 1-800-862-7020 or 876-5555. You can cook in your room using the microwave, coffee-maker and fridge provided.

Alabama Hills Hotel: 1920 South Main Street. ☎ 876-8700. Near the junction between the road to Death Valley and Route 395. Small, recently built, very comfortable hotel with swimming pool and a superb view of the Sierra Nevada. The prices are reasonable compared to the motels in the centre of Lone Pine.

BETWEEN LONE PINE AND YOSEMITE PARK

☗ **The Winnedumah Hotel**: 211 North Edwards. At Independence, a small town 15 miles (25km) north of Lone Pine, on the road to Yosemite Park. ☎ (619) 878-2040. Many actors have slept in this hotel, built in 1927, which has preserved its aura of the Old West. Gary Cooper stayed here. Bing Crosby sang in the shower here. Rooms with or without shower and WC, decorated with 1920s furniture. Doubles from $45.

BISHOP

Located 45 miles (70km) north of Lone Pine. Readers have recommended the following:

☗ The **Starlite Motel**: 192 Short Street. ☎ 873-4912. Inexpensive, with a small swimming pool.

☗ More comfortable, the **Mountain View Motel**, 730 West Line Street. ☎ 873-4242. Also has a swimming pool.

FILM FESTIVAL

– Each year, around mid-October, the **Sierra Film Festival** pays tribute to the American movie industry, with screenings of films, concerts, opportunities to meet actors, etc. Routes are suggested that guide you round Lone Pine's legendary movie history. You can visit the desert where Johnny Weissmuller became Tarzan, drive on the road driven by Tony Curtis in *The Great Race*, see the place where Robert Mitchum saved Hopalong Cassidy's life, and so on. For information: ☎ 876-4314.

DEATH VALLEY

Situated 130 miles (210km) northwest of Las Vegas, Death Valley is one of the lowest points in the northern hemisphere, plunging, at its lowest point, to 282ft (86m) below sea level. The sinister name came from the exclamation of a pioneer survivor expressing Mormon gratitude: 'Thanks be to God, we have gotten out of this Valley of Death.' This is a place where the temperature in summer is more than 105°F/40°C in the shade – actually though – there is no shade and you can fry an egg on the bonnet of your car! 1913 was a good year for records: that year alone witnessed the highest temperature (135°F/57°C) and the lowest (17°F/–9°C). During the summer of 1994, the temperature remained above 130°F/49°C for 31 days.

Relative air humidity is close to zero and, if you sit at the wheel of a car with no air-conditioning, you will be losing more than a litre of water an hour in perspiration. For this reason it's more than just wise to take reserve supplies of water – at least 7 pints (4 litres) per person. Don't even dream about hitching across Death Valley: it's out of the question.

The lunar grandeur of the landscape reflects a region that has been scorched by the sun but still shows incredible diversity. There are mountains, canyons, seas of salt, fields of cacti, palm groves and sand dunes, craters and other geological wonders. If you want to take some decent photographs, remember that it's only at dawn and at the end of the day that the rocks take on any colour. And, more importantly, the heat is less stifling.

Stay on the made-up roads. If your vehicle breaks down, don't leave it under any circumstances, as someone will always come along and help, sooner or later. This advice, which is provided by the tourist information office, is not to be taken lightly: the 'Missing Persons' posters in the information centres can make you shiver in spite of the heat.

The desert is inhabited by a rich variety of wildlife: lynx, coyotes, snakes and that 'beep-beep' cartoon bird, the roadrunner.

TIP
This journey is very hard on car engines, so, most importantly, you should check your radiator thoroughly before you leave. Don't let the engine overheat (switch it off from time to time if necessary). Throughout your crossing of Death Valley, however, you'll be able to find tanks of water for topping up you car radiator (they're marked 'radiator water only'). Note also that the price of petrol is a lot higher in Death Valley.

USEFUL ADDRESSES

Visitors' Center: on Route 190, approximately 300 yards from the Furnace Creek Ranch. Open 8am–7pm. ☎ (760) 786-2331. Lots of useful information on the state of the roads (from time to time, even in high summer, sections of the road are carried away by floods), current temperatures, and advice about driving in the desert. There's an interesting (free) museum with numerous displays, including the animals of the desert, period objects and everyday scenes from the lives of the pioneers and the miners, information about the geology of the region, and so on. Other information offices are located at Lone Pine (*see above*), Shoshone (*see below*) and Emigrant (after the western entrance).

■ **Grocery stores**: at Furnace Creek Ranch and Scotty's Castle. Open 5.30am–8.30pm.

■ **Petrol pumps**: at Furnace Creek (7am–7pm), Scotty's Castle, north of the Valley (9am–5.30pm), Stovepipe, between Furnace Creek and Emigrant (7am–8pm) and Beatty (in Nevada).

■ **In an emergency**: ☎ 911 (available at any time)

■ **Showers and swimming pools**: at Furnace Creek Ranch and Stovepipe Wells. Make your booking at hotel reception desks. Expect to pay a small charge.

WHERE TO STAY, WHERE TO EAT

BAKER

At the intersection of Route I-15 and Route 127, 50 miles (80km) south of Death Valley. This is a grim little town, of no particular interest except that it possesses the world's biggest thermometer, which measures 134ft

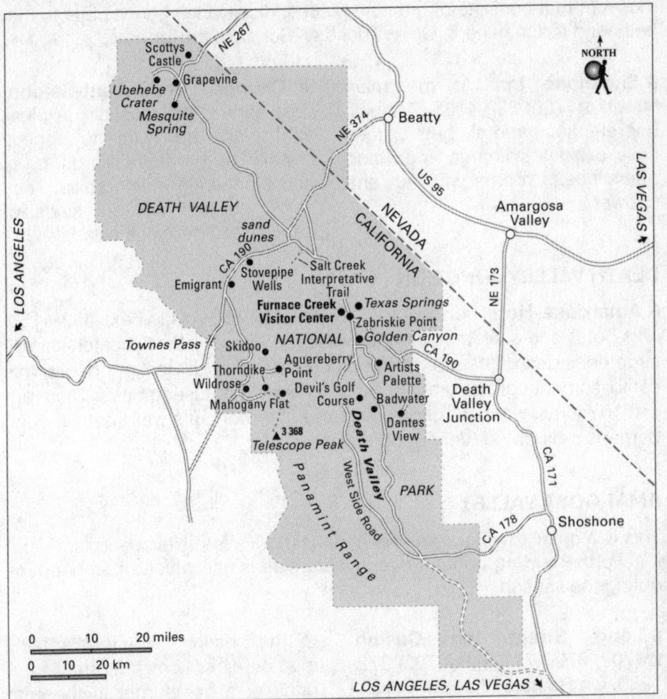

DEATH VALLEY NATIONAL PARK

(41m) in height. It was built to commemorate the year 1913, when the temperature reached 134°F (57°C) in Death Valley – an all-time record for the United States. After Baker, it's desert and more desert for quite a long way, so remember to fill up with everything!

Bun Boy Motel: Gateway to Death Valley. ☎ (760) 733-4363. Near to the service stations. Good views of the desert. Quiet, comfortable, clean double rooms with bathroom.

Next door, the **Bun Boy Restaurant**, a good place, in a pleasant setting.

SHOSHONE

If you want to pass through Death Valley from the south, you can spend the night at Shoshone, which is on Route 127, just before the intersection with Route 178. This tiny village has a very nice *Baghdad Cafe* ambiance (if you've seen the movie). After it, there's 60 miles (100km) of desert!

The vilage has a Death Valley information centre (the opening hours depend on how energetic the rangers are feeling) and also a little museum that consists of bits and pieces, displaying various objects that belonged to the miners. Open Tuesday–Sunday 9am–4pm.

☗ **Shoshone Inn**: in the main street. ☎ (760) 852-4335. A small, unpretentious motel, but it does have a small swimming pool and offers cheap rooms with fan and shower.

✕ **Crowbar Restaurant-Saloon**: next door to the museum. A pleasant place still with its original decor. The bar has billiards, darts and pioneering memorabilia. They serve burgers with all kinds of sauces and delicious salads.

DEATH VALLEY JUNCTION

☗ **Amargosa Hotel**: on Route 190. ☎ (760) 852-4441. Fax: 852-4138. This hotel is in a white hacienda with blue windows that is astonishingly large considering the size of the place it's in. Marta Becket opened this establishment right next to her theatre (*see* 'What Else to See'). There are just 10 rooms, with air-conditioning and bathroom. It's well kept although perhaps a bit dated. Very good welcome.

AMARGOSA VALLEY

This is a small town outside the national park – into Nevada in fact – but it's worth knowing about if everywhere else is full, which often happens during the season.

☗ **Long Street Inn Casino**: ☎ (702) 372-1777. Fax: (702) 372-1280. On Route 373 at the California–Nevada border. Not actually very close to Death Valley: it'll take you 45 minutes to get to Furnace Creek. This is a very recent establishment, where the slot-machines will give you a (pale) foretaste of Las Vegas. It's in the middle of the desert, with a wonderful view of the mountains. The rooms are very comfortable and clean and many have two double beds. There's a swimming pool and a pretty pond at the rear. The place has a launderette and even a hairdresser. Expect to pay between $45 and $65, according to the season. The food's fairly mediocre, so consider having a drink or a hamburger in the cafe opposite. The clientele consists of long-distance drivers and regulars. You may get the impression of being in a time-warp here.

☗ **Desert Village Motel**: between Route 373 and Mecca Road to Amargosa Valley. ☎ (702) 372-1405. Rooms with double bed, drawing room, kitchenette and bathroom, all for $45. Very friendly welcome. You can eat in the restaurant. You're really at the ends of the earth here, but it's a very practical solution in an emergency.

IN THE VALLEY

It's impossible to camp in summer because of the heat. An oven would definitely be cooler.

☗ **Furnace Creek Campground**: right beside the Furnace Creek Ranch. Open all year. Fairly shaded. No showers, but many facilities just nearby, such as a cafe, swimming pool, post office, showers, service station, grocery store . . . and bistro. It's frequently full up.

☗ **Mesquite Spring Campground**: in a dead-end a few miles south of Scotty's Castle. Very isolated and quite small. Open all year.

☗ **Wildrose Campground**: far away from everything and in a region of no interest. Poorly equipped, but it's free. Open all year.

☗ There are five other **campgrounds** in the Valley: at Thorndike and Mahogany Flat (both open all year) and three others that close in summer: Sunset, Texas Spring and Stovepipe Wells (on concrete!).

☆☆ MODERATE

☗ **Panamint Springs Resort**: at the western entrance to Death Valley on Route 190. ☎ (702) 482-7680. Fax: (702) 482-7682. Postal address: P.O. Box 395, Ridgecrest, CA 93556. A wild spot, with a view of the Valley. The resort is a typical big Western house. Some rooms have air-conditioning, all have a bathroom. They also have a bar and restaurant, open until 10pm every day. On the other side of the road is a rather rough-and-ready camping area.

☆☆☆☆ SPLASH OUT

☗ **Furnace Creek Ranch Resort**: at Furnace Creek Village, in the heart of the Valley. ☎ (760) 786-2345. Freephone: ☎ 1-800-366-0099. Not to be confused with the Furnace Creek Inn, which is still dearer. A quite exceptional place because, after hours of nothing but desert, you find yourself in a real oasis! In fact the 'ranch' is actually a village, with bungalows, shops, a small supermarket, an ironing service, a post office, a cash machine and . . . a museum. As well as all this, there's a swimming pool and a tennis court (floodlit at night). Of course, all of this is eminently touristy, often packed, and the reception you get reflects this. But the accommodation is sufficiently well dispersed among the greenery to be peaceful. There are two options: motel rooms ($125) or bedroom cabins (less expensive). On the eating side, there's a saloon and four restaurants (not great, and quite expensive) – Mexican, Italian, steakhouse and coffee shop. Bike hire at the service station. You can also camp here, mainly in campers, but you get the additional benefit of the swimming pool.

☗ **Stovepipe Wells Village**: on Highway 190, between Panamint Springs and Furnace Creek. ☎ 786-2387. The setting is quite amusingly Western. Use this one only if those listed earlier are full, because the prices are a bit higher. One big advantage is the swimming pool. There's also a restaurant, a grocery store, a service station and a camping area here. Non-residents can use the swimming pool and the showers for a small charge.

WHAT TO SEE IN DEATH VALLEY

If you want to leave the made-up roads, make very sure you find out from the Visitors' Center about the state of the trails. Whenever you leave your car for a stroll on foot, take a hat and some water with you.

TO THE SOUTH

★ **Zabriskie Point**: about 5 miles (8km) after Furnace Creek, on Route 190 towards the Death Valley junction. This place was made famous by Antonioni's film *Zabriskie Point* and it's one of the most fascinating geological phenomena in the Valley. You really have to get there at sunrise, before the tourists come swarming up in their cars. Olympian peace and magical colours are guaranteed. The view of the neighbouring hills, with the ravines cut into them by storms, gives an absolutely unique landscape. The rock has a marvellous range of hues, ranging from green through pink to orange.

★ **Twenty Mules Canyon**: right after Zabriskie Point. Away from Route 190. The one-way circuit is not made-up, but it's in reasonable condition. This is a narrow road tucked away in rocks the colour of Zabriskie Point – a really magnificent run.

★ **Dante's View**: well off Route 190, after Zabriskie Point. From the top of this promontory you have a superb view of a large section of Death Valley, looking out over the whole valley from a height of 5,580ft (1,700m). The last mile, which rises with a gradient of 14 per cent, is rough on cars. It's better to switch off the air-conditioning, otherwise you run the risk of the engine boiling.

★ **Golden Canyon**: 2 miles (3km) south of Furnace Creek Ranch on Route 178 as you go towards Shoshone. Arrive very early if you want to avoid the worst of the heat. This is just a short journey on foot (about 1.5 miles / 2.5km) in a beautiful canyon with interesting geological formations. You'll need some water, a hat and sunglasses.

★ **Devil's Golf Course**: along Route 178, between Artist Drive and Badwater. An immense stretch of salt – so white it's almost blinding – right out there in the middle of the desert. There are strange forms on the ground, carved out by the wind as it eats into the blocks of soil and salt.

★ **Badwater**: at the side of Route 178, a pool of stagnant water. You are at the lowest point in the United States here, 282ft (86m) below sea level. Someone got the job of climbing the rocky wall overlooking the road in order to set up a poster showing the exact position of sea level!

★ **Artist Drive**: just before Golden Canyon, as you return from Badwater. This is one to tour on the way back, because it's a one-way loop. In an natural amphitheatre, mineral pigments have added a mass of colours to the volcanic rocks: the reds, pinks and yellows have been produced by iron, the green has come from mica, and the purples and violets from manganese. Another treat for the eyes (and your camera!).

GOING NORTH

★ **Salt Creek Interpretative Trail**: on the road leading to Scotty's Castle, 500 yards (460 metres) off Route 190. A quite unreal ramble on a board walk (a raised path is essential so to avoid damaging the flora). Many explanations are given of the flora and fauna of the area.

★ **Sand Dunes**: still on the road leading to Scotty's Castle. Take the little road on the left after the main junction. These sand dunes have been created by the winds, which meet at this precise point in the valley, bringing fragments of rock from the neighbouring mountains, grain by grain.

★ **Scotty's Castle**: guided tour every hour 9am–5pm. Not more than 25 people per tour, so there's often a long queue (the waiting time is displayed at several points in the valley). Scotty, who bore the illustrious name of Walter Scott, was a skilful swindler back in the early 20th century. He managed to convince a man called Johnson, an insurance magnate, that he had located a goldmine in Death Valley and succeeded in persuading him to part with a fortune to invest in exploiting it. One day, Johnson came to see for himself and realized he had been tricked. But the millionaire, who was chronically ill, found the very dry desert climate beneficial to his health, so instead of taking vengeance on Scott, he went as far as to pay him a monthly pension. Johnson went on to build a real palace, right in the middle of the desert.

This large building in Spanish style cost a fortune. Nothing was too good for the place, with antique furniture bought in Europe, wrought iron and other precious materials. But the Stock Market crash in 1929 meant that the castle was never finished. As for Walter Scott, he passed his days living alone in a shack right in the middle of the desert, and having repented his past as a swindler, he went down in American history.

★ **Ubehebe Crater**: is 5 miles (8km) west of Scotty's Castle. This beautiful crater, 2,625ft (800m) wide and 500ft (162m) deep, was created by a volcanic explosion. You can go down into it.

★ If you go beyond the crater and continue along the track for 25 miles (40km), you'll reach **Racetrack Valley**, an astonishing phenomenon that looks exactly as though the ground has been marked by a number of huge wheels. But no vehicle has passed this way – in fact, the marks have been left by great blocks of stone that have quite simply rolled over the ground, pushed along by the wind.

★ And, if you still have any time left, there's **Natural Bridge**, **Mushroom Rock**, **Keane Wonder Mine**, and plenty of canyons.

WHAT ELSE TO SEE

★ **Amargosa Opera House**: at Death Valley Junction, on Route 190. Marta Becket is an astonishing woman. One day, this New York dancer's car broke down in this small village, isolated from the world. She discovered the desert – and decided to live here. So, since 1968 (between October and May), dance shows, ballets, plays and pantomimes have been presented here every Monday and Saturday at 8pm, for an admission price of $10. The walls are decorated with a huge fresco painted by Marta. ☎ (760) 852-4441.

★ If you're staying in Furnace, the **ancient forges at Wildrose** (in the west of the Valley) are sort of interesting, but they're simply not worth the extra round-trip of 124 miles (200km), not to mention the risk of overheating your engine. On the other hand, they are on your route if you're leaving the Valley going west.

FROM DEATH VALLEY TO LAS VEGAS

If you'd like to go to Las Vegas the long way round instead of following Route 95, here's an unusual but much longer itinerary.

From Amargosa Valley, follow Route 95 to Tonopah, then take Route 375 to the intersection with Route 168. The road runs across the open range, so watch out for cattle! You are in fact avoiding the famous 'Area 51' by using Highway 375, the **Extra-terrestrials Road**.

Base 51 is a large military area that comprizes Nellis Air Force Range and Nevada Test Site. The secrecy surrounding it (this is where they test stealth aircraft) has sent a section of the American population off its collective trolley and many are convinced that spacecraft and extra-terrestrials are being concealed here.

At **Rachel**, a village with 100 inhabitants (mostly in mobile homes, plus one or two proper houses), there's a UFO centre housed in a caravan, and a Research Center. This is spot-on for any remaining *X-Files* devotees. Have a drink in the Little Ale'Inn (the name's a pun on 'little alien' – geddit?), where the photographs decorating the walls of the cafe demonstrate the boss's passion for flying saucers. But he also has business sense as he sells T-shirts, badges and other trinkets. The US Air Force doesn't seem to mind his activities, judging by the number of military personnel monopolizing the billiard table – although it *is* the only bar for 60 miles (96km) in any direction!

LOS ANGELES AND SOUTHERN CALIFORNIA

LOS ANGELES

AREA CODE: 213

For maps of Los Angeles *see* the colour map section, which includes a general map; Downtown (map I); Santa Monica and Venice (map II); Hollywood (map III); Hollywood and Beverly Hills (map IV).

Los Angeles, 400 miles (640km) from San Francisco and 130 miles (210km) from San Diego, is spreading out further every year thanks to the tentacles of its freeway network. You could almost say that it sweeps away everything in its path. It's a metropolis that is both rich and energetic, creative and lively, yet there are inevitably a number of social and ethnic problems at the city's very core, making it a place of contrasts and contradictions – riches, bright lights and glamour . . . poverty, squalor and dust.

Los Angeles is a conglomeration with no true centre, an immense jigsaw puzzle of 80 districts – Hollywood, Downtown, Venice, Santa Monica, South Central, Chinatown, Koreatown and others – each independent of the others but part of a greater whole.

LA has often been described as an endless sea of concrete, but this is unfair. The truth is quite different – what strikes you about the city right from the word go are the stretches of green space and the constant presence of the natural landscape. Then there's the feeling that the desert is so close – yet there are a great many trees, and the freeways that furrow across town have wild grasses scattered along their banks. Leaving aside the giant high-rise buildings of Downtown, where people work but no one lives, Los Angeles looks like a suburban landscape stretching out on all sides as far as the eye can see. The street grid is regular – almost provincial – and the little timber houses with their neat gardens testify to a real quality of life.

When LA is called inhuman, it's because of the traffic, the earthquakes, the fires, the floods and (in some districts) the crime. Even this picture is neither completely true nor entirely false. To get around the traffic problem, for example, it's best just to avoid the rush hours, when the place is grid-locked. Outside rush hours, the city becomes almost easy to conquer, as long as you study a map carefully before setting off.

This large and unlovable place is largely misunderstood and it's best not to try to love it until you get to know it. The people here work hard, go out rarely and go to bed early and sport has become a new religion. What's more, they find beauty in what actually works, in what's functional and innovative.

With its 14 million inhabitants, LA is getting ready to become the capital of the economic empire of the Pacific, the new centre of a world that encompasses the western United States and a large part of Asia (Japan, China, Taiwan, South Korea, Indonesia, the Philippines, Malaysia, Australia, etc.). Los Angeles is also the place where the Far West meets the Far East. In less than a century, the fastest city in the West has become the cradle of a culture capable of being exported all over the world. It all began with the Hollywood dream factory, where many of the elements of today's 'lifestyle' started out before spreading all round the world – such things as roller-skating, bodybuilding and even jogging. This process is still going on.

LA is the end-point of the conquest of the West and the arrival-point of Route 66, which begins in Chicago and ends in Santa Monica, at the edge of the Pacific. Despite its growing pains, LA still carries the American dream, hands outstretched.

But it is an unexpected turn of events that has made this arid strip of desert into the world's third largest city in less than a century!

KEY FACTS

If New York is the Big Apple, LA is the Big Nipple.

the late French film director, Louis Malle

AREA

Measuring strictly within its administrative boundaries, the city covers 450 square miles (1,165 square kilometres), which puts it in second place in the list of the biggest cities in the United States. But Los Angeles County, or 'Greater Los Angeles', is nearly 10 times larger: 4,036 square miles (10,452 square kilometres). Broadly speaking, LA County is shaped like an anvil. The dimensions of this immense metropolis, bounded by the Pacific in the west and south, the hills of Hollywood and Beverly in the north, and the desert in the east, immediately give the astonished backpacker a new set of measurements to reckon with. As the crow flies, it measures 50 miles (80km) from west to east, or from Malibu to Euclid Avenue, level with Highway 83! From north to south, again in a straight line, the distance between the San Fernando Valley and the tip of Point Fermin in the San Pedro district, near the port of LA, is about 35 miles (60km).

POPULATION

In 1995, the city had approximately 3.5 million inhabitants, Los Angeles County had 9.2 million, and Greater Los Angeles 14 million. In world ranking, 'the Big Nipple' takes third place after Mexico City and New York (which has more than 18 million inhabitants including its extensive suburbs). After LA, come Tokyo, Shanghai and Sao Paulo. To give you a ballpark notion of size, an upper-crust district like Beverly Hills numbers only 32,600 people. Santa Monica is a sort of middle-sized city with almost 90,000 inhabitants, but it's still only a district. Contrary to popular belief, the inhabitants of Los Angeles (known as Angelenos) don't live packed together like sardines, but enjoy plenty of space: the population density in LA is 6,830 inhabitants per square mile, as against 23,494 in New York.

ETHNIC GROUPS AND LANGUAGES

In this bustling Tower of Babel on the Pacific, nearly 120 languages and dialects from every part of the world are spoken. Nearly half (49.7 per cent) of the population is white. The second-largest group consists of members of the Hispanic community, originally from Mexico and Central America: they form a quarter of the population of LA and are often called 'Chicanos', but this is a pejorative term, so know it – don't use it! With 3.6 million inhabitants, the Hispanic community of LA represents the third-largest Hispanic 'city' in North America, after Mexico City and Guadalajara.

While American English is the official language, information in Spanish is very often seen in public places, so if you've ever picked up a few words of Spanish, they'll be useful to you here.

– **Latino district**: this is in Downtown, around Olvera Street, the Hispanic cradle of the city, but many Spanish speakers also live in the areas east of Downtown. In any case, East Los Angeles is the heart of the *barrio*, a conglomeration of several little districts enclosed by Lincoln Heights and Whittier Boulevard. This is the 'Latino' capital of the US.

– **Chinatown**: Asians make up 8.4 per cent of the population of LA. Among them are the Chinese – California's oldest Asian community. Although 72 per cent of them have taken on American nationality, they still remain faithful to their country of origin. Hsi Lai, the biggest Buddhist building in America, bears witness to the importance of this community, which controls 15 per cent of business in LA's Chinatown. Chinatown is north of Downtown and not far from the Mexican district (around North Broadway Boulevard). It is much smaller than the Chinatown in San Francisco – but just as lively.

– **Little Tokyo**: this is the Japanese district of LA, bounded by First, Alameda, Third and Los Angeles Street. This district has the largest Japanese community living outside Japan.

– **Koreatown**: the Korean district of LA stretches between Hollywood and Downtown or, more precisely, between Wilshire and Western Avenue, Pico Boulevard and Freeway 110. The dynamism and spirit of enterprise of Korean immigrants are reflected in the multitude of shops of every kind that they control. All the shop signs are written in Korean.

– **Little Saigon**: the people living here are almost exclusively Vietnamese, accepted into the US as political refugees after the Vietnam War. Very much an outlying district, Little Saigon is in Orange County, in the district of Westminster, along Bolsa Street and bounded by Beach Boulevard and Bristol Street.

–**Afro-American areas**: Afro-Americans represent approximately 8 per cent of the population of LA. The poorest live in the districts of South Central and Watts, a sort of immense ghetto that has been taken over by drugs, violence and gang law.

CLIMATE

This isn't the Promised Land, though it may well look like it. In official terms, the climate of Los Angeles forms part of the temperate subtropical zone, which is the Mediterranean type. The city has 186 days of sunshine a year, with an annual rainfall of just 15 inches (38cm) which comes in the form of occasional showers.

The result of this is marvellous – immense palm trees (where else do you get palms as tall as this?), cypresses, eucalyptus trees, cacti just like you get in the desert (which, of course, begins at the gates of the city), and orange trees right in the heart of the city. In summer as in winter, people leave their jackets at home and wear T-shirts whenever possible.

The climate of LA, like that of southern California in general, is so good that it immediately captivated the movie industry pioneers, who found themselves able to shoot outdoors throughout the year. The weather here is broadly similar to that on the North African Atlantic coast, in Casablanca, for example. In LA, you also get the benefit of having the ocean on one side and the desert on the other.

The consequence of this type of climate is that you can come here at any time of the year. Nevertheless, there are some differences between summer and winter:

– **November–March**: the mean temperature is 65–70°F/18–19°C in the day and 45–50°F/8–9°C at night. Don't forget to take a jumper or a light jacket.

– **May–June**: a sort of 'in-between season', milder than in summer (75°F/ 23–25°C daily average). June is known for its famous 'June gloom', when mornings are obscured by smog, a mixture of fog and smoke (actually, it's pollution). The sun makes an appearance in early afternoon and the blue sky returns to light up the city for the remainder of the day.

– **July–September**: these are the hottest and driest months of the year, with average daily temperatures around 80°F/27–28°C (65°F/16–17°C at night). In July, the weather is almost the same as in Málaga in southern Spain, though LA nights are a little cooler. In August, the sunshine is as strong as in Southern Portugal, Algeria or Corsica. The weight of the air is stifling, alleviated just a little by breezes blowing in from the Pacific. There's no rain at all at this time of year.

SOME STATISTICS

- Did you know that in Los Angeles there are 19 TV studios, 88 radio stations, 11 universities (including the famous UCLA) and a multitude of film production companies – the five 'Majors' (MGM, Columbia, Warner, Universal and Paramount) and a host of little 'Minors'? The movie industry provides employment for 60,000 people.
- And did you know that the crime rate for Los Angeles is lower than that

COLOUR MAPS

101
Santa Barbara
Ventura
14
San Fernando
Burbank
CHANNEL ISLAND
NAT'L PARK
Beverly Hills
S. Monica
Hollywood
Santa Cruz
Island
Acanapa I.
Santa
Rosa
Island
LOS ANGELES
Anaheim
Long Beach
Disneyland
Santa Barbara
Island
Laguna
Beach
Santa
Catalina
Island

130° 0
120° 0
110° 0
100° 0
90° 0
50° N
CANADA
WASHINGTON
Seattle
Portland
OREGON
MONTANA
Helena
NORTH DAKOTA
Bismarck
MINNESOTA
Boise
IDAHO
SOUTH DAKOTA
Pierre
Minneapolis
WYOMING
IOWA
40° N
Bodega Bay
Napa
Reno
NEVADA
Carson City
S. Lake Tahoe
Sonoma
Sacramento
San Francisco
Salt Lake City
Cheyenne
NEBRASKA
Des Moines
Lincoln
Yosemite
Palo Alto
San Jose
Monterey
Carmel
UTAH
Denver
COLORADO
Kansas City
Lone Pine
Big Sur
Sequoia N.P.
Death Valley
KANSAS
CALIFORNIA
San Luis Obispo
Solvang
Santa Barbara
Page
Las Vegas
Monument Valley
Grand Canyon
Los Angeles
Anaheim
Flagstaff
OKLAHOMA
Oklahoma City
Palm Springs
ARIZONA
Albuquerque
San Diego
Phoenix
NEW MEXICO
Tucson
Bisbee
30° N
Dallas
TEXAS
Houston
PACIFIC OCEAN
Tropic of Cancer
MEXICO
RUSSIA
150° 0
ALASKA
Fairbanks
60° N
Anchorage
BERING SEA
Juneau
500 miles
500 km
Aleutian Islands
158°
Kauai
Oahu
Maui
PACIFIC OCEAN
20°
500 miles
200 km
Hawaii
20° N

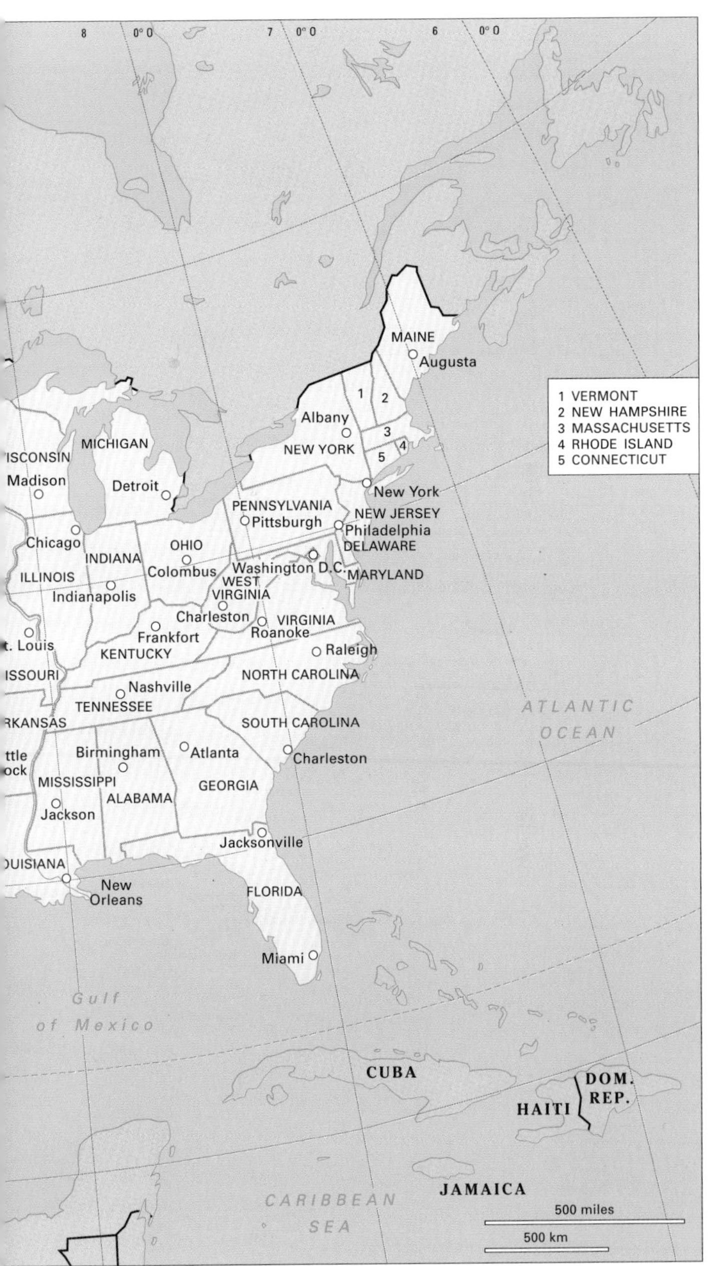

THE UNITED STATES

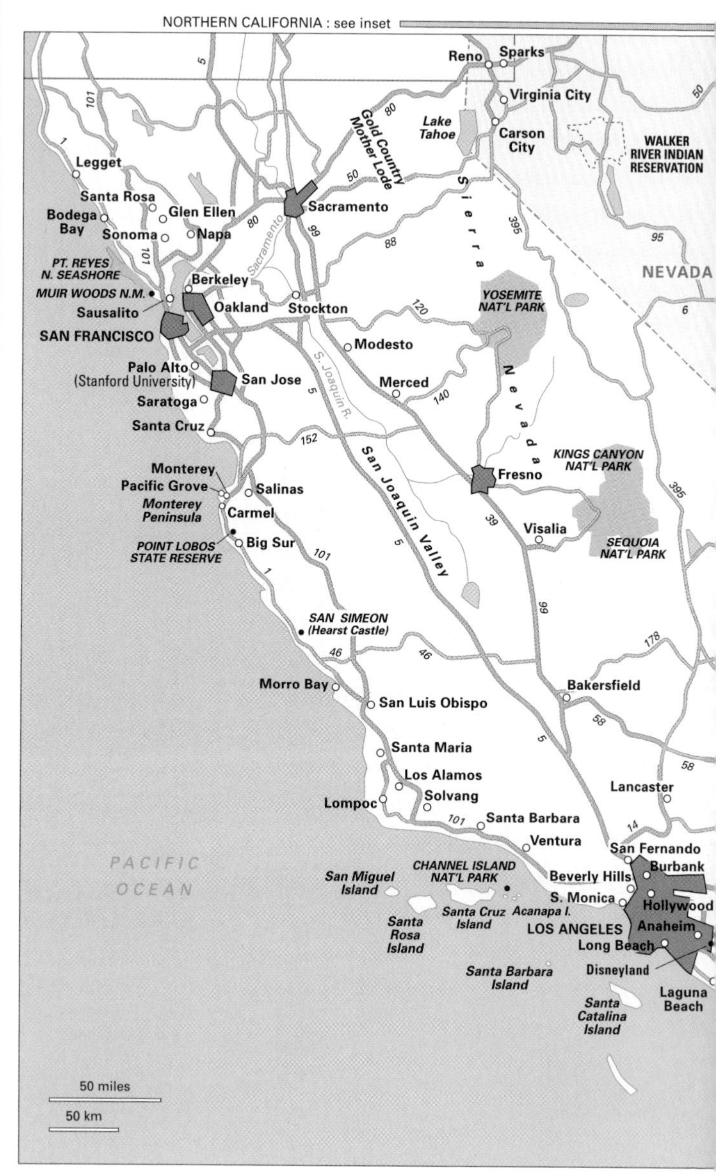
NORTHERN CALIFORNIA : see inset
Reno
Sparks
Virginia City
Carson City
Lake Tahoe
WALKER RIVER INDIAN RESERVATION
Gold Country Mother Lode
Sierra
Nevada
NEVADA
Legget
Santa Rosa
Glen Ellen
Bodega Bay
Sonoma
Napa
Sacramento
PT. REYES N. SEASHORE
MUIR WOODS N.M.
Sausalito
SAN FRANCISCO
Berkeley
Oakland
Stockton
YOSEMITE NAT'L PARK
Modesto
Merced
Palo Alto
(Stanford University)
San Jose
Saratoga
Santa Cruz
S. Joaquin R.
San Joaquin Valley
Monterey
Pacific Grove
Monterey Peninsula
Salinas
Carmel
POINT LOBOS STATE RESERVE
Big Sur
Fresno
KINGS CANYON NAT'L PARK
Visalia
SEQUOIA NAT'L PARK
SAN SIMEON
(Hearst Castle)
Morro Bay
San Luis Obispo
Bakersfield
Santa Maria
Los Alamos
Solvang
Lompoc
Lancaster
Santa Barbara
Ventura
San Fernando
Burbank
PACIFIC OCEAN
San Miguel Island
CHANNEL ISLAND NAT'L PARK
Beverly Hills
S. Monica
Hollywood
Santa Rosa Island
Santa Cruz Island
Acanapa I.
LOS ANGELES
Anaheim
Long Beach
Santa Barbara Island
Disneyland
Laguna Beach
Santa Catalina Island
50 miles
50 km

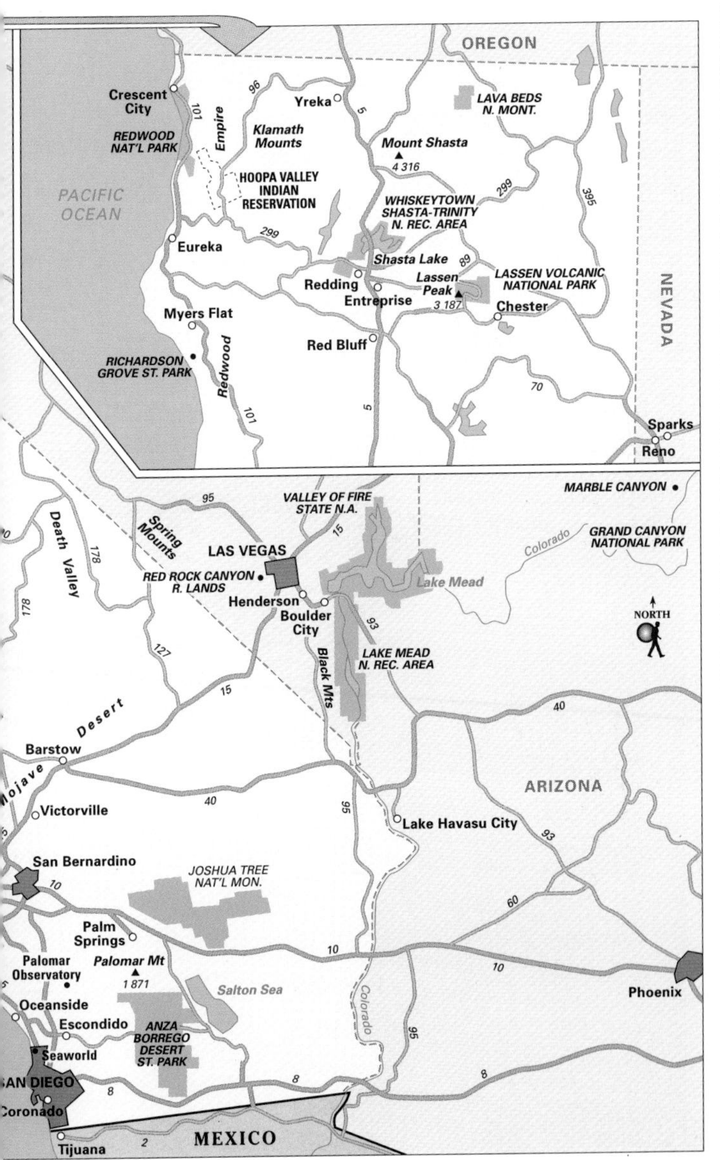
OREGON
Crescent City
REDWOOD NAT'L PARK
Empire
Klamath Mounts
Yreka
LAVA BEDS N. MONT.
Mount Shasta
4 316
HOOPA VALLEY INDIAN RESERVATION
PACIFIC OCEAN
WHISKEYTOWN SHASTA-TRINITY N. REC. AREA
Eureka
Shasta Lake
Redding
Lassen Peak
LASSEN VOLCANIC NATIONAL PARK
Entreprise
3 187
Chester
NEVADA
Myers Flat
Red Bluff
RICHARDSON GROVE ST. PARK
Redwood
Sparks
Reno
MARBLE CANYON
VALLEY OF FIRE STATE N.A.
Spring Mounts
Death Valley
LAS VEGAS
GRAND CANYON NATIONAL PARK
Colorado
RED ROCK CANYON R. LANDS
Lake Mead
Henderson
Boulder City
NORTH
Black Mts
LAKE MEAD N. REC. AREA
Mojave Desert
Barstow
ARIZONA
Victorville
Lake Havasu City
San Bernardino
JOSHUA TREE NAT'L MON.
Palm Springs
Palomar Observatory
Palomar Mt
1 871
Salton Sea
Phoenix
Oceanside
Escondido
ANZA BORREGO DESERT ST. PARK
Seaworld
SAN DIEGO
Coronado
MEXICO
Tijuana

CALIFORNIA

LOS ANGELES (AREA MAP)

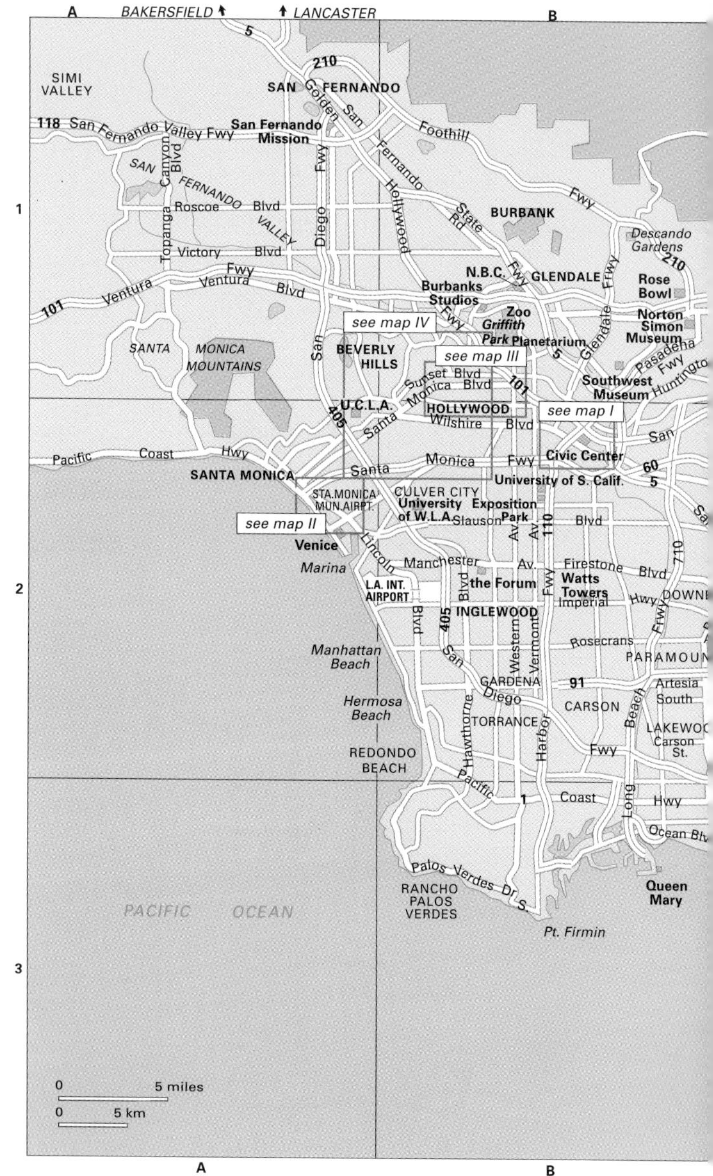

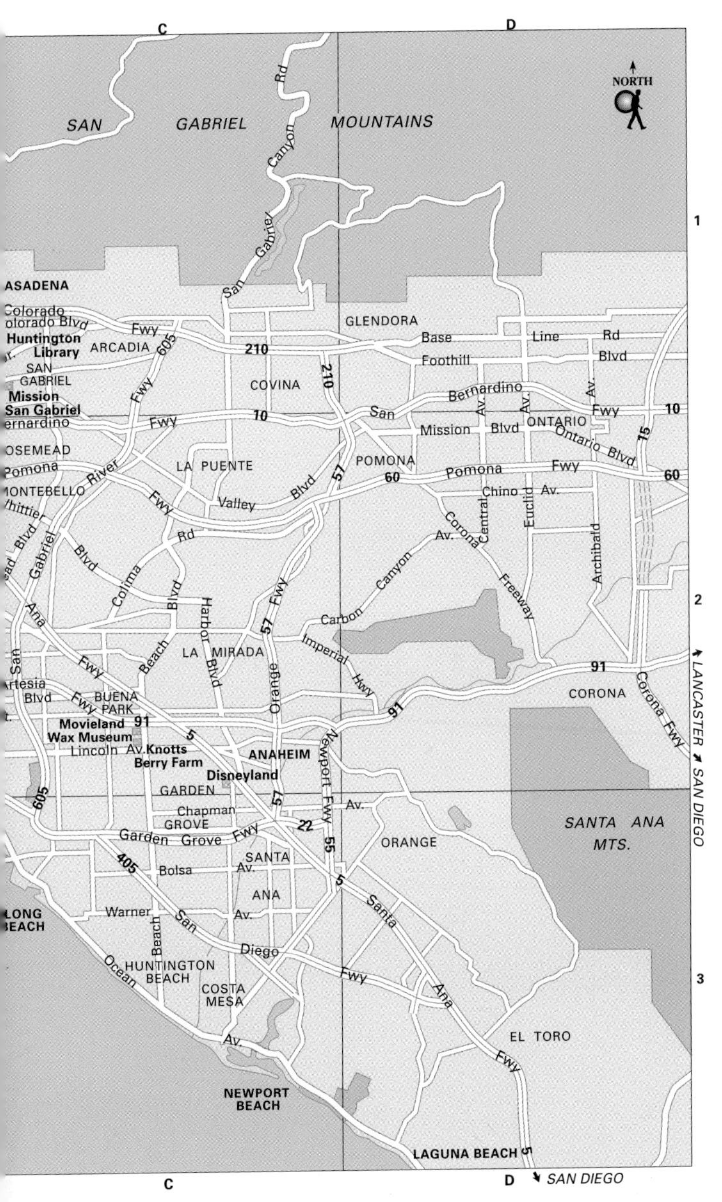

LOS ANGELES (AREA MAP)

DOWNTOWN LOS ANGELES (MAP I)

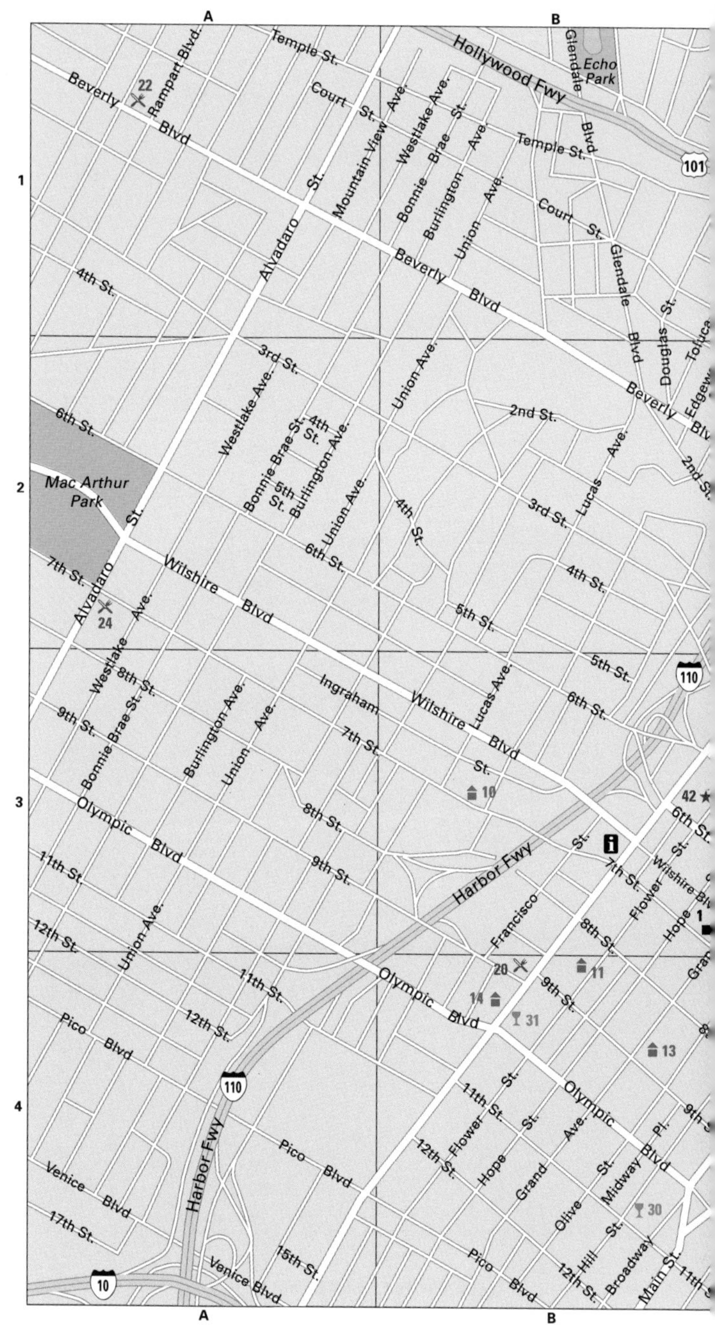

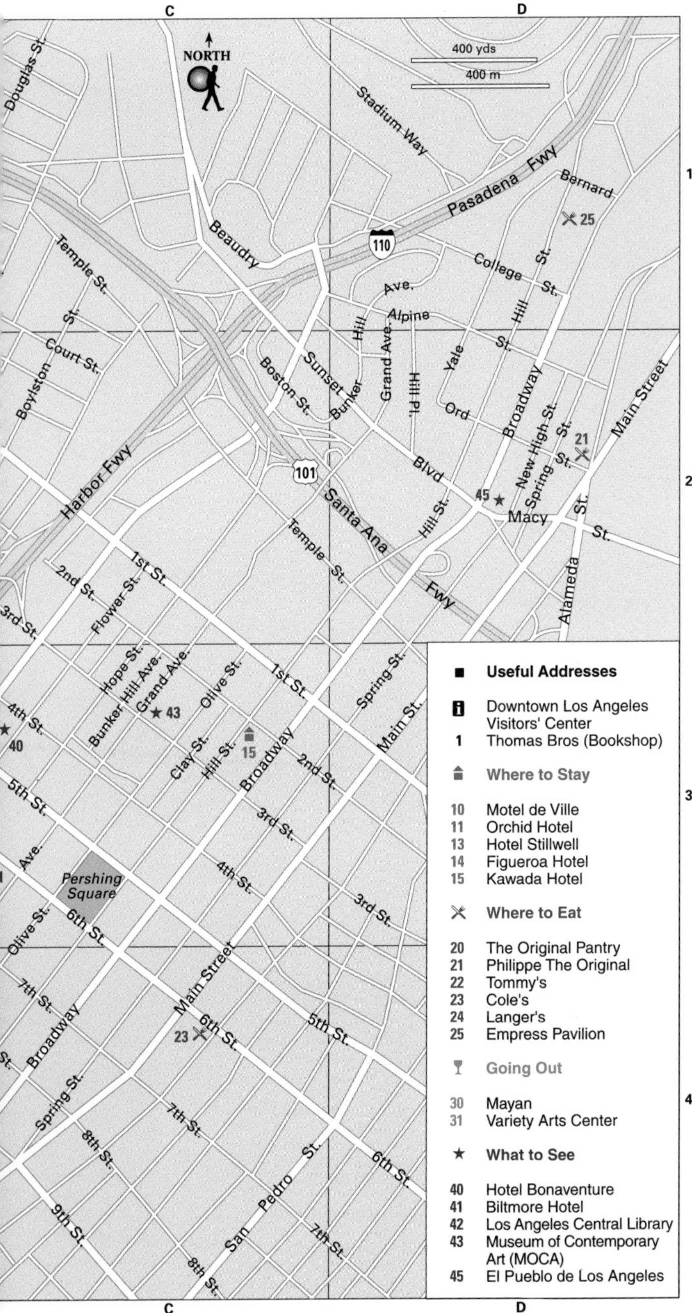

DOWNTOWN LOS ANGELES (MAP I)

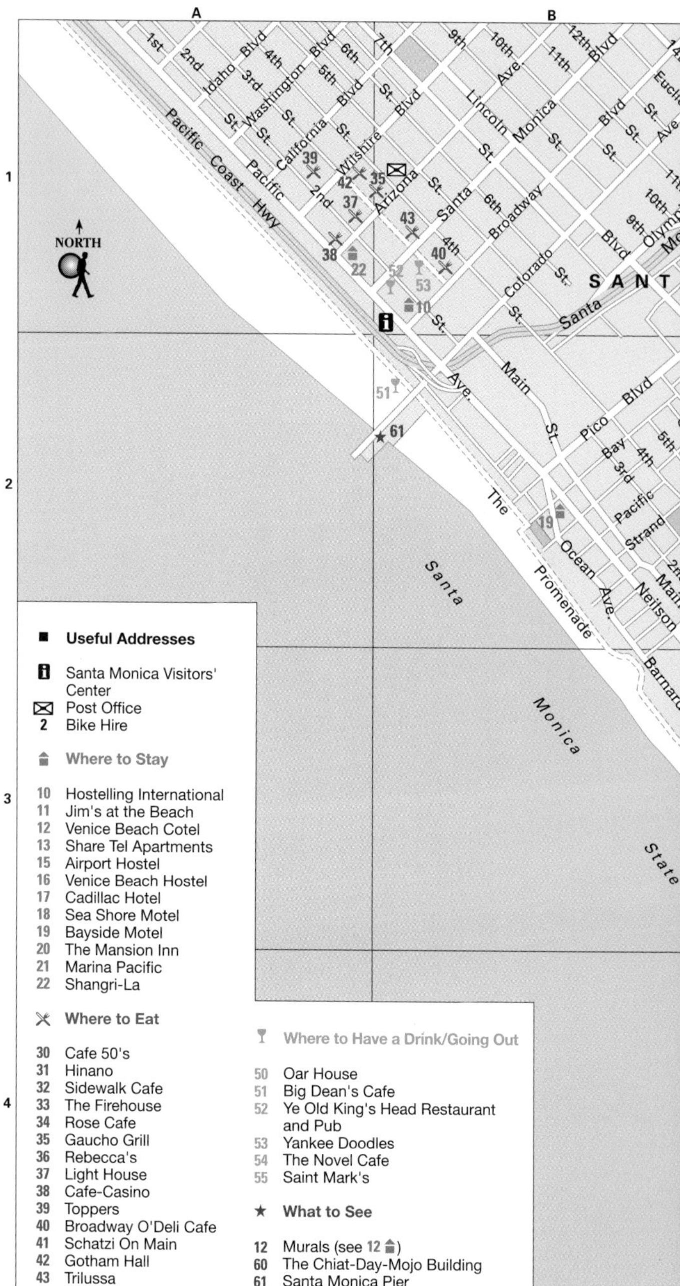
A
B
1
2
3
4
NORTH
1st
2nd
Idaho
3rd
4th
Washington
5th
6th
7th
9th
10th
11th
12th
14th
Euclid
Blvd
Ave.
St.
California
Wishire
Arizona
Lincoln
Monica
Santa
Broadway
Colorado
Olympic
Pacific Coast Hwy
Pacific
Main
Pico
Bay
Pacific
Strand
Neilson
Barnard
The Promenade
Ocean Ave.
SANTA
Santa Monica State
39
42
35
37
43
38
22
40
52
53
10
51
61
19
Useful Addresses
Santa Monica Visitors' Center
Post Office
2 Bike Hire
Where to Stay
10 Hostelling International
11 Jim's at the Beach
12 Venice Beach Cotel
13 Share Tel Apartments
15 Airport Hostel
16 Venice Beach Hostel
17 Cadillac Hotel
18 Sea Shore Motel
19 Bayside Motel
20 The Mansion Inn
21 Marina Pacific
22 Shangri-La
Where to Eat
30 Cafe 50's
31 Hinano
32 Sidewalk Cafe
33 The Firehouse
34 Rose Cafe
35 Gaucho Grill
36 Rebecca's
37 Light House
38 Cafe-Casino
39 Toppers
40 Broadway O'Deli Cafe
41 Schatzi On Main
42 Gotham Hall
43 Trilussa
Where to Have a Drink/Going Out
50 Oar House
51 Big Dean's Cafe
52 Ye Old King's Head Restaurant and Pub
53 Yankee Doodles
54 The Novel Cafe
55 Saint Mark's
What to See
12 Murals (see 12)
60 The Chiat-Day-Mojo Building
61 Santa Monica Pier
A
B

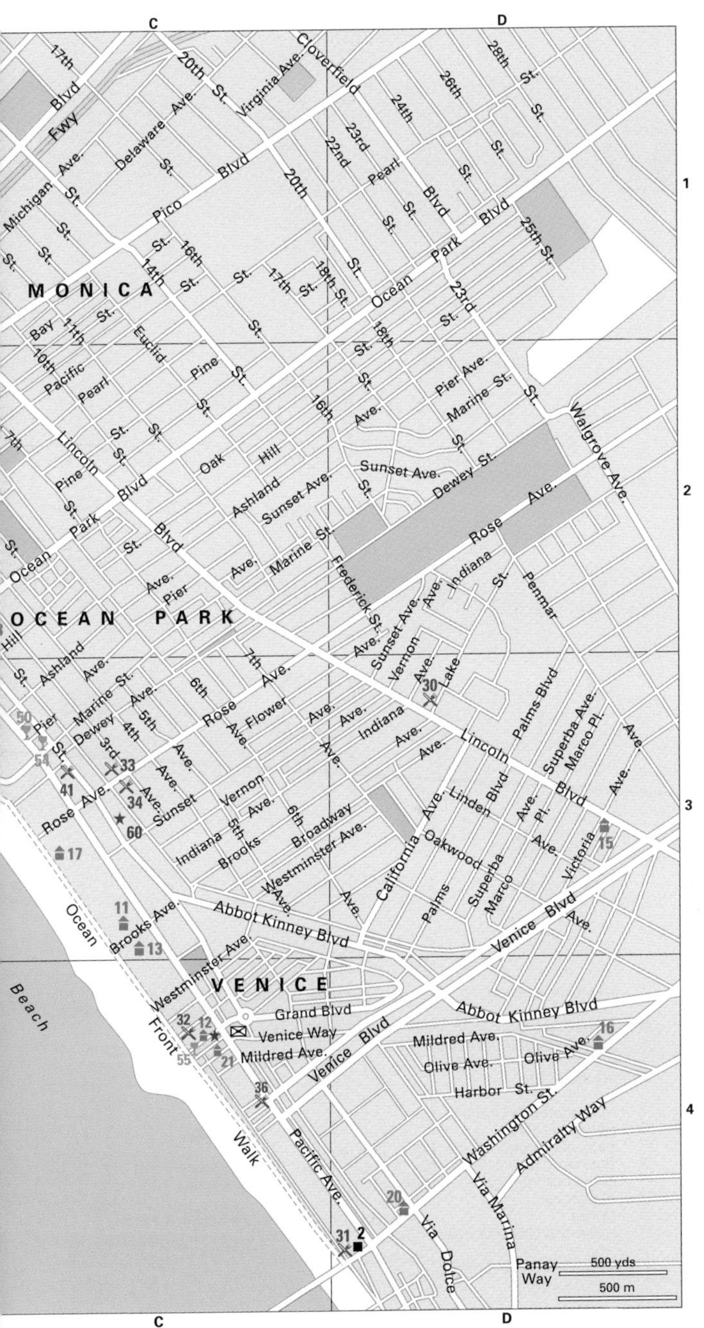

LOS ANGELES – SANTA MONICA AND VENICE (MAP II)

LOS ANGELES – HOLLYWOOD (MAP III)

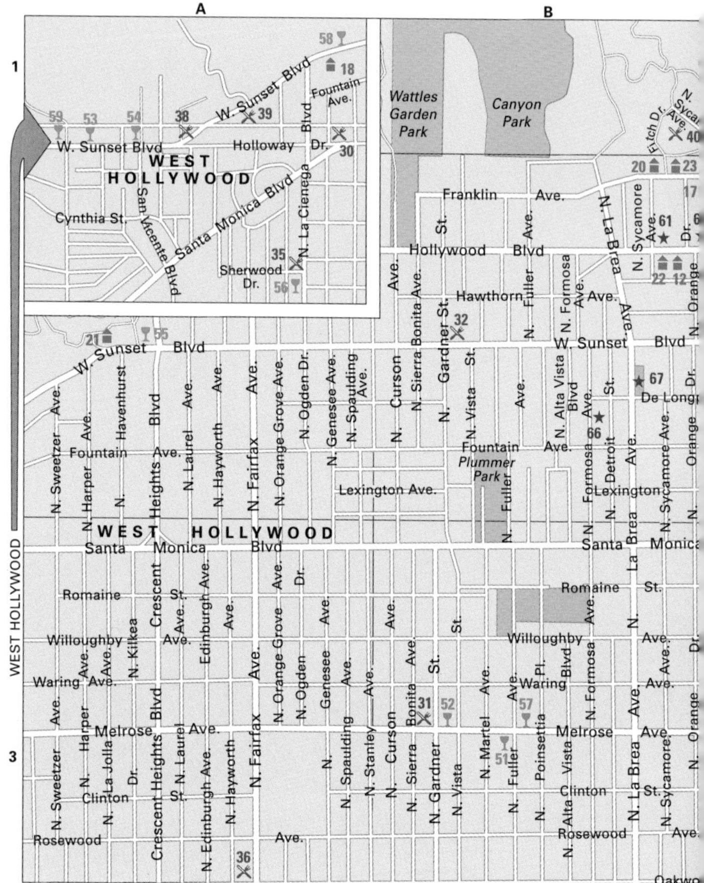

■ **Useful Addresses**

i Hollywood Visitors' Information Center
1 Collectors Book Store

Where to Stay

10 Hollywood Hills Hostel
11 Hollywood YMCA
12 Student Inn International Hostel
13 Hollywood Downtowner Motel
14 Hollywood International Hostel
15 Budget Inn
16 Dunes
17 Hollywood Celebrity Hotel
18 Clarion Park Sunset Hotel
19 Hollywood Metropolitan Hotel
20 Highland Gardens Hotel
21 Chateau Marmont
22 Hollywood Roosevelt
23 Magic Motel
24 Liberty Hotel

Where to Eat

30 Barney's Beanery
31 Johnny Rockets
32 Toi
33 The Old Spaghetti Factory
34 The Musso and Frank Grill

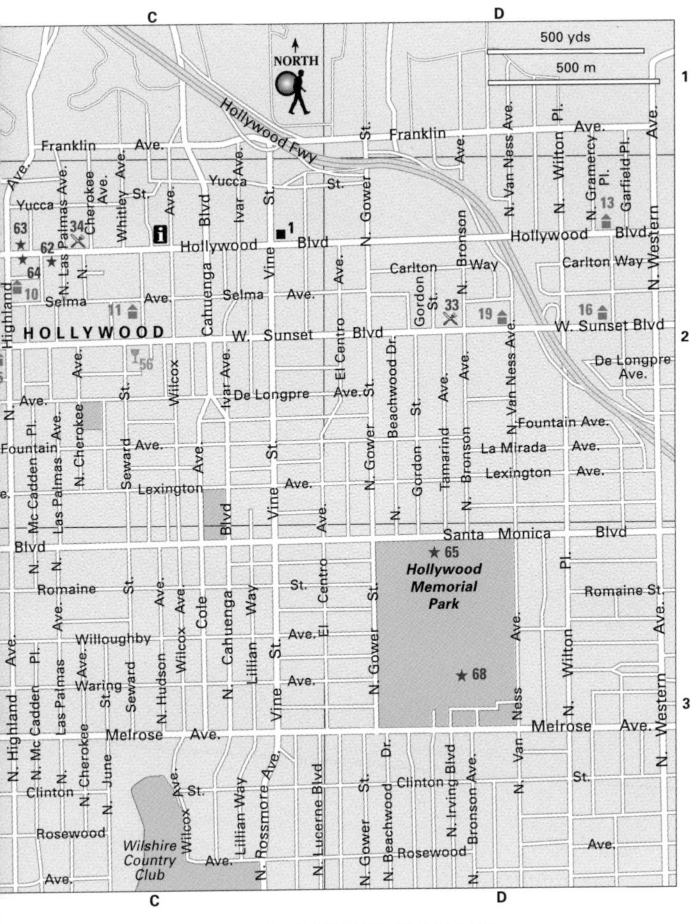

LOS ANGELES – HOLLYWOOD (MAP III)

35 Cafe Maurice
36 Canter's
37 Citrus
38 Spago
39 Le Dôme
40 Yamashiro

Where to Have a Drink/Going Out

51 Vienna Cafe
52 Caffè Luna
53 Roxy
54 Whisky a Gogo
55 Coconut Teaszer
56 Gate
57 The Grounding Theater
58 The Comedy Store
59 Billboard

★ **What to See**

60 Mann's Chinese Theatre
61 Entertainment Museum
62 Egyptian Theater
63 Hollywood Wax Museum
64 Guinness World of Records Museum
65 Hollywood Cemetery
66 French Village Movie Set
67 Charlie Chaplin Studios
68 Paramount Studios

LOS ANGELES – HOLLYWOOD AND BEVERLEY HILLS (MAP IV)

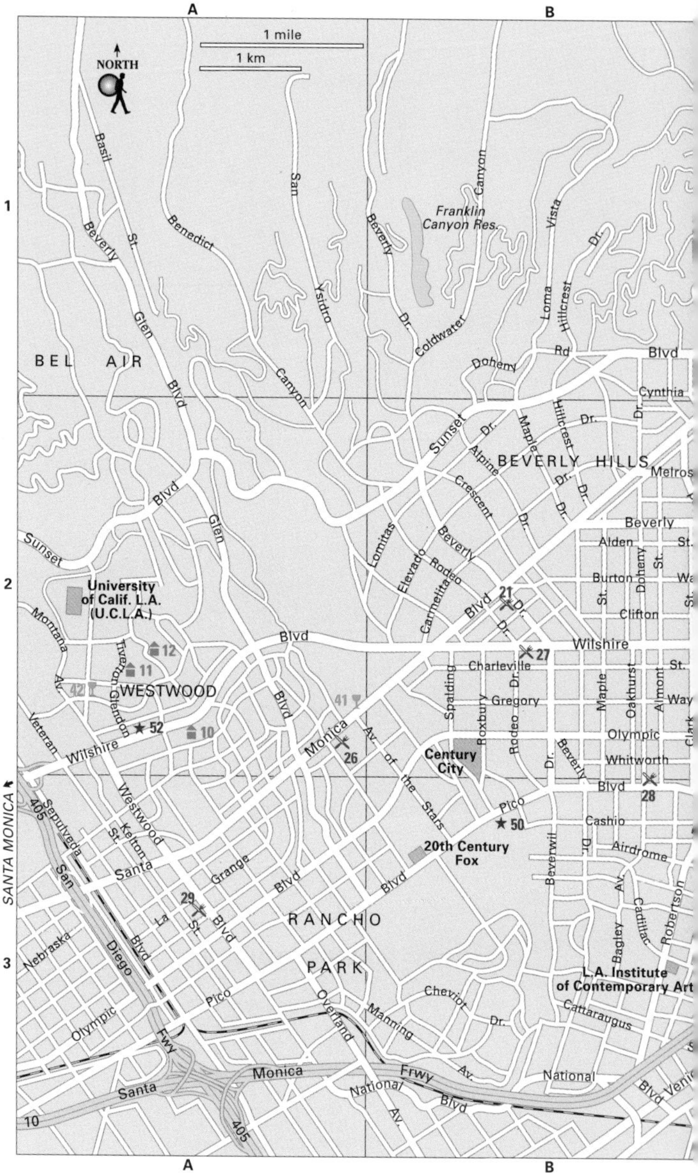

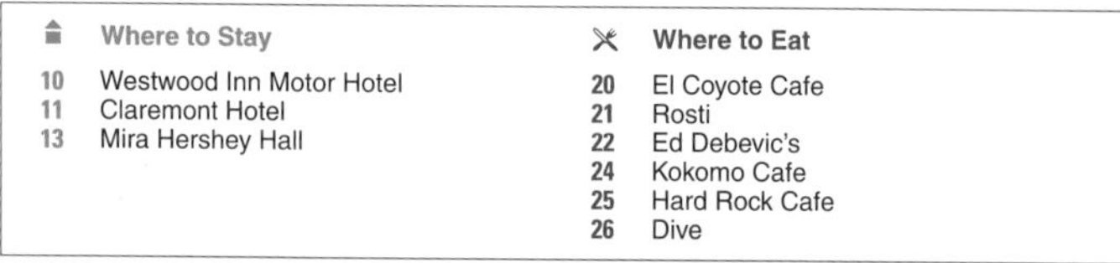

Where to Stay

10 Westwood Inn Motor Hotel
11 Claremont Hotel
13 Mira Hershey Hall

Where to Eat

20 El Coyote Cafe
21 Rosti
22 Ed Debevic's
24 Kokomo Cafe
25 Hard Rock Cafe
26 Dive

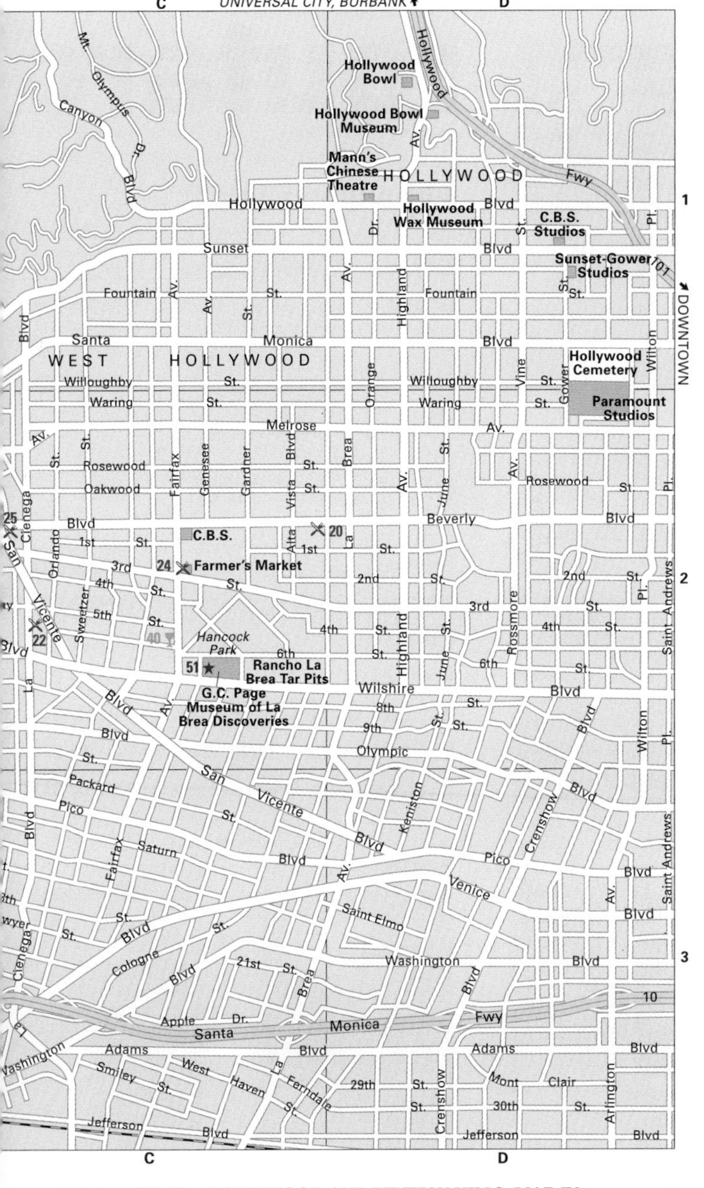

LOS ANGELES – HOLLYWOOD AND BEVERLY HILLS (MAP IV)

27 Planet Hollywood
28 Milky Way
29 Shamshiri

Where to Have a Drink/Going Out

40 Molly Malone's
41 Lunaria
42 Maloney's on the Campus

★ **What to See**

50 Museum of Tolerance
51 Los Angeles County Museum of Art
52 The Armand Hammer Museum of Art and Cultural Center

for New York (9,272 crimes a year per 100,000 inhabitants, as against 9,667 in New York)?

• The city of LA seems to attract East-Coast Americans like a magnet. Statistics show that an average of 85 New Yorkers leave the 'Big Apple' every day to set up home in Greater Los Angeles.

A BRIEF HISTORY

– **1542**: the Portuguese navigator João Cabrilho (Juan Rodriguez Cabrillo) was the first European to set eyes on Los Angeles, which he studied from on board his ship. The fires of the Native Americans formed such a layer of smoke above the land that he called the place *Bahia de los Fumos*. Cabrilho was an unconventional explorer, as he made discoveries but never sought to set up colonies.

– **1769**: while all of California was in the hands of the Spanish, its governor, Gaspar de Portola, led an expedition to explore Monterey Bay. He travelled across what is now the present-day city with the aim of establishing a chain of interlinked Franciscan missions and *presidios* (forts) along *El Camino Reàl* (the Royal Road) that would consolidate the Spanish grip on California. By the end of the 18th century, 21 missions had been created this way, including two that are now in the suburbs of Los Angeles: San Gabriel Arcángel (1771) and San Fernando Rey de España.

– **1781**: on 4 September, a group of 44 *vecinos pobladores* (settlers), most of them of mixed African, Native American and Hispanic race, founded an embryo colony that they called *El Pueblo de Nuestra Señora La Reyna de Los Angeles del Río Porciùncula,* naming it after the saint whose feast day in their calendar had fallen on the previous day. A bit of a long-winded name for a small village that would go on to become the centre of LA!

– **1822**: Mexico gained its independence from Spain and inherited California, which it then controlled. Los Angeles was then a series of immense ranches where horses and cattle were raised. The *rancho* Rodeo de Las Aguas later became Beverly Hills, the *rancho* San José became the city of Pomona while the *rancho* San Vicente y Santa Monica gave birth to the famous seaside town of Santa Monica.

– **1835**: LA became a totally separate city *(ciudad)* and the capital of Alta California. The Mexican governor continued to live in Monterey.

– **1846**: as a consequence of the war between the United States and Mexico, Los Angeles, like the rest of California, joined the US and became an American city. While San Francisco to the north was living through the Gold Rush (**1848–56**), the less affluent and less well known Los Angeles earned its living from agriculture and plantations. Everything changed with the opening, in **1885,** of the Santa Fe railroad line – LA's economic lift-off had begun.

– **1886**: Horace and Daeida Wilcox, two immigrants, bought a large property near the city, turning it into a prosperous farm, with fruit trees, and other crops divided up into plots. The central avenue of this new property was called Prospect, but it was later to become Hollywood

Boulevard. Mrs Wilcox called her farm Hollywood, a name that she had picked up from her neighbour in the train. Though not a very original name, it was made famous when the movie empire was born and developed in the middle of the apricot, orange and eucalyptus trees.

For more of the Hollywood story, *see* 'What to See' *below*.

AND, MORE RECENTLY . . .

On 29 April 1992, in Simi Valley (a white and reactionary county of LA, and Ronald Reagan territory), an all-white jury acquitted the white police officers accused of beating up a black motorist, Rodney King. Unluckily for them, an amateur video-maker had filmed the scene and his tape was broadcast all round the world. In response to the scandalous acquittal, South Central, one of the poorest districts in LA, erupted into violence and attacked all the symbols of the consumer society with pillage and arson. The disturbances went on for two days, with more than 40 deaths and damage amounting to millions of dollars. It was an event waiting to happen, given the immense frustration that had built up within the Afro-American and Hispanic communities in the wake of the cancellation of social welfare programmes, police racism, unemployment and the ever-growing gap between the incomes of the rich and the poor.

It was not as though there had been no warning signs in recent years, for example depicted in such movies as the remarkable *Boyz 'n' the Hood* by John Singleton and Spike Lee's *Do the Right Thing*, which depicted the disastrous ghettoization of the Afro-American community and clearly showed the fuse that was ready to explode.

The Simi Valley jury was the spark that finally lit that fuse. Three months later, in July 1992, the Californian Supreme Court appealed against the verdict and brought the police officers back into court. And, on 17 April 1993, in the second trial of the same policemen, two of them were found guilty. This verdict was met with relief. A sociologist analyzed it this way: 'The rebels have taken revenge on their own district – they've destroyed their own properties. Next time, they'll hit Beverly Hills! They have very little political awareness or organizing ability, but things won't stay that way forever.' The American ghettos have come to the end of their tether.

THE EARTHQUAKE OF 1994

At 4.30am on 17 January 1994, an earthquake measuring 6.6 on the Richter scale awoke the sleeping city, and some thought that the 'Big One' had finally arrived. The earthquake, whose epicentre was in the San Fernando Valley, some 19 miles (30km) from LA, killed 51 people and injured 3,000 more. It left 9,000 homeless, affected almost 3,000 buildings and seriously damaged the infrastructure of the highways – a vital element in the region's economy. The resulting bill was somewhere between $15 and $30 billion. But it still wasn't the dreaded 'Big One'.

Having become accustomed to seismic shocks, the inhabitants of LA soon played this catastrophe down, reserving most of their irritation for the additional time it now took to get to work. Business, after all, is business, and it must go on! That's how they think out here – a month after the event, they were giving it no further thought.

ARRIVING AT THE AIRPORT

– A **No. 607 bus** during the week will drop you Downtown. Or you can take the free 'C shuttle' to the terminal, then get a No. 42 bus, or a No. 439, which is faster, to Downtown.

– The **Airport Service** bus serves Downtown as well as Beverly Hills, Hollywood, West Los Angeles, Pasadena, Long Beach and Universal City.

– **Hotel Reservation Center**: inside LA Airport, before you pick up your luggage. This has many advantages. There's a 30 per cent reduction on the cost of your room, because the Center can assure the hotels of bookings. Tell the operator the number of your chosen hotel: they'll call directly to book a room, even after 6pm (the usual cut-off point for phone reservations). This is a good service if you arrive late in LA and haven't reserved ahead.

– **To get to your hotel**: free shuttles provide a connection between the airport and certain hotels (including youth hostels), provided, of course, you call as soon as you arrive.

– The big **car-hire companies** have offices and large parking lots outside the airport. To get there, take one of their regular shuttles from the exit. These minibuses, which have the name of the company painted on them, will drop you at the hire office without charge.

GETTING AROUND LOS ANGELES

ORIENTATION

The first thing to do is to get a good map of LA or, better still, a street atlas of the city (*see* 'Maps and Guides' *below*). Always know where you're going before setting off, study the map closely to work out your destination and the route you'll be following. When travelling by car in LA, you must also be very clear about your itinerary, the names of the exits and the numbers of the freeways to follow, and you have to know how to make the connections. Otherwise, you'll get lost the first time you go out in your car. Logic, organization and foresight are better than impulse, improvization and rough navigation in a place the size of LA!

Learn the following key routes across this over-sized metropolis:

– **Interstate 5 (the Golden State Freeway)** crosses the city from the north (from San Francisco) to the south (to San Diego), via Downtown.

– **Interstate 10 (the Santa Monica Freeway)** crosses the city from west to east, from Santa Monica to Arizona and Nevada.

– **Interstate 405 (the San Diego Freeway)** cuts the city from north to south, parallel with Interstate 5, but lying further to the west.

– **Route 1 (Pacific Coast Highway)** runs along the Pacific shore to the north and south of LA.

MAPS AND GUIDES

The *City Map of Los Angeles and San Fernando Valley* (Rand McNally) has the merits of being well made and inexpensive. But the street index isn't easy to use. The most practical solution is the backpacker atlas of the streets of LA. The least expensive (but not the most detailed) is the *New Revised Gousha Street Atlas of Greater LA* (published by Gousha).

The most complete and precise street atlas is the *Thomas Guide to Los Angeles County*. It costs about $26, but will be of such service that it's worth it, especially if you're staying for a week or more. The *Thomas Guide* is on sale in most bookshops and some service stations. It's revised and updated every year, so make sure they give you the latest edition.

CAR HIRE

Once you realize that some of the interesting places can be up to 20 miles (30km) from the centre, you quickly see that the city is a nightmare for anyone without a car. LA is the only place where it is advisable (if not essential) to hire a car. If you get three or four people together, you'll break even very quickly and a serious gain in time – like several days – is guaranteed (*see* 'Orientation' *above* for notes on how to get around by car). Outside the rush hours, a car is very practical. You'll be astonished to find how easy it is, and how well signed the roads really are!

■ **Alamo**: 9020 Aviation Boulevard, Inglewood, not far from LAX. ☎ 649-2245. Freephone for reservations: ☎ 1-800-327-9633. Fax: (310) 649-2245. These are the lowest and most competitive rates of all the big agencies. The cars are new, with automatic gearbox and air-conditioning, and are always in good condition. Unlimited mileage. There's a regular shuttle minibus between LAX and the company's parking lot.

■ **CAFLA Tours**: 7100 Hayvenhurst Avenue, Suite 111, Van Nuys, CA 91406. Freephone: ☎11-800-636-9683 or (818) 785-4569. Fax: (818) 785-3964. Website: www.cafla-tours.com. Run by a competent, dynamic team, this highly recommended agency undertakes to get you a car (less than six months old and of any category) or a motorbike (including a Harley-Davidson) at the best price. It offers rates that are in fact often lower than those quoted by the big American hire companies for the same cars. There's no point in going down there in person, because the agency is a long way from the airport. Just call them.

– The small hire companies: the many independent agencies, scattered around the edge of the airport, generally offer better rates than the big hire companies (Avis, Hertz, Budget, National, Alamo, etc.). But the other side of the coin is that they have fewer cars available for their clients, they aren't overhauled as regularly as those provided by the big companies and, lastly, it isn't always possible to take a car from point A and return it to point B at the end of your trip. Check first.

■ **Holiday Payless**: 6355 Westchester Parkway. Near the airport. ☎ 645-2100.

■ **Lucky-Rent-a-Car**: 8620 Airport Boulevard. ☎ 641-2323. Fax: 310-6411. Website: www.

luckyrentacar.com. Good reputation and excellent prices. There's a direct free line to call if you're at the airport (in the baggage area), as well as transport that will take you to pick up the car.

■ **Rocket**: 4820 West Century Boulevard. ☎ 674-1820. Near the Tivoli Motor Hotel. Services and prices are OK.

■ **Avon Rent-a-car**: 8459 Sunset Boulevard, West Hollywood. ☎ (213) 650-26-31. Website: www.shooshani.com. Hire to young people aged 18–25 (a very rare service!) in return for a daily additional charge (which is very large if you're under 20).

■ **Enterprise Rent-a-car**: offices at the airport. ☎ (310) 649-5400. Interesting prices. Weekend Specials.

■ **Oldies Car Rental & Tours**: 502 Washington Boulevard, Suite 489, Marina del Rey, at Venice. ☎ (310) 823-6312. Fax: (310) 823-3052. With or without driver, hire of cars that were the queens of the highway in the 1960s! For anyone who can afford it, this is a fabulous way to explore LA and its surrounding area.

MOTORCYCLE HIRE

If you're travelling alone or in a pair, this is probably the most pleasant means of travel. Unfortunately, the obligation to take out one or even two additional insurance policies makes it very costly. You need to bear this in mind, of course, and you must have a motorcycle licence.

PARKING LOTS: HOW TO USE THEM

Read the notices at parking lots very carefully. They often differ very markedly from each other and the parking they allow is very precisely spelled out. Occasionally, parking is allowed free for one hour (the cops quite frequently take note of car numbers as they patrol their beats, in order to catch out anyone outstaying their time). Many places have parking meters, but these are subject to restrictions. For example, you may have to remove your car during the rush-hours, i.e. 7–9am and 4–6pm. This will be indicated in some way. Fines are very swiftly slapped on by highly mobile but almost invisible teams of omnipresent agents, and cars are towed away with great haste. Make a careful note of the days and times of street cleaning, which, of course, change from street to street: parking is prohibited at these times. The worst thing about LA is that you don't have the option of walking.

– A red line on the edge of a pavement means parking is prohibited.

– A green line means parking is allowed for just 20 minutes.

– A white line means you are only allowed to stop in order to set down or pick up passengers.

BY BUS

If you're very poor, the bus can be an option, but it's not really recommended. It's true that buses go everywhere but, unfortunately, they are very slow because they rarely use the freeways. Bus-stops are indicated by a white-and-orange RTD sign.

Several bus companies cover the LA area: **MTA** buses depart from Downtown, **Big Blue Buses** cover all of the western part of the city

(Westwood, Santa Monica) and **Culver City Buses** go from Culver City to Santa Monica and Westwood.

Consider buying a ticket with a transfer which, for 25 cents extra, lets you get off once or twice en route until the time marked at the bottom of the transfer.

Travelling by bus is also a question of organization. You have to prepare your itinerary carefully.

Information and timetables are available from **MTA Bus Information**: Arco Plaza, 515 Flower Street (level C). In Downtown. Open 8am–3.30pm. ☎ 626-4455. Freephone: ☎ 1-800-COMMUTE Using the same number, you can call and say, 'I'm *here* and I want to go *there*' and, amazingly they'll tell you what bus to take, where to change, etc. It's good to familiarize yourself with the MTA Rapid Buses, which stop only at big junctions and so can help you save quite a bit of time.

– **Hollywood office**: 6249 Hollywood Boulevard. Open Monday–Friday 10am–6pm: closed 2.30–3.15pm. Beside the old Pantages Theatre and the Equitable Building. One little tip: Hollywood is a good connection point for bus devotees – there are the beaches, UCLA, Universal Studios, NBC, Beverly Hills and the Hollywood Bowl (for concerts).

There's a reduction for students below the age of 18.

Have the exact fare ready before boarding the bus. The driver won't give you any change.

Greyhound Terminal: 1716 East 7th Street, at the corner of Alameda. ☎ 620-1200. Faster than the MTA bus to get to Hollywood, Santa Monica and Anaheim (Disneyland). The cafe in the terminal is not expensive. The district is quite dangerous in the evening. To get to Downtown, take a No. 60 bus going west to the Hilton Hotel.

USEFUL PLACES AND INFORMATION

TOURIST INFORMATION

There are three main tourist information offices – one in Hollywood, another Downtown, and the third in Santa Monica. Here, they're called Convention and Visitors' Bureaux.

Downtown Los Angeles Visitors' Information Center (map I, B3): 685 S Figueroa Street (between Wilshire and 7th Street). ☎ 689-8822. Open daily, 8am–5pm (8.30am on Saturday). Closed Sunday.

Hollywood Visitors' Information Center (map III, C2): The Janes House, Janes Square, 6541 Hollywood Boulevard. ☎ 689-8822. Open Monday–Saturday 9am–5pm. A charming Victorian house at the end of a sort of mini shopping mall. This house bears the name of three sisters who ran a primary school in the early days of Hollywood, a school that taught the children of Cecil B. De Mille, Charlie Chaplin and Douglas Fairbanks Jnr. The welcome is very friendly and they have abundant information about Los Angeles and environs, as well as information about tours of the movie studios and guided tours of Beverly Hills. Grayline/Starline Tours give amusing commentaries on the houses of the stars.

🛈 Santa Monica Visitors' Center (map II, B1): 1400 Ocean Avenue, between Broadway and Santa Monica Boulevard. ☎ (310) 393-7593. Open daily, 10am–5pm in summer and 10am–4pm in winter.

– **For full information**: ☎ 411 or 555-1212. Hotels, stations, banks, restaurants, or even if you've lost your friend's phone number. They're very efficient.

POST OFFICES

✉ In Hollywood: 1615 Wilcox Avenue. ☎ (213) 464-2194. Open Monday–Friday 8am–5pm (1pm Saturday).

✉ In Santa Monica (map II, B1): at the junction of 5th Street and Arizona. ☎ (310) 576-2626. Open Monday–Friday 9am–6pm (1pm Saturday).

TELEPHONE AREA CODES

It's important to distinguish between these, especially when phoning a hotel.

– **213**: for Downtown, Hollywood, Huntington Park, Vernon, Montebello

– **310**: for Malibu, Pacific Coast Highway, Westside, Westwood (UCLA) Southern and Eastern Los Angeles County

– **818**: for Northern Los Angeles County, including the San Fernando Valley and Pasadena

– **714**: Orange County

– **619** and **670**: San Diego County

– **805**: Ventura County

MONEY, CURRENCY EXCHANGE, BANKS

– There are many **cash dispensers** (ATMs) that accept foreign credit cards. Note that there's a ceiling on how much you can withdraw, if you rely on using cash a lot.

■ **American Express**: 404 S Figueroa. ☎ 627-4800. Within the Hilton (Thomas Cook) and the Hotel Bonaventure. Open Monday–Friday 9am–5pm, Saturday 10am–5pm.

■ **American Foreign Exchange**: World Trade Center, 350 S Figueroa. ☎ 626-0255. To change traveller's cheques that aren't denominated in dollars.

■ **Bank of America**: 525 S Flower Street. ☎ 228-4069. You can obtain dollars on presentation of your Visa card. Also at the **First Interstate Bank.**

■ **Round-the-clock exchange**: 6565 Hollywood Boulevard. ☎ 464-2718. Closed Sunday night (5pm–8am). Only for emergencies, because the rates of exchange are not as favourable as in the banks.

EMERGENCIES

– All hospitals have an emergency service. Dial **911** for an ambulance.

■ **24-Hour Pharmacy**: Kaiser Pharmacy, in the Los Angeles Medical Center, 4861 Sunset Boulevard. ☎ 667-8301.

■ **Free Clinic**: 8405 Beverly Boulevard. ☎ 653-1990. Open 10am–10pm. Advisable to call for an appointment.

AIRLINE COMPANIES

■ **American Airlines**: ☎ 1-800-433-7300

■ **Alaska Airlines**: ☎ 1-800-426-0333

■ **C.I.E.E.** (American charters): 1093 Broxton Avenue, Office 224. Westwood (near UCLA)

■ **Continental Airlines**: ☎ 1-800-525-1700

★ **Northwest Airlines**: ☎ 1-800-225-2525

■ **Southwest Airlines**: ☎ 1-800-435-9792. Offers a year-round 'Two for One' deal, but there is a limited number of places, so reserve ahead.

■ **United Airlines**: ☎ 1-800-521-4041

■ **US Airways**: ☎ 998-6622. Famous Californian company that offers many connections via San Francisco. They also have a useful pass for many cities in the West.

TRAVEL AGENCIES

■ **CAFLA Tours**: 7100 Hayvenhurst Avenue, Suite 111, Van Nuys, CA 91406. ☎ (818) 785-4569. ☎ 1-800-636-9683. Fax: (818) 785-3964. Website: www.cafla-tours.com. Individual service, advice and excellent rates. Tailor-made holidays that include activities in Native American territory and rafting on the Colorado River, plus car hire, motorbikes, campers, boats, houseboats, small planes, etc. Ideal for groups. A good place for anyone who wants to know what they're letting themselves in for before they arrive in the country. Call before coming here because it's a long way from the centre.

■ **Chez E.T. Surf**: 904 Aviation Boulevard, Hermosa Beach. Eddy Talbot ('E.T.') welcomes you cordially and gives you information and the necessary advice about surfing.

■ **Heliclass**: ☎ 1-800-998-4354. This agency offers helicopter flights over LA. The cost is high but the experience is amazing. For $120 per person, you can go on a sortie that includes 30 minutes in a helicopter, taking off from Van Nuys airport, flying over the Santa Monica Hills, Beverly Hills, central Hollywood and Downtown, then returning by passing over Griffith Park, Hollywood Hills (Madonna's home) and Universal Studios. You can even get a 'maiden flight' certificate.

NEWSPAPERS, MAGAZINES AND BOOKS

– Get the free 140-page *LA Weekly*, which lists everything that's going on. Look out for money-off vouchers in the display advertisements. The magazine can be found piled up more or less everywhere in public places.

– There's also a monthly called *Where in LA* that tells you everything about Los Angeles: attractions, museums, films, restaurants, and everything is classified by district. Website: www.wherela.com/where

■ **Collectors Book Store** (map III, C2, **1**): 1708 N Vine Street. ☎ 467-3296. Close to the intersection of Vine and Hollywood Boulevard, at the historic heart of Hollywood. This is like Ali Baba's cave, full of treasures of every kind, aimed at movie buffs: old film posters, photos of actors, books. You can even buy film or TV film scripts here.

■ **Thomas Bros** (map I, B3, **1**): 603 W 7th Street. ☎ 627-4018. In the heart of Downtown. Travel bookshop with a large selection of maps and tourist literature.

MISCELLANEOUS

■ **Quality Electronic**: 7761 Santa Monica Boulevard. One of the few shops where you can find a transformer that converts from 220V to 110V.

WHERE TO CAMP

There are several campgrounds at **Anaheim** (*see* 'Anaheim').

Valencia Travel Village: 27946 Henry Mayo Road (Highway 126), Valencia. ☎ (805) 257-3333. About 30 miles (50km) north of LA via Route 405 and Route 5, then take exit 126 West towards Ventura, making it 30 minutes from LA by car, and 5 minutes from Six Flags Magic Mountain. This is one of the most beautiful campgrounds in the Los Angeles region, in the foothills of the San Fernando hills, and well into the countryside. Nevertheless there's a certain amount of noise from heavy goods vehicles during the night. The campground is impeccably clean, very well equipped and pleasantly cool. There are three swimming pools, launderette and grocery store.

Malibu Beach Park: 25801 Pacific Coast Highway (Route 1). ☎ (310) 456-6052. Between Malibu Canyon Road and Coral Canyon Road, just 30 minutes from Santa Monica. Good view of the ocean.

WHERE TO STAY

NEAR THE AIRPORT (AREA CODE 310)

Unless you have to catch an early flight, there's little point staying in the airport area and even less if you don't have a car. You're a long way from the city and you can't do anything much on foot. On the other hand, it's very useful if you're flying into LA late or taking off early in the morning, as lots of hotels provide a free shuttle. Ask for information when you reserve ahead.

☆☆ MODERATE

☗ **Marletta's Motel**: 4849 W Century Boulevard, at Inglewood. ☎ 677-7500. This is just over a mile (2km) east of the airport. Take Bus No. 117. A small, unpretentious motel with TV in the rooms. The rooms for four are reasonably priced. Chinese restaurant.

☗ **Tivoli Motor Hotel**: 4861 W Century Boulevard, at Inglewood. ☎ 677-9181. Fax: 677-5578. A little more expensive than Marletta's, but there's a swimming pool, TV and telephone, and the price is still moderate for LA. Free shuttle to and from the airport, provided you don't require it too late in the evening.

☗ **Royal Comfort Motel**: 4230 W Century Boulevard. ☎ (310) 419-8041. ☎ 1-800-BUD-HOST. Not much further away than the Tivoli and a little cheaper. Friendly welcome. The rooms are clean and spacious. There's a jacuzzi and a parking lot. Morning coffee is free, but it's nothing to get excited about.

☗ **Caesar's Motor Hotel**: 4652 W Century Boulevard, Inglewood. ☎ (310) 671-6161. Fax: 672-4310. The rooms are quiet, as they overlook an interior courtyard where there's a swimming pool. Airport shuttle every 30 minutes. Same prices as the Royal Comfort.

DOWNTOWN (AREA CODE 213)

Certain parts of this district are rather dangerous in the evening. After dark, for example, avoid MacArthur Park, which is a meeting place for drug dealers and gangs. But there are many buses that will take you to interesting places. Among the things you find here are bars and great nightspots. From the airport, take a No. 42 bus to Olive Street.

☆ BUDGET

☗ **Motel de Ville** (map I, B3, **10**): 1123 W 7th Street. ☎ 624-8474. Fax: 624-7652. From the airport, take the Airport Transit Bus to the Hilton Hotel. If you leave the Harbor Freeway (Route 110) coming from the south, take the 6th Street exit, or take the 8th Street exit coming from the north: it's not very far. Nothing particularly luxurious, but it is clean. Rooms cost roughly the same as at the Orchid Hotel and prices only go up by a few dollars in summer. There's air-conditioning, a coffee shop and a small swimming pool. With 62 rooms, there's every chance you'll get one but, in high season, you may want to book. Reduction if you pay by the week.

☗ **Orchid Hotel** (map I, B4, **11**): 819 S Flower Street. ☎ 624-5855. Freephone: ☎ 1-800-874-5855. Fax: 624-8740. From the airport: Shuttle Bus C to the parking lot, then a No. 439 bus. Right at the centre of Downtown, this small, well-run hotel has pleasant rooms that are among the cheapest in the area. The surrounding townscape is part of a programme of urban regeneration and the district is progressively becoming a better place to be. The hotel offers reasonable comfort, with air-conditioning and clothes-washing facilities. There's even free coffee.

☗ **Cecil Hotel**: 640 S Main Street, near 7th Street. ☎ 624-3841. Gigantic 700-room hotel where maintenance is at a very average level. Private showers and private TV. Small safety deposit box can be had by the day. Some rooms are better than others. Charges by the week are attractive (less than $100 including tax). Note that this is a rough district in the evening, so keep the name for emergencies only.

☆☆–☆☆☆ MODERATE TO EXPENSIVE

☗ **Park Plaza Hotel**: 607 S Park View Street, level with 6th Street. ☎ 384-5281. No. 18 bus to 5th Street. Ask the driver to stop in front of the hotel. This is a magnificent art-deco building – perhaps one of the finest in LA, surrounded by gardens. This was a prestige hotel when it opened in the 1920s, and the interior is breathtaking. There's a grand staircase lit by gigantic chandeliers. In its heyday, Eleanor Roosevelt and Bing Crosby stayed here. Later patrons have included Charlton Heston, Sylvester Stallone, Richard Pryor and Robin Williams. Dozens of films and TV movies have been made here, including: *Harlem Nights* with Eddie Murphy, *Psycho III* with Anthony Perkins, *Wild at Heart, Bugsy Malone, The Bodyguard, Hook, Chaplin* and *Stargate*, and there are display panels showing these, in the lobby.

These days, the hotel is showing signs of age and the district doesn't really feel too safe after dark, so this is a place that will appeal to those who like unusual architecture or a slightly decadent atmosphere, or whose dream is to get first-hand experience of bygone days as seen in *Sunset Boulevard*. There's a swimming pool and gymnasium in the basement, both free. Ask for a room on an upper floor for a good view of Downtown. All the rooms have been undergoing a total refurbishment.

☗ **Hotel Stillwell** (map I, B4, **13**): 838 S Large Avenue, Los Angeles, CA 90017. ☎ 627-1151. Freephone: ☎ 1-800-553-4774. Fax: 622-8940. This place is very comfortable and well located. There are 250 rooms, all with bathroom, air-conditioning and TV, and all recently renovated, so it's very good value for money. Pleasant ground-floor cafe, offering predominantly Mexican and Native American cuisine, and a plush bar (Hank's) with a quiet atmosphere. The 'Starving Students Special' breakfast is inexpensive and copious – it's available 7–10am.

☆☆☆ EXPENSIVE

☗ **Figueroa Hotel** (map I, B4, **14**): 939 S Figueroa Street, level with Olympic Boulevard. ☎ 627-8971. Freephone: ☎ 1-800-421-9092. Fax: 689-0305. This is an old, 12-storey brick tower housing a 300-room hotel; its interior has been marvellously redecorated in Hispanic style with Mexican tiled floors, plants, and bright, attractive colours. The swimming pool is bizarrely coffin-shaped. Still, there's a jacuzzi. Rooms have TV, phone, air-conditioning and bathroom, and they offer an airport shuttle. Double rooms cost from $80.

☗ **The Inn at 657**: 657 W 23rd Street. ☎ 741-2200. Freephone: ☎ 1-800-347-7512. Two blocks away from the Route 110 (Harbor Freeway) exit and five blocks south of Route 10 (Santa Monica Freeway). Conveniently located on the DASH (the local transport service for Downtown), in a residential district in an interesting, socially mixed area right near Figueroa. The hotel is very large with a small garden and a parking lot. The exterior is nothing special, but inside, they have some charming suites that give good value for money. Suites (all non-smoking) cost between $80 and $110. They're really spacious – almost as big as apartments and with tasteful decor and furnishings. One suite can even be connected with another room, for families or couples travelling together. A lavish breakfast is included. Booking is very strongly advised: you'll be asked for one night's down-payment.

☗ **Kawada Hotel** (map I, C3, **15**): 200 S Hill Street. ☎ 621-4455. Freephone: ☎ 1-800-752-9232. Fax: 687-4455. In an old brick high-rise building that has been entirely refurbished. This is one of the cheaper small luxury hotels. Rooms have a small fridge, video, TV and air-conditioning, and some have a small kitchenette. Prices start at $70. On the ground floor is a new restaurant, the **Epicenter,** decorated with an earthquake theme (but they could have made it a bit more exciting!!).

VENICE AND SANTA MONICA (AREA CODE 310)

This is *the* nicest place to stay, because it's near the ocean and it has an atmosphere that's simply impossible to describe. The ideal thing to do is to hire a bike. Take a No. 33 bus south from Downtown, or a No. 333 on Spring Street and 6th Street. Or take the blue No. 10 bus for 'Santa Monica via Freeway' at the intersection of 5th and Flower. From Hollywood, on Highland Avenue and Hollywood Boulevard, take Route 420 south for Santa Monica Boulevard. Ask for a transfer. Then take a No. 4 west. Get off at 4th and Santa Monica.

A word of advice: don't leave anything in your car if you hire one. Try to park it in a safe place or leave it in your hotel parking lot. Note that Venice tends to become quite menacing in the evening, whereas Santa Monica has much less of a problem. Hotels in Venice are often expensive in relation to their quality.

☆ BUDGET

☗ **Hostelling International – American Youth Hostel** (map II, B1, **10**): 1436 2nd Street, Santa Monica. ☎ 393-9913. Fax: 393-1769. One of the best youth hostels in California. Very well situated, really close to the beach and Santa Monica Pier. To get here from the airport, take Shuttle Bus C to the City Bus Terminal. Then take the Santa Monica municipal No. 3 Blue Bus to the junction of 4th Street and Broadway. Walk two blocks west to 2nd Street, then turn right. It's a large ultra-modern building, with a shop at the entrance selling books, guides, maps and hiking equipment. Inside the hostel there's plenty of open space, a fountain and a terrace. The welcome is very good in spite of the number of arrivals and departures they have to handle. The dormitories have eight to 10 beds and you can hire sheets. There are also dormitories with six beds, a touch more expensive, 'family' rooms of four beds, with sheets supplied for $2 extra. Then there are 'private rooms' – doubles – at around $40 a night. The showers and toilets are impeccably clean. Breakfast is reasonable. CD jukebox in the dining-room. There's a launderette, luggage-lockers and a TV-and-video room. No alcohol is allowed, and no smoking either. There's a money exchange facility and they accept major credit cards. Many activities are arranged, including excursions to Disneyland and Universal Studios.

☗ **Jim's at the Beach** (map II, C3, **11**): 17 Brooks Avenue, Venice Beach. ☎ 399-4018. Fax: 399-4216. Small, very well-located hotel for backpackers, in a rather nice private house about 50 yards (45 metres) from the beach, on a little street squeezed between Ocean Front Walk and Pacific Avenue. A mural on the outside shows an athletically built Samson dismantling the Philistine temple at Gaza (you're in the cradle of bodybuilding here!). Friendly welcome and warm atmosphere, thanks to the personality of the master of the house, Jim de Cordova, an old adventurer with blue eyes and a Californian beard. There are six beds per room. There's also a sitting corner with TV and kitchenette. It's clean and the prices are reasonable, and the place is so much less anonymous than Hostelling International. The weekly charges are good and there's lots of information for backpackers.

☗ **Venice Beach Cotel** (map II, C4, **12**): 25 Windward Avenue, Venice. ☎ 399-7649 and 452-9889. To get there from the airport, take Shuttle Bus C, then the No. 3 Blue Bus to the intersection of Lincoln and Venice Boulevard. Then a No. 33 RTD Bus that goes from Downtown to Venice. Get off at the post office and walk towards the beach. In the historic heart of the district and surrounded by arcaded buildings in Californian–Byzantine style, the hotel is recognisable from the huge mural that covers its western wall, and it's right in among the action. Ring the bell downstairs and come up to reception on the first floor. There are lots of young people here from all over the world. The dormitories accommodate four to 12 persons, and they have some rooms for couples with or without bathroom, at the same price as an average motel. Lots of people passing through. Don't expect too much where cleanliness is concerned and you won't be disappointed. Credit cards accepted. There's a restaurant – the St Mark's – on the ground floor.

☗ **Share Tel Apartments** (map II, C3, **13**): 20 Brooks Avenue, Venice. ☎ 392-0325. Fax: 392-9804. Another good location, just 20 yards (18 metres) from Ocean Front Walk, so it's very close to the beach. Almost opposite Jim's at the Beach, in a small block with 20 dormitories (not apartments, as you'd think from the name), each having four to eight beds, with kitchen. The rooms are unisex. You have to pay a deposit on your keys. There's free transport from the airport if you call ahead. The downside? – the charges for services are a bit high, it's not amazingly clean, and the dormitories are cramped.

☆ BUDGET – BUT FURTHER FROM THE BEACH

☗ **Venice Marina Hostel**: 2915 Yale Avenue, Venice. ☎ 301-3983. Go to Washington Boulevard and walk down three blocks. From the airport, take No. 3 Blue Bus (North). Go to Washington Boulevard, just over a mile (2km) from the beach in a quiet district. This is a large timber-built residential-type house where the atmosphere is very 'all in it together'. The rooms have bunk-beds and mattresses on the floor (you choose!), and everything is very well looked after. Lovely kitchen, and the bathrooms are almost luxurious. Breakfast is included and food is provided in the kitchen if you want to eat in the evening. Cozy living room with TV. Washing machines. Just right for nostalgic Woodstock first-time-rounders!

☗ **Airport Hostel** (map II, D3, **15**). 2221 Lincoln Boulevard, Venice. ☎ 305-0250. Run by the same organization as the **Venice Beach Cotel**. From the airport, just call the hostel and they'll come and pick you up at no charge. The building, which has no particular charm, is on an avenue carrying heavy traffic. Dormitories with either six or 25 beds. Breakfast and dinner is served, and there's a kitchen and a launderette. Bike hire is possible, and there's a large parking lot. They also have twin-bedded rooms for around $32 a night.

☗ **Venice Beach Hostel** (map II, D4, **16**): 701 Washington Street, Venice. Just after Oxford Street. ☎ 306-5180. Free transport from the airport if you call ahead. Otherwise, take Shuttle Bus C, then the No. 3 Blue Bus to Washington Boulevard, then walk west towards the beach. The hostel is above Celebrity Cleaners. There's a little outside staircase. This is a private youth hostel run by backpackers for backpackers. The dormitories hold 20 to 30 beds – usually packed but fairly quiet, because they face the rear. There's a relaxed atmosphere and a friendly welcome – laid-back and far out! No launderette, but bikes are provided.

☆☆–☆☆☆ MODERATE TO EXPENSIVE

☗ **Cadillac Hotel** (map II, C3, **17**): 401 Ocean Front Walk, Venice. ☎ 399-8876. Fax: 399-4536. This place has two addresses (the other one is 8 Dudley Avenue), because the hotel is on the corner of Dudley and the promenade that goes along the front at Venice Beach. Fortunately, there's no access for vehicles. This large building, only three storeys high, built in 1907 and has quite recently been renovated. You'll know it straight away from its walls, painted in salmon pink and pale green, and from the old iron fire escape, which they've kept. The rooms, though a bit small, are tastefully decorated and each has shower, WC and TV. The outlook is either over the surrounding roofs or, more expensively of course, onto the beach and the ocean. Try No. 401 (the California Suite) or, even better, No. 402 (the Charlie Chaplin Suite) with its four corner windows. In the 1920s, Charlie Chaplin spent two weeks a year here, writing film scripts and reviews. The story goes that Chaplin used to rent six rooms in six different motels, so that he would be able to meet one of his six girlfriends at any time of the day or night. No. 402 was one such place. There's a superb roof-terrace that's ideal for enjoying a lazy day in the sun, admiring the colours of the sun setting over the Pacific, or counting the planes taking off in the distance. With a little luck and patience, you might glimpse the silhouettes of some dolphins. Costs from $50 to $80 for a double.

☗ **Sea Shore Motel** (map II, B2, **18**): 2637 Main Street, Santa Monica. ☎ 392-2787. Simple, reasonable and moderately priced.

☗ **Bayside Motel** (map II, B2, **19**): 2001 Ocean Avenue, Santa Monica. ☎ 396-6000. Fax: 451-1111. Modern, hospitable, and well kept overall. The rooms facing the interior are quieter. Expect to pay $60 (a bit more in summer). Parking lot at the back.

☆☆☆ EXPENSIVE

The Mansion Inn (map II, D4, **20**): 327 Washington Street (and Sanborn), Marina del Rey. ☎ 821-2557. Freephone: ☎ 1-800-828-0688. Fax: 827-0289. Not far from the beach, this is an impeccable hotel with comfortable rooms. Breakfast is served in a flower-filled courtyard. Almost in the minor luxury class and it costs from $80 a room (in midweek there's a $10 reduction).

Marina Pacific (map II, C4, **21**): 1697 Pacific Avenue ☎ 452-1111. Freephone: ☎ 1-800-421-8151. Pleasant hotel with a colourful, fresh interior, located just a few yards from the beach and right at the heart of things. Rooms from $85. The receptionist has a mind-boggling array of security monitors behind the counter!

☆☆☆☆ SPLASH OUT

Shangri-La (map II, A1, **22**): 1301 Ocean Avenue, Santa Monica. ☎ 394-2791. Freephone: ☎ 1-800-345-STAY. Fax: 451-3351. Level with Wilshire Boulevard. In the city centre and with views of the Pacific. The white facade is very modern in style. The rooms, recently redecorated, are in the same style. Film stars are prone to drop in. Studio (bedroom plus living-room) for the cost of a room in a three-star hotel ($100–$120).

HOLLYWOOD (AREA CODE 213) AND BEVERLY HILLS (AREA CODE 310)

Hollywood really no longer looks the way it did in its heyday, in the 1920s, 30s and 40s. In the little streets at right angles to Hollywood Boulevard (the eastern part, which is roughly between Highland Avenue and Western Avenue), there has been a proliferation of tacky sex shops and prostitutes. So be a little on your guard there, especially after nightfall. The western part of the same legendary boulevard (roughly everything west of Mann's Chinese Theatre) has stayed reasonably pleasant and safe.

☆ BUDGET

Hollywood Hills Hostel (map III, C2, **10**): 6772 Hawthorn Avenue. ☎ 850-7733. This is the most central and the best located of the backpacker hotels. If you go up Highland Avenue towards Hollywood Boulevard, this is the next-to-last street on the right before the intersection. It's well kept, clean and comfortable, despite what you might expect from the low prices. There are seven dormitories, each with six beds, and there's TV in the dormitory. Providing you want to stay for a minimum of three days, the cost is $15 a night. For this, everything is included, even the shuttle that comes to pick you up at the airport, provided you call ahead to warn them. There are also double rooms, costing $45. Like the dormitories, they are on the sides of the building, either overlooking the parking lot, which is at least quiet at night, or giving a glimpse of the street. So – no pretty views, but the atmosphere's good. There's no curfew and a membership card is not required. Free transfers for Venice Beach and Universal Studios, for a minimum group of five. The reception desk has plenty of useful information about LA and California.

⌂ **Hollywood YMCA** (map III, C2, **11**): 1553 N Schrader Boulevard. ☎ 962-4685 (ext. 216). One block from Hollywood Boulevard (between Sunset and Hollywood). From the airport, take the Airport Service Bus to the Roosevelt Hotel and walk six blocks east. It's a large, recently renovated building with swimming pool and gymnasium. While the single rooms seem affordable, the doubles (which are without bathroom) are expensive for what you get. The dormitories in the youth hostel in the same building, at their usual prices, are obviously less expensive. Undergoing renovation, so ought to get better.

⌂ **Banana Bungalow Hollywood**: 2775 Cahuenga Boulevard West. ☎ 851-1129. Freephone: ☎ 1-800-4-HOSTEL. Fax: 851-2022. In North Hollywood. By car: from Hollywood Boulevard, go up Highland Avenue. After the entrance to the Hollywood Bowl, turn left into Cahuenga Boulevard West. There's no special view from the rooms, and not much room to park. The bungalows have four to six beds per room (with bathroom), and there are double rooms that are less attractive and aren't always that clean. Overall, it's not expensive and breakfast is included, but it's not huge. Swimming pool, solarium and games room. Decent restaurant. Good weekly programme of activities, plus free transport to places, including Universal Studios, Disneyland, Six Flags Magic Mountain, the beaches.

⌂ **Hollywood International Hostel** (map III, B2, **14**): 6820 Hollywood Boulevard. ☎ 463-0797. Freephone: ☎ 1-800-750-6561. Well located, opposite Mann's Chinese Theatre. There are four-bed dormitories and double rooms. It's cheap and clean, but don't expect great luxury: the kitchen is minuscule and there's no privacy in the showers. A rendezvous for international backpackers.

⌂ **Student Inn International Hostel** (map III, B2, **12**): 7038 Hollywood Boulevard. ☎ 469-6781. Freephone: ☎ 1-800-557-7038. Very well located on the Walk of Fame. Under the same ownership as the Hollywood International Hostel. Run by young people who pay for their rooms by looking after both places. Small four-bed dormitories and double rooms. Hot showers. Kitchen facilities provided.

LOS ANGELES

☆☆ MODERATE

⌂ **Hollywood Downtowner Motel** (map III, D2, **13**): 5601 Hollywood Boulevard. ☎ 464-7191. Fax: 467-5863. Two blocks east of Hollywood Freeway (the 101). Probably the cheapest of the motels. In spite of being located on a boulevard that carries very heavy traffic during the day, the rooms are quiet, and have TV and air-conditioning. In July and August rates are a little higher, but it's good value for money. Heated swimming pool and free parking.

⌂ **Budget Inn** (map III, C2, **15**): 6826 Sunset Boulevard. ☎ 465-7186. Freephone: ☎ 1-800-405 MOTEL. Fax: 962-7663. Opposite the Hollywood School, this small motel with pink walls has quiet rooms that look out onto a courtyard at the rear, where there's a swimming pool. There's TV, and, more importantly, air-conditioning.

⌂ **Liberty Hotel** (map III, C2, **24**): 1770 Orchid Avenue ☎ 962-1788. They'll come to fetch you from the station or the airport. This is a small house in the shadow of the big Holiday Inn, situated in a peaceful street that runs at right angles to Hollywood Boulevard. Well situated, with large, clean rooms at reasonable prices. Nice welcome.

☗ **Dunes** (map III, D2, **16**): 5625 Sunset Boulevard. ☎ 467-5171. Freephone: ☎ 1-800-4-LA-DUNES. One block from the Hollywood Freeway (Route 101) exit. The whole place is in Mexican–Provençal style with palm trees and red-tiled roofs. They have about 60 rooms, all beautiful and spacious, with air-conditioning, satellite TV, adjustable heating, etc. Expect to pay about $50 for two.

☆☆☆ EXPENSIVE

☗ **Hollywood Celebrity Hotel** (map III, B2, **17**): 1775 Orchid Avenue ☎ 850-6464. Freephone: ☎ 1-800-222-7017; in California: ☎ 222-7090. Fax: 850-7667. Two blocks away from Hollywood Boulevard and North Highland. Small and charming, this is a 1930s-style hotel that's been completely renovated. The rooms are spacious and very comfortable, with dark colours and lots of art-deco furniture, costing from $60 with a fairly ordinary continental breakfast, which offers good value for money. Some attractively priced deluxe suites for three or four people, with small drawing room and a sleeper sofa. The welcome's polite. Parking lot.

☗ **Clarion Park Sunset Hotel** (map III, inset, **18**): 8462 Sunset Boulevard, West Hollywood. ☎ 654-6470. Fax: 654-6470 (ext. 555). Very well located, on the Strip (i.e. Sunset Boulevard), the liveliest area at night because of its clubs. But there's no noise in the rooms: the nicest ones look out onto the back, where there's a lovely swimming pool. This is a smart, well kept motel where prices are affordable and there's a useful parking lot. Every room has two double beds. This place is ideal if you're on a business trip and want to be at the heart of Hollywood. View of the city in the distance. Thai cafe on the ground floor.

☗ **Hollywood Metropolitan Hotel** (map III, D2, **19**): 5825 Sunset Boulevard. ☎ 962-5800. Freephone: ☎ 1-800-962-5800. Fax: 465-1380. A newish hotel containing large, very comfortable rooms, with those on the highest floors offering a superb panorama of LA. Beds are queen-sized. Right at the top, the Vista Restaurant serves continental breakfast, which is included in the price. Expect to pay about $80 for a room.

☗ **Highland Gardens Hotel** (map III, B2, **20**): 7047 Franklin Avenue. ☎ 850-0536. Fax: 850-124-712. Well located, near the centre of Hollywood. A legendary hotel graced in the 1950s by such stars as Frank Sinatra, Sammy Davis Jnr and Errol Flynn. It was here that Janis Joplin's body was discovered (room 105 for anyone with an interest in morbid trivia) and it's still a favourite haunt for many of today's stars. Modern, with pleasant rooms, equipped with kitchenette. The standard rooms at the front cost about $70; the ones on the patio at the rear are a little more expensive.

☗ **Magic Motel** (map III, B2, **23**): 7025 Franklin Avenue. ☎ 851-0800. Fax: 851-4926. Quite peaceful, despite its location near to the boulevard. Each room has a double bed, refrigerator and air-conditioning. For families there are rooms with two double beds, fitted kitchen and dining area for about $160. Small swimming pool. The welcome is very pleasant.

☆☆☆☆ SPLASH OUT

🏠 **Chateau Marmont** (map III, A2, **21**): 8221 Sunset Boulevard. ☎ 656-1010. Level with La Cienega Boulevard. The brochure claims that the architect was inspired by the French chateau at Amboise – what he lacked in accuracy he sure made up for in the fantasy stakes. This pseudo-manor house perched up on the hill has been welcoming the stars in their droves since it opened in 1927. Humphrey Bogart spent his weekends here, Clark Gable had an encounter with Jean Harlow and John Belushi succumbed to his ultimate overdose. Famous scriptwriters have rubbed shoulders with luscious starlets, and so on . . . It may be a little flashy, but the gothic reception lobby exudes opulence. There's a pretty swimming pool surrounded by trees. Prices are those of a good four-star hotel.

☆☆☆☆ SPLASH OUT MORE

🏠 **Hollywood Roosevelt** (map III, B2, **22**): 7000 Hollywood Boulevard. ☎ 466-7000. Freephone: ☎ 1-800-423-8263. Fax: 469-7006. Built in 1927 at the very centre of the birthplace of the movies, this astonishing palace has witnessed the love affairs and the extravagant antics of a very special social class – the one that brings together film producers, film stars and American literary giants. The very first Academy Awards ceremony was held here in 1927. There has been a meticulous restoration of the hotel's Spanish–Moorish decor, with its painted ceilings, wrought-iron grilles and white marble accessories. On the mezzanine floor, there's a display on the history of the cinema using photographs and collectors' items such as old cameras from the 1930s, radios that once broadcast at the time when the talkies were just beginning. You might find here the ghosts of Chaplin, Marilyn Monroe, Ava Gardner, Clark Gable and many others. A kind of nostalgia reigns here – and why not?

There's an incredible painting on the left-hand wall of the restaurant as you enter. It's a scene of the Battle of Austerlitz, featuring Napoleon Bonaparte, Erich von Stroheim and Douglas Fairbanks in cameo roles. In the background, a dead-drunk Charlie Chaplin is being consoled by Marion Davies, the long-time partner of Randolph Hearst (there was talk of a liaison between her and Chaplin, which nearly got him into big trouble!). The swimming pool decor was created by that great British painter and Californian expatriate, David Hockney.

WESTWOOD (UCLA) (AREA CODE 310)

☆ BUDGET

🏠 **Westwood Inn Motor Hotel** (map IV, A2, **10**): 10820 Wilshire Boulevard. ☎ (310) 474-3118. From the airport, RTD No. 560 bus at Gate C of the terminal, in the direction of UCLA. Get off at Veteran Avenue, then walk three blocks east. This motel, completely refurbished in 1999, is well situated for anyone wanting to stay near the university. It's in the business district, five minutes from Westwood Village. The rooms are spacious and comfortable. The rates are reduced if you pay by the week. There are rooms for four (two separate rooms) at unbeatable prices. Parking lot. One snag – and it's a big one – is that it's right next to a very noisy road.

☆☆ MODERATE

Claremont Hotel (map IV, A2, **11**): 1044 Tiverton Avenue. ☎ 208-5957. Fax: 208-2386. When you get to Wilshire, take Glendon Avenue towards UCLA, then turn into Tiverton Avenue. It's nice and quiet here, and you're very close to UCLA. The public rooms have a positively British charm. The rooms are large and have a TV. Prices start at $50 and it's very good value for money. Free coffee and tea. Friendly welcome.

Mira Hershey Hall (map IV, A2, **12**): 801 Hilgard Avenue. ☎ 825-3691. On the UCLA campus, this is a student residence that provides very clean double rooms. But you need to stay here for quite a while. Sanitary facilities are in the corridor. It's possible to hire a fridge. Communal kitchen. If you want to stay here during the summer, you must get a permit from one of the UCLA departments. The charges are quite high – $50 per person per night, from July to September.

ANAHEIM (DISNEYLAND) (AREA CODE 714)

About 25 miles (40km) southeast of Downtown. From here, you can get to three of the main attractions, which are close by – Disneyland, Knott's Berry Farm and the Movieland Wax Museum.

Leave the Santa Ana Freeway (Freeway 5) at Disneyland. You come on to West Katella Avenue, which is packed with motels. There are plenty of places to stay on Beach Boulevard, but arrive quite early in the morning if you hope to find a room.

CAMPGROUNDS

Disney Vacationland Campground: 1343 S West Street. ☎ 774-2267. Not far from Disneyland (which owns the campground). Quite expensive for a campground, but it's well equipped. You can use all the facilities of the Disneyland Hotel, including the swimming pool. – The **K.O.A. Campground** next door is for caravans only.

C.C. Camperland: 12262 Harbor Boulevard, Garden Grove. ☎ 750-6747. Freephone: ☎ 1-800-422-6746. One mile (2km) from Disneyland. Heated swimming pool, washing machines, etc. Expensive for a campground. There are lots of trees, so it's nice and shady.

☆ BUDGET

Motel 6: 2920 W Chapman Avenue. ☎ 634-2441. 2 miles (3km) from Disneyland. From Route I-5, take the Chapman Avenue exit. This place has a swimming pool and is often full up.

Motel 6: 1440 N State College. ☎ 956-9690. 5.5 miles (9km) from Disneyland. From Route I-5, coming from the north, take Highway 91 east, then the State College exit.

Skyview Motel: 1126 W Katella Avenue. ☎ 533-4505. Reasonable prices and very close to Disneyland. This is one of the cheapest in the area, although there are increases in summer.

Motel 6: 921 S Beach Boulevard. ☎ 220-2866. 4.5 miles (7km) from Disneyland. From Route I-5, going north, take the Katella Avenue exit, then carry on for 4.5 miles (7km). Then turn right for Beach Boulevard. There are about 50 rooms here; they have a swimming pool.

Motel 6: 100 W Freedman Way. ☎ 520-9696. The closest one to Disneyland, just two blocks away. Recently built. The motel has 227 rooms and a swimming pool. Booking is essential in high season. The restaurant serves breakfast and dinner.

Village Inn: 1750 S Harbor Avenue. ☎ 774-2460. Opposite Disneyland. Recognizable from a distance because it's very colourful and is shaped like a whale. Simple and well kept, with a reasonable degree of comfort. One of the cheapest, and their prices are almost the same in summer.

Gaslite Motel: 7777 Beach Boulevard, in the neighbourhood of Buena Park. ☎ 522-8441. Fax: 821-7203. Five minutes' walk from Knott's Berry Farm. From Route I-5 and Route 91, take the Beach Boulevard exit. Pleasant, not expensive and well kept.

☆☆ MODERATE

Alamo Inn: 1140 W Katella Avenue. ☎ 635-8070. One block from the entrance to Disneyland. Rather pleasant, and gives good value for money. Pretty swimming pool and jacuzzi.

Sir Ru Dimar Motel: 615 W Katella Avenue. ☎ 635-8110. One block from Disneyland. Colour TV, radio, phone and bathroom in your room. Swimming pool. One of the cheapest in high season.

Alpine Motel: 715 W Katella Avenue. ☎ 535-2186. Freephone: 1-800-772-4422. Fax: 535-3714. Five minutes' walk from the entrances to Disneyland. There's a swimming pool, they serve breakfast, and the rooms are air-conditioned. Friendly welcome.

HUNTINGTON BEACH (AREA CODE 714)

Forty minutes by car from the airport (and 20 minutes southwest of Disneyland), Huntington is a pleasant little town between Long Beach and Newport Beach, with 175,000 inhabitants and 21 miles (34km) of beaches! There are many good places for surfing and miles of cycle track.

☆ BUDGET

Colonial Inn Youth Hostel: 421 8th Street, Huntington Beach. ☎ 536-3315. Fax: 536-9485. Open all year. (Reception open 7am–11pm.) As its name indicates, this is a large timber-built colonial house with a veranda and palm trees. There are also some rooms for couples and families. Charges are by the week. They have washing facilities, there's an equipped kitchen, plus a luggage store. They'll give you a key for the night. The beach is three minutes away. Visa cards are accepted.

NEWPORT BEACH (AREA CODE 714)

Newport Channel Inn: 6030 W Pacific Coast Highway. ☎ 642-3030. Freephone: ☎ 1-800-255-8614. Not far from the ocean, a white-and-blue motel, on the right if you come from the south, level with 62nd Street, and next door to a military surplus store. Very good welcome. Well kept and very affordable. Comfortable rooms, looking out onto a peaceful inner parking lot rather than the street.

WHERE TO EAT

The thousands of restaurants in LA offer a more or less infinite variety of dishes, within the reach of everyone. The French restaurants are the most popular and, of course, the most expensive. American restaurants, other than snack counters, are a rarity. Their specialities are high-quality meat dishes and the typically Californian salads. You can't go to southern California without having at least one taste of Mexican or Chinese cuisine. Among the fast food restaurants are Tex-Mex places such as Taco Bell, La Salsa or El Pollo Loco, which serve simple and good dishes at lowish prices. It's worth knowing that all restaurants and shops selling food products are classified by a letter from A to D. This letter, which has to be displayed in the window, reflects the quality of the establishment's standards of service and hygiene.

DOWNTOWN (AREA CODE 213)

☆ BUDGET

✕ **The Original Pantry** (map I, B4, **20**): 877 S Figueroa, on the corner of 9th Street. ☎ 972-9279. This very popular restaurant has the unusual feature of having been open round the clock since it opened in 1924 (the locks must be completely seized up!). It is even featured in American record books. Today, it rather stands out in an environment that has completely changed, and smart new buildings have sprung up on every side. The house motto is 'Never closed, never without a customer'. The loyalty of the waiters is one for the record-books, too: there are 80 staff, and two have worked here for between 40 and 55 years, 12 for between 20 and 40 years, and another 24 for between 5 and 20 years, and so on. And it's an undeniable fact that plenty of people still come here to eat (they have 3,000 customers per day!). In front of the cash desk, you can idle away a happy hour counting the layers of worn linoleum. The Pantry was created by a former jailbird, so it goes without saying that the cuisine is good and portions are generous. They don't serve alcohol.

Talking of records, their consumption statistics are interesting: bread – 90 tons a year, 20 cattle and 2,400 eggs a day, 3,000 pigs and 2,300 lambs a year. Lastly, 220 cows donate their entire milk output to The Original Pantry every year. 30 tons of celery are nibbled as 'appetizers' and 15 tons of sugar are used for cooking and sweetening coffee. The dishwashers use 17 tons of washing powder every year! Every word is true.

✕ **Philippe the Original** (map I, D2, **21**): 1001 N Alameda Street, level with Main Street. ☎ 628-3781. Open daily, 6am–10pm.

Right next to the old Mexican district (El Pueblo de Los Angeles). This is an immense room where the style is retro but cozy. Fans rotate on the ceiling, there are large tables and the floor is strewn with sawdust. Mixed clientele, with office staff and blue-collar workers drinking side by side. It's an archetypal American restaurant, yet it was created, in 1908, by one Philippe Mathieu. So, you can sample the famous 'French dipped sandwiches' at very affordable prices. These were greeted as an extraordinary invention, if you go by the favourable newspaper reviews that decorate every wall. Servings are really generous. Good cakes.

✕ **Vim** (map I, off A2): 831 S Vermont Avenue. ☎ 480-8159. Open daily, noon–10pm. Some blocks south of Wilshire. This is a Spanish-speaking district but, in this part of the avenue, you'll find numerous Asian (mainly Korean) restaurants. Vim is one of the best known for the quality of its Thai cuisine and its pre-war (Korean war) prices. It's all bare walls and Formica tables. Basically, people come here to eat, including lots of families. Portions are generous. Taste the barbecue duck, pork ginger and black mushroom (cooked Thai-style), oyster omelette, delicious *pad Thai* (fresh shrimps). There's a long list of Chinese dishes, too.

✕ **Tommy's** (map I, A1, **22**): Beverly Boulevard and Rampart Boulevard. ☎ 389-9060. This restaurant has been occupying the whole corner of this street intersection since 1946 and sells the cheapest burgers in town (after McDonald's, of course). The crowds of people who pack the place in the evening give it an *American Graffiti* atmosphere. Maybe it's just because this cafe is open round the clock, or maybe it's also a matter of habits being passed on to succeeding generations. Whatever the reason, it's interesting to see Hispanic families queuing up then squashing up together along the narrow counters or eating in their cars. The success of the place allowed Tommy's to become a franchise and this has taken off like a rocket, but this one's the original – the place you come back to.

✕ **Cassell's**: 3266 W 6th Street. On the western edge of Downtown, two blocks from Vermont Avenue. ☎ 480-8668 and 387-5502. Open Monday–Saturday 10.30am–4pm. The business card says: 'World's best hamburger' – a slight exaggeration, perhaps, but it's indisputably the best in LA and everything's made on the premises. The freshness of the meat is legendary and the helpings are generous. But don't try to influence the cooking process or, even worse, ask for your burger rare, as you'll be treated with some scorn. So, order it with fried zucchini (courgettes) and, like Johnny Carson, Clint Eastwood, Liza Minnelli and the late-lamented Jane Mansfield (who, in *The Girl Can't Help It,* found Cassell's burgers 'divine'), serve yourself at the salad bar and try the tasty and original house sauces (homemade red relish, Roquefort cheese, etc.), which are included in the price of the hamburger. This spot is highly recommended!

✕ **Cole's** (map I, C4, **23**): 118 E 6th Street, level with Los Angeles Street. ☎ 622-4090. Open Monday–Friday 9am–7pm, (10pm Saturday). Closed Sunday. Founded in 1908, this is the oldest restaurant in Los Angeles. To one side is a very affordable self-service counter and to the other is a dark bar, with low lighting as the Americans seem to like it. Large selection of dishes: pastrami, turkey, roast beef, etc. served in generous portions. The mahogany counter has a fine patina – polished by the shirt-sleeves of generations. On the wall are photographs showing the building under construction in 1902. This bar has been part of movie history, having been used as a location for scenes from *Forrest Gump* and *Jumping Jack Flash*.

✕ **Langer's** (map I, A2, **24**): 704 S Alvaredo Street. ☎ 483-8050. Open 8am–4pm. Closed Sunday. Next to MacArthur Park. The district can be a bit tense in the evening, but it's worth braving it to visit this old deli, which offers a very long menu that includes delicious soups, 20 different types of pastrami, excellent corned beef, chicken in the pot, 'cheese blintzer', a 'smoked pastrami plate dinner', a large variety of cold fish specialities, and all the standard Jewish fare. The decor is traditional – leatherette-covered benches and Formica tables. There's a free parking lot right next door.

CHINATOWN (AREA CODE 213)

Chinatown lies north of Downtown, between Route 110 and Route 101. Not many tourists come here.

✕ **Empress Pavilion** (map I, D1, **25**): 988 N Hill Street. ☎ 617-9898. Right at the top of Chinatown, in the Bamboo Plaza. Open daily, 10am–2.30pm. This restaurant is on the first floor of a newish shopping centre that has its own parking lot, so show your parking ticket – it'll be deducted from your bill. A very large room and the setting's rather austere: no lanterns or other Chinese paraphernalia, just a few posters. The service is particularly efficient and quite friendly. People come here for the *dim sum,* which is one of the most highly reputed in LA. The waitresses scurry along with trolleys bearing a wide range of delicious and fragrant dishes. If you come here with someone else, you get more of a choice, for there are often four portions per dish. The menu contains no fewer than 166 dishes, including 37 based on fish or seafood, such as stir-fried clams with ginger and green onions, boiled shrimps in the shell, fillet of rock cod in crab meat sauce, deep fried oysters, etc. Prices are extremely reasonable. Get here before lunchtime – after that, the queue gets longer (although the wait isn't too bad).

HOLLYWOOD, SUNSET, MELROSE AND WILSHIRE (AREA CODE 213)

☆ BUDGET

✕ **Barney's Beanery** (map III, inset, **30**): 8447 Santa Monica Boulevard, between La Cienega and Sweetzer. ☎ 654-2287. Open daily, 10am–2am. One of the temples to the American hamburger: McDonald's pales, by comparison. First of all, there's an original menu in the form of a colour newspaper (which you can take away as a souvenir). A selection of over 150 burgers (if you're hungry and feeling flush, have No. 125!), and almost 100 omelettes of every kind. They also do Tex-Mex cuisine. with over 30 kinds of chilli. The clientele is what you might call 'colourful', the atmosphere is electric – it's all fun, and it's loud. There's a pool-table and 255 varieties of beer for anyone with a specialist knowledge! These include American labels as well as beers from all over the world, so if you want beer from Alsace or Japan, or if you fancy Congolese,

Salvadorian, Korean or Israeli beer – you've come to the right place! For reading matter there's a complete sheet of 'House Rules'. After you've looked through these, you may wonder whether it's OK to breathe!

✕ **Johnny Rockets** (map III, B3, **31**): Melrose and Gardner. ☎ 651-3361. Open Sunday–Thursday 11am–midnight, Friday and Saturday 11am–2am. This is a restaurant in the *American Graffiti* style with an entertainingly well reconstructed 1950s atmosphere. The waiters and waitresses occasionally sing in chorus, going through a fine repertoire of songs made famous by Fabian, Frankie Avalon, Chuck Berry, Ricky Nelson, Bobby Darrin and others. Young people, and nostalgic people who aren't all that young, squeeze in around the counter (nicer than on the terrace) to enjoy enormous burgers and crispy fries.

✕ **Seafood Bay**: 3916 Sunset Boulevard. At the junction with Santa Monica Boulevard to the extreme east of Hollywood. ☎ 664-3902. Open 11.30am–9.30pm (10pm Friday), 4–10pm (9.30pm Sunday). Worth the detour if you're into fish or seafood. This cafe, of rather modest appearance, serves nothing but fish and seafood, and the rates are very reasonable. It's also considered to be an 'inflation fighter' of a restaurant. At lunchtime, they serve inexpensive specials: light meals such as 'fresh fish sandwich', or 'squid spaghettini', or grilled sardines, or their own chowder recipe. They serve bouillabaisse, to which you can add lobster if you like. You can even order whitefish caviar or smoked oysters as a starter. They also have a huge number of seafood cocktails. Bear in mind before coming all the way here that it's a long way out, and the place is often fully booked, so reserve ahead.

✕ **El Coyote Cafe** (map IV, C2, **20**): 7312 Beverly Boulevard. ☎ 939-2255 or 939-7766. Open daily, 11am–10pm (11pm Friday and Saturday). This is the kitschest Mexican restaurant for miles. They've been doing it for 50 years – serving delicious Mexican dishes in dimly lit rooms that bring a certain degree of intimacy to the proceedings. The waitresses are dressed in national costume, as you'd expect. You could start by checking out the Margarita cocktail, which will set you up nicely. The whole place is very noisy and colourful. Although the food is decent enough, it doesn't have a great deal of finesse (what Mexican food does?!). This is a large restaurant that can serve several hundred people every day, with such things as chili con carne, tostada, tamales, enchilada ranchera, guacamole and tacos, all at unbeatable prices for LA (especially the 'combinations'). This explains some of their success, and the cheerful good-time atmosphere of the place undoubtedly makes its own contribution.

✕ **Toi** (map III, B2, **32**): 7505 W Sunset Boulevard (on the corner of Gardner and Sunset). Open 11am–4am. Here you can get American–Thai cuisine. The atmosphere and decor are very rock 'n' roll. They even have some famous regulars, including Quentin Tarantino, Juliette Lewis and various rock stars.

✕ **Rosti** (map IV, B2, **21**): 233 Beverly Drive. Restaurant and cafe offering simple Italian dishes. More expensive than a simple cafe, but it's good and the service is cheerful.

☆☆ MODERATE

✗ **Ed Debevic's** (map IV, C2, **22**): 134 N La Cienega. ☎ (310) 659-1952. If you're familiar with the one in Chicago, you'll already know what kind of nostalgic experience to expect here. It's a 1950s-style diner, and it's always packed. The decor is amusing and the service is attentive. You can get large burgers, chilli, salads and house desserts, none of it is very expensive. Souvenir menu with some tongue-in-cheek observations, such as: 'At Ed's, we promised you friendly and courteous service at reasonable prices. If we didn't succeed, please don't tell anyone.'

✗ **Canter's** (map III, A3, **36**): 419 N Fairfax Avenue. ☎ 651-2030. Open round the clock. Immense deli serving traditional Jewish food. Even at 3am, you'd think you were in the middle of the lunchtime rush. Very mixed clientele, ranging from quiet old insomniacs to noisy, extrovert showbiz folk. The waiters are in many cases as old as the establishment, or at least they look it. Service is not too swift. Menu as long as your arm, with all the favourite standards: hot corned beef and cabbage, lachs (smoked salmon) and cream cheese, chopped-liver-and-egg salad, blintzes and big sandwich 'specials'.

✗ **The Old Spaghetti Factory** (map III, D2, **33**): 5939 Sunset Boulevard, Hollywood. ☎ 469-7149. Open Monday–Saturday 11.30am–2pm and 5–10pm (11pm Friday and Saturday), Sunday noon–10pm. The decor is one of the most original in LA. At one time, this was the headquarters of Golden West Broadcasters, a production company that belonged to Gene Autry, the famous movie cowboy. The architectural features immediately hit you – Corinthian columns and a carved fireplace – you can have your dish of spaghetti in a breathtaking setting. It's '19th-century rococo', with red-and-gold velvet, excessively ornate furniture, cabled (twisted) columns, crystal chandeliers, and, strangest of all, beds cut in half and made into lovers' tables. The bar and the fittings behind it were made in France in 1909 and were then brought all the way out here. The food is less expensive than you might expect from the setting.

✗ **Larry Parker's**: 206 S Beverly Drive. Half a block south of Wilshire Boulevard. ☎ 274-9007. What with the 1950s decor, the cheeky attitude of the waitresses and the incredible list of dishes they offer (about 900 things on the menu!) this place is somewhere you shouldn't miss. Outside, there are a couple of rear passenger seats from old American automobiles and a machine at the entrance offers to measure the depth of your love for your partner. The place is open all night, so it's ideal for a snack whenever. Try out their Michael Jackson Hot Tuna Melt, or Mike Tyson's Favorite Buffalo Wings, or even Robin Williams Popcorn Shrimps.

✗ **Kokomo Cafe** (map IV, C2, **24**): Farmer's Market, 6333 W 3rd Street (and Fairfax). ☎ 933-0773. Access via 'Gate 9', on the 3rd Street and Fairfax side. Open summer 9am–7pm, Sunday 10am–6pm, winter 9am–6.30pm, Sunday 10am–5pm. Here's a chance to hang out among the snack stands and seafood stands in the Farmer's Market. Outside the season, there are more Americans here than tourists, and they come here to rediscover all the charms of the place – both the stalls and the many moderately-priced restaurants. The Kokomo is one of the most popular, and you can eat at the counter or at a table. On Sunday morning, there's even a waiting list for brunch! There's a large collection of portraits above the counter – it's just a pastiche of those famous restaurants that hang out photos of their most famous clientele. *These* pictures are of the staff and ordinary customers! They serve good soups and salads and, best of all, a great smoked BLT (a bacon, lettuce and tomato sandwich with smoked salmon). Free parking.

✕ The same proprietor runs the **Gumbo Pot**, a little further on (West Patio, Fairfax side: ☎ 933-0358), which claims to be the best Cajun restaurant in the city. This is probably a slight exaggeration, but if jambalaya or gumbo are new to you, it's a useful place for an introduction to Cajun cuisine.

☆☆–☆☆☆ MODERATE TO EXPENSIVE

✕ **Hard Rock Cafe** (map IV, C2, **25**): 8600 Beverly Boulevard, on the San Vincente intersection. ☎ 276-7605. Open daily, 11.30am–midnight. You can park in the parking lot at the Beverly Center for only $1 for three hours. The place is impossible to miss: there's a gigantic Cadillac suspended above the restaurant. Over the entrance are two enormous electronic advertising hoardings: one of them giving the world population figure to the nearest second and the other indicating the never-ending shrinkage of the world's tropical rainforests. Very pc! The music is non-stop and the place is heavily patronized by the young of West Hollywood and Beverly Hills. The name was inspired by the photograph of a Hard Rock Cafe (which was just a made-up name – there was no such place) that featured on the cover of the Doors album, *Morrison Hotel*. As for the decor, no expense was spared. There's a miniature NASA Space Shuttle, an array of gold discs, a fuel pump, Elvis Presley's motorbike, a Jimi Hendrix jacket, a positive orgy of Fender guitars . . . Get a copy of the brochure provided at the reception desk and you can go on a proper tour and spot such relics as guitars owned by B.B. King (he called it 'Lucille'), Bob Dylan and Chris Isaak, as well as Neneh Cherry's bra, Janet Jackson's jacket or the scooter from the Who film *Quadrophenia*. So this is the oldest and most authentic of all the Hard Rock Cafes on the planet (a planet obviously requiring emergency treatment!). To eat (in case you've forgotten it's a restaurant!) there's Californian salad, Famous Babyrock Watermelon Ribs and giant hamburgers. The prices are not bad.

✕ **Dive** (map IV, A2, **26**): 10250 Santa Monica Boulevard. ☎ 788-3483. From Freeway 405, exit at Santa Monica and travel east as far as the Century City Shopping Center. You can't miss the big yellow submarine on the right. Open daily, 11.30am–11pm (midnight Saturday and Sunday). How'd you fancy going for a giant sandwich at 1,000ft (300m) below sea level? The Dive is the place to do it. On the outside, what you see is a big, yellow, pot-bellied submarine. On the inside there are portholes, gangways, steel beams, and screens showing pictures of underwater fauna and flora. The whole effect works very well, and you really get the sensation of being in a submarine under dive conditions. The concept of the decor and special effects is the work of Steven Spielberg, so you won't need convincing about the impact that it all has. There are plenty of customers, so the hostesses at the door give you what they call a 'coaster'. This is a small electronic gizmo that blinks like crazy when your table is ready to order. So you can go off for a walk, visit the different levels of the submarine, or have a drink at the bar while waiting for a place to enjoy your sandwich. The Dive has reinvented the Submarine Sandwich. The bread (made by a French bakery) is terrific. There are also Italian specialities (pasta) and American ones (hamburgers). It's not cheap, but it's good.

✗ **Planet Hollywood** (map IV, B2, **27**): 9560 Wilshire Boulevard. ☎ 275-7828. Level with Rodeo Drive, in the middle of the most up-market shops in Beverly Hills. One of the chain owned by Stallone, Schwarzenegger and Willis. If you like this kind of restaurant, you'd do better to go to the Dive or the Hard Rock Cafe. Parking lot behind the restaurant.

✗ **Milky Way** (map IV, B2–3, **28**): 9108 W Pico Boulevard, on the corner of Doheny Drive. ☎ 859-0004. Open Monday–Thursday until 8.30pm. In the heart of the Jewish district. This is a Kosher vegetarian restaurant serving dairy products, whence the name Milky Way. The restaurant is run by Leah Adler, Steven Spielberg's mother, who presides over things in person. The decor is simple and restful, with white walls, a red-brick interior and flowers everywhere. Not a lot to be said about the menu – it's not wildly exciting. However, there are numerous photos of the child prodigy and stills from his movies all over the walls.

☆☆☆ EXPENSIVE

✗ **The Musso and Frank Grill** (map III, C2, **34**): 6667 Hollywood Boulevard. ☎ 467-7788 and 467-5123. Open 11am–11pm. Closed Sunday. Open since 1919, this is the oldest restaurant in Hollywood and it's a place where Hollywood's intellectuals and scriptwriters hang out – anyone who's anyone, in fact. It's been that way since the 1940s, when Ernest Hemingway, Dashiell Hammett, Aldous Huxley and William Faulkner regularly met here. Faulkner had the irritating habit of leaping over the bar to show his chums how to make a real mint julep. The place is famous for its roast dinners . . . and its overworked waiters; they serve a range of excellent Californian wines. There are two rooms – one is the restaurant, the other is more of a cafe with small booths and leather benches. If you aren't hungry, go anyhow and have a drink at the big, dark wooden bar where so many people have sorted out the world's problems! The daily specials, unchanged since the day they opened, are: Monday, chicken with noodles; Tuesday, corned beef and cabbage . . . and so on. Try the flannel cake, created by a former chef who gave 53 years of good and loyal service. The Hollywood ghosts haven't totally deserted the women's toilets, where you can find hair lacquer, hand cream and everything else you might need to beautify yourself even if you aren't a star.

✗ **Cafe Maurice** (map III, inset, **35**): 747 N La Cienega Boulevard (corner with Sherwood Street). ☎ (310) 652-1609. Decorated in Toulouse-Lautrec style, with a very French sort of menu, including an excellent entrecôte steak or their own grilled salmon recipe. The music mainly consists of French hits from the 1980s, and customers get up and dance whenever the mood takes them.

☆☆☆☆ SPLASH OUT

✕ **Citrus** (map III, C3, **37**): 6703 Melrose Avenue. ☎ 857-0034. Fax: 939-2694. Open noon–10.30pm (11pm Friday and Saturday). Closed Sunday. Booking is very advisable. This is one of those widely-talked-about restaurants that's incredibly fashionable, and it has all the right ingredients. The architecture and decor are very Californian – hi-tech and predominantly white, which gives a certain 'clean and healthy' feel, with splashes of colour provided by the paintings on display. The welcome is courteous and the atmosphere more laid-back than you might expect from the prices. The cuisine is rarely anything but first-rate. The recipes are elaborate, and the cakes are guaranteed to be delicious, as the French chef, Michel Richard, is a pastry whizz. You can watch the chefs at work, as there's just a pane of glass between the nickel-plated trappings of the kitchen and the dining room itself. Paradoxically, it has less charm and is less elegant than Le Dôme, but it's more expensive! Lunch is quite affordable, though.

✕ **Spago** (map III, inset, **38**): 8795 Sunset Boulevard (1114 Horn Avenue). ☎ 652-4025. Open daily to midnight. Spago is something of a mystery. It's been full up for more than 10 years and is unbelievably fashionable – despite its very banal setting, it's noisy, uncomfortable, and the cuisine, while good, is nothing special. You have to book several days or even a week or two in advance.

Probably the reason for its popularity is that there's a star or two here every evening (Tony Curtis is a regular visitor) and Spago has acquired a really big reputation as a place to 'see and be seen' (this is Hollywood after all!). The clientele is quite trendy, as you'd expect. One trick as good as any other for getting a table is to turn up early (6–7pm), purely on spec. It works – occasionally. If you get the choice, go for the room at the back. You'll be less visible, but it's more pleasant, with parasols, lush plants and less noise. The pizzas are always good and at prices that are still reasonable (try out the spicy chicken in particular). The menu's quite long, and includes some pasta dishes and a few specialities: for example, the parmesan risotto with *ragoût* of shrimps, lobster and scallops.

✕ **Le Dôme** (map III, inset, **39**): 8720 Sunset Boulevard (West Hollywood). ☎ 659-6919. Open noon–midnight. Closed Saturday lunchtime and Sunday. The frontage has nicely-balanced columns; inside, the decor is a great success – it's sophisticated and has a nice aura of intimacy. In the drawing room, the atmosphere is muted – soft as velvet – and there's an elegant, circular bar. Overall, the welcome is refined, but not at all snobbish. The menu offers tasty and imaginative dishes (seafood salad and succulent cockles in white wine). Excellent cakes. The prices are surprisingly reasonable for an establishment of this quality.

✕ **Yamashiro** (map III, B1, **40**): 1999 N Sycamore Avenue, which comes out on Franklin Avenue between La Brea and Highland. ☎ 466-5125. At the top of a hill, this superb Japanese pagoda offers a fantastic panorama of LA. An exact replica of a pagoda situated on the heights of Kyoto, Japan, this one was built in 1914 by two brothers who had made their fortune in the import-export trade. Several hundred craftsmen came from the Far East to work here. The interior garden is magnificent – and conforms to the rules of Zen. Quite an expensive place to eat, but you may be happy to just drink a *sake* or tea here. Outside, there are wonderful places to take a stroll, and in the grounds, you may come across a 600-year-old little pagoda next to a pond. The clientele tends to be rather smart. If you come by car, there's a valet to deal with it for you. Try to book a table on the terrace and enjoy the panoramic view. If you're walking home late in the evening, this district is not the most reassuring.

VENICE (AREA CODE 310)

☆ BUDGET

✕ **Cafe 50s** (map II, D3, **30**): 838 Lincoln Boulevard. ☎ 399-1955. Open daily, 7am–11pm (1am Friday and Saturday). Good little place, away from everything but really nice! Located at the intersection with Lake Street, which continues along Brooks Street as far as the ocean. Coming from Washington Street, on Lincoln, it's on the right, 200 yards (180 metres) after a large red sign ('The Boys'). There's a clock on the wall with the announcement that it's 'Time to eat'. As you can guess from the name (and the phone number), fans of Jimmy Dean and Marlon Brando will savour the 1950s decor and atmosphere, the walls decorated with old posters and discs and the old jukebox with its collection of 45s that can still thrill you. There's an autographed photograph of Roy Rogers, the singing cowboy movie star. As far as the food goes, they offer burgers, and such delights as Big Bopper's Special Scramble, Omelette Jerry Lee Lewis Whole Lotta Shakin' Goin' On, Fats Domino Triple Decker Delight or the Peggy Sue and, to finish up with, succulent Sweets For My Sweet. You could even try a Veal Sinatra. The music is great (if you hadn't guessed) and it's a place not to miss if you're a 1950s buff.

✕ **Hinano** (map II, C4, **31**): 15 Washington Street. Open daily to 1am. This place has sawdust on the floor and three pool tables where the games are fiercely contested. Interesting old photos on the walls. Good band. People stand at the counter to sink two-pint pitchers of beer. The atmosphere is quite rough-and-ready. Snacks include hamburgers, tamales and hotdogs.

☆☆ MODERATE

✕ **Paco's**: 4141 Centinela. ☎ 391-9616. Open daily, 10am–10pm. A bit of a way from the centre, east of Venice. Go up Washington, and it's at the intersection with Centinela. A Mexican restaurant that's very popular with local people. Pleasant rooms separated by little arches, lush plants, fishermen's nets and dried starfish. Try the chef's *tostada*, Paco's Burrito, and the *combinaciones mexicanas* (assorted specialities), which are quite interesting. Large selection of *platos regionales* (*pulpo ranchero*, *Cancún mojo de ajo*, *enchiladas del mar*, etc.). This Mexican food is '*mucho bueno*'.

✕ **Sidewalk Cafe** (map II, C4, **32**): 1407 Ocean Front Walk, at the end of Horizon Avenue. Right in the heart of Venice. ☎ 399-5547. Open Monday–Thursday 9am–11pm (midnight Friday), Saturday and Sunday 8am–midnight. There's a large terrace facing the beach, sheltered by a red-and-white canopy held up by seven metal Corinthian-style columns. It has an atmosphere that's a shade industrial, but it's one of the best places for people-watching you could imagine. Their salads and burgers are not cheap but the atmosphere is good. Francophile intellectuals may just be impressed to learn that one of the burgers is named after Marcel Proust, which ought to be good for the memory! Or you could grab a 'Pavarotti sandwich' or try the Jane Fonda dish. Or just settle for a drink. There's live music some evenings. In the restaurant, there's an interesting bookshop called **SWB** (☎ 399-2360).

✕ **The Firehouse** (map II, C3, **33**): 213 Rose Avenue, at the intersection with Main Street, next door to the School for Chocoholics, and opposite a giant statue of a clown dressed up as a ballet dancer in a blue tutu and a red hat. You can't miss it. ☎ 396-6810. Open 7am–11pm (8pm Saturday and Sunday). A former neighbourhood firehouse that has been converted into a coffee shop. The building's previous role is nicely echoed by the red decor and the scale models everywhere. Nice welcome. Traditional Californian cuisine.

☆☆–☆☆☆ MODERATE TO EXPENSIVE

✕ **Rose Cafe** (map II, C3, **34**): corner of Main Street and Rose Avenue. ☎ 399-0711. Open 11.30am–3pm and 5.30–10pm. This is the building with two big roses painted on its salmon pink walls. The interior is what you might call a tasteful cafeteria, with art on display, a shop selling crafts, and a clientele made up of all sorts: laid-back yuppies, intellectuals, artists and vegetarians. They serve a variety of salads, a bit on the expensive side. plus tacos, pizza, quiche, samosas, and some excellent pastries, chocolate cakes and tarts.

✕ **Rebecca's** (map II, C4, **36**): 2025 Pacific Avenue and North Venice. ☎ 306-6266. Open 6pm–1am. Closed Sundays and public holidays. Just a few seconds from Venice Beach. This is the rendezvous spot for the LA in-crowd and it's a place where you can dine in one of the most imaginative decors ever concocted by California's favourite son, the architect Frank Gehry. Suspended crocodiles and giant octopuses are illuminated from within and the whole place contains a mish-mash of styles, including totem poles that look like Arizona cactuses. Widely recognized as one of the great architects of the day, Gehry has given his creative genius free rein, as usual. As for the food, it's not bad, either. Besides the many tacos, burritos and ceviches, you can try genuine Mexican dishes like 'Tamale Chicken Fajitas and Potato', or 'Jumbo Scallops Tostada'. Not cheap, but well worth it. With a little luck, you may dine seated in comfortable creations made of soft green leather. Valet parking at the entrance. As you might guess, it's best to reserve ahead.

LOS ANGELES

SANTA MONICA (AREA CODE 310)

☆☆ MODERATE

✕ **Light House** (map II, A1, **37**): 201 Arizona Avenue. ☎ 451-2076. Between Wilshire and Santa Monica Avenue, almost on the ocean front. Open noon–9pm (9.30pm Thursday, Friday and Saturday); open Sunday only in summer. This is more like a cafe than a restaurant, but that's only the first impression – it's an extremely popular restaurant with an 'all-you-can-eat' policy, Japanese-style (it's run by Japanese-Americans). There's fresh sushi, crab, clams, mussels *au gratin*, squid, various fish (both raw and cooked), salads, giant shrimps, chicken *teriyaki*, spareribs, and much more. The place offers unbeatable value for money and the buffet is half the price at lunchtime. Get to it!

✕ **Cafe-Casino** (map II, A1, **38**): on the Arizona and Ocean Avenue intersection. Open 7am–10pm (11pm weekends). A very large cafe serving lunch and dinner specials in a pleasant, airy setting. The dishes are copious and the choice is interesting. They do good cakes. Terrace.

✕ **Toppers** (map II, A1, **39**): 1111 2nd Street. ☎ 393-8080: in the same street as the youth hostel. On the top floor of the Huntley Hotel, this restaurant offers free food, consisting of excellent Mexican dishes, every evening (5.30–7.30pm) for the price of a drink. The sunsets are also particularly worth seeing from up there.

☆☆–☆☆☆ MODERATE TO EXPENSIVE

✕ **Broadway O'Deli Cafe** (map II, B1, **40**): 1457 3rd Street Promenade, Santa Monica. ☎ 410-0616. Open daily, 7am or 8am–midnight (1am Friday and Saturday). This big brasserie serves up excellent Californian cuisine combining Eastern European-Jewish with French and Italian influences. It's also a catering firm, and the grocery section is impressive; they offer a wide range of French and Italian wines, bread worthy of the name, decent pastries and so on. They open early in the morning, so it's a good place to have breakfast after you've finished your jog along Santa Monica beach!

✕ **Gaucho Grill** (map II, A1–B1, **35**): 1251 Third Street. ☎ 394-4966. Open Sunday–Thursday 11am–11pm, Friday and Saturday noon–midnight. Good steakhouse; also serves Argentinian specialities. Large restaurant, with modern decor. Quite noisy.

✕ **Schatzi On Main** (map II, C3, **41**): 3110 Main Street. ☎ 399-4800. Fax: 399-6868. Opened by Arnold Schwarzenegger, this trendy new restaurant offers decent prices. Try their Austrian specialities, such as *Wiener Schnitzel*, *Bratwurst* or *Knackwurst*, or health-food dishes, or special bodybuilder menus if you're a flab-fighter! Brunch Saturday–Sunday 9am–3pm.

✕ **Gotham Hall** (map II, A1, **42**): 1431 Third Street Promenade. ☎ 394-8865. Open Monday–Saturday 5.30–11.30pm (midnight Thursday–Sunday). The decor is wild, with lots of metal, dark colours: very modern and classy. As soon as you get to top of the stairs, you can see why it won the award for the finest decor in California. Italian-American specialities, including coconut beer shrimps and crab-cakes. Servings are not very large and quite expensive, but the cuisine is quite refined. Large billiard room (with 17 mauve tables!). There's a disco on the mezzanine floor on weekends from 10.30pm, with mostly 1970s music.

✕ **Trilussa** (map II, B1, **43**): Santa Monica Boulevard, on the corner of Third Street. ☎ 319-1985. Trendy Italian restaurant. Here's where you go to find all the gilded youth of the area. Superb decor. The terrace, which faces the finest pedestrianized street in Santa Monica, fills up very quickly. Their cuisine is famous and the service meticulous.

MALIBU (AREA CODE 310)

✕ **Gladstone's**: 17300 W Pacific Coast Highway, Pacific Palisades. ☎ 454-3474. At the end of Sunset Boulevard where it hits the Pacific at Malibu Beach. This place is a real institution. Overlooking the beach, it's a rendezvous for surfers. You can drink or eat here. The food is OK, but it's mainly the atmosphere that attracts people, many of them tourists. The decor is pleasant yet unexpected, with hundreds of old photos on the walls. People mostly wear Bermuda shorts and T-shirts. The place is madly crowded. In the evening, on the glassed-in terrace, you can watch entranced by the Pacific rollers as they crash onto the beach, all cleverly lit by powerful spotlights. You'll sometimes have to queue.

✕ **Pier View**: 22718 Pacific Coast Highway. ☎ 456-6962. No. 434 bus from Downtown. If you're coming from Santa Monica, it's before Malibu jetty. This is the only restaurant in Malibu directly on the ocean-front, and it has a terrace. Friendly place, with sawdust on the floor and young staff giving fast service. It's ideal for breakfast and if you arrive early in the morning, you may get to see some dolphins. Booking is recommended for Sunday brunch. Breakfast is simple but there's plenty of it and the prices are reasonable given the surroundings.

WESTWOOD (UCLA) (AREA CODE 310)

☆ BUDGET

✕ **Shamshiri** (map IV, A3, **29**): 1916 Westwood Boulevard. ☎ 474-1410. Open daily, noon–10pm (11pm weekends). The setting is restful, the atmosphere peaceful. Some comfortable booths. Good Iranian cuisine and entirely reasonable prices. Massively frequented by people who migrated to LA following the Iranian revolution. Sample their *koodibeh*, *sabzi polo mahi*, *koresht bademjon*, and Iranian desserts.

PASADENA (AREA CODE 626)

✕ **Twin Palms**: 101 W Green Street, Old Pasadena. ☎ (818) 57-PALMS. Take Freeway 134 towards Pasadena. Exit at Orange Grove, on the right, then take the first on the left. The restaurant is on the corner of Green and Delacey. It looks just like a vast nomad tent, put down, as if by magic, on twin palms. All in all, it's an astonishing metamorphosis for what was a service station and has now become one of LA's trendiest restaurants, due perhaps to its proprietor, the actor Kevin Costner. The chef is French – so you can get such things as fish soup served with *rouille* (soft cheese with garlic) and croutons, *cassoulet* (meat-and-bean stew) and *bouillabaisse* (fish soup). During the week, small jazz and reggae groups liven up the evenings, and a gospel group plays at Sunday brunch. The profits from this brunch are going towards the restoration of a local church, the Friendship Baptist Church, which was seriously damaged by the 1994 earthquake, so you can eat lunch and do good at the same time.

WHERE TO HAVE A DRINK, LISTEN TO MUSIC AND MEET SOME OF THE LOCALS

VENICE (AREA CODE 310)

🍸 **Oar House** (map II, C3, **50**): 2941 Main Street, Santa Monica (administratively this is in Santa Monica, but the location is really Venice). ☎ 396-4725. Fax: 399-7514. Nothing conformist about this place, and no concessions to the 'clean and cool' look of the techno years! This is quite simply a good old psychedelic tavern, haunted by the ghosts of the California hippie era. A sign at the entrance warns: 'No walkmen, no flipflops, no rollerblades, no shorts below the knee'. Inside, confronted by some of the craziest bric-à-brac in LA, you may wonder if you're dreaming: there are buggies hanging from the ceiling, a tank(!) and heaven knows what else. Founded by two pilots, this bar was used as a film-set for the early scenes of *Easy Rider*. Happy hour is 4–8pm. Oldies night is on Monday, with music from the 1950s, 1960s and 1970s: DJ and dancing. The spirit of Route 66 is here, alive and well!

ON SANTA MONICA (AREA CODE 310)

🍸 **Big Dean's Cafe** (map II, B2, **51**): 1165 Ocean Front. ☎ 393-2666. At the end of Santa Monica Boulevard, opposite the wharf. This bistro is great in the late afternoon, when the surfers come in for a drink. It's on a terrace at the edge of the beach. Here you get music, beer and burgers in a very 'young Californian' atmosphere.

🍸 **Ye Old King's Head Restaurant and Pub** (map II, B1, **52**): 116 Santa Monica Boulevard. ☎ 451-1402. Between Ocean Avenue and 2nd Street, in the final stretch of the legendary Route 66 before it hits the ocean. This is one of the most popular English pubs in LA – the setting is plush and comfortable, and there's a fine portrait of Winston Churchill in among the many paintings, photos and engravings. There are even some of Ronald Reagan, done in the 1970s when he was Governor of California. They sell Watney's, John Courage and the like. The place is frequented by expatriates who will tell you all about their life as an illegal alien. There's no way you won't make new acquaintances here.

🍸 **The Irish Rover**: 3012 Santa Monica Boulevard. ☎ 828-3960. Yet another Irish pub – this one's small but nice. You can dance here without feeling like you're in a nightclub. Very good live music on Saturday night.

🍸 **Yankee Doodles** (map II, B1, **53**): 1410 3rd Street Promenade. ☎ 394-4632. Open daily, to 2am. This place is like a factory, but has great decor in brick, copper and leather. There's a long bar and about 20 billiard tables. People come here to be seen, to play, to have a drink, or to eat in an easy-going atmosphere. There's an interesting atmosphere and the band is good. Big TV screens show sports videos. The clientele is mixed, part trendies, part tourists on a spree. Standard menu: pizzas, salads and cakes.

ON HOLLYWOOD AND WILSHIRE (AREA CODE 213)

🍸 **Molly Malone's** (map IV, C2, **40**): 575 S Fairfax Avenue (between 5th and 6th Streets). ☎ (213) 935-1577. Between Wilshire Boulevard and

6th Street, not far from the Los Angeles County Museum of Art (LACMA). Open 5pm–2am. Irish pub selling good Irish draught beer – it's very lively, even during the week. The walls are adorned with oil portraits of famous Irishmen, and some infamous ones, including a fine and moving portrait of the playwright Brendan Behan, whose great-niece, Angela Hanlon, is the proprietress. Live music nightly, except Monday. On Tuesday, new and up-and-coming bands attract a clientele of Hollywood starlets and leading men. Music from 8.30 or 9pm. You can even dance. There's an admission charge on Tuesday and at weekends.

The Cat and Fiddle (map III, C2): 6530 Sunset Boulevard. ☎ 468-3800. Voted the best pub in Hollywood by the *LA Weekly*, this is a very nice place with a vast patio, complete with a small fountain with a gurgling water-jet tucked away in the greenery. The clientele is trendy. The place is worth checking out, especially at weekends. There's good beer and an excellent roster of bands.

Lunaria (map IV, A2, **41**): 10351 Santa Monica Boulevard. East of Beverly Glenn. ☎ 282-8870. This is a restaurant–bar, with a trendy clientele and a pleasant atmosphere, provided by jazz, blues and gospel groups. It's quite expensive, but you get the appropriate quality and quantity for the money.

ON MELROSE (AREA CODE 323)

Martini Lounge: 5657 Melrose Avenue. ☎ (323) 407-4068. One of the trendiest bars on Melrose Avenue. Different kinds of bands play each night. Thursday is reggae night, with a genuine Rasta atmosphere guaranteed. Multi-coloured hair, tattoos and piercings are *de rigueur*. Some specialist evenings feature gogo dancers.

Melrose Avenue is a great place for a stroll. In the old days, it was simply a link to the surrounding residential areas, but now the shops and restaurants on both sides of the avenue have become ultra-trendy: jazzy clothing, extravagant shoes and unusual nick-nacks. Even if you're not into window-shopping, there's always plenty to look at.

WESTWOOD (AREA CODE 310)

Maloney's on the Campus (map IV, A2, **42**): 1000 Gayley Avenue, on the corner with Weyburn Avenue. Very nice pub with good music. Giant TV screens, which (of course) show all the baseball games. Snacks, soup and salads at reasonable prices. Full to bursting in the evening.

COSTA MESA (AREA CODE 714)

Henry 'n' Harry's Goat Hill Tavern: 1830 Newport Boulevard. ☎ 548-8428. They sell 140 draught beers in this place, and the decor's amazing. Not far from Newport Beach.

WHERE TO HAVE BREAKFAST AND WHERE TO GET REAL COFFEE

Starbucks: more or less everywhere in the US, Starbucks is one of the few chains of coffee shops that offer something tasting better than old socks. They also do muffins and a large and rather good range of coffee.

WILSHIRE (AREA CODE 213)

✕ **Caffè Latte**: 6254 Wilshire Boulevard. A few seconds from the Museum of Art (map IV, C2). ☎ 936-5213. Fax: 936-4756. Open daily, 7am–9pm (10pm Friday), Saturday and Sunday 8am–3pm. Pleasant decor with a fresh feel, achieved by the use of white wood, soft colours and lots of plants. You're welcomed by a delicate aroma of coffee. They serve sandwiches, pancakes and muffins – all excellent, in copious portions and at very acceptable prices. Smiling, friendly service. Good rock music (mostly 1970s). At lunchtime the clientele is mainly local workers and the occasional stray visitor looking for a museum, as the exterior is rather anonymous. Vegetarian dishes. Taste the 'hot or sweet Italian' (scrambled eggs with sausages, basil, tomatoes and onions). Fresh pasta from 11am to 3pm, and also sesame chicken salad, *pomodora cruda*, *bruscietta* and green chilli stew.

MELROSE (AREA CODE 213)

✕ **Vienna Cafe** (map III, B3, **51**): 7356 Melrose Avenue. On the Fuller Avenue intersection. Open 7.30am–9pm. Very pleasant cafe with smiling welcome. Large choice of breakfasts, plus fruit juice and freshly pressed vegetable juices, including beetroot, celery and carrot. At lunchtime, there's simple, good cuisine (pasta, sandwiches and salads).

✕ **Caffè Luna** (map III, B3, **52**): 7463 Melrose Avenue. Italian menu offering an impressive selection. The service is a little slow, due to the place's popularity, but there's a good welcome. This restaurant stays open all night, as it's not far from the Hollywood night-spots, so it's the ideal place for a cappuccino in the small hours.

WHERE TO END THE EVENING

A coffee-house is the most relaxing of places when you need to get warmed up. Many are open during the day and close around 2 or 3am. They generally serve real coffee and can provide a genuine feast for culture vultures, putting on things like poetry readings. So although they can sometimes feel a bit posh, they're quite good fun. There's often a pile of books and magazines to relax with. Here's a selection of some of them.

ON WILSHIRE AND HOLLYWOOD (AREA CODE 213)

Onyx Cafe: 1802 N Vermont Avenue. ☎ 660-5820. Open until 1am (3am weekends). In an interesting district (East Hollywood, south of Griffith Park) that's inhabited by intellectuals and artists. It can be fun to split your evening between the art movie-house (Los Feliz Theater) and the Chatterton bookstore, one of the best in LA and right next door. The Onyx Cafe displays paintings by local artists. The atmosphere's very good and the coffee, drinking chocolate and cakes are great.

SANTA MONICA (AREA CODE 310)

The Novel Cafe (map II, C3, **54**): 212 Pier Avenue. No distance at all from the Venice boundary. ☎ 396-8566. Open 7am–midnight, Saturday and Sunday 8am–2am. A delightful bookstore and coffee shop where you'll find old, comfortable armchairs and shelves overloaded with ageing books. Good cakes. A very small terrace outside. The atmosphere might be lively or reflective, depending on the day, the hour, the state of the moon, and the good graces of Wei Dto, the Chinese god who's the guardian of books and is thought to protect the shop.

🍸 **Congo Square**: 1238 3rd Street Promenade. ☎ 395-5406. Open until 2am (3am Friday and Saturday). As the building is new, they've recreated the antique style artificially with odd bits of furniture and big armchairs. Here, relaxation is cultivated. Exhibitions of paintings, a clientele of trendy intellectuals, and most mornings the place is graced by students with their noses in their books. The music is good, and they serve many different varieties of coffee, tea and Italian sodas, as well as cakes, cookies and bagels.

THE BEST NIGHTCLUBS IN LA

Most of these clubs charge admission on Friday, Saturday and Sunday, which usually entitles you to one or two drinks. It's quite difficult, in fact, to map out the nightclubs of Los Angeles. As in New York, their existence is totally transient. Roughly speaking, there are three areas: Sunset for 'heavy metal', hard and other varieties of rock, Hollywood–Wilshire for standard, and Downtown for more trendy stuff.

DOWNTOWN (AREA CODE 213)

The Downtown clubs are regaining favour with the public since the district took a turn for the better. They are generally located in old public buildings, warehouses or former cinemas.

– **Mayan** (map I, B4, **30**): 1038 S Hill Street. ☎ 746-4287. Former cinema with a quite breathtaking Mayan–Aztec temple decor, particularly the facade, the ceiling and the bars. Inside, the space is enormous. Good selection of music.

– **Variety Arts Center** (map I, B4, **31**): 940 S Figueroa Street, level with Olympic Boulevard. Quite fantastic. An old-fashioned dance-hall of the kind that no longer exists in Britain. On Friday and Saturday from 8pm, you dance to a swing and foxtrot beat. It isn't really a smart place, but still it's better to wear jacket and tie. There are lots of advertising posters at the bar, plus souvenirs and photos of American singers of yesteryear.

– **Vertigo**: 333 S Boylston Street. ☎ 747-4849. Beside Route 110 (Harbor Freeway), some blocks north of Wilshire. Not an easy place to reach by car. The least trendy and smallest of the three. Giant video screen. Disco-funky music. You can even play blackjack in one corner.

WEST HOLLYWOOD

How on earth has the heavy metal phenomenon managed to last so long? There's still no sign of it fading away. It's one of the mysteries of LA. And why it should have established itself in West Hollywood, on the outskirts of Beverly Hills, to the great displeasure of the inhabitants of the area, is yet another mystery. As soon as night falls, Sunset Boulevard – level with Doheny Drive and Wetherly – is invaded by clones. You will see legions of Alice Cooper lookalikes, with painted faces and long hair. Eerily, they seem to come in twos, looking like hundreds of sets of twins, and dress in suggestive boleros, trousers or tights. The heavy metal clubs are lined up one after another, and beer cans and bottles litter the sidewalks or, spraying beer, spin through the air to land in someone's garden.

The dazed inhabitants of the area are always asking the police to crack down on the numbers of people who get drunk in their flowerbeds, so officers do sometimes prowl around quite aggressively, and occasionally cart troublemakers away. There's a good deal of tension and bad feeling among residents, although many of those involved are relatively thoughtful types and aren't real troublemakers. Their 'non-conformity' is mostly a matter of how they look.

Anyway, here are some nightclubs – the liveliest ones. But many more are sure to have opened up by the time you read this.

– **Roxy** (map III, inset, **53**): 9009 Sunset Boulevard. ☎ (310) 276-2222. Booking: ☎ 278-9457. Quite breathtaking – a real adrenalin experience.

– **Billboard** (map III, inset, **59**): 9039 Sunset Boulevard. ☎ (310) 274-5800. On three floors. Live techno music.

– **Whisky a Gogo** (map III, inset, **54**): 8901 Sunset Boulevard. ☎ (310) 535-0579. Music from 8pm. This is the oldest club in Hollywood (opened in 1964). And then there's **The Viper Room** (Johnny Depp's place, where River Phoenix died) at 8852 Sunset Boulevard ☎ (310) 358-1880.

– **Coconut Teaszer** (map III, A2, **55**): 8117 Sunset Boulevard. ☎ (213) 654-4773. There's plenty going on here, too. And there's a room for rock gigs with an 'underground' feel. Music starts at 8pm.

– **Gate** (map III, inset, **56**): 653 N La Cienega Boulevard. ☎ (310) 289-8808. If you're looking for beautiful Californians of either sex driving one of those legendary cars, you'll be in your element here, where Californian display takes on its purest form. Come well dressed, because there's a strict weeding-out policy at the entrance. And get here relatively early (around 10pm). The music is dance and techno.

– It's impossible to list all of the places on the streets adjacent to Sunset and those on the other boulevards, but they include **Madame Wong's**, **Club With No Name**, and **Troubadour** (9081 Santa Monica Boulevard).

– There are also many **gay bars and restaurants** on Santa Monica Boulevard, between Doheny Drive and Westmount Drive.

VENICE AND SANTA MONICA (AREA CODE 310)

– **Oar House** (map II, C3, **50**): 2941 Main Street. ☎ 396-4725. An excellent underground bar with disco some evenings (*see* 'Where to Have a Drink'). Every style of music: funk, soul, hip-hop, reggae, etc. Sophisticated lighting effects and sounds. Their motto is: 'Dance till you drop!' Every Monday is Oldies Night, with music of the 1950s, 1960s and 1970s.

– **Cock 'n' Bull Pub**: opposite 3000 Lincoln Boulevard. At the side of the road and with parking alongside. Quite a long way from the centre. This is an Irish pub where they have dancing on Saturday and Sunday evening, plus live music on Tuesday and Friday. Billiard tables, old jukebox, darts. A good atmosphere is guaranteed when the place is full.

– **Alligator Lounge**: 3321 Pico Boulevard. A nice place with an authentic atmosphere and good music.

WHERE TO HEAR JAZZ AND BLUES

On the radio round the clock, on 88.1 MHz.

– **House of Blues**: 8439 Sunset Boulevard. ☎ (213) 650-1451. Currently *the* fashionable spot on the Strip, dreamed up by Dan Ackroyd, the surviving Blues Brother. Externally, it has a weird appearance, but inside, the decor is New Age, and there's a big stage, a mobile bar and a restaurant. Brunch on Sunday morning. Best to book.

– **The Mint**: 6010 W Pico Boulevard. ☎ (213) 954-9630. Live rock, blues and jazz bands every evening from 8pm. Admission charge, which goes up at weekends. Food is served here.

– **St Mark's** (map II, C4, **55**): 23 Winward Avenue, Venice. On the ground floor of the Venice Beach Cotel. ☎ (310) 452-2222. Rhythm and blues and jazz, with an excellent list of gigs. The restaurant serves salads, pasta and pizzas at moderate prices (Tuesday–Friday 6–8pm there's pizza and pasta at two for the price of one). On Wednesday, it's Ladies Night, so there's no cover charge. Dancing until 2am.

– **The Baked Potato**: 3787 W Cahuenga, North Hollywood. ☎ (818) 980-1615. On the left, approximately 200 yards (180 metres) before Lankeshim Boulevard, up by Carl's Jnr Drive-Thru. Open 7pm–2am. Great atmosphere in this cafe, with live music provided by two groups every evening and they serve food here too. There's one dish on the menu: a giant baked potato accompanied by a multitude of sauces. At about $10, this is a pretty expensive potato, as you have to pay for two drinks as well as the admission charge.

LOS ANGELES

A CULTURAL EVENING

– **The Grounding Theater** (map III, B3, **57**): 7307 Melrose Avenue (and Poinsettia). ☎ 934-9700. This is currently the most imaginative theatre in LA, and much of its work is devoted to improvization. For the last 15 years the place has been playing to full houses and it's the place where Pee-Wee Herman came to fame. Booking is strongly recommended. Shows are normally at 8pm, daily except Sunday.

– **Hollywood Bowl** (map IV, D1): 2201 N Highland Avenue. Programme information: ☎ 850-2000. Superb concerts are given by the Los Angeles Philharmonic in summer. It's possible to buy tickets up to 1pm on the same day: ☎ 480-3232.

– **The Comedy Store** (map III, inset, **58**): 8433 Sunset Boulevard. ☎ 656-6225. One of the most famous stand-up comedy clubs. Call for programme details or look in the 'what's on' magazines. With a bit of luck, you could catch an evening with Robin Williams or Richard Pryor! Shows are usually at 10pm on Friday, 8pm and 10.30pm on Saturday; and 9pm Monday to Wednesday.

WHAT TO SEE

The nearest sights worth seeing are listed here, followed by a section-by-section guide to those farther out.

DOWNTOWN

As in most large American cities, the centre empties bit by bit at the end of the working day (around 5pm), and it can be quite dirty and even dangerous in the evening. As elsewhere, the centre is undergoing a process of recovery but it's certainly true that this has not progressed as fast in LA as it has in New York, where the gentrification process is all but complete. In some parts of town, there are plenty of skyscrapers occupying the space.

MAKE GOOD USE OF THE DASH

The DASH buses are an excellent way of getting around. For just a quarter, you have full use of three lines (A, B and C) that link all the Downtown points of interest as well as free transfers from one line to another at the junctions. it's a good idea to get a map of the lines going from Exposition Park to Chinatown. Full information: ☎ 1-800-2-LA RIDE.

★ **Hotel Bonaventure** (map I, C3, **40**): 5th Street and Flower Street. This place is an astonishing piece of architecture. The design is similar to the San Francisco Hyatt and brings to mind 1950s science-fiction decor. The view from the 35th floor is spectacular and it's worth going there just for the free ride in the glass elevator on the outside wall . . . remember the fight between John Malkovich and Clint Eastwood in *In the Line of Fire*? The rotating bar goes through one complete revolution every hour and is open 4pm–midnight.

★ **Biltmore Hotel** (map I, C3, **41**): 506 S Grand Avenue. Legendary and glamorous pre-war hotel. Take a stroll in the Main Galeria, whose eastern entrance is on 5th Street. The lobby of this luxury hotel is surreal, with an immense and elaborate ceiling painted by an Italian painter who also worked in The White House and The Vatican!

★ **Los Angeles Central Library** (map I, B3, **42**): opposite the Biltmore Hotel. It cost $215 million to restore the Central Library after it was severely damaged by fire in 1986.

★ **Museum of Contemporary Art (MOCA)** (map I, C3, **43**): 250 S Grand Avenue, level with California Plaza. ☎ 621-2766. Open daily, 11am–5pm (8pm Thursday). Closed Monday. Free on Thursday 5–8pm. Reduction for students. This museum tends not to exhibit artists who have already made their name, looking out for the latest developments and the most innovative approaches. And they don't wait for artists to die before acknowledging their talents! In the permanent collection, you can see works by Franz Kline, Tapiés, Fautrier, Rothko (*Untitled, Black on Dark Sienna on Purple, Red and Blue Over Red*), Morris Louis (*Pillar of Delay*), Nicolas de Staël (*Vue d'Agrigente, Les Joueurs de Football*), sculpture by Giacometti, Dubuffet, Alechinsky, Miró (*Personnages dans la nuit*). And also Mondrian, Jackson Pollock, etc. Well-stocked bookshop on the terrace, with works of art for sale.

★ **California Plaza**: new and successful piece of townscape. As well as the beautiful MOCA, look at the cheekily bevelled shape of the Wells Fargo building.

Not far away, the **First Interstate Tower** is currently the tallest tower west of Chicago.

★ **The Museum of Neon Art (MONA)** (map I, D4): 704 Traction Avenue. On a street intersecting with Alameda Street. Open Wednesday–Saturday noon–5pm. In an arty loft-dwelling district east of Little Tokyo. This is quite a small museum, contrasting with its powerhouse environment of banks and shopping complexes. It contains some huge neon signs that are worthy of Broadway, plus others that are more modest in size. Surprisingly, the museum was built with the proceeds of a one per cent levy imposed by the municipality on the city renovation programme, but its running costs are met from private funds.

★ **El Pueblo de Los Angeles** (map I, D2, **45**): on Olvera Street, at the northern end of Main Street. Along this little street are some adobe houses that were built during the Spanish period. The LA story began when 44 farmers set up here back in 1781. Since then, it has become an ultra-touristy area and the shops are overflowing with souvenirs in dubious taste. You can easily give it a miss, or you could console yourself by having something to eat at Philippe the Original (*see* 'Where to Eat'). Get there early to beat the plebs! While you're on Olvera Street, call in at Sepulveda House, which houses the Visitors' Center (open 10am–3pm; closed Sunday). Here you can see a film, *Pueblo of Promise*, on request. On the ground floor is a genuine little museum with antique furniture of the period. Pick up their nicely produced leaflet called *El Pueblo de Los Angeles Historic Park*, which includes a map.

Next door, you can see the **Avila Adobe** which, dating from 1818, is the oldest residence in LA. It was originally the Mayor's house. Open daily, 10am–5pm. During the war between the US and Mexico, it served as the US Army headquarters.

Other interesting buildings are the **Masonic Hall** (1858) and the **Fire House** (1884). There's a small information kiosk on the square.

There are free guided tours, Tuesday–Saturday at 10am, 11am, noon and 1pm. Gather at the Docent Office (near the Fire House, on the square). ☎ 628-1274. On the first and third Wednesday of every month, free two-hour bus tours of the oldest districts in LA are organized by an association called *Las Angelitas del Pueblo*.

★ **Little Chinatown** (pedestrianized) (map I, D2), between Hill Street and Broadway (around No. 945 North). Traditional and popular shops and 'wishing wells'. *See also* 'Where to Eat'.

★ **The Los Angeles Morgue Shop**: Los Angeles County Coroner's Department, 1104 N Mission Road. ☎ (213) 343-0786. Fax: (213) 221-9768. Open Monday–Friday 8am–4.30pm. Closed weekends. To get here: by car from Freeway 5, exit at Mission Road. By bus, starting from Downtown, take a No. 78 bus anywhere on Spring Street and get out at Workman. The bus stop is located right opposite the morgue.

What kind of place can this be? You may well ask – a gift shop in a morgue? Saddened by the dozens of bodies arriving daily, mostly young people killed in road accidents, and mostly casualties caused by drunkenness, the morgue authorities came up with an idea to finance a programme to combat drink-driving. And it seems to have worked, because the first year's profits financed an education programme that, among other things, includes photographic displays of the shattered bodies of some of the young victims. A Hitchcock imitator would probably have given the audience a peek into the refrigerated corpse cabinets as well. But, even if there may be some sensitivity lacking here, the initiative has a social and educational purpose.

In the shop on the second floor, you can buy all sorts of objects decorated with a skull or a silhouette in the shape of the outline in chalk drawn by the police on the ground around a corpse: T-shirts, ball-pens, pins, underpants, mugs, bath towels, watches, helmets and more. Well, this is America . . .

It isn't worth crossing the whole of LA by bus just to see this, but if you do have a car, it's worth the journey. Remember that you have to read between the lines to get the point.

★ PASADENA (AREA CODE 626)

This place, to the northeast of Downtown, has two buildings that you ought not to miss.

★ **Norton Simon Museum**: 411 W Colorado Boulevard. ☎ 449-6840. Open Thursday–Saturday noon–6pm. To get here by car from Downtown: come up Alvaredo, then take Highway 2 (North). Exit at Colorado Boulevard. Or take a No. 483 bus from Olive Street, between 6th and 7th Streets. Magnificent museum of art with quite an interesting architectural design. The building was initially intended to house a museum of modern art, which failed in 1975. The Norton Simon collection is remarkably well displayed here. Although much less well known than the MOCA and the LA County Museum of Art, it's well worth a visit. Here are its main treasures:

• **The room on the left of the entrance**: this gallery is mainly devoted to **French and European painting** and includes works by Courbet, Berthe Morisot, Pissarro, Boudin, Renoir, Juan Gris, Braque and Picasso, and a series of beautiful lithographs on the subject of bullfighting. There are also examples by Modigliani, Puvis de Chavannes, Manet, Seurat, Monet, Gauguin, Van Gogh, Cézanne, Matisse, Douanier Rousseau and Toulouse-Lautrec.

• **The Native-American sculpture department** displays marvellous small bronzes, a superb Bodhisattva in schist (2nd century BC) and a rare and lovely chess set with an ivory-encrusted marquetry board.

• **The room on the right of the entrance**: statues by Rodin, views of Venice by Guardi, works by Luca Giordano; Giovanni Paolo Pannini (a master of perspective and *trompe l'oeil*), Poussin, Chardin, Fragonard, Ingres, and portraits by Goya, Zurbarán, Rubens, Tiepolo, Ribera, Murillo, Rembrandt, Frans Hals, Canaletto's *The Piazzetta* and many more.

• **Modern section**: works by Klee, Kokoschka, Soutine, Diego Rivera, Kirchner.

• **Religious Primitives**: works by El Greco, *Madonna and Child with Book*, a superb canvas by Raphael, seven panels of an altarpiece by Bernardino Luini, and a beautiful polyptych by Pietro Lorenzetti.

• **In the basement**: contains drawings by Rembrandt, many works by Degas, especially some beautiful pastels, and paintings by Corot, Boudin, Sisley, Utrillo, and others.

★ **Huntington Library and Art Gallery**: 1151 Oxford Road. ☎ (818) 405-2141. Open 1–4.30pm. Closed Sunday, Monday and public holidays. Free parking. Northeast of Downtown, in the district of San Marino (towards Pasadena). This library has some very rare items, such as a Gutenberg Bible that was printed in Mainz in 1455. There's a small museum containing some interesting 18th-century French paintings and furniture. Lastly, there are magnificent botanical gardens: a tropical garden, a Japanese garden, a desert garden with hundreds of cacti, and a Shakespeare garden that contains all the flowers mentioned in his works.

WHAT TO SEE IN AND AROUND LOS ANGELES

HOLLYWOOD

(AREA CODE 213)

HISTORY OF THE MOVIE CAPITAL

IN THE BEGINNING WAS A PROMISED LAND . . . AND A COWSHED

When movies were born, Hollywood still looked like a little paradise. This peaceful locality near Los Angeles, backing onto a range of hills and next to the Pacific Ocean, was renowned for the mildness of its climate and for its wide horizon, wholly devoid of buildings. To arrive in Hollywood was to enter the Garden of Eden, the air deliciously scented with orange, eucalyptus and jasmine. Bougainvillea, roses, geraniums and lupins thrived and tall, elegant palm trees reached into a limpid blue sky. At night, coyotes could be heard howling in the canyons near the city.

One fine day in December 1913, Cecil B. De Mille, of the Famous Players Lasky company (later Paramount Pictures), arrived from New York with his movie crew. After passing along a wide, shady avenue called Vine Street, the group stopped at the 'studio' – a cowshed – a large, dark green wooden building, stained by the fruit falling from nearby trees. De Mille sent a telegram to his company's headquarters in New York: 'Request authorization rent cowshed in place called Hollywood for 75 dollars a month.' The authorization was not slow in coming, and enabled De Mille to film *The Squaw Man* (1914), the first American (silent) feature film.

So began the rush to the Promised Land of Hollywood. Pioneers of the cinema, movie directors and producers came running, drawn by the mildness of the weather that made it possible to film outdoors in summer and winter alike, and by magnificent lighting conditions, the low cost of real estate, the presence of an abundant workforce that was cheaper to hire than in New York, and the huge variety of locations in the surrounding area – city, ocean, mountain and desert.

A man of genius, D.W. Griffith, who had already been working since 1910, organized the first superproduction by filming *Birth of a Nation* (1915), followed by *Intolerance* (1916). These films were like nothing ever seen before. *Intolerance*, for example, had a cast of 5,000, filming took 16 weeks, and 76 hours' worth of film was shot, to end up as a movie only three hours long!

Hollywood was the birthplace of one of the earliest film genres of the silent cinema – burlesque (or slapstick) comedy. The pioneer was Mack Sennett, who made hundreds of short comedies for Keystone in a few humble shacks near Edendale.

Sennett himself launched the careers of a number of comedians, including Charlie Chaplin. Newly arrived from his native England, Chaplin invented his tramp character while ransacking the Keystone wardrobe. His triumph was immediate and spectacular. His cane, moustache and bowler hat – and his ridiculous walk – made him a world star in less than three years. Hired initially at $75 a week, Chaplin signed the movie industry's first million-dollar contract in 1917. This amazing deal made him a multimillionaire at the age of 28 and, in 1918, he set up his own studios at 1416 N La Brea (which are still there: *see* 'What to See'). Together with Douglas Fairbanks and Mary Pickford, two other prominent stars of the time, and with the participation of D.W. Griffith, Chaplin set up Associated Artists in 1919, further developing the image of Hollywood as the world's movie capital.

THE GOLDEN AGE OF THE DREAM FACTORIES

The era from 1920 to 1940 now stands out as the 'Golden Age' of the Hollywood movie. There were several reasons for this: TV had not yet come into existence; the American movie industry was young and vigorous, full of ambitious people with bright ideas; and people had adopted the movie-going habit, with an average of three visits a week. There was also the cult of star worship.

The first major film company, Paramount Pictures, headed by Adolf Zukor, was born at the end of World War I. During the Roaring Twenties, the Hollywood cinema industry transformed itself into the movie business, with Hollywood as its nerve centre, brain and driving force. The big production companies kept their offices in New York, but invested in building huge studios in Hollywood. The working arrangements, organization and production processes were so well tailored to producing maximum profitability that the studios very soon became known as 'dream factories'.

Almost 28,000 people were employed in Hollywood, including 170 directors and 350 scriptwriters. The latter, forever under pressure, supplied 500–700 scenarios each year. The writer Joseph Kessel described the Hollywood of the time as a 'working town' which, beneath a luxurious veneer, was just like a mining town, sitting empty from dawn to dusk while its population slaved away in the pits or on the production line. He pointed out that Hollywood made talking pictures in the same way that Henry Ford turned out automobiles.

Five large dream factories dominated the world of cinema. Most of the American studios had been founded by Jewish businessmen originally from Central Europe, who had come to try their luck in the United States towards the end of the 19th century. Their success is doubtless due in part to their deep desire for integration and a wish to be totally Americanized.

True to its slogan, 'More stars than there are in heaven', **MGM (Metro Goldwyn Mayer)** had a policy of collecting stars: Greta Garbo, Clark Gable, Marion Davies, Joan Crawford and Norma Shearer were all under contract.

Paramount had the irresistible Mae West, the sparkling Gary Cooper, the Marx Brothers, Bing Crosby, Bob Hope, Tyrone Power and the divine Marlene Dietrich.

Warner Brothers, run by the four Warner brothers, didn't have that many stars, but what they lacked in quantity they made up for in quality, with a stable that included Humphrey Bogart, James Cagney and Bette Davis.

It was not until 1935 that **Twentieth Century Fox** rose from the ashes to become the fourth of the Big Five.

The fifth was **RKO**, which had the inspiration to produce Orson Welles' masterpiece *Citizen Kane.*

After the Big Five came the Little Three: **Columbia**, **United Artists** and **Universal**. **Columbia** are now housed in the MGM Studios in Culver City having left their Hollywood studios, now called 'Sunset-Gower Studios', in 1972.

The largest and most impressive studio in the early days of the cinema was Universal City, set up by Carl Laemmle on wasteland several miles north of Hollywood. Each of these studios was like a city within the city, a fortress surrounded by high walls and heavily guarded. According to Kessel, who came out of his Hollywood experiences dazzled but crushed, everything was organized and hierarchical – even thoughts and inspiration were had to order.

The overlords of the dream factories were the producers. They exercised control over everything, intervening at every level in the making of a film, and selecting the subject, the author, the director, the actors and even the camera crew. Because of the extent of their power, they were nicknamed the 'Moguls'. One of these Hollywood Moguls, Irving Thalberg, Louis Mayer's right-hand man at MGM, was the model for F. Scott Fitzgerald's *The Last Tycoon.* A few independent producers succeeded in making a name for themselves in the shadow of the major studios. This was the case with Samuel Goldwyn and David O. Selznick, the producer of *Gone With the Wind* (1939).

The 1930s were marked by great directors like Frank Capra (a genius with thought-provoking comedies), John Ford (the 'Daddy of Westerns') and Howard Hawkes (the initiator of the *film noir*). With the 1940s came the era of the *film noir* and of pin-ups, and glamour girls replaced the academic beauties of pre-war times. Among the pin-up girls were the 'atomic star' Rita Hayworth, the swimmer Esther Williams, the smouldering Jane Russell, the torrid Lana Turner, the perverse Barbara Stanwyck, the bitch Bette Davis, the foreigner Ingrid Bergman, and 'the most beautiful animal in the world', Ava Gardner. Later on, of course, came Marilyn Monroe, the Hollywood star *par excellence.* All these stars, 'the best paid slaves in the world', lived in Beverly Hills, a short distance away from the studios.

There was yet another galaxy of geniuses when it came to directors: John Huston (*The Maltese Falcon, Night of the Iguana, The Asphalt Jungle*), Raoul Walsh (*High Sierra*), Billy Wilder (*Sunset Boulevard, The Seven-year Itch*), Joseph Mankiewicz (*Dragonwyck, All About Eve, The Barefoot Contessa*), Ernst Lubitsch (*Ninotchka, To Be or Not to Be, Heaven Can Wait*), and of course Alfred Hitchcock, the inventor of the cinema 'thriller'.

THE STATUETTE LOOKED LIKE UNCLE OSCAR

A slender knight in gold-plated bronze holds a sword upright, his feet resting on a reel of film. This prestigious statuette has been awarded every year since 1928 to the best film, director and a whole host of other categories.

But why the name 'Oscar'? Until 1931, the Academy Award had no name. An obscure librarian at the Academy, Margaret Herrick, gave the statuette its nickname because of its resemblance to her Uncle Oscar! Then the nickname entered the public domain on 18 March 1934 in an article by a local Hollywood reporter, Sidney Skolsky. The previously obscure Margaret went on to become the executive director of the Awards.

HOLLYWOOD TODAY

The reputation of Hollywood is still unequalled in the world. As many as nine people out of ten here earn a living in the film industry and nine out of ten dollars spent in that industry in the United States are spent in this one place. After a serious crisis for the studios with the arrival of television, their diversification into the production of TV programmes in the end saved them. Today, the existence of hundreds of American TV channels, which transmit for up to 20 hours a day, means that their future is assured for a long time to come.

The latest development in the American cinema industry is for the big-budget movies to be aimed at teenagers, who go to the cinema more often than their parents. Films for adults often have a hard time finding a producer. This implies a crisis not only for the cinema but also for the star system, because films aimed at a young audience rarely have much appeal to the big stars. Steven Spielberg has always said that he prefers to put his money into special effects rather than stars, and as things stand, the facts appear to support his approach.

The frenetic activity of the Hollywood studios, most of which, in reality, have always been located in Burbank, in the San Fernando Valley, made a huge contribution to propagating the American myth around the world.

At this point it's appropriate to mention the giant letters spelling out the name 'HOLLYWOOD' up on the hillside. The letters, which were in a sad state of deterioration for many years, have fortunately now been saved thanks to a national appeal sponsored by rock stars. Alice Cooper was the initiator of the rescue effort, insisting on financing the last 'O' himself, while David Bowie paid for the letter H. The first 'O' belongs to Russ Meyer. The giant sign, which was originally constructed in 1923, started out as a publicity stunt dreamed up by a promoter in order to sell houses in the Hollywood hills – it originally read 'Hollywoodland', but was shortened in 1945.

To get a photo of this legendary sign, take the Hollywood Boulevard exit on the freeway, turn into Franklin and then into Beachwood Drive.

The big Hollywood event of 1995 was the announcement of the setting up of a new multimedia company, **Dreamworks SKG**, by Steven Spielberg, Jeffrey Katzenberg (the No. 2 at Disney studios) and David Geffen (a music magnate). The founding of a new studio on this scale is all the more surprising because no new studio had opened up in Hollywood for 50 years. Spielberg and co. aim to make it the prototype 21st-century studio, producing films, TV films, animated cartoons, toys 'that will drive parents crazy' (according to Spielberg) and computer entertainment products.

USEFUL ADDRESS

Hollywood Visitors' Information Center (map III, C2): 6541 Hollywood Boulevard. ☎ 689-8822. Housed in a historic old house at the bottom of a street lined with shops. The welcome is good and there's plenty of interesting information.

WHAT TO SEE IN HOLLYWOOD

★ **Mann's Chinese Theatre** (map III, B2, **60**): 6925 Hollywood Boulevard, near Highland Avenue. ☎ 464-8111. First show 11.30am. This is without a doubt the most famous movie theatre in the world. The presentation facilities are perfect and it's where most grand premieres take place. And no, Sid Grauman wasn't Chinese. It was after travelling to China in 1924 that he had the idea of building this hall in Chinese style. For some reason it is spelled in the English way – 'theatre'.

★ **Footprints of the stars**: the greatest movie personalities are immortalized on this esplanade by their handprints and footprints in cement. Look out for those of the *Star Wars* robot R2D2, Donald Duck, Humphrey Bogart, Shirley Temple and Marilyn Monroe, as well as Arnie Schwarzenegger's enormous earth-grippers. Great stories often have a simple origin. It was a French mason, Jean Klossner, who put the first handprint into the cement. The proprietor of the theatre, Sid Grauman, asked him what the heck he thought he was doing. Klossner explained that it was important to leave his mark for posterity, in the same way as his ancestors had done when building Notre-Dame in Paris. That was all it took to give Grauman the germ of an idea, and he kept the practice going. Three new prints are added to the collection every year.

★ From here starts the **Walk of Fame**, a series of large stars that have been set into the sidewalk, each being assigned to the big movie, radio, TV and recording stars. There are now over 2,000 of them, and a new star is assigned every month. To find out the date of a ceremony, write to or call the Hollywood Chamber of Commerce, 6255 Sunset Boulevard (Suite 911), Hollywood CA 90028. ☎ 469-8311. Mickey Mouse, Bugs Bunny, Snow White and the Simpsons are the only imaginary personalities to have a star.

★ Hollywood seems to have got its second breath with the opening of the **Galaxy**, a very fine cinema complex at 7021 Hollywood Boulevard (on the Sycamore Street intersection). It is tinged with an art deco feel and there's an orgy of blue neon signs. At No. 6834 (and Highland Avenue) is **El Capitan**, another superb place with rich decor, dating from 1926. At No. 6712 is **The Egyptian Theater**, dating from 1922 (map III, C2, **62**), the first Grauman cinema in this district. Sadly, the usherettes are no longer dressed as Egyptian servants. On Hudson and Hollywood there are superb frescoes dedicated to Dolores del Rio, one of the first movie stars.

★ **Hollywood Wax Museum** (map III, C2, **63**): 6767 Hollywood Boulevard, one block away from Mann's Chinese Theatre. ☎ 462-8860. Open 10am–midnight (2am weekends). Old-hat and expensive, not worthy of the famous Movieland Wax Museum (*see* 'Around and About in Disneyland'). Among many others you can see John F.

Kennedy, Marilyn Monroe, Robert Redford, Clint Eastwood, Ronald Reagan, Dolly Parton, Katharine Hepburn, Sly Stallone, Michael Douglas and the Beatles.

★ **Guinness World of Records Museum** (map III, C2, **64**): 6764 Hollywood Boulevard, level with Highland Avenue. ☎ 463-6433. Open daily, 10am–midnight. Next door to and containing the same sort of material as Ripley's Believe It or Not! Odditorium. Contains examples of extreme human behaviour as well as the biggest, smallest, strongest and fastest from the natural world. The presentation is dull at times, but there are some eye-catching videos. There are also some interactive displays that might keep the children amused. To whet your appetite there's the parrot with the 800-word vocabulary, the man who dived from a height of more than 26 feet (8m) into just 1 foot (30cm) of water, the longest screen kiss (three minutes five seconds), the 153 roles played by John Wayne (only 11 of them non-starring ones) . . . and so on. Then there's the recipient of the greatest number of fan letters: Mickey Mouse, with nearly 800,000 in one year.

★ **Entertainment Museum** (map III, B2, **61**): 7021 Hollywood Boulevard. ☎ 465-7900. Open 10am–6pm. This is one of the newest museums on the Boulevard, and great for film buffs. There's a guided tour, and they start by getting you to create a film soundtrack. After that, there's a room containing costumes and props that have been used in various films: *Dante's Peak* and *Forrest Gump*, among others. You can also sit in the seats of the Starship Enterprise, or stroll through the reconstructed set of the American series *Cheers*.

★ **Frederick's of Hollywood**: 6608 Hollywood Boulevard. Open 10am–6pm, Sunday noon–5pm. Frederick's is the king of exotic underwear, and the display window contains items of erotic lingerie. Eccentricity and extravagant fantasies lie shamelessly, cheek by . . . er . . . jowl. Most of the major stars have shopped here for titillating negligees or saucy bras. The violet, mauve and pink facade on its own is worth the trip. When you get inside, there's what can only be described as an explosive range of fripperies. You even get a great alibi for visiting this establishment in the name of 'culture': at the rear of the store, there's a museum (admission free) and gallery where you can pore over some of the most famous undergarments of the 20th century: basques worn by Mae West and Madonna, Ingrid Bergman's corset, the bra worn by Marilyn Monroe in *Let's Make Love,* a bra autographed by Cher, a black satin nightdress that belonged to Garbo . . . and so on.

★ **Hollywood Cemetery** (map III, D3, **65**): 6000 Santa Monica Boulevard, also known as the Hollywood Memorial Cemetery, on the corner of Santa Monica Boulevard and Gower Street, a few blocks southeast of Mann's Chinese Theatre. This is where fans have come to weep over the graves of the likes of Rudolph Valentino, Douglas Fairbanks and Tyrone Power. The directors buried here include D.W Griffith, John Huston, and Cecil B. De Mille. Don't look here for Marilyn: she's buried in Westwood Village Cemetery (*see below*), which is more peaceful.

★ **Hollywood Studio Museum**: 2100 N Highland Avenue. ☎ 874-2276. Open Saturday only – phone for appointment. The only museum devoted to the silent cinema era, and housed in a one-time barn that served simultaneously as a set, wardrobe department and stable for

Squaw Man, Hollywood's first feature film, made by Cecil B. De Mille. The building was renovated some years ago, shifted from the Paramount Pictures plot on the corner of Vine Street and Selma, and set up here. It contains many objects and souvenirs from the early days of the movies.

★ **French Village Movie Set** (map III, B2, **66**): 1330 Formosa, level with Fountain Avenue. A hamlet of a few small houses grouped around a tree-shaded courtyard. This is the French Village Movie Set, one of the oldest sets in Hollywood and intended to represent a traditional village in deepest France. Built in 1920 by Charlie Chaplin for one of his films.

★ **Charlie Chaplin Studios** (map III, B2, **67**): 1416 N La Brea Avenue. On the corner of La Brea and Paul de Longpré Avenue. The studios are now occupied by AM Records and are not open to visitors. It's a long, low building, vaguely Anglo-Norman in style, right in the heart of Hollywood. Listed as an historic site, the studios have finally been saved from destruction. This is where Charlie Chaplin, already famous and a millionaire at the age of 28, had his own studios built in 1917 among fields of orange trees, lemon trees and tomatoes, and where he made the first eight films commissioned by First National (including *A Dog's Life* and *The Pilgrim*). At that time, the building housed the secretaries, the casting office, and the two-roomed bungalow, on the corner of Longpré Avenue, that was reserved for Chaplin. But to avoid the constant interruptions, he frequently took refuge in a one-roomed shack at the back of the studio. He worked here until September 1952, while living at 1085 Summit Drive in Beverly Hills.

★ **Hollywood shopping**: from N Highland Avenue to Cahuenga Boulevard, there are many original shops, as well as crazy clothing shops selling T-shirts and Hollywood gimmicks. Here's a small selection:

Starworld: 6665 Hollywood Avenue. Open daily, 11am–7pm. Autographs (Michael Jackson, Madonna, the Beatles, Elvis, etc.), photos, posters and scripts; everything's at prices that reflect the celebrity involved. This is a shop for the movie or music buff who's looking for a genuine souvenir of Hollywood – but without a serious budget, it could be a place for daydreaming!

Hollywood Toys and Costumes: 6600 Hollywood Boulevard, corner with Whitley Avenue. Open 10am–7pm, Sunday 11am–6pm. The biggest shop in LA for costumes, disguises, toys and masks. The range is incredible.

Ozzie Dots: 4635 Hollywood Boulevard. At the eastern end of the boulevard. Open 9am–6pm (5pm Sunday). Second-hand clothes of excellent quality – cast-offs from the stars. It goes without saying that they're a little more expensive than your traditional Oxfam selection, but they're worth a look. Disguises and wigs, too.

★ **Paramount Studios** (map III, D3, **68**): 5555 Melrose Avenue, in Hollywood (two blocks east of Vine Street, between Santa Monica Boulevard and Melrose Avenue). ☎ 956-17-77. Open Monday–Friday; two-hour tours start on the hour from 9am–2pm. It's all on foot. Not for children under 10.

The studios are featured in the movie **The Ghost of Hollywood**, but this movie focuses on the Paramount of the 'Golden Age' and has little to do with the present-day studios, so don't go expecting to experience the genial, creative atmosphere that reigned in the old days: things have changed, and you may come away disappointed.

It's worth noting that when films or TV programmes are in production, access to some studios is prohibited and the tour loses out to some extent. Nevertheless it's interesting to see some of the unsung movie heroes in action (the cameramen, the make-up ladies and the extras).

★ **Melrose Avenue shopping**: this is a long avenue south of Hollywood. It starts off in Beverly and disappears into the jungle of the Hollywood Freeway. But the most interesting section is between Alta Vista and Spaulding Avenue (map III, A3–B3). This has become the district that really swings in LA, with trendy shops and restaurants, one of the rare areas where people still walk around where Angelenos come to rediscover the joys of window-shopping. Here, you'll see bohemians, the bourgeoisie and the punk generation mingling happily together. By day and by night, it's a meeting place for the tattooed crowd and the devotees of every kind of body piercing. The average lifetime of these shops isn't long and new ones are always opening up, each more eccentric than the last.

🔒 **Wasteland**: 7428 Melrose. Open 11.30am–8.30pm, Sunday noon–8pm. The facade itself sets the tone of the place, which sells second-hand stuff, especially clothes. Not everything is worth the money, but studying the clientele can be fun.

🔒 **Vinyl Fetish**: 7305 Melrose. Open daily, 11am–9pm. A record shop specializing in punk, post-punk and industrial music. It's packed with hard rock and heavy metal gimmicks.

– **Johnny Rockets**: *American Graffiti*-style restaurant not to be missed (*see* 'Where to Eat, Hollywood').

★ **Pacific Design Center**: 8687 Melrose. ☎ (310) 657-0800. Closes 5pm. You can't miss this screaming blue building, otherwise known as the 'Blue Whale', right beside the antiques district of Melrose Avenue. It houses a very impressive contemporary design exhibition, with more than 50 showrooms displaying the most sophisticated products to be had in the world of kitchens, bathrooms and furniture.

★ **Barnsdall Park**: 4800 Hollywood Boulevard (between Edgemont and Vermont). In the east of the district, this beautiful park contains many facilities and activities, including the **Municipal Art Gallery**, which shows the work of contemporary Southern Californian artists. ☎ 662-7272, and the **Hollyhock House**. This bizarre art-deco building was the work of architect Frank Lloyd Wright, completed in 1921 and his first building in Los Angeles. Guided tours take place on Tuesday, Wednesday and Thursday every hour 10am–1pm; Saturday and the first three Sundays in every month noon–3pm. For information: ☎ 485-4580.

★ **Museum of Tolerance** (map IV, B3, **50**): 9786 W Pico Boulevard. ☎ (310) 553-8403. South of Hollywood, in the **Simon Wiesenthal Center**. Open Monday–Thursday 10am–4pm, Sunday 11am–5pm (closes 3pm Friday from April and October, and at 1pm from November to March). Closed Saturday and Jewish festivals. Free parking. Established in 1993, this museum is an educational presentation on racial conflict in America and the history of the Holocaust.

There's a guided tour, the initial (interactive) part of which is concerned with tolerance. It has many videos on the struggle for the rights of man, on racial discrimination in the US, and on the massacres in Rwanda and Bosnia and so on.

The second section is devoted to the Holocaust. They give you a passport bearing the photograph and name of a real child who was born in the 1930s, and whose all-too-real fate you discover at the end of the trip. The displays show the horrifying lack of reaction of many countries to the fate of the Jews caught up in the Holocaust.

GRIFFITH PARK (LOS ANGELES ENVIRONS MAP B1)

The largest municipal park in the world stretches between Freeway 101 and Route 5, north of LA. Open 6am–10pm. This land was donated to the city in 1896 by Griffith J. Griffith, a Welsh immigrant who, after making his fortune, took up residence here. Looking back on his years of extreme poverty, he stipulated in his will that his estate should become a place for leisure activities and rest. There are high hills, canyons, woods, footpaths and jogging trails, cycle tracks, horseback riding and the like, making it a haven of clean, fresh air right next to Hollywood. Mount Hollywood rises to 1,770ft (540m). Many parts of the park are still very wild, but there are miles of paths here. The **Los Angeles Zoo** and some interesting museums are also within the park, including a **Greek Theater**, **Bird Sanctuary**, the famous **Observatory** and the **Nature Museum**.

USEFUL ADDRESS

i Rangers' Visitors' Center: 4730 Crystal Spring Drive. East of the park, just before you get to the Gene Autry Museum. ☎ 665-5188. Open daily, 7am–5pm. Full information on Griffith Park, its many walks, etc. There's a map, also available from the Hollywood Visitors' Information Center, showing all the sites and museums.

★ Gene Autry Western Heritage Museum

4700 Western Heritage Way. ☎ (213) 667-2000. Open 10am–5pm. Closed Monday (except certain public holidays) and Thanksgiving, Christmas and New Year's Day. Located in Griffith Park, at the junction of Route 5 (Golden State Freeway) and Route 134 (Ventura Freeway). Take the 'Zoo' exit. The simplest way to get here from the city centre is to take the Los Feliz Boulevard from Western or Vermont and follow it until you're close to Route 5. Turn left on Crystal Springs Drive, and continue straight on towards the Zoo and the Museum: they are opposite each other.

The museum, which opened in 1988, is housed in a large Spanish mission-style building and bears the name of the famous star of Western movies. Gene Autry made 95 films between 1934 and 1953. He had a successful radio programme for CBS, *Melody Ranch*, which ran for 16 years, and his TV show, the *Gene Autry Show*, ran from 1950 to 1955. He recorded 635 songs and sold 40 million records. What's more, he holds the record number of stars on the Walk of Fame on Hollywood Boulevard.

So, you would expect to see a big museum about the history of the West here but this is history told from the point of view of the White Man. The museum's approach doesn't give any critical insight into the period, and the Native Americans appear only as elements of folklore. But don't deny yourself the pleasure of a visit: the collections are comprehensive, and there are some remarkable reconstructions. Allow a minimum of two hours to see it all – it's a fascinating museum, with displays of the highest quality.

The museum is divided into thematic sections:

• **Spirit of Discovery**: beautiful Chimayo carpets and Native American children's clothes; an interesting painting: *Passing Time, Eternal Beauty* by Wilson Hurtley (or a fantasy on the Grand Canyon); the inevitable gallery of weapons, with the story of gunmakers Smith and Wesson. Everything you ever wanted to know about firearms manufacture, plus documents, photos, advertising posters and decorated revolvers.

• **Spirit of Romance**: paintings, engravings, watercolours and charcoal drawings on how the West was won. Posters for Buffalo Bill's circus, kitsch furnishings, silverware with Native American motifs, art objects, etc. Theatre and opera shows in the West.

• **Spirit of Imagination**: an attractively reconstructed street in a Wild West town; fascinating videos about stuntmen in cowboy movies; and everything you can think of about Western movies: cameras, costumes, including the one worn by Clint Eastwood in *Pale Rider,* Steve McQueen's hat from *Tom Horn,* and hats once worn by John Wayne and Gary Cooper, toys (including Roy Rogers), ceremonial saddles, superb portraits of Sioux Indians. Finally, there's a movie and video theatre offering a presentation of the history of the West.

From here, you reach the rooms downstairs:

• **Spirit of Cowboys**: clothing, tools, stirrups, spurs, photos. You might even be astonished by the number of different kinds of barbed wire that have been used to divide the prairies.

• **Spirit of Community**: a superb gallery of Colts and rifles, souvenirs of Pat Garrett and Billy the Kid, photos of the deaths of the Dalton brothers, documents about the shoot-out at the OK Corral, a gambling saloon and mahogany bar, an 1873 fire engine, and a reconstruction of a saddler's shop.

• **Spirit of Opportunity and Conquest**: a remarkable reconstruction of a stagecoach, Native American clothing and craft products, dolls, toys, souvenirs of the pioneers, embroidery, furniture, domestic objects. A fresco evoking an angelic vision of the West. Not much sign of any acknowledgement of how any of this might have seemed to the Native Americans, though.

★ **Travel Town Transportation Museum**: Griffith Park, 5200 Zoo Drive. ☎ (213) 662-5874. Right at the north end of the park. Open daily, summer 10am–4pm (5pm weekends and public holidays), winter Saturday and Sunday 10am–4.30pm. Admission free. This is the biggest display of steam locomotives west of the Mississippi, with all kinds of vehicles dating from 1849 through to World War II. Some fire engines, too, and an impressive Union Pacific locomotive weighing 110 tonnes. A miniature steam train runs through the museum. Picnic area close by.

Further on are the **LA Live Steamers**, a club for scale-model fans. On the first Sunday of every month, 10am–5pm, they run a free trip on a miniature train.

★ **Loz Feliz Station**: if you haven't yet reached saturation point, there's something else for you to try out on Crystal Springs Drive (it's before the Visitors' Center and the Western Heritage Museum). ☎ 664-6788. Open 10am–4.30pm (5pm weekends). Next door, for the children, there's a track for ponies and a mini-ride in a stagecoach: mid-June–mid-September 10am–5pm, rest of year 10am–4.30pm. Closed Monday.

★ **The Observatory and Planetarium**: access via Vermont Avenue and Western Canyon Drive. From Downtown, take a No. 97 bus on Spring Street. ☎ 664-1191. Open daily, mid-June–mid-September. The Planetarium has room for 650 people and shows are at 1.30pm, 3pm and 8pm (plus 4.30pm weekends); in low season, they're at 3pm and 8pm (plus 1.30pm and 4.30pm weekends). Closed Monday. The shows last approximately one hour, and the one at 1.30pm is open to the under fives. It's worth going there at least once during the evening (before 10pm). On a dark night, if the weather is clear and the smog isn't too heavy, it's a magical experience. James Dean had a knife fight here in *Rebel Without a Cause*. For photographers, it's a great place to get a shot of the Hollywood sign up there on the hillside.

• In the Planetarium, the hoped-for starry sky may occasionally be replaced by a **laser show**, with a Pink Floyd soundtrack. Information: ☎ (818) 997-3624.

• The **Hall of Sciences** presents scientific experiments. In summer, it's open Sunday–Friday 1–10pm (Saturday opens 11.30am), winter Tuesday–Friday 2–10pm (Saturday from 11.30am, Sunday from 1pm). Closed Monday. Admission free.

• The public can use the giant **telescope** on clear evenings, from dusk until 10pm. Information: ☎ 664-1191.

★ **Bird Sanctuary**: Vermont Canyon Road. Open daily, 10am–5pm.

WHAT TO DO IN GRIFFITH PARK

– Many **sports** are practised in the park, including tennis, golf (four municipal courses), horse-riding and more. Bridle-paths have been specially designated.

■ Horses can be hired from the **Griffith Park Equestrian Center**: ☎ 840-9063. Information about the other centres is also available from the Visitors' Center.

■ **Sunset Ranch**: 3400 N Beachwood Drive. ☎ 464-9612. Any Friday evening, you can take a 'midnight ride' on horseback, across the Hollywood Hills and as far as Burbank, getting a panoramic view of LA with everything all lit up. You eat in a Mexican restaurant and get back around 11pm. It costs around $20 per person, not including the food.

– Hikes: it's very popular to get some oxygen into the lungs by setting out across the hills of Griffith Park and there are at least 50 miles (80km) of paths. Some of the tracks are shared with horse-riders. Ask at the Rangers' Visitors' Center for help with planning your route (☎ 665-5188). One of the most popular hikes goes over Mount Hollywood, starting from the parking lot at the Planetarium. The round-trip is around 6 miles (10km) and you get a fantastic panorama of the whole of LA.

GLENDALE

(LOS ANGELES ENVIRONS MAP B1)

WHAT TO SEE

★ Forest Lawn Cemetery

1712 S Glendale Avenue, Glendale. ☎ (213) 254-3131. 'The art of dying in California.' The most extravagant part of this cemetery is divided into four sections, each containing wildly insane chapels, sculptures, etc.

Above all else, this is a very large and pleasant **park**, and a big reservoir of oxygen. It's not in the least morbid, since most graves consist merely of plaques set level with the lawn. You can even tour around by car.

• Near the Freedom Mausoleum are the final resting places of **Walt Disney**, **Sammy Davis Jnr**., and the evangelistic preacher **Aimée Semple McPherson**, who, they say, had herself buried here along with a phone and a working line. Also nearby is the grave of **Errol Flynn**, who, they say, was buried with six bottles of whisky to keep him company.

• Inside the **Freedom Mausoleum** are the funerary urns of **Alan Ladd**, **Nat King Cole**, **Clara Bow**, and **Chico** and **Gummo Marx**.

• Right at the top of the **Court of Freedom**, you can see a reproduction in mosaic of the famous work by John Trumbull, *The Signing of the Declaration of Independence*. It contains 700,000 mosaic pieces in a total of 1,500 colours.

• At the **Great Mausoleum**, you can also see *The Last Supper*, after Leonardo da Vinci. Inside the Great Mausoleum, you can see the funerary plaques of **Clark Gable** and his wife, **Carole Lombard**, as well as that of David O. Selznick, the producer of *Gone With The Wind.* Tours start daily every half-hour, 9am–4.45pm. There's a superb stained-glass window.

UNIVERSAL STUDIOS

In the north of Hollywood. ☎ (818) 622-3801. To get there from Downtown, take a No. 420 bus on the corner of Hollywood Boulevard and Highland Avenue. Travelling by car, take Route 101 N on the corner of Hollywood Boulevard and Highland Avenue. Expect to take a good 15 minutes.

Open summer 7am–11pm, winter 9am–9pm. Closed Thanksgiving and Christmas. You can spend a whole day on this tour. Admission charge quite high. Reduction for children between three and 11 years and for Over 60s; free for children under three. Buy a two-day ticket and get a $4 reduction. If you're going in summer, be there as soon as it opens!

This tour of the studios of America's biggest production company includes a live experience of many attractions based on famous movies. It also shows you how sets are built, effects are achieved, and so on. Universal Studios was established in 1915, and organized tours began in 1964. To date, the Studios have seen more than 65 million visitors.

The trip is organized into two phases. It's best to arrive at opening time and rush (literally!) to the attractions on the lower level, then climb to the **Tram Ride** that takes you all through the studios, past the immense hangars, reconstructed streets and districts. In the afternoon, start with the **Entertainment Center**. However you play it, you'll have to queue at some time or other, but if you stick to this order, the waiting won't be so bad.

WHAT TO SEE

• **Jurassic Park**: this attraction cost the pretty sum of $110 million, which was twice as much as Spielberg's film! You travel on board a big raft among dinosaurs and other prehistoric monsters, and they look totally realistic. A 10,000-watt sound system supplies the roars of a 45-ton *Tyrannosaurus Rex*, which rushes forward to meet you – with its jaws open. The finale is guaranteed to give you a big thrill. Remember to protect your camera and camcorder: they just might get wet!

• **Backdraft**: there are two rooms designed to explain the tricks of the movie camera and show you the main spectacle, a huge fire inside a building. Bad luck, folks, it's a warehouse full of gas and petrol – and of course, you're stuck inside! The heat given out by the explosions is bad enough, so where's the fire brigade?

• **ET Adventure**: . . . you (and all the other visitors) enter a mysterious, dark redwood forest and you're asked to help ET, who is lost in the forest. This is a trip by bike and cable-car to the stars and to the Moon, where you're surrounded by characters from the film *ET – The Extra-Terrestrial* and pursued by all manner of bad guys (the cops, the FBI, the CIA, the Army, etc.). Finally, you wind up before the extra-terrestrial, and the brilliant light radiating from his heart illuminates you as a token of his gratitude. It's a truly emotional moment! This trip cost the trifling sum of $40 million, and Steven Spielberg, of course, made a big contribution to this show, which takes place inside the biggest studio ever built.

• **Terminator**: a recent attraction with a giant screen that you view through 3-D specs. Stunning special effects throughout.

• **The World of Cinemagic**: this is the large studio where you get to see the techniques and tricks used in famous movies. It can only be described as being both spectacular and amusing – the presenters certainly have a good sense of humour. You get to see inside three strong sequences, including the shower scene from Hitchcock's *Psycho*, thanks to which showers will never be the same again! The secrets of Hitch are revealed, including the revolutionary techniques he invented for *Vertigo*, *Rope*, *Rear Window*, etc. Try to get picked for the cast in the final scene of *Sabotage*, or 'How to Fall from the Top of the Statue of Liberty'.

You'll also be shown the techniques used in some scenes in *Back to the Future*. You might even be lucky enough to be put into that memorable De Lorean automobile. To finish up with, younger visitors are involved in creating a live soundtrack under the same conditions and time constraints as the professionals. In this studio, the audience participation makes the show great fun.

★ Later, the trip on board the **Tram Ride** gets you straight into the heart of things. As you pass from one studio to another, you'll see Norman Bates's motel and house, the street where *The Sting* was filmed, and lots more. It's a good idea to keep your eyes wide open because the studios are still in use every day for TV soaps and film sequences. You never know who you might see. Some parts are more interesting than others, of course, and some of the attractions are only open during the summer months. But, some of the sets are amazing. Here are the 'must-see's:

• **Earthquake**: your chance to survive an earthquake measuring 8.3 on the Richter scale. You're sitting comfortably, quietly travelling along in the San Francisco underground, when everything comes to a stop . . . the catastrophe and the nightmare begin. The underground tunnels collapse. Cracks open all around you. The street falls away, taking with it a large truck loaded with propane and this, needless to say, promptly explodes. The heat flushes your face and the shattered pipes cause terrible flooding. There are 145 seconds of earthquake and the emotional response is guaranteed. The show is in itself a great technical achievement, as everything on the set is designed to explode and shatter at least 200 times a day!

Ironically, the studio housing this attraction has been designed to withstand a genuine earthquake of force 8.3 – so this has to be the safest building in the world!

• **King Kong**: comfortably ensconced in an elevated railway, you're quietly travelling along above the roofs of New York when you encounter the dreaded King Kong. His breath will make your head spin: it smells of . . . bananas! He nearly catches you and your vehicle gets a good shaking. This is a stirring trip, and is definitely not suitable for very young children.

Some facts and figures: King Kong is 33ft (10m) or three storeys tall, weighs more than six tons (including 600lbs/270kg of fur) and is able to make 29 facial movements – computer-controlled ones. This means that he has the most sophisticated system of any animal in the world. And he's designed to appear 20 times an hour all year round! The reconstruction of New York has also been done with extraordinary attention to detail.

• By contrast, **The Crossing of the Red Sea** and **Jaws** are a little worn.

– At the exit from the Tram Ride, still more attractions await you.

IN THE ENTERTAINMENT CENTER

All the shows are at fixed times, so there are long queues in the afternoon, but they move along quite quickly:

★ **Back to the Future**: you're seated in the fantastic car invented by 'Doc' to travel in time. Sensations are guaranteed.

★ **Waterworld**: based on the Kevin Costner film. The special effects are breathtaking. Get here at least half an hour ahead of time if you want a place. Everything you can imagine: the bad guys, the famous smokers in search of Dryland, and the good guys. The stunts on the water are really impressive, as is the end-of-the-world setting. Six shows a day from 1pm.

★ **The Wild Wild Wild West Stunt Show**: a Western spectacle that pits two rival outlaw gangs against each other. The stunts and the gags are excellent, and there's plenty of brazen humour. In the short space of 15 minutes you see a succession of fights, explosions and collapsing sets. Seven shows a day, starting at 11am.

★ **Beetlejuice's Rockin' Graveyard Revue**: a very rock 'n' roll show lasting 25 minutes and starring Dracula, the Phantom of the Opera, the Bride of Frankenstein and Frankenstein's monster himself. The music is good, as are the special effects and the choreography, and there's a good dose of humour. Five shows a day starting at 1pm.

★ **The Blues Brothers**: these two arrive explosively in their car, then there's an outdoor concert with reprises of the legendary duo's hits.

★ **Lucy, a tribute**: a retrospective of the career of Lucille Ball, the red-headed actress of the 1930s and TV star of the 1950s and '60s.

★ Other attractions include **Animal Actors Stage**: a whole heap of famous animal movie 'actors' demonstrate their talents. All have an impressive number of films to their credit – the envy of many a human actor. Among others, you'll meet Lassie, and Einstein, the star of *Back to the Future.* Great for kids.

★ Then there's **The Flintstones** (super), **An American Tail**, with the mouse-hero Fievel, who's larger than life size. At the **Fievel Playland**, the kids will be literally dwarfed into Lilliputians as they slide along on a huge banana-skin toboggan or explore a giant slice of cheese!

– Wherever you go, you'll meet lookalikes posing as Groucho Marx, W.C. Fields, Marilyn Monroe, Clark Gable, Charlie Chaplin and so on.

WHERE TO EAT AT UNIVERSAL STUDIOS

✗ **Mel's**: famous 1950s-style diner for burgers and creamy milk-shakes.

✗ **Victoria Station**: smarter. Famous for its prime ribs, mixed salads and desserts.

✗ **Hard Rock Cafe**: in the pedestrianized area (at Universal City) in front of the studio entrance. You can't miss it – there's a 60ft (18m) electric guitar in front of the entrance. The decor is brilliant; the food is so-so.

– There are stacks of places to have a snack both outside and inside the studios. If you want to go out and come back in again, you'll need your hand stamped at the gate.

WHERE TO EAT IN THE AREA

✗ **Miceli's**: 3655 Cahuenga Boulevard. ☎ (818) 508-1221. Below Universal Studios. A good Italian restaurant, run by the same family since 1949. But the interest of the place isn't only in the food on your plate. Get this: the waiters are trained tenors, and when the mood takes them, they strike up rather good renditions of Italian operatic arias.

BEVERLY HILLS

(LOS ANGELES MAP IV)

Contrary to popular belief, Beverly Hills isn't just a district but an actual town of 32,000 inhabitants, with its own Town Hall and a separate administration from the rest of Los Angeles. Its constituents form one of the richest residential communities in the US – perhaps even the world. Since the start of the 20th century, film stars, recording stars and producers have tended to live in Beverly Hills, an incredible residential area buried in subtropical vegetation and right next to the dream factories of Hollywood. They work down in the plains, but they live in the hills, well away from the bustle of the big city.

Beverly Hills lies on a range of hills between Hollywood and Santa Monica. The district of Bel Air, extending to the west, is every bit as wealthy as Beverly Hills itself, which divides into two: upper Beverly Hills and lower Beverly Hills. The lower part stretches between Santa Monica and Sunset Boulevard, forming a large, regular grid of impeccably clean avenues, all fringed by tall, majestic palms and other exotic trees. This was where those early screen stars lived.

This area of Beverly Hills is almost flat. The real hills begin above Sunset Boulevard (renamed 'Suckette Boulevard' since the Hugh Grant affair). Nowadays, the stars tend to live outside Beverly Hills, in Santa Monica, Pacific Palisades, or Malibu, because the Pacific is so close at hand.

PRACTICAL ADVICE AND INFORMATION

– Get the detailed **Map of the Movie Stars' Homes** because, even though it may look like a tourist rip-off, it's currently the only map that will let you find your way quite easily through the maze of avenues and streets in Beverly Hills. Many shops in Hollywood sell it, as do strolling vendors along the sidewalks of Sunset Boulevard. This map gives lists of celebrities (deceased or still with us) together with the exact address, locating them on the street map. But remember that there are very frequent changes of address in this part of the world!

– **A simple tip**: house numbers are painted on the edge of the sidewalk, and that's the easiest way to find your bearings here, especially when you're driving.

– To find out all about the murders and suicides that have made Hollywood history over the last 80 years, get hold of **This is Hollywood** by Ken Schessler. It's an easy read, very comprehensive, with plenty of maps.

– All the houses are **private residences**, monitored by high-security systems, so don't try to get in or climb over any walls. You run the risk – in ascending order of danger – of a) setting off the most powerful alarms in the city, b) the immediate arrival of the cops, or c) being attacked by a pack of Dobermans or the like. The stars have a saying: 'if you want to live happily, live in hiding'!

– You will, of course, get a good look at the railings, the heavy entrance doors, the dustbins and the walls crumbling under the luxuriant vegetation, but only rarely might you get a glimpse the owners. Your imagination will have to fill in the gaps – just picture the heart-shaped swimming pools, moon-shaped bathtubs, sun-shaped bedrooms, castle-shaped dog kennels, and so on

– If you do come face to face with one of your idols, it's not advisable to try to approach them. Your move is just as likely to be interpreted as aggressive by their chauffeur or bodyguards.

– One way to see past the facades would be a place an ad in the *LA Times*, seeking a position as an au pair or helper. You might find you have a choice of millionaires to work for.

– **Guided tours**: of all the agencies offering guided tours of Hollywood and Beverly Hills, Grave Line Tours (PO Box 931654, ☎ 213 469-41-49) stands out because of its originality. They take you in a Cadillac – well, it's a hearse, as a matter of fact! The commentary includes many spicy anecdotes about the movie world (fantastic adventures, scandals, suicides, murders, etc.), and black humour abounds. You can also see the house where Marilyn Monroe had a brief affair with Yves Montand. Tours run daily, around noon, to the left of Mann's Chinese Theatre on Hollywood Boulevard, and last two hours 30 minutes.

WHAT TO SEE IN BEVERLY HILLS

★ **Rodeo Drive**: take a No. 20 or 22 bus from Wilshire Boulevard. The most expensive avenue in the world is located in Beverly Hills and you'll find all the major haute-couture fashion houses represented here.

Parking is possible in the surrounding streets, and you can use some public parking lots at no charge for the first two hours (until 6pm). That leaves you just enough time to go and do your shopping at the Rodeo Collection, an extremely smart shopping mall.

★ **The Regent**: 9500 Wilshire Boulevard. This is the hotel where *Pretty Woman* was filmed.

★ **Elvis Presley's house**: 144 Monovale Drive, between Sunset and Carolwood. The star lived here from December 1967 to March 1975. Then he sold the house to Telly 'Kojak' Savalas, who in turn sold it to Paula Meehan, the current owner, one of the richest women in the world. You can't see much from the street, unless the gate at the eastern entrance is open, in which case you can vaguely make out the famous terrace.

★ **Walt Disney's house**: 355 Carolwood Drive. The inventor of Mickey Mouse lived here until his death in 1966. Next door, at 375 Carolwood, is the home of Gregory Peck.

★ **Charlie Chaplin's house**: 1085 Summit Drive (on the corner with Cove). You can hardly see the house for the trees surrounding it. Built in 1922 in Hispanic style, it was nicknamed 'The Breakaway Home', for a comical reason quite worthy of a Chaplin comedy. In order to save money on the building work, Chaplin used carpenters from his studios, who normally made film sets. Not knowing how to go about constructing a solid, lasting structure, they made it in their normal (temporary) style. The result was that Charlie had hardly moved into his little palace when pieces of plaster started to fall from the ceiling, the floor began to creak and doors fell bizarrely from their hinges. Chaplin lived here until 1950, which you may see as a feat of stoic heroism. Then the house went through a number of hands, in particular those of the Philippines dictator Ferdinand Marcos and the Saudi arms dealer Adnan Khashoggi, who went on to give it to his daughter.

★ **The house of Mary Pickford and Douglas Fairbanks**: 1143 Summit Drive. 'Pickfair', combining the names of these early movie superstars, was the most famous residence in the Hollywood of the silent era. This huge 42-room mansion was the dream of all America. Unfortunately, it was sold to the singer Pia Zadora and her husband, the millionaire Meshulam Riklis, who immediately demolished it, to the great wrath of the various Beverly Hills conservation associations. A three-storey house now stands here.

★ **Bugsy Siegel's house**: 810 Linden Drive. Benjamin 'Bugsy' Siegel was known as 'the most dangerous man in America', and in the 1930s, he ran LA's biggest gambling and prostitution network. A gangster, but also a visionary who 'invented' Las Vegas, he was murdered in this house, which had been rented by his mistress, while he was sitting quietly in the drawing room. The story is told in the film *Bugsy*, with Warren Beatty.

★ **The house owned by Greta Garbo, David O. Selznick and Elton John**: 1400 N Tower Grove, at the top of one of the hills in Beverly Hills, on the corner with Seabright Drive. Even though the house itself, a kind of neo-French manor with two bronze lions in front of the entrance gate, is of no particular interest, the winding road that takes you up the hillside is really worth a look. There's a superb view of the whole city, or at least a large part of it: Hollywood, with the Pacific on the horizon. You're in a sort of sunny eagle's nest here, far from the bustle of LA. Greta Garbo and her lover John Gilbert lived in a Hispanic-style house that was later bought by David O. Selznick, the producer of *Gone With the Wind,* and then, much later, sold to the singer Elton John. Unfortunately, this house was destroyed in 1986, to be replaced with the present pseudo-manor house. Down below, in one of the canyons, is the villa of the late Cary Grant.

★ **Hugh Hefner's house**: 10236 Charing Cross Road. 'The Playboy Mansion' is a sort of big manor in the British style, with 23 rooms. This is where Hugh Hefner, the publisher of *Playboy*, has lived since 1971.

★ **The houses of Stan Laurel and Oliver Hardy**: always together in front of the cameras, Laurel and Hardy went home in different directions. Oliver Hardy lived at 621 Alta Drive in the lower part of Beverly Hills, while his pal Stanley had a house at 718 Bedford Drive.

★ **Harold Lloyd's house**: the greatest movie comedian before Chaplin had a superb house at 1225 Benedict Canyon.

★ **Alfred Hitchcock's house**: 10957 Bellagio Road.

★ **The Witches House (Spadena House)**: 516 N Walden Drive (corner with Carmelita), in lower Beverly Hills. Not to be missed on any account, this is yet another vestige of the silent movie era. Whereas all the surrounding houses vie with each other in opulence and luxury, this one looks like a house out of a fairytale: cranky, crooked, vaguely Bavarian in style, with a weird little garden surrounded by a no-less-anachronistic hedge of trees. It could be the witch's house from *Hansel and Gretel*. Originally, and until 1926, this strange house contained the offices of Irvin Willat Productions. According to movie fanatics, you can catch glimpses of it in certain 1920s silent films.

– **Other celebrities living in Beverly Hills**: Kirk Douglas, Phil Collins, Elizabeth Taylor, Ronald Reagan . . . and plenty more.

– **Celebrities living in Benedict Canyon**: Mickey Rourke, Jacqueline Bisset, Eddie Murphy.

★ **Bel Air**: one of the poshest districts of Beverly Hills, with Lionel Richie, Judith Krantz, Quincy Jones and Gene Wilder among those living here.

– **Further out, in Hollywood Hills**: on Mulholland Drive, you can find a row of houses that belong to the stars. Jack Nicholson is at No. 12850, Marlon Brando at No. 12900, while Burt Reynolds and Sharon Stone live in the vicinity.

★ **Sunset Plaza**: on Sunset Boulevard, just before Beverly Hills, this is a very upscale district with a number of restaurants and shops.

MIDTOWN

(LOS ANGELES MAP IV)

A district extending roughly south of Melrose to the Santa Monica Freeway, bounded to the east and west by Downtown and Beverly. Wilshire Boulevard forms its central backbone.

WHAT TO SEE

★ **Los Angeles County Museum of Art** (**LACMA**) (map IV, C2, **51**): 5905 Wilshire Boulevard, in Hancock Park, not far from the Farmer's Market. ☎ (213) 857-6110. Open Tuesday–Thursday 10am–5pm, Friday 10am–9pm, Saturday and Sunday 11am–6pm.

Some galleries are occasionally closed and most of the special exhibitions in the Ahmanson, Anderson and Hammer galleries have different opening times on Wednesday, Thursday and Friday: it's best to call the museum and obtain precise information rather than just going along on spec. From Downtown, you need a No. 20, 21 or 22 bus from Wilshire Boulevard, level with Flower Street.

This is the most important fine arts museum on the West Coast, with furniture designed by Eero Saarinen, a fine collection of Islamic art and masterpieces of contemporary Asian painting, plus 14 works by Degas and 10 by Cézanne.

• **The Anderson Building** is devoted to 20th-century art, with all the art movements represented.

– **On the third floor** are the permanent collections. Works include: *Portrait of Juñer Vidal* by Picasso (Blue Period, 1903); American paintings by Morgan Russell and Stanton McDonald-Wright; works by Braque *(Bateaux sur la plage* and *Nature morte au violon*); bronze heads by Matisse; Chagall *(Violoniste dans la neige*); Soutine, Rouault and Modigliani *(Jeune femme du peuple*); works by Fernand Léger, Juan Gris and Mondrian; Kandinsky's *(Untitled Improvization III)*; a superb Picasso *(Femme pleurant au mouchoir)*; Dufy's *Paris*; Man Ray and Dufield *(La Boîte dans la valise)*; works by Magritte, Max Ernst, Miró, Diego Rivera (the splendid *Day of the Flowers*), Nicolas de Staël *(Vue de Marseille)*, Jackson Pollock and Dubuffet.

– **On the second floor** is contemporary American painting and sculpture.

• In the **Hammer Building** are some beautiful works by Gauguin, temporary exhibitions, some Impressionists and several true masterpieces: *Madeleine à la flamme* by Georges de la Tour, *The Holy Family* by Rubens and Rembrandt's *Awakening of Lazarus*.

★ George C. Page Museum of La Brea Discoveries

5801 Wilshire Boulevard. ☎ 936-2230 and 857-6311. Open 10am–5pm. Closed Monday (except holiday Mondays) and Tuesday (except the first Tuesday of every month, when admission is free), and closed for Thanksgiving, Christmas and New Year's Day. Take the No. 20, 21 or 22 bus from Downtown.

This is a natural history museum, established at Rancho La Brea, an immense ranch which, at the turn of the 20th century, was discovered to contain a vast deposit of natural tar. Then came the discovery that the tar held thousands of creatures that had been preserved – mammoths, tigers, wolves, insects, birds, micro-organisms, plants, and . . . a woman. All of them were completely submerged in the mass of asphalt. This prodigious discovery inspired George C. Page, a millionaire philanthropist, to create the museum. He had left his native Nebraska at the age of 16 after tasting his first orange, and, inspired by the idea of a country that could produce such a delicious fruit, he went to California and made his fortune by selling tropical fruit to cold countries.

The presentation is quite remarkable, and has largely been designed for children: there are animated young mammoths, a chance to test your strength against the tar, and the laboratory itself, where work can be observed by visitors through a large window. The animals that were found date from between 10,000 and 40,000 years ago, and the most numerous examples are of the *Smilodon californius*, a kind of giant tiger with walrus-like fangs, the enormous *dire wolves* (*Canis dirus*), the 'short-faced' bear, American lions, horses, peccaries and bison.

The visit is in two parts: the museum and a guided tour of the pits (the excavation sites). Meet at the Observation Pit Wednesday–Sunday 1pm. The tour of the museum (with a film) begins at 2pm Tuesday–Sunday and also at 11.30am at the weekend.

In summer, you can even watch the palaeontologists working in Pit 91.

★ Farmer's Market

W 3rd Street and Fairfax. From Downtown, take a No. 16 bus at 5th Street. ☎ 933-9211. Open 9am–7pm, Sunday 10am–6pm. Founded in 1934 by 18 farmers as a place where they could sell their own products, it now has 160 stands offering an almost infinite variety of food products from the four corners of the globe. A modernization and enlargement project is in progress.

✕ There are many **restaurants** of all nationalities to be found here.

★ Wilshire Boulevard

From Downtown, going west, explore some of the most remarkable art-deco buildings in LA, as well as some interesting Victorian timber houses from the late 19th century.

• **Park Plaza Hotel**: a splendid 1924 art-deco building used many times as a film set. Take a look at the immense entrance hall and its breath-taking decor (*see* 'Where to Stay near the Airport').

• **Grier-Musser Museum**: 403 South Bonnie Brae (between 3rd and 4th Streets). A street two blocks away from MacArthur Park. ☎ 413-1814. Open Wednesday–Saturday 11am–4pm. A beautiful house in Queen Anne style (1898), and one of the few still existing in LA. The visit is doubly interesting because of the interior, and there are furnishings, watercolours, ancient porcelains, Victorian stained-glass windows, a collection of old postcards of the city, unusual domestic objects and a miscellany of other items.

• The **Magnin Wilshire** and the **Wiltern Center**: at 3050 and 3780 Wilshire Boulevard respectively. The Magnin dates from 1928 and is considered to be the finest art-deco building in LA. It also now houses a private library. Pretty interior decor. The Wiltern Center, built in 1931, has a bright green ceramic facade. There's a beautiful auditorium on the ground floor. Take a look at the schedule of performances so that you can get a chance to see the interior, which is really worth seeing.

WESTWOOD

(LOS ANGELES MAP IV)

From Downtown, take a No. 21 bus. Students heading for **UCLA** arriving from the airport would do better to take the Super Shuttle or the Coast Shuttle rather than the bus to the LAX terminal, which drops passengers some distance from the residential areas on campus.

The main thing about Westwood is that it's one of the oldest villages in LA. It used to be charming in every way, before the developers got their hands on it. The *Shopping Village*, a pleasant shopping district in Hispano-Mediterranean style, was built in the late 1980s. The Dome (Westwood and Broxton), the Tower (Westwood and Weyburn) and the ravishing Village Theater, at 961 Broxton Avenue (built in 1930) are the only symbols of this era still to remain.

At weekends, Westwood becomes very lively, with people thronging to its 250 shops, its cinemas and theatres, and its many cafes and restaurants.

Where to Stay / Where to Eat: *see* the sections 'Where to Stay' and 'Where to Eat in Los Angeles'.

WHAT TO SEE IN WESTWOOD

★ **The Armand Hammer Museum of Art and Cultural Center** (map IV, A2, **52**): 10899 Wilshire Boulevard. ☎ (310) 443-7000. Open Tuesday–Saturday 11am–7pm (6pm Sunday). Closed Monday.

This museum has a curious history. Armand Hammer, a millionaire industrialist, art collector, friend of Lenin and member of Los Angeles County Museum of Art's board of directors, was preparing to leave his rich collections to LACMA. But when he realized that the individual items would be dispersed, he created his own museum instead in order to keep them together. The result is an imposing museum, built in 1990 in an architectural style that perplexes many of its visitors. The collections are valued at around $300 million and include many masterpieces.

Among other things, you'll find the largest Daumier collection outside France, the only known Leonardo da Vinci Codex (*Pharmacopoeia*), *The Man in the Black Hat* and *Juno* by Rembrandt, works by Tintoretto, Rubens, Titian, Watteau *(Fête en l'honneur de Pan*), Ingres, Géricault, Gustave Moreau (one of his most beautiful works, *Salomé dansant devant Hérode*), Chardin, Boucher, Fragonard *(L'éducation de la Vierge*), Gauguin *(Bonjour Monsieur Gauguin*), Goya, Van Gogh *(L'Hôpital à Saint-Rémy*), Pissarro, Chagall *(L'Ange bleu)*, Mary Cassatt *(Reine Lefèvre et Margot*).

They put on prestigious temporary exhibitions, but it's worth noting that some galleries are taken over for these shows, with the result that some of the permanent collection is not on view. Ask for information beforehand.

★ **Marilyn Monroe's last house**: 12305 Fifth Helena, in the residential district of Brentwood, between Sunset Boulevard and San Vincente. Only for Marilyn fanatics, because the house, situated at the back on the left of the cul-de-sac, isn't open to visitors. There's a black railing covered with a tarpaulin that stops you seeing inside the property. Only if you are very tall will you be able to stand on tiptoe and peer over the top.

The actress was found dead on 5 August 1962, naked on her bed, with one hand lying mysteriously on the phone. She was 36 years old. It has never been agreed whether this was a case of suicide or murder, though she is reported to have swallowed 47 packets of Nembutal, a very powerful sedative. The villa, a humbler edifice than the luxurious residences of Beverly Hills, looks like a farmhouse in Provence, with its tiled roof and whitewashed walls. The small building at the back on the right is where her body was found. The window of her room is to the left of the turquoise door.

★ **The house of the O.J. Simpson 'affair'**: 875 South Bundy, south of San Vincente. Nicole Simpson, wife of O.J. Simpson the former American football star and movie actor, was murdered in this house. The crime itself and the trials that followed, totally gripped American and many European TV audiences while casting more doubt on the US justice system. Simpson was tried before two courts and was acquitted.

★ **Marilyn Monroe's grave**: Westwood Memorial Park, 1218 Glendon Avenue. On the corner of Wilshire Avenue and Glendon Avenue there are two towers, the Oppenheimer Tower and the tower of the Wells Fargo Bank. Just after the latter, before the second building on the left, there's a path leading to the cemetery, which is an island of calm hidden behind the towers. The grave, just a simple plaque in the wall, is located to the left of the entrance, after the first three 'sanctuaries of devotion'. Curiously, it's often covered with traces of lipstick – kisses sent to the Great Beyond by admirers of the tragic star.

The same cemetery contains the grave of **Natalie Wood** (on the central lawn – it's the most flowery one), **John Cassavetes**, **Truman Capote**, **Peter Lorre** and **Darryl F. Zanuck** (a simple plaque in the lawn).

★ **University of California at Los Angeles (UCLA)**: founded in 1929, the university started off as four buildings that now form its historic centre, around Dickson Plaza: the Powell, Kinsey, Royce and Haines Buildings, which were built in brick, in Romanesque style. The architect of Royce Hall took inspiration from the basilica of Sant' Ambrogio in Milan, while the Powell Library's designer copied the dome of San Sepolcro in Bologna as well as the main entrance of the church of San Zeno Maggiore in Verona.

Nowadays, the campus is immense, and is bounded by Le Conte Avenue, Gayley, Hilgard and Sunset Boulevard. To get here take a No. 20, 21, 22, 320 or 322 RTD bus. All run along Wilshire Boulevard; the No. 322 goes from Downtown to Santa Monica.

At UCLA, a cheap RTD Shuttle serves the main points of interest.

i You should definitely pay a visit to the **UCLA Visitors' Center**, Ueberroth Building on Le Conte Avenue, between Gayley Avenue and Westwood Plaza. ☎ 206-8147. This is a good source of information and they do a detailed map. Occasionally there's a film about the university. The walking tour, which takes approximately 90 minutes, begins at 10.30am and 1.30pm on weekdays: call to double-check the times.

• If you have a little extra time, there are many things to see, especially the smaller museums, such as the **Fowler Museum of Cultural History** (art and ethnography) beside Royce Hall. **Schoenberg Hall** has a small but rich collection of musical instruments. Right next to it is the **Inverted Fountain**, which is just like a mountain torrent. In the **Wight Art Gallery**, north of the campus in the **Dickson Art Center**, there are interesting temporary exhibitions (open Tuesday 11am–8pm, Wednesday–Friday 11am–5pm, weekends 1–5pm; closed Monday and school holidays). Next door are **Macgowan Hall** and the **Tower of Masks** in the theatre courtyard. Opposite is the **Franklin D. Murphy Sculpture Garden**, where you can find around 50 sculptures by Rodin, Miró and other artists. It's a popular picnic area for students.

Students' Store: Ackerman Union Building (B level) on Bruin Walk (any student will tell you where it is). ☎ 825-7711. You can find everything here: calculators, photographic film, T-shirts, books, etc. Generally open weekdays 7.45am–7.30pm (6pm Friday), Saturday 10am-5pm and Sunday noon–5pm.

✕ Inside Ackerman Union, there are two restaurants: the **Cooperage** (pizza, salad-bar and burgers) and the **Treehouse**, which is a bit more like a proper restaurant.

• On the outside is the huge **Bruin Bear**, the symbol of the university, and the **UCLA Athletic Hall of Fame**, which records everything worth knowing about the university's sporting history, its successes, big sports stars and so on.

VENICE

(LOS ANGELES MAP II)

Best seen at the weekend. This district at the edge of the Pacific got its name from the canals that once ran through it. A millionaire called Abbott Kinney had them dug after seeing Venice. Then a storm blew up, wiped out the buildings and filled in the canals. Undismayed, Kinney reconstructed bridges and buildings. In 1924, when the canals had been completed, the extravagant Californian went further and imported some authentic gondolas. Two Venetian gondoliers were hired to teach young Americans the art of oaring. Today there are still some Venice-inspired bridges and houses, mainly in Windward Street (the Venice Beach Cotel is a fine example), and there's also the Sidewalk Cafe on Ocean Front Walk.

Then, in 1929, oil was discovered, the whole area was drilled, the barely completed constructions were destroyed without a second thought, and most of the canals were filled in again. From the 1930s onwards, the district began to lose its tone, and became a popular place for modest dwellings lived in by ordinary people. The rediscovery of Venice has changed the tone of the place yet again.

This area is now a rendezvous for artists and dropouts. It's popular throughout the week because of its little shops (along the seafront) and also for its murals, the best of which are at to be found at the end of Windward Street (the west wall of the Venice Beach Cotel) and between Windward and Market Streets.

PRACTICAL INFORMATION AND WHAT TO DO

– Most of the action takes place in the area around the **Sidewalk Cafe** (map II, C4, **32**). Here, it's like full-time theatre, with most people deeply into some role-play or other. And you can, if you fancy it, have yourself photographed standing beside a bodybuilder on **Muscle Beach**.

– If you stroll along **Ocean Front Walk** you enter into a really busy marketplace where every conceivable small trader and street artiste co-exist, from Hindu masseurs to fortune-tellers, with jugglers, singers and tumblers thrown in for good measure.

– The **rollerskate** was born here. And you can hire a pair (although it's rollerblading nowadays) and shoot off along the beach. Anyone on foot usually makes way for the throng of skaters. It's an interesting sight and it's also great to have a go. You'll see the best of them performing some astonishing turns and moves, and some even have the skill to dance . . . and play football.

– **Bike hire**: Venice Pier Bike Shop, 21 Washington Street, very near the beach. They also hire rollerskates, rollerblades and tandems. Another outlet on the corner of North Venice and Ocean Front Walk. ☎ 650-1076. Open for hiring until 8pm.

– If you come by car, take a tip and don't park on the private parking areas of the houses beside the beach or in the nearby streets. Your car will be impounded before you know it. Once night falls, the street life also comes to a stop, and at night, there are the same safety problems here as in many other parts of LA. Romantic evening strolls here are best avoided.

Where to Stay and **Where to Eat**: *see* the sections 'Where to Stay' and 'Where to Eat in Los Angeles'. There are quite a few private youth hostels. Unfortunately, the area is a bit menacing in the evening, with a few junkies and dealers around.

WHAT TO SEE IN VENICE

★ **Murals** (map II, C4, **12**): you shouldn't leave LA and Venice without taking a good look at some of their beautiful murals. Some of these are real works of genius and their explosive colours have brought new life to bare stretches of wall among buildings that were rather run down. Thanks to the generous involvement of sponsors, including private companies and city authorities, art has been taken onto the streets.

On the west wall of the **Venice Beach Cotel** at 25 Windward Avenue, a luminous fresco signed by one R. Cronk shows a Venice that's as much fantasy as reality, a Californian version of Botticelli's *Birth of Venus*. On the left, under the window, the rollerblading, bearded guitarist with turbaned head, is Harry Perry, a local freak who you may well bump into on Ocean Front Walk, where he spends most of his time.

★ **The Chiat-Day-Mojo Building** (map II, C3, **60**): 340 Main Street. 200 yards south of Rose Street. Here's another typically Californian architectural folly, which houses the offices of the Chiat-Day-Mojo advertising agency – one of the trendiest on the Pacific coast.

The design was by Frank Gehry, the darling of the architectural avant-garde. To get into this little PR temple, you pass through a far-from-ordinary archway in the shape of a pair of concrete binoculars, which stands 50ft (15m) high. Each 'lens' contains a mini-conference room with a panoramic view through the eyepiece.

SANTA MONICA

(LOS ANGELES MAP II)

It's at Santa Monica, that the famous *Route 66* from Chicago finally hits the Pacific, and Santa Monica Boulevard is the last straight section of this legendary road.

A natural extension of Venice to the north, Santa Monica is traditionally much more of a residential district. It's one of the closest beaches to the centre, and in summer, it's hard to reach because of the traffic jams.

The city centre around the **Third Street Promenade**, has recently been the subject of a highly successful renovation, turning it into a very up-to-date meeting place for trendies of all kinds, with cinemas, bars and restaurants. The district is lively most of the evening, by contrast with the more low-life feel that Venice Beach takes on after dark.

To get to the centre of Santa Monica, you can choose from a number of buses: Nos. 4, 20, 22, 33, 304, 320, 322, 333 and 434.

WHAT TO SEE

★ **The Getty Centre**: 1200 Getty Center Drive, Santa Monica. Open Tuesday and Wednesday 11am–7pm, Thursday and Friday till 9pm, Saturday and Sunday 10am–7pm. Closed Monday, Christmas Day, New Year's Day, 4 July and the last Thursday in November. There's no admission charge, but it costs $5 to park your car and you have to book in advance. ☎ (310) 440-7332.

The enormously wealthy oil magnate J. Paul Getty never got the chance to see his own personal museum. Getty lived in England and he died in 1976, only two years after it opened, leaving a fund of $1.3 billion to fill it with works of art. This had the effect of causing chaos in the world's art markets – price was no obstacle and the museum's administrators were able to get anything they wanted. This brought some unfortunate consequences: the museum was unable to find enough works to spend all of its money on, and along the way, succeeded in buying a few magnificent forgeries!

This museum, one of the world's greatest cultural complexes, replaces the J. Paul Getty Museum at Malibu, which is closed until 2001 for renovation. The Malibu establishment was housed in a reconstruction of the Villa dei Papiri, a luxurious building near Herculaneum that was buried along with Pompeii when Vesuvius erupted. This Getty Center is perched on one of the hills of Santa Monica, overlooking Los Angeles.

THE WORK OF RICHARD MEIER

If you arrive on foot, you come to a futuristic-looking square at the foot of the hill, and from here, you travel to the museum on a tram. As you climb, look over towards the east. The museum is an imposing construction that combines glass and Italian travertine stone, cut to allow the raw surface to reflect all the variations of the light. It was designed to be visible for miles around, and you can't miss it from the San Diego Freeway or Interstate 405. The effect is amazing.

Spread over 104,000 square yards (87,000 square metres) and set in 11 acres (4.5 hectares) of gardens, the Getty Center, the work of the architect Richard Meier, includes an institute for art research as well as the museum, and constitutes what has to be the new Californian bastion of 'high culture'.

– In the **garden**, a gigantic bouquet of azaleas geometrically arranged in a pool, brings to mind a floating island – or perhaps Catalina Island?

– The **museum** has five pavilions, one at each of the four cardinal points, plus a fifth, intended to house temporary exhibitions. The pavilions are linked in a variety of ways – by courtyards, gardens, glass-covered walkways, and in the open air. Meier's idea was to guide the visitor through the galleries by means of a cunning game of hide-and-seek with the landscape, with the visitor's eyes drawn progressively by the amazing panorama of LA. One small bonus: the exhibition galleries now proceed chronologically, which wasn't always the case!

– At the end of the tour route is a terrace, a great spot for contemplating the view of the mountains of Santa Monica, San Gabriel and Downtown.

THE MUSEUM

The permanent collections have been transferred from the Getty Museum at Malibu and are spread over two levels:

• **On the ground floor**: Graeco–Roman antiquities, sculpture, photographs, manuscripts and drawings. The 'must-sees' are the superb French 18th-century furniture and reconstructions of a Regency drawing room dating from 1810 and a neoclassical drawing room from 1788. The New York artist Thierry Despont collaborated with Meier on the design of these 13 rooms.

• **On the first floor**: breathtakingly rich collections of canvases by a throng of great masters. It's impossible to mention everything as there are 22 galleries. Canaletto, Rembrandt, Van Dyck, Ruysdael, Rubens, Poussin, and Goya are all represented. Sketches by Watteau, Chardin, Boucher, Fragonard, Delacroix, Daumier, Millet (ink drawings, pastels, charcoals, etc.). More recent acquisitions are the celebrated *Irises* by Van Gogh and Cézanne's *Still life with apples*. The layout of the museum was specially designed around them, as well as Maurice Quentin de la Tour's famous pastel work, the *Portrait of Gabriel Bernard de Rieux*, which hangs in the south pavilion.

But the museum's masterpiece is *Christ's Entry into Brussels* (1889) by James Ensor, which occupies a whole wall to itself in the west pavilion.

The Center was created as a place for cultural exchange, so do take advantage of this by asking the curators about anything that especially interests you.

★ **Museum of Flying**: 2772 Donald Douglas Loop North, Santa Monica Airport. ☎ 392-8822. Open Wednesday–Sunday 10am–5pm. To get here from Santa Monica Freeway (Route 10), take the Bundy South or Centinela South exit. Then go two blocks towards Ocean Park Boulevard, turn right and go as far as 24th Street, which you turn into on the left and go all the way to the end, where there are signs indicating the museum. For devotees of old flying machines there are three floors of Spitfires,

Skyhawks, Skyraiders, Douglas DC3s, Burma Pascals and Dago Reds, plus films, videos, documents, models, bookshops and so on.

★ **Santa Monica Pier** (map II, B2, **61**): at the southern end of 3rd Street. Very lively and hugely popular in summer. **Palisades Park,** highly valued by the homeless of the area, begins here.

★ **Third Street Promenade** (map II, A1–B1): on either side of Santa Monica Boulevard and Arizona Avenue, Third Street has been turned into a luxurious pedestrianized precinct, with trendy cafes and restaurants, such as **Yankee Doodles**, a great cinema complex with seven screens, and plenty of sophisticated shops.

– At the end, on 3rd and Broadway, is **Santa Monica Place,** an immense shopping centre with a stack of different restaurants.

MALIBU

(LOS ANGELES ENVIRONS MAP A2)

Northwest of Santa Monica stretches the very long **Pacific Coast Highway**. Take it to reach **Malibu Lagoon**, a surfing centre of world-wide renown. The houses along the beach are among the most expensive in LA, valued at between $1 and 10 million, but in design terms they're not always up to much. Most are on stilts above a minuscule strip of sand, in locations that are probably described by realtors as 'very peaceful and romantic' – i.e. squeezed between the ocean and the highway. (You have to know how to suffer to be one of the beautiful people!)

As well as this, the traffic on the coast road is insane, while many areas are private property complete with security guards and big dogs.

– You might find some of the **beaches** interesting. **Topanga State Beach** is mainly for surfing. Higher up are **Corral Beach** and **Point Dume Beach** which, in general, are nice and not heavily frequented. Up in the north, **Zuma Beach** is very popular with the Angelenos: this one is for surfers and anyone else who's desperate for a swim.

– You can get further information on the beaches here by writing to the **Department of Beaches and Harbors,** 13837 Fiji Way, Marina del Rey, CA 90292. ☎ 305-9503. Fax: 821-6345. They know their 72 miles (115km) of coast by heart, including the 40 miles (65km) of beaches, and can tell you the beaches for surfing, any regulations governing the sports there, which beaches have lifeguards, anticipated changes of weather, and all that sort of thing.

– Alternatively, if you stroll along the coast of Marina del Rey (south of Venice), you'll find a **Visitors' Center** on the corner of Admiralty and Mindanao. ☎ 305-9545. Open daily, 9am–5pm. Tourist literature and more information about the beaches and surfing.

–The stars who live in **Pacific Palisades** include Tom Cruise, Steven Spielberg, Arnold Schwarzenegger, Michael Keaton and John Travolta.

– And **Malibu** is the home of Tom Hanks, John McEnroe, Mel Gibson, Charles Bronson, Dustin Hoffman, Pat Benatar, Bob Dylan, Whoopi Goldberg, Nick Nolte and Sean Penn.

✕ A little further north on Route 1, which goes along the coast, there's a great bar and coffee shop about level with Malibu Pier: the **Malibu Inn**. The restaurant dining room is filled with dozens of old photos of Hollywood stars, and more recent ones too, who have come here to savour the cuisine. The decor is very 'Western'. If you're travelling north one morning, this is a great place to stop for breakfast.

OTHER MUSEUMS AND PLACES TO SEE AROUND LOS ANGELES

★ **Southwest Museum**: 234 Museum Drive. ☎ 221-2164. Open Tuesday–Sunday 11am–5pm. Closed Monday and public holidays. Northeast of LA. Quite a long way from the city centre, between Glendale and Pasadena, some blocks west of Highway 110. RTD bus No. 83.

This is a very interesting museum for anyone with an interest in the art of the Native Americans, who live in territory as scattered as Alaska and South America. Founded in 1907, this is one of the oldest museums in LA; its large, luminous galleries display superb tunics, textiles, prehistoric painted pottery and wickerwork. There's a rich Meso-American and Pre-Columbian art section with pottery, textiles and Spanish colonial art. Educational programmes, including lectures, traditional dances and films are run throughout the year. The museum shop is well stocked.

– At the same time, you can visit the **Casa de Adobe** at 4605 North Figueroa. Take a No. 81 RTD. bus, if you're going straight there. This place is furnished and decorated like a residence of the Spanish period. It has a pretty kitchen with a clay oven and antique domestic articles. From time to time you can see Mexican dance shows there.

★ **Natural History Museum**: 900 Exposition Boulevard. ☎ 744-DINO and 744-3414. Open 10am–5pm. Closed Monday. Free admission on the first Tuesday of the month. South of Highway 10 and the University of Southern California (USC), some blocks west of Route 110, between Figueroa and Vermont. To get here, take a No. 40 or 42 bus from Downtown. Coming from the North, catch a No. 204 bus at Vermont. Coming from Santa Monica, get a No. 20, 22 or 320 bus and connect with a No. 204. From Venice, you need a No. 333 bus (Venice Boulevard).

This is the biggest natural history museum in the West, with rich collections of animals displayed in reconstructions of their natural environment. There are sections on reptiles and birds, as well as displays on minerals, fossils and dinosaurs, as well as temporary exhibitions on special subjects. And there's a **Discovery Center** for kids.

★ **California Museum of Science and Industry**: 700 State Drive, Exposition Park. Entrance at Exposition Boulevard and Figueroa. ☎ (213) 744-7400. Open daily, 10am–5pm. Free (except for the IMAX Theater). This is a contemporary museum of science and technology that tells you all about the conquest of space, earthquakes, energy, health, mathematics, economics, the planet's food supplies, and more.

• The **IMAX Theater** presents an extraordinary movie environment: the screen is five floors high, 75ft (23m) wide, with six-track sound. The image is 10 times larger than that of a 35mm film, so these films will almost literally take your breath away, with coverage of such things as incredible sporting exploits, spectacular volcanic eruptions and so on. A normal programme consists of four films. Call for their timetable: ☎ (213) 744-2014, 744-2015 (recorded message) and 744-2019.

• Next door is the **Aerospace Building**: open on the same days and at the same times. Admission is free. As you'd expect, this place is for anyone with an interest in old airplanes and space capsules.

★ **California African–American Museum**: 600 State Street, Exposition Park. ☎ (213) 744-74-32. Open daily, 10am–5pm. Free. This museum is devoted to African–American art, with displays of painting and sculpture, as well as temporary exhibitions. Decent bookshop.

★ **Pet cemeteries**: instead of having their pets treated chemically and converted into fertilizer (pets may not be buried in your garden, according to Californian law), many Angelenos have them buried in the two pet cemeteries on the outskirts of LA. The minimum cost is $150, to which you have to add a supplementary charge for a mahogany coffin. It's interesting to visit one of these cemeteries – they're quite unique. There's one on the Ventura Freeway, 20 miles from LA, but it's not easy to find – ask for directions when you're nearby. It's called **Los Angeles Pet Park**.

SAN FERNANDO VALLEY

(LOS ANGELES ENVIRONS MAP A1)

★ **The 94th Aero Squadron**: 16320 Raymer Avenue, Van Nuys. ☎ (818) 994-7437. To get here from LA, take Freeway 405 north, exit at Roscoe Boulevard, take a left on Roscoe, then another left on Woodley and a right on Raymer, and go right to the end of the road. Here, you'll find an unforgettable restaurant – it's a replica of a French farm during World War II, complete with planes, sandbags, jeeps and military trucks. And, a thoughtful touch, the waitresses are dressed up as nurses. All this should leave you feeling totally immersed in an atmosphere that says: 'the day after the Allied landings, somewhere in Normandy'. The outside terrace is right next to one of the runways of Van Nuys Airport – one of the world's busiest private airports.

The menu is relatively limited, but the Italian–Mexican–French–American cuisine is decent and the prices are reasonable. There's a buffet lunch at weekends or you can just have a drink on the terrace.

This is an airport where many student pilots learn to fly, and you may see the occasional spectacular landing.

FURTHER NORTH

★ **Six Flags Magic Mountain**: take Freeway 405 North (which then becomes Route 5 North) and exit at the Magic Mountain Parkway. You're then 35 miles (60km) northwest of Los Angeles city centre. The Gray

Lines buses call here. ☎ 481-2121. Open daily, 10am–10pm between Memorial Day and Labor Day; for the rest of the year, on weekends and during school holidays, open at times that seem to vary according to the number of visitors. ☎ (805) 255-41-00. The admission charge is high. It's advisable not to come here at weekends, because there are long waits for everything. Remember that you can pick up coupons from your hotel that will give you a reduction – some coupons cover up to six people if they're members of the same family. Make a really good mental note of where your car is parked, and use the free shuttle to get to the park.

The park has 40 attractions, including some that are totally unheard of in Europe, particularly the famous rollercoasters, which rotate through every possible axis. There's the **Revolution**, the only rollercoaster going through a 360° vertical loop, the **Colossus**, the biggest wooden rollercoaster in the world, and the **Viper** (in which you hang upside down), which performs phenomenal loops and leaves most people totally shattered! Don't miss **Superman**, **the Escape** – a carriage that accelerates from zero to 100mph (160kph) in seven seconds (equivalent to ascending a 41-storey tower). There's also the **Craft Village**, a 384-ft (117m) high **observation tower**, and the **Showcase Theater**, where stars put on variety shows. If you'd like to get a good idea of what it's like to go down the Colorado River in a boat, don't miss the **Roaring Rapids**: it's a lot of fun, but expect to get very wet!

– Next door, **Six Flags Hurricane Harbor** features 22 fountains that children seem to love, with each toboggan crazier than the last. Try **Black Snake Summit**, the highest in California, or **Bamboo Racer,** or **Reptile Ridge**. Open daily, from 10am, June to early September. A swimming costume is indispensable.

ANAHEIM (DISNEYLAND)

AREA CODE: 714

Twenty-five miles (40km) southeast of the centre of Los Angeles.

– **For all information**: ☎ 999-4565. From LA: ☎ 999-45-65. By post: Disneyland Guest Relations, PO Box 3232, Anaheim, CA 92803.

HOW TO GET THERE

BY BUS

From 6th Street, take the No. 460 **RTD bus**. It'll take 90 minutes and costs only $3. When you leave, you have to come down Harbor Boulevard, on the right as you come out of Disneyland. The stop is just three blocks away, or 10 minutes' walk. The **Greyhound bus** is faster than the RTD bus. Departures are frequent from the Downtown terminal at 208 E 6th Street, on the corner of Los Angeles Street (but note that there are no departures from Union Station). If you plan to arrive at the park around 8.30am, aim to leave LA at about 7am, because the next departure is not until 9am. The Greyhound terminal is about 20 minutes' walk from the entrance to Disneyland, on the other side of the Freeway, but don't leave your luggage at the Greyhound terminal, because the left-luggage office closes at 7.30pm. You can use the lockers at Disneyland itself, which can be found on the main square after the entrance.

BY CAR

Take the Santa Ana Freeway (Route 5) then the 'Disneyland' exit.

ONCE UPON A TIME . . . THE DISNEY STORY

Mickey arrived in Hollywood in 1928, but unlike many other characters, he didn't begin life on a strip cartoon. Mickey was an animated hero right from the start, although right up until the 1940s he played only supporting roles – the star in those days was Pluto. Disney himself was not an exceptional artist, and very soon gave up drawing. But he was a man of genius, able both to originate ideas and to implement them. His first brilliant idea was to give his heroes facial expressions that expressed their thoughts and feelings.

The story goes that Disney acquired a little mouse, which he named Mortimer. His wife insisted on renaming it Mickey, a much less high-flown name. Thus history was made. Later on, she was also not in favour of the name 'Donald' for the eminent duck, but this time Disney got his way.

For the ease of the studio artists, Mickey consisted of a number of circles: ears, head, eyes . . . even the buttons on his shorts. It's probably for this reason that he has no whiskers! As a character, Mickey is not always very courageous, but has the heroism of the good guy, and often sets about defending Minnie's honour. He is timid with girls, but nevertheless shows a certain nobility of character. In short, he's a respectable fellow and sets a good example to the children! Curiously, Benito Mussolini, the pre-war Italian dictator, prohibited all American comics except *Mickey Mouse*. The Nazis, by contrast, announced in 1931 that Mickey Mouse was 'an expression of the most contemptible ideal ever revealed to the world'. Could this be why the Allies used his name as their password during the 1944 Normandy landings?

Disney became convinced very early on that the future lay in the talkies. *Steamboat Willie* was the first animated cartoon to have a synchronized soundtrack, and it's still shown at Disneyland. Interestingly, the nasal voice of Mickey was produced by none other than Walt himself.

Another stroke of Disney's genius was his concentration on marketing and market studies before these subjects had been identified and named. He would take his crew out to the cinema whenever his latest animated cartoon was being shown. The reactions of the audience were duly noted, and a post mortem followed in which they would try to thrash out exactly why some gags worked and others didn't. Mickey was developed as a 'real' character, and if a child phoned Disneyland asking to speak to Mickey, the operator would reply sympathetically that he was unfortunately having a siesta.

Most of his other star characters were easier to find as they did not have to be invented. Disney quite simply looted children's fairytales that were in the public domain. *Cinderella* was taken from the fairy tale by Charles Perrault, *Alice in Wonderland* was borrowed from Lewis Carroll, the story of *Pinocchio* was written by Carlo Collodi, the boy Mowgli was a Rudyard

Kipling character, Captain Nemo had been created by Jules Verne and the *Hunchback of Notre-Dame* was written by Victor Hugo.

Walt Disney died on 15 December 1966 at the age of 65 and Disney World in Florida opened its doors in 1971.

THE MAGIC KINGDOM

TICKETS AND ADMISSION CHARGES

Don't forget that Unca' Scrooge McDuck is at the cash desk, so the admission charge is high, although it does allow you free and unlimited admission to all the attractions in the park. There's no charge for children under two. Small reductions are available for children aged three–11 years and for people over 60 (but not Saturday June–September).

You can buy one-, two- or three-day tickets to the Magic Kingdom, and it's OK to go out and come back in, but don't forget to have your hand stamped at the exit.

INFORMATION

– At the parking lot (where you have to pay), it's advisable to make a note of the exact **number** of your space and, also the **name** of the parking lot. You may not find it otherwise, at the end of a long day on your feet.

– There are lockers at the entrance, for a small charge.

– Strollers are available for hire.

EXTREMELY IMPORTANT: it's best not to come here at weekends or during the Christmas and New Year festivities, as the whole place is packed and you'll spend several hours in queues. Summer afternoons are not brilliant, either, and it's a good idea to check on the dates of American public holidays, because they're even more crowded than the weekends.

A HOT TIP: in summer, Magic Kingdom is generally open 9am–midnight. In fact, the gates open at 8am in order to deal with the queues. Between 9am and 10am, you should be able to trot swiftly round the most popular attractions. Starting on the left, these are **Indiana Jones**, **The Pirates of the Caribbean**, **The Haunted Mansion**, **Big Thunder Mountain Railroad**, and **Space Mountain**. This should reduce your queuing time by two or three hours!

– Then, when thousands of visitors seem to be coming from all directions, make for the less busy attractions such as **Liberty Square Riverboat** or **Tom Sawyer Island**.

– As all this makes for a very long day under the hot sun, you may wish to go back to the car for a siesta. Ask for a free re-entry stamp at the exit.

You can even leave the parking lot and return later (only on the same day, of course), but you'll need to keep your ticket.

– The winter timetable (9am–6pm) starts on Labor Day (the first Monday in September). There are no more parades, and some attractions are closed, but the prices stay the same.

WHAT TO SEE

The *Guide Map* provided by Disneyland shows you the location of all the sights. Grab a copy, to make sure you don't miss anything.

The houses lining Main Street are quite superb, and it's interesting to note that in building them, they used false perspective. This is a technique commonly used on movie sets – the second and third floors are made progressively smaller, giving an illusion of height and distance. This process was invented by the ancient Greeks and features in the Parthenon!

★ On **Main Street**, the **Penny Arcade** has lots of pre-war slot-machines. Some of these are superb, particularly 'Electricity Is Life'. They all take the good old penny, nickel, dime or quarter.

– Still on Main Street, there's a little movie theatre with six screens showing *Steamboat Willie*, the first animated cartoon with a soundtrack, made by Disney in 1928. A historic masterpiece.

★ On the right at the entrance are **The Walt Disney Story** and **Great Moments with Mister Lincoln**, a tribute to the 16th president of the United States.

★ **Space Mountain**: at Tomorrow Land. This ride is definitely *the* Disneyland hit, and it's a must. You are whisked into a thrilling interstellar journey seated at the controls of a space ship and you're propelled at high speed (actually reaching 30mph/45kph) through a dark night lit by a terrifying shower of meteorites. This is like being on a rollercoaster ride through space – the special effects are superb.

★ **Star Tours**: next to Space Mountain. This is a journey through space, created by George Lucas (*Star Wars*). It's quite a turbulent ride, and a very popular one, so expect to queue.

★ **Submarine Voyage**: a trip in a yellow submarine that goes off to explore the North Pole.

★ **Circle Vision**: a showing of the film *American Journeys* on a circular screen that enables you to explore America, its amazing landscapes and the people who live there. It's a superb spectacle, although some bits are rather nationalistic; the film may be an uncomfortable reminder of Disney's staunch support for Senator Joseph McCarthy.

★ **The Pirates of the Caribbean**: New Orleans Square. The sets for this ride are superb. You're out in a boat in the days when pirates roamed the seas. It's night and you pass through a string of fishermen's villages, populated by pirates of the most alarming kind. Suddenly, the shout goes up, guns fire and cannons boom, and another pirate ship hauls in alongside . . . Expect to get a bit wet on this one!

★ **Haunted Mansion**: Liberty Square. Don't say you're too scared, and don't waste time thinking up excuses for not going in: you just have to accept the invitation offered by this crowd of phantoms from the great beyond! Just picture yourself . . . crouched in a little carriage, threading your way through narrow, dark corridors and dusty rooms. You'll come across the dance of the phantoms, but beware the friendly vampire – who will happily suck your blood given half a chance. Screams, groans, ghosts, vampires . . . it all builds up to the scariest moment of all, when a dozen ghostly holograms join up to perform a slow, terrifying waltz (remember Polanski's *Dance of the Vampires*?). Go on – be brave!

★ **Indiana Jones Adventure**: Adventureland. As you'd expect, this is one of the biggest attractions. You make the journey in a kind of oversized jeep that whisks you into the maze below the accursed Temple of the Forbidden Eye. There are streams of lava, poisoned arrows, rotten vermin, menacing snakes, falling stones . . . all to be avoided at all costs. Just like in the film, really.

★ **Jungle Cruise**: the mysterious world of the tropical forest. Nothing is missing: wild animals, unfriendly natives – you name it.

★ **Big Thunder Mountain Railroad**: Frontierland. This is a crazy trip on board a runaway train – a small Wild West mining train that belches out smoke and steam as you rush through tunnels and down to the depths of the mines only to re-emerge in a Gold Rush town hidden in the heart of the red-rock mountain.

★ Still at Frontierland. If you really want to get into the atmosphere of the Wild West, go to the B-movie-style saloon, the **Golden Horseshoe Stage**. This is a cabaret show (done in good taste – for the sake of the children) and it's very popular (it's best to book your afternoon seat in the morning). Shows are at 11.15am, 12.45pm, 2.30pm, 4pm and 5.15pm, but check first because these times could change.

★ The popular **Mark Twain Steam Boat** has reopened following a $60 million renovation, and gives you a nice trip on a Mississippi riverboat.

★ **Splash Mountain**: Critter Country. A rollercoaster ride on a tree-trunk along a rushing river and heading towards . . . an unforgettable finale. The length of the queue tells its own story! This is the longest 'fall' anywhere in the world. Naturally, it's to be avoided by small children, pregnant women and anyone who might succumb to vertigo.

★ **Fantasy Follies**: Plaza Garden. For the tinies. Every hour, there are parades of life-size Disney characters all singing and dancing.

If you think Disneyland is just for kids, forget it – you ain't seen nothing yet!

WHERE TO STAY

See 'Where to Stay in Anaheim' in the Los Angeles section, where reasonably priced campgrounds and motels are listed.

WHERE TO EAT

Food is quite expensive at Disneyland. You aren't allowed to take food or drink in with you (what a surprise!), but this doesn't stop most visitors taking in something, discreetly hidden in their bags. There's a picnic area beside the main entrance, and anyone hooked on Coke and burgers will find them on sale here at the same prices as anywhere else. As health-food conscious as everyone else these days, the Disney brochure even lists restaurants where you can get spaghetti without sauce and non-fat frozen yoghurt!

✕ If you have any dollars left, enjoy a salad in the **Blue Bayou**, on New Orleans Square. There's probably not another restaurant anywhere with such fabulous decor – the setting is a Louisiana plantation under a brilliantly starry sky.

WHAT TO SEE NEAR DISNEYLAND

The **Town Tour Funbus** in Anaheim (☎ 365-1390) runs buses from Disneyland. Their No. 4 bus serves Knott's Berry Farm, Buena Park Shopping Center, Movie World and Movieland Wax Museum, stopping at many hotels in Anaheim. Departures are every hour 9am–6pm. There's a return journey from Knott's Berry Farm to the Disneyland area. If you're hard up, take the No. 802 RTD bus.

★ **Knott's Berry Farm**: 8039 Beach Boulevard, Buena Park, south of Santa Ana Freeway, 6 miles (10km) from Disneyland. ☎ (714) 220-5200. Open summer 9am–11pm (midnight Saturday and Sunday); winter 10am–6pm (10pm Saturday and 7pm Sunday).

This 151-acre (61-hectare) park started life as a roadside snack bar run by farmer Walter Knotts and his wife, Cordelia, who became famous for her chicken dinners and fruit pies (you can still eat them here today). At Knott's Berry Farm, everything's a whole lot more personal than its two rivals (Disneyland and Six Flags Magic Mountain) – they still have the stomach-churning rides, but the staff pay you a bit of extra attention.

Probably the most interesting of the attractions is the astonishing **Ghost Town**, which has a saloon, railroad station, trading post, gunshop, smithy, prison and even a seedy hotel! You can visit a mine, take a trip in an old steam train under attack, and even search for gold.

There's an interesting **Museum of the West**, where you can examine photographs dating from the Gold Rush, gold nuggets, cowboy tools, firearms, etc. The **Native American village** is also fascinating, with its authentic teepees, hogans, and traditional songs and dances. And there's an impressive figure-of-eight ride, shooting the rapids, etc.

✕ There are several restaurants here: the best and least expensive is probably the **Firemen's Brigade**. Here you can eat grilled meats at a big outdoor table. Or perhaps try one of Mrs Knott's 'chicken dinners'.

★ **Movieland Wax Museum**: 7711 Beach Boulevard. Near Knott's Berry Farm. ☎ (714) 522-1155. Open daily, 9am–9.30pm (10am in winter), but note that the cash desks close at 8pm. This is a really successful wax museum that has nothing in common with all the tacky places that tend to give this type of show a bad name. Opened in 1962 and inaugurated by Mary Pickford, the museum has 250 wax likenesses of famous actors, many of them astonishingly good, with each figure set in meticulously correct surroundings.

The models are generally posed in a scene from a film for which they are remembered, so you'll see scenes from such movies as *African Queen*, *Gone With the Wind*, *Rear Window*, *Singing in the Rain*, *Spartacus*, *West*

Side Story, etc. Some are highly evocative, such as Jean Harlow in *Dinner at Eight*, Gary Cooper in *High Noon*, Jerry Lewis in *Doctor Jerry and Mister Love*, and Kevin Costner in *Dances with Wolves*. Interestingly, the models are often dressed in costumes that were actually used in the films and have been donated by the stars or the studios. With a good nose for business, the organizers make you struggle past an array of opportunely positioned gift shops before you leave.

For lovers of the gruesome and the grotesque, there's a **Chamber of Horrors** featuring scenes from 15 classic horror films, including *The Exorcist* and *Halloween*.

★ **Ripley's Believe It Or Not**: 7850 Beach Boulevard. ☎ (714) 522-7045. Right opposite the Wax Museum and under the same management. A subsidiary of the famous 'Believe It Or Not', which is to be found in many American cities. If this is what you like – then you'll like this. The exhibits can be rather uneven but there are some spectacular videos and really strange phenomena.

★ **Medieval Times**: opposite Movieland Wax Museum. Shows on Monday, Tuesday and Thursday at 6pm and 8.30pm, Wednesday at 5pm, Friday at 6.15pm and 9pm, Saturday at 4pm, 6.30pm and 9.15pm, Sunday at 1pm, 4.45pm and 7.30pm. You get a medieval banquet with a jousting tournament – it's quite expensive and all rather 'American'.

★ **Crystal Cathedral**: 13490 Chapman Avenue, corner of Lewis Street. A few minutes south of Disneyland. You can see this extraordinary 230-ft (70m) glass cathedral from Freeway 5. It cost the modest sum of $10 million and was built in 1977 by Robert Schuller, America's most famous pastor, whose sermons are transmitted on dozens of TV channels to an audience of around 1.7 million. Even if you aren't in the habit, you might go to Sunday Mass (9am and 11am). It's a big show with its Hollywood-style production numbers. There are also organ concerts at lunchtime almost every day.

★ **Orange Drive-in**: a gigantic drive-in right beside Freeway 5, close to the Disneyland exit. Useful if you're thinking about staying in this area.

HOW TO BECOME A FIGHTER PILOT IN ONE DAY

– **Air Combat USA**: at Fullerton (North of Anaheim), Box 2726. ☎ (714) 522-7590. It's incredible: over 3,000 individuals, among them plumbers, computer scientists, teachers, farmers, nurses and students (only the pretty affluent ones, though), have so far flown a real fighter plane on a sortie hoping to shoot down the enemy.

After a briefing on the flight details, the apprentice Top Guns get their money's worth in the form of a flight with the pros, experiencing all the sensations that are the daily fare of a fighter pilot. Of course, you don't get to shoot off a real missile at your adversary, but you can zap them with a laser beam which, if you strike home, sets off a smoke generator. Such heady experiences do carry a certain cost, as you will have guessed: this can be anywhere between $400 and $2,300, depending on the options you select (extra engagements, steep climbs, loops, etc.). Take your pick! At the end, the new Tom Cruises leave, walking tall with a video of their exploits (which is included in the price).

ALONG THE COAST TO SAN DIEGO

★ LONG BEACH

★ **The *Queen Mary***: at Long Beach, the *Queen Mary* is one of the largest passenger ships ever built. From Downtown in Los Angeles, take the Blue Line, a tram that links Downtown with Long Beach. By car, follow the Long Beach Freeway (Route 7) right down to the southern end. Approximately 25 miles (40km) from the centre of LA. Take the Queen Mary exit. ☎ 435-3511. Open 22 June–Labor Day 9am–7pm (you have to buy your tickets one hour ahead); rest of the year 10am–6pm. Coupons giving reductions can be found in some hotels.

Launched in 1934, this ship was bought by the city of Long Beach and turned into a Museum of Navigation. The *Queen Mary*'s past is intimately linked with event-packed years, and she carried many illustrious passengers including Winston Churchill, Clark Gable and Greta Garbo.

Some of the scenes from the ship's heyday have been reconstructed, using wax figures: you see a young couple in the restaurant and get a glimpse into the ship's gaming room. The days of World War II are recaptured: the *Queen Mary* was requisitioned to carry troops. You can also tour the cabins and the bridge. The observation bar is a masterpiece of art deco and the swimming pool and the engine room are both worth a look. Some of the cabins have been furnished as hotel rooms in art-deco style and they're not enormously expensive. Reservations: ☎ (310) 432-6964.

> **TIP**: one excellent way to pay a visit here is to come for Sunday brunch, (11am–2pm). There are seven international buffets, with unlimited champagne. The cuisine is quite refined and portions are generous. The tour of the ship is included in the price of the brunch, which is extremely reasonable.

★ **Long Beach Museum of Arts**: 2300 E Ocean Boulevard. ☎ (310) 439-2119. Open Wednesday–Sunday noon–5pm (8pm Thursday). Closed Monday and Tuesday. Situated in a fine residence dating from 1912 that overlooks the ocean. Displays of contemporary painting, plus temporary exhibitions and videos.

★ **Shoreline Village**: on the other side of the bay, near Downtown and the Convention Center. A sort of (not-very-well- !) reconstructed fishermen's village, where the multicoloured timber shacks house souvenir shops and restaurants.

★ **Long Beach Aquarium of the Pacific**: 310 Golden Shores. ☎ (562) 590-3100. Opened to a rapturous reception from adults and children alike a couple of years ago. More than 10,000 fish from over 500 different species – and each more amazing than the last. The highlight of the visit is definitely the 15 or so 'heavyweights' . . . sharks, whales and the like. Don't miss it.

★ **Catalina Cruises**: 320 Golden Shores Boulevard. ☎ 1-800-338-8767 (information and reservations). Less than an hour away from the city you can get an island break on Catalina Island, arranging your schedule of activities in advance from a good menu of options. Various options are available, but the price includes transport by sea, the hotel room and activities such as golf, fishing, diving or climbing. There are also a casino, numerous restaurants and bars and just about everything you might need for a good mini-break.

✕ **Parker's Lighthouse** has a remarkable view of the *Queen Mary*. They serve a good Seaside Sunday Breakfast on the patio, 10am–1pm Sunday.

★ THE SOUTH COAST BEACHES

If you want to return to San Diego by car and you're not in a hurry, you can go along the Pacific Coast Highway as far as Dana Point, then rejoin the San Diego Freeway (Route 5). This is longer, but a very pleasant drive.

For some years this region has been attracting affluent Americans who have tired of Malibu or Santa Monica. There are superb beaches that extend for miles – such as **Seal Beach** and **Sunset Beach**, often a favoured haunt for surfers.

There are large seaside resorts like **Huntington Beach** or **Newport** Beach, and smaller ones like **Laguna Beach**.

Some beaches are equipped with showers and this makes them rather attractive as a place to stop for a few hours.

ADVICE ON SURFING

You may be surprised and disappointed to find that the waves here are often smaller than in Europe. It's just the opposite of what you'd expect, but still, they do vary according to season and location. In general, the beaches around Los Angeles aren't the best ones for surfing. You have to go either south or north to find good waves.

– **Going south**: take Freeway 405 or Route 1. **Huntington Beach** is good, and the place is something of a 'Surf City', and there's even a museum of surfing. At **Newport Beach**, you have to watch your timing. In summer, no surfing is allowed between noon and 4pm but there are many bathers and body-boarders around. There are some very beautiful beaches here but, inevitably, they're overcrowded in the summer. Further south, continuing along the Pacific Coast Highway as far as **San Clemente** and **San Onofre**, you'll find **state beaches** with paid parking. You can leave your car outside, and go in on foot. The simplest way is to follow the local surfers. There are other interesting sites at Encinitas and La Jolla, near San Diego.

– **Going north**: **Malibu**, of course, is a legendary city from the early days of surfing in California. There are good sites, but there are too many people there in summer. Continue along Freeway 1 until you get to the boundary of Los Angeles County and Ventura County: this is a well-known site, the **County Line**, a wild beach at the side of the road and at the foot of the mountains. Opposite, there's a snack bar where some scenes in *Point Break*. were shot. This is a rendezvous for surfers of all kinds and it's very easy to find. There are usually excellent waves with a rising tide. Furthest north is **Santa Barbara**, the hometown of Tom Curren, the world surfing champion, who now lives in Biarritz. As the hard-core surfers say, when there's a swell, you'll get superb 'glossy waves' here.

FROM LOS ANGELES TO LAS VEGAS

WHERE TO STAY AND WHERE TO EAT

KOA Campground: at Yermo. ☎ (760) 254-2311. Between Calico and Barstow.

Calico Motel: at Yermo (Highway 15 and Ghost Town Road). ☎ (760) 254-2419. Small, very cheap motel on the edge of the highway. Rooms are furnished in positively pre-war style but they're well kept.

✕ **Peggy Sue's**: next to the Calico Motel. ☎ (760) 254-3370. Last orders 10pm. An amusing little backpacker-style restaurant with a 1950s feel and a very nice atmosphere. An ample menu, with stuff ranging from the 'Buddy Holly Bacon Cheeseburger' to the 'Lana Turner Tuna Salad', via the 'Hank Williams Chilli Spaghetti'.

WHAT TO SEE

★ VICTORVILLE

This town, situated between LA and Barstow, is of no interest except for its museum, which is dedicated to Roy Rogers, who, for generations of Americans, was everyone's idea of 'the cowboy'.

Housed in an imitation cavalry fort at the side of the highway, the **Roy Rogers–Dale Evans Museum** celebrates Roy Rogers' long career. He made more than 100 films and hosted a TV show between 1935 and 1952. Dale Evans was his wife and co-starred in many of his movies. Open daily, 9am-5pm.

★ BARSTOW

The **factory outlet** at Barstow is a priority stop – if you're into shopping! There are around 100 brand-name shops (including Timberland, Ralph Lauren, Levi's, etc.) that offer savings of between 25 and 70 per cent . . . but only if you spend a lot of dough. As always, the goods are slight seconds. Open daily, 9am–8pm. On Route I-15, one exit before the city of Barstow if you're coming from LA.

★ CALICO

Calico is a real ghost town (though it's not such a great example!) situated east of Barstow, on Highway 15, (not Route 15). There are tours daily, 8am–sundown. In the 1890s, Calico was a prosperous town that owed its success to a silver mine whose annual production was worth nearly $86 million, and you can tour the place on the small train that once carried the precious ore. There's a campground in the vicinity, in the canyon, but there's not much shade to be had there.

If you like, you can dress up as a pioneer gold prospector in order to have your photo taken. And don't miss the leaning house – you'll think you've got gravity beaten!

This is an extremely touristy place, where every building is a souvenir shop, and the saloon sells burgers. Fossil collectors will find plenty of inexpensive specimens on sale.

★ THE REAL 'BAGDAD CAFE'

Tucked away in Newberry Springs, 46548 National Trail Highway. ☎ (760) 257-3101. Open daily, 6am–9pm. Website: www.kaiwan.com/-wem/bagdad.html

Do you remember the wonderful film *Bagdad Cafe*? – it featured the captivating voice of Jevetta Steele singing *Calling You*. Made by the German director Percy Adlon, the film won an Oscar for the best foreign film of 1989 and became the young people's cult film of the year. The motel and bar where the movie was filmed is right in the middle of the Californian desert, on Route 66 and away from Highway 40, which links Barstow and Ludlow. Exit at Newberry Springs, then drive for another 2 miles (3km), following the signs.

The 'middle-of-nowhere' atmosphere still pervades the place. Inside the bar, the walls are adorned with autographed photographs taken during the filming. The cafe sells all the standards items that you'd expect, plus excellent milkshakes.

Behind the cafe, there's still a piece of the famous tank that was carried on to the highway by a violent gust of wind. This place is a must if you're anything of a film fan: it's only 12 miles (19km) east of Barstow and you can get back onto Highway 15 without having to retrace your route.

SAN DIEGO

AREA CODE: 619

San Diego is 127 miles (205km) south of Los Angeles and 16 miles (25km) from the Mexican border at Tijuana. California's second-largest city in terms of population, San Diego was skipped by the railroad in the 19th century and therefore experienced no large-scale immigration compared to what happened in San Francisco or Los Angeles.

Facing the ocean, San Diego is a pleasant place. With a hot, dry climate and an exceptional location on two well-protected bays, it is a highly prized residential centre, with real-estate projects progressing explosively in the Downtown area.

PUBLIC TRANSPORT

– **Arriving at the airport**: the No. 2 bus serves Downtown.

– **Rainbow Ride Shuttle Service**: serves the city's hotels from the airport. ☎ 695-3830.

– **Greyhound** (map I, B2): 120 West Broadway, level with 1st Avenue.

– **Transit Store**: 102 Broadway Street. ☎ 233-3004 or 234-1060. Open

Monday–Friday 8.30am–5.30pm, Saturday and Sunday noon–4pm. Information on the timetables and routes of the San Diego bus and trolley services. You can also buy from here a one-day-pass ($5) or a four-day pass ($15). They also provide information about the Coaster, which links all the stations along the coast.

USEFUL ADDRESSES

Visitors' Center (map I, B2): 11 Horton Plaza, entrance in 1st Avenue. ☎ 236-1212. Website: www.sandiego.org. Open Monday–Saturday 8.30am–5pm, Sunday 11am–5pm. Friendly and efficient. Maps, brochures (including the useful *San Diego Official Visitors Planning Guide*), phone cards and booklets called *Sunny Money* or *Traveller Discount Guide*, which contain lots of money-off coupons.

✉ **Post office**: small office in Horton Plaza. The office in the centre with the best location is at 815 East Street. Open Monday–Friday 8.30am–5pm, Saturday 8.30am–noon.

■ **Times Arts Tix**: Center Broadway Circle, in the Horton Plaza. ☎ 497-5000. Open Tuesday–Saturday 10am–5pm. They sell tickets for the theatre or concerts. Buy them in advance or on the same day (50 per cent reduction on same-day purchases). They also sell discounted tickets for admission to the Zoo, Wild Park and Sea World.

■ **Bank of America**: 450 B Street. ☎ 230-6200. You can get cash here on your Visa card.

■ **American Express**: 258 Broadway. ☎ 234-4455.

■ **Thomas Cook**: Money Exchange, Horton Plaza. Freephone: ☎ 1-800-287-7362.

■ **Pharmacy**: Sharp Cabrillo Hospital, 3475 Kenyon Street. ☎ 221-3400. Closed midnight–7am.

■ **Car hire**: Rent-a-Wreck, 1904 Hotel Circle North. ☎ 228-8235.

■ **Mexican Consulate**: 1549 India Street (corner with Ash). ☎ 231-8414. Open Monday–Friday 9am–3pm.

BOOKSTORES

■ **The Store for Travellers**: 745 4th Avenue. ☎ 544-0005. In the Gaslamp District. Books, travel guides, maps and equipment of every kind.

■ **Upstart Crow**: in Seaport Village, 835 West Harbor Drive. ☎ 232-4855. Good store, which also operates as a coffee-house.

WHERE TO STAY

DOWNTOWN AND SURROUNDINGS

☆ BUDGET

Hostelling International – The Metropolitan (youth hostel) (map I, C3, **10**): 521 Market Street. ☎ 525-1531. Fax: 338-0129. Very central, in a building renovated in 1997. They provide 100 beds in dormitories for four or six persons, and four double rooms. No curfew (just as well, when you think of all the things you can do in the area). You can cook your meals here and do your laundry.

☗ **The Inn at the YMCA** (map I, B2, **11**): 500 West Broadway, very close to the Santa Fe station. ☎ 234-5252. Fax: 234-5272. Central, in a fine 1924 building. You don't have to have a youth hostel membership card. There are 225 rooms for one or two people (with communal bathrooms) at prices that seem very reasonable given the situation and the services they provide, which include a swimming pool, sauna and fitness room. Get breakfast in the Grand Central Cafe.

☗ **Grand Pacific Hostel** (map I, C3, **12**): 726 5th Avenue. ☎ 232-3100. Fax: 232-3106. Very central, right in the middle of the Gaslamp District, which is very lively in the evening. This is an old Victorian-style hotel furnished as a hotel for backpackers. The ambiance is warm and friendly and the welcome is excellent. The eight clean dormitories are each fitted with six beds, and there are eight double rooms. There are fans in the rooms. Breakfast is included in the price. There's a large communal kitchen, you can do your laundry and there are some bikes you can use at no charge. The cost of the evening meal is incredibly low and you don't have to do housework. There's a minibus shuttle to the beach daily, and another to LA on Monday and Thursday. In addition, the hostel organizes excursions at reasonable prices to Tijuana and into Mexico.

☗ **Jim's San Diego** (map I, D2, **13**): 1425 C Street. ☎ 235-0234. To get here, take a trolley beside the Greyhound station. Get off at City College, which is three blocks away. A private youth hostel in two Victorian-style residences. The small dormitories have four beds and everything's very well kept. Well-equipped kitchen plus washing machines. There's a pleasant patio between the buildings and a sunny balcony and little garden at the back. The manager knows the city thoroughly.

☗ **The Maryland Hotel** (map I, C2, **14**): 630 F Street. ☎ 239-9243. Fax: 235-8968. No distance at all from the city centre. This is a fine old building that's been entirely renovated and offers among the cheapest double rooms in Downtown. Attractive prices by the week. Good welcome. It's worth noting that, by arrangement with the city authorities, the hotel houses most of the city's mentally handicapped.

☗ **Golden West Hotel** (map I, C3, **15**): 720 4th Avenue. Level with G Street and not far from Horton Plaza. ☎ 233-7594/96. Fax: 233-4009. An old hotel dating back to 1913 that you really do have to see, if only for the reception lobby, which has an immense wooden counter – the kind you last saw in a 1920s movie. This place is rather retro – still, it's central. There are reductions if you pay by the week, so it's no surprise to find a lot of retired people here. The place is well kept, all in all. The rooms with washbasin are among the least expensive in the city. And for not much more money, you get your very own toilet. Colour TV.

☗ **The Baltic Inn** (map I, C3, **17**): 521 6th Avenue. ☎ 237-0687. About 20 minutes' walk from the Greyhound bus terminal. It's very central – just a few seconds from the Gaslamp district, which is the liveliest part of the city. It's a clean hotel, recently built, but has very little character. The rooms have WC, colour TV, fan and refrigerator; showers are on the landing.

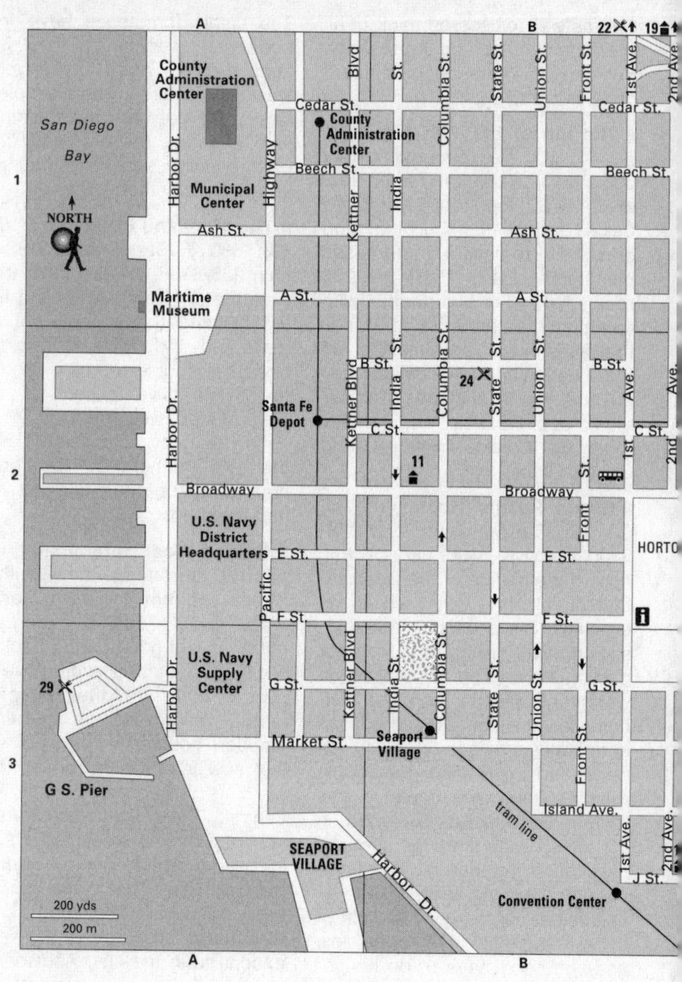

■ Useful Addresses

- Visitors' Center
- Greyhound Bus Terminal

Where to Stay

10 Hostelling International – The Metropolitan
11 The Inn at the YMCA
12 Grand Pacific Hostel
13 Jim's San Diego
14 The Maryland Hotel
15 Golden West Hotel
16 J Street Inn
17 The Baltic Inn
18 Days Inn Downtown

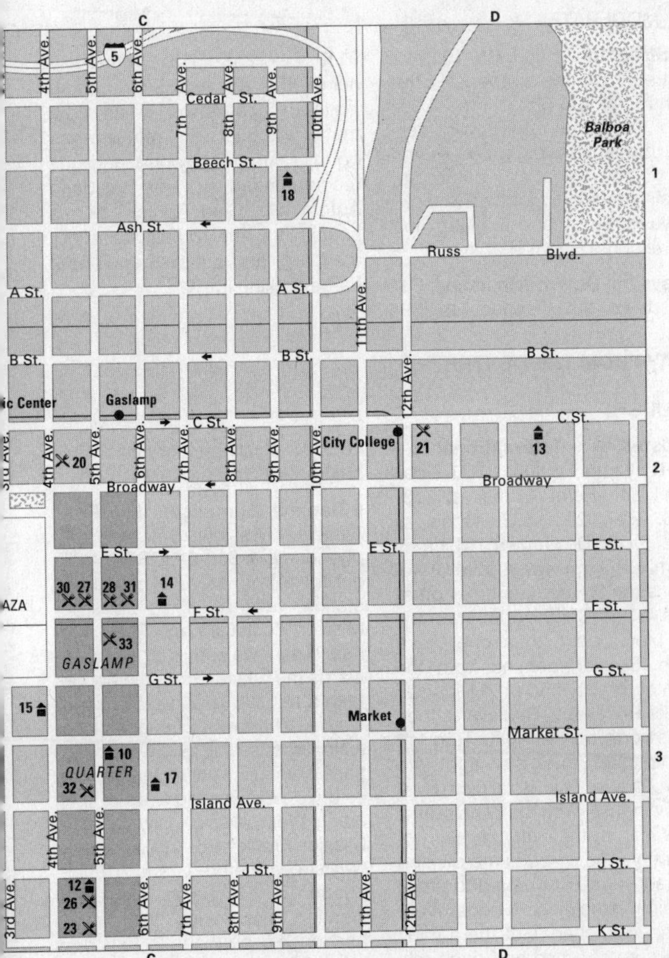

DOWNTOWN SAN DIEGO (MAP I)

19 Keating House Inn

Where to Eat / Going out

20 Eastern Chinese Restaurant
21 Gen Lai Sen
22 Hob Nob Hill
23 Hops! Bistro & Brewery
24 Karl Strauss' Old Columbia Brewery
25 The Jolly Roger
26 Dick's Last Resort
27 Croce's and Croce's Top Hat
28 Fio's
29 Fish Market
30 Patrick's
31 Bodie's
32 Blarney Stone
33 Olé Madrid

☆☆ MODERATE

J Street Inn (map I, B3, **16**): 222 J Street, on the corner of 2nd Avenue. ☎ 696-6922. Fax: 696-1295. In a large, rather characterless, modern building, 200 rooms with all conveniences – bathroom, TV, air-conditioning, fridge and microwave. The place is clean and the welcome is reasonable.

Days Inn Downtown (map I, C1, **18**): 1449 9th Avenue. ☎ 239-9113. Fax: 232-9019. On the corner of 9th Street and Beech Street, north of Downtown, in an area that's not bad. The motel offers good value for money and it's recommended by the American Automobile Club, which means something. The rooms are pretty standard, and are well equipped. Large parking lot.

AWAY FROM THE CENTRE

☆ BUDGET

Hostelling International – Elliott (youth hostel): 3790 Udall Street, at Point Loma. ☎ 223-4778. Fax: 223-1883. Open all year. From Downtown, which is 5.5 miles (9km) away, take a No. 35 bus (on B Street) and get off at Voltaire and Chatsworth. Then it's one block west, then one block south. By car: coming from the north of the city and from Highway 5, take Rosecrans Boulevard, then Chatsworth on the right. Turn left into Voltaire Street then right into Udall Street. This is a nice two-storey house with balconies in a pleasant district that's full of greenery. The 61 beds are divided between double rooms and small dormitories holding 10 beds. Well-equipped kitchen. Get there early to be sure of a bed and don't rely too much on booking by phone.

Ocean Beach Hostel: 4961 Newport Avenue, Ocean Beach, right on the edge of the beach. ☎ 226-9027. Fax: 223-7881. Freephone: ☎ 1-800-339-7263. To get there, just call them – they run a free shuttle. The style and price of the dormitories and double rooms are similar to those in a youth hostel. Breakfast is included; and you can do your laundry and cooking too. The welcome is very nice. Lots of small restaurants in the area.

Banana Bungalow: 707 Reed Avenue, Mission Beach. Freephone: ☎ 1-800-5-HOSTEL. To get there from the Greyhound bus station, take a No. 34 bus for Mission Boulevard and Reed Avenue. Then walk half a block towards the beach. From the airport, take a No. 2 bus as far as Broadway in Downtown. Change there to a No. 34 bus, and follow the directions above. By car, take Highway 5, drive west on Highway 8, then along West Mission Bay Drive to Mission Boulevard. Go up this to two streets before Grand Avenue. Though it may be in a splendid location overlooking the Pacific and on the promenade that runs alongside the beach for several miles, it's definitely not the best place in town. In fact, if you're a penniless but demanding backpacker, you should go to the previous entry. Here, there are six beds to a dormitory, though they're small and the covers are skimpy. There's a launderette and luggage lockers – and breakfast is free.

KOA Campground: 30601 Edgemere Avenue, at Chula Vista. ☎ (714) 427-3601. From Mission Bay, take Freeway 5. Continue towards the south and exit at E Street. Go up E Street as far as 2nd Avenue. Turn left, then go straight on. The campground is on the right. The facilities are clean and there's a swimming pool. On summer evenings, there are musical events with a band. You can get reductions for the Zoo, Sea World and Wild Animal Park if you show your campground ticket.

☗ **Campland on the Bay**: 2211 Pacific Beach Drive. ☎ 274-6260. Fax: 581-4206. Freephone: ☎ 1-800-422-9386 (7am–9pm). On Freeway 5, coming from the south, exit at Mission Drive and take Grand Avenue up to Olney Street, where you turn left and go along to the end. The campground is then on the left. It's well-situated but a bit expensive. Note that later arrivals have to take a position near the exit (which is expensive and its noisy). There's a swimming pool and the beach is beautiful. The restaurant is affordable.

☆☆ MODERATE

☗ **Pacific Sands Motel**: 4449 Ocean Boulevard. ☎ 483-7575. Fax: 273-7090. From Freeway 5, exit at Garnett Avenue, turn left into Mission Boulevard and take Hornblende Avenue on the right. The motel is at the edge of Pacific Beach, which is very beautiful, tucked away behind some palm trees. It's handy for families, because a room with two double beds costs less than $60, even in high season. The rooms are well equipped, with bathroom, TV and fridge – even a kitchenette – but the decor is a little spartan.

☗ **Ocean Manor Apartment Hotel**: 1370 Sunset Cliffs Boulevard. ☎ 222-7901. Level with Point Loma Avenue and in a residential district, this motel is right at the ocean's edge, just 50 yards (45 metres) from Sunset Cliffs (which are named for their famous sunset views). Take a No. 35 bus, which goes directly to Broadway. Some rooms have a kitchenette. A good place and very clean. Small swimming pool. Three days is the minimum stay.

☗ **Loma Lodge**: 3202 Rosecrans Street. ☎ 222-0511. Freephone: ☎ 1-800-266-0511. Just off the boulevard. Prices are reasonable and the rooms are spacious, with balcony and bathroom. The place is very well kept, although the small swimming pool isn't always very clean. Breakfast is included and there's free parking. The district is of little interest and there's some aeroplane noise.

☗ **The Crown City Inn**: 520 Orange Avenue. ☎ 435-3116. Freephone: ☎ 1-800-422-1173. Fax: 435-6750. This is the place if you want to stay on Coronado Island. It's a pretty motel in Mediterranean style with a red-tiled roof. The rooms are pleasant and comfortable and there's a swimming pool.

☗ **Radisson Inn National City**: 700 National City Boulevard. ☎ 333-3333. To get here from San Diego, take the I-5 South, exit at National City and take the first on the right. This large, modern motel is five minutes' drive from Downtown. Rooms are very comfortable and clean, with TV and air-conditioning. No breakfast provided.

☆☆☆ EXPENSIVE

☗ **Keating House Inn** (map I, off B1, **19**): 2331 2nd Avenue. ☎ 239-8585. In a beautiful residential district north of Downtown, this splendid Victorian house, dating from 1888, is surrounded by a leafy garden with jacarandas, roses and bougainvillea. The place has a touch of grace, a discernible taste for refined things. In fact, it's got style. It's advisable to book, because word is beginning to get around. The rooms are enticingly fitted out, and have descriptive names like 'the Rose Room', 'the Yellow Room' (which is done Japanese-style), or 'the Blue Room', which has the benefit of two corner windows. Probably the best one is at the end of the garden – a little cottage containing the two most expensive rooms ($75–85). The 'Butler's Room', which is the larger, has two beds and is quite charming. Both these rooms have their own bathroom – rather old-fashioned, but comfortable. The breakfasts are substantial.

☗ **The Avenida Inn**: 1315 Orange Avenue. ☎ 435-3191. Fax: 437-0162. Next to the famous Hotel del Coronado. A beautiful motel with every convenience. The rooms are quiet. Pleasant swimming pool. Costs $87–100 for a double room.

☆☆☆☆ SPLASH OUT IN THE OLD TOWN

☗ **Heritage Park B&B Inn** (map II): 2470 Heritage Park Row. ☎ 299-6832. Fax: 299-9465. Freephone: ☎ 1-800-995-2470. In the north of San Diego. Twelve rooms in a beautiful Victorian house on a leafy hill in an old residential district, so peace and quiet are guaranteed. The place is furnished in antique style and has a certain charm. They do a good 'homemade breakfast'. Double rooms cost $100–150.

WHERE TO EAT

DOWNTOWN

☆ BUDGET

✗ **Eastern Chinese Restaurant** (map I, C2, **20**): 1065 4th Avenue. ☎ 233-6090. Open 11am–8pm. Closed Sunday. This small Chinese self-service cafeteria occupies a very large room. It's clean, and they give you a good welcome. It's a godsend for anyone on a tight budget because the buffet is unlimited and the price is modest. The food's very decent, particularly the soup and the fish fritters. Purified fresh water.

✗ **Gen Lai Sen** (map I, D2, **21**): 1065 12th Avenue (and C Street). ☎ 239-5478 and 5479. Open daily, 10am–9.30pm. Next to a public garden and near a large parking lot. Great if you're staying at Jim's San Diego, because it's right nearby. This is a large Chinese canteen with a good reputation, and there's a vast choice on the menu – 157 dishes! The cuisine is Hakka (a Chinese minority group). Good value lunch and dinner specials.

✗ **Galaxy Grill** (map I, B–C2): 522 Horton Plaza. ☎ 234-7211. Open Sunday until 8pm. Right above the famous shopping centre. An entertaining bar and grill with great 1950s decor and atmosphere. The welcome is friendly. They serve sandwiches, burgers, wonderful salads and excellent milkshakes, as well as Brownie Hot Fudge Sundae, Death-By-Chocolate, Carrot Cake Supreme, and more.

☆☆ MODERATE

✕ **Karl Strauss' Old Columbia Brewery** (map I, B2, **24**): 1157 Columbia Street (corner with B Street). ☎ 234-BREW. Large cafe and bakery furnished in light-coloured wood. An unpretentious place offering a good selection of beers. Fine for a light meal at lunchtime.

✕ **Hob Nob Hill** (map I off B1, **22**): 2271 1st Avenue, on the corner of Juniper. ☎ 239-8176. In the north of Downtown and some way from the centre, but not hard to find. Open daily, 7am–9pm. This is one of the city's oldest restaurants, established in 1944, so it's something of an institution, with retro decor and family cuisine at very acceptable prices. The dish of the day is always substantial – dishes such as old-fashioned beef stew, gourmet breast of chicken curry or corned beef and cabbage. Try their speciality: braised domestic lamb shank. The salads are generous. The house wine is decent and they also do homemade cakes. Breakfast portions are ample.

✕ **The Jolly Roger** (map I, A3, **25**): Seaport Village (807 West Harbor Drive, level with Kettner Boulevard). ☎ 233-4300. Open 7am–10pm (11pm Friday and Saturday). To the south of the village. Fresh setting and pleasant atmosphere, with lots of plants, makes it a nice place for breakfast, among other things. Well known for their burgers and seafood. Prices are reasonable, even in the evening. In the morning, try Pigs in a Blanket or the avocado omelette. They also do a good chicken pot pie and fajitas. On the evening menu, there are meat specialities that include an interesting combination with prime rib. In the lounge, the happy hour is 4pm–7pm, with appetizers and draught beer at half price.

✕ **Dick's Last Resort** (map I, C3, **26**): 345 4th Avenue (between J and K Streets, with another entrance on 5th Avenue). ☎ 231-9100. Open daily, 11am–2am. An immense hall with a rip-roaring atmosphere at weekends, and hardly any more peaceful during the week. Here, they deliberately cultivate non-conformity. Don't forget to take away their menu which includes quotes like: 'You can't kill a man born to hang'. And 'Alka Seltzer and aspirin on the house!' Gangs of suburbanites vie with each other to make the crudest jokes. It must be said that the waitresses, too, get drawn into cracking some rough gags! Everything is punctuated by the sounds from a country or rock band that compensates for its defects with deafening volume. You'll gather that, in view of what things are like, what you get on your plate is of minor importance: Mae West Plate (chicken breast . . . ho, ho, ho!), Gulf oysters, etc. But the speciality here is a bucket of something, whether it's ribs, shrimps or crabs' claws. The atmosphere conveniently makes you forget that it isn't cheap, which is probably the point. There's a selection of 80 beers. The pleasant terrace makes a good refuge from the frenzy inside.

✕ **Baja Brewing Co.**: 203 5th Avenue, south of Gaslamp, just before the railway track. ☎ 231-9279. Open daily, 11.30am–10pm. Huge Mexican restaurant where the bar faces towards the barrels on the brasserie side. The place has a good reputation offering tacos and enchiladas at the counter, with a nice, cold Margarita. Alternatively, there's a good selection of *pescados* and *mariscos*. The service is very nice but a bit slow.

☆☆☆ EXPENSIVE

✕ **Croce's** (map I, C2, **27**): 802 5th Avenue, on the corner with F Street. Right in the middle of Gaslamp, the heart of the city. ☎ 233-4355. Open at lunchtime and in the evening to 11pm (midnight Friday and Saturday). Jim Croce was a successful songwriter whose compositions included *Bad, Bad Leroy Brown*, *Time in a Bottle* and *Operator*. He died in 1973. His wife opened this restaurant to honour his memory. There's a large portrait of him on the wall and assorted mementoes. The decor is quite sophisticated. There's a piano bar at lunchtime and in the evening. At lunch, it's very relaxed and casual, and the prices are accessible to all. In the evening, the clientele is much smarter, the atmosphere is more starchy, and the prices have almost doubled. So it's best to come here for lunch. There are some delicious salads and appetizers, such as Croce's Sampler, Buffalo Mozzarella and the Blinchikis (two superb blinis). There's live jazz or blues every evening.

✕ **Fio's** (map I, C2, **28**): 801 5th Avenue. ☎ 234-3467. At the heart of Gaslamp. Open 11.30am–11pm (midnight Friday and Saturday), Sunday 5–11pm. The setting is very elegant (superb *Palio* fresco) and the menu is guaranteed to be up to date. Cooking is done in the main room. Quite noisy. They serve Northern Italian food in a very refined way, with such dishes as *polenta a la montenara, osso buco, rotolino di mozzarella, piccata di vitèlla,* chicken Tuscan-style and *scampi arrosti*. In the ongoing, fierce struggle between the great Italian restaurants of San Diego, Fio's is undeniably winning on points. Although they don't welcome people with holes in their jeans, casual dress is what people wear. The prices are reasonable.

✕ **Fish Market** (map I, A3, **29**): 750 North Harbour Drive, level with G Street Pier. ☎ 234-4867. Here you get a nice view of the bay. There are two restaurants in one: a brasserie on the ground floor and a smarter place on the first floor (**Top of the Market**). Fish specialities in both. Prices are quite expensive, but it's a chance to eat shark, *mahi-mahi* and lots of other nicely prepared fish. Booking is essential at weekends, because the place is packed. You need to make it very clear which room you're booking for.

✕ **Hotel del Coronado**: 1500 Orange Avenue, Coronado Beach. ☎ 522-8000. Don't miss Sunday morning brunch, which is delicious and served in a vast dining room shaped like the hull of an upturned boat. The setting is elegant. Don't be put off by the long queue, because it goes down quite quickly, but remember to take your numbered ticket right away. The food is abundant and quite delicious – save a little room for dessert. Not all that expensive – you can expect to pay about $25. During the week, there's a buffet lunch. Dinner in the luxurious drawing rooms of the **Prince of Wales Grill**, however, is very expensive. The mahogany bar is massive. They have old photos of the Duke of Windsor and Mrs Simpson.

HILLCREST

☆ BUDGET

✕ **The Corvette**: 3946 5th Avenue. In Hillcrest, 2 miles (3km) from Downtown, but it's a straight run so the place is easy to find.

☎ 542-1001 and 542-1476. Open until 11pm. Bar and grill with a lively ambience, given over exclusively to the 1950s, but especially to the Corvette – one of the most famous automobiles of the period. The huge room supposedly holds 288 people – or 49 Corvettes (how do they know?). There's also a superb 1963 Corvette Roadster on display inside. The decor is great. Youngsters crowd in here at weekends to wolf down good hamburgers and a DJ spins some great rock 'n' roll music.

✕ **City Delicatessen**: 535 University Avenue, also in Hillcrest. ☎ 295-2747. Not far from The Corvette. Open 7am–midnight (2am Friday and Saturday). One of the largest delis anywhere, with layout and decor in the style of an old diner. The salads are enormous! Try the chopped liver or the whitefish. They do hot dishes at reasonable prices: chicken in the pot, corned beef and cabbage, mixed grill, eggplant (aubergine) casserole, etc. They also serve sandwiches and generous cold fish platters. A lunch special is served on weekdays. You can even find a calorie counter if you're worried about your figure, and there are little jukeboxes on the tables. This place is worth going out of your way for.

OLD TOWN

☆ BUDGET

✕ **O'Hungry's** (map II, B2, **2**): 2547 San Diego Avenue, opposite the Church of the Immaculate Conception. ☎ 298-0133. Open daily, 8am–11pm. This is the least expensive restaurant in this rather touristy area. They offer homemade soup and some affordable dishes, plus a salad bar, pancakes, spaghetti and sandwiches. The music is good: country, rhythm 'n' blues and rock. Beer is sold by the length of the glass: a half-yard and a yard!

☆☆–☆☆☆ MODERATE TO EXPENSIVE

✕ **Casa de Pico** (map II, A2–B2, **3**): Juan Street, inside the Bazar del Mundo shopping centre. ☎ 296-3267. Open 10am–9pm (9.30pm at weekends). This is an excellent Mexican restaurant, but go quite early or you might have to wait for an hour. Pleasant ambiance with an interior garden, sunshades and music. Copious dishes, mariachi band, waitresses in traditional costume. Try the *polo fundido, taco loco,* or the *tostada del mundo.*

✕ **Casa Bandini** (map II, B2, **4**): Just 100 yards (90 metres) from the Casa de Pico. ☎ 297-8211. Formerly the house of an adventurer, Juan Bandini, who had it built in 1829, it then became in succession a shop, an olive oil factory, a post office and a hotel, before finally becoming a restaurant. It's a beautiful adobe building with balconies and verandas. The atmosphere is a little less touristy than next door. Large pleasant garden with fountain and well-established plants. Decent Mexican food, at prices which are reasonable, all things considered. Good Sunday brunch. Booking is advisable.

WHERE TO GO OUT, HAVE A DRINK, OR HEAR SOME MUSIC

A lively part of the revival of Downtown is the emergence of some great music spots. Rock and blues sounds pour out onto the pavement from everywhere – it's like choosing from a musical menu as you walk along. Most nightspots are in the recently renovated Gaslamp District. During the week, there's almost never a cover charge.

🍸 **Patrick's** (map I, C2, **30**): 428 F Street. ☎ 233-3077. Opposite the Horton Plaza parking lot. This place is very dark and very lively. Every evening you can hear some remarkable blues, jazz and rock bands. Happy hour daily, 6–7.30pm (with 'finger munchies' on Thursday and Friday). There's a big blues festival on the first Friday of every month. Probably the best bar and the best atmosphere in Downtown San Diego.

🍸 **Bodie's** (map I, C2, **31**): 528 F Street, between 5th and 6th Avenue. ☎ 236-8988. A big rival of Patrick's. Great blues gigs on Thursday. Alternative rock on Friday and Saturday.

🍸 **Olé Madrid** (map I, C3, **33**): 753 5th Avenue. Music and dancing in the room at the back of the restaurant. The crowd is interesting but it isn't always easy to get in.

🍸 **Croce's Top Hat** (map I, C2, **27**): 820 5th Avenue. ☎ 233-4355. Beside Croce's restaurant. Inside, the decor is like an old cinema facade. Open to 2am. Nice atmosphere. Interesting cocktails. Excellent programmes of jazz and R'n'B.

🍸 **Johnny's MS 801** (map I, C2, next door to **30**, which is Patrick's): 4th Avenue and F Street. ☎ 233-1131. On Thursday, there's a 1950s–60s Oldies Night!

🍸 **Hops! Bistro & Brewery** (map I, C3, **23**): 310 5th Avenue (corner of K Street). Large, very lively room right in the middle of the Gaslamp District, attracting lots of young people. There's a huge, horseshoe-shaped bar, plus TV screens and music. They make their own beers here – 11 kinds in all, including Three-Peat Wheat and Sunset Red Ale (delicious). Laid out brasserie-style in the early evening. No live music. Happy hour is 4–7pm daily. Good cuisine at sensible prices.

🍸 **Blarney Stone** (map I, C3, **32**): 502 5th Avenue. ☎ 233-8519. Open to 2am. Excellent sessions of Irish folk music (Thursday, Friday and Saturday). Outside those sessions, it's not very animated. It's possible to get a meal here.

Alternatively, the rock ambiance is a little more electric in the bars at **Ocean Beach** (some are even a bit menacing) and there's a more friendly, Californian atmosphere in the bars of **Mission Bay** (between the Roller Coaster and Crystal Pier Water).

WHAT TO SEE

DOWNTOWN

As in most large American cities, the centre of San Diego became progressively emptier during the 1960s as people moved out to the suburbs. The district slowly became a place for dropouts and homeless people, and the buildings began to deteriorate. The city authorities have been addressing this problem for a number of years now, in an attempt to recapture something of the splendour of 100 years ago. The Victorian facades have been cleaned up and, in the Gaslamp District, restaurants, cafes and nightspots are opening up all the time. Magnificent city-centre refurbishments do not, of course, eliminate social problems, and at night, Downtown is still a meeting place for street people looking for a little warmth. Take care.

★ **Horton Plaza** (map I, B2): between Broadway and G Street, 1st and 4th Avenues. ☎ 238-1596. Shops are open 10am–9pm (6pm Saturday), Sunday 11am–6pm. The vast shopping centre is the work of architect Ernest W. Hahn. It consists of over 140 shops and restaurants and there are four department stores (including the famous Broadway and Nordstrom) spread over six levels. The levels are linked by a complex of overhead walkways. There are facades are of every colour, attractive plazas, and the whole thing is conceived in a mixture of Spanish, Byzantine and contemporary styles. There are often free lunchtime concerts on the plazas. On E Street and 1st Avenue, in front of the Doubletree Hotel, there's a beautiful luminous fountain. If you have a receipt for a purchase from a shop, your first three hours of parking are free of charge.

★ **Gaslamp District** (map I, C2–3): this historic district of San Diego extends over 16 blocks between 4th and 6th Avenues. You can join a tour of it any Saturday at 11am. Information: ☎ 233-5227. This is a really great place for strolling or just sitting on a terrace. It's packed at weekends. The area consists mainly of restaurants, cafes and nightspots, but there are also some interesting shops. On 5th Avenue there are two cigar shops and factories: the Cuban Cigar Factory is at No. 551 and another, which also runs a coffee-house, is at No. 560. The Barber College (at No. 635), set up in 1926, has an impressive array of old chairs – and you can have your hair cut here for a third of the normal price! Classic Cars can be found at No. 861. It's a magnificent second-hand car showroom with Corvettes, Cadillacs and so on.

★ **The Maritime Museum** (map I, A1): 1306 North Harbor Drive. ☎ 234-9153. Open daily, 9am–8pm. Not far from the city centre (level with A Street), on the wharf. Here you'll find a large number of boats of all sizes and ages. The main item is the world's oldest merchant ship, the *Star of India* (1863), as well as the *Berkeley*, a steam-ferry dating from 1898, and the *Medea,* a 1904 luxury yacht. Information is provided to visitors by enthusiasts – often retired seagoing types.

★ **Children's Museum** (map I, B3): 200 West Island Avenue, south of Downtown, near Seaport Village and the Convention Center. ☎ 233-5437. Open Tuesday–Sunday 10am–5pm. This place is great for two- to 10-year-olds, and many of the exhibits are interactive.

★ **San Diego Museum of Contemporary Art** (map I, A2): 1001 Kettner Boulevard, level with Santa Fe trolley station. ☎ 234-1001. Open Tuesday–Saturday 10am–5pm, Sunday noon–5pm. Collections of modern works of art in a building of surreal architectural style.

★ **Firehouse Museum** (map I, B1): 1572 Columbia Street, corner of Cedar Street. ☎ 232-3473. Open Thursday–Sunday 10am–4pm. Located in the city's earliest fire station, there are displays telling you all about firemen plus an exhibition of old fire-fighting equipment. Admission is free.

BALBOA PARK (MAP I, D1)

To get to Balboa Park, take a No. 7, 7A or 7B bus from Broadway. This park covers 1,400 acres (560 hectares) and is the location of the city's largest museums, all in a green setting, as well as the famous San Diego Zoo. The park was established in 1868, at a time when San Diego was only a village with a few thousand inhabitants. Today, it is a major lung for more than a million people. The buildings, in Spanish colonial-style, are the remains of buildings that were constructed for the great exhibitions of 1915 and 1935. They have been attractively restored and sit alongside others built later in the same style, amidst luxuriant vegetation, palm trees, tropical trees and ornamental pools.

Information Center: 1549 El Prado. ☎ 239-0512. Open daily, 9am–4pm. You can buy a Balboa Park Passport, which is valid for one week and you can visit all the museums in the park for about $20.

★ **San Diego Zoo**: ☎ 234-3153 and 231-1515. Open 9am–10pm (5pm in winter). Admission $15 ($6 for a child), but note that ticket prices increase frequently. After-dark shows for children take place at weekends, with a lower admission charge. This is the largest zoo in the world, and the site is superb – a sort of tropical forest with a natural canyon. More than 6,000 animals live here in near-recreations of their natural environment. The most striking animals to be seen include the superb white tiger, the koala bears, the famous proboscis monkeys (*Nasalis larvatus*), so named for their prominent, pointed noses, and the uakari, which are monkeys with bare, demonic faces. Don't miss the hippopotamus pool! If you're pushed for time, there's a bus that gives a tour of the most interesting spots.

★ **San Diego Museum of Art**: 1450 El Prado. Not much room in the parking lot at weekends. It's best to leave your car before you get to the access bridge. ☎ 232-7931. Open Tuesday–Sunday 10am–4.30pm. Free admission on the third Tuesday of the month. Interesting collections: Ingres, Corot, *La jeune bergère* by Bouguereau, *Le Miroir de la loue* by Courbet, *Sortie de théâtre* by Daumier, *La Sen'te du chou, Pontoise* and *Une rue à Auvers* by Pissarro, *Effet de neige à Limetz* by Monet, Boudin, *Femme peignant ses cheveux* by Renoir, Dufy, Vuillard, Max Beckmann, Sam Francis, Paul Klee's *March to the Summit*, and *Metropolitan Opera House*, a photomontage by David Hockney.

• **Portraits and landscapes of the 19th and early 20th century**: Thomas Moran, George Inness, Thomas Eakins, Raphaëlle Peale, William Merritt Chase, Mary Cassatt.

• **Asian arts**: Chinese pottery; 18th- and 19th-century Sino–Tibetan bronzes; superb Hayagriva and *Twenty-four Warriors of Koyo* by Tosa Mitsunori; prints by Hokusai, Kobayoshi Kiyochika.

• **On the first floor**: *L'église du village* by Vlaminck, *Portrait de Pierre Monteux* by Bonnard, *Le Garçon aux yeux bleus* by Modigliani. Plus Tiepolo, Vuillard, Simon Vouet, Zurbarán, *The Repentant Peter* by El Greco, *Marqués de Sonagra* by Goya, Bellotto, the remarkable *Mole from San Marco* by Canaletto, the splendid *Grand Canal and Rialto* by Guardi, David Tenier the Younger, Rubens, *Queen Henrietta Maria* by Van Dyck, Frans Hals.

• **Medieval art**: *Crucifixion* by the Master of Alfajarin, *Christ in Captivity* by Hieronymus Bosch, *Madonna and Child* by Adriaen Ysenbrandt,

Giorgione, Véronese, Carlo Crivelli, Luca Signorelli, *The Conversion of the Magdalene* by Bernardino Luini, Lorenzo Veneziano and more.

★ **Reuben H. Fleet Space Theater and Science Center**: 1875 El Prado. ☎ 238-1233 and 238-1168. Open daily, 9.30am–9.30pm (10.30pm Friday and Saturday). 10 minutes' walk from the Zoo. This is the place where kids can develop an interest in such topics as astronomy, fluid mechanics and electricity. Omnimax film screenings are shown several times a day, generally on astronomy or the conquest of space, and there's also a laser show.

★ **Museum of Man**: also on El Prado. ☎ 239-2001. Open daily, 10am–4.30pm. Free admission on the third Tuesday of the month. This excellent museum of anthropology is housed in a building in the style of a baroque Spanish church, with an ornamental facade and a conical bell tower. Craftsmen can be seen giving public demonstrations of their work.

★ Inside a long building, the Casa Balboa, are three other museums. The **Museum of Photographic Arts** ☎ 239-5262. Open daily, 10am–5pm (free admission on the second Tuesday of the month). Interesting temporary exhibitions. The **History of San Diego Museum** ☎ 232-6203. Open 10am–4.30pm. Closed Monday and Tuesday, except the second Tuesday of the month (when admission is free). This museum shows the history of the city from 1850 to the present day. And there's a small **Miniature Train Museum** ☎ 696-0199. Open Tuesday–Friday 11am–4pm, Saturday and Sunday to 5pm. This museum is free on the first Tuesday of the month.

★ **The Natural History Museum**: 1788 El Prado. ☎ 232-3821. Open daily, 10am–4.30pm. Free on the first Tuesday of the month. Here you can find out about the animals, plants and geology of southern California, Arizona, Baja California and the Sonora desert in Mexico. There's an interesting section on species that are threatened with extinction, plus a new room on desert ecology, with a seismograph that records the daily movements of the earth. The museum shop is well stocked.

– If you still have time left or are strongly motivated, you could also visit one of the following:

★ **Museum of Champions**: 1649 El Prado. ☎ 234-2544. Open daily, 10am–4.30pm (free on the second Tuesday of the month). Everything you could possibly want to know about more than 40 sports. Film shows.

★ **Museum of the Automobile**: near the Museum of the Air and the Museum of Space. ☎ 231-2886. Open daily, 10am–4pm (free on the fourth Tuesday of the month). Stunning collection of cars and motorbikes.

★ **Raza Cultural Center**: Park Boulevard. ☎ 235-6135. Open noon–5pm. Closed Monday and Tuesday. A display of work by native Californians – that is: Native Americans, Mexicans and Chicanos. Temporary exhibitions and an interesting shop.

★ **Aerospace Museum**: 2001 Pan American Plaza. ☎ 234-8291. Open daily, 9am–5pm (free admission on the fourth Tuesday of the month). Over 70 vehicles are displayed, from a hot-air balloon to the latest space shuttle. There's a hall of fame with all the great pilots of history. You'll also find, in the Theodore E. Gildred Flight Rotunda, the largest flight library and archives in the world, as well as a well-stocked gift shop.

★ **Timken Museum of Art**: 1500 El Prado. ☎ 239-5548. Open Tuesday–Saturday 10am–4.30pm, Sunday 1.30–4.30pm. Closed Monday, public holidays and September. Admission is free. This is another interesting art museum containing astonishing masterpieces including beautiful Russian icons and Gobelin tapestries.

– **Old Globe Theater**: ☎ 231-1941 or 239-2255. Plays Tuesday–Sunday. This is the oldest theatre in California and produces 12 plays each year.

ON CORONADO ISLAND

★ **Hotel del Coronado**: 1500 Orange Avenue. ☎ 522-8000. Go over the Coronado Bridge (paying a toll of $1 if you're the only person in your car) or take a No. 910 bus from Downtown. The view of the city from the bridge is magnificent. This hotel is not included here as a place to stay, but as a historic monument. You can take a guided tour: ☎ 522-8196.

This extravagant Victorian-style building has sheltered five American presidents and a whole litany of octogenarian millionaires, kings in exile and movie stars. At the time it was built, it was the second largest structure to use electricity – the largest being New York City! And it was here that Thomas Edison himself switched on the first Christmas tree ever to be lit by electricity – and here, too, that the future King Edward VIII met Mrs Wallis Simpson, a meeting that was to change the course of British history.

Since the hotel's opening in 1888, the history of the Coronado has been inextricably linked with political, economic and movie history. An extreme example of this occurred when Billy Wilder brought Marilyn Monroe, Jack Lemmon and Tony Curtis to film *Some Like It Hot* (1959). There was a certain amount of tension between the actors at the time of shooting, and Tony Curtis, when asked by a journalist what it was like to kiss one of the world's most beautiful women, replied that he would have 'preferred kissing Hitler'.

Consider savouring Sunday brunch here, or a buffet lunch during the week (*see* 'Where to Eat').

★ **The Ferry Landing Marketplace**: 1201 1st Avenue (and B Street). ☎ 435-8895. Open daily. Take the ferry from Broadway Pier (at the end of Broadway, in Downtown). There's a departure every hour 9am–10pm (11pm Friday and Saturday). Small supplement for bikes. This is the former ferry landing, now transformed into a shopping centre with cafes and restaurants. It's a popular place for family walks. There's a beautiful view of the bay and the architecture is interesting. It's quite touristy, of course, but still worth the trip.

TO THE NORTH OF THE CITY

★ **Old Town** (map II): you get here via the San Diego Freeway, Interstate 5. If you use public transport, nearly all the bus and tram lines go through the Old Town Transit Center. This Spanish-style district, with its adobe houses, in fact occupies only six blocks. Built in 1820, it was one of the very first settlements in California. Washington Square makes up the centre of Old Town and there are many souvenir shops and restaurants.

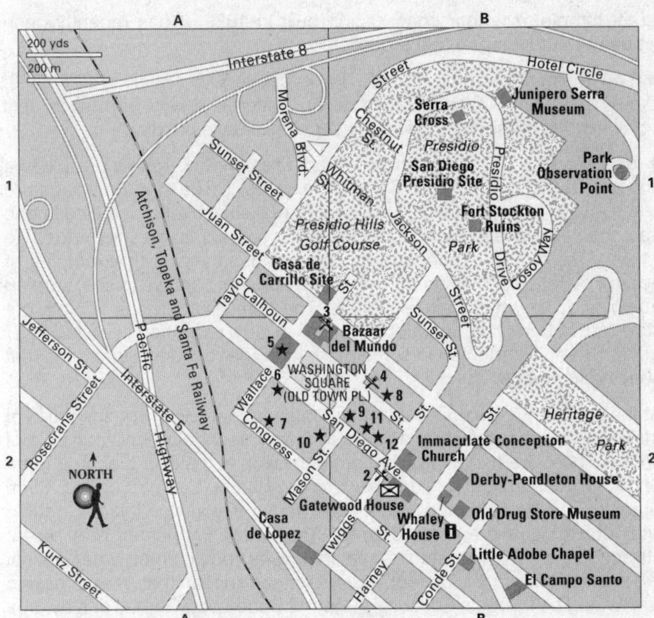

SAN DIEGO – OLD TOWN (MAP II)

■ Useful Address

- Visitors' Center

✕ Where to Eat

- **2** O'Hungry's
- **3** Casa de Pico
- **4** Casa Bandini

★ What to See

- **5** Congress Hall Site
- **6** Casa de Silvas-Machado
- **7** Casa de Stewart
- **8** Hazard Old West Museum
- **9** Casa de Estudillo
- **10** Mason St School
- **11** Casa de Pedrorena
- **12** Casa de Altamarino

Visit the **Bazar del Mundo** (2754 Calhoun Street), built as a copy of a Mexican marketplace, with shops around a courtyard decorated with pretty gardens. It's a pity that it's a bit too commercial. Get there at opening time (10am), so you can explore the remains of San Diego's earliest dwellings – the Casa de Machado Stewart (1830), the Machado y Silvas (1832), the Casa de Carillo (1820) and the Casa de Estudillo (1827). Guided tours are led by the park rangers at 2pm daily. Meet up at the Casa Machado y Silvas.

★ **Heritage Park**: 2455 Heritage Park Row. ☎ 299-6832. This splendid collection of old residences is situated on the hill overlooking the Old Town, and includes the very beautiful Sherman Gilbert House (1887). A little lower, overlooking the lawn, is San Diego's first synagogue, the Beit

Israel temple, a timber construction built in 1889. It has recently been renovated and is open to the public.

★ **The Serra Museum**: Presidio Park, above Old Town. ☎ 297-3258. Open 10am–4pm. Closed Monday. At California's very birthplace, this small historic museum is housed in a colonial-style building.

★ **Sea World**: 1720 South Shores Road, Mission Bay. Take a bus (almost any line) to Old Town Transit Center, then a No. 9. The trip from the centre takes 40 minutes. ☎ 226-3901. Open 9am–dusk (ticket office closes one hour earlier). In summer, opening hours are sometimes extended to 11pm. This is one of the world's largest aquariums, with examples of approximately 5,500 species. There are impressive shows to see, starring dolphins, killer whales and sea-lions. The admission charge is high, but it's worth it. Look out for coupons that give you a reduction of up to $5 per person – you'll find them in some of the San Diego tourist brochures that you find in motels.

At the entrance, pick up the practical little handout telling you the times of the shows and suggesting a route to follow depending on your time of arrival. There are two things that are unmissable: the Sea-Lion and Otter Show – remarkable and hilarious – and the Shamu Celebration at Shamu Stadium – a breathtaking killer-whale show! If you don't fancy getting wet, don't sit in the first 10 rows! The Shark Encounter is a recent attraction – it's a transparent tunnel that gives you an underwater view of the sharks. You do this on foot, except for one section that uses a moving walkway. The Penguin Encounter and the Coco Loco Games (a play area for children) are also great fun.

The latest novelty is The Wild Arctic: a simulated helicopter flight over the ice floes and an encounter with some polar bears. This is followed by a tour of the land base and encounters with bears, walruses and beluga whales.

Although this park is fabulous, we shouldn't forget that, for the animals, it's a beautiful blue prison and they really belong elsewhere. Twenty of them have died in the last 15 years and many have suffered from ulcerations caused by the reverberation of their sonars against the walls of their pools. Animal Rights organizations regularly air their views on this.

What's rather wearing is the large number of shops. Set aside some extra cash for the supplementary charges for the Bayride (the cable-car going over the bay) and the Skyride (the tower lift).

★ **The Scenic Drive**: this circuit, covering 52 miles (83km) and flagged by signposts marked with blue gulls, allows you to tour the city by car. It starts near Broadway, crosses Balboa Park, the Old Town, Mission Bay and Aquatic Park, goes over the top of Soledad Mountain to the Cabrillo National Monument, and returns to Broadway via Shelter Island. The drive at Santa Barbara is better.

★ **Cabrillo National Monument**: at the end of Point Loma. Accessible by bus No. 26. ☎ 557-5450. Open 9am–5.15pm. This monument is dedicated to the Portuguese explorer João Cabrilho (Juan Rodriguez Cabrillo), who discovered the coast of California in 1542. This is the third most frequently visited monument in the United States. There's a beautiful view of the bay from this hill (but not too early in the morning, because of the fog), and you can see the maritime infrastructure of the bay, plus ships and the distant heights of Mexico. From mid-December to mid-February you can watch the southward migration of the whales. An average of 30 go by each day, peaking at 200 a day in mid-January. Some agencies on North Harbour Drive (level with the Holiday Inn On The Bay) organize whale-watching trips.

THE NEW SAN DIEGO

Opposite the station, a spectacular architectural complex is taking shape. No fewer than 110 projects have been completed or are under way. In just a few years, Downtown has undergone an incredible metamorphosis. If you have an interest in modern architecture, these are the main gems:

★ **John Burham**: at 610 West Ash Street, whose facades reflect the whole district.

★ **Sunroad Pacific Tower**: on Ash, Columbia, Beach and State. It just looks marvellous.

★ **Columbia Square**: 1230 Columbia Street. Projects forward like the prow of a ship.

★ **One Courthouse Plaza**: on the corner of C Street and State. Again, the approach is particularly original.

★ **Wyndham Emerald Plaza**: 400 West Broadway. The eight bevelled towers resemble the pillars of the Giant's Causeway in Northern Ireland. This is particularly impressive at nightfall, when illuminations turn them emerald green.

★ **Great American Plaza**: 600 West Broadway. This project, with towers with bevelled tops at various angles, cost a mean $200 million.

★ **Koll Center**: 501 and 601 West Broadway. One of the city's most colossal achievements.

★ **The Courtyard**: 601 Front Street. An impressive 40-storey tower with a domed roof.

★ **Hyatt Regency**: West Harbor Drive. The top is bevelled rather in the style of an electric razor.

★ **One Harbor Drive**: 100 Harbor Drive. A daring piece of architecture. Two towers combining rounded shapes and horizontal lines. The roof is U-shaped.

SHOPPING

Seaport Village: 849 West Harbor Drive (level with Kettner Boulevard). A shopping mall reflecting the life of this part of the port one hundred years ago. The design and the space itself are pleasing, with timber houses surrounded by lush vegetation. The shops are open 10am–9pm (10pm June–August). For information: ☎ 235-4014. Make sure you go to Upstart, a friendly bookstore and coffee shop. Some nice restaurants too (*see* 'Where to Eat Downtown').

Horton Plaza Center: in the centre of Downtown, on Broadway. The latest shopping mall, with 140 shops on five levels and avant-garde architecture (*see* 'What to See Downtown').

Pannikin: 675 G Street. ☎ 239-7891. Open 9am–5.30pm, Saturday and Sunday 10am–5pm. Large, old-fashioned shop selling coffee, tea, mugs, teapots and all kinds of kitchen gadgetry.

World Market: 4th Avenue, on the corner of J Street. A large hall with all sorts of things: crockery, decorative objects and odds and ends. But the most interesting thing is the food department, where you'll find lots of sauces and other products, including in particular a very large selection of wines.

TO THE NORTH OF SAN DIEGO

LA JOLLA

AREA CODE: 619

This seaside resort and residential area has become famous for its luxurious shops and art galleries, principally along Prospect Street. It's also well-known for the seal rock – a flock of seals have set up home on the beach, not far from the city centre, and the presence of all those tourists doesn't seem to bother them at all.

WHAT TO SEE

★ **San Diego Museum of Contemporary Art**: 700 Prospect Avenue, La Jolla. ☎ 454-3541. Closed Monday and the second week of August. Interesting works by contemporary American artists. You can get a joint ticket combining this visit with the branch in the city centre.

★ **Stephen Birch Aquarium-Museum**: Expedition Way. Located in the Scripps Oceanographic Institute, a department of the university. From Interstate I-5, exit at La Jolla Village Drive and take the third on the left. You can also get there by bus: take a No. 34. ☎ 534-6933. Open daily, 9am–5pm. The layout is excellent, with a superb terrace opening out on the ocean. You get a good survey of the local marine fauna in the section on the right as you enter. Aquarium 19 is breathtaking. The section on the left is more of a teaching area. Look out for the deep-diving simulator, where you can study the species according to the different depths of their normal habitat.

WHAT TO SEE IN THE AREA

★ **Wild Animal Park**: 15500 San Pasqual Valley Road, at Escondido. ☎ (760) 234-6541. Open Monday–Wednesday 9am–5pm; open until 8pm Thursday and 10pm Sunday. Not to be confused with the Zoo, which is located in San Diego. The Wild Animal Park is 25 miles (40km) northeast of the city. Take Freeway 15, exit at Via Rancho Parkway and follow the signs for a further 6 miles (10km). Admission is quite expensive, but this place is one of a kind.

This gigantic wild animal park covers 1,800 acres (730ha) and contains animals living in conditions that are similar to their natural habitat. Some birds, for example, live in freedom near a faithfully reconstructed African village. Be sure not to miss the condors, and there's falcon training and, of course, elephants. There's a 5-mile (8km) monorail circuit that gives a good tour of the park.

There are numerous shows, so here are some times to help you organize your trip: Bird Shows are at 11am and 4.30pm; Rare and Wild America Shows at 1pm and 4pm; Elephant Shows are at noon (and 3pm weekends only). Monorail tours start every 30 minutes, 9.30am–4pm. Feeding times for animals at the Animal Care Center are at 11am and 4pm. You can see baby animals at the Petting Kraal, 9.30–10.45am, and for some great photographs, take in the Hawk Talk at 11.30am and 2.30pm. You can take photos up very close. Finally there's Photo Caravan Tours: if you book, you can take a trip in a safari truck in order to be able to photograph animals from quite close range. On Friday nights you can camp in the park among the enclosures (not inside them, of course), but there are only a very few places.

RAMONA

AREA CODE: 760

This is the first 'Western' city, 35 miles (57km) east of San Diego, on the road to Julian. The long Main Street is lined by some examples of typical 19th- and early-20th-century buildings. It doesn't justify a detour, but it *is* on the road to Julian.

WHAT TO SEE

★ **G.B. Woodward Museum of the Ramona Pioneer Historical Society**: 645 Main Street. Open Friday–Sunday 1pm–4pm. ☎ 789-7644. An interesting little museum, with covered wagons, old machinery, a blacksmith's shop, collections of old implements, women's clothes from the days of the pioneers, furniture, rare documents, etc.

JULIAN

AREA CODE: 760

The favourite excursion of San Diegans. A little old Western mining town with many painted timber houses – so it's very touristy, of course, and accommodation here is expensive, but it's very pretty! If you pass through here, check out the apple pie, the local speciality. One of the nicest is sold at **Mom's** (2119 Main Street), which also serves snacks.

★ The **Julian Pioneer Museum** is an interesting little regional museum at the entrance to the village, on the right as you come from Ramona.

★ **Eagle Mining Corporation Goldmine**: a few hundred yards from the city centre. ☎ 765-00-36. Open 10am–3pm. From Main Street, take C Street heading north and carry on along it right to the end of a dirt track.

It's badly signed. This is an authentic site, where nothing has changed since the mine closed in 1941, so the facilities are pretty rudimentary. Allow one hour for your visit (including 30 minutes actually in the mine), during which you'll get detailed explanations and a demonstration of panning for gold as it was done in the days of the Gold Rush. This visit is especially interesting if you haven't seen the ghost mines in northern California, where the Gold Rush mostly took place, from 1848 to 1856.

THE ANZO BORREGO DESERT

AREA CODE: 760

Two hours by car from San Diego is this genuine and beautiful desert. It's not very well-known (and, of course, there are quite a few more of them in the West), but this is one of the most extensive in the United States. To get here take Highway 8, then Route 67 and Route 78 as far as Santa Isabel. Next, take Route 79, then Routes S 2 and S 22 to Borrego Springs. A slightly different route is to take Highway 15 North, then Route 78, etc. In March and April, an incredible flowering takes place. Here you'll find 12 varieties of cactus, palm groves and many kinds of animal: 200 different types of bird, including the famous 'beep-beep' roadrunner and the golden eagle, as well as deer, puma, foxes, racoons and iguana.

USEFUL ADDRESSES

ℹ Visitors' Center: Borrego Springs. ☎ 767-4205. Open 1 October to 31 May daily, 9am–5pm; 1 June to 30 September 10am–3pm weekends and public holidays. There's a superb exhibition about life in the desert, all richly documented, and they can tell you everything there is to know about all the possible walks and excursions.

■ Borrego Springs Chamber of Commerce: 622 Palm Canyon Drive. ☎ 767-5555. Open 10am–2pm. You can write for information about the area. There are half-a-dozen motels, some of which are affordable.

WHAT TO DO

★ **The most popular trips**: Borrego Palm Canyon (two hours), Glorieta Canyon (only interesting in the spring), Font's Point to see the sunrise or sunset, the Borrego Badlands and more. All of these are not far from the Visitors' Center.

PALOMAR MOUNTAIN STATE PARK

To the north of Julian, the park is a great place to explore nature in the wild. It's possible to camp here. At the entrance (you pay an admission charge) you'll get a plan of the footpaths and a leaflet to help you learn to recognize the animals from the tracks they leave on the ground.

Dominating the park, is the **Mount Palomar Observatory**, which is famous for the size of its giant telescope – the mirror is 16ft (5m) in diameter and weighs 14.5 tonnes. It has a reach of one million light-years! The observatory and museum are open 9am–4pm. ☎ (760) 742-2119. Admission is free.

Watch your fuel gauge, as there's no filling station in the mountains.

SOUTH OF SAN DIEGO

TIJUANA

You don't need a visa to go to Tijuana, but you do need to have your passport with you so you can get back into the United States. As a matter of fact, you can enter Mexico on foot without showing any document, but you won't get back again that easily!

Be aware that hire cars are not allowed across the border without special authorization. There are very large parking lots at the border, on the American side. In any case, you have to take out special insurance cover at customs.

The simplest way to cross is by the Blue Line trolley on C Street, in the centre of San Diego. This will take you to Tijuana for just a few dollars. The journey takes 45 minutes.

The city boundary is 16 miles (25km) from San Diego. Frankly, it's nothing special: the buildings are low and were built in a rush, as in many such cities that have grown too fast. The place has become a bit squalid, if not dirty and dangerous. On Saturday night, Californians cross the border to go to the bars and enjoy themselves in an atmosphere that's hard to describe. There's no need to change your dollars into pesos, because everything in Tijuana is bought or sold in dollars. If you speak Spanish, you may be able to do some good deals here.

This little excursion into Mexico is useful from the shopping point of view – you can get clothes, jewellery and alcohol, but remember that you're only allowed one bottle of tequila! On the road to Ensenada, just over a mile (2km) from the border, there's a large market selling craft products.

Take note that it's inadvisable to drink anything alcoholic in the street, even if you have it hidden in a paper bag, and especially if you're an unmistakable *gringo*. It's not unheard of for people to suddenly get to know the wrong side of a cell after a bad beer decision. If this should happen to you, point out quickly that you're a friendly foreigner – it might help!

If nothing else, being in Tijuana gives you a useful insight into the strained relations between Mexico and the United States – it takes a month to earn in Mexico what you can earn in a week in Tijuana . . . or a day in San Diego.

BETWEEN SAN DIEGO AND TIJUANA

■ **San Diego Factory Outlet Center**: 4498 Camino de la Plaza, San Ysidro. ☎ (619) 690-2999. Open daily, 10am–8pm (7pm Saturday, 6pm Sunday). Coming from San Diego via Interstate I-5, turn right at 'Last US Exit' and follow Camino de la Plaza, which is signed one block further on. This large shopping mall has 35 factory shops, including Levi Strauss, Nike and Ray-Ban. The prices are very attractive, but all the goods are slight seconds.

PALM SPRINGS

AREA CODE: 760

About 150 miles (240km) from Los Angeles, Palm Springs is regarded as the place of rest and recreation for the better-off citizens of America's large cities. According to legend, it owes its success entirely to the impatience of Marlene Dietrich. In 1932, she is said to have had thrown out two actors who were hogging the city's only tennis court. They reacted by setting up their own club, The Racquet Club, and inviting all their showbiz friends to the opening. The stars have flocked here ever since. Today, more than 50 private clubs make up the backbone of the 'city', and the stars' houses, surrounded by the inevitable high walls, are spread out amid a total of 85 golf clubs.

Arriving in the city is quite surprising – it seems that, in a bowl right in the middle of the Californian desert, you come across a real oasis. This was achieved by diverting the waters of the Colorado River, as they did at Las Vegas. In summer, the temperature can go as high as 120°F/55°C so there's relatively little atmosphere. On the plus side, the hotels are much cheaper then.

USEFUL ADDRESS

Visitors' Center: 2781 North Palm Canyon Drive, to the north of the centre. ☎ 778-8418 or freephone: ☎ 1-800-34-SPRINGS. Website: www.palm-springs.org. Open daily, 9am–5pm. They're friendly and efficient here, and offer maps and brochures, including a well-produced Visitors' Guide, and information about trips into the desert, and so on. Hotel reservations in 80 of the city's establishments can be made free of charge, and they can get you fantastically low rates in summer.

WHERE TO STAY

From early June to late August, the prices charged by the big hotels are reduced by as much as half, so you can afford great luxury for the usual price of a motel. The Hyatt, for example, can cost less than $50!

☆–☆☆ BUDGET TO MODERATE

Palm Canyon Inn: 1450 South Palm Canyon Drive, not far from the firehouse. ☎ 320-7767. One of the best-value-for-money places, considering its situation very near the centre. The rooms are unpretentious but clean, with TV and kitchenette. Small swimming pool and jacuzzi.

Budget Host Inn: 1277 South Palm Canyon Drive. ☎ 325-5574. Fax: 327-2020. Beautiful rooms with TV, air-conditioning, refrigerator and coffee maker. Pleasant swimming pool.

Days Inn Tropics: 411 East Palm Canyon Drive. ☎ 327-1391. Fax: 323-3493. A little set back from the main boulevard. The rooms are motel-type, but well kept. There are two decent-sized swimming pools. Breakfast is included.

WHERE TO EAT

☆☆–☆☆☆ MODERATE TO EXPENSIVE

✕ **Jeremiah's Steak House**: 1201 East Palm Canyon Drive, in the middle of a parking lot. ☎ 327-1469. In a room where everything's made of wood, deep benches are laid out in semi-circles. They serve excellent food, with a pleasant salad bar. The bar's OK, with TVs tuned in to baseball games.

✕ **Las Casuelas Terraza**: 222 South Palm Canyon Drive. ☎ 325-2794. This is one of the oldest restaurants in Palm Springs in a very pretty white house with green shutters. Good Mexican specialities. The terrace in the evening is very pleasant. Some evenings there's musical entertainment, so it's always full and booking is advised.

☆☆☆☆ SPLASH OUT

✕ **Marriot Desert Springs**: 74855 Country Club Drive, at Palm Desert. Travelling via Route 111, take Country Club Drive on the left and follow it for approximately 4 miles (6km) or, from Highway 10, take the Country Club exit. ☎ 341-2211. Fax: 341-1872. In this crazy resort, everything is built around the theme of water: ponds, waterfalls, fountains, etc. There's an immense lobby in the form of an atrium, from which water-shuttles take you to the various restaurants attached to the hotel. You can choose from Italian, Japanese, Californian, fish, etc. with the menus displayed at each landing-point. The short boat trip enables you to see the pink flamingos as you pass by. There are five swimming pools and two 18-hole golf courses. It's just the thing if you aren't afraid of luxury and, out of season (i.e. in summer) and during the week, you can get a room from $120.

WHERE TO GO IN THE EVENING

It all happens around South Palm Canyon Drive, between Andreas and Baristo Road.

Ice House: 262 South Palm Canyon Drive. This bar serves frozen alcohol – crushed ice, flavoured with alcohol, fruit juice or cordials. The drinks have such exotic names as 'Purple Orgasm', 'Blue Devil', 'Sex in the Desert' or 'Zombie' and there are a few appetizers. It's a large space, open to the outside, with a billiard table in one corner. Good entertainment.

🍸 **Peabody's Coffee Bar**: 134 South Palm Canyon Drive. Good music and a more interesting clientele than the Ice House.

WHAT TO SEE AND DO

– **Golf**: Palm Springs is a paradise for golfers, so it would be a pity not to grab the opportunity, if you're keen on the sport. Some golf courses are public and you can do a round for $25–40 as long as you're happy to tee off at 6am; otherwise, it'll cost you $70–80. Details from the tourist information office.

– **Celebrity Tours**: 4751 East Palm Canyon Drive, Suite C. ☎ 770-2700. Tours lasting one hour or 2 hours 30 minutes are run daily. They take you round some of the city's famous places, passing in front of the houses of the stars – though it's interesting to note that some of the stars have only been here once or twice!

– **Aerial Tramway**: approximately 6 miles (10km) north of the city: take Tramway Road on the left above Palm Canyon Drive. Cars have difficulty just getting to the parking lot, because it's more than a bit steep here. In only 14 minutes, you climb from 2,600ft (800m) to more than 9,200ft (2,800m). A cable-car service runs from 10am during the week, 8am at weekends, approximately every 30 minutes. There's snow on top in winter and you can ski there. In summer, there's a good choice of walking routes in Mount San Jacinto Park.

WHAT TO SEE AND DO IN THE AREA

★ **Joshua Tree National Park**: Approximately 31 miles (50km) north-east of Palm Springs. Don't miss the fields of windmills at the exit from the city: they'll probably bring back memories if you saw the movie *Rain Man*.

Joshua Tree National Park is a magnificent desert nature reserve with a wide variety of landscapes and animal species, including coyotes, pumas and kangaroo rats, living in an environment of cacti and giant rocks. There are also numerous joshua trees – which gave their name to an album by U2. Also known as the yucca cactus and a plant not a tree, it grows to 30ft (9m) and is distinguished by its grotesque shape. Note that it's very hot here – all the safety rules apply for travel in the desert.

– **Entrance to the park**: if you arrive from Palm Springs, follow Park Boulevard for 3 or 4 miles (5 or 6km). Access is via West Entrance Station. The ticket, which costs $10, is valid for a week. Keep it safe, because they'll ask you for it at the exit!

ℹ **Visitors' Center**: 74485 National Park Drive, at 29 Palms, at the north entrance to the park. ☎ (760) 367-7511. Open daily, 8am–5pm. The brochure is well produced.

★ **Hidden Valley**: one of the first stops if you enter from the west. According to legend, cattle-rustlers hid their booty here. There's a short hiking route in this valley, which is disguised by huge blocks of rock.

★ **Key's View**: at an altitude of 5,250ft (1,600m), there's a superb view of the park and the mountains.

★ **Cholla Garden**: a strange garden made up of hundreds of cacti.

If you fancy staying here, there are at least two campgrounds, some motels and one moderate-priced hotel: **Joshua Tree Inn B&B**, Route 62 leading to 29 Palms. ☎ (760) 366-1188.

NEVADA

LAS VEGAS

AREA CODE: 702

Located 270 miles (440km) northeast of Los Angeles and 560 miles (900km) southeast of San Francisco, Las Vegas is anchored in a sun-blasted desert plain in the extreme south of the State of Nevada.

Whether you come here to have fun or get a tan, to gamble your money away or to get married (or divorced), you should try to arrive either at sunset or after dark so you can see 'the Strip' with its thousands of flashing neon signs. The Strip is what they call the long Las Vegas Boulevard, which runs across the city from north to south. Some say that it got its name because there was a good chance of losing your shirt here after gambling all your money away. Another reason for arriving at night is that the heat is pretty unbearable during the day.

ONE CITY, SEVERAL STYLES

Since the early 1990s, the city has been gripped by building fever. Cranes tower into the sky and buildings sprout from the ground like mushrooms after a shower of rain, each more way-out than the last. Several giant amusement parks have been created on the Strip: the Adventuredrome (which used to be called the Grand Slam Canyon) at the Circus Circus Hotel, the MGM Grand Adventures Theme Park, Treasure Island, and the Stratosphere Tower. This has probably been done with the aim of attracting families, the new and promising clientele on which Las Vegas, in a quest for respectability, is beginning to place a lot of emphasis.

The official line is that the people in charge of economic development would like to make the town 'a multi-purpose place of welcome'. In plainer terms, Las Vegas has for decades been building a sinful reputation based on gambling, money and sex but is now trying to clean up its image. Over a period of several years, it has been transforming itself into an immense 'show city', not unlike Disneyland and Hollywood. The objective is already close to being achieved. Oscar Goodman (nicknamed 'The Big O'), the new plebiscite mayor who won his place in 1999 with 64 per cent of the vote, is very keen to make his town respectable. (There may be a slight irony here, given his 30 years of service as a lawyer to the Mafia.)

Families wandering down the Strip is now a daily sight. But the city is voracious and wants still more. Fearing the legalization of gaming in more American states (42 already) and in order to protect itself from competition, Las Vegas has begun to develop an ever-more-luxurious hotel infrastructure. It presents itself these days in many guises: as a gaming metropolis, an artistic, theatrical and musical showcase featuring some of the world's most amazing spectacles, and still as a fairground. The city is also busy promoting itself as a convention centre.

A BRIEF HISTORY

Las Vegas owes its existence to the construction of the railroad in 1905. Situated right in the middle of the desert, the valley of Las Vegas (Spanish for 'the prairies') was, in 1840, a camping place for the caravans that travelled along the old Spanish trail from Santa Fe to California.

Under the constitutions of the various states of the Union, generally of either Puritan or Catholic persuasion, divorce and marriage were difficult matters. Long waiting periods and serious reasons were required. Nevada showed itself to be more liberal in this domain. There was a need to be able to fix up marriages for cowboys and pioneers with the least possible fuss or delay, such transient individuals staying only briefly in the area. Where divorce was concerned, the only thing demanded by the authorities was that you were a resident of the state, and this could be acquired in just six weeks. So someone hoping for a divorce needed only to spend a holiday of 42 days in a Las Vegas hotel in order to qualify. And the range of 'serious reasons' was usefully extended: Nevada provided a good one by inventing the notion of 'mental cruelty'.

Marriage in Las Vegas is still an extremely simple formality and it isn't even necessary to show a period of residence. It's enough for two people to turn up and fill in a form. So, each year, Las Vegas welcomes hundreds of thousands of Americans and foreign tourists who, while pushed for time, nevertheless wish either to tie the knot of marriage or pull it asunder.

The attitude of the authorities to gambling undoubtedly sprang from their liberalization of the divorce laws. They needed to keep their 'clients' occupied during their 42 days of leisure. So, in 1931, all forms of gambling were allowed without any prior formality. It all began around the hard core of the old city, in Fremont Street. This historic street, named after John Fremont, a famous explorer of the American West during the 19th century, has accumulated many firsts. The first hotel in Las Vegas, the Nevada Hotel, opened its doors here in 1906 – today, it's the Golden Gate Hotel (map II, A1, **22**). Fremont Street was also the first street to be paved, in 1925. The first gaming licence was granted in 1931 to the Northern Club. The first neon sign was installed at the Boulder Club in 1934. More than chemin de fer or roulette, the symbol of Nevada is the slot-machine. These were born during the Prohibition era, starting out as sweet machines that underwent something of a modification.

BUGSY SIEGEL – GANGSTER AND VISIONARY

Everything escalated with the arrival on the scene of 'the most dangerous man in America', a certain Benjamin Siegel, known as 'Bugsy'. This super-rich Jewish gangster, an unusually violent man, was not lacking in ideas. He controlled the biggest gambling and prostitution networks in Los Angeles. Obsessed by the movies, and driven by his own yearning for power, he sent his trusted representative, one 'Little Moe' Sedway, to Nevada. Moe spotted a small establishment, El Rancho Vegas, which Bugsy bought with financial assistance from 'Boss' Meyer Lansky. Bugsy then built the Flamingo, the first 'giant' casino in Las Vegas. Opened at Christmas 1946, this started as a financial disaster.

Shortly afterwards, Bugsy died when he was shot in the eye at the house of his mistress in Beverly Hills. The previously dormant Flamingo was transformed into a goose that laid ever more golden eggs. Success for the city followed. The Flamingo still exists today, though it is now outclassed by a new generation of mega-casinos. The Flamingo's story was told in the film *Bugsy,* with Warren Beatty taking the title role.

DAZZLING EXPANSION

At a time when no social security fund existed in the United States, the trades unions collected funds for their own retirement schemes. The powerful Teamsters Union accumulated enormous sums in cash, which they then needed to invest. The union's links with the Mafia led it to invest in the casinos of Las Vegas from 1945 to 1946. Apart from their enormous profits, these enterprises had and still have one very great advantage – almost all the money that comes in from gambling is in the form of cash.

In 1966 the millionaire Howard Hughes opened up a virulent campaign against the Mafia. His objective was not to hunt down the masters of the city but to break their monopoly on gambling for money. He put pressure on the elected officials of Nevada to ensure that any enterprise quoted on the Stock Exchange could legally obtain the licence required to open a casino. The patrons of the casino-hotels then witnessed the arrival of a new type of investor – the powerful hotel chains, such as Hilton and Mirage, and even commercial companies like ITT.

BABYLON, REVISED BY DISNEYLAND

Las Vegas is the uncontested most outrageous city in the United States – even more so than New York City or LA. Some people even say that you can't have a proper understanding of the country until you've been here. In Las Vegas, everything's possible – it even snowed once, in 1973. Las Vegas brings together all the contradictions and follies of America – architectural excess, orgies of electrical consumption, more food than you can eat, gigantic hotels . . . It invites a frenzy of getting and spending, offers lightning marriages and quickie divorce and reveals something of the murky empires of the Mafia in alliance with the glitzy world of showbiz . . . It has to be admitted, this is an awful lot for a country so assiduously puritan – but that's where its 'Sin City' nickname comes from.

In spite of – or because of – all of this, Las Vegas is a place you should see, if only once, even though it quickly begins to depress anyone with a European sensibility. Behind the wonderful decor, the sub-text can be terrible – you see processions of lost old folk and young people hooked on slot machines. People without a dime mingle with those who are loaded, gamblers stand in long lines almost transfixed, and all of this against the deafening background noise of the inescapable one-armed bandits (see p. 424).

There is an atmosphere here that's quite unique, and, at least superficially, the avenues of flashing neon can look enchanting. The cost of living is much lower than you might expect, if you know how to fix things.

So, take this tip: organize yourself one wild night, then get the hell out and head for the wide open spaces again before the degenerate city gets a grip on you!

KEY FACTS ABOUT LAS VEGAS

– **Population**: about 1,200,000, which accounts for three-quarters of the total population of Nevada. The city's population has doubled in the last 10 years.

– **Number of visitors**: more than 30 million every year. This represents about 7 or 8 per cent of the population of the United States.

– **Economy**: the hotels and casinos are the main employers, accounting for 25 per cent of the city's direct employment. Every new hotel room generates an additional 2.5 jobs on average. The average occupancy rate of the hotels is about 87 per cent, which is a record for the United States.

– **Casino profits**: in an average year, the casinos of Nevada make about $8 billion or nearly three times as much as the foreign debt of a country such as Mali. Las Vegas accounts for 6.3 billion of this. Almost 50 per cent of the profits made by Hilton in the United States is obtained from its two Las Vegas hotel-casinos.

– **Gamblers' winnings**: the biggest jackpot ever won amounted to $27.5 million. That was in 1998, at the Palace Station. On average, more than 50 people each year win over $200,000.

– **Marriages**: the city has about 50 chapels carrying out wedding ceremonies. In 1995, 101,755 marriage licences were issued at Las Vegas and Laughlin.

THE WORLD'S BIGGEST HOTELS

As evidence of the city's galloping megalomania, 18 of the 20 biggest hotels in the United States are located in Las Vegas. This crazy hotel hit-parade is headed by the brand new Venetian, which has an unbelievable 7,000 suites. The more modestly sized MGM Grand Hotel & Theme Park has a mere 5,005 rooms, the Luxor over 4,400 rooms, the Excalibur has 4,032 rooms, the Flamingo Hilton, 3,642, and so on.

To get some idea of the size of this place, add together the total number of rooms in the town's six main hotels (the Venetian, MGM, Luxor, Excalibur, Mandalay Bay and Flamingo Hilton) and you have the total capacity of all the hotels in San Francisco and San Diego put together! And you still haven't seen it all. The Luxor has been expanded by 1,950 rooms in two twin towers attached to its great smoked glass pyramid, the Circus Circus has added 1,000 rooms, and Caesar's Palace another 1,300! Some of these giants have only just emerged from their plastic wrappings, such as the New York-New York (2,035 rooms) and the Bellagio (3,000 rooms), the Paris–Las Vegas Casino Resort (2,500 rooms), or the new Aladdin / Planet Hollywood.

According to the Convention Center, the total available hotel capacity of

Las Vegas now totals over 120,000 rooms. Come to think of it, the idea of sleeping under the stars actually begins to feel quite attractive!

THE CLIMATE OF A DESERT ZONE

In summer, with some differences in detail, Las Vegas has approximately the same weather as Khartoum, in the Sudan. In contrast to California, which is in a temperate subtropical zone, the city of Las Vegas is at the heart of a vast desert where the climate is arid, hot and dry. The annual rainfall is only 25 inches (10cm). The sun is in the sky all day long for 211 days in the year and puts in some kind of appearance for at least 320 days.

– **June to September**: this is the hottest period of the year. The days are torrid. The mean temperature is 105°F/40°C, but it's a little cooler at night 73–75°F/24–25°C).

– **November to March**: A funny old winter, this, when the temperature hovers around 55°F/13°C during the day. The air is much more breatheable at this time of year than in the middle of summer. All the same, you'll need to take a jacket with you.

TIP
In summer you have to watch out for your sinuses, because of the abrupt contrast between the torrid temperature outside and the very cold air-conditioning inside the casinos and hotels.

ARRIVING IN LAS VEGAS

McCarran Airport (map I, B3) is 1 mile (1.5km) from the Strip. The air traffic it carries makes it the tenth most heavily frequented airport in the world, with 840 flights a day on average.

The minute you arrive at the airport you're likely to feel gripped by the city's passion for gambling. Hundreds of slot-machines are installed right there in the airport's waiting rooms and they even have them in the baggage reclaim area.

– There's plenty of information available from the tourist information office at the airport, including various publications that give you money-off coupons.

– From the airport, five private **shuttle bus** companies serve the main Downtown and Strip hotels. Allow about $4 for the Strip and $5 to get to the town centre.

– If there are three or four of you, a **taxi** will work out slightly cheaper ($12–15 for the Strip depending on distance and time of day, $15–19 for Downtown). You could even treat yourselves to a **limo** ride for only a few dollars extra!

Bus no. 108 (Paradise/Swenson) leaves every 30 minutes between

5.10am and 1.20am and is the only one that goes to the airport ($1). It runs into the town centre via the Hilton on the outward journey and the Convention Centre on the return, crossing the Strip at the Sahara.

USEFUL ADRESSES AND INFORMATION

Visitors' Centre (map I, B2): in a branch of the Las Vegas Convention Centre, on the other side of Paradise Road. If they try and make you pay for the parking lot, say that you are going to the Visitors' Centre and you should be allowed in for free. To get information by post, write to 3150 Paradise Road, Las Vegas NV 89109-9096. ☎ 892-0711 or 892-7575. Fax: 892-7692. Website: www.lasvegas24hours.com. The centre is open every day (including weekends) 8am–5pm. It offers myriad brochures on the hotels, restaurants, casinos and excursions in the region. The *Las Vegas Showguide* gives a full list of shows. For novices, there is a gaming guide detailing the thousand-and-one ways to lose your money at baccarat, craps, roulette, etc.

Greyhound Station (map II, A2): in Downtown, 200 Main Street, on a level with Carson Street. ☎ 382-8009. Freephone: ☎ 1-800-231-2222. Departures to Los Angeles every 2 hours on average, with seven buses per day to San Diego, six to Phoenix, five to Laughlin, four to Denver and only two to Salt Lake.

■ Car hire: the majority of big and smaller companies are present at McCarran airport. Check the newspapers for good deals.

Alamo: ☎ 263-8411 or freephone 1-800-327-9633

Avis: ☎ 261-5595 or freephone 1-800-831-2847

Budget: ☎ 736-1212 or freephone 1-800-527-0770

Dollar: ☎ 739-8408 or freephone 1-800-800-4000

Hertz: ☎ 736-4900 or freephone 1-800-654-3131

National: ☎ 261-5391 or freephone 1-800-CAR-RENT

■ **Currency exchange**: 3025 Las Vegas Boulevard South. ☎ 791-3301. Open Monday–Friday 8.30am–5pm.

– There are cash dispensers in practically every casino. Just remember to have a bit of self-control!

– There's an excellent **local radio station** on 105.5 FM for listening to yesterday's hits – and today's, too – while you're waiting in a traffic jam.

– **Airport information**: ☎ (702) 261-5743

– **Metro Police**: ☎ (702) 795-3111

– **Weather**: ☎ (702) 736-3854

– **State of the roads**: ☎ (702) 486-3116

PUBLIC TRANSPORT

– **CAT** (Citizens Area Transit) provides a service across the whole town within a 12-mile (20km) radius. The buses generally run from 5.30am to 1.30am, every day of the week. Some of the busiest lines even run 24 hours a day (including the 301, which runs non-stop up and down the Strip). The normal fare is $1 (exact change required), or $1.50 for the 301 and the 302. If you're planning to stay a few days you could buy a bag of 40 tokens (you need two per journey) for $15 or a monthly pass for $20. For further information call CAT: ☎ 228-7433.

– From the **Greyhound**, if you're going to the Las Vegas International Hostel, take the Strip bus (301) southbound, which runs every 10–15 minutes. For the Las Vegas Backpackers Hostel, located to the east of Downtown, take the 107 from the DTC building (four blocks north of Greyhound, behind the post office building). Try and carry your backpack like a suitcase, as they don't allow backpacks on the buses.

– **Las Vegas Strip Trolley**: runs up and down the Strip approximately every 15 minutes between the Stratosphere Tower to the north and the Luxor to the south between 9.30am and 2am. The cost is $1.40 per trip (exact money required). For information ☎ 382-1404.

– **Monorails**: several of these little suspended trains provide a free link between the hotels and casinos under the same ownership. Consequently, there is one between the Mirage and Treasure Island, between Bellagio and the Monte Carlo, between Bally's and the MGM, as well as between the Mandalay Bay and the Excalibur with a stop at the Luxor. They all have different opening times, but they generally function between 8am or 9am through until 1am or later (4am in some cases).

All the casinos have free parking lots in order to make things as easy as possible for players. Travelling by car is a good alternative to taking the bus or having to walk in the hot sun.

WHERE TO STAY

Another special feature of Las Vegas is that the hotels don't look like hotels. In fact, every hotel also operates as a casino, although the casinos don't always operate as hotels.

One snag is that this isn't always very peaceful (if, for example, your room is directly above the gaming tables); and the reception desk is somewhere in the middle of an expanse of one-armed bandits.

An advantage is that room prices are low, for the US. This may just be a ploy to draw you into the casinos. There are over 120,000 rooms in the city, and this will rise to 130,000 before too long. If you can't find what you're looking for here, you're being a bit picky!

IMPORTANT: outside the rush period and at weekends, when Americans flock to Las Vegas in their tens of thousands, the big hotels sometimes work out to be less expensive than the motels listed here. Don't be shy to ask around before making your selection. Some, on the other hand, require you to stay at least two nights and to reserve the day before in summer. In any case, it's best to avoid coming at the weekend. If you're lost in a shorts-clad human tide, dodging between whole flotillas of cars, it is much more difficult to enjoy the free attractions and you will almost certainly find yourself in long queues to get something to eat.

From Sunday evening to Friday morning, prices in both hotels and restaurants are much more attractive. You must make sure, however, that there are no major conferences scheduled for your visit, as this seems to cause prices to triple. You can check with the Convention Center to find out just when the town is expecting to be overrun with computer analysts or dentists . . . If you arrive by bus or by car, stop in a restaurant or a fast-food outlet where you may be able to pick up some coupons giving reductions on hotels and motels. It's not surprising that in the US some advertisers use the phrase 'at Vegas prices!' to mean 'cheap'.

On parking, it's worth remembering that every hotel in town will have its own private parking lot. Even if you're not staying at the hotel, you can often get the valet parking attendant to park your car for you, in exchange for a few dollars. This is obviously better than driving around looking for a parking place by yourself.

– **Information and reservations**: ☎ 1-800-233-5594. This freephone number will give you up-to-date information on the availability of hotels, and the best prices, on the Strip and Downtown, as well as in other towns in Nevada. You can make a reservation using a credit card.

– There is also another freephone service, run by the Convention and Visitors' Bureau: ☎ 1-800-332-5333 (every day).

DOWNTOWN (THE AREA AROUND THE RAILWAY STATION)

☆ BUDGET

The less luxurious casinos attract a more working-class clientele. The hotels associated with these casinos are quite cheap. From June to September and on weekends, it is best to reserve ahead.

Las Vegas Backpackers Hostel (map I, B1, **2**): 1322 Fremont Avenue, to the east of Downtown. ☎ 385-1130. Freephone: ☎ 1-800-580-8958. Fax: 385-4940. E-mail: vegasbackpackers@hotmail.com. One night in a six-bed dormitory costs $15 or only $12 in an eight-bed dormitory, breakfast included (toast, pancakes, etc.). Double rooms are also available at $35 weekdays and $50 weekends. All major credit cards are accepted. Take bus 107 or phone from the Greyhound station to be picked up. Situated to the east of Downtown, this private youth hostel was once a motel, which means you can still enjoy the use of a swimming pool and jacuzzi. All the dormitories (converted from the old bedrooms) have a private bathroom, air-conditioning and cable TV. The doors are painted with the flags of different countries and each room is guaranteed to have matching decor before long. Plus there's a pool table, laundry room, pay-as-you-go access to the Internet and a free shuttle service to the Strip. There's even free beer every Friday and Saturday night! You can have a barbecue on the terrace and the doors remain open all night. Inexpensive restaurant next door. Guests can take advantage of trips organized to Los Angeles at least three times a week (usually Wednesday, Friday and Sunday) at a cost of $36 a ride. The price includes a drop-off wherever you choose.

☗ **Gold Spike Casino** (map II, B1, **10**): 400 East Ogden (and Little Street). ☎ 384-8444. Fax: 384-8768. Freephone: ☎ 1-800-634-6703. Barely two blocks from the big time, this hotel has no charm but is modern and clean. It's one of the cheapest in the city and breakfast is free. All rooms have a phone, TV, air-conditioning and bathroom. Interesting that prices are the same all year round. They don't take reservations for Saturdays.

☗ **Western Hotel Bingo Parlor** (map II, B2, **11**): 899 East Fremont Avenue, level with 9th Street. ☎ 384-4620. Fax: 385-4047. Freephone: ☎ 1-800-634-6703. Even cheaper than the Gold Spike Casino but slightly further away from the centre, a standard double costs $20 with telephone, TV, air-conditioning and bathroom. The rooms in the annexe are smaller and a bit gloomy (there are 16 with shower). In the gaming room, the ambiance is 'deep West', so you could be rubbing shoulders with policemen, lorry-drivers and the like.

☗ **Ambassador East Motel** (map II, I B2, **14**), at 916 East Fremont (☎ 384-8281), is almost opposite the Western Hotel Bingo Parlor, and is under the same ownership. The prices are identical. The rooms are bigger but avoid those in the oldest wing – when we say old we mean old.

☗ **Budget Inn** (map II, A2, **12**): 301 South Main Street. ☎ 385-5560. Freephone: ☎ 1-800-959-9062. Fax: 382-9273. Slightly more expensive than the places listed above, costing from $29 during the week and $45–$65 at weekends. This is one of the few hotels that is not also a casino and it's situated only 50 yards (45 metres) from the Greyhound station. Good welcome. The rooms are clean, with shower, WC, TV and phone.

☆☆–☆☆☆ MODERATE TO EXPENSIVE

☗ **Lady Luck** (map II, A1, **13**): on the corner of Ogden Avenue and 3rd Street, in the heart of Downtown. ☎ 477-3000. Freephone: ☎ 1-800-523-9582. Fax: 477-7021. The double rooms vary between $35 and $40 during the week but go up to $45–$99 at the weekend. A casino on a human scale, offering good value for money and frequented by a very middle-class clientele.

☗ **Four Queens** (map II, A1–2, **15**): 202 East Fremont Avenue. ☎ 385-4011. Fax: 387-5133. Freephone: ☎ 1-800-634-6045. Prices change all the time: they can be as low as $39 during the week while soaring to $99 or more on a Friday and Saturday. The average is around $59 for a double. Right in the centre, on the town's most lively street, this mid-range luxury casino offers 700 comfortable rooms.

☆☆☆ EXPENSIVE

☗ **Golden Nugget** (map II, A2, **16**): 129 East Fremont Avenue. ☎ 385-7111. Fax: 386-8362. Freephone: ☎ 1-800-634-3454. Website: www.goldennugget.com. In summer, prices are lower: from $44 during the week, $79 at weekends. If you plan carefully, this is an opportunity to stay in a palace for next to nothing. Note, however, that prices triple at the busiest times. Right in the heart of Downtown, this luxury hotel-casino eschews vulgarity in any form, including the use of cheap materials. The most expensive marbles and fabrics were used in its decoration (for a more detailed description, *see* 'The Casinos, Downtown' *below*.) The luxury entrance hall is superb. The hotel also has three excellent restaurants and a cafe, and probably the city's finest facilities in terms of swimming baths and relaxation. Reserved for residents of the hotel, there's an elegant spa, which includes a marvellous pool with a wave machine.

ON THE STRIP (LAS VEGAS BOULEVARD) AND NEARBY

☆ BUDGET

Las Vegas International Hostel (map I, A1, **1**): 1208 Las Vegas Boulevard South. Level with Charleston Boulevard. ☎ 385-9955. This used to be a small motel, now converted into a youth hostel. It costs around $12 for members and $14 for non-members. Six private rooms at $26 for two. The dormitories have four or six beds, each with a shower and toilet. Could do with a bit more in the way of heating in winter. Cooking facilities are provided. The Youth Hostel offices are open 7am–11pm. There's quite a comradely atmosphere, and no curfew. They give you a key to get back in whenever you want. There are washing machines, and you can get Internet acess for $6 per hour. A decent place – the cheapest in Las Vegas. Very good for backpackers travelling alone. For two, it's better to go to a motel and pay a few dollars more. The hostel arranges excursions.

☆☆ MODERATE

There is a fairly good choice of attractively priced options in this category. All you have to do is to decide where you would actually prefer to spend the night.

Rodeway Inn (map I, B3, **4**): 187 East Tropicana Avenue. ☎ 795-3311. Freephone: ☎ 1-800-228-2000. Fax: 795-7333. From $40 weekdays to $70 at weekends (apart from special occasions when prices can soar). With a coupon you can even get a room for $32–34. Excellent value for money. Opposite MGM, right next to the Motel 6. Free use of a small swimming pool and jacuzzi, and washing machines available for guests' use. Although not very big, the rooms are comfortable. There are two restaurants right on the spot: Carrows (suitable for families) and Jeremiah's Steakhouse.

Vagabond Inn (map I, A2–3, **8**): 3285 Las Vegas Boulevard South. ☎ 735-5102. Freephone: ☎ 1-800-828-8032. Fax: 735-0168. Rooms start from $44 (single) or $49 (double) weekdays and $56–$59 at weekends. Some rooms have recently been renovated, with fridge, microwave and balcony overlooking the swimming pool (heated in winter) and are a little more expensive – up to $70. The Vagabond Inn is ideally situated opposite Treasure Island and offers good value for money. There are shuttles to the airport 7.30am–10.30pm.

Somerset House Hotel (map I, A2, **9**): 294 Convention Center

Drive. ☎ 735-4411. Freephone: ☎ 1-800-336-4280. Fax: 389-2388. 200 yards (180 metres) from the Visitors' Center. Although not as smart looking as the Rodeway and the Vagabond, it has 104 very clean, comfortable rooms, all equipped with a coffee-maker. Some also have a fridge, cooker or kitchenette. Good value for money.

Howard Johnson (map I, A1. **10**): 1401 Las Vegas Boulevard, next to the Little White Chapel, to the north of the Strip. ☎ 388-0301. Freephone: ☎ 1-800-446-4656. Prices from $49 (single) to $59 (twin beds) weekdays and up to $99 at weekends. This good chain motel, which is built around an attractive swimming pool, has comfortable bedrooms with cupboard, fridge and coffee-maker. There's a Cuban restaurant, the Florida Cafe, open 7am–10pm every day.

Wild Wild West Gambling Hall & Hotel (map I, A3, **5**): 3330 West Tropicana Avenue. ☎ 740-0000. Freephone: ☎ 1-800-777-1514. Fax: 736-7106. From $29 during the week and up to $59 at the weekend. Good value for money. Set slightly away from the Strip, this motel has a huge parking lot, a swimming pool, a small laundry and a small adjacent casino. Some rooms have a view of the towers of New York-New York. Shuttles run to the airport in the morning and to the Strip around the middle of the day.

Motel 6 (map I, B3, **3**): 196 East Tropicana Avenue. ☎ 798-0728. Freephone: ☎ 1-800-466-8355. Rooms cost $46 weekdays and up to $70 at weekends. Close to the Strip and near the airport. Try to check in early in the morning, as it is often full at weekends and during holiday periods (despite the fact that it has nearly 600 rooms). Swimming pool. Handy location, right by the MGM, Excalibur, and Luxor. A bit on the expensive side given the general level of comfort. Mini-market opposite reception.

Tam O'Shanter Motel (map I, A2–3, **6**): 3317 Las Vegas Boulevard. ☎ 735-7331. Freephone: ☎ 1-800-727-DICE. Fax: 735-2372. From $46 during the week up to $65 at the weekend. This partially renovated 1970s motel is next to the Vagabond Inn. It's well located (opposite Treasure Island), but considerably less attractive. A possible second choice if you are arriving on a busy weekend.

☆☆☆ EXPENSIVE

Excalibur (map I, A3): 3850 Las Vegas Boulevard, on the corner with Tropicana Avenue. ☎ 597-7700. Freephone: ☎ 1-937-7777. Fax: 597-7040. Website: www.excalibur-casino.com. Impossible

Where to Stay

- **1** Las Vegas International Hostel
- **2** Las Vegas Backpackers Hostel
- **3** Motel 6
- **4** Rodeway Inn
- **5** Wild Wild West Gambling Hall & Hotel
- **6** Tam O'Shanter Motel
- **8** Vagabond Inn
- **9** Somerset House Hotel
- **10** Howard Johnson

Where to Eat

- **20** Gilley's
- **21** Dive
- **22** Sfuzzi
- **23** Smith & Wollensky

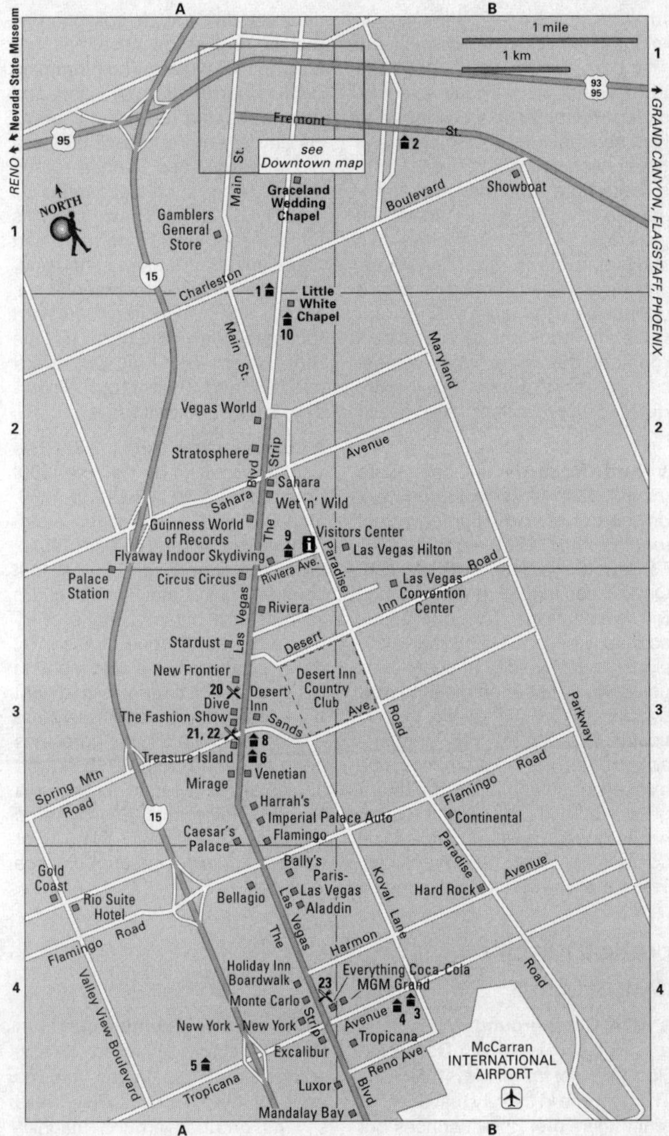

LAS VEGAS – THE STRIP (MAP I)

to miss – from a distance, you might take it for a mini-Disneyland! The best deal in Las Vegas: $49 from Sunday to Friday evening, except during school holidays and high season. All the mod cons and the service you would expect from a major hotel, and medieval atmosphere by the bucket-load! An incredible 4,032 bedrooms, two swimming pools, six restaurants, a chapel to get married in, etc. It is possible, and even strongly advisable to book ahead to ensure a room at this price whatever the day and time of year. For a more detailed description, *see* 'Casinos'.

☗ **Hard Rock Hotel and Cafe** (map I, B3): 4455 Paradise Road, on the corner with Harmon Street (behind the MGM). ☎ 693-5000. Freephone: ☎ 1-800-HRD-ROCK. Quite reasonably priced during the week (from $75) but prices soar at weekends to $155 – obviously best avoided at such times unless you are set on meeting new people, the young crowd in particular. With its 340 very comfortable rooms, it could almost be classed as intimate and boasts a giddy rock 'n' roll decor. Guitar necks even replace handles on some of the slot-machines. There's a showcase dedicated to Jimi Hendrix and a collection of guitars and stage costumes belonging to the stars. The swimming pool is surrounded by sand and palm trees and has several jacuzzis and a water chute. There is a big performance venue ('The Joint') where such legendaries as Bob Dylan, James Brown and Yes have been known to perform, and major events are often scheduled. For information and reservations ☎ 693-5066. Website: www.hardrockhotel.com. Shuttles to the Strip 10am–7pm (Sunday–Wednesday) and 9am–11pm (Thursday, Friday and Saturday).

☗ **Luxor** (map I, AB3): 3900 Las Vegas Boulevard. ☎ 262-4000. Freephone: ☎ 1-800-288-1000. Fax: 262-4405. One of the architectural successes of Las Vegas. From the airport you glimpse the life-size sphinx that stands guard in front of a pyramid that's every bit as big as the one at Giza. By day, it sparkles like a gold ingot; in the evening, it becomes midnight blue. Inside the pyramid there are 2,526 rooms, and the hotel has been extended, with two buildings alongside the pyramid containing a further 1,950 rooms. Slightly more expensive than the Excalibur. For a more detailed description, *see* 'Casinos'.

OUTSIDE THE CITY

CAMPGROUNDS

☗ **KOA Campground**: 4315 Boulder Highway, level with Desert Inn Road (east of the city). ☎ 451-5527. The only one in the city that accepts tents: there are 12 tent spaces but the ground's very hard and there's no shade. It does, however, have a swimming pool, jacuzzi, showers and launderette and there are free shuttles to the Strip.

☗ There are two **campgrounds** at Boulder City, 19 miles (30km) southeast of Las Vegas, on the edge of the Colorado River, and several grounds around magnificent Lake Mead, between Las Vegas and the Grand Canyon. Get a list from the tourist information office at Las Vegas.

WHERE TO EAT

Backpackers will be delighted to learn that Las Vegas is, without any doubt, the city with the lowest prices in the US for eating! The casinos vie with each other for your custom, so that it's possible to find yourself in front of a buffet offering all you can eat for $4, to get yourself a royal dinner for $5 and even a champagne brunch for $6! Of course, to get to the dining room you have to run the gauntlet of beckoning slot-machines but this doesn't seem to put off the punters, who crowd in at all hours of the day. Record attendance levels were recorded by Circus Circus, which served as many as 17,600 people in one day. The cooks do their best, but quality is sometimes questionable. Some casinos, rather than offering set-price buffets, prefer themed dining (seafood, exotic, etc.) which at the top end of the range can cost as much as $15. If you are very hungry this can still be worthwhile. As you will have guessed, most of the places that we recommend in this section are in fact casinos.

If you can't take the noise of the one-armed bandits any more, you can fall back on the standard fast-food outlets, which, under the pressure of competition, also give useful reductions! Don't forget to pick up fun coupons wherever you can find them (in hotels, inside newspapers), which relate to all kinds of promotions in the casinos (more details below). The casinos listed are those that most often offer cheap rates in their restaurants. But you'll find that plenty of others are advertised on specific dates in the local press or on giant posters on the Strip.

BUFFETS

✕ **Main Street Station** (map II, A1, **28**): on Main Street on a level with Ogden in Downtown. ☎ 387-1896. Its promo material declares that it was voted the best buffet in Las Vegas for 3 years running. Good-value breakfast ($5) served 7–10.30am; lunch ($9.50) 11am–3.30pm; dinner ($10) 3.30–10pm. This is a pleasant setting, built to resemble a Victorian-style station.

✕ **Golden Nugget** (map II, A1–2, **16**): 129 East Fremont Avenue. ☎ 386-8121. Breakfast 7–10.30am; lunch 10.30am–3pm; dinner 4–10pm, all at unbeatable prices. Half-price for children aged four–10, except on public holidays. Champagne brunch on Sunday 8am–10pm. On arrival in the main gaming room, look for signs indicating **The Buffet**. This is the cheapest restaurant in the hotel and is considered the best buffet in Las Vegas, although hotel guests are given priority. You won't believe how fast the queues form!

As well as the buffet, the hotel has two superb restaurants: **Stefano's**, which has perhaps the most 'sophisticated' decor, serving delicious cuisine from northern Italy and excellent affordable wines, and **Lillie Langtry's**, with late-19th-century decor and fine Cantonese cuisine. There is also a pizzeria and, near reception, the Carson Street Cafe, open 24 hours a day and with some good special offers on Chinese dishes for famished night owls.

✕ **Circus Circus** (map I, A2): 2880 Las Vegas Boulevard. ☎ 734-0410. One of the cheapest breakfasts in town, served 7–11.30am; lunch served noon–4pm, at an unbeatable price; dinner 4.30–10pm (11pm on Saturday), and it's hardly any more expensive. On Friday, there's seafood at the same price. An absolutely gigantic buffet is located at the back of the gaming room. At least 10,000 people eat here every day, and basically, you can help yourself to as much as you can carry, although quantity should never substitute for quality. Not for the faint-hearted though – some people won't be thrilled by the heat or the crowds, either. On the menu: salads, chicken, steak and ribs. The choice is very small and it's all very American in taste.

✕ **Luxor** (map I, A3–B3): 3900 Las Vegas Boulevard. ☎ 262-4000. The buffet in the basement (**Pharaoh's Pheast**) is open continuously 6.30am–11pm and is among the town's best known. Slightly more expensive than the previous entries: breakfast at $7.50; lunch at $8; dinner at $11.50. On top of that, the decor is unusual: you find yourself in the middle of an archaeological dig. A statue is half buried in the ground and others stand around majestically, while tools lie about here and there.

✕ **Mirage** (map I, A3): 3400 Las Vegas Boulevard South. ☎ 791-7111. Breakfast 7–10.45am; lunch 11am–2.45pm; dinner 3–9.30pm and champagne brunch on Sunday 8am–3.45pm. Reduced prices for children under 10. A good buffet, with salmon and prawns among other things.

– There are also eight restaurants in Mirage. They are not particularly cheap but some of them are worth it just for their exceptional decor. Among these, don't miss the marvellous **Kokomo's** (seafood and meats) in the middle of a tropical jungle, or the **Moongate** Chinese restaurant and the **Mikado** Japanese restaurant, both with a superb starry sky. Even if you don't eat there, it's still a feast for the eyes.

✕ **Monte Carlo** (map I, A3): 3770 Las Vegas Boulevard South, next to the New York-New York and almost opposite the MGM Grand Hotel. ☎ 730-7777. One of the latest grand hotel-casinos. Its buffet, less expensive than the one at the Rio, is breathtaking. It's very good and copious too! The decor is North African – Morocco-style.

✕ **Harrah's** (map I, A3): 3475 Las Vegas Boulevard South, opposite Caesar's Palace. ☎ 369-5000. Their breakfast is famous for its gigantic **Fresh Market Square Buffet**, served 7–11am; lunch 11am–4pm; dinner 4–10pm. Champagne brunch on Saturday and Sunday 10am–4pm. The interior decor is quite nice, with its giant vegetables and fruits; the quality of the food is good, which explains the sometimes rather long queues. **Joe's Bayou** restaurant serves Cajun cuisine from Louisiana in a more sophisticated setting.

✕ **Excalibur**: (map I, A3). 3850 Las Vegas Boulevard South, on the corner of Tropicana Avenue. *See also* 'Where to Stay'. ☎ 597-7777. Freephone: ☎ 1-800-937-7777. Fax: 597-7009. The **Round Table** buffet on the first floor is very attractive. Cheap breakfast, 6.30–11am. Expect to have to queue, though, as it's always very crowded. If you've had enough of buffets, you can find a decent little breakfast at the **Cafe Expresso**.

✕ **Village Seafood Buffet**: 3700 West Flamingo Road, in the hotel **Rio** (map I, A3) at the intersection with Valley View Boulevard. ☎ 252-7777. Lunch 11am–3pm Monday–Friday; dinner 6–10pm (11pm Friday and Saturday and from 4pm Saturday and Sunday). Weekend brunch for $24. Possibly the most refined bistro-type buffet in Las Vegas. Attentive service. Daily delivery of seafood and fish, all very well prepared. Despite the price, the queues can be quite something.

✕ **Stratosphere Tower** (map I, A2): 2000 Las Vegas Boulevard South. ☎ 380-7777. Breakfast 7–11am; lunch 11am–4pm; dinner 7–11pm. Salads, roast beef, soup, traditional American food and some interesting Chinese specialities. A bit canteen-like in style but they have amusing lamps in the shape of hot-air balloons.

✕ **Sahara** (map I, A2): 2535 Las Vegas Boulevard South. ☎ 737-2111. A fairly modest hotel-casino compared with its neighbours. It has to be said that the buffet is the least expensive if not the best in town: $4 for breakfast (6–11am), $5 at lunchtime (12 noon–3pm) and $6 in the evening (6–10pm). Weekend champagne brunch, served from 8.15am, costs $8. Some Italian and Asian specialities. Having said that, the restaurant dining room is quite canteen-like and the food itself is nothing exceptional.

✕ Other casinos where the prices are attractive, include, in no particular order: **Imperial Palace** (Emperor's Buffet), **Flamingo Hilton**, **Boardwalk Casino – Holiday Inn**, and **Bally's** (Big Kitchen).

☆☆ MODERATE

✕ **Gilley's** (map I, A2, **20**): in the New Frontier Hotel, 3120 Las Vegas Boulevard South. ☎ 794-8200. Open from 10am. This big saloon is famed throughout Las Vegas because of its mechanical steer! On Thursday evenings there are free rides for women and all drinks cost $1. On other days you can enjoy the dance floor and shake your stuff to the strains of Country and Western – live on Tuesday, Wednesday and Thursday (9pm) and on Friday and Saturday (10pm). If you are feeling peckish, barbecues are the house speciality. Right next door, the Mexican restaurant **Margarita's** (a *tortilleria*) provides a good 'South-of-the-Border' menu at only $10 and Margaritas at $1.

✕ **Dive** (map I, A2, **21**): 3200 Las Vegas Boulevard, next to the entrance to the Fashion Show Mall. ☎ 369-2270. Open Sunday–Thursday 11.30am–10pm, (11pm Friday and Saturday). Allow around $15 per person. Like the Dive bar in Los Angeles, dreamt up by Spielberg, the unusual look takes its inspiration from the interior of a submarine. The gaudily coloured building is carefully designed to maintain the illusion: you even have to pass through a hatch to get to the restaurant. Decent, typically American cooking, without any great imagination.

✕ **Planet Hollywood** (map I, A3): 3500 Las Vegas Boulevard, in the forum of Caesar's Palace. ☎ 791-7827. Fairly wacky decor – much better than in the one in Beverly Hills. The bar is a particular masterpiece. Otherwise the food is not so bad, and much the same as ever – pastas, salads and sandwiches for $7–10, chops etc. up to $20. Good cocktails.

☆☆☆ EXPENSIVE

✕ **Sfuzzi** (map I, A2, **22**): 3200 Las Vegas Boulevard South, opposite Diva on the other side of the entrance to the Fashion Show Mall. ☎ 699-5777. Open every day 11.30am–3pm for lunch (noon on Sunday) and from 5pm for dinner. Expect to pay around $15–$20 per person. The *trompe-l'oeil* facade reminds you of Venice. This is a good Italian restaurant in an agreeable setting and with a direct view over the Strip, which makes a pleasant change from the usual run of buffets and neon signs. Salads, pizzas and *pannini*, pasta, delicious grilled salmon served with a lemon sauce are just a few of the choices on the menu. No hassles, gentle background music; all in all it's a very pleasant spot to take a break from the madness outside. Good (but expensive) wine list.

✕ **Pekin Market** (map I, A3): 3555 Las Vegas Boulevard South, on the first floor of the Flamingo Hilton, on the Strip opposite Caesar's Palace. ☎ 733-3111. Open 5.30–11pm. Closed Thursday and Friday. A la carte dishes range from $11 to $20. Elegant Oriental decor with a small octagonal aquarium under a starry ceiling, plus attentive Chinese waiters. Mouth-watering menu: smoked duck, prawns in spicy sauce, chicken cooked with lemon or orange, etc. This is a perfect venue for a romantic meal, with its quiet atmosphere and intimate arrangement of tables. It's not exactly cheap but is reasonable compared to a similar sort of place in Europe.

✕ **Smith & Wollensky** (map I, A3, **23**): 3767 Las Vegas Boulevard South, opposite the Monte Carlo. A grill-room on one side and a chic restaurant on the other in the same building. This name, held in high regard in New York, Miami and New Orleans, specializes in wonderfully juicy pieces of meat. Main dishes in the restaurant will cost you at least $30 per person, but it is truly excellent. Very good tuna in mustard sauce and grilled salmon, in the $20–$25 range. The house speciality, crackling pork shank, is definitely worth a try. A very full wine list but with very high prices too. An ideal setting for a special occasion of some kind. **Wollensky's Grill**, which is also a delicatessen, is less expensive: you can expect to pay about $10–$25 per head depending on whether you just want a simple burger or sandwich or some grilled meat. Open for lunch (11.30am–4pm) and dinner (from 5pm).

✕ **Mortoni's** (map I, B3): 4455 Paradise Road, inside the Hard Rock Hotel. ☎ 693-5047. A meal will set you back a good $20 per person, not including wine. This excellent Italian cafe-restaurant, twin to the **Mortoni's** in Los Angeles, offers a wide choice of salads, pizzas and pastas in a chic and trendy setting.

THE CASINOS

Don't go to bed early, because Las Vegas is all about what happens after dark. Leave your luggage at the hotel or in the left-luggage office at the Greyhound station, located on Main Street, and go from casino to casino as your fancy takes you. This is a very American sport that even has a name – they call it 'casino hopping'.

There is no likelihood of this string of neon signs and slot-machines ever going away – at the last count, there were 1,530 casinos in Clark County alone. The current kings of this entertainment world include Arthur Goldberg, President of Park Entertainment Corp (the biggest gaming company in the world, with 18 casinos in the United States, Uruguay, and Australia including the Paris–Las Vegas, the Flamingo and Caesar's Palace), Sheldon Andelson (the owner of the luxurious Venetian) and Steve Wynn (who promotes the Bellagio and the Mirage). All three promise highs and thrills beyond the punters' wildest expectations, and live out their conviction that Las Vegas is 'where it's at'.

On Friday, beginning at 3am, swarms of planes deliver 'red-eyes' – that's what they call the people who rush to Las Vegas for a weekend. There's a good reason why the locals don't gamble: they know that only occasional gamblers – those who come for one or two days and then leave – ever win. Dedicated gamblers end up losing everything. This is in accordance with the law of big numbers!

Gambling is prohibited to anyone under 21, and some floors of the casinos are also out of bounds to this age group. It's as well to remember that cameras are generally very much frowned on, as the anonymity of players needs to be protected. It's very common for casinos to contain both a gaming room and an auditorium for shows. The admission charge to the first is clearly zero. They often also give you a free drink when you start to play, so if you do the rounds of the casinos, you can easily enjoy a fair amount to drink for absolutely nothing.

In principle, there's a code of 'decent dress' whether you're visiting a casino or spectating at a show, but everyone seems to disregard this, especially the staff of the casinos. You have to be looking really grimy to get thrown out of a casino!

Why are there never sunshades around casino swimming pools? Because it's so hot that the clients don't stay out very long but go straight back into the air-conditioned gaming rooms to cool down. Some people claim that the air-conditioning in the casinos is loaded with oxygen, which acts as a stimulant and reduces your need for sleep. There's nothing surprising about this when you realize that every last detail has been carefully planned in order to maximize profits. Even the noise levels in the casinos and the gaming rooms are planned – noise makes people spend. Psychologists are consulted on every tiniest point. Their opinions are sought on the decor of the gaming halls and the bedrooms, the music, the styling of the lifts, the shape of the seats and even the colour of the tokens. Of course gambling can become an illness, and in just the same way as with drugs, people become addicted to slot-machines. More people in Las Vegas are affected by this plague than by cocaine or heroin.

It's said that the casinos will give a plane ticket to any major customer who loses everything – so that they can get home. The expectation is that this will tempt them to tighten their belts still further in order to return as quickly as possible. The sheer number of cash machines in the gaming rooms makes the task of stripping people of their last cent even easier.

Finally, you may notice that the least visible sign in a casino is the one saying 'Exit'!

THE TWO CASINO AREAS

There are two distinct areas in Las Vegas: the Strip and Downtown.

THE STRIP

This is the name given to Las Vegas Boulevard – it's a word that suggests someone taking it all off, and this is obviously one reason why there are so many squalid brochures advertising shows with totally naked girls. But it's most likely that 'Strip' refers to the strong likelihood of losing everything at the tables, including your shirt, somewhere along this boulevard. The Strip is where you find the most luxurious casinos and there are some really mind-boggling structures lined up along its 4-mile (6km) length. It feels a bit like a nature reserve for weird creatures that are close to extinction.

In the following section, the casinos on the Strip are listed from north to south.

Bus 301 runs along the Strip as far as Downtown every 15 minutes, 24 hours a day.

★ **Circus Circus** (map I, A2): 2880 Las Vegas Boulevard South. ☎ 734-0410. Freephone: ☎ 1-800-444-2472. Website: www. circuscircuslasvegas.com. Situated between Desert Inn Road and Sahara Avenue. This place is in the shape of a circus big-top. Built in 1968, this great Las Vegas classic has recently topped the 3,700-room-mark. In fact it is a strange mixture of casino, funfair and circus. The mezzanine floor above the slot-machine hall serves as a show area where circus acts are performed for free. You can see trapeze artists, acrobats and clowns doing their stuff every hour from 11am to midnight (there's a programme displayed at the venue). According to its promoters, it is the biggest 'permanent' circus in the world.

– On the same floor is the delightful **play area**, reserved for children. While you are trying your luck down below, they can squander the last of your savings. The pocket money lost at church fetes has nothing on this! Children are not allowed into the casino, so they win fluffy toys using tokens bought by the dollar – a cunning ruse!

At the other end of the casino, in the middle of the shopping arcades, a large amusement park has been installed: the **Adventuredrome** (previously the Grand Slam Canyon), with rollercoasters, climbing wall, dinosaurs, etc. For more details, *see* 'Entertainment'.

★ **The Venetian** (map I, A3): 3355 Las Vegas Boulevard South, opposite the Mirage. ☎ 733-5000. Freephone: ☎ 1-800-494-3556 or 1-800-2VENICE. This has to be the craziest project that Las Vegas has ever seen. When completed, it will constitute the largest hotel in the world, with 7,000 suites each boasting a sumptuous surface area of 700 sq ft (65 sq m) as well as a four-poster bed, large-screen TV, and an Italian marble bathroom. The casino measures nearly 120,000 sq ft (11,000 sq m), there are 15 restaurants, 90 very chic shops, the biggest conference centre in the United States, and nearly 10,000 employees!

This is a simply staggering project of unprecedented luxury, which clearly couldn't be accommodated in just any old setting – so, the whole thing is a reproduction of the city of Venice, with St Mark's Square (and, to cap it all, 3,000 pigeons are trained to fly over it five times a day!), a Grand Canal that's 400 ft (365m) long and spanned, of course, by the Rialto Bridge, with genuine gondolas, the Doges' Palace, and so on. The developer's ambition was to make a real copy, not a cheap imitation, and all the materials have been imported from Italy (including 3,000 tons of marble). Perhaps he also wanted to ensure that The Venetian lives on even after Venice itself has sunk into the sea.

To entertain tourists, some of the employees are dressed as Napoleon (in a slight error of casting), Casanova, Marco Polo or Florentine beauties.

Inside, there's a magnificent *trompe-l'oeil* gallery leading to the casino reception. This also houses Madame Tussaud's (admission $12.50) where you can see celebrities associated with Las Vegas, such as Siegfried and Roy (*see below* under 'Mirage') and Liberace, as well as stars like Elvis Presley, Cher, Paul Newman and Mohammed Ali.

Inevitably, the cost has vastly exceeded that of any of its predecessors: phase 1 cost $2.5 billion, with only half the suites completed, but the developers have projected that they will be in profit by the year 2005, which seems like a good enough return on the investment!

★ **The Mirage** (map I, A3): 3400 Las Vegas Boulevard South, opposite the Venetian. ☎ 791-7111. Freephone for reservations: ☎ 1-800-827-6667. Fax 791-7448. Website: www.themirage.com. The proprietor of the Golden Nugget invested $630 million in this fantastic folly. In broad daylight, it resembles a giant ingot of refined gold and it has 28 floors and over 3,000 rooms, serviced by 7,500 employees. The lobby is covered by an 88-ft (27-m) high glass atrium designed as a tropical greenhouse, and there are 2,200 slot-machines installed just next door. The gardens and the huge swimming pool look like a lagoon in the South Seas, with lakes, caves and waterfalls hidden amidst 1,000 palm trees. What's more, each night after dark, volcanic eruptions can be seen every few minutes, above the waterfalls overlooking the avenue. In true American style, smoke and spectacular flames belch out of the crater. Make sure you go before midnight if you don't want to miss the spectacle.

There is also a large, exotic aquarium behind the reception desk, containing some amazing fish including two white-tipped sharks. The real stars of the Mirage, however are Siegfried and Roy's white tigers, which have been performing in the casino for more than 10 years. If you want to catch a glimpse of one, you can do it for free – just turn left as you enter the casino and follow the signs to the 'White Tigers'.

However, most of the animals spend the greater part of the day in the Secret Garden of Siegfried and Roy, ($10 admission); open 11am–5.30pm (from 10am weekends and public holidays). For the price you will also see some white lions (the youngest were born there), an Asian elephant and some black panthers . . . and you can watch a little dolphin show. You may just decide to hang onto your cash so that you can buy one of the lovely white fluffy toy tigers they sell.

A free monorail will take you to Treasure Island. Very useful.

★ **Caesar's Palace** (map I): 3570 South Las Vegas Boulevard. ☎ 731-7110. Freephone: ☎ 1-800-634-6001. Website: www.caesars.com. On the corner of Flamingo Road. This illuminated facade is one of the finest to be seen. They haven't learned about restraint here: more than 6,000 people are employed in looking after 2,500 rooms, 11 restaurants and three casinos! The waitresses are dressed in Roman togas (ultra-short ones, of course). The club **Cleopatra's Barge** is kitted out like a Nile barge in Ancient Egypt. The gardens house an immense swimming pool that's almost worthy of staging Olympic events – it's shaped like a Roman shield. The 1,186-seat auditorium attracts World Championship boxing matches, and motorcycle shows take place in the hotel stadium.

Forum Shopping is one of the most unusual shopping malls in the world. It's a reconstruction of an avenue in Ancient Rome, with columns, immense arches, exuberant fountains and statues, just like in Julius Caesar's time. The colour of the sky changes according to the hour of the day, clouds are projected onto the ceiling, and stars appear at night. There's a fountain near the entrance that includes a the statue of Bacchus, the god of wine and drunkenness. Every hour on the hour, a crash of thunder sounds and the god starts to speak, while a phalanx of lesser beings springs to life around him. OTT or what?

At the other end of the mall, the Atlantis fountain harbours a vast aquarium, so there's another show on offer here every hour. On your way you pass the feet of a gigantic Trojan horse.

There are pretty shops, especially MGM and Just For Feet, which display a large selection of trainers, caps and T-shirts. You can try the trainers out on a track inside the shop! When they're not too busy, the shop assistants are often to be seen on the counters, bopping along to Village People and the like – the atmosphere is guaranteed. In front of the Warner Bros shop (it's called *Warnerius Fraternius Studius Storius*, which is not first-class Latin!) Silvester and Bugs Bunny wear togas. The forum also contains a **Planet Hollywood**; *see* 'Where to Eat'.

★ **Bellagio** (map I, A3): 3600 Las Vegas Boulevard South. ☎ 693-7111. Freephone: ☎ 1-800-987-7111. Opened in 1998, this gigantic hotel complex (3,000 rooms and nearly 8,000 employees), was built in place of the old, totally demolished Dunes. It takes its inspiration from the architecture of the village of Bellagio, which overlooks Lake Como in Northern Italy. From the outside, the hotel may not be among the most beautiful, but the village is magnificent, with its shops and restaurants directly overlooking the mini-lake (not so small, in fact, since it occupies an area of 8.5 acres (3.5 hectares). Don't miss the sight of its extraordinary fountains while enjoying the strains of opera or 'Singing in the Rain' in the background. The place is undoubtedly top of its class. There are shows every 30 minutes 3–6.30pm and every 15 minutes 7pm–midnight.

Inside, the Bellagio is the height of luxury. It has an entrance hall with a mosaic-tiled floor, a strange ceiling decorated with what are probably water-lilies, an artificial garden with pergolas, luxury boutiques and 16 restaurants, six of which are four-star. The rooms are attractive and the biggest suite measures a barely conceivable 888 sq yds (743 sq m)! The best is yet to come, however: the hotel museum's collection of paintings by famous artists (although entrance costs $12) – some of the rare originals in town, given how you could talk for hours about the town's commercial artifice. This amazing collection, with an estimated value of some $300 million, was put together by the proprietor, Steve Wynn. It began in 1996 with the almost random purchase of a Manet, followed by a Gauguin, a Van Gogh, a Degas, a Cézanne, a Matisse, a Picasso and, more recently, some American abstracts: Jasper Jones, de Kooning, Pollock, etc. Wynn, far from being distracted from his business interests, hires his collection to his company for a mere $480 million per year!

To round off your visit, you can always treat yourself to lunch or dinner in the hotel's most highly rated gastronomic restaurant – the **Picasso**, which features 10 originals by the great artist displayed on its walls, so watch where you squirt that ketchup! It's quite clear why the Bellagio cost $1.7 billion! It is here that you can see the Cirque de Soleil troupe perform their show 'O' – it's one of the best-known in Vegas.

The monorail runs to the Monte Carlo and Caesar's Palace.

Paris–Las Vegas Casino Resort (map I, A3): 3845 Las Vegas Boulevard South, near Bally's Hotel. ☎ 739-4111. Freephone: ☎ 1-800-BONJOUR. Having already got the Egypt of the Pharaohs, Imperial Rome, New York, Monte-Carlo and a tropical island . . . all that was needed was France's 'City of Light' to make Las Vegas the artificial city to end all artificial cities. And see how she shines! This 34-floor casino-hotel houses 2,916 bedrooms, 4,200 employees, 2,200 slot-machines and 80 gaming tables . . . and just about all of Paris's most familiar sights, including the Arc de Triomphe, the Champs-Élysées, the Opéra-Garnier, the Musée d'Orsay, part of the Louvre, Parc Monceau, the façade of the Hôtel de Ville, the shops of Rue de la Paix and, of course, the Eiffel Tower – in miniature, at only 490 ft (150m) high, but still sporting 50 floors, and topped with its Jules Verne restaurant.

The casino was opened in 1999 by the project's sponsor, Line Renaud, the French consul in Los Angeles, Catherine Deneuve and Charles Aznavour. If you want to get married at the top of the Eiffel Tower, it will set you back a mere $2,500, but for that, you get the honeymoon suite included in the package. Even the Seine is there (fed by water from the canyons), and boat trips are available. To complete the illusion, 500 cooks 'imported' from France work in the establishment's 10 restaurants (eight of them French) under the direction of a French chef, Eric Scullier. So any American who dreams of Paris but can't afford the air-fare has only to get himself to Las Vegas.

★ **Monte Carlo** (map I, A3): 3770 Las Vegas Boulevard South, almost opposite MGM Grand Hotel and next to New York-New York. ☎ 730-7000. Freephone: ☎ 1-800-311-8999. Website: www.monte-carlo.com. The cream-coloured silhouette of the Monte Carlo's 32 floors make an impact from quite a distance. This mammoth, which has little architectural extravagance apart from the two false Brandenburg Gate-style neoclassical doors with a fountain and sculptures, offers 3,014 rooms and 259 suites. It was vaguely inspired by the famous casino in Monte-Carlo, and cultivates a 'European' slant. However there is nothing exciting enough to merit a detour – a quick glance in passing will do and you needn't worry that you've missed much.

Inside, there's a pub-brasserie with enormous copper vats at the back. The one thing worthy of mention is the buffet, which is excellent (*see* 'Where to Eat'), and the Lance Burton show (*see* 'Mad Entertainment and Mega-shows').

Monorail to the Bellagio.

★ **New York-New York** (map I, A3): 3790 Las Vegas Boulevard South, between the Monte Carlo and the Excalibur and opposite the MGM. ☎ 740-6969. Freephone: ☎ 1-800-NY-FOR-ME. Website: www.nynyhotelcasino.com. This one's more than just good-looking, it's a stunner! Opened in 1997, the New York-New York (with 2,035 rooms) was the first of the new generation of extravagantly designed hotel-casinos to see the light of day. For a cool $460 million or so, the architects put together a dozen of the most beautiful Manhattan tower blocks and, of course, the Statue of Liberty, Brooklyn Bridge and Grand Central Station. You can pick out the Empire State Building (this one has 42 floors) and the Chrysler Building, plus a series of apartment buildings in every style and colour.

The interior is designed to evoke New York's districts – Broadway, Chinatown, Greenwich Village and Little Italy, and the rollercoaster is fabulous. Look out for the 'Mowtown' (sic!), where imitation Supremes do a singing act, and the airshafts that spout steam in front of the lifts.

★ **MGM Grand Hotel and Grand Adventures Theme Park** (map I, B4): 3799 Las Vegas Boulevard South, opposite New York-New York on the corner of Tropicana Avenue. ☎ 891-1111. Freephone for reservations: ☎ 1-800-929-111. Website: www.mgmgrand.com. For several years the MGM was the biggest hotel in the world – until the Venetian seized the crown. This smoked-glass monster with its 5,034 rooms, employs almost 8,000 people. By the time it opened in 1993, the MGM had cost $1 billion. It's a big rival to Caesar's Palace – the stars of showbiz and TV appear here regularly, as well as those associated with boxing (Sylvester Stallone filmed *Rocky IV* here).

Although the swimming pool, with its multiple pools meandering among the palm trees is very pleasant (reserved for hotel guests), the casino itself (one-and-a-half times bigger than the one at Caesar's Palace) is nothing special. The unfortunate truth is that the MGM is simply outclassed by its rivals. You will have to settle for the huge golden lion that mounts guard in front of the building, and the giant screens showing James Bond films and the like around the clock. While you are there, the **Rainforest Cafe** is worth a detour for lunch or dinner – enjoy a salad or grill in a 'real' virgin rain forest, enlivened by gorillas and elephants trumpeting under a starry sky.

Apart from 'Skyscreamer', where they drop you, supported only by a rope, from a height of 246ft (75m) – not, we hope, too soon after your meal – the amusement park is also disappointing, while at the same time being quite expensive.

★ **Excalibur** (map I, A3): 3850 Las Vegas Boulevard South, on the corner of Tropicana Avenue. ☎ 597-7700. Freephone for reservations: ☎ 1-800-937-7777. Fax: 597-7040. Website: www.excalibur-casino.com. *See also* 'Where to Stay – on the Strip'. This is an extraordinary wedding-cake version of a medieval castle on the theme of King Arthur.

You'll spot this casino-hotel by its unusually shaped towers and its gold, red and blue turrets that glitter in the night. From a distance you'd think it was a giant Lego construction.

The architects studied 20 Scottish and English castles for their inspiration. The outer walls contain some 4,000 rooms. The staff roam around in period costume, and knights in armour confront each other in the corridors. This little medieval extravagance cost just $290 million – a pittance by comparison with some of the others. On the first floor is a shopping mall decorated with dragons, dolls, etc. And, for a memorable wedding, you could rush down to the Canterbury Wedding Chapel. The hotel will even hire you crowns and period costumes!

★ **Luxor** (map I, A–B3): 3900 Las Vegas Boulevard South, next to the Excalibur and very near the airport (visible from the terminal). ☎ 262-4000. Freephone: ☎ 1-800-288-1000. Website: www.luxor.com. *See also* 'Where to Stay – on the Strip'. The Luxor hotel-casino covers 47 acres (19ha) and has over 4,400 rooms, including some in an annexe. It's a life-size reproduction of the pyramid of Giza; an immense sphinx, also full-size, stands guard at the entrance. The atrium, the biggest in the world, could house nine Boeing 747s stacked on top of each other! The elevators, which they call 'inclinors', follow the building's oblique 39° inclines. It's an experience not to be missed. At night, from the apex of the pyramid, a powerful beam of light sweeps the starry Nevada sky. They say this beam has been seen from an aeroplane 250 miles (400 km) away in Los Angeles.

Not quite all of the decor is true to the Egyptian theme – if you're well travelled, you may find yourself standing before a combination of India and the Middle East. In fact, the architect who designed the entrance must have seen a bit too much Indiana Jones, because it's quite clearly a Mayan pyramid. Still . . . The **Luxor Museum**, (admission $5) dedicated to Tutankhamun, contains a cardboard reconstruction of his tomb and some approximate replicas of the treasures discovered inside. The curious might find it worth a quick glance, but Egyptologists are far better off at the Metropolitan Museum in New York or even the British Museum. There is also a 3-D IMAX screen (costs $9 and runs every two hours, 10am–midnight) and the '**In Search of the Obelisk**' attraction, which isn't up to much and has more to do with sci-fi than with archaeology.

★ **Mandalay Bay** (map I, A3): 3950 Las Vegas Boulevard South, the most southerly of the casinos, after the Luxor (to which it is linked by a monorail). ☎ 632-7777. Freephone for reservations: ☎ 1-800-632-7000. Website: www.mandalaybay.com. One of Las Vegas's most recent casinos (it was officially opened in March 1999), there is nothing particularly special about this vast, 3,700 room Asian-tropical block. There are a few fountains in the shape of elephants, a number of swimming pools languishing among the palm trees (one of which has a wave machine), a sandy beach and a few rooms decorated in the Gothic, Oriental or Indian style (no one seems quite sure why) – but there it stops. This is nothing exceptional in comparison with the others. The '**Treasures of Mandalay Bay Museum**' (entrance $6), open 2pm–midnight every day, contains a collection of banknotes and coins, including two genuine $100,000 bills!

★ Other original production numbers include: the **Rio** (map I, A3), on a carnival theme, with red and violet neon signs illuminating its walls; the **Sahara** (map I, A2) with Oriental decor; and the **Tropicana** (map I, B3) which has a **Gaming Museum**, open 8am–9pm (midnight at weekends).

The developers have plenty more projects in the pipeline. The totally revamped **Aladdin** is now open, with 2,600 rooms and a 7,000-seat theatre (the old Aladdin was completely destroyed in 1998): 3667 Las Vegas Boulevard South ☎ 877-333-9474. Website: www.aladdincasino.com. It is linked to the new **Music Hotel** by a leisure complex and the **Desert Passage** shopping mall.

– The eccentric and latterly reclusive millionaire Howard Hughes, who owned part of Las Vegas, spent the last years of his life on the top floor of the **Desert Inn** (map I, A2) but would not receive any visitors – he was terrified of catching germs!

DOWNTOWN

This is where you'll find the most popular casinos. The stakes are much smaller. The clientele have little money or have already been ruined by the casinos on the Strip!

The city centre conceals one of the most beautiful establishments in the whole city, the Golden Nugget. Above all, however, the district is much more human in dimension than the Strip, where the casinos are spread over a distance that's tiring for any pedestrian. The really big kick in Las Vegas is to go up Fremont Street at night: there's a deluge of colours, and an unimaginable cascade of neon signs (*see* 'Fremont Street Experience' *below*).

★ **Golden Nugget** (map II, A1–2, **16**): 129 East Fremont Avenue. ☎ 385-7111. Freephone for reservations: ☎ 1-800-634-3454. Website: www.goldennugget.com. Although it's in Downtown, this is considered to be the best casino in the city, along with Caesar's Palace. It holds the world record for the greatest number of slot-machines and has a reputation for the sharpest customer awareness in Las Vegas. The decor and style of the building are near perfect. The marble comes from Italy and all the carpets in the corridors are hand-woven, at a cost of $600 per square metre! Just changing the flowers every day costs $1,000.

On the ground floor, beyond the north lobby, there's a showcase with a collection of unusually-shaped nuggets, including one of the biggest in the world – hence the casino's name. It was discovered in Australia, only 8 inches (20cm) below ground level, in October 1980, near Wedderburn, Victoria, by a family who were prospecting near their trailer. The thing weighs almost 66lbs (30kg). There's also a superb watch chain, made using more than two pounds (1kg) of gold.

DID YOU KNOW?

Some time ago, a truck driver who lived in a flea-bitten motel Downtown won $3 million at the Golden Nugget casino. The boss made out the cheque immediately and offered him a bed in one of the best rooms. He asked him whether he would like anything else. The happy winner replied, 'Yeah! I wanna burger an' a beer!'

★ **Main Street Station** (map II, A1, **28**): Main Street, on a level with Stewart. ☎ 387-1896. This brand new casino symbolizes the renaissance of Downtown. Inspired by a Victorian station, it features attractive decor, with a glasswork ceiling, caryatids and a vast bronze wild boar in the bar. Beer brewed on the premises. The atmosphere can be a bit feverish. It's a good place to eat as well, and was voted 'best buffet in Las Vegas' for three years running (*see* 'Where To Eat').

★ **Binion's Horseshoe Club** (map II, A1, **27**): Fremont Avenue, between 1st Street and Casino Center. ☎ 382-1600. You can have your photo taken free, standing in front of a million dollars in 10,000-dollar bills! This is also one of the best places for sampling the feverish atmosphere of the gambling game. Poker tables have wads of $100 notes piled up

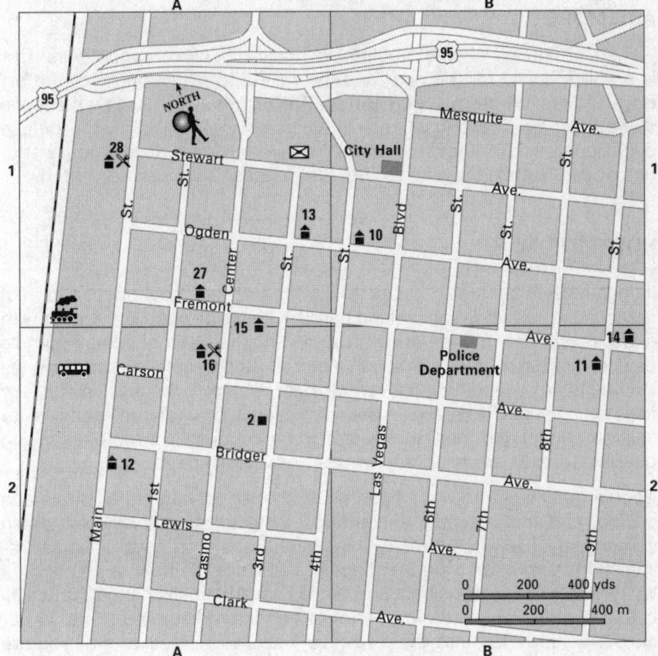

DOWNTOWN LAS VEGAS (MAP II)

■ Useful Addresses

- Greyhound Bus Station
- Post office
- 1 City Hall
- 2 County Courthouse (Marriage Bureau)
- 3 Police Department

Where to Stay

- 10 Gold Spike Casino
- 11 Western Hotel Bingo Parlor
- 12 Budget Inn
- 13 Lady Luck
- 14 Ambassador East Motel
- 15 Four Queens
- 16 Golden Nugget

Hotel-casinos

- 20 El Cortez
- 22 Golden Gate Hotel
- 27 Binion's Horseshoe Club
- 28 Main Street Station

on them, and the maximum stake is $2.5 million. Since you can never be too careful, all the games are recorded on video. If you find yourself lacking in motivation, you should take a stroll past the wall that gives onto Fremont Street, which features a gallery of portraits of the casino's happy winners, indicating the sum won (the majority of winnings are still on the modest side – thousands rather than millions of dollars).

AND MORE . . .

– There are hotels where gamblers play only with nickels and dimes. This is an opportunity for the poor and the ruined to play along with the big boys. At the **Western Hotel Bingo Parlor** (map II, B2, **11**), someone staked just one cent in March 1986 and won $95,172! Some people occasionally make a few hundred or a few thousand dollars on a bet of one or two cents – but you can bet that it doesn't happen very often.

HOW TO PLAY

If you've never set foot in a casino, don't panic: the most popular form of gambling in Las Vegas is shaking hands with a slot-machine, known with good reason as a 'one-armed bandit'. It's a disconcertingly simple device: just slip in a coin and push a button – it prevents the strain injuries you might get from pulling a lever. It's best to stick to those taking one- or five-cent coins. There aren't many of them (look for the 'pennies' or 'nickels' signs) and they quickly become occupied, but the ones taking quarter, $1 or $2 coins will ruin you at breakneck speed.

People often seem to win a handful of coins shortly after they arrive at a casino, and this naturally encourages them to stake everything again immediately. Beware! After winning small amounts several times, re-investing them and losing them again, you'll start to believe you're on a lucky streak. So, you pull out a note and ask for small change . . . It's all calculated: the majority of one-armed bandits redistribute 95 to 98 per cent of what is fed into them to give you the impression that you are enjoying a run of luck. That's the way to end up broke, while the casinos end up rolling in money. The whole secret of success is to know when to stop: either after losing only an amount you decided on in advance and don't mind sacrificing, just for the thrill, or immediately after winning just one pile of coins, if you've been lucky.

The other gambling opportunities available in the casinos tend to attract specialists and require a more substantial investment. There are all sorts here: roulette, craps, blackjack – even a race book, with entire walls of TV monitors showing what's happening at the race-tracks.

THE RULES: LEARNING TO PLAY

– **With a book**: to understand the basics of all these games, get the small *Las Vegas Gaming Guide* from the tourist information office.

You can also take one of the many courses provided by the casinos.

– **'Live' courses and lessons**:

• **New York-New York**: will give you free lessons on how to play – but not how to win: Monday–Friday at 2pm. For further information ☎ 740-6969.

• At **Caesar's Palace**, where the gaming rooms are immense, you can take free lessons in craps, blackjack, poker, baccarat and roulette, Monday–Friday 11am–5pm. ☎ 731-7110 for details of sessions. You can also see the giant slot-machine with a handle one metre long – it even works!

'FUN COUPONS'

A great dodge in Las Vegas for backpackers who are penniless but still want to enjoy themselves is to collect free or half-price 'fun coupons' for the casinos. There are also coupons for free drinks and breakfasts, and even packets of tokens, which have no monetary value but are accepted by slot-machines. It's worth taking advantage of them, as long as you know when to stop!

Unfortunately the fun coupons are becoming more and more difficult to find. You will probably have more luck in the Downtown casinos (ask the cashiers) as they try to tempt customers away from the Strip. Failing this, try the Gray Lines Tours stations or some of the service stations. Coupons are also occasionally to be found in the reception areas of some of the hotels in the centre. Pick up as many as they'll let you carry away and plan a route on the basis of the coupons you've scrounged. You can then check out the casinos one by one. Among the most interesting coupons are the ones given out by the Lady Luck Casino in Downtown, and those from the Hard Rock Hotel near the Strip.

Many casinos also offer coupons that get you meals – breakfast to supper – at prices that challenge any competition. You can have lunch or dinner for something like $5.

All in all, as long as you don't gamble, Las Vegas is definitely one of the cheapest cities in the United States!

MAD ENTERTAINMENT AND MEGA-SHOWS

Get a copy of *Today in Las Vegas*, *Showbiz* or *Tourguide* – all are free newspapers that you can pick up at the airport, in most hotels, and in certain casinos. They will keep you up to date with the attractions and shows of the week.

Inevitably, the casinos have enough money to attract the world's biggest stars. You may chance on shows starring the likes of Dolly Parton, Willie Nelson, Kenny Rodgers or Chuck Berry.

FREE SHOWS

– **Treasure Island** (map I, A2–3): 3300 Las Vegas Boulevard, next to the Mirage. ☎ 894-7111. A free attraction lasting 15 minutes, every 90 minutes, 4–11.30pm (in winter there's no 11.30pm show except on Friday and Saturday). Shows may be postponed if there's too much wind. Check the timetables carefully. In the evening, it's wise to get there at least 20 minutes before the start to beat the crowds.

The architecture of the hotel, impressive though it is, is totally overshadowed by the incredible decor of Treasure Island, reconstructed on the very edge of the Strip. It's a fine homage to Robert Louis Stevenson, author of the eponymous adventure novel. There's an immense pirate skull on the giant sign at the side of the boulevard. Buccaneers Bay has been reconstructed at a cost of $170 million, and the imagineers dreamed up a pirates' bay, with two big pools bordered by a tumble of rocks, fake houses, and palm trees. On the left, the pirate ship *Hispaniola* lies in wait for the British frigate, HMS *Britannia*, a superb 18th-century ship approaching with all sails set. The British sailors and pirates, all in costume, scream, leap, fall into the water, fire cannonballs and fight like very devils in the course of a naval battle that's every bit as grand as a full-scale Hollywood production.

– **Fremont Street Experience** (map II, A1): ☎ 678-5777. Website: www.vegasexperience.com. Right in the heart of Downtown, this is an astonishing *son et lumière* musical show, presented hourly every evening (check the timetables). The street is covered for its entire length with an immense mechanical roof, 89ft (27m) high, 1,400ft (416m) long, with a total area of 4 acres (1.5ha), and decked out with 2.1 million light bulbs. These are lit over a six-minute cycle to form astonishing figures and patterns in more than 65,000 combinations, all different, all magic. Everything is controlled by 31 invisible computers. This is a fabulous cybershow that features the emblematic Las Vegas cowboy couple, Vic and Vickie, in neon lights.

SHOWS CHARGING ADMISSION

Except for the most popular weekend periods, it is generally possible to get tickets for shows the night before. To be on the safe side, book two days in advance. *O*, at the Bellagio, is the exception to this rule.

– ***Siegfried and Roy* at the Mirage** (map I, A3). Currently the show with the biggest reputation in Las Vegas. The erupting volcanoes at the entrance to the Mirage are absolutely nothing compared to this show. The special effects were created by Steven Spielberg and George Lucas and the original music is by Michael Jackson. The 'two greatest magicians in the world', Siegfried and Roy (of German origin) have been appearing at the Mirage for more than 10 years now (for several tens of millions of dollars) and have more than 4,000 shows under their belts. They pull some pretty amazing stunts – like making one of their 19 lucky white tigers disappear from the stage. Sometimes it's even an elephant! This is a spectacle not be missed, so catch it if you can.

A seat is expensive (about $90), although this does include two drinks. There are two shows daily, 7.30pm and 11pm except Wednesday and Thursday. To book seats in advance, go to the ticket office any time between 8.30am and 11pm or, if you're staying at the Mirage Hotel, you can call them to find out whether there are seats available: ☎ 1-800-792-7777.

– ***Mystery* at Treasure Island** (map I, A2–3): reservations in person 8am–11pm, and by phone: ☎ 894-7722. Shows are at 7.30pm and 10.30pm, except Monday and Tuesday. It's expensive ($70) but fabulous. The Cirque du Soleil troupe from Quebec chose to come and live here in 1994, and they've put together a wonderful show. In total there are over 70 actors, dancers, singers, musicians, jugglers, acrobats and clowns from all over the world. They do circus acts, of course, but their costumes and the choreography make the whole thing enchanting. Highly recommended!

– ***O* at the Bellagio** (map I, A3): ☎ 693-7722. Freephone: ☎ 1-800-488-7111. This superb aquatic ballet is performed by members of the Cirque du Soleil troupe and uses the circle to create a theme of infinity. It has played to packed houses for almost two years now and features no fewer than 75 actors and over a million gallons of water (6 million litres) on the stage! For the slightest chance of getting to see it, reserve tickets several days in advance, or even before your arrival in Las Vegas through a tour operator. At $100, seats are more expensive than for any other show in Vegas. Performances every day (except Wednesday and Thursday) at 7.30pm and 10.30pm.

– ***King Arthur's Tournament* at the Excalibur** (map I, A3): in medieval style, the Excalibur organizes King Arthur's Tournament, which, as you can imagine, is a historic, costumed reconstruction of the lively medieval festival, with jousting, dancing . . . and dinner. In fact, it's the story of King Arthur and the Knights of the Round Table, told with lasers and mysterious clouds of smoke, ending up, of course, in a superb wedding. To make things more medieval, you eat without cutlery: not a bad idea, really, it cuts down on the washing up. It's quite expensive. Two shows daily at 6pm and 8.30pm. ☎ 597-7600. Freephone: ☎ 1-800-937-77-77.

– ***Lance Burton* at the Monte Carlo** (map I, A3): one of the most famous magicians in the United States. His show is more traditional than Siegfried and Roy, but less phoney than David Copperfield. He flies, too, with his convertible! This show is much more affordable, with tickets around $40. Two shows: 7.30pm and 10.30pm Tuesday–Saturday, with autographs after the second one. ☎ 730-7160 or freephone: ☎ 1-800-386-8224.

– ***Star Trek: The Experience* at the Hilton**: 3000 Paradise Road (map I, B2). ☎ 697-8700. For fans of the TV series. If you have always dreamed of being Spock or an evil extra-terrestrial with a wart-covered nose, now is your chance. All the effects are produced by means of interactive videos and virtual reality technology. Sceptics or the impoverished (entrance $15) should stick to admiring the decor in the shops and the bar (the Starfleet Lounge) and the Cardassian Restaurant. Open every day 11am–11pm.

SHOPPING MALLS, SHOPS, SOUVENIRS

The shopping malls in Las Vegas are exceptional, especially Forum Shopping and the Fashion Show Mall. You can also find original shops with attractive prices.

Forum Shopping (map I): *see* Caesar's Palace *above* in 'Casinos on the Strip'.

Fashion Show Mall (map I, A2): 3200 Las Vegas Boulevard South, corner of Spring Mountain Road. ☎ 369-8382. An immense, typically American shopping mall of the kind normally found in the suburbs. Open Monday–Friday 10am–9pm, Saturday 10am–7pm, Sunday noon–6pm.

Belz Factory Outlet World (off map): 7400 Las Vegas Boulevard South. ☎ 896-5599. Open Monday–Saturday 10am–9pm. About 3 miles (5 km) to the south of Tropicana Avenue and the Excalibur and Luxor casinos. This store basically sells designer clothing for adults and children, shoes, bathroom-ware, games, luggage, etc. at what claim to be factory prices.

Gamblers General Store (map I, A1): 800 South Main Street. ☎ 382-9903. Freephone: ☎ 1-800-322-CHIP. Open every day 9am–5pm. The shop for gamblers, selling packs of cards, slot-machines, anything and everything to do with the world of gambling, and, of course, books. The welcome is good and the goods are not expensive.

Boulevard Mall: 3528 South Maryland Parkway, on the corner of Twain Avenue, east of the Strip. The most recent and one of the biggest shopping centres in the city. Open 9am–10pm (10am–8pm Saturday and Sunday).

Everything Coca Cola (map I, A–B3): 3785 Las Vegas Boulevard South. Open Sunday–Thursday 1am–midnight, (until 1am on Friday and Saturday). Identifiable by the immense glass bottle, which houses an elevator. If you haven't yet handed over half your cash to the Coca Cola corporation as a result of the heat of the desert, now is the moment to spend a few dollars more on useless gadgets. For $3.50 you can look at some old advertising posters and gorge yourself on Coke.

A few great shops include: **The Sharper Image** and its surprising gadgets, **Disney Store**, which has great decor, the inexpensive **Gap** clothing stores and **Bonanza**, which markets itself as 'the biggest souvenir shop in the world'.

– In all the casinos, **playing cards** are used only once. Near the slot-machines, you can buy professional packs of cards with the name of the casino printed on them. At $2 these make nice, inexpensive presents.

MUSEUMS

★ **Nevada State Museum and Historical Society** (off map): 700 Twin Lakes Drive, west of Downtown. ☎ 486-5205. Open 9am–5pm. Admission charge is modest ($2), and free for under 18s. To get there, take the 515 to Lorenzi Park: Twin Lakes Drive borders it to the west. Bus 106 or 208. There are sections dedicated to the history of the region, from the Anasazi tribe through to nuclear testing, and others about ethnography, anthropology, geology, flora and fauna. All the varieties of cactus, insects, reptiles and wild animals to be found in Nevada are included, in excellent showcases. There is even a magnificent specimen of the mammoth discovered in Utah. Also very interesting displays of Native American craftwork, pottery, finely-wrought basketwork, weaving and painting, and temporary exhibitions on special topics. A well-stocked bookstore.

★ **Las Vegas Natural History Museum** (off map): 900 Las Vegas Boulevard North, to the north of Downtown. ☎ 384-3466. In principle this is open daily, 9am–4pm. Admission costs about $5.50 (adults) and $3 (4–12s). This little natural history museum, which periodically plays host to excellent national touring exhibitions, is above all aimed at the inhabitants and schools of the region. However, there is plenty for outsiders to enjoy, including the attractive section dedicated to dinosaurs. There's a life-size reconstruction of a Tyrannosaurus, the largest carnivorous dinosaur, with animation and real roars! Also a Triceratops, whose eyes move – but don't worry too much, because this beast was a herbivore.

Elsewhere, there are aquariums and displays on shark ecology, naturalized animals from Nevada and Africa and fossils retracing the evolution of the species, etc.

★ **Imperial Palace Auto Collection** (map I, A3): 3535 Las Vegas Boulevard South. ☎ 731-3311. Open daily, 9.30am–11.30pm. Here you can see 250 superb cars, most of them American. They have the largest exhibition of Duesenbergs here and one of the finest collections of presidential cars, including those from Herbert Hoover to Richard Nixon, plus Nicholas II of Russia's Rolls Royce, Emperor Hirohito of Japan's Packard, Adolf Hitler's Mercedes, and the car that once belonged to Howard Hughes. Terrified of microbes, he had an air filter installed that cost more than the car itself. You have to pay an admission charge, but there are 'fun coupons' that will get you free admission.

★ **Las Vegas Liberace Museum** (off map): Liberace Plaza, 1775 East Tropicana Avenue, to the east of the Strip. ☎ 798-5595. Open Monday–Saturday 10am–5pm (1pm–5pm Sunday). A museum dedicated to the late Liberace – one of the most famous celebrities of the American stage. He was an idol in Las Vegas and a very popular pianist. Here you can see one of the most fabulous piano collections in the world, as well as his incredible wardrobe, his stage jewellery and the extraordinary custom-built cars that were often used as stage-props.

★ **Guinness World of Records Museum** (map I, A2): 2780 Las Vegas Boulevard South. ☎ 792-0640. Just to the north of the Circus Circus Hotel. Officially open 9am–8pm, but they don't always keep to these hours. You'll see the world's tallest man, most tattooed lady, fattest man . . . or smallest bicycle. OK for kids, but there's nothing there that isn't to be seen in the one in LA, and other places.

WHAT TO DO

– **Adventuredome** (ex-Grand Slam Canyon): in the Circus Circus Hotel (map I, A2). ☎ 794-3939. Open from 10am. An air-conditioned theme park covering 5 acres (2ha) under a vast dome. More for teenagers than adults. There's a 125-foot (38m) rock-climbing face (made artificially of sandstone), tunnels, grottoes, caves and waterfalls, designed to remind you of the canyons of the American West – the park's official theme. The scenic railway, 'Canyon Blaster' is incredible while on 'Rim-Runner', you slide down a 90-foot (27m) cascade into a pool of water. Further on there are animated dinosaurs Another top attraction is the 'Hot Shot Laser Tag', a high-tech interactive game in an arena lit by ultraviolet lights. There is also a whole series of attractions for younger children.

– **The Stratosphere Tower** (map I, A2): 2000 Las Vegas Boulevard South. ☎ 380-7777. Freephone for reservations: ☎ 1-800-99-TOWER. Website: www.stratlv.com. You have to see this one after nightfall. It's the tallest monster in Las Vegas – at 1,150ft (350m) high, it's a mixture of water tower and concrete vase, topped by a circular observatory. This observation tower, the biggest of its kind in the US, was built by developer Bob Stupak.

At the foot of the tower, there's yet another hotel-casino with 1,500 rooms and suites. From the lobby, to gain access (for $6) to the lift leading to the top of the tower, you go through a shopping mall built on a Parisian theme. The escalators climb up through the feet of the Eiffel Tower towards the Champs-Élysées and you even go under the Arc de Triomphe to get to the toilets. After that comes Chinatown and, finally, the lift itself. In no time at all you are propelled to the top of the Stratosphere, where there is a panoramic restaurant offering a superb view over the ocean of lights and multicoloured casinos that is Las Vegas. The blue-and-pink Stardust, the green MGM, the red-and-purple Rio.

To crown it all, Stupak has managed to install rollercoasters ('High Roller') on the roof of the observatory, and, in particular, an insane attraction known as the Big Shot. In a 'strato-second', the Big Shot can propel a dozen passengers, firmly strapped into their seats, to the top of a 170-ft high (50m) metal column at a speed of 45 mph. You go up and down three times and it's a bit like being in an ejector seat. Up on this antenna, which feels like of the tip of a rocket being launched, you can experience all the powerful sensations felt by the Nasa astronauts, so it's a good training session if you're thinking of taking off for the moon. Not advisable for people who suffer vertigo, have weak hearts or suffer from claustrophobia, nor for expectant mothers. The $14 package includes ascent to the Stratosphere and the two attractions. For the future, Stupak is planning to construct a 50-ft high (15m) mechanical gorilla that will climb the tower carrying up to 60 people.

– **Wet 'n' Wild** (map I, A2): 2600 Las Vegas Boulevard South. ☎ 734-0088. Open end of April to early October 10am–6pm in May, the last two weeks of August and in September, 10am–8pm in June and early August, 10am–10pm in July. If you fancy a change from the casinos, this offers all imaginable forms of water games including the 'Banzai Boggan' and the 'Royal Flush'. Or there's the 'Black Hole', which will blow your mind! There's even a beach with artificial waves – you'll need trainers or sandals as the sand can be burning hot! It may seem a bit expensive, but if you look in the papers and brochures, you can find coupons giving a decent reduction.

– **Flyaway Indoor Skydiving** (map I, A2): 200 Convention Center Drive. ☎ 731-4768. Website: www.flyawayindoorskydiving.com. If you are a beginner at high-sensation activities or have always dreamed of making a parachute jump, you can experience a 3-minute free-fall – or rather a 'hover' – in a gigantic wind tunnel where the winds reach more than 110 mph (176 kph). It costs $35 a shot, $55 for two goes or five for $100, which seems pretty expensive considering the short time you get. The price includes a short, preparatory session lasting around 20 minutes.

HOW TO GET MARRIED IN LAS VEGAS

Clark Gable married Carole Lombard in Las Vegas in 1939 and so the city started its route to international fame as the place for quick marriages. Since those days, a great many celebrities have got married here, including Mickey Rooney, Bing Crosby, Elvis Presley and Priscilla, Frank Sinatra and Mia Farrow, Bruce Willis and Demi Moore, Brigitte Bardot and Roger Vadim (but not to each other), and many more.

Contrary to legend, more weddings than divorces (10 times as many) are celebrated in Las Vegas. In 1998, a total of 108,717 weddings took place, more than 3,000 of them on St Valentine's Day. That's an average of 298 weddings a day, or one every 4 minutes, 50 seconds.

You can get married in all sorts of ways: while sitting at the wheel of your car, in a helicopter, or even in the hot-air balloon built specially for the purpose by the proprietor of the Little White Chapel. At the Graceland Chapel, there's an Elvis Presley lookalike to conduct the wedding and in the Excalibur's Canterbury Chapel, the tone is medieval, with costumes to match. And anyone who has ever dreamed of Ancient Rome might want to head straight for Neptune's Villa in Caesar's Palace.

However, the prize for originality must still go to a couple who renewed their marriage vows a few years ago on a bunji-jumping platform before leaping into thin air.

REQUIREMENTS FOR CIVIL MARRIAGES

There are very few requirements needed in order to get married in Las Vegas. You must be aged 18 or over, though 16–17-year-olds may get married if a parent is present or if consent is given through a notarized affidavit. Proof of age is required up to the age of 21.

You need to get a marriage licence in advance. These can be obtained from: **The Marriage Licence Bureau** (map II, A2): County Courthouse, 200 South 3rd Street (1st Floor), Las Vegas, NV 89155-1601. ☎ 455-4416 (office hours) or 4415 (after hours / recorded information). Fax: 455-4929. On the corner of Carson Street. The office is open Monday–Thursday 8am–midnight, and does not close at all from Friday 8am to Sunday midnight. Try to avoid going on a Saturday, as it's very, very busy. A license costs $35 and you have to pay in cash.

At least one additional witness must be present. Divorcees are required to produce evidence of the date and place of the final decree. No blood tests are required, nor is any documentation necessary other than a passport giving proof of your date of birth and nationality.

Afterwards, the marriage must be registered in your home country through the usual channels. Check out the website: www.lasvegas.com for further information and a list of suitable wedding venues.

Married couples can also download a certificate of their marriage from the Internet by going to www.co.clark.nv.us. It costs $7, and you pay by Visa or MasterCard.

THE PROCEDURE

The cheapest way to marry is to go to the **County Courthouse** (*see above* for details) (this is the Las Vegas city hall) to get the marriage licence. Then for the ceremony proper, you can choose between the chapel and the civil registry office (which is just across the way at the Commission of Civil Marriage at 309 South 3rd Street). A full list of weddings is there to be consulted.

A civil wedding is the fastest and cheapest. A wedding in a chapel in cowboy or rock-star fashion, though, is really worth the experience. At both ends of the Strip an astonishing number of chapels (getting on for 50), each more kitsch than the one before, offer wedding trips at all prices. The average is between $35 and $50 but with the addition of optional extras this amount can soon soar. If it seems a bit expensive, you can always ask to get married on credit.

More recently, 'Fast Weddings' have been introduced . . . you don't even have to get out of the car, as a pastor will marry you in just a couple of minutes, for a symbolic fee. But on the assumption that good traditions haven't gone completely out of fashion, these are the two 'nicest' chapels in Las Vegas:

– **The Little Church of the West** (off map): 4617 Las Vegas Boulevard South. ☎ 739-7971. Freephone: ☎ 1-800-821-2452. Level with Russell Road, two blocks south of the Luxor and on the other side of the road. It's open 8am–midnight. Although it has relocated several times since it was founded in 1943, this is still the prettiest church in the city, built in timber and set among a small grove of trees. This real haven of peace in the concrete-and-neon jungle has even been classified as a historic monument! It was here that Elvis got married in the film *Viva Las Vegas*. Since then, many stars have been wed in the Little Church of the West, including Dudley Moore, Judy Garland, Mickey Rooney, Telly Savalas, Bob Geldof and Paula Yates, Richard Gere and Cindy Crawford. If their track records are anything to go by, it may not be the best place to get hitched!

Hiring the chapel will cost you around $55, but this includes the cost of the limousine – generally a white Cadillac. The chauffeur picks you up at your hotel, and you give the lady organizer the licence issued by the County Courthouse. She gives the bride a bouquet of flowers (costing from $10 upwards), then leads you along the corridor to the music of a harmonium ($25 for the organist) or, for those who are broke, a cassette ($8)! On handing over the rings, you are then entitled to a sermon from the pastor: a gratuity at the end of the ceremony is appreciated, but discretionary. You are also entitled to congratulations from the curious watchers who have gathered in front of the church door. There are bell noises at the exit, but these are free. And let's not forget the main item: after the fateful 'I do' – the pastor encourages a moderate amount of kissing. If you've forgotten your camera, you can stump up $50 for photos of your unforgettable moment.

– **A Little White Chapel** (map I, A1): 1301 Las Vegas Boulevard South. ☎ 382-5943. Freephone: ☎ 1-800-545-8111. Open 24 hours a day. All in white, as its name indicates. Tiny and with a naively sentimental sort of decor, this has been the best-known church in Las Vegas since Joan Collins set American hearts throbbing with her wedding here. Michael Jordan, Bruce Willis and Demi Moore followed suit. The drive-through option is the cheapest, at only $45. The hot-air balloon option may be more romantic but it is also more expensive.

EXCURSIONS

■ **Gray Line Sightseeing Tours** organize day-trips to the Grand Canyon. The cheapest option, at $149, includes the return journey, the walk itself and lunch. For an extra $65, you can add a light aircraft flight over the canyon. It is also possible to go down the Black Canyon by raft for $79 (the total excursion lasts seven hours) and you get a unique view of the Hoover Dam. There are also visits to Bryce Canyon for $129. Book at least 24 hours in advance: ☎ 384-1234. Freephone: ☎ 1-800-634-6579. Fax: 632-2118. They also run many other excursions: ask for details.

Other companies offer similar excursions at comparable prices.

One is **Valen**: ☎ 735-4947; freephone: ☎ 1-800-487-2252.

■ **Eagle Scenic Airlines**: 275 East Tropicana Avenue, Las Vegas. ☎ 638-3300. Freephone: ☎ 1-800-634-6801. Fax: (702) 739-8065. Website: www.scenic.com.

This private company organizes various flights departing from Las Vegas: night flights over the city, flights over the Grand Canyon (1 hour 15 minutes), and Bryce Canyon, as well as day-trips to Monument Valley (travelling by plane as far as the Grand Canyon). Note that it's very hot in the planes in summer. Reservations must be confirmed 24 hours before departure.

Las Vegas International and the Las Vegas Backpackers Hostel both organize trips to the Grand Canyon. *See* 'Where to Stay'.

THE ROUTE BETWEEN LAS VEGAS AND GRAND CANYON VILLAGE

★ **Hoover Dam**: located 34 miles (54km) from Las Vegas on Highway 93. ☎ 294-3523. Fax 294-3585. Website: www.hooverdam.com. The visit costs $8 and you also pay for parking. This immense dam, 728ft (222m) high, was opened on 30 September 1935 by President Roosevelt. It was then the biggest in the world, even bigger in terms of volume than the largest of the Egyptian pyramids. Around 5,000 labourers took part in its construction, and 96 were killed.

The purpose of the dam is to prevent flooding that could be caused by unpredictable rises in the level of the Colorado River. It also produces electricity for Nevada, Arizona and California and provides irrigation for all the crops in this desert region, which has the unfortunate effect of reducing the river to little more than a trickle for the Mexican peasants further downstream. They don't have much to thank Uncle Sam for. It also supports the Lake Mead reservoir (which has 546 miles/880km of shoreline) which also provides the water supply for 25 million people, including the whole Las Vegas area. Guided visits lasting 35 minutes take place frequently, from 8am to 5.15pm. During the busy season, these queues sometimes look never-ending. The lake also offers various water sports.

★ **Kingman**: 100 miles (160km) to the southeast of Las Vegas. This is a small town with a big reputation! The historic Route 66 passes through here on its way from Chicago to Santa Monica, although the stretch that passes through the town is called Andy Devine Avenue, named for an obscure B-movie actor who was a local boy. The motels, restaurants, cafes and museums make constant reference to Route 66.

A long time ago, the town was the last stopping-place for the pioneers before they crossed the Black Mountains. Be sure to take a look at the town centre with its law courts (a fine building in dressed stone) and Masonic temple. If you feel like it, you can also have a look at the **Mojave Museum of History and Arts**, at 400 West Beale Street. Open 9am–5pm weekdays (1pm–5pm weekends). Admission is by donation.

✕ **Dambar & Steakhouse**: 1960 East Andy Devine Avenue. ☎ (520) 763-3523. Lunch 11am–3pm; dinner until 10pm. 'Early-bird' reduced prices 3–6pm. Expect to pay $5–$8 at lunchtime, a little more in the evening. This place is Route 66's ode to cowboy culture! It's a fake red barn at the side of the road, with every conceivable gimmick: cow on the roof, wagon-wheels against the walls and, inside, sawdust on the floor. At the bar, the seats are cow-coloured (with black-and-white patches). They serve a good selection of salads, burgers, sandwiches and grilled meat and chicken is a special favourite (all freshly killed, according to the menu!). Oven-hot cookies are served at the start of the meal and the beer is homemade. The helpings are very generous and the service is friendly. In fact it's recommended – if you're going that way.

✕ **Mr D'Z**: 105 East Andy Devine Avenue. ☎ 520-718-0066. This one's difficult to miss, with its blue Cadillac sign and its pink-and-green walls. This American 1960s-style snack bar – at which Jack Kerouac might well have stopped when he was on the road – serves excellent burgers, sandwiches, salads and chips. They even give you free Coke refills. A good place to go.

☗ **Quality Inn**: 1400 East Andy Devine Avenue. ☎ (520) 753-4747. Freephone: ☎ 1-800-869-3252. A double room costs $59 every day of the week. This comfortable chain motel has a good collection of objects on the 'Route 66' theme, which helps to make it less obviously part of a chain.

☗ **Motel 6**: 424 West Beale Street. ☎ (520) 753-9222. Freephone: ☎ 1-800-4-MOTEL-6. Fax: 753-4791. Double rooms cost $48. The place is traditional and well maintained, with a friendly welcome. Swimming pool. Reservation advisable at weekends.

☗ **Hill Top Motel**: 1901 Andy Devine Road. ☎ 520-753-2198. Good reception. There's a launderette and a small swimming pool. Really, this is just another motel among many, and a bit run-down maybe. But it's cheaper than the two above.

★ **Oatman**: This town is tucked away in the mountains, on the old Route 66, 25 miles (40km) to the southwest of Kingman. In times gone by, it boasted the biggest gold mine in Arizona, discovered by Joe Jeneres, a Mexican prospector. After a series of ups and downs, the unprofitable mine was finally closed in 1998, although tours are still possible. The descendants of the donkeys used by Jeneres to transport the gold-bearing soil can nowadays be seen wandering around freely.

Little more than a ghost town, it was given a new lease on life by the arrival of the movie industry and tourism. Several Westerns were filmed here, the best known of which was *How The West Was Won*. Apart from that, Clark Gable and Carol Lombard found no better place to spend their wedding night than here in the old Oatman Hotel. At weekends, duels are staged and Western music played – but there is still a long way to go to revive the place, with only 150 inhabitants as compared to the 3,500 of a hundred years ago.

Chamber of Commerce: P.O. Box 423, Oatman AZ 86433. ☎ (520) 768-6222. Website: www.rippers.com/oatman/home.htm.

★ **Hackberry**: about 19 miles (30km) northeast of Kingman, on Route 66, Hackberry is a big, forgotten village. If you're feeling nostalgic about Route 66, you should stop here and have a look at the Old Route 66 Visitors' Center. Here you can meet the owner, Robert Walmir, who's an erudite philosopher with a good sense of humour, and who knows his subject by heart. Nearby is a roomful of memorabilia, especially on James Dean and Marilyn Monroe.

★ **Seligman**: 156 miles (252km) from Las Vegas, on Highway 40, before you reach Williams. This is in the middle of nowhere, in 'deepest America'. In fact, between Seligman and Flagstaff, you're actually driving on the legendary Route 66.

Delgillado's Snow Cap Cafe: on the main road on the right as you exit from the city heading for Flagstaff. There's an old white Chevrolet Impala convertible, covered with garlands and with a Christmas tree on the back seat, and more old bangers slumbering in the yard, near the cabin where the toilets are. Inside, the cafe is plastered with banknotes, hundreds of business cards and other miscellaneous objects – it's a real hotch-potch, but rather fun. It's a good place for a quick sandwich or one of their excellent, refreshing milkshakes before heading off again. The TV and telephone seem to be in the toilets. The owner's very friendly. Just next door, his brother Angel has set up the Route 66 Visitors' Center in what was an old hairdressing salon (he used to be a barber) – an improbable mixture of a museum, a junk-store and a souvenir shop . . . worth a look though.

RENO

AREA CODE: 702

It is a quiet little town . . . Everything is sharp to the eye at this altitude, the sky is immaculate . . . It is a clean town . . . It is a prospering town . . . One can see immense distances here . . .

Arthur Miller, *The Misfits*

Reno is like a mini version of Las Vegas – it's less cosmopolitan, more provincial, and much less crazy. But just like its sister city in the southwest of Nevada, the Americans like to come here for a weekend slumming it. They go gambling in the casinos, spending their dollars and having fun. They get married – and divorced. The formalities for getting married here are now very straightforward, compared to those for getting a divorce, yet even that is pretty simple. Nowadays, a divorcing couple must reside in the state of Nevada for at least six weeks before they can start proceedings. Still, for many people, Reno remains the world capital of divorce.

Reno and Las Vegas have reversed their roles. In the 1930s, Reno was a city of vice, gambling and prostitution while Las Vegas was a very well-behaved place. Then, in the 1940s and 1950s, their roles swapped, with Las Vegas becoming a real Babylon while Reno quietened down. Nowadays, while Reno looks for all the world like a big city (with its population of 135,000) dedicated to gambling, it's just a contented little place on a burbling river. It's known, with some justification, as 'the biggest little city in the world'.

USEFUL ADDRESS

Visitors' Center: 300 North Center Street. ☎ 1-800-367-736. Website: www.renotahoe.com. Located in the hall of the National Bowling Stadium.

WHERE TO STAY

☆ BUDGET

Mizpah Hotel: 214 Lake Street, on the corner with 2nd Street. ☎ 323-5194. One of the most central of the budget hotels. This brick-built hotel dates back to 1922 and is listed as a historic monument. The decor is old-fashioned, but rooms are simple and clean, with shower and WC. Costs around $30 a night for two people during the week in summer and it's a bit more expensive at weekends.

☆☆ MODERATE

Travelodge: 655 West 4th Street. ☎ 1-800-255-3050 or 329-3451. Very well located right next to the casinos. Friendly welcome. The rooms are impeccable, and have every convenience. There's a swimming pool and parking lot. This place definitely offers the best value for money in Reno, in this category.

WHERE TO EAT

The buffets in the **casinos** offer the best value. They serve good food at moderate prices on an 'all-you-can-eat' basis.

The buffet in the **Eldorado** is considered to be the best in the city. A little less expensive, but good all the same, is the buffet at **Fitzgerald's**.

WHAT TO SEE AND DO

★ **The Reno Arch**: in the city centre, on the corner of Virginia Street and Commercial Row. Spanning the street; the arch commemorates the revival of the Downtown area after years of economic stagnation. It was restored in 1987. The arch features in the Whoopi Goldberg film *Sister Act.*

★ **The Silver Legacy Casino**: between 4th and 5th Streets. This is the finest of all the casinos. Its roof, in the form of a postmodern dome, is visible from some distance, especially at night. Inside, a huge oilrig has been reconstructed at its original size, symbolizing the silver mines that made the region prosperous in the 19th century.

– **Reno Rodeo**: held annually in mid-June. One of the most spectacular in the country. Information from the Visitors' Center.

IN THE RENO AREA

★ PYRAMID LAKE

Located 35 miles (56km) north of Reno. Allow an hour for the drive. A beautiful lake with the purest of waters, situated on land belonging to the Paiute Indians. At an altitude of 3,730ft (1,137m) and in an almost desert landscape, the lake is surrounded by rock-covered mountains and arid ochre-coloured hills. The sky is bright blue and the nights are exceptionally starry. There are also some hot springs. The made-up road goes along the western shore (heading north) as far as Pyramid Site – beyond that, it's a dirt road.

ℹ If you want to spend a day in the reservation, or even just to spend some time at the water's edge (there's a little beach), you have to buy a 'day-use permit', costing $5, at the **Dunn Hatchery Visitors' Center**. This is on the left side of the road, before the village of Sutcliffe on the western shore. It's signposted. Great place to camp, especially in the evening. Take heed – the Native American rangers are very strict about the permit.

■ For more information contact **Pyramid Lake Ranger Station** ☎ (702) 476-1155.

★ VIRGINIA CITY

This is a famous mining town dating back to the days of the Gold Rush, situated about 22 miles (36km) southeast of Reno and 38 miles (60km) east of Lake Tahoe. Founded in 1859 on the side of a hill, the town is still in an excellent state of preservation, and there are many old timber-and-brick buildings still standing, stretched out along a typical Wild West street (C Street). The writer Mark Twain lived here at the time of the Gold Rush.

The city has been listed as a National Historical Landmark, and today lives mainly on the proceeds of the tourist trade.

– Lots of shops and small private museums, although not all of them are in the best of taste.

– Lots of old saloons, such as the **Old Washoe Club** with its beautiful bar and the **Delta Saloon**, which contains the famous 'suicide table'.

– The **Chollar Mine** offers a 30-minute tour.

– The famous **camel races** take place in September, on the weekend following Labor Day.

– There's not much choice of places to stay: they're not cheap and a bit over-rated.

ℹ **Chamber of Commerce and tourist information office**: ☎ (702) 847-0311.

★ CARSON CITY

This is another legendary city and the capital of the state of Nevada, situated 30 miles (48km) south of Reno. It was named after Kit Carson, who was one of the great pioneers of the Wild West but also a fierce and determined enemy of the Native Americans.

– The town offers the **Kit Carson Trail**, which takes you on a picturesque stroll through the history and folklore of the Old West.

– There's nothing exceptional to see except some nice old houses and the **Krebs-Peterson House** at 500 North Mountain Street.

– From the road, you can get the strange experience of seeing the silhouette of **John Wayne** in one of the windows of the house used as a location for some scenes of his last film, *The Shootist*, made in 1972.

ℹ Convention and Visitors' Bureau: 1900 South Carson Street. ☎ (702) 687-7410. Freephone: ☎ 1-800-NEVADA-1.

IN SEARCH OF *THE MISFITS*

Among the many film masterpieces by director John Huston, *The Misfits* has become a cult. Arthur Miller's play was turned into a screenplay in 1961 and was filmed in the area around Reno. It tells the story of a joyful, sexy divorcee, Roslyn (played by Marilyn Monroe – who was married to Miller at the time) and three unhappy men, who might be described as 'cowboys without a cause', leading lives without aim or direction.

The first, Gay (Clark Gable), is divorced. The second, Perce (Montgomery Clift), is looking for a soulmate. The third, Guido (Eli Wallach), is a widowed and desperate car mechanic. Naturally everything suddenly springs to life when Roslyn appears. Fuelled by this ray of hope, the three gallants regain their lust for life with Roslyn becoming their adored muse. The four, semi-revellers, semi-bohemians, set off in search of adventure. Everything goes well until the day Roslyn falls in love with Gay, resulting in rivalries between the men.

During the filming, Marilyn was taking drugs and medication and eventually had to be hospitalized. Filming was halted and her husband, Arthur Miller, fell into the arms of a movie trainee. The tenacious John Huston nevertheless completed his film, somehow even finding the time to win a camel race in Virginia City!

A rich and serious work, full of hidden symbolism, and touching on the profoundest subjects, *The Misfits* was the last film ever made by each of the three Hollywood superstars. As if a curse had been placed on their roles as misfits, Monroe and Gable both died within months of the making of the film.

LOCATIONS WHERE MEMORABLE SCENES WERE FILMED

★ **The bridge on the Truckee River**: in Reno. After leaving court following the finalizing of her divorce, Roslyn stops on this bridge with her old friend Isabelle, who tells her, 'If you throw your ring in there, you'll never have another divorce.' Embarrassed, Roslyn touches her ring as though to protect it. Isabelle says: 'Go on, kid. Everybody does it. There's more gold in this river than in the Klondike.' Roslyn won't do it and they go for a drink in the bar of a casino, to celebrate their freedom. The rest of the adventure is just about to start.

★ **Dayton**: 38 miles (60km) southeast of Reno, Dayton is on Highway 50 between Carson City and Silver Springs. Arthur Miller described it as 'the last free town in the West: no cops, no law . . . you never know what to expect in this place'. Roslyn, Gay, Perce and Guido come here to see the Dayton rodeo. But, before it begins, the motley crew calls in at a crowded saloon where the juke-box is hammering out some thunderous music. Innocently keeping time with the music, Roslyn displays her divine form and sets the men aflame. All this almost triggers off a general brawl.

The saloon where this unforgettable scene was filmed is now called the 'Old Corner Bar'. Coming from Carson City via Highway 50, at the entrance to Dayton there's a junction with traffic lights. Go left onto Main Street; you'll find the bar 100 yards (90 metres) further on, on the right, at the intersection with Pike Street.

On the walls are portraits of Monroe and Montgomery Clift. There's a long bar with video-poker consoles, drunks in broad daylight, a huge mirror behind the bottles and, between the two, a tattooed but friendly cowboy barman. In accordance with local custom, a good customer has to sign his name on a dollar bill and give it to the barman, who then sends it flying to the ceiling on a dart.

★ **The mustang hunt**: this is the final scene, and possibly the most gripping. Without money or jobs and already quite deranged, the lonesome cowboys hit on an idea for filling their pockets without too much effort. They set out to hunt down the last wild horses in Nevada, the famous mustangs, to sell them to the abattoirs for a good price.

They use an old plane and a truck to capture the mustangs, but Roslyn is horrified by the hunt. An unrelenting struggle follows, in the solitude of the desert, between one rebellious woman and a trio of men possessed by their pride. The action takes place in a region 'so sinister that it becomes almost supernatural', wrote Miller. 'There is no tree, no bush, no pool of water . . . Gradually a perverse beauty grows out of the place.'

The exact location of this scene is a place called **Stagecoach**, located 12 miles (19km) east of Dayton on Highway 50. Before you reach Stagecoach, which is straight ahead, a sign on the right bears the significant name 'Breakheart Road'. This stony road is full of potholes, but it is possible to drive a car along it provided you keep the speed down to walking pace. It leads to the middle of nowhere. About 3 miles (5.5km) from the junction with Highway 50, you reach a strange depression, arid and chalky, called **Dry Lake**. This is where Marilyn Monroe appears in the distance as a small, dark dot, screaming alone in the vastness. In Huston's film, the desolate landscape appears to be even more vast than it is in reality.

'Now there is only the sky full of stars, and absolute silence.' This is the last line of the film.

ARIZONA

PHOENIX

AREA CODE: 602

This city is spread out so much that it's almost possible to pass through it without noticing. Phoenix is a funny place – the bane of hitchhikers, being 44 miles (70km) long and 30 miles (50km) wide. It's extremely hot here in summer – you might even say burning hot – but the climate is really pleasant during the rest of the year, which explains the number of retired people here. It seems to be almost totally made up of bungalows, with the exception of Downtown.

The fact that the city grew out of the middle of a stifling desert was because of the existence of the Salt and Verde rivers. Since the end of World War II, it has gone from strength to strength, as more and more land has been reclaimed from the desert. The city seems to attract both schemers and dreamers, as in Arizona anything seems possible. But if this rate of growth continues, Phoenix will one day have to face up to two crucial problems: too little water and too much pollution. There are cars everywhere, running on the innumerable freeways, and an incredible amount of water goes on irrigating golf courses, filling swimming pools and helping gardens to grow.

To visit the places of interest in Phoenix, you'll find that a car is essential. In the evening, Downtown is truly dead. Whatever you do, try not to arrive on a Sunday, as there are few or no city buses. If you're a walker, your best bet is to make a few friends at the youth hostel – the city might then seem to have a few attractions. Otherwise, you might be put off by the town's vastness, the heat, and its relative lack of charm – and be off on the road again in double-quick time.

On the other hand, some of the suburbs are almost pleasant, particularly the area around Scottsdale, which is about 25 miles (40km) to the north, or Tempe, a trendy district that is swarming with students. Sun City in the western suburbs, on the other hand, is home to more than 15,000 retired people. Apparently every single inhabitant is at least 50 years old and children aren't allowed to live there during the school year. It takes all sorts.

ORIENTATION

Washington Street divides the city into northern and southern sections. Street names are preceded by an 'N' in the northern section, and the numbers go up as you go north. It's the same for the southern section, where the prefix is an 'S', and the numbers rise as you travel south. **Central Avenue** separates the town into east and west. The numbering system follows the same centrifugal logic. All roads located east of Central Avenue are called 'Street', while those in the west are called 'Avenue'. It may seem simple, but it's remarkably easy to get it wrong!

ARRIVING AT THE AIRPORT

The airport is 10 minutes by taxi from the city centre. The **Alfa Taxi** company has done a deal with the youth hostel, so the journey isn't expensive.

USEFUL ADDRESSES

Visitors' Office: the main office is right in the centre of town at the Arizona Center, 400 East Van Buren Road, Suite 600 on the 6th floor. ☎ 254-6500. Open Monday–Friday 8am–5pm. A second office is located at the corner of Adams and 2nd Street, on the ground floor of the Hyatt Hotel. Same telephone number. Open Monday–Friday 8am–4.30pm. There are also information centres at the airport terminals.

Arizona Tourist Office: 2702 N 3rd Street, Suite 4015. ☎ 230-7733. Freephone: ☎ 1-800-842-8257. Can provide full information about Arizona.

✉ **Post Office**: Central Avenue, level with Fillmore Street, in the centre. Another at 4949 E Van Buren. Quite a long way from the centre.

✉ Poste restante: 1553 E Buckeye Road: also a long way from town.

■ **Banks**: some that change money include **Bank of America**: 101 N 1st Avenue. ☎ 597-5000. **First Interstate**: 100 W Washington. ☎ 528-1000. **American Express**: Biltmore Fashion Park, 2508 E Camelback Road. ☎ 468-1199. AmEx offers currency exchange and other services.

Greyhound Terminal: 5th Street and Washington Street, in the centre. ☎ 271-2222. Freephone: ☎ 1-800-231-2222. There are four buses per day for Flagstaff (travel time: 3 hours 30 minutes), eight buses for LA (6–8 hours), about 15 buses for Tucson (about 2 hours), about eight buses for Dallas (a 24-hour trip), and 12 buses for El Paso (an 8-hour trip).

Greyline-Nava-Hopi: also goes to Flagstaff (three times a day). ☎ 495-9100. Departs from Terminal 2 at the airport. Buy your tickets at the Arizona Shuttle kiosk. This is useful if you want to go direct to Flagstaff without passing through Phoenix itself.

City Bus Terminal: Washington Street, at the corner of Central. Ask for a route map: it's a complicated system. Note that no urban buses run on Sunday. ☎ 253-5000. You probably won't need to use the bus much, given how much time it can take, but note the violet DASH buses in the city centre: these cover Downtown regularly and cheaply.

■ **Auto drive-away**: 3530 E Native American School Road. ☎ 952-0339. Phone ahead.

– **Amtrak**: there haven't been any trains passing via Phoenix for some years now.

– **Information about events in the city**: ☎ 252-5588.

– **Radio KDKB**: on 93.3 FM. Rock classics only.

WHERE TO STAY

Summer in Phoenix is so hot that many hotels lower their prices to attract customers. A luxury hotel may then become affordable. Most of the cheaper places are located along E Van Buren Road, between 24th and 35th Streets. The reason they aren't expensive is that this is the dodgiest area in town, and, therefore, somewhere that you might want to avoid. In a car, you'll be relatively safe as the hotels are not far away from the centre and they're quite safe. On the other hand, it's advisable to refrain from taking a stroll around the area after the sun goes down.

☆ BUDGET

Metcalf House Youth Hostel: 1026 N 9th Street. ☎ 254-9803. From the City Bus Terminal, take a No. 7 bus to 7th Street, then walk two blocks. In the evening, go by taxi. Alpha Taxi offer a good price from the airport to the youth hostel. This is a lovely brick-built house with a surrounding lawn. Open all year round. The common-room is pleasant, and pleasingly tidy, there's a little courtyard at the back, a kitchen is available, and there's a washing machine. There's a choice of accommodation: either an inexpensive dormitory or a room at a motel price. Unfortunately, it's a bit far from the centre. Non-members are accepted, but have to pay more. If you can play the piano well, you can get a reduction of 50 per cent by playing in the lounge in the evening for everyone's pleasure! You can hire a bike, and it's possible to buy a cheap car and resell it here at the end of your stay. If you're interested, ask the owner.

YMCA: 350 N 1st Avenue, between Van Buren Road and Fillmore. ☎ 253-6181. Blue or red bus from the City Bus Terminal. Open all year. This place has one big advantage – it's located right in the centre. It's one of the cleanest YMCAs in the country. They only have single rooms and it's more expensive than the youth hostel. Very safe. You can't book, but they'll tell you on the phone whether they're full or not. Another bonus: you can use the swimming pool and the fitness center, which costs next-to-nothing. Special weekly rates.

☆☆ MODERATE

Most of the motels are on Van Buren, a large but rather seedy avenue leading out from Downtown.

Budget Lodge Motel: 402 W Van Buren. ☎ 254-7247. A cheap motel near the city centre. It's clean and pleasant and has a token swimming pool.

American Lodge: 965 E Van Buren. ☎ 252-6823. Rooms with air-conditioning and cable TV. Completely redecorated not long ago. There's a swimming pool and prices are very reasonable. One of the most suitable hotels in the area.

Motel 6: 2323 E Van Buren Road. ☎ 267-7511. At the corner of 24th Street. Unremarkable but comfortable enough.

Motel 6: 6848 Camelback Road. ☎ 946-2280. The best Motel 6 in the city, this one is located in the residential district of Scottsdale. Good value for money.

PHOENIX

☆☆–☆☆☆ MODERATE TO EXPENSIVE

Travelodge: 2900 E Van Buren Road. ☎ 275-7651. Provides the same services as those in the 'Moderate' section, but it's a little better. One notch above a Motel 6.

☆☆☆ EXPENSIVE

San Carlos: 202 N Central Avenue. ☎ 253-4121. Charming European-style hotel in the middle of Downtown, next to the museums. It's expensive but genuinely good, offering very tempting discount prices in summer that bring this luxury establishment within the reach of almost everyone. They say that a ghost lives around here somewhere, but he doesn't play nasty tricks. Excellent service and well-presented rooms.

Ramada Downtown: 401 N 1st Street, on the corner of Polk Street. ☎ 258-3411. Downtown, close to the museums. This place has large, beautiful rooms and a big swimming pool. Not expensive for four.

Days Inn: 3333 E Van Buren. ☎ 244-8244. Excellent place in motel style. Where the cars used to be there's a grassy area and a swimming pool. This gives it an almost family atmosphere, which is quite rare for a chain hotel.

BED AND BREAKFAST

There are several associations in Arizona but the B&Bs in Arizona aren't cheap. ☎ 860-9338. Freephone: ☎ 1-800-266-STAY.

WHERE TO EAT

The best restaurants are always a little way from the centre, so here, you may easily have to travel 3–6 miles (5–10km) to reach a place with any quality.

☆ BUDGET AND UNUSUAL

Organ Stop Pizza: 1149 E Southern Avenue. ☎ 813-5700. Large restaurant-pizzeria with a monumental organ – one of the biggest in the world, they say. Various organists take it in turns to play here each evening at dinner-time, from 5pm until 9pm or 10pm. This is a rare experience – don't miss it!

☆–☆☆ BUDGET TO MODERATE

Planet Hollywood: 2402 E Camelback Road. ☎ 954-7827. Open daily, 11am–midnight. On display are the bra worn by Marilyn Monroe in *Bus Stop* and the cape worn by Douglas Fairbanks in *Zorro*. This restaurant, opened as one of the first in the Planet Hollywood chain by Arnold Schwarzenegger, Bruce Willis and Sylvester Stallone, is a must for movie buffs. They serve American cuisine in a cult decor, and you end up sitting between James Dean's letters and the costumes from *Terminator II*. There's also a bar. The place is always packed.

The Spaghetti Company Restaurant: just beside the university in Old Tempe, at 111 Mill Street, on the corner of 4th Street.

☎ 966-3848. Open daily, 11am–10.30pm and a little later at weekends. Going to this place gives you a chance to explore the Old Tempe district, which has been nicely refurbished. The restaurant decor is attractive – all varnished wood, with some beautiful objects and antiques. One big plus is to get to have your meal in a replica of one of the old trams that ran through Phoenix in the good old days. There's a lengthy lunch menu and prices are very reasonable: pizzas, salads, sandwiches and savoury snacks. In the evening, the menu's longer still but the prices are still good: veal Marsala, cheese Manicoti, excellent spaghetti, lasagne, etc.

✕ **Bobby McGee's**: 8501 N 27th Avenue. ☎ 995-5982. Open 5pm–10pm (11pm Friday and Saturday). In the north of the city. If you're coming from the centre, take Highway 17 and exit at Northern Avenue. This enormous restaurant is decorated in turn-of-the-century Old West style, with engravings, stained-glass windows and tiffany lamps. Even the waitresses are in costume. There are several rooms and a bar. Happy hours with free buffet are 4–8pm. The menu is good and they also do smaller dishes, all cheaper than you'd expect. Try the favourites (*Mahi Mahi Macadamia*), charbroiled dishes (delicious *teriyaki*) or the specialities (prime rib of beef, sautéed seafood). If you've ordered a main course, you can serve yourself at the salad bar, which looks fresh and plentiful. Booking is recommended. There's also a lively and young nightclub in an adjoining room. Admission is free if you've eaten in the restaurant.

Another **Bobby McGee's** is at 1330 W Southern. ☎ 969-4600.

✕ **Garcia's**: Peoria Avenue and 33rd Avenue ☎ 866-1850. Open 11am–10pm (11pm at weekends). Take Highway 17 and exit at Peoria. Quite a well-known Mexican restaurant. The decor's colourful, as you might expect. They offer very decent cuisine and prices are reasonable. There's an inexpensive lunch during the week. Specialities include enchiladas, fajitas combo, chili relleno and Garcia's *Chimichanga*. Booking is advisable.

✕ **Lombardi's**: 455 N 3rd Street, on the ground floor of the Arizona Center, near the fountain. ☎ 257-8323. Open all day to 11pm. There's a shady terrace and good Italian cuisine with big servings. The decor is classy and relaxed. Very popular at lunchtime with the office workers of the district. Pleasant service.

✕ **The Fish Market**: 1720 E Camelback Road. ☎ 377-3474. Open daily, 11am–9.30pm (10pm at weekends). Fish and more fish, in all its forms, from marinated *ceviche* to *sashimi,* grilled or smoked. An unpretentious room with a bar, where the walls are hung with some superb photographs of fishing scenes. A smarter and more expensive restaurant is on the first floor.

✕ **Big Apple**: 3757 E Van Buren Road ☎ 275-2107. This is a restaurant with a real cowboy feel. Each waitress packs a Colt on her hip, there's sawdust on the floor, and there's Country music to add to the atmosphere. A good place for breakfast, because it's very near where all the hotels are, and it's definitely an entertaining place to start your day. The omelettes are generous.

✕ **Rawhide**: *see* 'What to See in the Area'.

✕ **Minders Binders**: *see* 'Where to Have a Drink'.

PHOENIX

☆☆☆☆ SPLASH OUT

Vincent: 3930 E Camelback Road. ☎ 224-0225. Open daily except summer Sundays, 11.30am–2.30pm and 6–10pm. Take the best American and international cuisine, add a great French chef – and you'll get Vincent. Once at The Ritz in Chicago, this chef is daringly imaginative. The restaurant setting is pleasant, without pretension, and the service is impeccable – one of the best restaurants in the US. Each dish will cost about $25. Booking is recommended.

WHERE TO HAVE A DRINK (AND HAVE A GOOD TIME . . .)

Minders Binders: 715 South McClintock Drive, Tempe. ☎ 966-1911. Open daily, 11am–1am. Take Apache Boulevard to McClintock, it's very close to the corner. It's a grand, old timber-built house painted in striking colours. The setting inside is way-out – a bit of a bazaar, with weird stuff hanging from the walls and ceiling: whaleboats, stuffed mules, sleighs, one bearing a lewd Father Christmas, a real stagecoach, a corn-husking machine, caribou heads and hundreds of other things, as well as some superb collages. Great rock music at full blast, and cheap beer.

The clientele are mostly young students. You can eat here, too, and there's a sense of humour on the menu: Beefy Brotherly Love sandwiches, Curley QQQ, Gadzook Zuchs, burgers, etc. Daily specials are listed on flyers. For example, on Sunday 8pm–midnight, a beer costs 75 cents. There's a large bar, video games and a dance floor on the first floor. Happy hour is 4–7pm Monday–Friday. You can play mini-basketball and table football. A band plays upstairs on Friday and Saturday evening 9pm–1am, and you can dance and everything! Behind the restaurant is a 'beach' where students play volleyball. A really good place.

Toolies Country Saloon and Dance Hall: 4231 W Thomas Rd. ☎ 272-3100. Open daily to 1am. Bands every evening 8pm–1am. Free admission on Sunday, Monday and Tuesday, and sometimes Wednesday. Every Thursday 6–9pm, there's a great party. You just pay the admission charge and every drink costs only a silver coin, which means you can pay with any single coin except a copper one. You're in a temple of Country music here: it's huge, full of atmosphere and there's lots of space. There are people playing billiards, others dancing the 'two-step', and at the back you can watch live greyhound racing on giant screens and place bets. It's a truly cult place – you might almost call it a course of study in the habits of the last cowboys. So, yank on your tight Wranglers, jump into your cowboy boots, whistle up a taxi – and yeeehaa!

Chars Has the Blues: 4631 N 7th Avenue ☎ 230-0205. This is just a little white house that's hardly visible, but blues fans know the place well. Every evening 9pm–1am, they feature some excellent blues bands of every kind. There's a small admission charge on Friday and Saturday, but it's free the rest of the week.

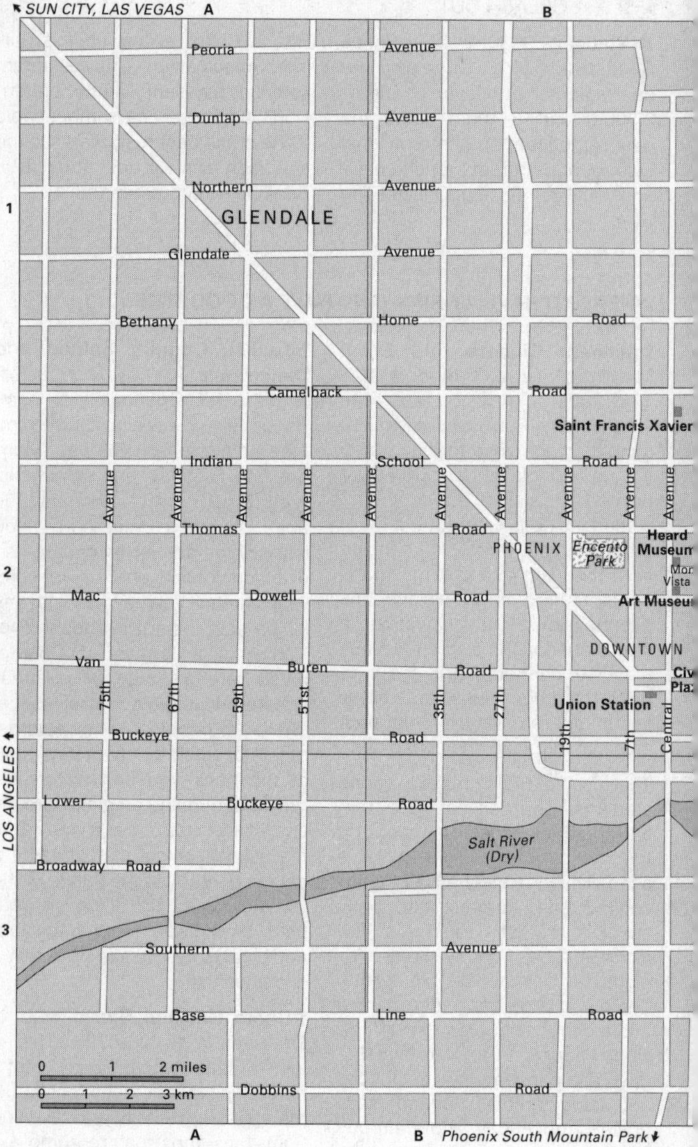

SUN CITY, LAS VEGAS
A
B
Peoria Avenue
Dunlap Avenue
Northern Avenue
1
GLENDALE
Glendale Avenue
Bethany Home Road
Camelback Road
Saint Francis Xavier
Indian School Road
Thomas Road
PHOENIX
Encanto Park
Heard Museum
Mon Vista
2
Mac Dowell Road
Art Museum
DOWNTOWN
Van Buren Road
Civic Plaza
Union Station
75th Avenue
67th Avenue
59th Avenue
51st Avenue
35th Avenue
27th Avenue
19th Avenue
7th Avenue
Central Avenue
Buckeye Road
LOS ANGELES
Lower Buckeye Road
Salt River (Dry)
Broadway Road
3
Southern Avenue
Base Line Road
0 1 2 miles
0 1 2 3 km
Dobbins Road
A
B
Phoenix South Mountain Park

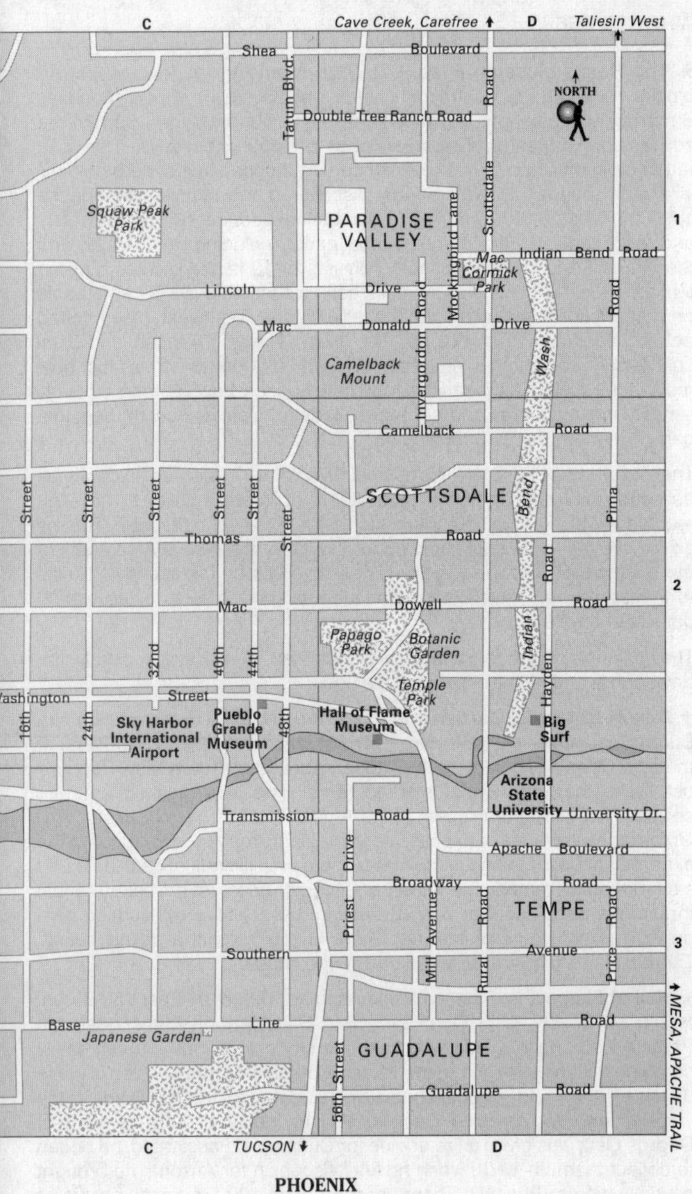
C
Cave Creek, Carefree
D
Taliesin West
Shea
Boulevard
Tatum Blvd.
Double Tree Ranch Road
Road
NORTH
Scottsdale
Squaw Peak Park
PARADISE VALLEY
Mockingbird Lane
Mac Cormick Park
Indian
Bend
Road
Lincoln
Drive
Road
Road
Mac
Donald
Drive
Camelback Mount
Invergordon
Wash
Camelback
Road
SCOTTSDALE
Street
Street
Street
Street
Street
Street
Bend
Pima
Thomas
Road
Road
Mac
Dowell
Road
Papago Park
Botanic Garden
32nd
40th
44th
Indian
Hayden
Washington
Street
Temple Park
16th
24th
Sky Harbor International Airport
Pueblo Grande Museum
48th
Hall of Flame Museum
Big Surf
Arizona State University
University Dr.
Transmission
Road
Apache
Boulevard
Drive
Broadway
Road
Priest
Avenue
Road
TEMPE
Road
Southern
Avenue
Mill
Rural
Price
Base
Line
Road
Japanese Garden
GUADALUPE
Street
Guadalupe
Road
56th
C
TUCSON
D
MESA, APACHE TRAIL
1
2
3

PHOENIX

WHAT TO SEE

★ **The Heard Museum** (map, B2): 22 E Monte Vista Road. About 10 blocks north of the centre of Phoenix. ☎ 252-8840. Open Monday–Saturday 9.30am–5pm (8pm Wednesday), Sunday noon–5pm. Free admission Wednesday 5–8pm. Closed on public holidays. This is a remarkable museum of Native American art, housed in a superb colonial villa. The founder, Harvey Heard, discovered the richness of Apache culture in the late 19th century. He also took the concession for the hotels and restaurants in many of the national parks, including Death Valley and the Grand Canyon. The museum consists of 10 large galleries housing temporary exhibitions plus a main gallery that displays a remarkable permanent collection relating to the tribes of the southwest, their habitat, pottery, fabrics and traditions. The Hopi, Navajo, Apache and Zuni cultures are presented in an informative way that demonstrates just how much they differ. It's clear that our conceptions have tended to over-simplify these cultures and put them all, quite mistakenly, into the same bag.

The everyday objects are quite beautiful. There's also an exceptional collection of *kachinas*: these magnificent dolls were given to boys on reaching puberty, to initiate them into their future role in the tribe. There's an excellent audio-visual show about the life of the Native Americans of the southwest. The whole experience is overlaid by the sound of Native American music. There's a small sculpture garden. Also a fascinating display of cradles.

The galleries of modern Native American art demonstrate clearly the development of native art across the ages.

★ **Desert Botanical Garden** (map, D2): 1201 N Galvin Parkway. On Van Buren Road, level with 56th Street. ☎ 941-1225. In Papago Park, east of the city. Open daily, 8am–8pm October–April; 7am–10pm May–September. Take the No. 3E bus marked 'Zoo'. This is a gigantic open-air collection of cacti from America and Africa. Ask for the very useful *Trail Guide* at the entrance. It explains how the plants managed to adapt to the extreme rigours of the desert climate. There are all kinds of cacti here and each is quite remarkable: creepers, squat ones, short-haired ones, thread-like ones, etc. It's very interesting, but try to avoid coming here during the hot hours of the day. Right at the back is a desert house. There's also a picnic area and a cafe in the shade.

★ **Hall of Flame** (Fire Fighting Museum; map, D2): 6101 East Van Buren. ☎ 275-3473 (ASK-FIRE). Open 9am–5pm, Sunday noon–4pm. Located in Papago Park, quite a long way from the city centre, but you can easily combine this trip with one to the Desert Botanical Garden, which is close by. This is the world's biggest museum dedicated to firemen. Some of the vehicles are really amazing. Back in 1955, an industrialist by the name of George Getz was given a fire engine for Christmas. Fascinated, he began to collect them. In 1970, when he left Wisconsin for Arizona, he brought his collection to Phoenix. There are more than 100 fire-fighting vehicles on show. The oldest item dates from 1725, and exhibits range from the Rumsey pump that was used to fight the great fire of Chicago in 1871, to the superb, sparkling Seagrave pump of 1928. Then there are the tools, accessories and uniforms, plus some interesting photographs and documents. There's even a control room that can send genuine live calls to fire stations.

★ **Phoenix Art Museum** (map, B2): 1625 N Central Ave, on the corner of McDowell Road. ☎ 257-1222. Open 10am–5pm (9pm Wednesday). Opens noon on Sunday. Closed Monday and public holidays. Free admission, except to the temporary exhibitions. Completely renovated not long ago. This is a very interesting museum of art. It has a good selection of bronzes by Rodin, Sino-Tibetan art, ancient lithographs, engravings by James Ensor, Goya, Gavarni, Daumier, etc.

There's a splendid American section on the Old West and the Native Americans, and a restored Spanish colonial house. All kinds of art are represented, from Latin American to the Renaissance, from the baroque period to modern art. In this last gallery is the work of Tápies, Paul Guerrero, David Bates, Jim Waid, and a unusual Frida Kahlo, as well as examples of the work of Picasso, Magritte, Karel Appel and others.

There are more paintings, by Georgia O'Keeffe, Joseph Stella, Rousseau, Vuillard and Dufy, as well as painters of the Flemish School. There's the 18th-century French School, in Boucher, Élisabeth Vigée-Lebrun and Quentin de La Tour. Finally, there are works by Corot, Millet and Delacroix.

SCOTTSDALE

★ **Taliesin West** (off map, D1): 12621 Frank Lloyd Wright Boulevard. ☎ 860-2700. Open daily, 8–11am June–September, 10am–4pm the rest of the year. Northeast of Scottsdale, some way from the city centre. The guided tours are obligatory and last 1, 1 hour 30 minutes or 3 hours (there are no 3-hour trips in summer). High admission charge. In 1938, Frank Lloyd Wright, one of the country's greatest architects, decided to build a university of architecture right on the edge of the desert, where students could spend the winter. The students didn't live in the actual buildings. Their first task was to build their own bungalows around the main structure – with their own hands. The idea here was to be integrated with nature to the maximum possible extent, according to the principles of 'organic architecture'. What's more, a rather surreal lifestyle was organized on this unconventional campus. Music also played a large role because Lloyd Wright believed that, like architecture, it should be completely rhythmic and balanced.

The first tour takes you round his office, the theatre where evening entertainments were organized, the cabaret and the cinema auditorium. You have to remember that, back in 1938 there was no electricity and no telephone here, and, as the city wasn't as extensive, the location was some way out in the desert. It's an exciting tour if you find this kind of approach appealing. If you reckon the trip is too expensive and the site too far from the centre, you could visit instead the Baltimore Hotel on 24th Street and Missouri Avenue. This was Frank Lloyd Wright's other great project in Phoenix. The hotel, built in 1929 in art-deco style, is well worth a look. Close by, the white house on the promontory once belonged to William Wrigley, the inventor of chewing-gum.

★ **The residential district of Scottsdale** (map, D2): many large, beautifully designed mansions, principally on Scottsdale Avenue. On 5th Avenue, there are shops selling Native American crafts, jewellery and turquoise. You will find things here that are no more expensive than on the Navajo or Hopi Native American reservations.

TEMPE AND THE UNIVERSITY DISTRICT

Tempe lies near the airport and south of Papago Park. It's a pleasant, youthful place, because, of course, it's home to the university. In fact, it's the fourth-largest town in the state, with approximately 150,000 inhabitants. It has the Big Surf Aquatic Park, which has artificial waves for surfers, and a nice restaurant, Minders Binders (*see* 'Where to Eat').

★ You might want to go and see the university and its **Gammage Center of the Performing Arts** (Mill Avenue and Apache Road). One of the last big projects by the architect Frank Lloyd Wright, the university incorporates interesting little museums that you should visit if you have time: Geology (minerals, fossils, etc.), Fine Arts (American 19th- and 20th-century painting), on Mill Avenue and 10th Street.

★ Stroll round **Old Tempe**, which is a very well restored district that's nice and lively, with plenty of young people. Some interesting buildings and good restaurants.

WHAT ELSE TO SEE, IF YOU HAVE TIME TO SPARE

★ **Arizona Hall of Fame Museum**: 1101 W Washington. ☎ 542-4675. Admission free. Open Monday–Friday 8am–5pm. A trip here is always interesting. First and foremost, it's a fine, early 20th-century building situated in a large garden. It was for a long time the home of the Carnegie Public Library. Today, you can see temporary exhibitions on the history of the citizens of Arizona and there's a Hall of Famous Women and the Woman of the Year.

★ **Greyhound racing**: Greyhound Park, 3801 E Washington Street. ☎ 273-7181. Daily at 7.30pm, plus Tuesday afternoon, September–May.

★ **Heritage Square**: between 6th Street and Monroe, in the middle of Downtown. If Phoenix has a historic centre, this is it. A small square, some old houses – and that's about it. There's also a sweet little museum on the square: the **Arizona Doll Toy Museum**, open Tuesday–Saturday 10am–4pm and Sunday noon–4pm.

★ **Pueblo Grande Museum** (map, C2): 4619 E Washington Street. ☎ 495-0901. This is the ancient site of a Honakan Native American village, of which only a few uninteresting ruins remain. To make matters worse, the whole thing is located right next to the airport runways.

WHAT TO DO

– **Salt River Recreation**: 30 miles (50km) northeast of Phoenix on the Salt River, near Bush Highway and level with Usery Pass Road (Tonto National Forest). Open daily, mid-April to mid-September, 9am–4pm. This consists of shooting the 'rapids' while floating downstream on some truck tyre inner-tubes. Phoenix gets very hot in summer, and the water isn't polluted, so these are two good reasons why the sport is so popular. It isn't inherently dangerous, although you have to obey some sensible rules, namely, wearing trainers to protect yourself from submerged rocks, wearing a hat and covering your body with sun-block. The inner tubes can be hired on the spot for a few dollars and the price includes the return upriver by bus as many times as you like. This means that you can shoot the rapids several times, as the hire of the inner tube is valid for the whole day. Each shooting trip takes about two hours.

– **Trips by hot-air balloon**: several companies offer similar services, with some minor differences. The trip lasts one or two hours, and can be with or without champagne. Here are a few names:

Desert Balloon Flight: ☎ 991-3666. Freephone: ☎ 1-800-HOT-AIR-8

Balloon Tours: ☎ 502-6999. Freephone: ☎ 1-800-831-7610

The Hot Air Balloon Co: ☎ 461-8689. Freephone: ☎ 1-800-84-FLY-US

WHAT TO SEE IN THE AREA

★ **Rawhide**: 23023 N Scottsdale Road. ☎ 502-1880. 12 miles (20km) north of Phoenix via Scottsdale Road. In summer it's open daily, 5–10pm; the rest of the year it's open at weekends from 11am. Free admission. This is a reconstruction of a city in the West in the 1880s with a saloon, a prison, a goldmine and even quite an interesting museum. The restaurant is famed for its steaks, which you eat seated at big tables. Try the amazing game in which chickens challenge you at noughts and crosses – they'll beat you every time! Live show and cowboy shoot-out. It's hyper-touristy, of course, but enjoyable all the same.

★ **Arcosanti**: at Cordes Junction, 65 miles (104 km) north of Phoenix on the road to Flagstaff (Interstate 17, Exit 262). ☎ 632-7135 and 254-5309. Open daily, 9am–5pm. Guided trip every hour 10am–4pm (it's free, but donations are very welcome – say about $5). Four people is the minimum. This futuristic city was begun in 1970 by the architect Paolo Soleri as part of a movement that called itself 'Arcology' (a combination of 'architecture' and 'ecology'). Soleri wanted to reconcile man and his environment, taking inspiration from solar energy and termite habitats. The result is astonishing and many professionals find it inspirational. Some concerts are held here. Interesting if you're keen on architecture. Cafe open daily, 8am–4pm.

If you're interested in Soleri's work, you may also enjoy a visit to **Cosanti,** at Scottsdale, Paradise Valley (6433 Doubletree Ranch Road). ☎ 948-6145. Open daily, 9am–5pm. There are futuristic buildings and structures here, too, but more oriented towards ecology. They also cast bells of a very refined modernistic style here.

☗ You can spend a night (maximum of two nights) in one of the studios in the middle of the city of Arcosanti. Allow $20 per person. You will then be able to be look in on the evening gatherings of resident students and architects.

★ Go by car over the trail that links **Tortilla Flat** with **Lake Roosevelt**. The landscape is superb: desert, cactus, canyons, and a road carved out of a mountain. Allow five hours.

TUCSON

AREA CODE: 520

Tucson is one of the oldest of the Spanish cities, although it's been American since 1853 and very little of the original town remains. The city is quite spread out, which means that the places of interest are widely scattered, but there's a pleasant local atmosphere. You might not, however, want to spend a week here as in many areas, it's completely dead in the evening. The climate is very hot and dry. You'll find plenty of opportunities to meet Native Americans in town. The area around Tucson is also the place where you'll see the giant saguaro cactus.

The city is chiefly interesting for its fascinating Museum of the Desert. All in all, it's a bit like Phoenix – only smaller.

USEFUL ADDRESSES

Metropolitan Tucson Convention and Visitors' Office: 130 South Scott Street. ☎ 624-1817. Website: www.arizonaguide.com/visittucson. Open daily, 8.30am–5pm. In the centre of town. Good welcome and an excellent range of information. You can get a city map here and also telephone hotels.

✉ **Post office**: 150 S Church Street and 141 S 6th Avenue Downtown.

■ **Auto drive-away**: ☎ 323-7659.

Amtrak: 400 E Toole (and 5th Avenue). ☎ 623-4442. Freephone: ☎ 1-800-872-7245. Two or three trains a week for Los Angeles, Phoenix and El Paso.

Greyhound: 2 S 4th Avenue ☎ 792-3475. Downtown. Between Broadway and Congress. Around 15 buses for Phoenix, the same for Nogales on the Mexican border, four for San Diego, three for Bisbee and maybe 10 for LA.

– The *Tucson Weekly* and the *Tucson Lifestyle* are two lively magazines that are full of information about the city.

ARIZONA

WHERE TO STAY

CAMPGROUND

Gilbert Ray Campground: on the left, just before you get to the Desert Museum. This place is in the middle of the desert, among thousands of giant cacti. It's rough and ready – and pretty wild. It's also free. No sanitary facilities, no kitchen, nothing at all in fact. But you're either a cowboy or you ain't!

☆ BUDGET

Congress Hotel: 311 East Congress. ☎ 622-8848. Downtown. Close to the Greyhound terminal and Amtrak. An old Western-style hotel (1919) that's been well restored and still retains some of its old-fashioned charm. It serves as a local youth hostel and hotel. John Dillinger, the notorious bandit, slept here. The hotel still has a 'borderlands' ambiance. There are hostel rooms and hotel rooms; the former have bunk beds, take two persons and are smaller. It's clean, very cheap – and you might even get a 1940s radio in your room. Bar and ground-floor nightclub, which attracts the local youth. It's the nicest place in the city.

☆☆ MODERATE

University Inn: 950 North Stone Avenue ☎ 791-7503. Freephone: ☎ 1-800-233-8466. A small traditional motel, not too far from the centre, with a small swimming pool. Impeccable rooms. Good value.

Most of the budget and moderate hotels are along Interstate 10, level with exit 258, on a small road that runs parallel with the highway and their cheerful neon signs are visible from a long way off. All the chains are represented there: Motel 6, Travel Inn, Quality Inn, Super 8, etc.

Motel 6: 1222 S Freeway. ☎ 624-2516. The rooms have been nicely redecorated; and prices are moderate in summer. Take a room at the back to get some quiet and enjoy the sunset view.

☆☆☆ EXPENSIVE

Quality Motel: 475 N Granada. ☎ 622-3000. Fax: 623-8922. This charming place consists of low, pink buildings in Mexican style surrounding a pleasant swimming pool. Right in the centre yet very quiet. Price is the same as for a three-star hotel.

WHERE TO EAT

Plenty of options in the Mexican district. Even though there's hardly anyone in the streets in the evening, there's a livelier atmosphere in the bars of this district.

El Torero: 231 E 26th Street (west of S 4th Ave). ☎ 622-9534. Open 11am–11pm at least. Closed Tuesday. Probably the best of the city's popular Mexican restaurants and run by the same family since 1956. Pleasant setting and good welcome. Try their combination dishes: tostadas, chimichangas, burros, tamales, and the many house specialities (*carne con chile verde,* fish and crab *topopo* and *carne seca y tortilla).*

El Dorado: 1949 S 4th Avenue ☎ 622-9171. Serves Mexican food and seafood. Good reputation. Traditional music on Friday, Saturday and Sunday.

Congress Cafe, Cup Cafe: in the Congress Hotel, 311 East Congress. ☎ 622-8848. Open daily, 9am–1am. Just a few little tables, frequented by the young people of the area. Perfect for a peaceful breakfast, in a cool 'Californian' atmosphere. Good omelettes; snacks in the evening.

Maya Quetzal: 429 N 4th Ave, near 6th Street. ☎ 622-8207. Open lunchtime and evening; closed Sunday. A small, old-fashioned Guatemalan restaurant that creates its authentic atmosphere with photos on the walls and brightly coloured tablecloths. The cuisine is inexpensive and authentic – more subtle than Mexican.

✕ **Delectables**: 533 N 4th Ave, between 5th and 6th Streets. ☎ 884-9289. In this quietly trendy district, this restaurant is a cool place to eat, providing a varied menu that crosses many frontiers: houmous, *tabouleh*, smoked trout, exotic salads, quiches, etc. Nice service.

✕ **Cafe Magritte**: 254 E Congress. ☎ 884-8004. Open to 10pm and later at weekends. Closed Monday. A cafe with a name like this should be a little surrealist. This one has paintings on the walls and a nice atmosphere; the food is pleasant and quite modern. They serve some vegetarian dishes, large salads and some concoctions that are pleasing if not original.

WHERE TO HAVE A DRINK

🍸 **Congress Hotel**: 311 East Congress. ☎ 622-8848. This is the best place in the city for the kind of music you get here. Lots of different kinds of people frequent it and the atmosphere that's generated is quite 'cool'. OK if you want to have a wild time, a drink or just a chat with friends.

🍸 **Wild Wild West**: 4385 W Ina Road. ☎ 744-7744. Admission charge varies according to the group. The total opposite to the Congress, with a strong 'Country' ambience. Billiard tables, shoeshine boys – a real cowboy place.

🍸 **The Rock**: 136 N Park Avenue ☎ 629-9211. Usually open on weekend evenings. Modest rock, reggae and other groups do their best to generate a lot of noise in an atmosphere that fluctuates between awful and excellent. Not many people are around in summer when the students are on vacation.

🍸 **Berky's on the 4th**: 424 N 4th Avenue ☎ 622-0376. Another bar where you can have your eardrums damaged by obscure second-rank musicians for a small fee. Open every night except Wednesday.

– One place you must go in the evening is **4th Street**. This is an area that's a bit marginal and away from the cutting edge, where you'll find a comfortable mix of restaurants, nightspots and bars.

WHAT TO SEE

Two places in particular that you should visit are the Old Tucson Studios and the Arizona Sonora Desert Museum. Both are really good, but unfortunately they're 12 miles (20km) outside the city to the west. Hitchhike rather than go by bus, or take the Grayline tour, or form a group and make a deal with a taxi driver to deliver you to the museum around 9am and come back to pick you up in Old Tucson at an appointed time. You can do the distance between the two sites (2 miles/3km) on foot, strolling across the cactus-filled plain. It feels as if you might see John Wayne at any moment. This area has often been used as a film and TV location, including *The Little House on the Prairie*.

★ **Old Tucson Studios**: 201 S Kinney Road. ☎ 883-0100. Open daily. Columbia Pictures reconstructed this small, late 19th-century Old West town in 1939. The studios unfortunately burned down almost totally some years ago, but they've been restored to their former glory and are now open to visitors again. All the houses and cabins have been used as sets in more than 200 Westerns. The first was *Arizona,* in 1939, with Jean Arthur and William Holden; others include *Rio Bravo, El Dorado, Joe Kidd* (Clint Eastwood) and *Judge Roy Bean* (Paul Newman). Everything is as you'd expect – a typical main street with a bank, prison, saloon, etc. There's a Mexican village, a railroad station and even a Chinese street. There's also a Museum of Medicine in which you can view an alarming array of equipment used by doctors and charlatans at the time of the Old West. There's a gunfight every couple of hours: a faithful reconstruction of a classic movie scene.

★ **Arizona Sonora Desert Museum**: 2021 N Kinney Road. 2 miles (3km) beyond Old Tucson on the same road. ☎ 883-1380. Open 8.30am–5pm; from Memorial Day to Labor Day (the summer months), 7.30am–6pm. Admission is expensive, except for children, but it still seems like good value for money. You may wonder how you can have a desert museum when, by definition, there's not a lot in a desert – but they've managed it. An amazing 1,300 species of wild animals, snakes and birds can live in the desert. The Cactus Garden has more than 300 varieties of rare plants. Have a look also at the 'Grassland Soils', where the desert subsoil is magnified 100 times. As a finale, you enter a stalactite cavern made more impressive by the superb lighting. Try to arrive as early as possible, because the animals are more lively in the morning.

★ **The University of Arizona Museum of Art**: Speedway and Park (in the centre of the block of houses). ☎ 621-7567. Open winter Monday–Friday 9am–5pm, Sunday noon–4pm; summer Monday–Friday 10am–3.30pm, Sunday noon–4pm. Closed Saturday. Free admission. The museum houses a collection of European and American art, but it's best known for its collection of about 60 works by Jacques Lipchitz, one of the greatest sculptors of the art deco period.

There's a Summer Arts Festival with a good atmosphere. Theatre, dance, opera, etc. ☎ 621-1162. Tickets from the Drama Building, Park and Speedway.

★ **Arizona Historical Society**: 949 E 2nd Street. ☎ 628-5774. Open Monday–Saturday 10am–4pm (opens noon Sunday). This large museum presents the history of Arizona, from the time the Spaniards ruled to the present day. Conquistador armour, stagecoach, reconstruction of a mining gallery with its machinery, etc.

★ **Tucson Museum of Art**: 140 N Main Street. ☎ 624-2333. Open 10am–4pm (opens noon Sunday). Closed Monday in summer. The museum displays interesting collections of Pre-Columbian art, furniture, Spanish and contemporary paintings.

★ **4th Avenue**: around 5th and 8th Streets, has loads of shops selling really nice antiques, second-hand goods and bric-a-brac.

WHAT TO SEE IN THE AREA

★ **Pima Air and Space Museum**: 6000 E Valencia Road. ☎ 574-9658. Open daily, 9am–5pm (ticket counter closes 4pm). Take Interstate 10 East, Valencia Exit, then travel for about 2 miles (3km). More than 300 planes of every kind, civilian and military, from 1940 onward, are on display here, including some bizarrely shaped military planes that you've probably never seen anywhere else. You can explore the site in a small tourist tram, with a running commentary provided.

★ You can supplement this trip by visiting a **Titan rocket launching site**, now disused, some 25 miles (40km) south of Tucson. On Interstate 19 South (Exit 69). ☎ 625-7736. Open May to October, by appointment only.

★ **Sabino Canyon**: open daily, 9am–5pm. ☎ 749-2861. For motorists only, because it's quite a long way off (20 miles/30km) northeast of Tucson. Take the East Speedway to Wilmot, turn north and follow the signs for Sabino Canyon. It's a small national park that's most notable for its canyon. Admission is free for walkers, who can choose from two trails. Most visitors join the small open bus trip that goes for several miles into the canyon. Departures are every hour through the week and every 30 minutes at weekends, 9am–4.30pm. Pleasant, but avoid the high temperatures in the middle of the day. A second minibus takes walkers to the starting point of several hiking trails.

★ **The San Xavier del Bac Mission**: take Interstate 19, exit 92. You can see this white mission building from the highway, level with the exit – it's in the distance in the middle of the desert. Follow the San Xavier Road and it's signed. It's about 6 miles (10km) south of Tucson. ☎ 294-2624. Open daily, 9am–6pm. This magnificent Spanish mission, known as 'the White Dove' and the most beautiful in the US according to some, is located on the Tohono O'odham Native American reservation. The mission was founded in 1692 by Father Eusebio Francisco Kino, who named it after the Apostle of the Indies. It was built in 1783, on Native American territory, at a time when missionaries were setting up in the region.

The mission's architectural style shows a subtle mixture of Byzantine, Moorish and Renaissance influences, which, curiously, give it a certain unity, however contradictory this may appear. Its interior frescoes were restored by some of the artists who helped to renovate the Sistine Chapel. The nave consists of several domes and a cornice ornamented with geometric friezes. Two lions, donated by a Spanish family in the late 18th century, stand guard at the entrance to the choir. In the south transept, there's a St Francis Xavier in wood, on which the faithful hang thanksgiving plaques.

★ **Biosphere 2**: from Tucson, follow Oracle Road, which becomes Highway 77, to the north as far as Oracle Junction. From there, keep going north for a few miles and you'll see signs for Biosphere 2 on the right. The journey takes about one hour. Open daily, 9am–5pm. There's an obligatory guided tour lasting two hours. Regular departures. Admission is very expensive. Maps are handed out at the entrance.

Biosphere 2 (Biosphere 1 being Planet Earth) was an astonishing ecological adventure and a very well-publicized scientific experiment that set out to prove that it was possible to reproduce the terrestrial ecosystem. Eight 'researchers' were sealed into a glass pyramid in the middle of the Arizona desert to demonstrate that they could live in a closed vessel containing a reconstructed natural environment (tropical forest, farm, savannah, mini-ocean, etc.). This greenhouse, with an area of 167,440 square yards (140,000 square metres), cost $200 million and was intended to shed light on certain current mysteries, such as the greenhouse effect and acid rain. The first experiment began in September 1991 and ended two years later. But barely three months after the project began, the occupants of the biosphere needed to top up the air supply, even though they had intended to stay there for two years without any external input. In fact, the micro-organisms that take in oxygen and give off carbon dioxide stood up better than the plants that give off oxygen, so the balance was slanted, causing physiological difficulties for the 'passengers'. In addition to this, several varieties of cockroach had started to proliferate and destroy the harvests, forcing the inhabitants of the biosphere to restrict their food intake. Twenty per cent of the 3,800 vegetable and animal species disappeared and the equilibrium of the ecosystem was seriously compromised. In spite of denials by the people on the site, it had to be regarded as a failure. Then the American press broke the discreetly eulogistic veil around it and revealed the enterprise's rather murky underside – it seems the whole thing was like something out of a James Bond story – an attempt to create a means of human survival surviving on Mars after planet Earth destroys itself!

The actual reasons for the failure are still not clear, but there's no doubt that nothing worked the way it had been planned – a pity, because at the outset, everyone believed in this project and, in the end, the image of ecology has suffered a heavy blow.

A second stage in the experiment took place, from March to September 1994, after which it became necessary to try and generate some profit from the affair, and the site was opened to visitors. The billionaire behind the project will at least be able to recover his investment soon, thanks to the hefty admission charges.

The trip is a bit disappointing, mainly because you're not allowed into the Biosphere 2 enclosure. You have to content yourself with watching two rather feeble films that sort of explain the experiment. You only get to see the laboratory, which is actually a sort of mini-biosphere where tests were made before the 'full-size' adventure was attempted. The only feature of any interest is the biosphere 'lung', which was used to introduce air into the interior of the environment. What *are* worth seeing around the site are the sculptures by Tony Price. This artist started off in the Marines, doing paintings of generals. Today, he uses fragments of metal from the Los Alamos research centre to construct pacifist sculptures in what he calls a 'post-destroy' style. Around 20 of them are spread around the site of Biosphere 2.

Biosphere Inn Hotel: beside Biosphere 2. ☎ 896-2347. Pleasant and quiet little hotel with a superb view of the Canyon del Oro and the Santa Catalina Mountains. Packages in summer include dinner, breakfast and, of course, a trip to Biosphere 2.

Canyon Cafe: on the site. The food is mediocre, but there's a beautiful view of the valley.

TOMBSTONE

AREA CODE: 520

Tombstone ('the town too tough to die') lies 60 miles (100km) south-east of Tucson along Interstate 80. This was a mining town with a reputation for violence in the days of the Wild West, and many of the old buildings from that time still exist. Although it had a big reputation, Tombstone is a tiny town, mainly famous as the location of the famous gunfight at the OK Corral. The memory of Wyatt Earp, Doc Holliday and the Clanton clan still pervades the streets, and the old cemetery on Boot Hill, where the dead were buried with their boots on, still gets many visitors. Each grave, dating from 1880–1900, tells you not only the name of its occupant but also how he died, and – sometimes – who killed him.

Tombstone was founded by a silver prospector called Ed Schieffelin, who had been told: 'Don't go there, you'll only find a tombstone'. But he discovered a rich seam, which attracted other miners, and he called his city 'Tombstone'. When the town reached a certain size, an enterprising publisher set up its first newspaper and called it, naturally enough, *The Epitaph*. Tombstone has suffered two heavy blows: in 1887, the mines were flooded, and the courthouse was relocated to Bisbee in 1929.

Tombstone never became a ghost town, despite the closure of the mines. It might have vegetated, but it did survive, which explains the exceptional state of preservation of the buildings.

And, of course, the American genius for stage-setting means that there are daily reconstruction gunfights on Main Street, while heavies disguised as cowboys burst into the saloons with their Colts drawn.

GUNFIGHT AT THE OK CORRAL

This famous episode in the history of the West actually took place – on 26 October 1881. It was immortalized in two films: *Gunfight at the OK Corral*, directed by John Sturges (with Kirk Douglas and Burt Lancaster), and *Doc Holliday,* directed by Frank Perry (with Stacy Keach). Sheriff Wyatt Earp, his two brothers Virgil and Morgan, as well as 'Doc' Holliday, a dentist with a drinking habit who also went on to become a legend, went out to arrest the Clanton and McLaury brothers, who were notorious bandits. The shooting lasted just 30 seconds, during which the two McLaury brothers died in a blaze of bullets. Three members of the Earp group were slightly wounded. One of the Clanton brothers died shortly afterwards, but not until he had asked someone to take his boots off, as he had promised his mother he would try his best not to be buried with them on.

Sheriff Wyatt Earp died in his bed in Los Angeles in 1929, at the age of 80, having changed his occupation in the meantime to real-estate agent.

THE ORIGIN OF THE EXPRESSION OK

There are a number of stories about where this expression comes from. Some say that it comes from a political club in Pennsylvania that supported the presidential candidate Martin Van Buren in 1836, in the small town of Kinderhook. The club was called 'Old Kinderhook', which quickly became abbreviated to OK. As the club was very fashionable, 'OK' quickly came into use to indicate something very good. In the club itself, everyone was an OK member and therefore one of the best. This easily used expression spread like wildfire to all the states of the Union, and, before long, to the rest of the world as a way of saying that things are great, or that there's no problem.

Another theory goes that the expression originated during the American War of Independence. When the numbers of dead and wounded were recorded in the regiments' files, if there were no victims, '0 Killed' was abbreviated to OK. The expression would rapidly have come to mean that all was going well.

WHO WAS 'RUSSIAN BILL'?

Russian Bill appeared in Tombstone one fine day in 1880. He was a lanky man with elegant clothes and beautiful manners, but he carried a glistening Colt on his hip. It was clear from the outset that he was an outlaw – he certainly acted the part well, and spoke the way outlaws would speak. He associated with the worst crooks in the city, particularly Curly Bill, who was a notorious bandit. He did everything he could to be accepted onto the scene, even caring for wounded gang members and giving them refuge and cover. But eventually Curly Bill grew tired of his act and advised him to stop playing games because he'd never make it as an outlaw. Disappointed, Russian Bill left for New Mexico and joined a gang led by Zeke Murillo, another bandit of some repute. But he had no credibility there either and they only made fun of him.

Deeply upset, he made up his mind to go it alone, and started off by stealing a horse, but, as he stayed around in the area, the horse was quickly recognized and the sheriff came and arrested him. So Russian Bill spent his first night as a horse thief in the prison at Shakespeare, in the company of Sandy King, a well-known killer. They were tried in the dining room of the city's grand hotel and were sentenced to be hanged. The execution was wonderfully diverting. Russian Bill was in a merry mood and thanked the hangman and the crowd with refined politeness. How could they guess that he was finally achieving his lifelong dream – of being recognized as a real outlaw? Some time later, it emerged that he was one William Tattenbaum, a member of one of the greatest families of Russian aristocrats.

USEFUL ADDRESSES AND INFORMATION

Visitors' Center: on the corner of Allen and 4th Streets. ☎ 457-3929. Open daily, 9am–5pm.

✉ **Post office**: on Allen Street.

■ **Bank of America**: Allen Street, between 5th and 6th Streets. Open Monday–Saturday 9am–2pm.

– **Gunfights in the street**: Monday–Saturday 2pm.

WHERE TO STAY

There are not many motels or hotels here. Nearly all of them are along Route 80, which along this stretch is called Fremont Street. If it's charm you want, keep going until you reach Bisbee.

CAMPGROUND

Tombstone KOA Campground: as you enter the city, on the right. ☎ 562-2486. Large and comfortable. Open all year. Rents out small timber bungalows and camping spaces. They even have picnic tables.

☆☆ MODERATE

Trail Rider's Inn: 13 N 7th Street, at right angles to Fremont Street. ☎ 457-3573. A nice-looking family motel, with its two carts on a patch of lawn out front. Accommodation is in little brick-built houses packed in alongside each other, and only a whisker off the main road. But it's the most pleasant motel in the area by far.

Tombstone Motel: 502 E Fremont Street. ☎ 457-3478. A straightforward enough motel. Every room is different, so the quality can be fairly variable. Look at a few rooms before taking one.

Lorian Motel: on Fremont Street, between 4th and 5th Streets. ☎ 457-2272. A rather unremarkable motel with reasonable prices.

Best Western: as you come into the city, on the right. ☎ 457-2223. By far the most expensive of the city's hotels, yet it isn't really the nicest, nor the best located, nor the most comfortable.

WHERE TO EAT

Blake's Char-Broiled Burgers: 511 Allen Street. ☎ 457-3646. Open daily, 11am–4pm. Tiny room, where little old ladies feed you generous, genuine burgers, accompanied by fries. It's a fast-food restaurant with a family atmosphere.

Big Nose Kate's Saloon: 417 E Allen Street. ☎ 457-3107. The town's most 'Wild West' place, where they have plenty of Country music concerts. It's full of cowboys (some real, some pseudo), and the atmosphere really takes you back 100 years. The food here consists of pizzas, sandwiches and burgers, but people seem to come mainly for the ambiance.

Nellie Cashman: on the corner of 5th Street and Toughnut. ☎ 457-2212. Serving daily, 7am–9pm. This place was opened back in the good old days of the mid-19th century by Nellie, a woman full of character who provided a welcome, and housing, for miners. It's an excellent place – a sort of family guest house that has held onto its old-time atmosphere. They serve tremendous hamburgers, not at all greasy. Try the ones with *jalapeños* (mild Mexican peppers). It's the sort of place where you find fabric tablecloths and serviettes; the service is charming and the prices won't scare you. If you're by yourself, you can pass some time playing Solitaire. This is a popular game in many places and they'll give you a set to play with.

Nora's Olde-Fashioned Ice-Cream Parlor: 104 4th Street, almost on the corner of Allen Street. Just what it says it is.

WHAT TO SEE AND DO

The city has retained its original downtown area, with some streets intersecting at right angles, so that the places of interest are close to each other. Nevertheless, you'll need at least two to three hours to do a tour, and the cemetery's a little way outside the city. If you buy all the visitor coupons at the Historama at the same time, you get a small discount.

★ **Tombstone Historama and site of OK Corral**: Allen Street (and 3rd Street). The Historama is a show lasting 30 minutes, presenting the history of the region with the aid of a revolving model. There's a performance every hour 9am–4pm. Nearby, you can visit the site of the gunfight at the OK Corral. They put on a fairly sketchy re-enactment of the gunfight between Wyatt Earp, Doc Holliday and the Clanton and McLaury brothers. The relics of the stable, with a buggy and carriages are on view, along with the hearse that they used to move the Clanton and McLaury bodies.

In one of the shacks there's a beautiful exhibition of photos by Fly, who was an accomplished photographer of the Old West at the end of the 19th century. It movingly brings to life the Native Americans and the surrender of chief Geronimo, who gave himself up after being promised that American justice would be lenient. In fact, he was taken to Florida, where he spent the remaining 23 years of his life in prison, where he eventually died worn down by grief and alcohol. General Crook, who carried out the negotiations, has left his name to history as a result of his failure to keep his word – the word 'crook' meaning a swindler from that time onwards. There are some alarming photographs, including one of a hanged man and one of a Native American woman whose nose was cut off as a punishment for adultery.

– '**Wild Bunch Show**' on the first and third Sunday of every month. '**Vigilante Show**' on the second, fourth and sometimes fifth Sunday in the streets of the city. Get details from the tourist office.

★ **Crystal Palace**: at the corner of Allen and 5th Streets. This establishment has had virtually the same appearance since 1880, when it was the most popular of the city's 100 or so saloons. It stayed open for business until 1963, when it was bought and restored by the Commission for Historic Monuments. Thanks to photographs, the reconstruction of the famous mahogany bar was carried out with great accuracy. The bar had many famous customers, including Virgil Earp, Judge Wells Spicer, who conducted the inquiry into the gunfight at the OK Corral, Dr Harry Matthews, who examined the bodies, Dr George Goodfellow, a famous retired Army surgeon, as well as a good many desperadoes. Goodfellow enjoyed a notoriety that's hard to believe. He treated all gunshot wounds within a radius of 60 miles (100km), lost $20 in a bet with Geronimo, and was a friend of Porfirio Diaz, the Mexican president. Finally, he negotiated the Spanish surrender after the war over Cuba in 1898. This last solemn occasion has gone down in history because of the number of bottles of gin consumed during the talks.

★ **Bird Cage Theater**: 6th and Allen Streets. Admission charge. Open daily, 8am–6pm all year round. This might even be the most moving part of the visit. It's a honky-tonk theatre where professional cardsharps, hard-up miners and others down on their luck crowded in to watch lewd shows and play poker. Somehow, it's in a complete state of preservation. From 1881 to 1889 it never closed, not even for a minute, and was the scene of 16 gunfights. The walls still bear the scars of the 140 bullets. The stage is in ruins, the original wallpaper is still on the walls, and in among all the dust, all the city's memorabilia are on show – gaming tables, old posters, clothes of the period, weapons, various domestic objects, the instruments belonging to 'Doc' Holliday the dental 'surgeon', etc. There's even a rather curious 'merman' (kind of half man, half fish) in a small showcase on the right-hand wall (nothing like the sirens that we learned about at school!). It was found in the China Sea and somehow ended up in an Arizona brothel.

You can see the box used by 'Russian Bill', who came here regularly to down a few drinks and make use of 'the other facilities'. The boxes in the first balcony communicated with the stage, where a bevy of beauties from all parts would be seated in cages and singing the song: 'I'm Only a Bird in a Gilded Cage'. These boxes enabled potential clients to observe the girls from below. When a man made his choice of a girl, she would pull the curtain and her 'beau' would ascend. Each box contained a makeshift bed. As a rough estimate, the price of such a visit varied between $10 and $30 depending on what was on the menu.

★ **Rose Tree Inn Museum**: 4th and Toughnut Streets. ☎ 457-3326. This is a house full of history that has been turned into a charming little museum. Very fine original period furniture in a good interior, but the main feature is the world's largest rosebush (recorded in the Guinness Book of Records). This dates back to when a young Scottish wife living here was sent some rose shoots from home. She planted one of them on the terrace, and it flourished. At the back of the garden, a staircase allows you to view this huge specimen from above.

★ **Boot Hill Graveyard**: at the northern entrance to the city, on the left when you arrive. Open all day every day. Admission free. A few dozen modest graves are all that remain of the old Tombstone, when very few people lived to a ripe old age. Some of the gravestones footnote the cause of death: the one for George Johnson, hanged in error, is one that nobody misses.

★ **Tombstone Epitaph**: 5th Street. Open daily, 9am–5pm. You can visit the offices of this famous newspaper, even though there's almost nothing to see. Western fans can even take out a subscription: it's now a monthly publication. You can buy a special edition on the OK Corral gunfight, which contains the minutes of the inquiry and the trial.

★ **The Court House**: Toughnut and 3rd Streets. ☎ 457-3311. Open daily, 8am–5pm. Built in 1882. One of the few stone buildings of the era, and it still has the gallows standing in the courtyard. Inside, there's a well-run little museum displaying many old objects and paraphernalia that once belonged to Ed Schieffelin, the silver prospector who made Tombstone what it was. There are further collections upstairs, as well as a courtroom.

At the other end of the same street is the Fire House.

★ **The Town Hall**: on Fremont, between 3rd and 4th Streets. Built in the same period as the Court House and still in use. Pretty facade.

– And why not go on a little **stagecoach trip**? Two companies offer their services: the Tombstone Stage Coach Line, daily, 9am–5pm ☎ 457-

3191; or Tombstone Historical Tours ☎ 457-3018. You'll see their stagecoaches running regularly through the centre.

BISBEE

AREA CODE: 520

About 25 miles (40km) south of Tombstone. If you're fascinated by the Old West, this little old mining town is really worth going to see. What Tombstone was for cowboys, Bisbee was for miners. And while you go to visit Tombstone, it's at Bisbee that you'll stay. Situated almost on the Mexican border, Bisbee is on the slopes of a beautiful, curiously verdant valley. It has a pleasant, almost European feel, and most of the buildings date from the late 19th century. An enormous crag, Castle Rock, overhangs the city. The panoramic view as you arrive from Tombstone is rather good – actually, the road itself is quite spectacular. And, unlike most American cities, there are practically no motels here but mostly bed and breakfast places, which add to the charm of the place. You can go around Bisbee on foot, or on horseback if you're feeling like a cowboy.

A BRIEF HISTORY

For a long time, this was a very wild area. No one dared to set foot in this valley, at an altitude of 5,250 feet (1,600m), and overlooked by the Mule Mountains, as it was occupied by ferocious Apaches who defended their territory very effectively.

Nevertheless, in 1877, an Army patrol in pursuit of rebellious Native Americans discovered the valley and, more importantly, found a spring with a high lead content. This was an indication of the presence of rich seams of precious metal, perhaps of silver, though in fact the area turned out to be mostly rich in copper. Two years later, 53 claims had already been recorded.

Bisbee was born and its population rapidly grew to 25,000 (there are now 8,000 inhabitants). The mines flourished, then went into crisis, but it wasn't until 1975 that the last mine closed, which explains why this town is in no way a ghost town. In view of the prices of certain metals, it has even been rumoured that certain mines may reopen. Whatever happens, the inhabitants are determinedly struggling to keep their city alive.

USEFUL ADDRESSES

Visitors' Center: 7 Main Road. ☎ 432-5421. Open 9am–5pm, Saturday and Sunday 10am–4pm. Good information on the city. The tourist office keeps a list, with photographs and prices, of all the Bed & Breakfast places in the city.

✉ **Post office**: at the bottom of Main Street.

■ **Bank of America**: 1 Main Street.

■ **Cash dispenser**: at the city's main car park, on the left just as you arrive in the centre.

WHERE TO STAY

☆ BUDGET

YWCA: Box 968, Bisbee 85603. ☎ 432-3542. Right in the centre of Old Bisbee. The welcome is good, but the place is rather decayed. Definitely one for the desperately broke. Take your sleeping bag . . . and some disinfectant.

☆☆ MODERATE

The Inn at Castle Rock: 112 Tombstone Canyon Road. ☎ 432-4449. Below the road from Tombstone, right opposite Castle Rock. A huge Victorian residence with long balconies, which used to be a miners' lodging house. The proprietor is an artist and his canvases brighten up the whole house. The ground floor has one curious feature – in the middle of the restaurant is what looks like a well. It's 10ft (3m) wide and 66ft (20m) deep and in fact used to be an entrance to one of the silver mines. After being flooded, it served the city as a well for 15 years. The rooms are not very large and have no air-conditioning, but each is in a different style, prettily furnished and with a bathroom. A pleasant rest and reading room has a panoramic view of the city. They serve a large and excellent breakfast that you can eat outside if you wish. Everything is homemade and the quality is great. A romantic place, and worth a small additional expenditure: you'll pay $80 for two, with an all-you-can-eat breakfast included.

Main Street Inn: 26 Main Street. ☎ 432-5237. Right in the centre, a former miners' hotel that has been turned into a B&B. Eight rooms, some very large, but some with no window. Some could easily accommodate families of four or six. The decor is simple and in good taste and there's a fairly wide range of prices.

The Bisbee Inn: 45 OK Street. ☎ 432-5131. There are about 20 rooms in this big brick-built hotel building, all tastefully done up. This one is cosy and well kept.

– There are plenty of other places some distance from the centre. The tourist office has a list. Here are two that are worth trying:

The Curry Home: 608 Powell. ☎ 432-4815. Lots of charm.

The Mile High Court: 901 Tombstone. ☎ 432-4636.

☆☆☆ EXPENSIVE

Copper Queen Hotel: 11 Howell Street. ☎ 432-2216. Fax: 432-4298. Built in 1902 by the Phelps Dodge Mining Company at a time when mining fever was at its height. Initially the headquarters of the company, the building then became a hotel for mining executives. Today, the place has been very well restored, and still has much of its old flavour. There are over 40 beautiful rooms, many of them furnished in the style of the era. Teddy Roosevelt slept here (in room 406) as did John Wayne, who used to have a ranch in the area and would call into town from time to time. He'd hardly be able to get two or three drinks at the bar before a crowd of fans would rush in to see the great man and beg for his autograph. Some might have expected John to have got angry, thrown a few punches or even whipped out his Colt to cool down the worst troublemakers . . . but he always reacted with good humour. Rooms here are expensive, but not horrendously so, so if you arrive in late afternoon and the hotel isn't full, you may even be offered a reduction. The Copper Queen Saloon and Dining Room are charming.

WHERE TO EAT

☆ BUDGET

✕ **Pastabilies**: 21 Main Street. ☎ 432-3155. Open daily (except Monday) until 9pm (closes earlier on Sunday). Enormous salads and good, inexpensive pasta dishes. Mainly a place for lunch. Very nice service. There's a cheap special every day. And every Tuesday, if you order the most expensive pasta dish, you get a second one free of charge.

✕ **Cornucopia**: 14 Main Street. ☎ 432-3364. Only open at the start of the week and at weekends 10am–5pm. Cute little tea salon with garden tables. Homemade pies, vegetarian sandwiches and fresh fruit juices.

✕ **Miner's Diner**: 1 Brewery Gulch. Mainly a place for breakfast. Pancakes and omelettes.

☆☆☆ EXPENSIVE

✕ **Inn at Castle Rock**: *see* 'Where to Stay'. This hotel restaurant is the town's new smart place to eat. Dine indoors or on the attractive terrace: inventive cuisine that blends European influences with American daring. The end result is original, but usually successful.

WHERE TO HAVE A DRINK

🍸 **Stock Exchange Bar** (The Brewery): 15 Brewery Gulch. ☎ 432-9924. As its name indicates, this used to be the Stock Exchange for the local mining industry. The enormous blackboard that covers all of the back wall is a reminder of its past life. There's a good, lively scene on Friday and Saturday evening, with dancing to local bands. Billiards, too.

ARIZONA

WHAT TO SEE

★ **Copper Queen Tour**: departs from the Queen Mine Building. ☎ 432-2071. Tours lasting a bit over an hour, start at 9am and 10.30am, noon, 2pm and 3.30pm every day. They'll fit you out with a yellow oilskin and a safety helmet, but be sure to wear warm clothes as the temperature drops to 50°F (10°C). There are about 143 miles (230km) of galleries criss-crossing this mine, which closed in 1943. The mine was sunk after two soldiers discovered a vein of silver in 1877, although in fact it ended up producing copper. The guide takes you along a gallery in a small train. They are often former miners, so they know the ropes pretty well. In the 19th century, mules were used to pull the wagons; these creatures spent an average of 18 years underground and were never taken back to the surface, for fear that they might go blind or, quite simply, refuse to go back down. The first automatic machine put into operation was called the 'widowmaker' because of the large amount of dust it gave off and the ensuing medical problems.

★ **Bus tour of the city**: departures from the Queen Mine Building are at 10.30am, noon, 2pm and 3.30pm. The trip takes about 75 minutes and also goes via the **Lavender Open Pit Mine**, one of the biggest open-cast copper mines, which closed in 1975.

★ **The Mining Museum**: in the centre. ☎ 432-7071. Open daily, 10am–4pm. The museum is housed in a residence dating back to 1897, which was once the mining company headquarters and Masonic Lodge Hall. It gives an interesting dip into the history of the mines at Bisbee, with a collection of black-and-white photographs, scientific instruments and information about everyday life. It's worth remembering that, in its heyday, Bisbee was larger and more prosperous than San Francisco. There's an interesting section that describes the Army's 1917 operation to deport striking miners to a camp in the middle of the New Mexico desert.

★ **Mulheim House**: 207 B Young Blood Hill. Right at the top of the town. Opening times are irregular, so check at the tourist information office. This is a typical house of the region.

★ **Take a stroll on foot**: on the slopes of the city, along Copper Queen Plaza, Main Street, Subway, Howell, Opera, Brewery, OK Street and Naco Road, to view the picturesque residences and public buildings, including the old prison, the opera house, the post office, the Covenant Presbyterian Church and many more. The tourist office has brought out a town map (*Bisbee, a Walking Tour*) listing all the landmarks.

★ **If you like ghost towns and mining camps** and have some time available, there's plenty in the region for an in-depth visit. The Arizona Office of Tourism has a brochure listing the main points of interest, but be aware that these places are often much less spectacular than Tombstone or Bisbee. You'll need to be strongly motivated.

FLAGSTAFF

AREA CODE: 520

Located 140 miles (225km) from Phoenix, 130 miles (210km) from Lake Powell and 80 miles (130km) from the Grand Canyon, this city is at quite a high altitude, and surrounded by wooded mountains. The climate is mild, and very pleasant after the furnace of the desert, but it's cool in the evening.

Although the city is spread out over some distance, Flag (as it's familiarly known to hardened travellers) has a nice centre, with elegant early 20th-century buildings and an atmosphere that's half-cowboy, half-European. There are music bars, small popular restaurants, pretty shops, and even a few youth hostels in the centre. In short, an excellent port-of-call for a few days, and also an ideal point of departure for the Grand Canyon and the whole surrounding area.

Curiously, everything is much less expensive here and there's no lack of motels. Long goods trains trundle through and give off a deep and deafening howl. Not a place for insomniacs!

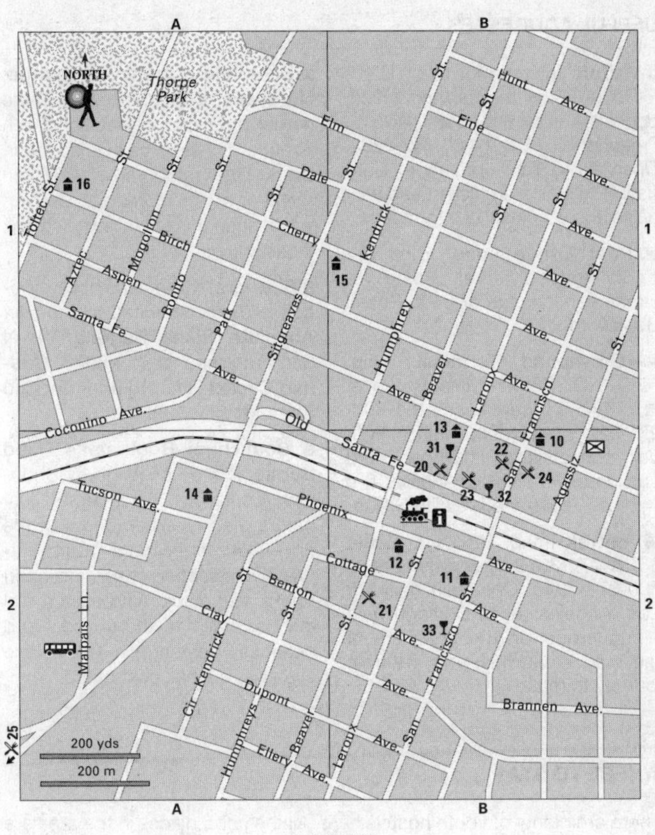

FLAGSTAFF

Useful Addresses

- Visitors' Information Center
- Post office
- Greyhound Bus Terminal
- Amtrak station

Where to Stay

10 Monte Vista Hotel
11 Grand Canyon International Hostel
12 Dubeau International Hostel
13 Youth Hostel
14 Family Inn
15 Dierker House Bed & Breakfast
16 Birch Tree Inn

Where to Eat

20 Alpine Pizza
21 Macy's European Coffee House
22 Kathy's Cafe
23 Hong Kong Cafe
24 Cafe Express
25 Furrs Cafeteria

Where to Have a Drink

31 Charly's
32 The Monsoon's
33 The Mad Italian

USEFUL ADDRESSES

Visitors' Information (map, B2): 1 E Route 66, in the railway station, opposite Leroux Street. ☎ 774-9541. Freephone: ☎ 1-800-842-7293. Open daily, 7am–6pm (5pm Sunday). The staff are efficient and very polite; there's plenty of information.

Post Office (map, B2): 104 North Agassiz Street. Poste restante services are at 2400 Postal Boulevard.

Greyhound Terminal (map, A2): 399 South Malpais Lane. ☎ 774-4573. Freephone: ☎ 1-800-231-2222. South of the station. Four daily connections with Phoenix and Tucson, seven with Los Angeles, five with Las Vegas and five with Gallup.

Amtrak (map, B2): 1 E Route 66. ☎ 774-8679. Freephone: ☎ 1-800-872-7245. One train daily for Los Angeles and Chicago (via Albuquerque). In the great era of the Wild West, this was *the* train journey to make.

■ **Bank and currency exchange**: **Northwest Bank** (map, B1): at the corner of Leroux Street and Birch Avenue, it has a cash dispenser. **Bank One** (map, B1), on Birch Avenue, at the corner of Beaver, will change currency, and also has a cash dispenser.

■ **Bike hire**: this means of locomotion is perfectly suited to the city. **Absolute Bikes Rentals**, 18 N San Francisco. ☎ 779-5969. **Cosmic Cycles**, 113 N San Francisco Street. ☎ 779-1092.

■ **Bookshop**: **Bookman's Used Books**, in the Longs Drugs Shopping Center on Milton Road, just before the university (south of the city). Open daily, 9am–10pm. Impressive selection of second-hand books and discs. Also sells travel guides, maps of the country and beautiful postcards. The place even has a small post office.

WHERE TO STAY

There are plenty of youth hostels here. All the good places in the area are listed in order of preference.

REALLY BUDGET

Grand Canyon International Hostel (map, B2, **11**): 19 San Francisco Street. ☎ 779-9421. E-mail: info@grancanyonhostel.com. Website: www.grandcanyonhostel.com. Just beside the Dubeau, but much cleaner and quieter. Very pleasant. Rooms are small, but very well kept, and they cost $25–$35. Dormitories for four persons. You can do your own cooking. Free coffee and fruit in the morning. If you phone, they'll even come and pick you up at the bus terminal. They also organize day trips to the Grand Canyon and Sedona.

Youth Hostel (map, B1–2, **13**): on the first floor of the Weatherford Hotel at the corner of Leroux Street and Aspen Avenue (Downtown), opposite the train station. ☎ 774-2731. Reception open 7–10am and 5–10pm. In a late 19th-century building. They offer dormitories for four to eight persons if you're pretty broke, and singles for those with a bit of money. Same prices as the private youth hostel, but the rules are stricter. You can do your own cooking here. Curfew at 1am.

☆ BUDGET

Dubeau International Hostel (map, B2, **12**): 19 W Phoenix, Avenue Downtown, beside the station. ☎ 774-6731. Freephone: ☎ 1-800-398-7112. Fax: 774-4060. E-mail: dubeau@informagic.com. In what was once a brick-built motel, this is a meeting place for American and foreign backpackers. Not at all expensive (allow about $13 for a dormitory place and $26 for a room). Kitchen, launderette and various facilities. A little jumbled (well, actually it's a real shambles), but a truly pleasant ambiance. Breakfast is free. They also organize trips to the Grand Canyon.

Family Inn (map, A2, **14**): 121 South Milton Road, A2 86001. At exit 195B on Interstate 40, south of Downtown (0.5 mile/1km from the centre). ☎ 774-8820. This unpretentious motel is open round the clock. Everything in blue and white, the rooms are well kept and it's not too far from the centre. Air-conditioning, big beds and cable TV. Very good prices for four.

Monte Vista Hotel (map, B2, **10**): 100 N San Francisco Street. Freephone: ☎ 1-800-543-3068 or 779-6971. Fax: 779-2904. In the old centre of Flagstaff, this hotel has welcomed the likes of John Wayne and Clark Gable. Some scenes in *Casablanca* were even filmed here. The rooms have kept their 1927 decor, with period mirrors and furniture that makes a nice change from motels, although the place has become a bit run down, the welcome is only average and it's not very cheap (allow about $60). Groups play in the bar on the ground floor every evening.

☆☆ MODERATE

The great majority of motels charging reasonable prices are in the east of the city, strung out for about 3 miles (5km) along the legendary Route 66: **Red Roof**, **Relax Inn** and others. Of average quality and often at very similar prices. The prices change almost daily, depending on the level of demand.

☆☆☆ EXPENSIVE

Dierker House Bed & Breakfast (map, B1, **15**): 423 W Cherry Avenue ☎ 774-3249. Three blocks north of Route 66, in a quiet, wooded residential district, and yet very close to Downtown. A very pretty private house, comfortable, and kept by a charming lady. It's a no-smoking establishment. It's almost twice as expensive as a motel but, if you can afford it, it's worth the money. There are only three rooms, with shared sanitary facilities. A large breakfast is served at 8am precisely. Call ahead, as it's often full.

Birch Tree Inn (map, A1, **16**): 824 W Birch Ave, on the corner of Toltec Street. ☎ 774-1042. Freephone: ☎ 1-800-645-5805. A superb B&B in a nice big house in a peaceful residential district. Five rooms, two of which share a bathroom and one of which is huge. Cosy and comfortable, with a carpet so thick your feet seem to disappear into it. Expensive (more so than the previous entry), but it's an ideal place for 'cocooning' in peace. Large lounge and a veranda for taking some air, a drink, or both. Oh yes, there's also a jacuzzi.

CAMPGROUNDS

☗ **Woody Mountain Campground**: 2727 W Route 66, exit 191 from Interstate 40. ☎ 774-7727. 2 miles (3.5km) west of Flagstaff. Superb, large campground, in the middle of a big pine forest. Quality equipment. Small and well laid out. Swimming pool. Nice, but noisy at night because of the passing trains.

☗ **Fort Tuthill Campground**: 3 miles (5km) south of Flagstaff on US 89A, which runs parallel to Route 17 towards Sedona. ☎ 774-3150. Open May–October. Isolated in a small park, in the middle of a pine forest. The equipment is simplified to the extreme and you pay extra for the showers.

☗ **Flagstaff KOA**: 5803 N Highway 89. About 5 miles (3km) from the centre, to the northeast of the city. ☎ 526-9926. Surrounded by trees. Lots of people here, rather on top of each other. It's comfortable but a bit expensive.

AT SEDONA

☗ **Sedona RV Resort**: 6701 W Highway 89A. ☎ 1-800-547-8727 or (520) 282-6640. At the exit from the city, just 3 miles (1.5km) west of the centre. This is a well-equipped campground, spacious and clean and no more expensive than elsewhere. Spaces for tents and mobile homes. They also hire out bungalows. Extra features: swimming pool, playground, small restaurant, grocery store.

WHERE TO EAT

☆–☆☆ BUDGET TO MODERATE

✕ **Alpine Pizza** (map, B2, **20**): 7 N Leroux Street, near the station and the official youth hostel. ☎ 779-4109. Open 11am–11pm (midnight Friday and Saturday). An interesting and relaxing place. The pizzas are succulent and gigantic. If you're only peckish, the nine-inch one will be plenty big enough. Alternatively, you can buy slices. They serve wine and beer. Pocket-sized terrace.

✕ **Macy's European Coffee House** (map, B2, **21**): 14 S Beaver Street. ☎ 774-2243. This place injects a touch of California into your herbal tea. Superb vegetarian dishes and lovely fresh cakes. A beautiful place that distinguishes itself by friendliness and quality.

✕ **Kathy's Cafe** (map, B2, **22**): 7 N San Francisco Street. ☎ 774-1951. Open daily, 6.30am–3pm. The decor is quite good but the benches aren't so comfortable. Try the omelettes or the Navajo taco. Breakfast with homemade rolls.

✕ **Hong Kong Cafe** (map, B2, **23**): 6 E Route 66. Opposite the station. Open 8am–9pm. A large 1950s-style room where they serve a large American breakfast. At lunch and dinner, it's cheap but quite unremarkable Chinese cuisine.

✕ **Cafe Express** (map, B2, **24**): 16 N San Francisco Street. ☎ 774-0541. Open daily, 7am–10pm (11pm weekends). A peaceful vegetarian place with an ambiance somewhere between an art gallery and a literary cafe. Good for a snack.

✕ **Furrs Cafeteria** (map, off A2, **25**): 1200 S Milton Road, a mile (2km) before the junction with Interstate 40 so it's away from the centre. Lunchtime and evening, there's an all-you-can-eat buffet for a low price. Food not particularly great, though. The fluorescent desserts must be made on Mars!

☆☆☆ EXPENSIVE

✕ **Black Barts**: 2760 East Butler Avenue ☎ 779-3142. Open 5–9pm (10pm weekends). Only any use if you have a car, because it's a long way from the city centre. Gigantic steak-house in a sort of reconstructed saloon. The 'retro-Western' decor is quite successful. Relaxed, friendly ambiance, but very touristy all the same. The special feature of the place, believe it or not, is that the waiters and waitresses, all of whom are students at the University of Flagstaff, take it in turns to accompany your meal with songs and music! And they regularly get together into an ensemble to perform a short extract from a musical comedy. Some of them are very talented. People must come mainly for the show because the cuisine (mainly grilled meats, including the chef's BBQ chicken), although excellent, isn't cheap.

✕ **Horsemen Lodge**: at the exit from the city on Highway 89 N towards Wupatki, about 8 miles (13km) from the centre on the left-hand side. ☎ 526-2655. Open evenings only. Closed Sunday. In a sort of log cabin at the edge of the forest, you can get the best steaks in town, in a Western atmosphere.

WHERE TO HAVE A DRINK

IN THE CENTRE

🍸 **Charly's** (map, B2, **31**): 23 N Leroux Street, just next to the youth hostel. One of the best spots in the city to get carried away by the sound of jazz or blues.

🍸 **Monte Vista Hotel Bar**: 100 N San Francisco Street. ☎ 779-6971. Freephone: ☎ 1-800-543-3068. Fax: 779-2904. One of the top musical spots in Flag. All kinds of music, but it's all good stuff.

🍸 **The Monsoon's** (map, B2, **32**): 22 E Route 66, level with San Francisco Street. ☎ 774-7929. Wooden floor, stone walls, billiard tables and old-style fans to keep the temperature down. Hot ambiance some evenings

🍸 **The Mad Italian** (map, B2, **33**): 101 S San Francisco Street. ☎ 779-1820. Open daily, 11.30am–1am. Big student bistro with a U-shaped counter that lets you see everybody. They serve sandwiches and salads. Happy hour 4–7pm. Groups on Thursday. Giant TV screen and billiard tables. Not as good as the others listed here.

ARIZONA

NEARBY

🍸 **The Museum Club (The Zoo)**: 3404 E Route 66. ☎ 526-9434. Open Tuesday–Sunday 9pm–1am. Just 3 miles (5km) from the centre, on the left-hand side of Route 66. Look for the big red neon guitar. Since 1936, this place has been providing the best Country music in the whole area. Its other name (The Zoo) comes from its having been the home of a taxidermist who evidently left his place in its present state, judging by the number of trophies on the walls. These patient beasts have been listening to Country music for over 60 years! Admission is free on Tuesday or Sunday; towards the weekend, the ambiance is at its hottest. All the cowboys in Flag are there!

WHAT TO SEE

★ **Lowell Observatory**: on a hill about 3 miles (5km) west of the centre. ☎ 774-3358. Go directly west on Santa Fe and climb to the top of the hill. Several trips take place daily between 9am and 5pm. Call for exact times.

In 1896, one Mr Lowell had constructed an enormous, elegant telescope so that he could observe what he believed to be a network of canals on Mars, although this turned out to be an optical illusion. A second telescope was designed in 1928 to observe the other planets. The two telescopes are still in use today for taking photographs and carrying out research tasks. The tour includes a slide-show, a visit to the room containing the big telescope, the historic library containing superb ancient measuring instruments, as well as the second telescope. The most interesting time to visit is on a summer evening when you can actually look through the telescope. Viewing sessions are usually organized at 8pm, 8.45pm and 9.30pm Monday–Saturday (check the times, which will vary with the season). What happens during these sessions is, of course, directly related to the prevailing weather conditions, and depending on the configuration of the celestial vault at the time, you're likely to observe a mass of stars, the planets Jupiter, Saturn and Mars, or simply the Moon.

★ **Museum of Northern Arizona**: 3 miles (5km) north on US 180 (the road to the Grand Canyon). ☎ 774-5213. Open 9am–5pm. Half-price for students. A museum plan is given out as you enter. This museum, tucked away in the pine forest, has a superb collection of pottery, small and large. In fact, the local potters systematically produced miniatures, although the reason for this is not known, and at least 50 examples are on display. The museum has tried to set out the history of the Native Americans in the region over the last 15,000 years. The different tribes had their own characteristic patterns and there are many examples that show this. One display focuses on the importance of corn in Native American cultures, and there are photographs of Hopi headgear, a collection of Zuni animal fetishes, Katsina dolls, etc. The collection of Hopi, Navajo and Zuni jewellery is also very interesting, and there's a gallery of modern art and exhibitions of Native American paintings. There's also a reasonable museum shop that sells books, jewellery, and CDs of Native American music.

★ **Pioneer Museum**: a bit before you get to the Museum of Northern Arizona, on the right side of the road. ☎ 774-6272. Open 9am–5pm. Closed Sunday. An amusing little museum about the pioneering life, with photographs, tools and everyday objects of the time. Two exhibits of special interest are an impressive iron lung and a doctor's surgery.

★ **Gene's Shoe Hospital**: 111 North Leroux (which is the same street as Alpine Pizza). A Western shop (lassoes, belts, flags, etc.) that's not too expensive. And, as a bonus, there's a good chance you'll see some 'real' Native Americans come here to shop.

EVENTS

– **Native American Festival**: at the Museum throughout the summer, in theory, you can experience Navajo, Zuni and Hopi songs and dances. Call for information about dates.

– **Annual rodeo**: one weekend in mid-June. Great ambiance. A Western small-town festival where everyone knows everyone else.

– **Festival of the Arts**: throughout July, on campus. Classical concerts.

– **Rodeos at Prescott**: the weekend nearest to 4 July.

WHAT TO SEE IN THE AREA

★ **Sedona**: 26 miles (40km) south of Flagstaff via US 89A. This is a superb one-day excursion, especially if you manage to slip in a picnic stop on the bank of the river. The road to it runs through a dense forest before dropping down into a canyon flanked with reddish-orange rocks, and following the meanderings of Oak Creek. The Coconino National Forest, as it's called, contains several small, basic, boy-scout style campgrounds (Flatpine, Bootlegger and others) deep in the pine forest. You can even buy wood to build your fire. These campgrounds are well signposted at the side of the road. A little further along the same road, you can pull in at Slide Rock State Park; this charges for admission and is only open during the day. There are some natural pools here where you can swim, and the environment is fantastic. After a good snack, a little splash and a brief siesta, you move on to Sedona.

This city, where the artist Max Ernst lived for some years, has become a New-Age Mecca. Hyper-trendy and hippyish, it attracts very rich Californians. The whole region around Sedona is quite simply superb. It's not surprising that it should have become a focal point for a commercial sector dealing in mystic products.

But, although the region is rather special, Sedona itself is not of great interest. It has expanded at high speed and seems rather touristy. The New Age seems to have become a market niche for all manner of salespeople, and there are shops that stock junk at sky-high prices all along the main street. In little more than a decade, a number of centres for spirituality, relaxation, and reflection have opened up here. The hotels are mostly very luxurious and very expensive.

The region itself – and here we're speaking of the natural environment rather than the city – has for thousands of years been regarded by the Native Americans as an important centre for the convergence of the Earth's energies: they came here long before it became fashionable, and are still coming. But of course the Native American rapport with nature has always been genuine. These zones of confluence, of magnetism, are known as vortices, and there are several of them within a radius of a few miles.

★ **Bell Rock**: located a few miles south of the city, this is the best known vortex point in the region. Ask at the tourist office exactly how to get there, as the route isn't at all complicated but it's quite hard to describe! The rock is a beautiful outcrop on top of which you can stretch out and simply relax. With a little bit of faith and if prepared to take it seriously (jokers out for a giggle needn't bother), some people have managed to experience some kind of detachment from the body, like distancing themselves from the mental and the physical process. Some emerge from the experience quite shaken, while others merely pretend. Clearly, it's something extremely intimate, and a certain amount of openness of spirit is required. In 1987, a rogue started charging people $75 to sit on Bell Rock. According to him, as soon as you sat down there, you would go straight up to the Andromeda galaxy. People actually paid. Hmmm. Access is now free, however. Even if it doesn't work for you, the site is really very beautiful, giving you a view of the sweep of red rock formations that frame the city.

★ On your way to Bell Rock, be sure to see **The Chapel of Holy Cross**, just 2 miles (3km) south of the city. This curious church, set into the rock, was built in 1953 from a design by Frank Lloyd Wright. You really must have a look at this astonishing structure – it's totally integrated into the natural surroundings in a remarkable way, yet you can still see that it's a striking piece of modern architecture. The end of the nave is a wall of glass, constructed so that the altarpiece is the natural rock.

★ **Tlaquepaque Shopping Center**: in the city centre, Tlaquepaque is a superb Mexican village unlike any you'll ever find if you go to Mexico: it's so clean and pretty, with flower-filled terraces and sparkling fountains. The shops and restaurants are very expensive – but you haven't gone there to spend money, so take in the atmosphere. There are lots of art galleries here, evidence of the fact that more than 300 painters live round about.

★ **Wupatki National Monument and Sunset Crater**: to get from Flagstaff to the Grand Canyon or to Navajoland, you can take a loop via Wupatki National Monument instead of going on US 89. It's a really beautiful road, and the detour only takes an hour. It crosses the park, meets Wupatki Monument, then rejoins US 89. There's an admission charge. Coming from Flagstaff, the first thing you see is Sunset Crater, which last erupted several centuries ago. In itself, it's not particularly exciting. Next, you come to the Wupatki site, which is a collection of rather modest ruins scattered about. These ruins were once occupied by the Anasazi, the ancestors of the present-day Native Americans. Although the surrounding area is tempting, don't venture too far off the track – there are rattlesnakes about.

★ **Meteor Crater**: this is 35 miles (56km) east of Flagstaff, on the US 180. Take exit 233. The site is 5 miles (8km) from the main road. ☎ 526-5259. Open 6am–6pm in summer. High admission charge. This is the largest meteor crater in the world, which is, of course, quite spectacular, at 4,150ft (1,265m) in diameter and 570ft (175m) deep. Must have been some meteor! Right at the rim of the crater there's a museum with some impressive photos of lunar craters and information about the Apollo missions. The place has also been used as a training camp for astronauts.

The display tells you that this meteor, composed of nickel and iron, impacted about 49,000 years ago, travelling at a speed of 40,000mph (64,000kph) and causing a huge explosion surmounted by an enormous mushroom cloud. More than 300 million tonnes of rock were pulverized and scattered to the winds, which explains why nothing has been found at the bottom of the crater. The meteor is thought to have probably been part of an asteroid that became detached because of its incredible speed.

There's also a video called *The Future Belongs to the Brave,* which is a tribute to the crew of the shuttle that exploded. In a few short minutes, this film really succeeds in encapsulating the 'American spirit'.

★ **Walnut Canyon National Monument**: 15 miles (24km) east of Flagstaff on Interstate 40. Open all summer 8am–5pm. Admission charge. This is a narrow canyon thick with pine trees where there are hundreds of cave dwellings of the Sinagua tribe, who lived here around the 12th century. Only the ruins remain. A small museum explains the culture, and two short but rather nice little trails have been laid out for visitors to explore the canyon. Island Trail, which is undoubtedly the more atmospheric of the two, dives into the canyon itself and goes round in a loop. Rim Trail simply runs along the fault line. Pick up a map from the reception desk.

★ **Petrified Forest National Park**: about 100 miles (160km) east of Flagstaff, on Interstate 40. Petrified tree trunks in a lunar landscape made up of volcanic rock. This is probably better than the petrified forest on the road to Calistoga in the Napa Valley.

★ If you're interested in Native American civilization, there are other cave dwellings to look at, 26 miles (42km) to the southeast, at **Montezuma Castle**. Some of these dwellings are actually perched up on the cliff face.

SUGGESTED ITINERARY, STARTING IN FLAGSTAFF

Flagstaff is an excellent point of departure for exploring some of the most beautiful sites in the US as well as some Native American reserves. The suggested itinerary goes round a loop and can be completed in about a week. Many places have no bus service, and hitchhiking is risky because there are not many cars and the heat is intense. This means you have to hire a car.

The route takes in the following: Flagstaff to Grand Canyon Village on US 264 (which crosses the Hopi and Navajo reservations). Then US 191 for Canyon de Chelly to Monument Valley via Kayenta, Page and Lake Powell, then Bryce Canyon, Zion Canyon, Las Vegas and Flagstaff.

Buy a detailed map of Arizona. You can extend the route by departing from Canyon de Chelly via US 40 for Santa Fe, Taos, Durango and Mesa Verde. Then return to the main itinerary via Monument Valley.

– **Bus to Grand Canyon Village**: Nava-Hopi Tours (Gray Line). ☎ 774-5003. Freephone: ☎ 1-800-892-8687. Return trip on the same day.

– Two of the youth hostels mentioned organize day bus trips to Lake Powell, the Grand Canyon and Sedona. Check when you get there.

Do you hold a Greyhound 'Ameripass'? You won't be able to get to the Grand Canyon free. Some private tour operators organize tours departing from the Greyhound Terminal in Flagstaff ($25). One snag is that the trip to the canyon has to be done in about four hours, which you may think is not much time.

THE GRAND CANYON

AREA CODE: 520

The main entrance to the Grand Canyon National Park is about 81 miles (130 km) from Flagstaff, 275 miles (440 km) from Las Vegas and 487 miles (780 km) from Los Angeles. The Grand Canyon is one of the world's greatest geological phenomena – the jagged contours of the vast plateau stretch from the south of Utah to the north of Arizona, scoured out by the Colorado. Over thousands of years this river has carved its way through both soft and hard rock, creating a meandering course along a distance of 291 miles (466 km). The canyon is up to 5,250 feet (1,600m) deep in places, and has an average width of 19 miles (30 km). Prior to the construction of the Glen Canyon dam in 1963, the river swept down 500,000 tonnes of sand a day.

According to geologists, the canyon has been in existence alongside several seas, deserts and mountains as high as the Himalayas. The sand all around it is substantially of marine origin. Mixed with sediment, it gradually agglomerated to form sandstone and schist. In the Mesozoic period, under pressure from the continental plates, the Colorado plain gradually lifted to form a plateau. This then tilted as the Rockies were formed further east. The river began to erode the surface as it flowed along, exposing more and more geological layers. The oldest, at the very bottom, dates back 1.7 billion years. The canyon is a unique geological formation, and on a single visit it's possible to see two-fifths of the Earth's history.

Because of the great differences in altitude, five of the seven major climatic zones occur along the Grand Canyon. At the bottom of the gorge, at around 3,280 feet (1,000m) above sea-level, the presence of cacti indicates a dry, sub-tropical climate. At 3,940 feet (1,200 m), even though a hot climate still predominates, oak and mahogany trees are the proof of that the climate is moving towards the temperate. Higher up, there are pines and finally, at around 8,200ft (2,500m) the climatic zone is almost like that in Canada, with pine and fir forests, especially on the north side. These differences have resulted in a considerable bio-diversity, including a recorded 1,500 plant species, 305 bird species and 76 different species of mammal. Squirrels are a very common sight, but be careful of them as they sometimes bite. Deer are also quite common.

It's worth taking a jumper or even a waterproof as it often rains in the canyon, even in summer.

A BIT OF HISTORY

The first hunters are thought to have settled in the Grand Canyon region around 11,000 years ago, during the great migrations of tribes from Asia across the Bering Strait during the Upper Palaeolithic era. However, archaeologists have only discovered human traces dating back to the second millennium BC. These were fragile animal figurines made of twigs, which had been hidden away in cracks in the rock.

Agriculture seems to have first appeared around the beginning of the first millennium – an idea probably imported from Central America. Around 500 AD, a tribe took up residence in the Grand Canyon, the Anasazis, also known as the Pueblos and the 'basketmakers', which refers to the large number of woven baskets discovered in the places where they lived. Living in low, smoky, semi-subterranean dwellings, they were still basically dedicated to hunting, along with the cultivation of maize. Some 2,000 inhabited sites have been recorded along the length of the canyon, which they then shared with the Cahoninas tribe. Although for a long time these tribes were believed to have been peaceful, it now appears that this was far from the case. A recent study has proved conclusively that the Anasazis indulged in cannibalism . . . and not only for ritual purposes.

In the 13th century, the Pueblo culture reached its height. Their dwellings had become veritable apartment complexes (which would later earn them their Spanish name, as *pueblo* means 'town'), their religious ceremonies were celebrated in subterranean ritual rooms known as *kiva*, they had begun to cultivate beans and squash, and they used their pottery to barter with neighbouring tribes as far afield as the Pacific Coast. However, towards the end of the 13th century, for reasons that remain unclear (probably drought, maybe war), the Anasazis suddenly disappeared. They are thought to have resettled further east, in what is now the homeland of the Hopi, who are thought to be their descendants.

In the 14th and 15th centuries, several tribes moved into the region: the Cerbats, ancestors of the Hualapais and the Havasupais (who still live in certain remote corners of the canyon) followed by the Paiutes and the Navajos.

In 1540, the beginning of the conquest of the west was marked by the 'discovery' of the '*Gran Cañón*' by García López de Cárdenas, one of the members of Francisco de Coronado's expedition, which had set out in search of the Seven Cities of Gold of Cibola. Prevented from advancing northwards, the conquistadors returned to Mexico empty-handed to face a court martial. The first colonists arrived at the end of the 16th century and Santa Fe was quickly established as the base for Spanish colonization in the American West.

With the opening of the Santa Fe Trail in 1821, linking St Louis to New Mexico, a wave of Anglo-Saxon trappers, merchants and adventurers of all kinds invaded Spanish territory and another slice of the cake fell into the hands of the rapidly expanding United States. The Grand Canyon became American in 1848 when it was purchased from a defeated Mexico. Army expeditions were quickly sent in to explore this virgin territory. In 1858, an unknown lieutenant wrote the following report: 'The region is definitely not of the slightest interest . . . Our troop was the first and without doubt will be the last to visit this place, which offers nothing of value'. Ten years later, Major Powell made his incredible odyssey down the Colorado, opening up the whole of the southwest to colonization. The 'Palefaces' had arrived, the 'Indians' had gone to ground and tourism had taken its first determined steps.

The Grand Canyon was declared a national park in 1919. By the turn of the 20th century a canny entrepreneur, Fred Harvey, had already built a hotel catering for the needs of city dwellers with a yearning for wide open spaces. History has proved his business acumen to be sound.

HOW TO VISIT THE GRAND CANYON

There are three good ways of exploring the Grand Canyon; by plane (fantastic, but expensive, noisy and environmentally unfriendly), by raft (the method most in keeping with the natural environment, although you need to book well in advance) and, of course, on foot. Anyone wanting to undertake the hike under their own steam will need to be very fit, but it is the least expensive method and offers the most spectacular views. A further plus is that the further you go, the more chance you have of escaping the crowds. If you are only intending to spend a few hours there, try and arrive two hours before sunset.

– A word of warning: trying to view the Canyon from the viewing points can prove rather frustrating, as it's impossible to appreciate the sheer size and scale of what you can see, and the large number of visitors (around 5 million every year), makes it difficult to enjoy the view in peace and quiet. Try and get as far out of the village as possible – the various viewing points dot the rim for several miles. Cars are banned in spring and summer along West Rim Drive, to the west of the village. However, a new public transportation system, currently under construction (*see* 'Grand Canyon Village'), will mean easy access to all parts of the canyon without causing long-term damage to the natural environment. The Visitors' Center, which is also being developed, provides free brochures and very good maps of the area to help you find your way around. The different viewing points are well marked: Maricopa Point, Mohave Point, Pima Point, Yavapai Pont, etc.

It is interesting to note that although the two sides of the Grand Canyon are relatively close together as the crow flies, to get from one to the other by road is a journey of 215 miles (345km).

HOW TO GET THERE

FROM FLAGSTAFF

Nava-Hopi Bus (Gray Line): ☎ (520) 774-5003. Freephone: ☎ 1-800-892-8687. Service runs from mid-May to the end of October only. Tickets can be bought at the Amtrak station. Two departures a day in summer via Tusayan, at 7.30am and 2.30pm. The trip takes about 2 hours depending on the route. The 7.30am bus stops off at Williams, departing again at 8.20am. The return journeys from the Grand Canyon, at Maswick Lodge, are at 10.30am and 5pm. The second one stops at Williams. It's advisable to buy your ticket on arrival. $12 single from Flagstaff and $9 from Williams. It's half-price for children aged 5–15 and free for younger ones.

FROM WILLIAMS

One train daily leaves this small city, 93 miles (41km) west of Flagstaff, for the Grand Canyon. What's original about it is that *The Grand Canyon Railway* is a locomotive that dates back to 1920, so in high season, you can make the journey on a magnificent steam train. The unique machine dates back to 1923 and is a real Great West museum piece. For the rest of the year, a more modern diesel version replaces the old train.

Departures leave Williams at 9.30am, arriving at Grand Canyon Village at 11.45am; the return trip starts at 3.15pm, returning to Williams at 5.30pm. The service runs all year round (except 24–25 December). For information: ☎ (520) 773-1976. Freephone: ☎ 1-800-THE-TRAIN. Fax: 773-1610. Website: www.thetrain.com. It's advisable to buy your ticket in advance and get there about 1 hour 30 minutes before departure. The return trip costs $50–$120 depending on what class you travel. One-way tickets are also available.

FROM TUSAYAN

Grand Canyon Tusayan Shuttle (Cassi): ☎ 638-0821. Website: www.canyonairportshuttle.com. Bus service between Tusayan and Grand Canyon Village (Maswick Transportation Center) via the IMAX dome, the airport and Babbitt's General Store. Every hour 10.15am–3.15pm from mid-March to October, with extra services at 9.15am and until 7.15pm from June to August. It costs a very reasonable $4 and is free for under-16s if accompanied by an adult.

A light railway is to be put into service between Tusayan and the new Visitors' Center at Mather Point towards the end of 2000 (or thereabouts). The park authorities are talking about making it obligatory – visitors would then no longer be able to take their own cars into Grand Canyon Village.

FROM LAS VEGAS

– **Gray Line Bus**: 1550 S Industrial Avenue ☎ 384-1234. Freephone: ☎ 1-800-634-6579. It's a full and very long day's excursion with the option of a flight over the canyon. Quite pricey.

– **Eagle Scenic Airlines**: 275 E Tropicana Avenue ☎ 638-3300. Freephone: ☎ 1-800-634-6801. It's expensive, but ideal for discovering one of the most sumptuous landscapes in the world. For safety reasons and to protect the environment, flying over the Grand Canyon is restricted to a general look at the landscape, and it's no longer possible to go down into the gorges. You leave Las Vegas and, after flying for 90 minutes, you land near Grand Canyon Village. The best seats are the two at the back. You can buy a return or a one-way ticket. It's very popular in summer, so booking is advisable.

Don't forget that both of the **youth hostels** in Las Vegas also offer excursions to the Grand Canyon.

AT THE GRAND CANYON

Transcanyon Shuttle operates a daily shuttle service in summer between the South Rim and the North Rim. This is very useful if you're thinking of crossing the canyon on foot. The journey takes 5 hours. For information ☎ 638-2820.

★ THE SOUTH RIM

The South Rim is by far the more popular of the two, and 90 per cent of visitors make this their only port-of-call. It's the official entrance to the Moqui National Park, on Route 180 as you come from Flagstaff.

The admission charge is $20 per car, valid for seven days, unless you've already bought the 'Golden Eagle' Pass, and $10 for anyone coming by bus, bicycle or on foot.

GRAND CANYON VILLAGE

AREA CODE: 520

Grand Canyon Village is an artificial village situated at the South Rim of the Canyon that was built purely to meet the needs of tourists. Due to a vast increase in visitors to the area in recent years, however, a major restructuring project has been underway since 1995 to accommodate the annual figure of nearly 5 million visitors and to protect the local environment from long-term damage. In October 2000, the **Canyon View Information Plaza**, a gigantic new visitors' transit and orientation centre situated near Mather Point, was officially opened. This was the first major step in the project which is due to be completed in 2010. Further developments designed to facilitate a visit to the Canyon will include light railway transportation and the implementation of the Greenway system for visitors on bicycle and foot. As private vehicles are no longer allowed access to the Canyon, visitors will need to leave their cars in designated parking areas and take a connecting shuttle bus service to continue their visit. For more information on the latest developments in the area, check out the website: www.nps.gov/grca/mgmt/.

USEFUL ADDRESSES AND INFORMATION

TOURIST INFORMATION

🅸 This Visitors' Center is scheduled to close by the end of 2000 and will be replaced by the **Canyon View Information Plaza** which is situated near Mather Point (East Rim Drive). The **Visitors' Center** (🅸) is in the east of the village. You can pick up plenty of leaflets and information. ☎ 638-7888. Open daily, 8am–5pm (in winter), 8am–7pm in summer. Ask them about the guided walks, films and free sets of slides.

Get hold of a copy of the *Grand Canyon Magazine* (free) in Tusayan or the park itself, it is an excellent source of information about the park and the activities available, and is peppered with plenty of practical tips. For information in writing, contact the Superintendent, Grand Canyon National Park, PO Box 129, Grand Canyon, AZ 86023, USA. Visit the website at www.thecanyon.com/nps.

TRANSPORT

■ **Railway station** (map, **2**): Santa Fe Railway Depot

■ **Garage** (map, **5**): open daily, 8am–5pm. ☎ 638-2631

■ **Gas station**: the gas station in Grand Canyon Village has closed, so you will need to go back to Tusayan for fuel. The nearest gas station is the one at Moqui Lodge.

– **State of the roads**: ☎ 638-7888 (recorded information)

MISCELLANEOUS

■ In the event of a problem, a **doctor** is available at **Grand Canyon Clinic** (map, **4**), to the south of the Village. ☎ 638-2551 or 638-2469. On duty 8am–5.30pm during the week and 9am–midday on Saturday. Alternatively, contact any of the rangers.

■ **Bank** (map, **9**): The only bank, **One**, is situated next to the Post Office and Babbitt's General Store ☎ 638-2437. Open Monday–Thursday 10am–3pm, Friday 10am–5pm. It will change traveller's cheques and some foreign currency. There's a cash machine that takes Visa, MasterCard and American Express.

■ **Babbitt's General Store** (map, **3**): a big supermarket, ideal for stocking up on provisions, with a good range of camping equipment. Open every day 8am–8pm.

■ The **Post office** is open Monday–Friday 9am–4.30pm and Saturday 11am–3pm. A stamp machine is available 5am–10pm.

■ **Launderette** (map, **6**): near the Mather campground. Open 6am–9.45pm in high season. Shorter hours the rest of the year.

■ **Public showers** (map, **7**): coin-operated (75c for 5 minutes). Open 6am–10pm in summer.

AT TUSAYAN

– There's a **post office**, a **gas station**, a **grocery store**, public **telephones**, and a **Versateller** cash dispenser (in the IMAX dome) that accepts Visa cards.

WHERE TO STAY

In the Village, of course, accommodation is often fully booked, so you need to reserve months in advance in the high season. You have a small chance all the same if you get to the Visitors' Center early in the morning, as there's always the possibility of a last-minute cancellation.

All the hotels, restaurants and campgrounds form an exclusive concession that was granted to a man called Fred Harvey. At the close of the 19th century, this great man began his career as a dishwasher in a restaurant in Kansas. He very soon realized that he could turn the Native American regions to good account. Grand Canyon Village was on the railroad line from Santa Fe that brought the pioneers out to the West. The women who worked in Fred Harvey's restaurants and hotels acquired a solid reputation – they weren't afraid of hard work and they were good at their job. Their reputation was so good that 'to marry a Fred Harvey's girl' came into the vocabulary. Times have changed somewhat and the present staff seem overwhelmed with work.

HOW TO BOOK A ROOM / SITE AT A CAMPGROUND

– **Rooms**: a single organization deals with reservations for all the lodges in the park (three older ones and four more modern, motel-style ones). Although this may seem straightforward enough, it can be a laborious process. From Britain, you can try faxing 00-1-303-297-3175, or telephoning (00-1-303-29-PARKS). It's probably easiest to use the website: www.amfac.com, because they often take ages to respond and are often fully booked for the foreseeable future. Payment is accepted by international money order or a cheque drawn on an American bank, so this is a real obstacle course. If you succeed, you can feel really proud.

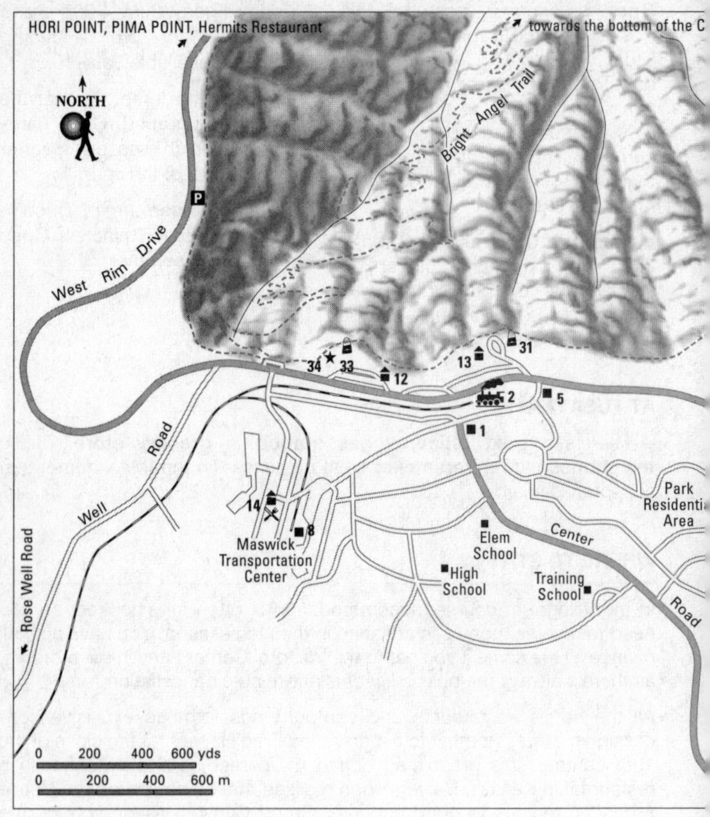

■ Useful Addresses

- ℹ Visitors' Center (closing end of 2000)
- ✉ Post office
- 1 Rangers Station
- 2 Santa Fe Railway Depot
- 3 Babbitt's General Store
- 4 Grand Canyon Clinic
- 5 Garage
- 6 Launderette
- 7 Public showers
- 8 Backcountry Office
- 9 Bank

Where to Stay

- 10 Mather Campground

Visitors arriving in the Grand Canyon with no accommodation booked will have to hope for a cancellation. Try phoning 638-2631 for same-day reservations. More rooms are available out of season.

Don't forget to allow for the 6.38 per cent local tax in addition to the prices given here.

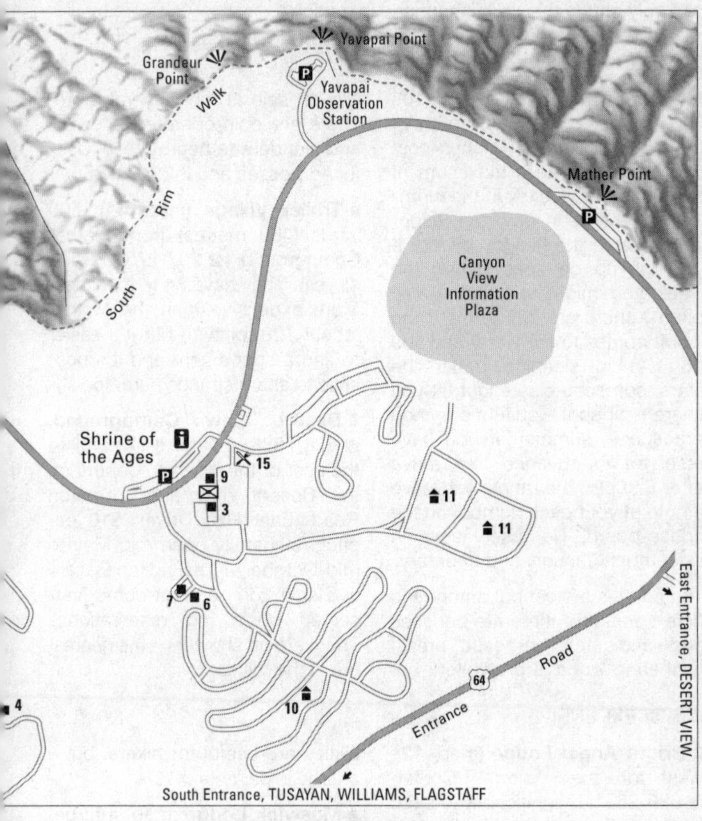

GRAND CANYON VILLAGE

11 Trailer Village
12 Bright Angel Lodge
13 El Tovar Hotel
14 Maswick Lodge

Where to Eat

3 Babbitt's General Store
14 Maswick Lodge Cafeteria
15 Yavapai Lodge Cafeteria

★ **What to See**

2 Santa Fe Railway Depot
31 Hopi House
33 Lookout Studio
34 Kolb Studio

– **Sites in campgrounds**: to reserve a pitch in the Mather Campground, contact the Biospherics service on freephone: ☎ 1-800-365-2267. They deal with reservations for all the American national parks, so you'll need to specify which one you want.

If you are planning a **trek** lasting several days, you'll need a permit. You can only obtain this on the spot and in person.

CAMPGROUNDS

☗ **Mather Campground** (map, **10**): 500 yards (460 metres) south of the Visitors' Center. Pitches cost $12 and can take a maximum of two tents. Arrive early in the morning or reserve in advance, especially during the holiday period. If you roll up on spec during the week you might still find a free pitch – there are 320 in all. If the worst comes to the worst and you don't mind sleeping under the stars, someone else might let you share their spot – quite a common practice in summer. If you have reserved in advance and arrive after 6.30pm, the ranger will leave a note of your pitch number on the notice-board. No reservations in December, January and February.

The pitches are set out among the pine trees, and there are benches and dedicated barbecue areas. Gathering wood is prohibited, but it is on sale at the General Store. There are coin-operated showers and launderette nearby (*see* 'Useful Addresses and Information').

☗ **Trailer Village** (map, **11**): 500 yards (460 metres) from Mather Campground. ☎ 297-2757. Open all year. They have 84 tent pitches. More expensive than the Mather (about $20 for two) but it's easier to find a space here and it's possible to share spaces here, too.

☗ **Desert View Campground**: ☎ 638-7888. 26 miles (42 km) to the east of the Visitors' Centre, on the Desert View and Cameron Road (East Rim Drive). $10 per pitch. Generally open mid-May to mid-October. The pitches are available on a first-come-first-served basis (no reservations). There are no showers – the nearest are in the Village.

☆☆☆ EXPENSIVE

☗ **Bright Angel Lodge** (map, **12**): west of the Visitors' Center. ☎ 638-2631. Magnificently located on the cliff edge. Standard rooms are $60, $70 for the old bungalows with open fireplaces but no central heating, $100–$120 for the new rooms overlooking the canyon. Built in 1935, it's the most affordable hotel in the park, with rustic log-cabin decor. You haven't a hope in summer unless you book. The constant flow of visitors means that peace and quiet are in short supply. The left-luggage facilities are useful for hikers, but a charge is payable.

☗ **Maswick Lodge** (map, **14**): behind the Maswick Transportation Center, by the Backcountry Office (which issues the trekking permits). Not the best of locations, as it's well set back from the rim, but at $60 the somewhat 'rustic' bungalows are the cheapest in the park along with those at the Bright Angel. The rooms range from $75 to $115 depending on which wing they are in.

☆☆☆☆ SPLASH OUT

☗ **El Tovar Hotel** (map, **13**): a stone's throw to the east of Maswick Lodge. The rooms are the most expensive in the park and the most in demand, costing $115–$130 for a standard room and up to $280 for the most exclusive suite, which offers an unbeatable view of the Grand Canyon. This chic hotel dating from 1905, clad throughout in wood and roofed in clapboard, is named after the conquistador Don Pedro de Tovar, a member of the Coronado expedition. For almost a century it has played host to the vacationing American gentry. Worth a quick visit even if you're not a guest.

TUSAYAN

There's no sign to tell you you've arrived in Tusayan, a small village with not much style. But it does have one big advantage: it's just over a mile (2km) from the entrance to the Grand Canyon park, and 8 miles (13km) from the bottom of the gorges. It's the closest village to the site. Markedly more expensive than the other towns, but there's nothing you can do about it. You are, after all, at the Grand Canyon. Developers are well aware of this and hotel complexes are now mushrooming. Prices given here are for the high season (June–September). They are considerably lower the rest of the year (10–30 per cent depending on the hotel).

CAMPGROUNDS

Ten-X Campground: 2 miles (3.5 km) to the south of Tusayan, in the Kaibab National Forest. Open mid-May to the end of September. ☎ 638-2443. $10 a pitch on a first-come-first-served basis. No showers but a pleasant setting.

Camper Village: on the right as you head out of Tusayan going north. ☎ 638-2887. A two-person pitch is $19. There are often free spaces – unsurprising since the site is noisy and not particularly nice and you have to pay for the showers. OK as a last resort if you can't find anywhere else. You can also hire a tepee (not a very big one) for $19.

☆☆ MODERATE

Seven Mile Lodge: ☎ 638-2291. A modest building with only 20 rooms, but it's pleasant nonetheless. Doubles cost $68 in summer. This is the cheapest and gives the best value for money in the area. You get a cheery reception on arrival. No reservations – rooms are allocated on a first-come-first-served basis, but opening hours can be a little unpredictable.

☆☆☆ EXPENSIVE

Moqui Lodge: although it's just outside the entrance, this is still classified as one of the national park's lodges and is run by Amfac. For reservations: ☎ 1-303-29-PARKS. Fax: 1-303-297-3175. Website: www.amfac.com. For postal reservations, *see* 'Where to Stay – How to Book a Room'. Open from the beginning of April to the end of October. The cost, inclusive of a good breakfast, is $94 for one or two people ($12 per extra person). There is plenty of space; the wooden buildings are set among pine trees. The nearest fuel pump to the park is here, plus a fairly pricey Mexican restaurant (Moqui's Cantina) and stables offering horses for hire.

Rodeway Inn (Red Feather Lodge): on the left-hand side of the road if you're coming from Flagstaff or Williams. ☎ 636-2414. Freephone: ☎ 1-800-538-2345. Fax: 638-9216. One of the least expensive places in Tusayan in this category, costing from $89 in summer in the oldest wing (where the rooms and beds are smaller), up to $109 in the new wing. Swimming pool and jacuzzi. The welcome is far from effusive.

Quality Inn: ☎ 638-2673. Freephone: ☎ 1-800-221-2222. Fax: 638-9537. Comfortable and welcoming but quite expensive, at $118–$168 for a double room in summer. The least expensive rooms have coffee makers, while the suites all have a fridge and a microwave. There's a swimming pool, a jacuzzi, and a good restaurant (*see* 'Where to Eat').

Best Western Grand Canyon Squire Inn: PO Box 130, Grand Canyon, AZ 86023. ☎ 638-2681. Freephone: ☎ 1-800-622-6966. This is the only real resort in the area, with a swimming pool, tennis, bowling, jacuzzi, hairdresser and so on. Needless to say, it doesn't come cheap – the rooms are $135–$150 in high season and this increases still further over particularly busy weekends.

WILLIAMS

Williams is 57 miles (91km) south of Grand Canyon Village and 26 miles (41km) west of Flagstaff at the junction of Interstate 40 and Route 64. Far more authentic than Tusayan, this little Old West town in an area with a markedly cooler climate is surrounded by pinewoods. It has a lively centre and lots of reasonably priced motels (all the national chains), and as it's just under an hour by car to the site of the Grand Canyon, it makes an excellent staging point. If you're coming from California, there's no point in pushing on to Flagstaff. Best to stay here and continue to Grand Canyon Village next day.

Williams Visitor Information Center: in Railroad Avenue, on the corner of N Grand Canyon Boulevard. Open 8am–5pm.

In Williams, stop off at the headquarters of **Route 66 Magazine**, 326 W Route 66. ☎ 635-4322. Fax: 635-4470. Basically, it's a shop selling souvenirs and old magazines related to America's most famous road. The route is mapped on the wall, with all the legendary points of interest marked along the way. Open every day 6.30am–8pm.

Red Garter Bed & Bakery: 137 W Railroad Avenue. ☎ 635-1484. Freephone: ☎ 1-800-328-1484. Website: www.redgarter.com. An old brothel, from which it derives its name. Open from mid-February to the end of November, 6–11am and 4–8pm. At other times, John, the proprietor, is often there anyway, so try knocking at the door. Prices are the same all year round, including weekends (this is unusual enough to deserve a special mention): one room is $65, another $85 and the remaining two $105, each with its own bathroom. The most attractive (also one of the more expensive) with its own lounge, is the 'Best Gal's Room', which overlooks the street – the girls would have stood in the window to entice potential clients. Opened by a German in 1897, with a saloon on the ground floor, the bawdy-house continued to function until 1941. At one time, it even boasted an opium den that was run by a Chinaman. The 'bakery' is on the ground floor and it's where guests can take breakfast. Reservations are advisable, although they sometimes have a room free in July and August. No children allowed.

☗ **Motel 6**: 831 W Bill William Ave, on the way into town coming from the west. ☎ (520) 635-9000. Freephone: ☎ 1-800-4-MOTEL-6. Fax: 635-2300. A double room costs $59 in summer. This motel occupies what was once a quality chain store, spread across two buildings, and this gives it more spacious rooms than the average Motel 6. There's an indoor swimming pool and a jacuzzi.

BETWEEN THE GRAND CANYON AND PAGE

☗ **Cameron Trading Post**: 54 miles (87km) north of Flagstaff on Highway 89, and 57 miles from Grand Canyon Village. PO Box 339, Cameron, 86020 AZ. ☎ 679-2231. Freephone: ☎ 1-800-338-7385. Fax: 679-2350. Website: www.camerontradingpost.com. A motel-restaurant-shop that's run by Navajos. Pleasant rooms across a wide range of prices – from $59 in winter to $74 in summer for a single and $69–$89 for a twin. Reserved rooms are only held until 7pm. The dining room is attractive, but the restaurant is very touristy. They serve some Navajo dishes – tacos and stew, for example, but they get lost among the burgers and the steaks. Not too pricey ($5–$7). The shop is immense and sells some beautiful souvenirs.

WHERE TO EAT

GRAND CANYON VILLAGE

✕ **Maswick Lodge Cafeteria** (map, **14**): west of the Visitors' Center. Open daily, 6am–10pm. A self-service where you can eat your fill for $5–$8. The place is full to bursting in summer, so you have to queue up for your pasta or cheeseburger, but at least it's quite cheap (for the Grand Canyon).

✕ **Yavapai Lodge Cafeteria** (map, **15**): opposite the Visitors' Center, near the post office and the general store. Nothing particularly exciting but the dishes are relatively cheap ($3–$6) and there's a choice of salads, sandwiches, hamburgers, pizzas and the other usual stuff. Also does breakfast. Open every day 6am–10pm.

If you prefer to do your own food shopping, **Babbitt's General Store** (map, **3**), is 200 yards (180 metres) from the Visitors' Centre and just opposite the Yavapai Lodge Cafeteria. Open every day 8am–7pm. It also has a very reasonably priced cafe-cum-delicatessen that serves hot dogs and sandwiches for $2–$3, grilled chicken for only slightly more, and a wide variety of desserts. Excellent for a cheap but satisfying meal on the hoof.

☆☆☆ EXPENSIVE

✕ **Arizona Steakhouse**: beside Bright Angel Lodge, on the cliff. Open 4.30–10pm. Meals for around $15–$20. Attractive views if you get there early, but the setting lacks warmth. It feels like a cafeteria – hardly surprising since it is one during the day, when they sell excellent ice-creams. You sometimes have to wait a while to be served.

TUSAYAN

There's not much choice in Tusayan on the food front, although things are beginning to improve. Prices are on the expensive side. If you're short on money or time, head for McDonald's, Taco Bell, Wendy's or the Stix Canyon Food Mart.

✗ **Yippee-Ei-O Steakhouse**: ☎ 638-2780. Opposite the IMAX (on the other side of the road). The best restaurant in Tusayan. Filling snacks for $7–$8 and a full meal for $12–$20. The restaurant now takes Visa. The portions are generous but it's a bit expensive (which is only to be expected in this neck of the woods). The atmosphere is warm and the place is always packed out. The serving staff all wear stetsons. You can eat meat, meat and more meat (sometimes rather average sort of meat), chicken roasted over a wood fire and several Mexican dishes.

✗ **Quality Inn Restaurant**: on the other side of the road, inside the hotel. ☎ 638-2673. From April to October they offer a good buffet with a wide choice. Breakfast ($6.50) is served 6–9am, lunch ($8) until 2.30pm and dinner ($15) until 9.30pm. You can get sandwiches or burgers ($7–$9) or a big salad ($13–$14). The good quality meat dishes are more expensive ($16–20) and there's a wide selection of relatively cheap desserts.

✗ **Cafe Tusayan**: on the other side of the road, just before the IMAX if you're coming from the south. Open every day 6am–10pm. Prices are – once again – on the high side: breakfast is $7–$10, meat and fish dishes in the evenings cost $12–$20. Sandwiches, salads, burgers and Mexican are also on offer. The place is neither bad nor brilliant and it doesn't take credit cards.

WILLIAMS

✗ **Old Smoky's Pancake House**: on the way into the town on the western side, nearly opposite the Safeway supermarket. ☎ 635-2091. Open 6am–1.30pm. Quite a cosy setting. A good place for breakfast, with a large choice of fresh, home-baked bread. A bit pricey all the same ($8–$10 per person).

✗ **Old "66" Coffee House**: 246 W Route 66. ☎ 635-2572. Hot dogs, burritos and tacos for just a few dollars. The interior is an incredible junk-shop with all sorts of Route 66 memorabilia and 'antiques' from the 1950s and 1960s. Try the prickly-pear milkshakes.

☆☆ MODERATE

✗ **Pancho McGillicuddy's**: 141 W Railroad Avenue, in an old, listed brick building dating from 1893 (the old Cabinet Saloon), next door to the Red Garter B&B. ☎ 635-4150. Open in summer, noon–8pm. In times gone by, the street was nicknamed 'Saloon Row'. The decor is rather 'Mexico-meets-the-Rockies'. The walls are bristling with stuffed animals; long-haired goats, pronghorn and a bison sporting a sombrero. This mix-and-match is also evident on the menu, where burritos, tamales, enchiladas and tacos appear alongside steaks, spare-ribs, burgers and BBQ dishes. Prices are very reasonable (a good meal for around $10). Wide choice of beers and Margaritas in every conceivable flavour. You can eat on a rather pleasant patio, where there's live music from 5.30pm.

Rosa's Cantina: 106 S 9th Street, to the east of the town centre. ☎ 635-0708. Open 11am–10pm. Far superior to Pancho McGillicuddy's in the authenticity stakes – real Mexican dishes (and sandwiches), with copious Mexican portions and warm Mexican smiles from the waiting staff. The prices aren't Mexican – but they're still quite reasonable.

☆☆☆ EXPENSIVE

✕ **Rod's Steak House**: 301 E Bill Williams Avenue ☎ 635-2671. Freephone: ☎ 1-800-562-5545. Opposite the Econolodge. Open 11.30am–9.30pm. This place is difficult to miss – there's a steer on the roof and another at the entrance (with a cow for company). This meat-eaters' paradise has been building up its reputation over more than 50 years. The steaks are superb although, needless to say, not particularly cheap. Good value for money all the same.

There is no justification for the prices at **Max and Thelma's** restaurant in Williams station, especially as the immense dining room feels far too much like a station concourse.

FREE SHUTTLE BUS SYSTEM

A free shuttle bus operates from mid-March to mid-October (exact dates change from year to year) and this ensures a regular service between different points in the village and the viewing points along the West Rim Drive (as far as the Hermit's Rest terminal) and the East Rim Drive (Yaki Point and the South Kaibab Trail, since they are no longer accessible by private vehicle). These buses stop several times en route. Passengers can board and leave freely at each stop. It's an excellent way to explore the Grand Canyon, and you can alternate between periods of sitting and spells of walking. Bus times and a map of routes are given in *The Guide*, available from the **Visitors' Center.** Once the Visitors' Center has moved, the service will be extended further and will run all year round. The buses are very crowded between 11am and 4pm.

– **For the West Rim Loop**: access is prohibited to vehicles in summer throughout the entire period when the shuttles are in operation, with the exception of vehicles carrying disabled passengers. The bus starts at the West Rim Interchange, at the western exit from the village at the junction of Well Road and West Rim Drive (about 300 yards from Bright Angel Lodge). It's very well signposted. Buses leave every 10–15 minutes, from one hour before sunrise through to one hour after sunset. The bus stops eight times along the way at the most interesting sites and travels as far as the terminus of the vehicle route, which is Hermit's Rest – the point of departure of the Hermit hiking trail. Hermit's Rest is 8 miles (13km) west of the village. If you don't get off the bus, the return trip takes 90 minutes.

– **Village Loop bus**: operates from one hour before sunrise until 10.30pm, with departures every 15 minutes. This free shuttle bus continuously links the Visitors' Center, the hotels, the restaurants, the campgrounds and Yavapai observation station to the east of the village.

– **Yaki Point / South Kaibab**: since this superb East Rim Drive viewpoint has recently been closed to private vehicles, the best means of access is the shuttle bus. This service also operates from one hour before sunrise to one hour after sunset, and picks up passengers at the Maswick Transportation Center, Bright Angel Lodge and Yavapai Lodge. The buses run every 30 minutes. If you want to start your journey into the canyon by the South Kaibab Trail any earlier, you'll have to take a taxi (Fred Harvey Taxi: ☎ 638-2631); if you miss the last bus, it's an extra one hour's walk back to the Village.

WHAT TO SEE AND DO

★ **Santa Fe Railway Depot** (map, **2**): this little log-built station was built in 1909. It looks like an 'Old West' type of thing for tourists, but still – it's better than a concrete station. The train is still in service and shuttles between Grand Canyon Village and the station at Williams (*see* 'How To Get There').

★ **Hopi House** (map, **31**): in Grand Canyon Village, opposite the El Tovar Hotel. This is an ordinary shop, but the Hopi architecture has been completely respected. They sell Native American artefacts . . . made in China.

★ **Lookout Studio** (map, **33**): a stone-built house dating from 1914, and looking out across the chasm of the Grand Canyon. It was already a souvenir shop at the beginning, in hot competition with Hopi House and the Kolb Studio. Americans have never been slow to spot a commercial opportunity. Some of the items on sale are not even local – but the view is superb.

★ **Kolb Studio** (map, **34**): a timber-built house clinging to the cliff. The Kolb brothers set up shop here in 1904 and they began systematically photographing everything they saw, especially the mule drivers. These days, it's a bookshop specializing in the Grand Canyon. In the basement, an exhibition space houses a good collection of old photographs and some more recent views of the canyon.

Yavapai Observation Station: about 0.25 mile (500m) to the west of the new Visitors' Center. Open 8am–6pm. There are some sublime views from this observation station, which also houses a small exhibition of fossils. If you want to know more about the forces of nature that created the canyon, sign up for the Geology Walk, which happens every day at 1pm. The trip, accompanied by a ranger, lasts about an hour. There is also a Sunset Walk, which leaves one hour before sundown (times are posted in the Visitors' Center). If you look carefully, you can even see a tiny section of the Colorado.

Mather Point: Another beautiful viewpoint. The new **Canyon View Information Plaza** is located here.

WEST RIM DRIVE

This is where you leave your car and transfer to one of the park shuttles (*see* 'Free Shuttle Bus System'). There are long queues in summer and you should allow plenty of time if you want to see the sunset.

The first stop is **Maricopa Point**, from where there is a good view of the Bright Angel Trail leading down to Indian Gardens and the bottom of the canyon. At this point, the Rim Trail, which follows the crest (from Mather Point, to the east of the Village, as far as Hermit's Rest, right at the end of West Rim Drive), ceases to be surfaced. The journey towards the west is consequently easier, although the stretch to Hermit's Rest is nearly another seven miles (11 km). Unless you are very hardy, the best idea is to do some of the journey on foot and some of it by bus. Shortly after Maricopa are **Hopi Point** (toilets) and **Mohave Point**, offering some magnificent panoramas over the canyon. 1.25 miles (2km) further on, at **The Abyss**, the cliffs of the Great Mojave plunge impressively for more than 3,200 feet (1,000m) straight down to the Colorado. The excursion continues via **Pima Point** and ends up at **Hermit's Rest.** This takes its name from a solitary Quebecois, by the name of Louis Boucher, who grew vegetables there in the 1890s while prospecting in the neighbourhood. Another 150 yards (140 metres) further on is the start of the **Hermit Trail**, an uneven, way-marked track that leads to the **Santa Maria Springs**, 5 miles (8km) away. If you're coming back up on the same day, you need to turn around at this point.

EAST RIM DRIVE

Unlike the West Rim Drive, the East Rim Drive is still open to private vehicles, with one or two exceptions. This is because it's the road that leads to Cameron, to the east of the park, going in the direction of Page and Lake Powell, as well as leading to the North Rim. Again, there are some fabulous viewpoints offering truly amazing panoramas of the canyon at sunset.

Yaki Point: This viewing point, offering some of the South Rim's most beautiful views, is the only part of the East Rim Drive that's closed to cars (except for those carrying disabled people). The car park was no longer big enough to cope with the flood of visitors, so access is now via the shuttle bus (*see* 'Free Shuttle Bus System'). If you are passing through and don't want to return to the Village to take the bus, there's a 20–30-minute walk to be done here. There's a small car park nearly opposite the fork in the road. Don't be tempted to park on the roadside, as your car will soon be towed away. This is one of the prettiest of all the panoramas, as there's an orange light reflecting off the rock-faces as you drive eastwards.

The bus also stops at the beginning of the South Kaibab Trail, which leads down to Phantom Ranch via Cedar Ridge.

As you continue eastwards, there is one viewing point after another – some are official stopping places, but others, often unsignposted, are almost as impressive. From **Grandview Point**, which is one of the most famous, a path goes down towards a halfway plateau, to the Last Chance copper mine, which was worked in the last few years of the 19th century. The miners used the trail to bring up the ore on muleback. Further on, **Moran Point** provides a magnificent view over Hance Canyon and the Colorado, and the road runs very close to it at this point.

Tusayan Museum: 21 miles (34 km) from Grand Canyon Village, on the way to Cameron. Open every day 9am–5pm but sometimes closed between November and February due to staff shortages. Admission is free. This interesting little museum is dedicated to Anasazi culture and to the Hopi tribe, generally considered to be their descendants. On display are photographs, documents, jewellery and everyday objects; there's also a display on the Navajos. Right next to the museum are the remains of a little, 800-year-old '*pueblo*', believed to have been inhabited by some 30 people. Two partly-buried secret ceremonial sites (*kivas*) were discovered there, though they are not particularly spectacular. There are guided tours at 11am and 1.30pm, starting at the museum.

The excursion along the East Rim Drive ends with two more viewing points: first **Lipan Point**, from which you can see the Colorado and then **Desert View Point**, which is famous for its Indian-inspired tower built in 1932. The view from the top (small admission charge) is much the same as the one from below – the river winding majestically between outcrops and cliffs. Beyond Desert View, the road turns off towards Cameron.

TUSAYAN

★ **Grand Canyon Imax**: in Tusayan, at the southern entrance to the park. ☎ 638-2468. Open from 1 March to the end of October 8.30am–8.30pm, the rest of the year 10.30am–6.30pm. A film of the history of the Grand Canyon is shown every hour on the giant screen with special effects. It's well executed but fairly expensive for 35 minutes of cinema ($8, no credit cards).

★ **Flying over the Grand Canyon**: many companies offer flights over the Grand Canyon by helicopter or plane from Tusayan Airport, just before the entrance to the park. Almost immediately after take-off you are actually over the Grand Canyon. Prices vary, depending on the number of people, the duration of the flight and the time of day. At around midday, for example, it costs less because there's a heat haze and visibility is less good. The helicopter is much more expensive than the plane.

– **Grand Canyon Airlines**: ☎ 638-2463. Freephone: ☎ 1-800-528-2413. Fax: 638-9461. About $75 for 50 minutes.

– **Eagle Scenic Airlines**: ☎ 638-3300. Freephone: ☎ 1-800-634-6801.

– **Air Grand Canyon**: ☎ 638-2686. Freephone: ☎ 1-800-247-4726. Fax: 776-8099.

There's the more family-oriented **AirStar Airlines**, which also provides helicopter flights. Many people prefer these to plane flights and they are not as noisy as you might think. You get a better view but it is more expensive. Competition, as ever, is fierce.

Other companies offering helicopter flights:

– **Kenal**: ☎ 638-2764. Freephone: ☎ 1-800-541-4537. Fax: 638-9588.

– **Papillon**: ☎ 638-2419. Freephone: ☎ 1-800-528-2418.

Both companies offer 'Super-Saver' fares between 11.20am and 1.20pm (20 per cent less than at other times of the day). It's a good idea to ask, as they don't always tell you about these savings.

ADVICE IF YOU'RE GOING TO THE BOTTOM OF THE CANYON

– First of all, go to the **Visitors' Center/Canyon View Information Plaza** and discuss the various possible itineraries with the rangers.

– For all information, to book for a hiking trip, and for one of the 'basic' campgrounds located in the Grand Canyon, you can write to the **Back Country Reservations Office**, PO Box 129, Grand Canyon, AZ 86023.

– If you plan to spend the night in the canyon, you must buy a permit ($20 plus $4 per person). They are only available by post from the above address or on the spot (not by telephone). It is advisable to reserve at least four months in advance. The Back Country Office, in the Maswick Transportation Lodge, is open 8am–noon and 1–5pm. You do not need a permit if you are planning to return the same day or if you sleep at Phantom Ranch.

– Don't forget that a trip on foot into the canyon takes things in the opposite order to what you're used to with mountaineering. First you go down when you're fresh, and then you come back up again, when you're . . . knackered!

– Allow at least eight hours for the descent into the canyon and the return hike to the top. If you're very fit it may only take four hours to get down to the Colorado and back, but on average, people take seven or eight hours. Consequently, it is often preferable to spend a night at the bottom and tackle the ascent first thing in the morning when it is cooler and the cliffs are swathed in a magnificent array of colours in the light of the rising sun.

– For the descent, take only provisions and water (at least 1 gallon/4.5 litres per person), plus some packets of salt, which are on sale at the top (the salt is very important). The temperature can reach 115°F/49°C in high summer, so you must watch out for dehydration. Apart from that, limit your equipment to the absolute minimum. Lighten your load if possible by using the left-luggage facilities at Bright Angel Lodge (*see* 'Where to Stay').

– In order to protect yourself against the sun, it's vital to cover your whole body, including your arms, and to wear a wide-brimmed hat. Smother any exposed parts with a factor 25 or 30 sunblock.

– All the walking trips in the canyon can be done without a guide, but leaving the trails is strictly forbidden.

– If you'd like to eat or sleep in the cabins at **Phantom Ranch**, at the bottom of the canyon, you'll have to book a long time in advance, especially in summer. ☎ (303) 297-2757. Or you can go directly to the Bright Angel transportation desk at Bright Angel Lodge, between 6am and 7pm (*see* 'Where to Stay').

– The same applies if you want to camp at the bottom of the canyon at Phantom Ranch. A very heavy fine will be levied if you set up without a permit. The campground at the bottom of the gorge has a nice atmosphere in the evening.

ITINERARIES IN THE CANYON

You will pass through several geological eras as you travel through the 4,900ft (1,500m) of altitude, so the landscape is absolutely fantastic. Ultra-light equipment is essential. Remember that while you *can* complete the descent to the bottom of the Grand Canyon and the climb back out again in one day, it's dangerous and the rangers advise against it.

FIRST ITINERARY: BRIGHT ANGEL TRAIL

This is the most popular trail of all, twisting down from Bright Angel Lodge to the bottom of the canyon. Note that the distances given below refer only to a one-way trip and you should bear in mind that you have to be in good physical shape before going on this hike; the route is long (especially the way back) and the climb is hard. If you want a foretaste of the canyon without going all the way to the bottom, you could walk as far as Indian Gardens and Plateau Point (*see below*). The various stages in the itinerary are as follows:

– 1.5 miles (2.5km): **water** at the first resthouse, May–September.

– 3 miles (5km): **water** at the second resthouse, May–September.

– 4.5 miles (7km): **Indian Gardens**. Allow four to six hours for the return journey without making any stops. It can easily be done in a day as long as you don't overreach yourself, although it is also possible to camp here. This is a real oasis about half-way down, and where there are often deer in the evening. Also a water fountain and toilets.

– 6 miles (10km): **Plateau Point**. This is an easy path on the intermediary plateau from Indian Gardens, but note that it is a dead-end. Well worth pushing on this far, as there's a superb view over the river. An excellent place to stop before setting out on the ascent. The view is more beautiful half-way down the path and you may perhaps decide not to continue right to the bottom of the gorge. In any case, if you have got this far you won't really have time – since you'll need to go back along the path to Indian Gardens before continuing the descent to the Colorado. From there, the return to the upper plateau (4–6 hours' walk) is particularly difficult in the full heat of the summer sun.

– 8 miles (13km): **Colorado River**. The last part of the descent, from Indian Gardens to the Colorado, is fairly steep. If you have time, you might decide to spend the night at the campground on the plateau before continuing. Otherwise, the descent from the South Rim can easily be done in a day (particularly if you leave out the detour via Plateau Point). The river doesn't come into view until almost the last moment. After following the banks for a while you cross a big iron bridge, which brings you to Phantom Ranch (and the Bright Angel campsite). No swimming as the current is very strong.

☗ It's a good idea to rest and sleep at **Phantom Ranch**, at the bottom of the canyon, after a 'stroll' of 8 miles (13km) from the South Rim. It's quite expensive to have a shower and sleep in this impeccable, air-conditioned dormitory (outside, in August, it's 105°F/40°C at night) as it costs $21 per person – but that's not bad considering how

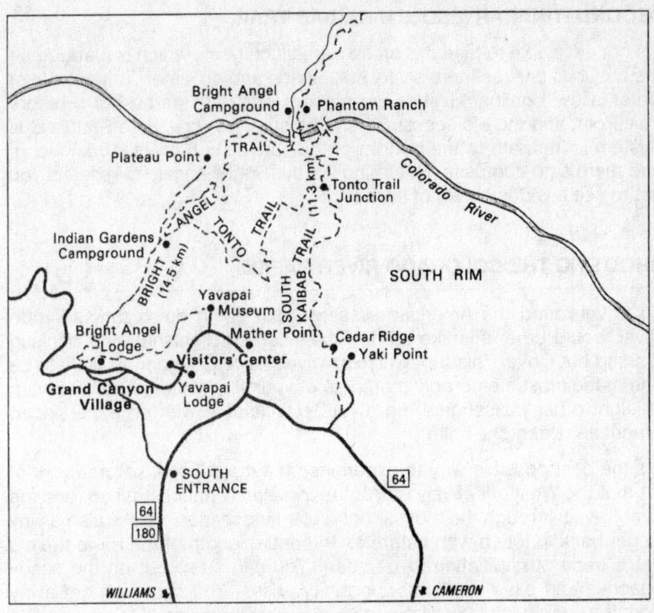

WALKS IN COLORADO (EAST RIM)

isolated it is. A good (although short) night's rest means you can get underway again the following morning at 4am and be back at the top by midday. Food at the bottom of the gorge is quite pricey. Breakfast is $12, a picnic lunch $7.50 and the two dinner options (stew or steak) cost $17 and $27 respectively. Reserve a minimum of a few hours in advance if you want to eat in the hostel or sleep in the dormitory at Phantom Ranch, and several weeks in advance (months in busy periods) for other accommodation. For further information, *see* 'Advice if you're going to the bottom of the Canyon'.

☗ If you go right down to the bottom and climb back via the North Rim, be prepared for a two-day climb in conditions that can at times be arduous. There's a **campground** on the trail. Get information from the rangers before organizing your trek.

Fancy jogging across?

The record time for jogging across the Grand Canyon, from the South Rim to the North Rim – a distance of 21 miles (33.5km) – is just three hours.

SECOND ITINERARY: SOUTH KAIBAB TRAIL

It's not advisable to take this steep and difficult trail, which is harder than the previous one, as there's very little shade and no water. Take plenty of water (allow 1 gallon/4.5 litres per person). The path starts shortly before Yaki Point and there's access by shuttle bus only (*see* 'Free Shuttle Bus System'). The path to the bottom of the canyon is 6 miles (10 km) long, and there's no campsite. Returning via the Bright Angel Trail means you get to see a wider variety of scenery.

SHOOTING THE COLORADO RIVER RAPIDS

To travel round the American West without going down the Colorado River would be a little like touring the Scottish Highlands and drinking nothing but Coke. This trip, which involves no real danger, is likely to be one of the most memorable moments of your life. You do the trip with up to eight other passengers, on a rubber inflatable with an experienced American pilot at the helm.

It's the best possible way to experience the magnificent natural work of art that the West effectively is. You're completely unconstrained, and the river travels through the most spectacular landscapes. This is also a way to get back in touch with nature as the entire length of the route there's not a trace of civilization to be seen. You can sleep out on the sandy beaches and eat when the opportunity arises. You can even get away from the river for a stroll, where there are other landscapes to admire. Out West, the rivers are inevitably punctuated by rapids, which adds to the thrill.

These river trips are organized and led by specialist American companies. Your travelling companions are likely to be a complete mixed bag of nationalities and types, which somehow adds to the attraction. Trips last from one day to one week and it won't be terribly expensive.

– Note: descents of the Colorado River canyon depart from Marble Canyon (Lee's Ferry) near Page (in Arizona), which is upstream, and not from Grand Canyon Village. You can also do the descent of the Colorado from Moab, which is further north, in Utah.

– **An important detail**: it's practically impossible to get a place without booking two months in advance. *See* Visitors' Center under 'Useful Addresses'.

SHOOTING THE COLORADO RIVER RAPIDS WITH NATIVE AMERICANS

Offered by the only company belonging to a Native American tribe, this excursion is the cheapest of the one- or two-day rafting trips. The Colorado crosses the territory of the reservation and the whole south bank of the Grand Canyon is the property of the 'people of the great pines' – the Hualapai. Although there were more than 100,000 of them in the 1800s, there are only around 1,100 today. For several years, a handful of these Native Americans has taken to business in the American style, organizing short rafting trips inside the gorges of the Grand Canyon. They look after all the logistics and cook you a giant breakfast at the bottom of the canyon, on a beach of fine sand where you spend a night in the open air (or in a tent if you prefer). A fantastic expedition.

– **Hualapai River Runners / Hualapai Reservations**: PO Box 538, Peach Springs, AZ 86434. Freephone: ☎ 1-888-255-9550. Fax: (520) 769-2372. Website: www.arizonaguide.com/grandcanyonwest. Reservations are also taken for the new Hualapai Lodge in Peach Springs, on the old Route 66. It's quite sensible to sleep there the night before your trip.

WHAT TO TAKE ON A TRIP DOWN THE COLORADO RIVER

– A light tent or bivvy bag (storms are frequent in summer). You can generally hire a sleeping bag and a tent on the spot.

– a light waterproof

– sunscreen

– mosquito repellent

– hat

– sunglasses

– swimming costume

– shoes that you can wear in water

– long-sleeved shirt

THE HAVASUPAI RESERVATION

Just over 30 miles (50 km) as the crow flies to the west of Grand Canyon Village, the Havasupai reservation encompasses a vast tract of land adjoining the national park, on both sides of the river Havasu, which runs into the Colorado. To the west is the immense Hualapai reservation, with which the Havasupai have close connections. In times gone by, the tribe was semi-nomadic, cultivating their fields within the canyon in summer and hunting along its banks in the winter. Today, there are only about 430 members of the tribe, making it one of the smallest tribes in the United States. The majority live in the single village of Supai, which can only be reached on foot or on horseback. The path is 8 miles (13 km) long and descends fairly steeply into the gorge (allow 3–4 hours' walk).

The reservation is open to tourists and is very well known for its delightful waterfalls and the turquoise pools formed by the river Havasu. These natural features gave the tribe their name – Havasupai means 'people of the emerald water'.

There is a fairly expensive hotel in the village of Supai, the **Havasupai Lodge** (no credit cards and you need to reserve well in advance). 2 miles (3km) further on, nearer to the waterfalls, is a campsite with 400 pitches. For all information, contact Havasupai Tourist Enterprises, Supai, AZ 86435. ☎ 448-2141 for the tourist office or ☎ 448-2111 for information on accommodation.

★ THE NORTH RIM

Shunned by the tourist masses (only 10 per cent of visitors to the Grand Canyon come here), the North Rim nevertheless has its own attractions. Depending on what you want to do, you may prefer it to the South Rim.

On the plus side: it's much less crowded and much more intimate, the road going there is fringed by forests of fir trees and wide prairies, and it's higher in altitude, at 7,900 feet (2,400m) as against 6,600 feet (2,000m) at the South Rim. The trail going down to the Colorado is more pastoral, even shaded in places.

On the minus side: it's more difficult to get to, the altitude means cooler nights, the view is a little less impressive and it's often closed until the beginning, or even the middle of May. Trekkers have to make a choice: the trail down to the bottom is 14 miles (23km) long from the North Rim, whereas the distance from the South Rim is only 9 miles (14km). If you want to go down and come back up using the same trail, the latter is therefore the better option. If, on the other hand, your intention is to go down one side and climb up the other, go down from the north. It's your choice.

USEFUL INFORMATION

✉ **Post office**: at Grand Canyon Lodge

■ **Camper Store**: at the entrance to the North Rim Campground. Open 8am–8pm. Quite limited range of goods, but they also sell wood and some camping items.

■ **Shower and washing machines**: 100 yards (90 metres) from the North Rim Campground. Open daily, 8am–8pm.

– At the entrance to the park, get the little park journal, which describes all the routes, as well as having a map of the canyon.

WHERE TO STAY

There's a campground and a lodge within the park, near the canyon.

North Rim Campground: very near the canyon, on the right, 1 mile (1.5km) before the end of the road. It closes on 15 October. Situated under great majestic pines, it is quiet and well equipped and operates a system of payment by envelope. There's a shower and washing machine (available daily, 7am–9pm) and a grocery store nearby. Make your booking with Biospherics (*see* 'How to Book a Room / Site at a Campground').

☆☆☆ EXPENSIVE

Grand Canyon Lodge: booking well in advance is advised: ☎ (801) 586-7686. Open 14 May–21 October. The Lodge is right on the edge of the cliff, so there's an impressive view from the terrace. Sunrise and sunset here are quite unique. The accommodation is in nice little well-equipped timber shacks that are spread out in a green space. Quite expensive, but very good value for money and as romantic a place as you could wish for. There's also a restaurant: with very good cuisine at reasonable prices.

Kaibab Lodge: 18 miles (29km) north of the North Rim. ☎ 638-2389. Open May–October only. This lodge has a good reputation and has a 'trapper' atmosphere. The welcome is good and the prices are fairly reasonable (about $60 for a couple), which makes it more expensive than the Grand Canyon Lodge. It's often full during the summer rush. The restaurant is average and expensive.

WHERE TO STAY OUTSIDE THE PARK

☗ **De Motte Park Campground**: 5 miles (8km) north of the park boundary, in the Kaibab National Forest. It's managed by the Park and is open in summer only. It's cheap and well equipped. No booking.

☗ **Jacob Lake Campground**: just 45 miles (72km) from the park. This, too, is open in summer only. Freephone: ☎ 1-800-283-2267.

WHERE TO EAT

✕ **Canyon Lodge Cafeteria**: serves breakfasts at modest prices. The meals in the restaurant are delicious, but more expensive. The view through the large bay windows overlooking the canyon is breathtaking.

WHAT TO DO

– **Bright Angel Trail**: this short, 15-minute trail starts from Grand Canyon Lodge and goes out along a narrow rock-face shaped like the prow of a ship. The view is indescribable – see it at both sunset and sunrise.

– **Transept Trail**: joins the previous trail, but starts from the North Rim Campground.

– **North Kaibab Trail**: starts about a mile (1.6km) north of the campground and is signposted. This trail goes right to the bottom, down to the Colorado River. Since the whole thing is about 14 miles (23km), most visitors content themselves with a small section of it. For a half-day walk, you can go down as far as the small bridge in 1 hour 45 minutes (but allow 2 hours 30 minutes for the return). If you want a whole day's trek (6–8 hours), you can go to Roaring Springs and back, which is 9 miles (15km) in all. If you want to go right to the bottom, discuss it with the rangers. You must book your place in a campground in advance. Some people do the descent in a day, but the rangers advise you to take two days. The climb back up via the South Rim takes a day.

– **Cape Royal**: about 23 miles (37km) from the campground. A small trail leads to a platform that looks out over the canyon and it's the only point on the North Rim from where you can see the Colorado River. The panorama is amazing.

– **Imperial Point**: another viewing point, different again from the others.

THE NATIVE AMERICAN RESERVATIONS

If you'd like to meet the Native Americans (don't call them Indians – the term has been completely replaced), it's not difficult as they're everywhere.

Bear in mind that the Native Americans will just be the way they are, so don't be in a hurry to decide that they're 'not very welcoming' or 'reserved' if they don't roll out the red carpet for you. They won't be trying to please or attract you.

Leave all your stereotypes behind, and above all, learn to live in Native American time.

If a Native American invites you in, you'll realize that he doesn't open his mouth unless he has something to say, that he's averse to negative turns of phrase, and that you'll need to speak the same kind of English as the Native Americans use.

In his novel *Sacred Clowns,* Tony Hillerman took inspiration from something that really happened: in John Ford's film *Cheyenne Autumn*, the Cheyenne were in fact played by Navajos, although the Navajos don't normally have anything to do with the Cheyenne. When the scenes were shot, the 'pseudo-Cheyenne', speaking in tones and making expressions that perfectly suited the script, exchanged coarse jokes in Navajo and made remarks that bore no relation to the film, which of course weren't in the script!

THE NAVAJO

The Navajo reservation is the largest Native American reservation in the US. Situated in the northern part of Arizona and extending into Utah and New Mexico, it is both the territory of about half of the 150,000 members of the Navajo nation, and the setting for those marvellous scenic pearls called Monument Valley and the Canyon de Chelly.

From the Grand Canyon, Route 64 heading east leads to Navajo territory. From Tuba City, you have a choice: Route 160 to Kayenta and Monument Valley, or Route 264 (which crosses the Hopi reservation) for Chelly or Gallup. These sections are dealt with later. You'll need to fill up with fuel, and cash, as there's no bank at either reservation. The Hopi reservation is set within the much larger Navajo reservation. The two tribes have difficulty living together without clashing, because their cultures are totally different: the Hopi are sedentary farmers while the Navajo are traditionally nomadic hunters.

The Navajo customarily will not look you in the eye when speaking to you. This is initially quite disconcerting, but just do likewise. The Navajo don't eat fish, which they believe to cause choking, and they have no interest in competing with their neighbours. Nor do they believe in the hereafter – after death comes oblivion.

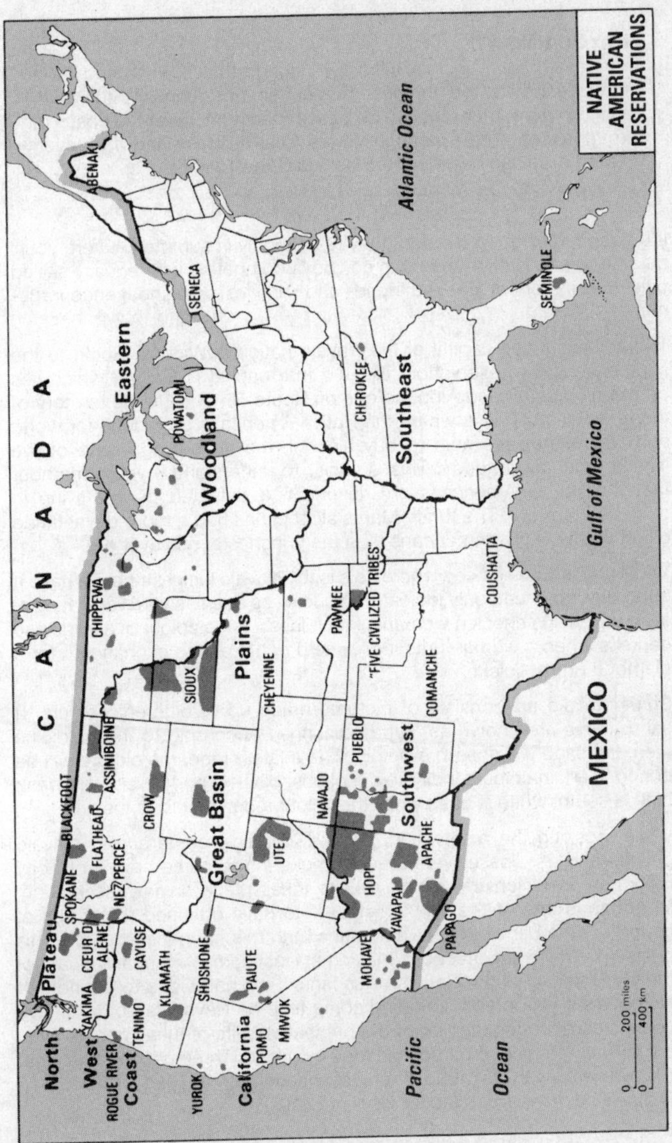

NATIVE AMERICAN RESERVATIONS

NATIVE AMERICAN RESERVATIONS

DID YOU KNOW?
The Navajo have such a difficult language that it was used as a secret weapon by the American Secret Services during World War II, enabling secret messages to be transmitted right under the noses of the Japanese. The operation was a total success and they even created a Navajo battalion, the Navajo Code Talkers.

It's good fun to go to a rodeo (they're held only in summer), where you'll be able to see Native American cowboys competing with equally skilled palefaces in front of amused friends and relatives, who shout encouragement.

The administrative capital of the Navajo nation is Window Rock, to the southeast of the reservation. But the true capital is Gallup, which lies between Flagstaff and Albuquerque on Route 66, outside the territory of the reservation. This is where the Native Americans go to look for work, and where they are able to buy alcohol, the underlying cause of the Native American tragedy. This is easier to understand if you remember that the Native Americans are, in effect, a defeated people living in occupied territory. The White Man's alcohol has had a more devastating effect on the Native Americans than the Winchester rifle ever did.

You'll see turquoise everywhere: this is the Navajo lucky stone. To have a good day, you need only look at a turquoise as soon as you wake. It also, allegedly, helps check a woman's faithfulness. If the colour of a turquoise darkens when a woman puts it on, she'd better ask to exchange it for a diamond pretty quick!

Some Navajo art consists of pictures made up of different colours of sand, these are known as 'sand paintings'. According to the medicine men, the sand will absorb evil spirits. At a later stage, the picture will be buried. Certain colours indicate directions: black is north; yellow is west; blue is south; white is east, while the colour red symbolizes the sun.

While crossing the reservation, you will certainly come across Navajo police vehicles. These were made famous in the crime novels of Tony Hillerman, in which the action always takes place on the reservation. Hillerman is one of the few 'palefaces' to have obtained the status of honorary member of the Navajo nation, and this happened because his bestsellers have succeeded in making at least some Americans aware of the social reality of the Native Americans. It's a good idea to get hold of his novels if you intend spending some time on Navajo land. It will give you a clearer understanding of the present-day life of these people, who are virtually displaced persons in their own land. Three popular titles are: *Skinwalkers* (with its atmosphere of witchcraft), *A Thief of Time* and *Dance Hall of the Dead* (about Hopi magic).

THE HOPI TERRITORY

AREA CODE: 602

Entirely surrounded by Navajo territory, the Hopi reserve is home to only 10,000 souls. Despite the beauty of its landscapes and although a small road, Route 264, runs across it, the reserve receives relatively few tourists. In fact, the Navajo seem to monopolize the available visitors, who travel to visit Monument Valley and the Canyon de Chelly. In the Hopi territory, you will at least find some peace and quiet, and the Hopi way of life, which is less affected by tourism than that of the Navajo, seems a little more authentic. Excellent farmers, the Hopi have some very advanced techniques for cultivation on arid terrain. The reservation covers three plateaux, or *mesas*. There's a village of little houses made of stone perched on every plateau.

Their oral tradition seems to confirm that the Hopis, who are known to have originally come from Tierra del Fuego, really are the closest descendents of the ancient Anasazis, who suddenly disappeared towards the end of the 13th century. When the Spanish invaded, they brought with them the terrible plague of smallpox, and the ensuing epidemic killed off two-thirds of the Hopi population. Using the horses imported by the Europeans, the Navajo, fierce warriors, carried out fearsome raids on the Hopi.

Hopi women are renowned for their curious hairstyle, known as the 'butterfly'. A great Hopi culinary tradition is *piki* bread – this is a pancake made from maize and it's green in colour. The few bread ovens that have been handed down from their ancestors are now used only during summer festivals.

It is not possible to go and watch Hopi religious ceremonies, which often take place in their ceremonial caves (*kivas*), as their religion is still secret. This, at least, is something that the whites can't steal from them. Hopi dolls or *katchinas* are at the heart of their religion. Symbols of supernatural spirits, the dolls are used for educating their children in traditional beliefs.

WHERE TO STAY

TUBA CITY (NAVAJO TERRITORY)

☆ BUDGET

Greyhills Inn Hostel: as you come in from the west on Route 160, be careful not to go towards the city centre. Continue straight on towards Kayenta to a small bridge – not much more than a metal walkway that crosses the road. The hostel is the first on the left and is well signposted. Reservations: ☎ 283-4450, or write to Hotel Management Program, Greyhills Academy High School, PO Box 160, Tuba City, AZ 86045. Open all year. At weekends, closed until 4pm. They have very well kept double rooms for rent in a school residence, costing about $46 for two. If you have a Youth Hostelling Association card it costs $22 for one and $32 for two in a private room. Communal bathroom. Good place for meeting people and a good welcome.

☆☆☆ EXPENSIVE

Tuba Motel Quality Inn: Main Street and Moenave Avenue ☎ 283-4545. Freephone: ☎ 1-800-644-8383. The only hotel in town. Rooms are large, comfortable, and well decorated. It's expensive for two ($90 for one bed and $95 for two), but curiously not much dearer for four ($110). Remember that you also have to add on the local tax, which is 14 per cent. The Mexican–American restaurant next door (The Hogan) has a decent enough salad-bar. Also next door is a Native American shop. Built in 1870, the trading post was a commercial link between the Native Americans and the Palefaces in the heyday of the Old West.

SECOND MESA

☗ **Campground**: you can camp beside the motel at the Hopi Cultural Center. There's no infrastructure or equipment, but the space is free. This is the only place in the reserve where camping is allowed.

☗ **Motel at the Hopi Cultural Center**: on the left-hand side of Route 264, about 5 miles (8km) before Second Mesa. Keep a sharp eye open for a brown wooden sign. ☎ 734-2401. Fax: 734-2435. This is the only hotel in the Hopi reservation, run exclusively by Native Americans. It's quite expensive, but every room has a double bed, WC and private bathroom. Under 12s go free. The place is often full. There's a Hopi museum and cafe in the same building, where you can get breakfast.

WHERE TO EAT

✕ **The restaurant at the Hopi Cultural Center** is good and cheap. There are salads plus American dishes, but this is a good chance to try Hopi cuisine: chilli, pancakes and doughnuts with honey. Note, however, that there's no alcohol. The nearest beer is way off the reservation: about 80 miles (130km) away, but the distance makes the most insipid American beer seem like the finest drink in the world.

WHAT TO SEE

Note: taking photographs, whether of the landscape or of the inhabitants, is absolutely prohibited on Hopi territory – they've had quite enough of other folk making money out of them. And you can't record their music, draw their villages or their dances, or even take notes. They take this ban seriously, and so should you.

★ **Walpi**: this is the most beautiful and astonishing of the Hopi villages. It's up on the heights of First Mesa, away from Route 264, on the left as you come in from the west, and not easy to find, because it's poorly signed. It's a little after Polacca, coming from Second Mesa (at the exit from Polacca going up Walpi). Imagine a stone-built village without any water or electricity, perched on the hillside and inhabited by only eight Native Americans! At the foot of Walpi, the plains stretch as far as the eye can see. The village, date unknown but certainly earlier than the 15th century, looks as though it hasn't changed a bit since it was built, with its crooked little houses, a well, and crumbling old stairways.

Note: your tour must be in the company of a Native American guide. You have to leave your car at the entrance to the village and go to the **municipal office.** Open 9.30am–5pm (in principle). For information: ☎ 737-2670. Free, but it's a good idea to leave a donation for the community – they do need it. The tour lasts 40 minutes. There's some beautiful pottery on sale in the village, made by local craftsmen.

★ Other villages to visit if you have time: **Shungopavi** and **Mishongnovi** (Second Mesa) and, above all, **Old Oraibi** (Third Mesa). This is thought to be the oldest inhabited village in the US, since it was probably built a century before the birth of Christ.

★ **Hopi Museum**: in the cultural centre at Second Mesa. Open Monday–Friday 8am–5pm; Saturday and Sunday 9am–3pm. Closed weekends in winter. Admission charge. The museum brings together the history of the Hopi, based on evidence from archaeological digs, and displays traditional crafts, such as pottery, basket-making and jewellery. Marvellous collection of photographs by Edward Curtis, who spent his life photographing the Native Americans.

– Find out about the **dances**. These take place almost every weekend. They are very important for the Hopi and every village organizes demonstrations of dancing that are open to the public (although not all of them are). One of the best known is the Snake Dance. The Hopi, dressed in jeans, arrive in their big, dilapidated cars. The older generation sit on folding stools around the village square drinking Coke. Suddenly, a group of about twenty dancers, musicians and clowns turn up wearing costumes and masks. You might not understand much of what is going on, but it's very absorbing and gives you the impression of what life was like over a hundred years ago.

CANYON DE CHELLY

AREA CODE: 520

A Spanish place-name, approximately pronounced 'Canyon di Ché', this place is halfway between Gallup and Monument Valley, right in the middle of the Navajo reserve. You can get here via Chinle, a big, sprawling village on Route 191.

The canyon is a magnificent fault line that cuts through the desert plain as though it had been slashed by a giant dagger. Apart from its undeniable beauty, the major point of interest is its scale. In contrast to the Grand Canyon, where you can't help but feel shaken by its gigantic size, this is a canyon that you can take in at a single glance. You can clearly see how the rocks have been eroded, how the river-bed was formed, and how the people living in this curious valley have organized their lives. On the floor of the canyon there are tiny, verdant fields.

Unlike other canyons, this one has been inhabited for thousands of years. Here there are the ruined villages of the Anasazi, who were the first occupants of the region and whom the Navajo refer to respectfully as their ancestors. The unusual feature of these villages, like those at Mesa Verde National Park in Colorado, is that they were built in caves, flush with the rock face. You can also see a number of pictograms engraved on the rock.

The light here is at its most glorious in the late afternoon. The canyon is also the place where the infamous Kit Carson won his final battle against the Navajo, having starved them out.

In order to get a clear idea of how the canyon is laid out and how to get around it, call at the Visitors' Center.

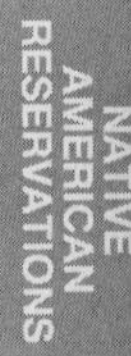

USEFUL ADDRESSES

ℹ Visitors' Center: at the entrance to the park. ☎ 674-5500. Open 8am–6pm (5pm winter). Nearby are a small **Native American Museum** and a 'hogan', a traditional Navajo dwelling. Rangers give explanatory talks, and a Camp Fire Program takes place around a wood fire at 9pm each day, sometimes with Navajo music. Admission is free. Ask for the programme of events, and for a map of the canyon, which will help you keep your bearings while walking.

■ **Justin's Horse Rental**: in the park, at the entrance to South Rim Drive. ☎ 674-5678. Riding is on Native American horses and it's charged by the hour (two hours minimum). A very pleasant ride. Only the 7am rides go all the way to the bottom of the canyon. It's advisable to book the previous day. The horses that they use are small, which is fine for beginners.

■ **Canyon Hiking Service**: 440 yards (400 metres) from the Visitors' Center, at the start of South Rim Road in the park. Ernest Jones is a guide authorized by the National Park Service. A devotee of the canyon, he organizes a variety of trips for hikers, including both day- and night-time walks. Booking is essential. Reasonable prices.

WHERE TO STAY

Cottonwood Campground: 0.5 mile (1km) south of the Visitors' Center. It's free and no booking necessary as it's first-come-first-served. Shaded, very quiet and pleasant. There are tables and toilets. Mobile homes are not accepted. Sometimes mosquitoes in summer. There's no shower, but you can have one for $1 at the Chapter House in Chinle, 1 mile (1.5km) before the Visitors' Center (open Monday–Friday 8am–5pm).

☆☆☆ EXPENSIVE

Holiday Inn: ☎ 674-5000. Fax: 674-8264. On the left, 500 yards (460 metres) from the Visitors' Center as you come from Chinle. A recent building, in Native American style, with a restaurant and a Native American shop. Navajo dances are performed in the evening beside the swimming pool Monday–Friday.

Thunderbird Lodge: just over 0.5 mile (1km) south of the Visitors' Center. Booking is strongly advised in summer: ☎ 674-5841. Native American-style architecture in brick tones. The lodge is less expensive than the motel, but it still comes close to the price of a three-star hotel. Truck tours of the canyon are available, and the half-day one is probably long enough.

Canyon de Chelly Inn Best Western: at Chinle. ☎ 674-5875. Less well located than the others because it's near the road, right in the centre. It's comfortable, but doesn't have a lot of charm. Restaurant and indoor swimming pool. Cheaper than the Thunderbird, but pretty pricey all the same.

– If everything's full up, your next best bet is in Gallup, just over the border in New Mexico.

NAVAJOLAND

WHERE TO EAT

✕ **Cafeteria at the Thunderbird Lodge**: a self-service with standard dishes and some Navajo specialities. Open 6.30am–9pm. Reasonable food and not very expensive.

WHAT TO SEE

The Canyon de Chelly National Park is in fact two canyons joined at the western end: the Canyon del Muerto (North Rim Drive) and the Canyon de Chelly proper (South Rim Drive). A road follows the contour of each rim of the canyon.

There are three ways to tour the site:

– Take one of the two roads that go around both canyons (Route 64 or Route 7) and enjoy the viewpoints, which give breathtaking views of the canyon. This is the simplest route but, unless you have powerful binoculars, you'll have difficulty distinguishing the Anasazi ruins, never mind the pictograms! If you don't have a lot of time, you can approach the canyon from above only, via the road. The most beautiful viewpoints can be found on the road that goes along the South Rim.

– Only one trail is open to you if you want to go to the bottom of the canyon on your own: the **White House Trail**. It leaves Route 7 South Rim from one of the viewpoints (see the map issued at the Visitors' Center). You'll need about two hours for the return trip. You won't need a guide, but make sure you take a supply of water, and a hat to ward off the heat. This marvellous 3-mile (5km) trail ends at a river that you can cross by a ford in order to reach one of the most beautiful ruins in the canyon. This is **White House**, an old village built in adobe and suspended from one of the canyon walls. Don't forget to obey the prohibition on going elsewhere: the Navajo rangers are watching!

– More expensive, but also more worthwhile, is to do a **group visit** with a Navajo guide. This is the only way to really see both canyons, because (with the exception of the trail described above) they're out of bounds unless you are accompanied by a guide. There are two reasons for this prohibition: first, some Navajo families still live at the bottom of the canyons, cultivating patches of land. And second, and more important, damage to the ruins and the pictograms has endangered the precious legacy of the Native Americans. It is for this reason that the Navajo prefer to keep control over the site, which in any case belongs to them and not, as you might suppose, to the national parks.

The guided tour is carried out either on horseback, on foot, or in a 4x4 vehicle. For contact details *see* 'Useful Addresses'. Two routes are available: a half-day route (3 hours 30 minutes) lets you tour part of the Canyon del Muerto and the Canyon de Chelly. You'll see a dozen Anasazi villages and several pictograms. This costs about $32 per person. Don't forget your hat; water is provided. The whole-day trip lets you see the whole of both canyons, including Spider Rock, which hangs out over the Canyon de Chelly. The tours on foot and in a 4x4 are options provided by the Visitors' Center. A Navajo guide is placed at your disposal and you decide on your route in consultation with him. For the 4x4 trip, you have to have your own vehicle.

– Alternatively, some 4x4 tours are also offered by **Thunderbird Lodge**, using their vehicle. In summer you'll need to book your place (*see* 'Where to Stay').

MONUMENT VALLEY

AREA CODE: 435

Remember those great Westerns *Stagecoach, Fort Apache, Rio Grande,* and *She Wore A Yellow Ribbon*? In the foreground you had the hero on horseback and in the background a set of astonishing peaks of red rock, sometimes reaching heights of 1,000–1,300ft (300–400m). Well, that's Monument Valley, one of the most extraordinary natural phenomena in the whole of America. The play of colours, varying from pink to violet, is especially gorgeous at sunrise and sunset, and you could be forgiven for imagining that you were in the middle of a Western film-set. The landscape hasn't changed at all since the days when the Pony Express passed through.

The valley is also populated by Navajos, who live by agriculture and sheep farming as well as by selling crafts, silver jewellery and woven blankets. Even now they live, as their ancestors did, in hogans made of wood, twigs and clay, and carry out their daily work in accordance with their ancestral traditions, taking part in the rites still kept up by the medicine man, and creating sand paintings. To see more, go and have a drink in the Golden Sands, for example, one of the pubs in Kayenta.

HOW TO GET THERE

There's no access by bus. There's a small admission charge ($2.50), even if you have a 'Golden Eagle' card. The entrance to Monument Valley is on Route 163, between Kayenta and Mexican Hat, just after you leave Arizona and enter Utah. At the crossroads if you're coming from the south, one road bears off left to Goulding's Lodge, the other to the reservation. Note that there's no admission to the park after 6.30pm.

It's helpful to get a fix on distances and travelling times. The following distances will help you plan your visit to Monument Valley.

DISTANCES FROM PRINCIPAL PLACES

– **Arches National Park** (Utah): 149 miles (240km) (from the entrance)

– **Bryce Canyon National Park** (Utah): 269 miles (433km) (from the entrance)

– **Canyon de Chelly** (Arizona): 109 miles (175km), via Route 59 (the shortest way)

– **Canyonlands** (Utah): 138 miles (222km) (from The Needles)

– **Capitol Reef National Park** (Utah): 189 miles (305km)

– **Flagstaff** (Arizona): 180 miles (291km)

– **Grand Canyon Village** (Arizona): 186 miles (300km)

– **Kayenta** (Arizona): 24 miles (38km)

– **Las Vegas** (Nevada): 386 miles (621km) (via St George)

– **Mesa Verde National Park** (Colorado): 119 miles (193km) via Bluff

– **Mexican Hat** (Utah): 21 miles (33km)

– **Moab** (Utah): 144 miles (232km)

– **Page** (Arizona): 119 miles (192km)

– **Panguitch** (Utah): 267 miles (430km)

– **Salt Lake City** (Utah): 376 miles (605km) (via Moab)

– **St George** (Utah): 270 miles (435km)

– **Zion National Park** (Utah): 240 miles (387km)

TIME DIFFERENCE

There's a time difference of one hour between Arizona and neighbouring Utah. When it's 5pm at Kayenta, Arizona, it's 6pm at Monument Valley, Utah. Bear this in mind when organizing bookings and trips.

MONUMENT VALLEY AND THE MOVIES

Monument Valley is a legendary place in the history of the cinema. If the image of its ochre and red rocky peaks towering over an immense desert plateau has become known around the world, it's thanks to the many Westerns made there by John Ford. Of the 140 films shot by Ford between 1917 and 1966, nine were made in Monument Valley, the most sumptuous of all natural sets. 'I'm a peasant who makes peasant movies', he liked to say.

It all began with an encounter in 1938 between Harry Goulding and John Ford. Goulding, who lived at Goulding's Lodge in Monument Valley, showed photographs of the site to the director. Fired with enthusiasm, John Ford immediately decided to make *Stagecoach* there, in 1939, with John Wayne in the main role. After World War II, during which he served in the US Navy, Ford returned to Monument Valley in 1946 to shoot *My Darling Clementine* with Henry Fonda and Linda Darnell. This film, which revived the story of the OK Corral, has been filmed about 50 times by Hollywood. Ford gave John Wayne the starring role in three of his most famous Westerns, all shot at Monument Valley: *Fort Apache* in 1948; *She Wore A Yellow Ribbon* in 1949; and *Rio Grande* in 1950.

These three masterpieces form a trilogy glorifying the US Cavalry. Naturally, the Native Americans were always left to pick up the pieces. It was in these Westerns that John Wayne forged his legend as 'Man of the West' – he was frank, unceremonious, not an intellectual giant, perhaps, but fearless, honest and resolute – in short, the archetypal American good guy. And Monument Valley became a legendary place in movie history.

Continuing in the same vein, and carried along by his international success, John Ford made further use of his favourite setting. In 1950 he filmed *Wagon Master* here, and in 1956 came *The Searchers*, with John Wayne and Natalie Wood. *Sergeant Rutledge* followed in 1960 and *Cheyenne Autumn* in 1964, with James Stewart and Carroll Baker. Ford frequently used the Navajos as extras, and a local medicine man, Hosteen Tso, served as weatherman during the shooting.

This raw natural setting still continues to attract movie directors. In *The Eiger Sanction* (1975), Clint Eastwood is seen anxiously climbing the 895-foot (273m) expanse of Totem Rock, and it was used as a location for scenes in *Back To The Future III* and *Forrest Gump*. Nowadays, Monument Valley also receives film crews for a seemingly endless succession of advertisements.

USEFUL ADDRESSES

ℹ Monument Valley Visitor Center: 800 yards (730 metres) beyond the entrance to the park. ☎ 727-3287. Fax: 727-3353. Postal address: Monument Valley Navajo Tribal Park, PO Box 360289, Monument Valley, Utah 84536. Open daily, 8am–5pm October–April, 8am–7pm July and August and 8am–6.30pm May, June and September.

Here are the golden rules for getting along with the locals in Native American territory: don't be in too much of a hurry, stay polite, and always keep in good humour.

There's a counter with a complete list of the companies providing 4x4 tours and trips on horseback. In this centre you can also see a small exhibition on Navajo traditions, and there's a cafeteria and snack shop, clean toilets, a stamp machine, a souvenir shop, as well as an ice-machine (costing $2 per bag).

There is a **cash machine** in Monument Valley at the Conoco station, next to Goulding's Lodge, and a big, brand new **supermarket** just opposite.

Kayenta Visitor Center: in Kayenta, on route 160, in the direction of Tuba City and Page, between the Conoco station and Burger King. ☎ 697-3572. They offer organized tours of the valley but they aren't really up to much.

There's a **cash machine** in Basha's supermarket behind the Visitor Center. There's a **Coin-op Laundry** in town, on the right-hand side of route 163, as you come in from the south, just after Cafe Amigo. It's open 6am–10.30pm.

WHERE TO STAY AND WHERE TO EAT

IN MONUMENT VALLEY (UTAH)

☆–☆☆ BUDGET TO MODERATE

Mitten View Campground: beside the Visitor Center, inside the park. ☎ 727-3287. A pitch in this extremely well located campsite costs $10. That's a bargain – if you can ignore the large numbers of visitors who start to converge from 8am. As would be expected in the middle of the desert, there's not much shade and it's very dusty when the wind gets up. Sanitary facilities and showers in the form of a traditional Navajo hogan. They don't take bookings – it's just first-come-first-served.

Monument Valley Campground: at Goulding's Lodge, opposite the road that leads to the entrance to the tribal park. A short way beyond the lodge and the Conoco station on the left. ☎ (801) 727-3235 or 727-3231. Fax: 727-3344. Open mid-March to the end of October only. A pitch costs $14 for two ($3 for each extra person). This place is quieter and more comfortable than the Mitten View Campground. The campsite is clean and has numerous pitches. It also offers a laundry, a little snack-bar, a small covered swimming pool and hot showers. You can reserve by telephone without paying a deposit – they will hold your pitch until 5pm, but no later.

Agnes Gray B&B: near the entrance to the tribal park (just over a mile (2 km) before the crossroads, as you come from Kayenta). Postal address: Navajo Basket Weavers, PO Box 360137, Monument Valley, Utah 84536. This is an opportunity to spend a night in an authentic Navajo hogan that sleeps up to 15 people. A fairly basic level of comfort – you sleep on mats and sheepskins laid on a beaten earth floor, or bring a sleeping bag – it's all very clean. Although the hogan is designed to remain cool during the day and retain heat at night, nocturnal temperatures can sometimes be on the chilly side. The owner lives in a trailer behind the hogan, and she's part of a co-operative of Navajo basket weavers. She can provide dinner and breakfast (reserve in advance). This is an interesting experience, especially with the views that you get of the sun rising and setting over Monument Valley. Prices for meals and accommodation vary depending on the number of people – generally around $30 per person per night.

✕ **Haskeneini Restaurant**: inside the Visitor Center, in the park. ☎ 727-3312. Open 7am–9pm. The name can also be transcribed as Hashké Neiniih. This is a big cafeteria that offers local specialities such as Navajo tacos (in fried bread instead of tortilla) and lamb stew, as well as various sandwiches, classic burgers and Mexican snacks. Apart from the steaks and fried chicken, everything costs around $4–$6. Credit cards are accepted.

☆☆ MODERATE

☗ ✕ **Goulding's Lodge** (and **Campground**): PO Box 360001, Monument Valley, Utah 84536. The famous Monument Valley Lodge is about 6 miles (10km) to the west of the Visitor Center. If you are coming from Kayenta, rather than turning right towards the park, turn left. It is signposted. ☎ 727-3231. Freephone: ☎ 1-800-874-0902. Fax: 727-3344. Website: www.gouldings.com. Open all year round. Several houses clustered together at the foot of a red cliff, facing out over stunning countryside – they remind you of an oasis in the heart of the desert. Here you'll find a motel, a restaurant, a swimming pool and a campground. The motel has housed whole convoys of directors, actors and movie stars. John Ford always used the same room, though it was very much more spartan then than it is now. The rooms are very comfortable – all are equipped with coffee machines and video players and have balconies opening onto the desert. There are a few videos for hire from reception ($3 each) of some of the great Westerns filmed in Monument Valley, so this is an excellent opportunity to see some of the masterpieces of the American cinema, right on the spot where they were filmed. The cost of a room changes frequently: from 1 January to 14 March it's reasonable ($62 for a double), then it gradually rises and from 1 June to 15 October, prices double to a hefty $128, although it is still worth it. Don't forget to add on the local tax, which is 17 per cent. Reservations are required up to eight months in advance for the busiest periods (May–October) although if you are lucky, you might get a place at the last minute. One-day or half-day excursions from the motel into the park.

☗ ✕ **Fire Tree Bed & Breakfast**: Diane Harris. ☎ 727-3228. Website: www.natureworksbooks.com. Postal address: PO Box 360417, Monument Valley, Utah 84536. Some miles to the west of Goulding's on the partially metalled track that runs round the Oljato mesa. Access from either side. The shortest route is to continue along the road for 4 miles (6km) after the campsite, although this is also the sandiest and least well-signposted approach. The second option is longer but more clearly marked: 11 miles (17.5 km) on a good road as far as the Oljato Trading Post, then another 3 miles (5km) after it becomes a track.

Diane Harris settled in this amazing spot 30 years ago and now runs a B&B in a Navajo hogan made of cedar branches. It sleeps two (or four at a pinch) and there are all mod cons, with air-conditioning, heating, fridge, and lots of carpets. By night you can see the stars gleaming through the opening in the roof. In the main house, there's a big, circular living room with magazines and books, and the bathroom is here. The place is open all year round, and she quite often has a vacancy, because it's so remote. Don't be put off by this – it's a really amazing place and gives a glimpse of the other side of American life. In the low season (November–March) the hogan costs $80 and April–October it's $115. It's advisable to telephone ahead. If Diane is 50 miles (80km) away in Kayenta doing her shopping, you might miss her!

✕ **Goulding's Stagecoach Restaurant**: next-door to Goulding's Lodge. Good food combining Western, Mexican and Navajo influences. Open all day 6.30am–9pm. A good meal will cost you $12–$20 per person, with drinks on top. It also serves breakfasts, such as *huevos ranchos*, with chilli and Navajo bread. Wide choice of desserts. A superb view out over the immense plain.

AT KAYENTA (ARIZONA) (AREA CODE 520)

☆–☆☆ BUDGET TO MODERATE

Rooms with local families: at Kayenta, the cheapest and most authentic places to stay are in what they call 'overnight accommodation'. This scheme was set up to tackle the shortage of accommodation in the summer months. Most of the addresses given below are, however, markedly more rudimentary than the majority of American B&Bs. A lot (but not all) are in the form of trailers. Their owners are either Navajo or American, and are not particularly well off. Some B&Bs are quite hard to find as the unsurfaced back-streets of Kayenta are like a rabbit-warren. When you phone, the proprietors will give you exact directions, and often come and fetch you. If everywhere you try is booked up, try ringing the Police Department, where they will be able to tell you if there are free rooms anywhere.

Sandy Yazzie Tsosie: ☎ (520) 697-8695. Fax: (520) 697-2160. Postal address: PO Box 1625, Kayenta, AZ 86033-1625. E-mail: SYTsosie@excite.com. As you head north on the 163, turn left just before the Best Western at an S-bend in the road. Then follow the mud track downhill to the right. Turn left almost immediately after a high brown fence. It is a small, pink, wooden house, 300 yards (275 metres) further on and to your right.

Sandy is a charming Navajo who delights in talking about her culture. She claims to prefer European guests to Americans, who she says are less interested and complain more. The three beautiful carpets adorning the lounge were woven by her mother. Her house is immaculately maintained. You have the choice of three rooms: one has a private bathroom ($72 from June to October and $62 for the rest of the year, including tax), the other two rooms share a shower room ($52/$62). If you're a single person, deduct $10. Pay by cash or traveller's cheques (no credit cards). She does not provide breakfast. Call before 6pm if you will be arriving late.

Navajo B&B (Yà'àt'ééh): ☎ 697-8200. Postal address: PO Box 634, Kayenta, AZ 86033. This B&B is run by a Navajo couple, Greg and Bertha. Ideal for anyone who wants to know more about Navajo customs and their land.

Greg works in a mine in the evening and conducts guided tours of Monument Valley during the day. He knows masses about the region, the history and the customs of his people. The Saganeys only have one room available in their big trailer, with three single beds and a private bathroom at a cost of $55. Yà'àt'ééh means 'Welcome' in Navajo.

☗ **Roland's B&B**: ☎ 697-3524. Fax: 697-2382. Postal address: PO Box 1542, Kayenta, AZ 86033. On the right hand side of the 163 heading up towards Monument Valley, shortly after the Amigo's Cafe (there is a large sign advertising Roland's Navajoland Tours). Roland, a Navajo who organizes excursions to Monument Valley, and his family, have three rooms in a large, very well maintained trailer that looks like a real house. The most expensive are $55 (one bed) and $65 (two beds). You can also sleep in a tepee on a plot of land behind the house for $20. Reservations can be made without a deposit and you can pay by cash or traveller's cheques.

☗ **Petty and Vernon Clarkson's**: 212 Canyon Drive. ☎ (520) 697-8221. Postal address: PO Box 948, Kayenta, AZ 86033. Canyon Drive is the first on the right just past Amigo's Cafe. Petty's B&B would not be to everyone's liking, and at first glance could be described as a bit of a shambles. In the road there's a camper van that sleeps two or four ($55). There's another one in what was once a garden ($65), and there is a third room with a bathroom in the main house, which is, in fact, a trailer ($55). The air-conditioned camper vans have a shower, kitchen, mini-lounge and fridge. Petty and Vernon work for the Fire Department (as well as on film and ad shoots in Monument Valley). They are not there very often and may have to leave in an emergency. Consequently they can't take reservations. Cash and traveller's cheques only. Petty and Vernon are adorable and very tolerant – children are welcome (this is fairly unusual in American B&Bs).

☗ **John A. Bornefeld's**: 244 Aspen. ☎ (520) 697-3737. Fax: as telephone. Postal address: PO Box 848, Kayenta, AZ 86033. On Canyon Drive, go past Petty and Vernon Clarkson's (*see above*) and take the first left fork. It is almost immediately on your left. John has lived alone in his mobile home for more than 20 years and works nights in a coal mine. He is very welcoming and comes to collect you if you phone in advance to ensure you don't get lost on the way. He has two very small rooms available, with a shared bathroom and old TVs. They are both the same price – $30 for two from November until April, $50 for the rest of the year (sometimes only $40 if there are not a lot of people in town). John can provide his guests with a map of Monument Valley and lots of useful information.

✕ **Amigo Cafe**: ☎ 697-8448. 200 yards (180 metres) or so on the right after the intersection of Routes 163 and 160 going towards Monument Valley. Breakfast is served until 11am, then a set menu for the rest of the day until 9pm. All dishes cost $5–$7 ('lunch specials' $3–$4, served 11am–2pm). Closed Saturday and Sunday. Credit cards are not accepted. The outside may be nondescript, but the interior is neat. This is a small, cosy place and Richard and Esther Martinez are very kind and hospitable. They offer good Mexican, Navajo and traditional American dishes. Try, for example their mega-sized Navajo burgers.

✗ **Golden Sands Cafe**: ☎ 697-3684. On the left behind the Best Western, about a mile (2 km) or so after the intersection of Routes 160 and 163 as you go towards Monument Valley. Open weekdays 6am–10pm, Saturday 6am–2pm. Steaks, omelettes, soups, sandwiches, hot dogs, chillis, drinks, all $2–$5. It's an old wooden house in the Western style; the walls are decorated with old photographs, a bison skin and various Native American tribal artefacts. Frequented, among others, by Navajos out from the town. Simple, clean and inexpensive.

✗ **The Blue Coffee Pot**: ☎ 697-3396. Just after the Route 160 and Route 163 intersection, going towards Page. You can't miss it – the octagonal restaurant's design is inspired by the blue coffee pots that the Navajos used to be keen to buy from the trading-posts. Open weekdays 6am–9pm, closed weekends. Good for an inexpensive snack ($4–$5), it serves a wide choice of sandwiches, some Mexican specialities and steaks in the evening. No credit cards.

✗ **Burger King**: ☎ 697-3534. Near the Blue Coffee Pot, on the road out of Kayenta in the direction of Page. Fast-food restaurants are not usually listed but this one is different. It houses a small but interesting exhibition dedicated to the Navajo 'Code Talkers'. In 1942, a Marine of Navajo origin suggested that his tribe's little-known and structurally complicated language be used as a code, to transmit secret messages in the Pacific. After several tests, the idea was adopted. About 150 Navajos served in the Marines during World War II as 'Code Talkers'. Just to be on the safe side, the Navajo language was not declassified by the army until 1968!

☆☆☆ EXPENSIVE

Best Western (Wetherill Inn): to the north of the town, on Route 66 in the direction of Monument Valley. ☎ 697-3231. Fax: 697-3233. E-mail: wetherill@gouldings.com. The hotel owes its name to John Wetherill, who established Kayenta's first trading post in 1910. It's cheaper than the Holiday Inn and almost as good. A double room costs $98 from May to October and the price gradually comes down to $55 in January and February. The rooms are very comfortable and equipped with coffee machines.

Holiday Inn: in the centre of Kayenta, at the intersection of US 160 and US 163. ☎ 697-3221. Fax: 697-3349. This costs as much as Goulding's in high summer ($129 plus tax), so it's perhaps a bit overpriced, even if the rooms are comfortable, nicely decorated and well-kept. Prices go down by almost half, from 1 November. The restaurant has a Navajo hogan-style and pueblo-style decor, serving good Navajo cooking on an 'all-you-can-eat' basis, and this includes as many trips as you like to the salad bar. Swimming pool.

So basically, the choice of accommodation is between these two, a B&B or Goulding's Lodge unless you want to go to Mexican Hat, just across the state boundary into Utah, where the hotels are nicer and cheaper too.

AT MEXICAN HAT (UTAH)

Mexican Hat is 21 miles (34km) northeast of Monument Valley. It's a pleasant village – not much more than a few houses clustered along the river. It's advisable to reserve several weeks in advance.

☗ **The San Juan Inn and Trading Post**: on the way into Mexican Hat, immediately on the left after you cross the bridge over the San Juan River. ☎ 683-2220. Fax: 683-2210. Freephone: ☎ 1-800-447-2022. The hotel charges the same prices all year round: $66 for two, with double or twin beds. Not the cheapest around but unquestionably the nicest, for only a few dollars more. You can squeeze three or four people into a room. To book, just call and give your credit card number. You must then arrive before 6pm or call again to warn them you'll be late. You can reserve without leaving a credit card number but you must arrive before 4pm. Prices increase from $70 to $74 for telephone reservations.

The **San Juan Restaurant** is next to the river, and is open 7am–10pm. Good food and large portions. A few Navajo specialities (stew and fried bread, tacos), Mexican dishes and the usual sandwiches and hamburgers, as well as apple pie. Good value for money. With the exception of the grilled meat that they serve in the evening, everything costs around $6. At the back of the dining room, there is a small, well thought-out display of the plants used by the Navajo to obtain the magnificent natural dyes used in their carpets.

☗ ✕ **Burch's Indian Trading Company Motel**: it's impossible to miss this big wooden hotel as you arrive in Mexican Hat. ☎ 683-2221. Fax: 683-2246. They have comfortable double rooms from $50 in summer, and only slightly more for three people ($54) or four ($58). The Mexican–American restaurant is pleasant, with large portions of very good food.

☗ ✕ **Mexican Hat Lodge**: ☎ 683-2222. Fax: 683-2203. More expensive than the others but you're paying for the typically Western decor and communal areas. The prices stay the same all year round – $60 for a single bed and $70 for a twin. The lodge also houses a steakhouse – with a display of John Wayne photographs, a pool table, a large cowboy-style lounge and even a table tennis table.

☗ ✕ **Canyonlands Motel**: in the centre of the village. ☎ 683-2230. Try this one if the others are full. It costs $46 for a single, $52 for a double, including tax. The welcome may be only lukewarm.

AT BLUFF (UTAH)

As you round a hill, a broad expanse of green suddenly appears – this is the oasis known as Bluff, a town with only 290 inhabitants. Further away from Monument Valley (an hour by car), and nicer than Mexican Hat, Bluff is 52 miles (83km) northeast of Monument Valley, on Route 191 going towards Blanding, Canyonlands Park and Moab. Over the last few years, the hamlet has become a popular hiking centre – it's a good starting point for excursions to see the Native American rock carvings, making the descent of the San Juan River, hiking, etc.

It's as well to note that the restaurants at Bluff close at 9pm. If you've been watching the sunset at Monument Valley around 7.30–8pm, you'd better get a move on or you won't find a restaurant still open at Bluff.

Recapture Lodge: at Bluff. ☎ (435) 672-2281. Fax: 672-2284. E-mail: jimnluhook@sisna.com. Peaceful, attractively decorated hotel, with swimming pool, jacuzzi and washing machines. The rooms are decent and the prices at the hotel are reasonable: $44–$48 for a double. Excellent welcome. Slide-shows are organized by an archaeologist from the village every evening in season.

The Pioneer House B&B: ☎ 672-2446. Freephone: ☎ 1-888-637-2582. E-mail: rmcbluff@sanjuan.net. Website: www.pioneerhouseinn.com. On the corner of Mulberry and N 3rd East (the turning after the Phillips 66 station). Dating from 1898, this big wooden house, built by a couple of Mormon settlers, was one of the first to have been erected in Bluff. There are five big rooms at $70 in the main wing and a few other smaller ones in the wing added in 1950 for $54. Prices are the same all year round and include a good breakfast. Reservations are recommended May–September. Thomas and Kelly, the owners, were an archaeologist and hiking guide respectively for a long time before they opened their B&B. They know the region like the back of their hands and organize tailor-made excursions – the degree of luxury (and the price) varies depending on the client's individual requirements. They have a friend who organizes descents of the San Juan River (Charlie at Wild Rivers Expeditions. ☎ 1-800-422-7654).

Calabre B&B: 127 W 4th Street. A small wooden house, in a quiet road on the left as you come into town from the south. ☎ 672-2252. Fax: 672-2445. E-mail: calabre@sanjuan.net. A reasonably priced, unpretentious B&B costing $45 for one, $50 for two and $60 for three, including breakfast. There are only two rooms that share a bathroom. Delightful garden, with humming birds. Under 10s not allowed.

Kokopelli Inn: right next to Recapture Lodge, Highway 191. PO Box 27. ☎ 672-2322. Freephone: ☎ 1-800-541-8854. Fax: 672-2385. Perfectly decent rooms, albeit small and without much charm. $50 for a double and $5 per additional person. A reasonable alternative if you arrive late and everywhere else is full. Friendly welcome.

Cow Canyon Trading Post Restaurant: Route 191. ☎ 672-2208. Rigged out like an Old West cabin, it's very well decorated, and has a terrace overlooking the valley, at the foot of the trees. Refined home cooking. Good value for money.

Cottonwood Steakhouse: ☎ 672-2282. A Western-style building made all of wood. It's on the right-hand side of the road if you're coming from the south. Open 11am–2pm for lunch and from 6pm for dinner (except Monday). The lunchtime menu includes all the Western classics at reasonable prices ($13–$20). There is plenty to satisfy carnivores on the evening menu. It's possible to eat on the terrace, under a large tree that is decorated with horseshoes.

Twin Rocks Cafe: 913 East Navajo Twin Drive. On the way to Bluff coming from Mexican Hat. As its name indicates, the cafe is located right below the enormous twin peaks that overlook the village. Open 8am–10pm Monday–Saturday. The building is a brand new timber cabin where you can have breakfast or dinner on a beautiful terrace well away from the road. Good service and decent food.

TO THE WEST OF KAYENTA

If you travel from Monument Valley to the Grand Canyon (or the other way round), you can spend the night at Tuba City, a small town on Route 160, 72 miles (115km) southwest of Kayenta (*see* 'Where to Stay in Navajo Territory').

▲ **Anasazi Inn – Tsegi Canyon**: 12 miles (20km) west of Kayenta on Route 160, in the direction of Tuba City and Page. ☎ (520) 697-3793. Fax: 697-8249. This big white-and-turquoise roadside motel belongs to Native Americans but is managed by non-Native Americans. It has 59 rooms with air-conditioning. Prices vary depending on season – on the expensive side in summer ($80 for a single, $90 for a twin), reasonable mid-season ($60–$70) and fairly cheap in winter ($40). There is an inexpensive cafe-restaurant next door.

▲ **Free campground**: in the Navajo National Monument Park, 20 miles (32km) west of Kayenta on Route 564, which branches off from Route 160. The campground is just beside the Visitor Center. Very well arranged, with shade, washing facilities, tables and individual barbecues. No showers, though. Arrive early in summer, as it fills up.

HOW TO TOUR MONUMENT VALLEY

A trail starts off from the Visitor Center – it's rather bumpy but is still accessible to all vehicles.

– **Taking the trail**: this dusty track winds between the gigantic blocks of stone scattered across the floor of the Hidden Valley desert, forming a 17-mile (27km) circuit. Note that the trail is only accessible 7am–6.30pm. At the entrance they'll give you a map, which is sketchy but readable, that marks the things they advise you to see. You'll need at least two or three hours to do the trip in your own vehicle, assuming you don't exceed the speed limit of 15 mph (24 kph). This can be a nuisance, if you are in a 4x4 open-top vehicle, as lots of dust is kicked up by the wind and other vehicles.

– One of the most beautiful places at sunset is John Ford's Point, and it's possible to go and view it by car. There's an admission charge of $2.50 per person, which you pay at the entrance to the site.

– **Excursions by minibus**: you can get information from the Visitor Center. Plenty of companies have stands just next-door, in the parking lot; and the itineraries they offer and their prices are almost all the same. There's quite a difference between the trip by minibus (10 passengers, no commentary) and the one by 4x4 (for two or three people, with a commentary given by the driver). This option is probably better, even though it is more expensive. These trips usually last about 2 hours 30 minutes. Accompanied by a Navajo guide, you go round the standard circuit that's accessible to everyone. The trip to see Mystery Valley, which is closed to individuals, takes four hours ($40 per person). Roland's

Navajoland Tours) is recommended (you'll find them in the parking lot or in Kayenta, – *see* 'Where to Stay'): they know Mystery Valley well and you can see Anasazi ruins as well as the natural arches and bridges. Alternatively, you can approach the Navajo living in Monument Valley and visit a traditional hogan. It's very touristy, of course. If you want to book a trip you can also go to Goulding's Lodge, but that's more expensive than doing it directly while you're on the spot.

For a tour by 4x4, try Monument Valley Simpson Tours. E-mail: simpson@worldonline.nl.

– **Trips on horseback**: More and more people are offering horseback riding in the immediate vicinity of Monument Valley. The stables listed below are some of the original ones and have a good reputations.

– **Ed Black**, PO Box 310155, Mexican Hat, Utah 84531. ☎ (435) 739-4285. Freephone: ☎ 1-800-551-4039. Not very well signposted. Beyond the parking lot, take the trail leading to Monument Valley for about 100 yards (90 metres), then continue straight ahead and the corral is on the left, down below. It's essential to reserve ahead: ☎ (818) 785-4569. Fax: (818) 785-3964. The shortest trip with a Navajo guide lasts about 90 minutes. This is the cheapest option – it costs $30 for a circuit round Mitchell Hill, the one closest to the access road (on the right). This is enough to immerse you in the Western ambiance without leaving you walking like a cowboy for the rest of your holiday. Exceptional, absolute quiet. Avoid the hot hours of the day. The ideal time to start is 6pm. Remember to take water and a hat. This excursion is feasible for children over eight, even if they have no previous experience. Ed Black also runs a two-day trip to the plateau of the Rain God, with Native American food and a night in the open air (or a tent, if you prefer). Sleeping bags are available for hire at a reasonable price. There are some exciting moments to be had for beginners and experienced riders alike, but avoid wearing shorts or swimming costumes, which will soon start to chafe. Ed's nephew, Roy Black, also offers horseback excursions: 2 hours to Horse Canyon (Navajo ruins and a stone arch) for $35, a similar circuit with an additional detour to see the rock-carvings costs $40, or you can do a full day's ride (8 hours) around Mystery Valley for $100. For information: ☎ 739-4226. Freephone: ☎ 1-800-749-4226.

WHAT TO SEE

★ **Monument Valley Museum**: in the grounds of Goulding's Lodge (*see* 'Where to Stay and Where to Eat'). Open 7.30am–9pm, April–November. Entrance fee $2. This is where Harry Goulding and his wife Leone (nicknamed Mike), founded Monument Valley's first trading post in 1928, having set up home here four years earlier looking out over what could be the eighth wonder of the world. Accepted by the Navajos, whose way of life had so attracted them, their first dealings with them involved trading finished products for local ones. In order to publicize Monument Valley (then unheard of by most people) and to earn some extra cash (which had been very short since the start of the Great Depression), Goulding travelled to Hollywood hoping to meet up with John Ford. He waited three days in the great man's office before finally managing to show him photographs of Monument Valley. Impressed,

John Ford immediately decided to go there to shoot his next Western, *Stagecoach*. That was in 1939 – the movie legend of Monument Valley had been launched.

– The museum is spread out across two floors, and you visit the warehouse, the lounge, living room, bedroom, kitchen and photograph room. What they call the 'shooting room' was originally decorated like a saloon, then it was used as dining room for the crew shooting the film *Harvey Girls*. This room is now filled with souvenirs of the films that were shot in Monument Valley. These include documents and photographs of John Ford and his friend John Wayne, who were both of Irish origin, and a number of stills from *Stagecoach*, *Rio Grande*, *Fort Apache*, *Cheyenne Autumn*, etc. Just behind the museum is what was Goulding's old shed, once used for storing sweet potatoes. In 1949, it was transformed into 'Captain Brittles' quarters' for the film the *She Wore A Yellow Ribbon* with John Wayne. Nothing has been touched since.

Earth Spirit Theatre: at Goulding's Lodge, just behind the museum. There's a 20-minute slide-show of Monument Valley every evening in summer at 6.10pm, 7.10pm and 8.10pm. Entrance fee $2 (free if you have booked an excursion through Goulding's). Some great images.

WHAT TO SEE IN THE AREA

★ **Navajo National Monument**: about 30 miles (50km) to the west of Kayenta. Take Route 160 in the direction of Tuba City and Page. Then fork right after about 20 miles (32 km) and follow Route 564 for 9 miles (14km). It leads to the Navajo National Monument. Admission is free. Despite their name, these magnificently preserved ruins are not Navajo but Anasazi (the forebears of the Hopis). This ancient tribe must have taken refuge in the canyons either in periods of war, or because their fields on the higher plateaux were suffering a major drought. The Navajos discovered the villages after they were abandoned at the end of the 13th century, and it was the Navajos who coined the name: Anasazis, in the Navajo language, means 'other ancient people'.

Leave your car at the Visitor Centre (where there's an attractive display of Anasazi pottery and utensils, followed by a short film on the site's history), take the **Sandal Trail** just behind the centre. This trail follows a very pleasant little surfaced track and it's a one-mile (2 km) round trip that takes a total of 30 minutes. As you reach the furthest point, the **Betatakin Canyon**, which branches off the immense Begi Canyon, suddenly becomes visible – and it's spectacular. Using the telescope at the viewpoint, you can admire a natural alcove that is 460 feet (140m) up, where the Anasazis built one of their stone-and-adobe villages. It's a superb sight. It's thanks to the beams that the ancient tribesmen used, that is has been possible to establish the age of the Betatakin houses, using carbon-14-dating, and a study of the rings in the wood reveals the years of drought. The first houses seem to have been constructed around 1250–60 only to be abandoned 40 years later. The village is so well hidden that the Americans only rediscovered it in 1909.

It's possible to go down into the canyon to visit it between May and September, but you need to book a place at the Visitor Center. The 5-mile (8km) round-trip takes about five hours and you must be accompanied by a ranger. Like the Grand Canyon, there is a steep descent, which makes for a tough uphill walk on the return journey. Departure time is 8.15am and the group is limited to 25 people. You spend around an hour at the site. It's impossible to reserve by post or telephone so you need to get there as early as possible (the best option is to spend the night at the campsite).

There is another village in the canyon, **Keet Seel** (meaning 'broken pottery' in Navajo), but it's invisible from the track. This one is the bigger and better preserved of the two and was the first to be discovered in 1894. It seems to have been occupied a little earlier and abandoned around 1286. Once again, the only way to get to it is on foot. It's a 17-mile (27km) round-trip, but you can spend the night next to the site on a primitive camping ground (no water). Only 20 people are admitted each day. They go down alone and meet up with the ranger at the village. As with Betatakin, permits are free but in this case you can reserve in advance: ☎ (520) 672-2366. Fax 672-2345. Book two or three months in advance in high season.

The dates when the site is open change from one year to the next, so telephone in advance to check.

Campground: next to the Visitor Center. Free. The site is shaded and the facilities are clean. For information, *see* 'Where to Stay'.

★ **Natural Bridges National Monument**: on US 95, about 30 miles (50km) north of Mexican Hat. These three natural arches, despite being among the longest in the country, aren't especially worth the detour unless you're going up to Lake Powell, where you can get a ferry.

★ **Goosenecks**: about 6 miles (10km) from Mexican Hat. If you're in the area, this is worth going to see. You get to a splendid viewpoint that looks out over the San Juan River as it meanders through a black, bare landscape.

TRIPS BY PLANE

■ **Grand Canyon Airlines**: PO Box 186, Grand Canyon, AZ 86023. ☎ (602) 638-2407. Flights over the Grand Canyon and Monument Valley. Not cheap.

■ **Scenic Airlines**: 241 E Reno Avenue, Las Vegas, Nevada 89119. ☎ (702) 739-1900. Freephone: ☎ 1-800-634-6801. Flight over the Grand Canyon and Monument Valley. Expensive, but an exceptional trip.

PAGE AND LAKE POWELL

AREA CODE: 520

The spectacle of enormous red cliffs sweeping down into Lake Powell may not be quite as astonishing as the Grand Canyon, but it's still well worth seeing. Many films have been made around here, including *Bandolero* with James Stewart, *Wanda Nevada* with Peter Fonda, *The Planet of the Apes*, and *Maverick* with Mel Gibson. It was also used as a location for some of the scenes in *Superman*.

Page is a small town with a population of 8,000, perched on Manson Mesa, a desert plateau overlooking the southern shore. The lake is just over 2 miles (3km) from the city centre on Route US 89. According to a survey in *Newsweek*, Page is considered to be America's third-nicest small town!

It's an ideal base – it's never too hot here because of the altitude (4,300ft/1,310m). There's a lot of water, whose temperature, in August, is 79°F/26°C. The excursion possibilities in the surrounding area are almost endless, and everything feels magnified by the wide open spaces.

A BRIEF HISTORY

Until 1884, this was Navajo territory. According to a Native American belief, this was 'the place where trees die of fright'. The spirits had taken refuge there, causing the humans to move out. This may be why, even today, there are still so few trees in these vast desert landscapes. The city is wholly artificial – it's a new town, a place of pioneers, right out in the middle of nowhere.

There was almost nothing here until 1957, when the federal government decided to build an enormous dam, at Glen Canyon, that would regulate the flow of the Colorado and allow the production of a good supply of electricity. The dam created the second largest artificial lake in America, and an oasis of green in an arid desert. Houses sprang up to accommodate the crowds of workers and foremen employed on this vast project, and for a long time, Page was a city made up only of workers. It was described as 'the largest truck stop in the United States'. Things have changed a great deal since then. Once the dam was finished, the trucks gave way to water skis, 4x4 tours and boat tours.

HOW TO GET THERE

Most of the following destinations are in what is sometimes called the 'Great Circle', which includes sites that are an average of two hours' drive in any direction from Page.

DISTANCES TO PRINCIPAL PLACES

- **Arches National Park** (Utah): 268 miles (432km)
- **Bryce Canyon National Park** (Utah): 150 miles (243km)
- **Canyon de Chelly** (Arizona): 200 miles (321km)
- **Canyonlands National Park (Needles area)** (Utah): 254 miles (409km)
- **Capitol Reef National Park** (Utah): 267 miles (430km)
- **Flagstaff** (Arizona): 133 miles (214km)
- **Grand Canyon North Rim** (Utah): 129 miles 208km)
- **Grand Canyon South Rim** (Arizona): 139 miles (224km)
- **Kanab** (Utah): 75 miles (120km)
- **Kayenta** (Arizona): 97 miles (156km)

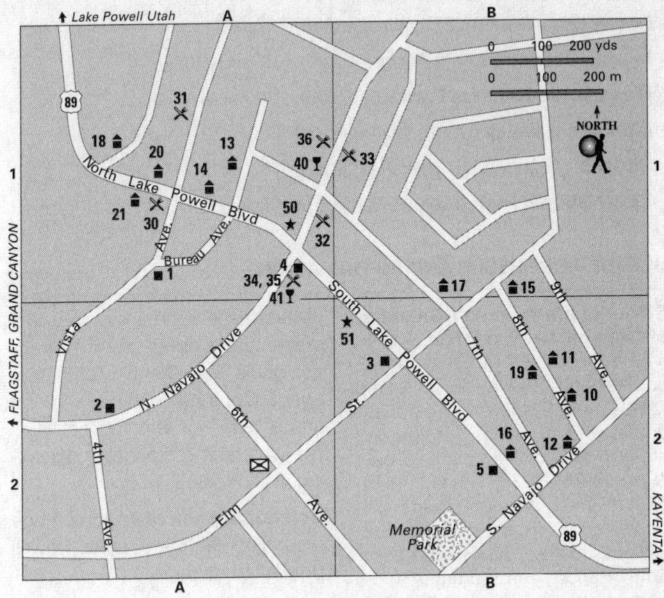

PAGE – TOWN CENTRE

■ **Useful Addresses**

- ✉ Post office
- 1 Police station
- 2 Hospital
- 3 National Bank of Arizona
- 4 Chamber of Commerce
- 5 Launderette

Where to Stay

- 10 Lake Powell International Hostel
- 11 Uncle Bill's Place
- 12 Bashful Bob's Motel
- 13 Navajo Trail Motel
- 14 Page Boy Motel
- 15 Lulu's Sleep Ezze
- 16 Econo Lodge
- 17 Super 8 Motel
- 18 Best Western Arizona Inn
- 19 Red Rock Motel
- 20 Best Western at Lake Powell
- 21 Best Western Weston Inn

Where to Eat

- 30 Glen Canyon Steak House
- 31 Ken's Old West
- 32 Stromboli's
- 33 Cactus & Tropicals
- 34 Beans Coffee House
- 35 Dam Bar & Grill
- 36 Bella Napoli

Where to Have a Drink

- 40 Windy Mesa
- 41 Gunsmoke Saloon

★ **What to See**

- 50 Powell Memorial Museum
- 51 Fatali Gallery

- **Las Vegas** (Nevada): 277 miles (446km)
- **Marble Canyon / Lee's Ferry** (Arizona): 38 miles (61km)
- **Mesa Verde National Park** (Colorado): 220 miles (354km)
- **Monument Valley** (Utah): 122 miles (196km)
- **Phoenix** (Arizona): 267 miles (429km)
- **Zion National Park** (Utah): 111 miles (179km)

USEFUL ADDRESSES AND INFORMATION

Tourist Information / Chamber of Commerce (Page map, A1, **4**): 644 N Navajo Drive (Dam Plaza), on the corner of Navajo Drive and Lake Powell Boulevard. Postal address: PO Box 727, Page AZ 86040. ☎ 645-2741. Freephone: ☎ 1-888-261-7243. Fax: 645-3181. E-mail: chamber@page-lakepowell.com. Open Monday–Saturday 8.30am–7.30pm; also 9am–6pm Sunday, in summer. Very competent and welcoming staff, and plenty of information available.

Carl Hayden Visitors' Center: about 2 miles (3km) north of Page on Route US 89, near the Glen Canyon Dam. (☎ 608-6404). Open daily, 8am–5pm (7pm in summer). You can see a big relief model of the Colorado plateau here, as well as information and an audio-visual presentation about the construction of the dam. Plenty of stuff, too, about boat trips on the lake, hiking and a range of sporting activities like waterskiing, canoeing, kayaking, fishing, etc.

■ **National Bank of Arizona** (Page map, B2, **3**): 58 S Lake Powell Boulevard. ☎ 645-2441.

Superwash Laundromat: (Page map, B2, **5**), on the Safeway Plaza (along Lake Powell Boulevard). Machines cost $1.25.

Navajo dancing: in summer, every Monday, Tuesday, Thursday and Saturday at 7.30pm, in front of the City Hall. Free of charge.

WHERE TO STAY

You have to arrive early in the morning in season to be sure of finding a room.

The city has about 10 B&Bs, although none has any sign to identify it. The tourist office can provide a list with the relevant phone numbers. You call up and the proprietor gives you the address so you can have a look at the rooms – but you needn't feel obliged to take one.

CAMPGROUNDS

Page Lake Powell Trailer, Motel and Campground: 849 Coppermine Road, (S Highway 98). ☎ 645-3374. Fax: 645-2588. On the way into Page from the direction of Kayenta. A tent pitch costs $15 – the same price as at the Wahweap marina (*see* 'Where to Stay at Lake Powell'), which is a much pleasanter site. Here, there's not much shade and it's almost exclusively full of camper vans. They have coin-operated hot showers ($3.50), a launderette (open 6am–8pm), swimming pool and jacuzzi.

☆ BUDGET

Lake Powell International Hostel (Page map, B2, **10**): 141 8th Avenue. ☎ 645-3898. Fax: 645-1263. This is one of the nicest hostels in the whole of the West. From the outside, it doesn't look anything like a youth hostel, but more like a few low houses surrounded by lawns, strung together in a line along a quiet street. When the dam was under construction this was where the site foremen lived. Today, it's occupied by backpackers from all over the world. You can sleep in one of the dormitories, which have four, five or six beds; this is the cheapest option, and costs $12–$15 depending on the season. The private rooms, although more expensive, are still affordable, ranging from $25 in winter up to $40 in summer (including tax). Suites cost $40–$70. This set-up is much more welcoming than motel rooms: they have large, comfortable studios, that are well decorated and fitted with a kitchenette. Covers and sheets are supplied. There's no curfew and no age limit. A launderette is available, and there's self-service tea and coffee at all times. The hostel is run by Jeff and Kate (he's American, she's English) – they're affable, lively and full of humour. They receive their guests like good friends. They've fallen in love with the region and know it like the back of their hands – so they can tell you a lot about the hidden places on Lake Powell, including where you can get a boat or take a swim, plus all the tours you can do by car within a two-hour driving radius from Page. Through them, too, you can get decent reductions on boat hire at Wahweap Marina.

☆☆ MODERATE

Almost all the addresses in this category are clustered around the same road (8th Avenue). This was an estate built originally to house the labourers when the dam was being built, and it's now an established residential area.

Uncle Bill's Place (Page map, B2, **11**): 117 8th Avenue. ☎ 645-1224. Freephone: ☎ 1-800-944-8270. Fax: 645-3937. E-mail: unclebillsplace@webtv.net. Website: canyon-country.com/uncle bill. Here, you feel like a guest in a family home, the atmosphere's so convivial. There are 12 rooms, starting at $36 for a double without en-suite. There are also some rooms-cum-apartments ($69 for four, $108 for six, in summer). Prices are generally lower out of season. There are laundry facilities and a barbecue.

Bashful Bob's Motel (Page map, B2, **12**): 750 S Navajo Drive. ☎ 645-3919. E-mail: bashfulbob motel@webtv.net. One of Page's finest, with doubles for $39 ($5 extra per additional person). This group of cabins was also built for the dam construction foremen. Each cabin has two rooms, two doors, a kitchenette and a bathroom. There's a small garden at the back and a quiet street at the front. Good welcome. Bob, despite the name, isn't all that bashful. Free Internet and e-mail access. Often full, so it's worth reserving ahead.

Red Rock Motel (Page map, B2, **19**): 114 8th Avenue. ☎ 645-0062. Website: www.redrock motel.com. Unpretentious but clean and well kept. Slightly more expensive than the others – starting at $49 for a double (some have a kitchen for the same price) up to $65 for a suite with two bedrooms, lounge and kitchen. All the rooms have coffee machines. Reductions November–March.

Lulu's Sleep Ezze (Page map, A2, **15**): 105 8th Avenue, on the corner with Elm Street. ☎ 608-0273. Freephone: ☎ 1-800-553-6211. E-mail: midiehl@yahoo.com. Attractive, brand new rooms in a well-kept house without any particular charm. For the area, the price is very reasonable: $43 for a single, $63 for four (two doubles). Very friendly welcome.

Navajo Trail Motel (Page map, A1, **13**): 800 Bureau Avenue, in the centre of Page. ☎ 645-9508. A little off the road, behind the Page Boy Motel. This is one of the least expensive motels in the city ($39 for a double). It's very simple, tidier than it used to be, and has colour TV. The air-conditioning sometimes breaks down, so check this out. Don't take a room on the same side as the reception building – it's noisy. The ones in the annex building (**Navajo Trail Motel 2**) are better but are poorly soundproofed. Only recommended as a last resort.

Page Boy Motel (Page map, A1, **14**): 150 N Lake Powell Boulevard. ☎ 645-2416. Freephone: ☎ 1-800-551-9005. A classic motel, right in the centre, lacking in character but not too expensive – $50 for two, including tax. There's a swimming pool surrounded by a patch of lawn. The rooms overlooking this side have bay windows, making them light and airy. Delightful Navajo welcome.

☆☆ MODERATE

Econo Lodge (Page map, B2, **16**): 121 S Lake Powell Boulevard. ☎ 645-2488. Freephone: ☎ 1-800-553-2666. On the main road. An unremarkable but reasonable motel that costs $54 for a double. Two buildings at right angles to the road, with a parking lot between them. Mini-swimming pool.

Super 8 Motel (Page map, B1, **17**): 75 S 7th Avenue. ☎ 645-2890. Freephone: ☎ 1-800-800-8000. The rooms are comfortable – but the prices are prohibitive. In summer, a double costs $75.

☆☆☆ EXPENSIVE

Canyon Colors Bed & Breakfast: 225 S Navajo Drive. ☎ 645-5979. Freephone: ☎ 1-800-536-2530 or 691-9191 (mobile). Fax: as telephone. E-mail: canyoncolors@webtv.net. This family-run B&B in a residential area to the south of the town centre has two pleasant rooms at very reasonable prices considering what they offer – $75 for two in summer for the Paisley Room ($50 from mid-October to mid-April) and $85 for the Sunflower Room ($60). Both have en-suite bathrooms (Sunflower has a spa bath), cable TV, video player with a wide choice of films, as well as a fridge – and there's a swimming pool. Credit cards are accepted.

Best Western Arizona Inn (Page map, A1, **18**): 716 Rimview Drive. ☎ 645-2466. Freephone: ☎ 1-800-826-2718. Fax: 645-2053. On the way out of Page, right next to the town's two other Best Westerns. This hotel is the only one where some rooms have a distant view of the lake. These rooms are more expensive ($92). The others are more reasonable, particularly for a hotel of this quality – a single room is $69 and a twin is $79. Of all the Best Westerns in Page, this one is the nicest. Swimming pool and jacuzzi, shuttle buses to the airport. When Mel Gibson was filming *Maverick*, he stayed in one of these three Best Westerns but they won't tell you which one!

☗ **Best Western Weston Inn** (Page map, A1, **21**): 201 N Lake Powell Boulevard. ☎ 645-2451. Freephone: ☎ 1-800-637-9183. Fax: 645-9552. The cheapest of the three Best Westerns – $63 for a single, $68 for a twin. Swimming pool and jacuzzi.

☗ **Best Western at Lake Powell** (Page map, A1 **20**): 208 N Lake Powell Boulevard. ☎ 645-5988. Freephone: ☎ 1-888-794-2888. Fax: 645-2578. Good value for money in winter but prices go up by half in April and then double for the summer – $75 for a double, $85 for a bigger room with a fridge and microwave. Heated pool and jacuzzi, shuttle bus service to the airport. Coffee and tea available in reception.

WHERE TO STAY AT LAKE POWELL

There's a charge to get into the Wahweap Marina. An entry pass costs $5 per car, valid for one week, or $3 per person if you arrive on foot or by bike. The 'Golden Eagle' pass is accepted.

☗ **Wahweap Campground Trailer Village**: 100 Lakeshore Drive, Wahweap. ☎ 645-1059. No bookings. Just 4 miles (7km) from Page, this is a well-arranged campground on the shore of Lake Powell, close to Wahweap Marina. A pitch costs $15. Get there early in summer (before 2pm) to bag a good shady space (in theory you can't choose – they allocate them to you – but you can always give it a try). The location is magnificent, facing the steep cliffs that plunge down into the lake. Free tables and BBQ facility. You can swim in the lake. There's a beach near the marina and several easily accessible, quiet coves. Coin-operated showers ($2 for 15 mins) 0.5 miles (1km) away, where the camper vans are parked.

☗ **Wahweap Lodge**: Freephone: ☎ 1-800-528-6154. Fax: 269-9408. This is a pleasant hotel at the heart of the Wahweap Marina. It has a swimming pool, jacuzzi, plus a shop; the restaurant has a beautiful bay window facing the lake. The various buildings clustered along the water's edge make it feel more like a good motel than a cosy lodge. You pay extra for the location – $150 for a double room with a view of the parking lot and only $10 more with a view of the lake. Be clear about your requirements when booking. John Travolta stayed here while shooting a film on location – probably in the best room of all! Out of season, prices drop by 30 per cent.

WHERE TO STAY BETWEEN PAGE AND FLAGSTAFF

☗ **Anasazi Inn**: Gray Mountain Trading Post, at Gray Mountain, a small village in the middle of nowhere on Route 89, 45 miles (72km) north of Flagstaff and 90 miles (145km) south of Page. ☎ (520) 679-2214. Fax: (520) 679-2334. A Navajo-style motel like the Cameron Trading Post but much cheaper, although it will still set you back $75 (including tax). The rooms are comfortable, with TV and telephone. Adjacent swimming pool and restaurant.

WHERE TO EAT

IN PAGE

☆–☆☆ BUDGET TO MODERATE

✕ **Cactus & Tropicals Garden and Cafe** (Page map, A2, **33**): 809 N Navajo Drive. ☎ 645-6666. Open Monday–Saturday 7am–5pm (closed Sunday). The new mayor of Page is also the owner of this pleasant cafe-cum-snack-bar offering a range of sandwiches, bagels, muffins and fresh orange juice for a few dollars. Nice terrace where you can have breakfast and listen to the fountain tinkling in the background. Also plants for sale (which explains its name) and a whole range of natural products. Good welcome.

✕ **Beans Coffee House** (Page map, A1, **34**): 644 N Navajo Drive. Dam Plaza. Right next to Gunsmoke Saloon and the Chamber of Commerce. Open Monday–Friday 6am–5pm (7am Saturday). This cafe and coffee bean shop is also very good for reasonably priced breakfasts. There's a big sofa to relax on while you savour the delightful smell of a good expresso. Internet-access (paying).

✕ **Strombolli's** (Page map, A1, **32**): 711 N Navajo Drive. ☎ 645-2605. Open Monday–Saturday 11am–10pm and (noon Sunday). Closes early if there aren't any customers and later if it is very busy. Lovely big wooden terrace and tasty Italian snacks – enormous pizzas and *calzones*, pasta and salad, all costing $9–$15.

☆☆☆ EXPENSIVE

✕ **The Dam Bar & Grill** (Page map, A1, **35**): 644 N Navajo Drive. Dam Plaza (on the corner of Navajo and Lake Powell). ☎ 645-2059 or 645-2161. Open Monday–Saturday 11am–midnight (last orders 11pm) and Sunday 3pm–midnight. At lunchtime there is a limited choice of sandwiches, burgers and fried chicken for $6–$8. You can eat on the terrace. In the evening, it becomes more upmarket, there is a wider choice of dishes and prices increase. Big salads ($7–$9), pasta ($15–$18), all sorts of steaks ($20–$25), ribs and a few fish dishes. Fish and chips is the cheapest option ($12). If you have to wait for a table, you could have a drink in the sports bar, which serves a range of cocktails. They are on the pricey side, but you can keep the glass – it's included in the price! Good welcome.

✕ **Ken's Old West & Glen Canyon Steak House** (Page map, A1, **31**): 718 Vista Avenue, on the corner of Lake Powell Boulevard. ☎ 645-5160. Opens at 4pm. Genuine cowboys meet up in this astonishing all-timber house, which is welcoming even though it's quite dark inside. Their concerts (usually Country music) are famous – the music begins at 8pm, on weekends only. The restaurant offers meat and seafood dishes and a help-yourself salad-bar. Great atmosphere but fairly expensive. Allow $15–$25 per person. It's advisable to make a reservation for the evening earlier in the day.

✕ **Glen Canyon Steak House** (Page map, A1, **30**): 201 N Lake Powell Boulevard. ☎ 645-3363. Opens at 5.30pm. Same proprietor as the previous entry, and similar prices, too, although perhaps a bit cheaper. The decor is western, with half-closed wooden shutters and blinds. Relaxed atmosphere. They serve breakfast, lunch and dinner and the 'specials' buffet is a reasonable price. Despite its name, this steakhouse also offers some good Californian salads (Louis crab, Teriyaki chicken), seafood and fish. Allow $15–$20 per person for a good dinner. The main dishes include a soup and an 'eat as much as you can' salad-bar. At lunchtime, there are simple sandwiches or burgers at about $7–$8. Music in the evenings.

✕ **Bella Napoli** (Page map, A1, **36**): 810 N Navajo Drive. ☎ 645-2706. Open evenings only, from 5pm. This fairly authentic Italian restaurant makes a pleasant change from the ubiquitous burger/rib/steak-style eateries. Classical music in the background, engravings on the wall and Chianti bottles hanging from the ceiling. $10–$20 per person for a main dish, served with a salad or soup and warm bread rolls. 'Early Bird' menu costs $7, from 5–7pm (and you still get a tablecloth and real napkin).

WHERE TO HAVE A DRINK

🍸 **Gunsmoke Saloon** (Page map, A1, **41**): 644 N Navajo Drive. Dam Plaza, next to the Dam Bar & Grill (the same building) and the Chamber of Commerce. ☎ 645-1888. Open daily 7pm–1am (closed Monday). The place is impossible to miss as it has a large covered wagon outside and an awning like the roof of a stagecoach. Pool, live music (especially Country) every evening except Sunday. Dance floor.

🍸 **Windy Mesa** (Page map, A1, **40**): 800 N Navajo Drive. ☎ 645-2186. Opens at 9pm (closed Monday). All kinds of people come to this place to hear good rock and Country music. Admission charge $1. The atmosphere isn't always very restful. Billiards.

ON LAKE POWELL

✕ **Wahweap Lodge (Rainbow Room)**: ☎: 645-2433. Website: www.visitlakepowell.com. A great place to have a salad when the sun's beating down outside. The 180° view of the lake and the canyon is superb, and the prices are reasonable. Breakfast costs $6–$7. There's a buffet at lunchtime, salads, sandwiches, burgers and other snacks for around the same price. Also a few dessert options. Some good fish on the evening menu (trout, salmon and catfish) although prices are fairly high ($14–$20). Also the usual steak and grilled chicken. Dinghies, house-boats and jet-skis for hire.

✕ **The Canyon King**: ☎ Freephone: ☎ 1-800-528-6154. Every night the *Canyon King* – a Mississippi-style paddle-boat – spends 2 hours 30 minutes cruising around the lake. The buffet on board is very popular, so booking is recommended. It departs at 5pm in April and from mid-August to the end of October, and at 6pm in summer.

WHAT TO SEE

★ **Powell Memorial Museum** (Page map, A1, **50**): Lake Powell Boulevard and North Navajo. ☎ 645-9496. Fax: 645-3412. Open

8.30am–5.30pm Monday–Saturday; 10am–4pm Sunday. This museum doubles up as an information centre, with displays of documents and souvenirs relating to the history of Lake Powell and Page. You'll find information here about the Native Americans and the construction of the great dam, but it chiefly pays tribute to John Wesley Powell (1834–1902), the man who, travelling by boat, first discovered what is now called Glen Canyon. Born in New York State in 1834, of English parents recently emigrated to America, Powell spent his childhood in Jackson, Ohio. When he reached adulthood he was one of the first volunteers to enlist under Lincoln's banner in the Civil War, and lost his right arm as the result of a wound.

After the war, he became a teacher of geology, but people continued to call him Major Powell. He then became an explorer and, with four boats and nine companions, he set out to travel along a large part of the Colorado River. On 24 May 1869, they left Green River in South Wyoming and spent more than three months (99 days) tracing the course of the Colorado. The exploratory journey, with only two boats and six men, ended on 29 August 1869 at the place where the Virgin River flows into the Colorado, at the eastern end of what is now known as Lake Mead, near Las Vegas. This journey of 1,094 miles (1,760km) constituted a great first in the history of the American West.

Today, flooded by the construction of the dam, Glen Canyon has become an immense lake, but it bears the name of the intrepid explorer. He certainly deserved the honour. In front of the museum is a rock that bears the fossilized footprints of a *saurischia therapod* dinosaur, dating back around 170 million years.

★ **Fatali Gallery** (Page map, B2, **51**): 40 South Lake Powell Boulevard. ☎ 645-3553. Website: www.fatali.com. Open 11am–6pm in winter and 9am–9pm in summer. This private gallery contains an exhibition of the best photographs by Michael Fatali. Over the years, this well known photographer has hunted down the most interesting geological formations and clefts in the canyons from northern Arizona to southern Utah. The prints are out of the range of ordinary budgets but entrance to the exhibition is free. There is another gallery in Springdale, Utah.

★ **The Glen Canyon Dam**: 2 miles (3km) north of Page, on Route US 89, going towards Kanab and the Wahweap Marina. You can visit the dam on a free, one-hour tour that starts out from the Visitors' Center. Tours leave every 30 minutes 8.30am–5.30pm (except noon). At a height of 705 feet (215m), this is the fourth tallest dam in the US.

★ **View of Lake Powell**: there's a very beautiful viewpoint beyond the dam when you're coming from Page. Follow the track that leads off from the right-hand side of the road. At sunset, the view is amazing.

★ **Navajo Village**: ☎ 645-2741. Information also from the Page Chamber of Commerce. This is a mock-up of a typical Navajo village, recreating the life of the Native American at the turn of the 19th century. There are craftsmen at work, and you can enjoy Navajo food around a wood fire while learning a wealth of interesting facts about the Navajo culture and its main customs. Traditional dancing.

★ LAKE POWELL

The lake straddles the northern part of Arizona and the southern part of Utah. It took 17 years to fill this lake with water after the opening of the Glen Canyon Dam in 1957. Those 17 years bear witness to the immensity of the site. It's the second largest artificial lake in the US and its many arms plunge deep into the land. In total, including carved-out creeks and secondary canyons, it has a shoreline of 1,957 miles (3,150km) – longer than the entire western coastline of the United States!

It was originally a long, deep canyon cut into the plateau by the Colorado River. The latter was first discovered by Major Powell in 1869 (*see* Powell Memorial Museum). 'So we have a curious ensemble of wonderful features – carved walls, royal arches, glens, gulches, mounds and monuments. From which of these features shall we select a name? We decide to call it Glen Canyon', noted John Wesley Powell in his logbook. 'Glen', of course, means 'narrow valley' in English, derived from a Gaelic word. It's in memory of Powell's exploratory journey of 1869 that the lake now bears his name. Glen Canyon was largely submerged with the construction of the dam. The waters reach a depth of 3,697ft (1,127m) in places, when the lake is full. In summer, the temperature of the water hovers around 76°F/26°C.

There are some beaches here as well as a multitude of wild creeks where you can have a really good dip or play at being a pioneer. The wild features of the landscape are striking. It may be an artificial lake yet the water and the rock look so beautiful and so harmonious that it's hard to believe that this is a recent creation.

★ One of the most popular sites with visitors to Lake Powell, 50 miles (80km) east of Wahweap Marina, is **Rainbow Bridge National Monument** in Utah. Classed as a national monument in 1910, this is an enormous arch of ochre-and-pink rock, called 'Navajo sandstone', at the bottom of a rugged canyon. It stands 272 feet (83m) high. To get there, you need to take a boat (☎ (520) 608-6404. Website: www.nps.gov/rabr) from a landing-stage that's about 50 miles (80 km) away, so allow around 4 hours for the return journey. After leaving the boat, there's a walk of a few hundred yards. This primitive bridge, with its rainbow shape, looks like something from a film-set – perhaps *The Raiders of the Lost Ark*. For the Navajos, this natural arch is a holy place, full of legend and spirituality, so respect their religious beliefs by not walking under it.

★ Exploring the lake takes time. There are small ports on the northern and southern shores to welcome anyone moving around by boat. For details of boat trips, *see below*.

★ **Antelope Canyon**: This gorgeous canyon is just over 6 feet (2m) wide and 656 feet (200m) long – like a sabre slash through the surface of the red-grey sandstone plateau. The ochre walls are astonishingly sculpted, resembling cloth fluttering in the wind or perhaps weird mineral waves. The colour of the rock changes according to the angle of the sun. Try to see it between noon and 2pm, which is when the canyon gets the most light, and the rocks take on an extraordinary orange hue. Discovered in 1931 by a young Navajo shepherdess, the canyon is named after the numerous pronghorns (a type of antelope) that used to inhabit the region. It is actually divided into two sections: Upper Antelope Canyon, which attracts the majority of visitors and Lower Antelope Canyon, on the other side of the road, which can only be visited with a guide.

Antelope Canyon is 6 miles (9km) to the east of Page. To get there, take Route 98 towards Kayenta. There's a modest $5 entrance fee. Email: antelopecanyon@page.az.net. The site is open May–October, 8am–5pm. It is closed in winter and during stormy weather because of the risk of flooding, which could be very dangerous. In 1997, an accident led to several deaths in Antelope Canyon. Some tourists were walking through the canyon when a violent and unexpected storm broke out. The walkers were swept away and drowned by a torrent of water as it rushed down the canyon. So avoid going there if there's any doubt about the weather.

The canyon itself is 3 miles (5km) further on beyond the point of entry, and you have to go along a sandy track unsuitable for normal cars although accessible in a 4x4. Visitors have two other alternatives – either join a 4x4 tour organized by one of the three agencies in Page (quick and relatively inexpensive – at $27 per person). There are several departures each day and the trip lasts around 1 hour 30 minutes. Contact Lake Powell Jeep Tours (☎ 645-5501) at 104 South Lake Powell Boulevard, Scenic Tours (☎ 645-5594) at 48 South Lake Powell Boulevard or Antelope Canyon Tours (☎ 645-9102). The latter also offers a special 'photographic' excursion lasting five hours ($44).

The best option is probably to go directly to the site and hire the services of a Navajo guide. For $12.50 per person, they offer a shuttle service to the canyon, with departures about every 30 minutes, or more frequently if there's enough demand. This is cheaper and in some ways more useful, and, since Antelope Canyon is on Navajo territory, it seems the most appropriate way to visit. The standard of living among the Native Americans is so much lower than that of any other ethnic group that income in any form is much appreciated. Transport is in the shape of a big-wheeled covered pick-up truck and you remain in the canyon for between 1 hour and 1 hour 30 minutes depending on the frequency of departures. For further information ☎ 698-3384 or 698-3285.

If you wish to visit Lower Antelope Canyon, you need to cross to the other side of the road. Here, the services of a Navajo guide are obligatory, as access to the site is more difficult and part of the descent is via ladders.

Photographers are advised to use 400 ASA films or preferably a tripod.

BOAT TRIPS ON LAKE POWELL

Don't miss this on any account! Taking a boat trip is by far the best way to explore Lake Powell and get a close-up view of its innumerable fantasies of nature. There are natural bridges (including the Rainbow Bridge, up in Utah), sculpted walls, stretches of red-sand desert, gorges and ravines.

– **Organized boat tours**: a number of companies offer all sorts of tours of the lake at a wide range of rates that depend on the time you spend there. Information from the Chamber of Commerce at Page (*see* 'Useful Addresses and Information'), or go directly to the Wahweap Marina, 4 miles (7km) northwest of Page, from where the excursions depart.

■ **Wahweap Lodge** offers an All-Day Rainbow Bridge Cruise. Information and bookings: ☎ 645-1070. Freephone: ☎ 1-800-528-6154. Website: www.visitlakepowell.com. It's expensive, of course (nearly $100 a day), but useful if you have the money and don't want to wait. Departures from the Wahweap Marina at 7am, 8am, 10am, 12.30pm and 1.30pm in summer, less frequently in April, May and October and just one trip a day (11am) from 1 November to the end of March. A half-day works out at practically the same price ($69) and unlike the previous option does not include lunch. Half-day trips generally leave Wahweap Marina at 7.30am or 8.30am, returning at 1pm or 2pm.

– **Hiring a motorboat**: If you want to go out on the lake under your own steam, don't hire just any old boat, take a Livingstone. Livingstones are small, 30HP motorboats that are suitable for anyone who wants to do a spot of fishing. But it's impossible to get up to Rainbow Bridge with an ordinary boat, so take a powerboat with an outboard motor. These powerful vessels have 115 or 150HP motors and can seat nine people. They're fantastic fun, but expensive – around $230 per day in summer (plus tax, plus $11 insurance and around $70 for petrol). From mid-October to mid-May, prices drop by almost 50 per cent but are still fairly expensive – $136. If possible, find other people to split the cost. If you're not already part of a big group, you should easily find willing participants on the spot in the summer. You could also try putting the word out at the Youth Hostel and you generally get a reduction if you make the booking through Kate. You don't need any kind of driving permit and they're easy to drive.

It's a good idea to book before your trip or as soon as you arrive (at least 48 hours in advance in August). To hire on the same day, you can try your luck by going along early in the morning (from 7am) to the Wahweap Marina. The boats for hire are beyond the campground (on the Utah side). ☎ 645-2433. Freephone: ☎ 1-800-528-6154. Before you leave the boat is inspected and a check-list drawn up (like for a hire car). It is particularly worth checking the propeller – the source of most disputes. If you need help, ask to speak to an instructor. You must bring the boat back by 4pm (5pm in summer) otherwise you lose your deposit. It's advisable to pay in cash, as credit cards are debited then re-credited at the end of the day – currency exchange charges imposed by your bank could mean that you end up paying extra.

– **Advice**: it's important to get hold of a good map of the lake and a copy of the *Glen Canyon Lake Powell Magazine*, a small but very comprehensive free guide that provides plenty of useful information about the lake and the boat trips. The glare is intense when you're out on the water in the sun, so it's vital to take something to cover your arms and legs, plus a pair of sunglasses and a hat. And don't forget water and provisions.

Take good note of the weather forecast. Strong winds can blow up out of nowhere during the day. If you're at all bothered by the thought of finding yourself on the lake with a gale blowing, then hire the more powerful type of boat.

Also, pay attention to the sheriff. If you come into the port making a big wash, the sheriff will be after you with his siren screaming. And let's face it, getting a fine for speeding on Lake Powell would be pretty embarrassing.

Houseboat hire: this is also possible at Wahweap Marina. Hiring a houseboat is a great (albeit expensive) way to explore the lake in peace. It costs from $511 for three days out of season in a 40-foot (12m) boat (which will take six people, or eight at a tight squeeze). From mid-May to mid-October, the same thing will cost $850. The bigger the boat and the more mod cons on offer, the higher the price. It's advisable to book well in advance.

Wilderness River Adventures specialize in descents of a calm stretch of the Colorado (no rapids) from Lake Powell to Lee's Ferry, passing through Marble Canyon. Information from Wahweap Lodge or from Wilderness, 50 South Lake Powell Boulevard (opposite the Safeway supermarket). ☎ 645-3278. Freephone: ☎ 1-8000-528-6154. From mid-May to mid-September, the trips, lasting from 9am to 3.15pm cost $72. A half-day trip costs $49 (one departure at 7.30am and another at 1.30pm). At other times of the year (March to mid-May and mid-September to the end of October, there is a single departure at 11am, returning at 3.30pm.

WHAT TO DO

– **Flight over Lake Powell**: with Scenic Air. ☎ 645-2494. Freephone: ☎ 1-800-245-8668. Website: www.scenic.com. Just over a mile (2km) from the centre of Page, near the Municipal Airport. If you can afford it, the 30-minute air trip over Lake Powell is fantastic. The little plane goes up the lake to Rainbow Bridge or you can extend the flight to Monument Valley, with a flight time of 2 hours 30 minutes.

– **Classic Helicopters** (☎ 645-5356) offer similar tours by helicopter. From $39 for 10 minutes, or $95 for the 30-minute ride to Rainbow Bridge. The price of the trip includes pick-up and drop-off at your hotel.

– **Walks**: a 14-mile (22km) trail will take you all the way to Rainbow Bridge. Ask for a brochure at the Visitors' Center. Escalante Canyon is one of the most beautiful places to walk in the area, and Paria Canyon, Dark Canyon and Grand Gulch are also very beautiful.

WHERE TO TAKE A DIP

– **In Lake Powell**: there are many beaches tucked away at the ends of creeks and on the shores, and they are often accessible only by boat. Near Page, there are fewer beaches and they're well hidden. Those that actually are signposted serve as points of departure for boats, so the water there is not always very inviting. Between Page and Glen Canyon Visitors' Center, very close to the dam, there's a narrow, unsurfaced road on the right. It's accessible to vehicles and leads to a rocky creek. The water here is clean and the rocks are smooth and painless to walk on. The appropriately named Warm Creek Bay is an ideal place for a swim, and waterskiing is also available. Padre Bay is also highly recommended.

NEAR PAGE

Horseshoe Bend: spectacular views down to a tributary of the Colorado, easily accessible from Page. Take the Flagstaff road out of Page, as far as Mile Marker 545. On the left you will see a big white P painted on a rock. Just after, on the right, is the start of a dirt track. Follow it for 300 yards (275 metres), as far as the parking lot. From there, it's only a 10–15 minute walk over the hill. Photographers will find the best light is early in the morning (but not too early when everything is in the shade).

Lee's Ferry: 24 miles (39 km) to the south of Page, route 89A (which leads to the North Rim of the Grand Canyon) drops down towards the Colorado at the place where the first ferry across the river was opened at the end of the 19th century. It is named after its first operator, John D. Lee. It was only two years after Major Powell's expedition to Glen Canyon. This was the only crossing point between Arizona and Utah for over 60 miles (100km).

It was mainly Mormon pioneers who crossed at this point, although in fact it would have been 3 miles (5 km) upstream of the current bridge. They were following the 'Honeymoon Trail', as many of them had civil weddings in Arizona or Colorado and then went on to St George in Utah for a religious ceremony in the church. As the Mormons were barely tolerated outside of Utah, there were no churches nearer to hand. It was not until the end of the 1920s that the flow of people stopped.

Nowadays, there is a modern bridge over the river and Marble Canyon, parallel to the Navajo Bridge, opened in 1929. Like everything over 50 years old in the United States, it is listed! A little way after that, a turning off to the right leads to Lee's Ferry, skirting the huge Cathedral Rock and taking you very close to another strange, hanging rock. From the end of this road there are several pleasant walks, and you can even climb up into Paria Canyon – an unusual hike taking several days and ending up back in Utah.

Lee's Ferry is the departure point for most of the raft descents of the Colorado.

Cathedral Wash: this is a walk of about two hours, through a narrow canyon. Don't risk it in stormy weather.

River Trail: you can follow an ancient cart-track for a mile (1.5km) along the Colorado.

Paria Canyon: this exceptional walk, for experienced hikers only, offers some fabulous landscapes with numerous clefts in the canyon to explore. The walk takes three to six days, depending on fitness and the time available. It links White House or Buckskin Gulch, on route 89, in southern Utah to Lee's Ferry. The traditional point of departure is 41 miles (66km) to the west of Page. Paria Canyon is very narrow higher up and broadens out as you descend. You need to cross the river in a number of places – and sometimes the only way forward is along the river bed itself. Summer (when there are more storms) is best avoided, in favour of spring or autumn. For a taster, you could simply enjoy a day's climb up the canyon from Lee's Ferry (departure from behind Lonely Dell Ranch).

If you don't have two cars at your disposal and you are staying at the Page Youth Hostel, have a word with Kate. She may have the time to drop you at the start of the walk and she usually only charges the price of the petrol.

WHERE TO STAY

Lee's Ferry Campground: ☎ 355-2234 (the ranger's station). Open all year round and costs $10 per pitch. It's on the left, shortly before the ranger's station. The pitches are small and don't have much shade, but there are normally plenty of spaces available – you can choose your own spot. A good base if you are planning a day trip up the Paria Canyon or if you are going to do other walks in the area. Some pitches have canopies – very handy when it rains. There are toilets but no showers.

Marble Canyon Lodge: at the intersection of route 89A and the road leading to Lee's Ferry, just after the bridge. ☎ (520) 355-2225. Freephone: ☎ 1-800-726-1789. Fax: 355-2227. Comfortable rooms, $64 for a single, $69 for a twin (including tax). There are also apartments with two rooms, a kitchen and a dining room, for $133. Out-of-season vouchers available from the Page Chamber of Commerce. These offer discounted lodging for two people including dinner (reservations possible) for $60. There is a trading post next to the hotel, which was established in the 1920s, and a cafe-restaurant, open every day 6am–9pm.

INDEX

Note: page numbers in *italics* refer to maps

INDEX